LOWE'S Home Plans

Country Homes

HOMES FROM 828 TO 4,237 SQ. FT.

Home Plans - Country Collection - This book is a collection of best-selling country-style plans from some of the nation's leading designers and architects. Only quality plans with sound design, functional layout, energy efficiency and affordability have been selected.

These plans cover a wide range of architectural styles in a popular range of sizes. A broad assortment is presented to match a wide variety of lifestyles and budgets. Each design page features floor plans, a front view of the house, and a list of special features. All floor plans show room dimensions, exterior dimensions and the interior square footage of the home.

Technical Specifications - At the time the construction drawings were prepared, every effort was made to ensure that these plans and specifications meet nationally recognized building codes (BOCA, Southern Building Code Congress and others). Because national building codes change or vary from area to area some drawing modifications and/or the assistance of a professional designer or architect may be necessary to comply with your local codes or to accommodate specific building site conditions. We advise you consult with your local building official for information regarding codes governing your area.

Blueprint Ordering - Fast and Easy - Your ordering is made simple by following the instructions on page 290. See page 289 for more information on which types of blueprint packages are available and how many plan sets to order.

Your Home, Your Way - The blueprints you receive are a master plan for building your new home. They start you on your way to what may well be the most rewarding experience of your life.

House shown on front cover is Plan #531-0299 and is featured on page 62. Photo Courtesy of Greg Marquis and Associates.

Lowe's Home Plans Country Homes is published by Home Design Alternatives, Inc. (HDA, Inc.) 4390 Green Ash Drive, St. Louis, MO 63045.

Artist drawings shown in this publication may vary slightly from the actual working blueprints.

CONTENTS

Extras Available With The Lowe's Signature Series Home Plans 4-5

Lowe's Signature Series Home Plans 6-162

Designer Series Home Plans ... 163-285

Our Blueprint Packages Offer... 286

Other Helpful Building Aids 287

Home Plans Index 288-289

What Kind Of Plan Package Do You Need? 289

To Order Home Plans 290

Current Printing 5 4 3 2

LOWE'S

Signature
SERIES

Home Design Alternatives is proud to bring you this unprecedented offer of our Lowe's Signature Series featuring our most popular residential plans. Never before has there been a compilation of home plans offering such unique services as you will find in this publication.

Home Plans included in the Lowe's Signature Series are indicated by the Lowe's Signature Series logo shown above, and are found on pages 6 through 162.

One of the main reasons for purchasing home plans from a publication such as this is to save you time and money. And, you will discover the extra benefits of the unique services offered through our Lowe's Signature Series of Home Plans.

Besides providing the expected beauty and functional efficiency of all our home plans, the Lowe's Signature Series offers you detailed Material Lists, Customizing Kits, free Estimated Material Pricing and a free Fax-a-Plan Service. This combination of services are not to be found in any other home plan book or magazine on the market today.

Free Estimated Material Pricing

When selecting the home plan that's right for you, the cost of materials can play a major roll. Staying within your budget is easier when choosing a plan from the Lowe's Signature Series. We provide free estimated material pricing on home plans you've selected. Call us at 1-314-770-2228. This unique service is provided "around-the-clock" to enable us to better serve you.

Fax-a-Plan™ Service

Our free Fax-a-Plan service offers the ideal option for those who have interest in several home designs and want more information to help narrow down the selection. Rear and side views for designs in the Signature Series are available via fax, along with a list of key construction features (i.e. roof slopes, ceiling heights, insulation values, type of roof and wall construction) and more. Just call our automated FAX-A-PLAN service at 1-314-770-2228 available 24 hours a day - 7 days a week and the cost is FREE.

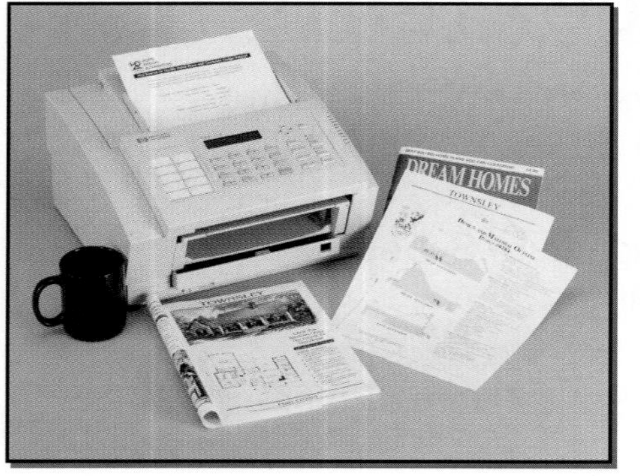
DREAM HOMES

Material Lists

To enhance the quality of our blueprint packages, we offer one of the most precise and thorough material lists in the industry. An accurate and detailed material list can save you a considerable amount of time and money. Our material lists give you the quantity, dimensions, and descriptions of the major building materials necessary to construct your home. You'll get faster and more accurate bids from your contractors and material suppliers and you'll save money by paying for only the materials you need.

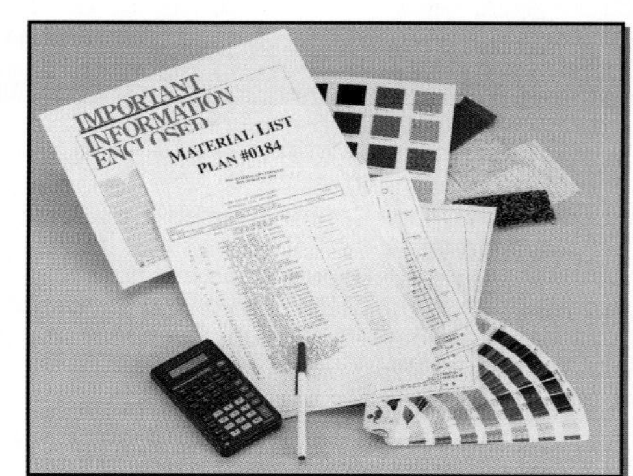
IMPORTANT
INFORMATION
MATERIAL LIST
PLAN #0184

How You Can Customize Our Plans Into Your Dream Home

Get exactly what you want with the help of our exclusive Customizer Kit™ and discover unlimited design possibilities available to you when building a new home. The Customizer Kit, available with any of the Lowe's Signature Series Plans, allows you to alter virtually any architectural element you wish, both on the exterior and interior of the home. The Kit comes complete with simplified drawings of your selected home plan so that you can sketch out any and all of your changes. To help you through this process, the Kit also includes a workbook called "The Customizer," a special correction pen, a red marking pencil, an architect's scale and furniture layout guides. These tools, along with the simplified customizer drawings, allow you to experiment with various design changes prior to having a design professional modify the actual working drawings.

Before placing your order for blueprints consider the type and number of changes you plan to make to your selected design. If you wish to make only minor design changes such as moving interior walls, changing window styles, or altering foundation types, we strongly recommend that you purchase reproducible masters along with the Customizer Kit. These master drawings, which contain the same information as the blueprints, are easy to modify because they are printed on erasable, reproducible paper. Also, by starting with complete detailed drawings, and planning out your changes with the Customizer Kit, the cost of having a design professional or your builder make the required drawing changes will be considerably less. After the master drawings are altered, multiple blueprint copies can be made from them.

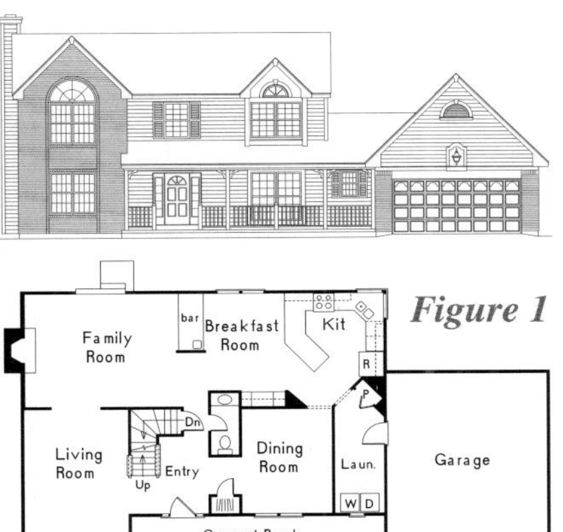
Family Room
bar
Breakfast Room
Kit
R
P
Dn
Living Room
Up
Entry
Dining Room
Laun.
W D
Garage
Covered Porch
Figure 1

If you anticipate making a lot of changes, such as moving exterior walls and changing the overall appearance of the house, we suggest you purchase only one set of blueprints as a reference set and the Customizer Kit to document your desired changes. When making major design changes, it is always advisable to seek out the assistance of an architect or design professional to review and redraw that portion of the blueprints affected by your changes.

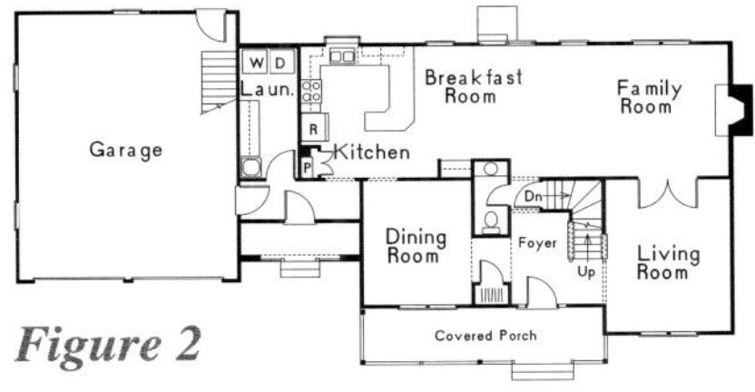
Garage
W D
Laun.
R
P
Kitchen
Breakfast Room
Family Room
Dining Room
Dn
Foyer
Up
Living Room
Covered Porch
Figure 2

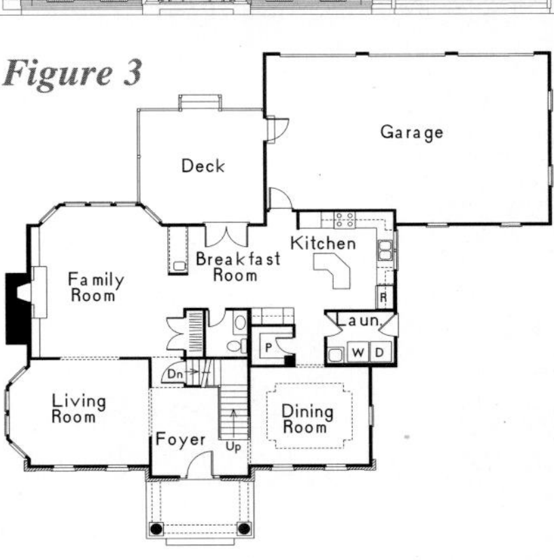
Garage
Deck
Kitchen
Breakfast Room
Family Room
R
Laun
P
W D
Dn
Living Room
Dining Room
Foyer
Up
Figure 3

Typically, having a set of reproducible masters altered by a local designer can cost as little as a couple hundred dollars, whereas redrawing a portion or all of the blueprints can cost considerably more depending on the extent of the changes. Like most projects, the more planning and preparation you can do on your own, the greater the savings to you.

Finally, you'll have the satisfaction of knowing that your custom home is uniquely and exclusively yours.

Examples of Customizing

Thousands of builders and home buyers have used the HDA Customizer Kit to help them modify their home plans, some involving minor changes, many with dramatic alterations. Examples of actual projects are shown here.

Figure 1 shows the front elevation and first floor plan for one of HDA's best-selling designs.

Figure 2 shows how one plan customer made few but important design changes such as completely reversing the plan to better accommodate his building site; adding a second entrance for ease of access to the front yard from the kitchen; making provisions for a future room over the garage by allowing for a stairway and specifying windows in place of louvers, plus other modifications.

Figure 3 shows another example of an actual project where the design shown in Figure 1 was dramatically changed to achieve all of the desired features requested by the customer. This customized design proved to be so successful that HDA obtained permission to offer it as a standard plan.

Affordable Atrium Ranch

Rear View

Plan #531-0710

Price Code D

Total Living Area: 2,334 Sq. Ft.

Home has 3 bedrooms, 2 baths, 2-car garage and walk-out basement foundation.

Special features

- Roomy front porch gives home a country flavor
- Vaulted great room boasts a fireplace, TV alcove, pass-through snack bar to kitchen and atrium featuring bayed window wall and ascending stair to family room
- Oversized master bedroom and bath features a vaulted ceiling, double entry doors and large walk-in closet

Lower Level
557 sq. ft.

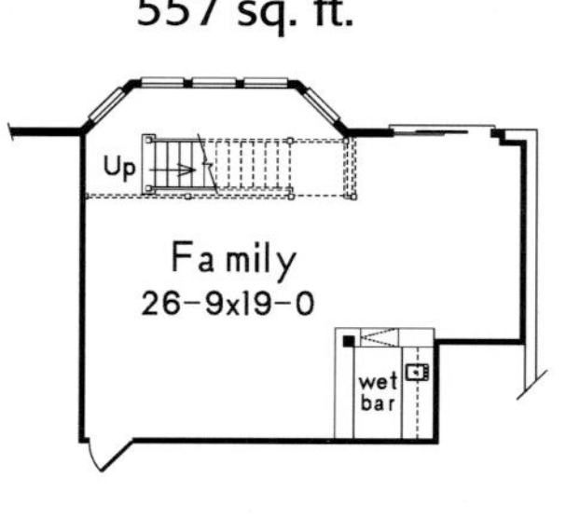
Up
Family
26-9x19-0
wet bar

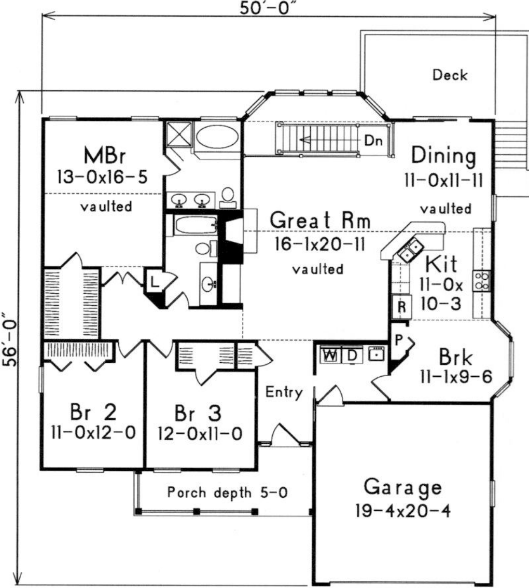
50'-0"
Deck
Dn
MBr
13-0x16-5
vaulted
Dining
11-0x11-11
vaulted
Great Rm
16-1x20-11
vaulted
Kit
11-0x
10-3
R
L
P
W D
Brk
11-1x9-6
56'-0"
Entry
Br 2
11-0x12-0
Br 3
12-0x11-0
Porch depth 5-0
Garage
19-4x20-4

First Floor
1,777 sq. ft.

TO ORDER BLUEPRINTS USE THE FORM ON PAGE 290 OR CALL TOLL-FREE **1-800-DREAM HOME** (373-2646)

Charming House, Spacious And Functional

LOWE'S

Signature SERIES

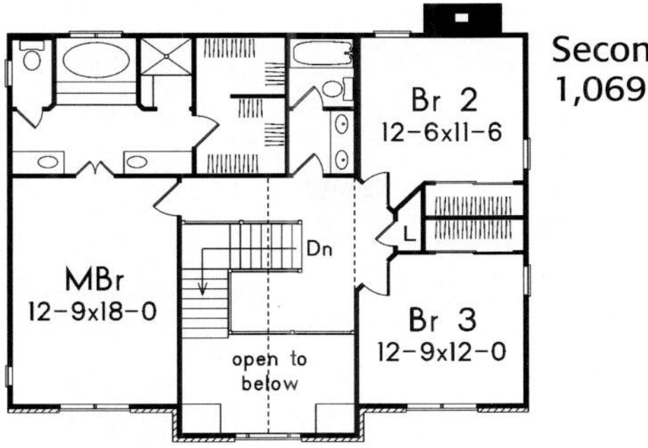
Br 2
12-6x11-6
MBr
12-9x18-0
Dn
L
Br 3
12-9x12-0
open to
below

Second Floor
1,069 sq. ft.

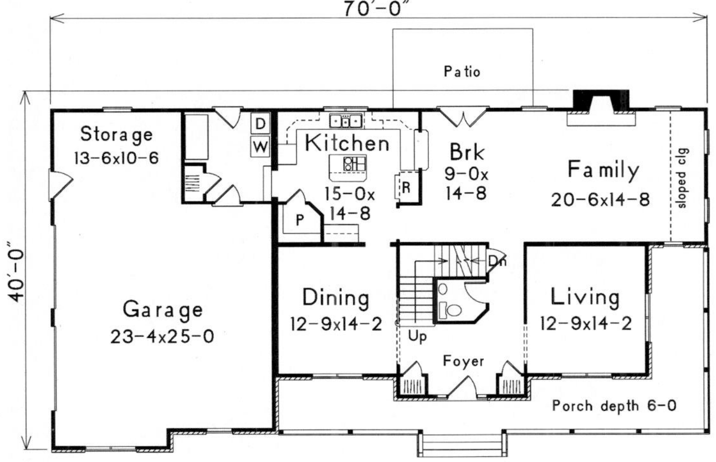
70'-0"
40'-0"
Patio
Storage
13-6x10-6
D
W
Kitchen
15-0x
14-8
Brk
9-0x
14-8
R
P
Family
20-6x14-8
sloped clg
Garage
23-4x25-0
Dining
12-9x14-2
Dn
Up
Living
12-9x14-2
Foyer
Porch depth 6-0

First Floor
1,436 sq. ft.

Plan #531-0449

Price Code D

Total Living Area: 2,505 Sq. Ft.

Home has 3 bedrooms, 2 1/2 baths, 2-car side entry garage and basement foundation, drawings also include crawl space foundation.

Special features

- The garage features extra storage area and ample work space
- Laundry room accessible from garage and the outdoors
- Deluxe raised tub and immense walk-in closet grace master bath

LOWE'S

Signature SERIES

Practical Two-Story, Full Of Features

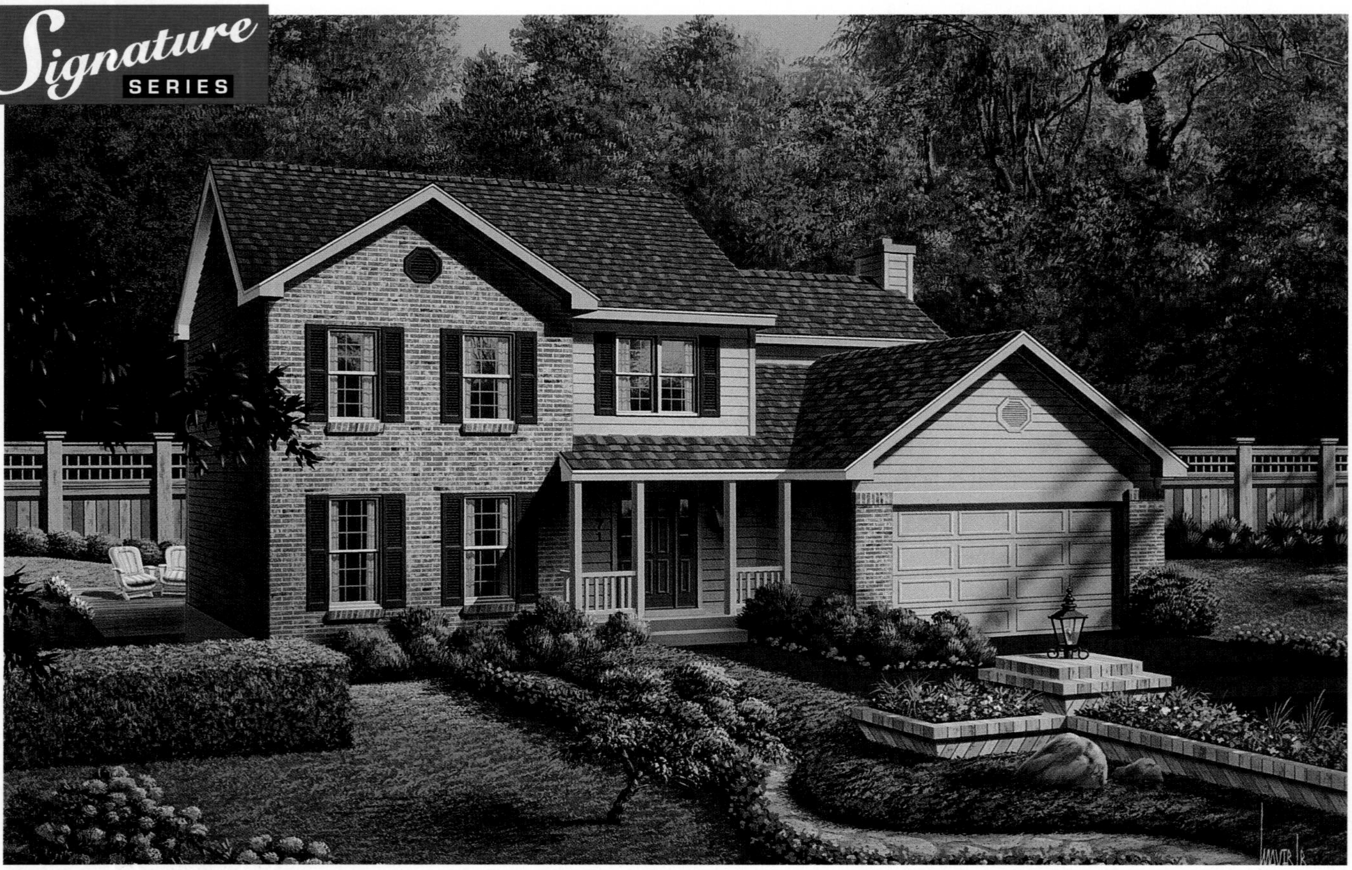

Plan #531-0171

Price Code C

Total Living Area: 2,058 Sq. Ft.

Home has 3 bedrooms, 2 1/2 baths, 2-car garage and basement foundation, drawings also include crawl space and slab foundations.

Special features

- Handsome two-story foyer with balcony creates a spacious entrance area
- Vaulted ceiling in the master bedroom with private dressing area and large walk-in closet
- Skylights furnish natural lighting in the hall and master bath
- Conveniently located second floor laundry near bedrooms

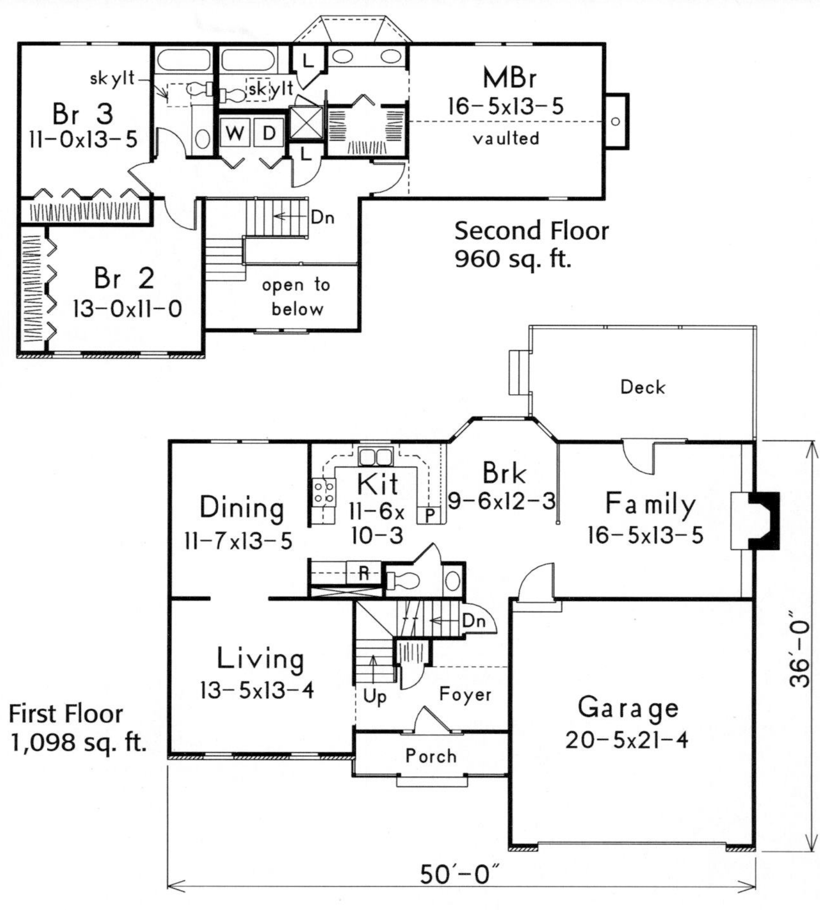
skylt
skylt
Br 3
11-0x13-5
W
D
L
L
MBr
16-5x13-5
vaulted
Dn
Br 2
13-0x11-0
open to
below
Second Floor
960 sq. ft.
Deck
Dining
11-7x13-5
Kit
11-6x
10-3
P
Brk
9-6x12-3
Family
16-5x13-5
R
Dn
Living
13-5x13-4
Up
Foyer
Garage
20-5x21-4
Porch
36'-0"
50'-0"
First Floor
1,098 sq. ft.

Picture Perfect For A Country Setting

LOWE'S

Signature
SERIES

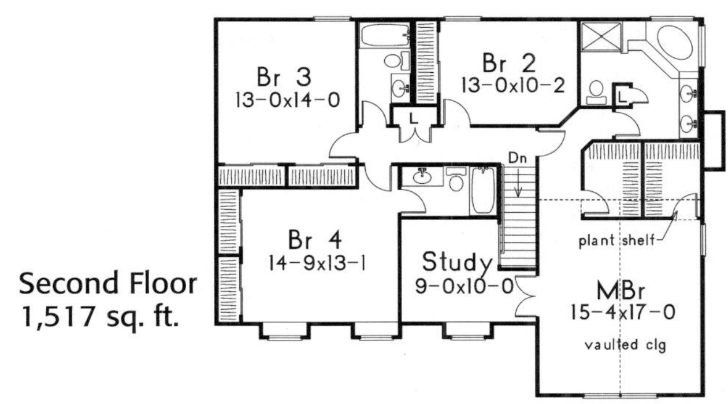
Br 3
13-0x14-0
Br 2
13-0x10-2
L
L
Dn
Br 4
14-9x13-1
Study
9-0x10-0
plant shelf
MBr
15-4x17-0
vaulted clg

Second Floor
1,517 sq. ft.

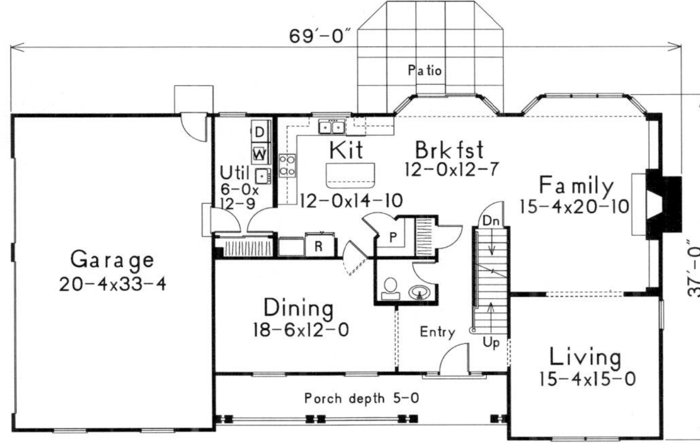
69'-0"
Patio
Kit
Brkfst
12-0x12-7
Family
15-4x20-10
D
W
Util
6-0x
12-9
12-0x14-10
P
Dn
R
Garage
20-4x33-4
Dining
18-6x12-0
Entry
Up
Living
15-4x15-0
Porch depth 5-0
37'-0"

First Floor
1,450 sq. ft.

Plan #531-0728

Price Code E

Total Living Area: 2,967 Sq. Ft.

Home has 4 bedrooms, 3 1/2 baths, 3-car side entry garage and basement foundation.

Special features

- An exterior with charm graced with country porch and multiple arched projected box windows
- Dining area is oversized and adjoins a fully equiped kitchen with walk-in pantry
- Two bay windows light up the enormous informal living area to the rear

Columns And Dormers Grace Stylish Exterior

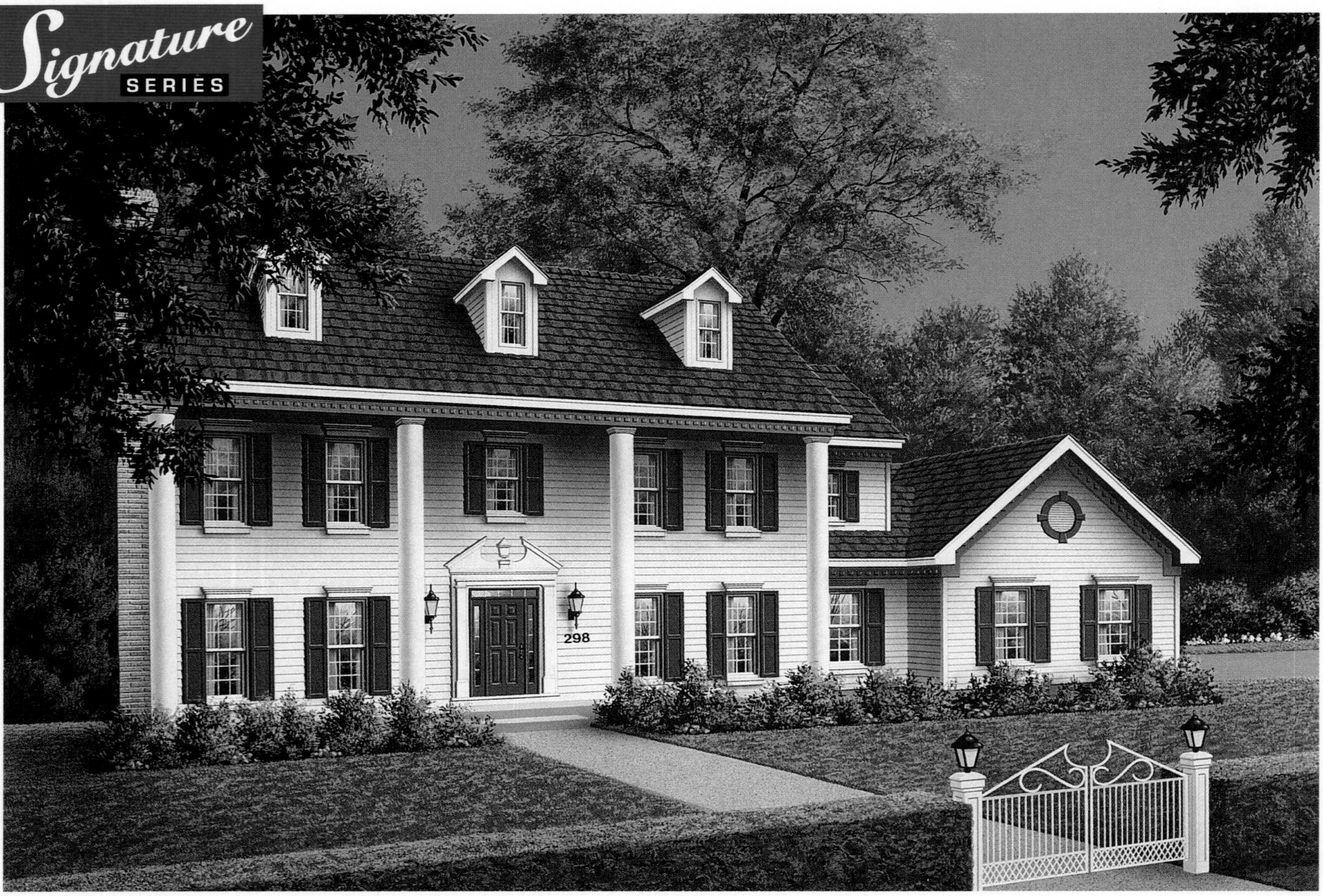

Plan #531-0298

Price Code F

Total Living Area: 3,216 Sq. Ft.

Home has 4 bedrooms, 4 1/2 baths, 3-car side entry garage and basement foundation.

Special features

- All bedrooms include private full baths
- Hearth room and combination kitchen/breakfast area create large informal gathering area
- Oversized family room boasts fireplace, wet bar and bay window
- Master bath with double walk-in closets and luxurious bath

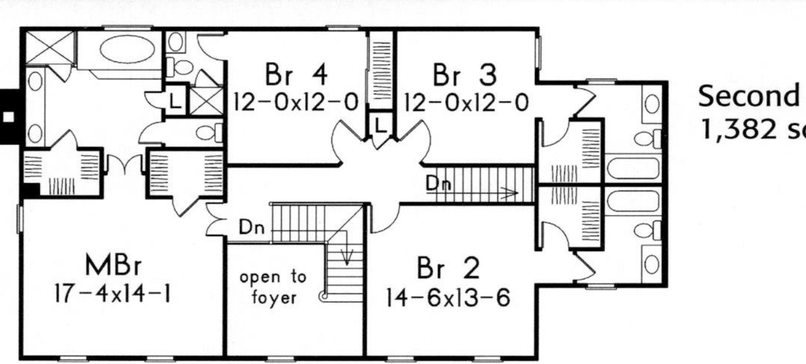
Br 4
12-0x12-0
Br 3
12-0x12-0
L
L
Dn
Dn
MBr
17-4x14-1
open to foyer
Br 2
14-6x13-6

Second Floor
1,382 sq. ft.

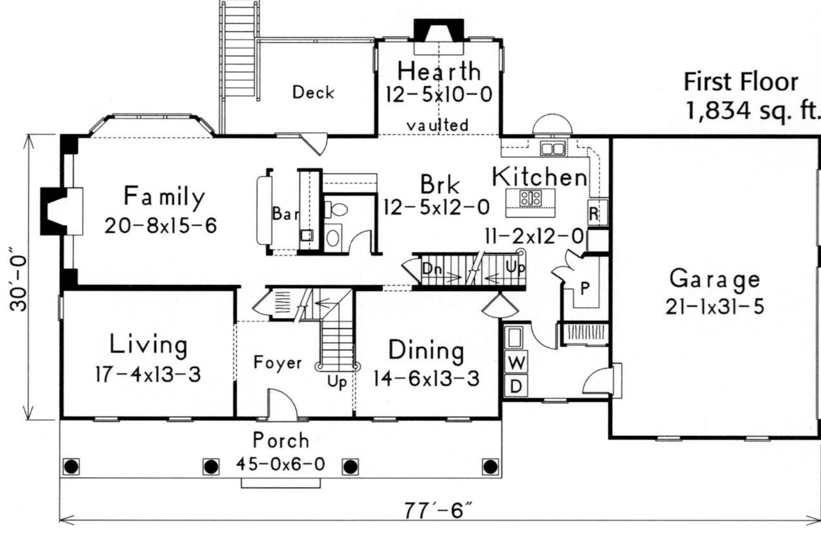
Deck
Hearth
12-5x10-0
vaulted
Family
20-8x15-6
Bar
Brk
12-5x12-0
Kitchen
11-2x12-0
R
Dn
Up
P
Garage
21-1x31-5
30'-0"
Living
17-4x13-3
Foyer
Up
Dining
14-6x13-3
W
D
Porch
45-0x6-0
77'-6"

First Floor
1,834 sq. ft.

Five Bedroom Home Embraces Large Family

LOWE'S

Signature
SERIES

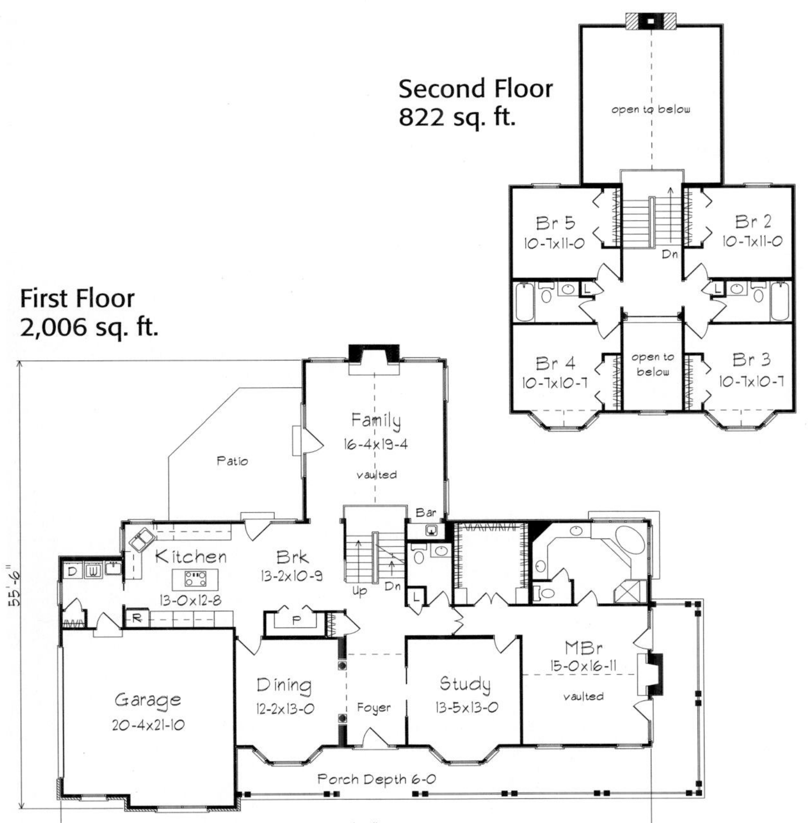
Second Floor
822 sq. ft.
open to below
Br 5
10-7x11-0
Br 2
10-7x11-0
Dn
Br 4
10-7x10-7
open to below
Br 3
10-7x10-7
First Floor
2,006 sq. ft.
Family
16-4x19-4
vaulted
Patio
Bar
Kitchen
13-0x12-8
Brk
13-2x10-9
Up
Dn
MBr
15-0x16-11
vaulted
Garage
20-4x21-10
Dining
12-2x13-0
Foyer
Study
13-5x13-0
Porch Depth 6-0
55'-6"
70'-6"

Plan #531-0417

Price Code E

Total Living Area: 2,828 Sq. Ft.

Home has 5 bedrooms, 3 1/2 baths, 2-car side entry garage and basement foundation, drawings also include crawl space and slab foundations.

Special features

- Popular wrap-around porch gives home country charm
- Secluded, oversized family room with vaulted ceiling and wet bar features many windows
- Any chef would be delighted to cook in this smartly designed kitchen with island and corner windows
- Spectacular master suite

LOWE'S

Classic Ranch Has Expansive Porch

Signature SERIES

Plan #531-0690

Price Code A

Total Living Area: 1,400 Sq. Ft.

Home has 3 bedrooms, 2 baths, 2-car garage and basement foundation, drawings also include crawl space foundation.

Special features

- Master bedroom is secluded for privacy
- Large utility room with additional cabinet space
- Covered porch provides an outdoor seating area
- Roof dormers add great curb appeal
- Vaulted ceilings in living room and master bedroom
- Extra storage in garage

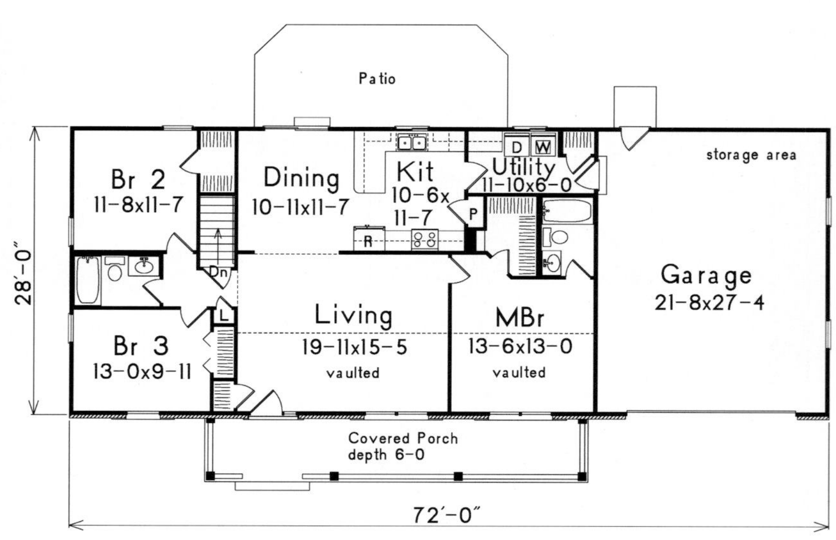
Patio
Br 2
11-8x11-7
Dining
10-11x11-7
Kit
10-6x
11-7
D W
Utility
11-10x6-0
storage area
P
R
Dn
28'-0"
Garage
21-8x27-4
L
Living
19-11x15-5
vaulted
MBr
13-6x13-0
vaulted
Br 3
13-0x9-11
Covered Porch
depth 6-0
72'-0"

 TO ORDER BLUEPRINTS USE THE FORM ON PAGE 290 OR CALL TOLL-FREE **1-800-DREAM HOME** (373-2646)

Impressive Victorian Blends Charm And Efficiency

LOWE'S

Signature
SERIES

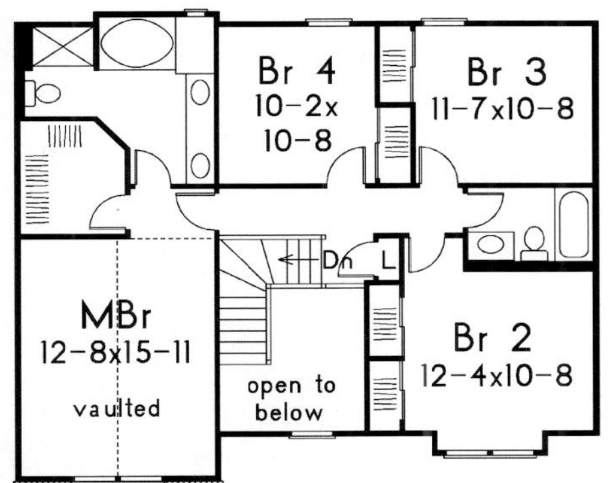
Br 4
10-2x
10-8
Br 3
11-7x10-8
MBr
12-8x15-11
vaulted
Dn
L
open to
below
Br 2
12-4x10-8

Second Floor
1,003 sq. ft.

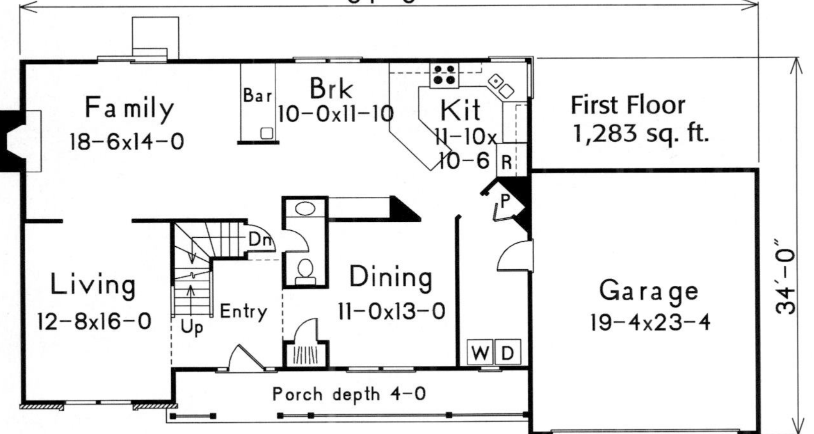
64'-0"
Family
18-6x14-0
Bar
Brk
10-0x11-10
Kit
11-10x
10-6
R
P
Dn
Living
12-8x16-0
Up
Entry
Dining
11-0x13-0
W
D
Garage
19-4x23-4
34'-0"
Porch depth 4-0

First Floor
1,283 sq. ft.

Plan #531-0138

Price Code E

Total Living Area: 2,286 Sq. Ft.

Home has 4 bedrooms, 2 1/2 baths, 2-car garage and basement foundation, drawings also include crawl space and slab foundations.

Special features

- Fine architectural detail makes this home a showplace with its large windows, intricate brickwork and fine woodwork and trim
- Stunning two-story entry with attractive wood railing and balustrades in foyer
- Convenient wrap-around kitchen with window view, planning center and pantry
- Oversized master suite with walk-in closet and master bath

Distinctive Country Porch

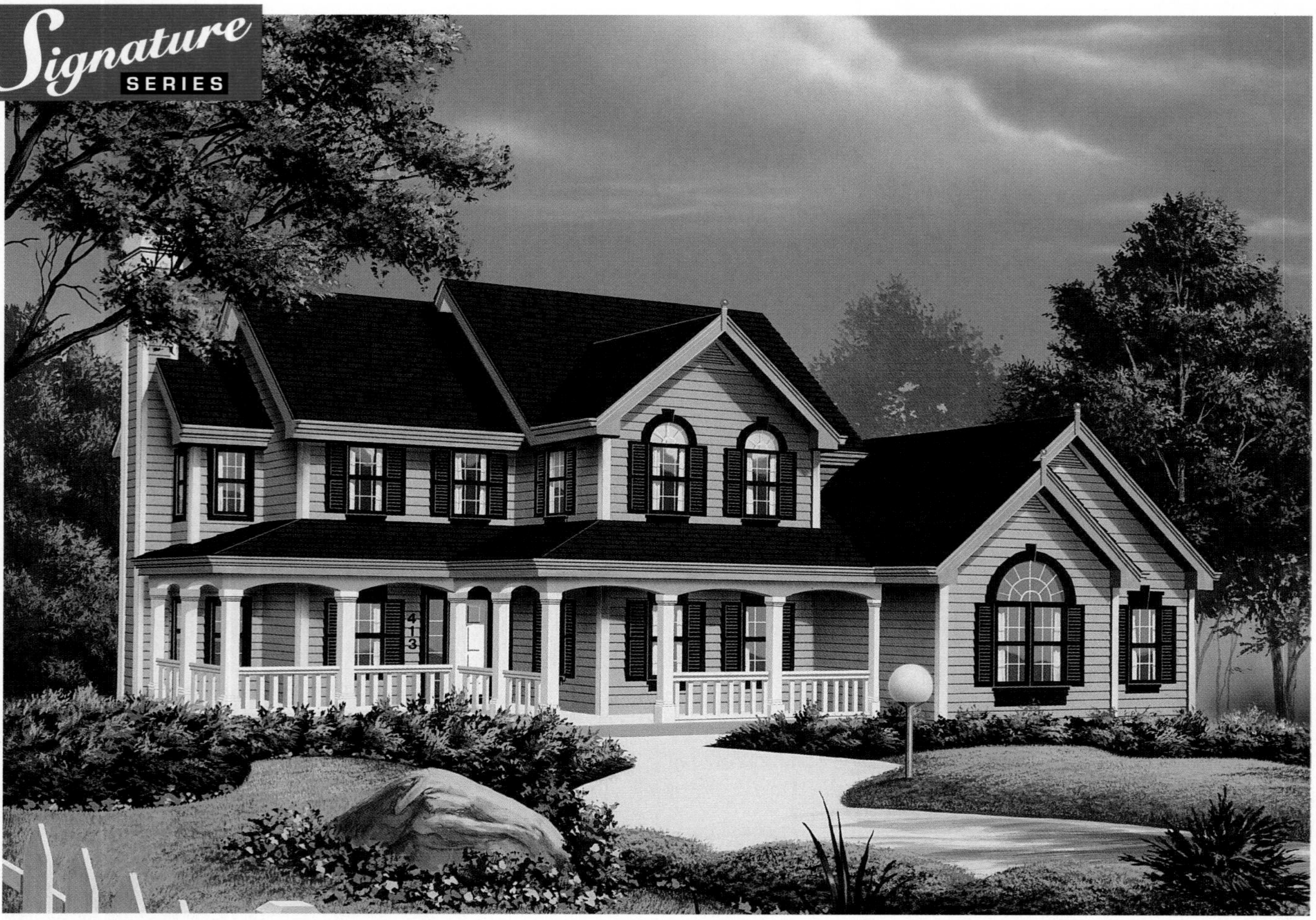

Signature SERIES

Plan #531-0413

Price Code C

Total Living Area: 2,182 Sq. Ft.

Home has 3 bedrooms, 3 1/2 baths, 2-car side entry garage and basement foundation.

Special features

- Meandering porch creates inviting look
- Generous great room has four double-hung windows and gliding doors to exterior
- Highly functional kitchen features island/breakfast bar, menu-desk and convenient pantry
- Each secondary bedroom includes generous closet and private bath

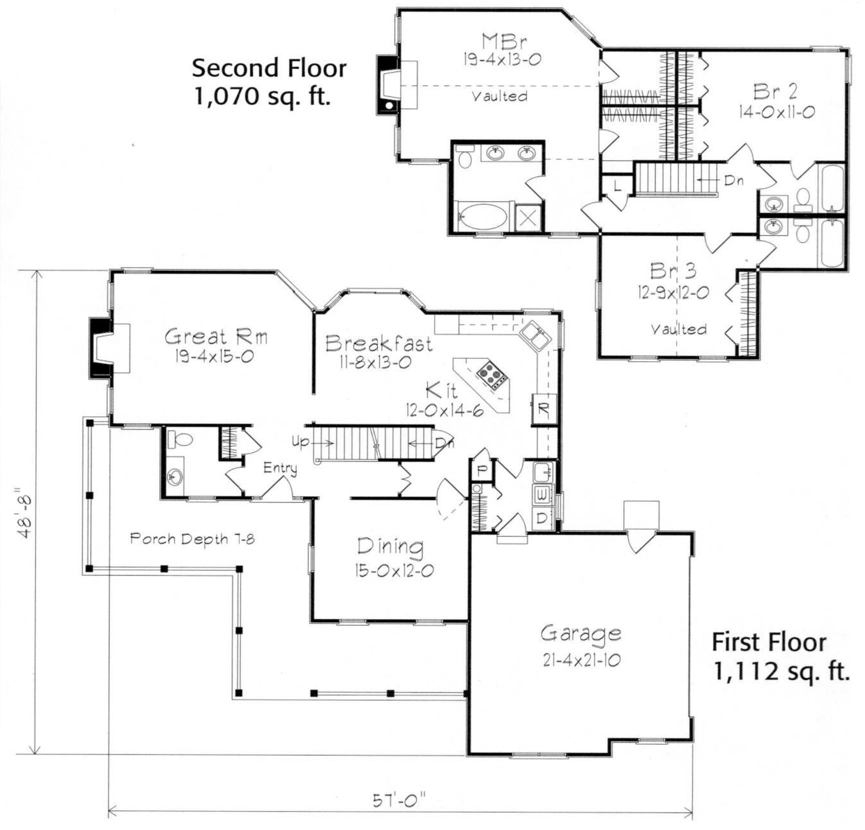

Second Floor
1,070 sq. ft.
MBr
19-4x13-0
Vaulted
Br 2
14-0x11-0
Dn
Br 3
12-9x12-0
Vaulted
Great Rm
19-4x15-0
Breakfast
11-8x13-0
Kit
12-0x14-6
Up
Dn
Entry
Porch Depth 7-8
Dining
15-0x12-0
Garage
21-4x21-10
48'-8"
57'-0"
First Floor
1,112 sq. ft.

Private Breakfast Room Provides Casual Dining

LOWE'S

Signature
SERIES

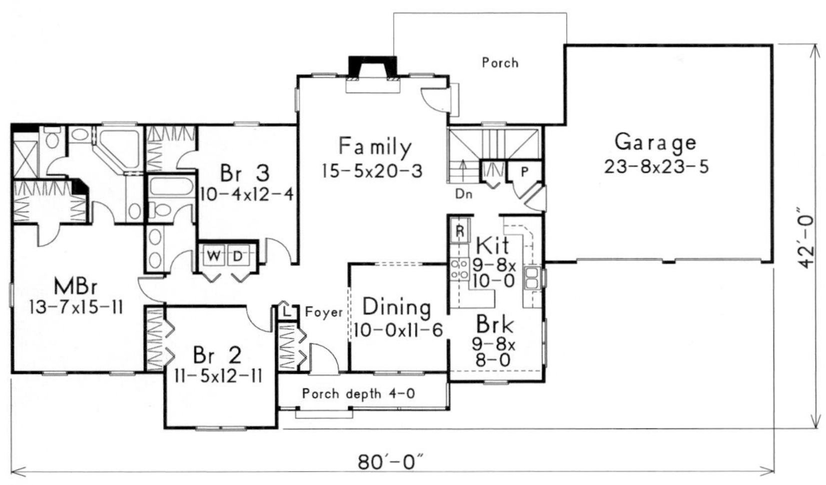
Porch
Family
15-5x20-3
Garage
23-8x23-5
Br 3
10-4x12-4
Dn
P
R
Kit
9-8x
10-0
W D
MBr
13-7x15-11
Foyer
Dining
10-0x11-6
Brk
9-8x
8-0
Br 2
11-5x12-11
Porch depth 4-0
42'-0"
80'-0"

Plan #531-0450

Price Code B

Total Living Area: 1,708 Sq. Ft.

Home has 3 bedrooms, 2 baths, 2-car garage and basement foundation, drawings also include crawl space foundation.

Special features

- Massive family room enhanced with several windows, fireplace and access to porch
- Deluxe master bath accented by step-up corner tub flanked by double vanities
- Closets throughout maintain organized living
- Bedrooms isolated from living areas

Small Ranch For A Perfect Country Haven

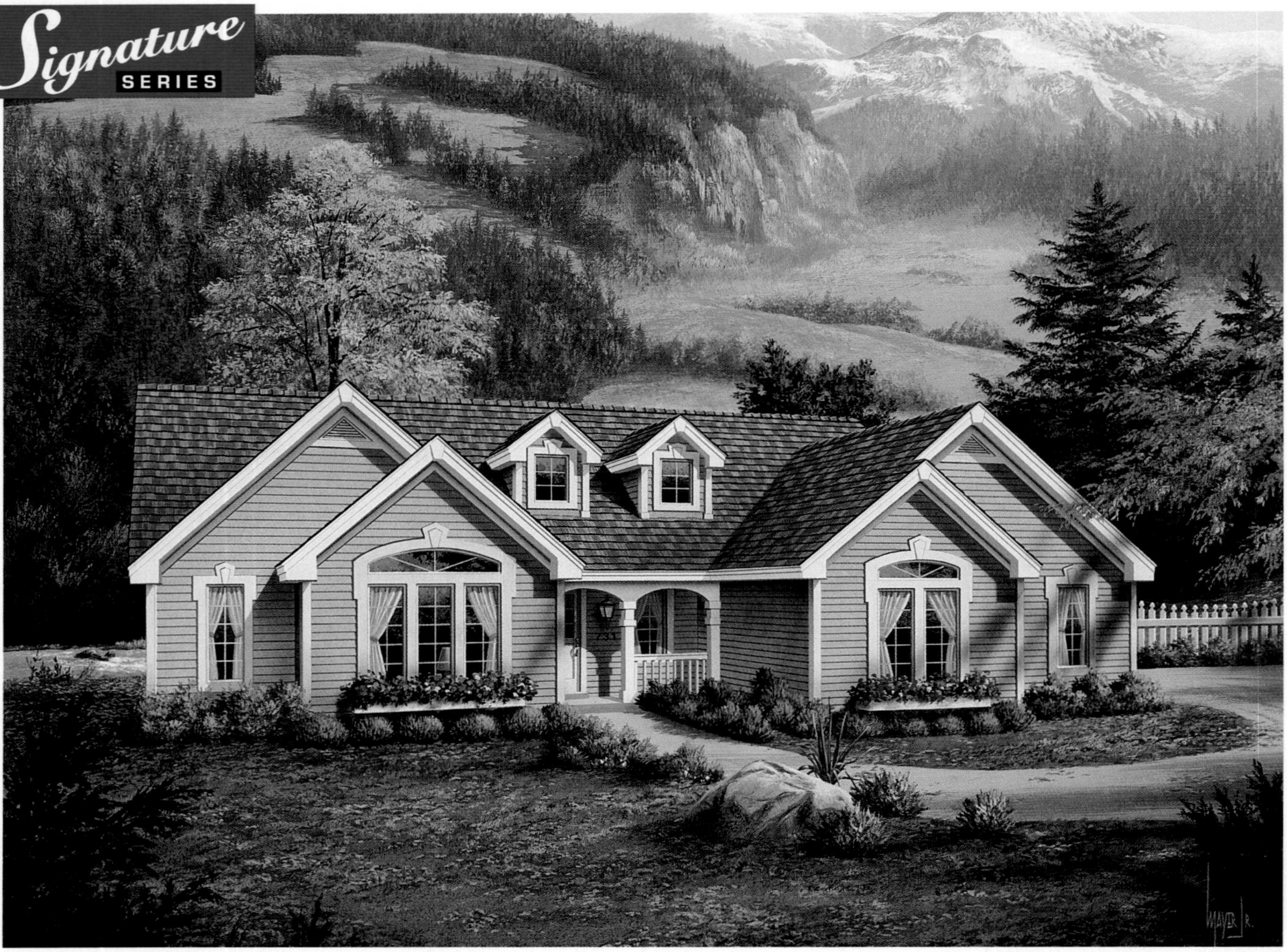

Signature SERIES

Plan #531-0731

Price Code B

Total Living Area: 1,761 Sq. Ft.

Home has 4 bedrooms, 2 baths, 2-car side entry garage and basement foundation.

Special features

- Exterior window dressing, roof dormers and planter boxes provide visual warmth and charm
- Great room boasts a vaulted ceiling, fireplace and opens to a pass-through kitchen
- Master bedroom is vaulted with luxury bath and walk-in closet
- Home features eight separate closets with an abundance of storage

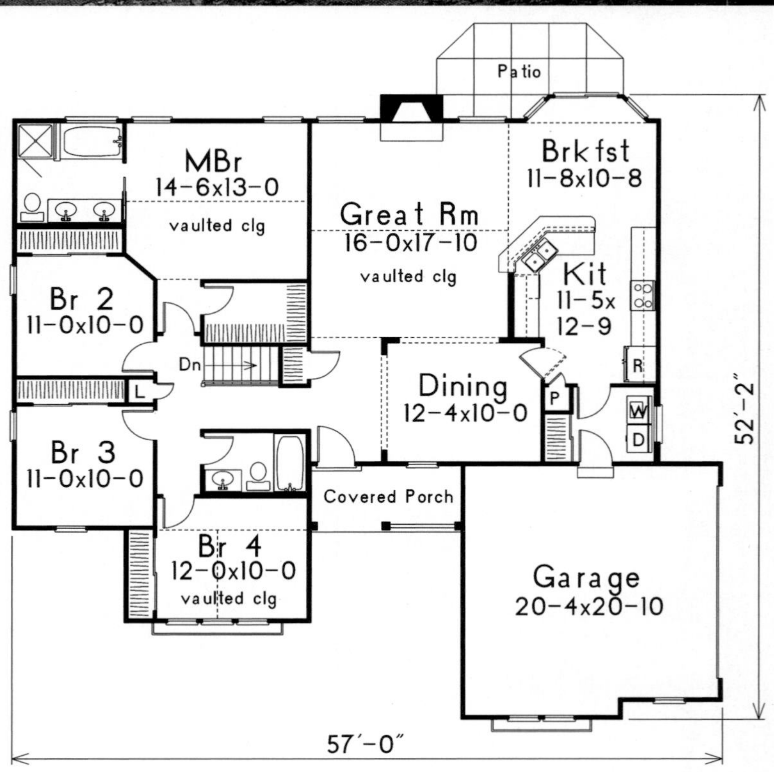
Patio
MBr
14-6x13-0
vaulted clg
Brk fst
11-8x10-8
Great Rm
16-0x17-10
vaulted clg
Kit
11-5x
12-9
Br 2
11-0x10-0
Dn
L
Dining
12-4x10-0
P
R
W
D
Br 3
11-0x10-0
Covered Porch
Br 4
12-0x10-0
vaulted clg
Garage
20-4x20-10
52'-2"
57'-0"

Fireplaces Add Warm Cozy Feeling

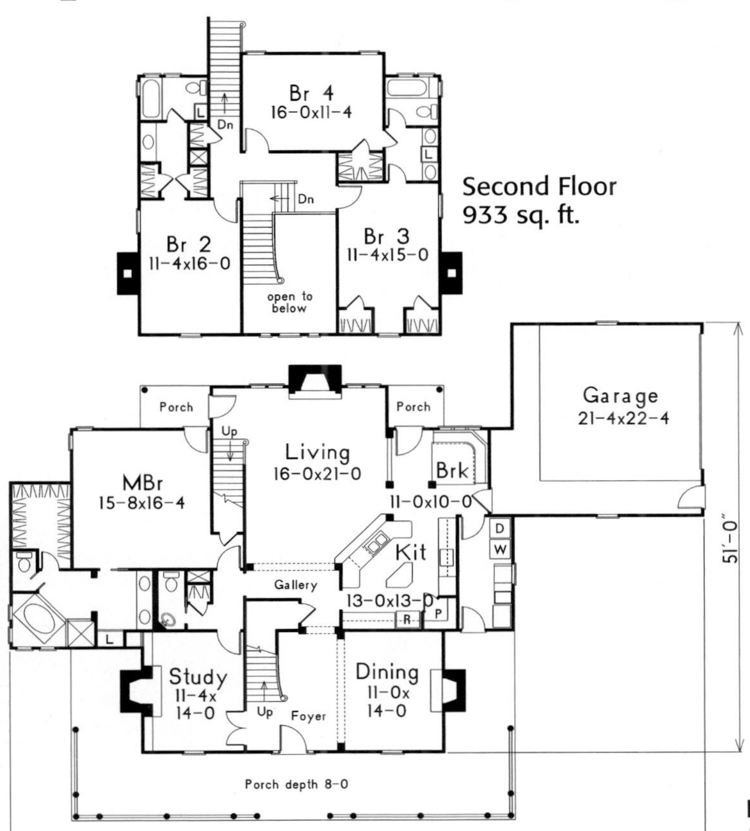
Br 4
16-0x11-4
Dn
L
Br 2
11-4x16-0
Br 3
11-4x15-0
open to below
Second Floor
933 sq. ft.
Porch
Porch
Garage
21-4x22-4
Up
Living
16-0x21-0
MBr
15-8x16-4
Brk
11-0x10-0
Kit
13-0x13-0
D
W
Gallery
R
P
L
Study
11-4x
14-0
Up
Foyer
Dining
11-0x
14-0
Porch depth 8-0
51'-0"
79'-4"
First Floor
1,999 sq. ft.

Plan #531-0232

Price Code F

Total Living Area: 2,932 Sq. Ft.

Home has 4 bedrooms, 3 1/2 baths, 2-car side entry garage and slab foundation.

Special features

- 9' ceilings throughout home
- Rear stairs create convenient access to second floor from living area
- Spacious kitchen has pass-through to the family room, a convenient island and pantry
- Cozy built-in table in breakfast area
- Secluded master suite with luxurious bath and patio access

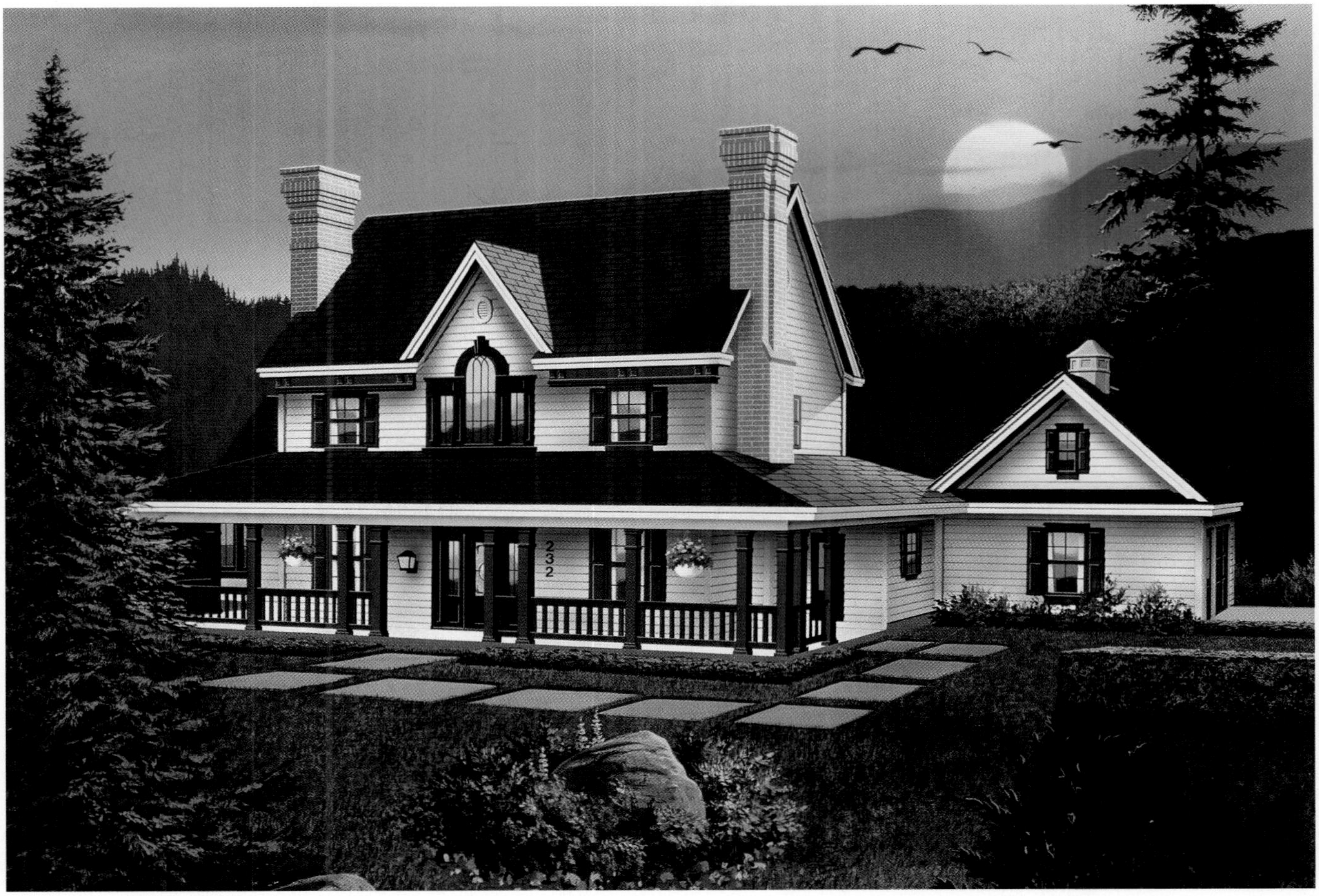

Tranquility Of An Atrium Cottage

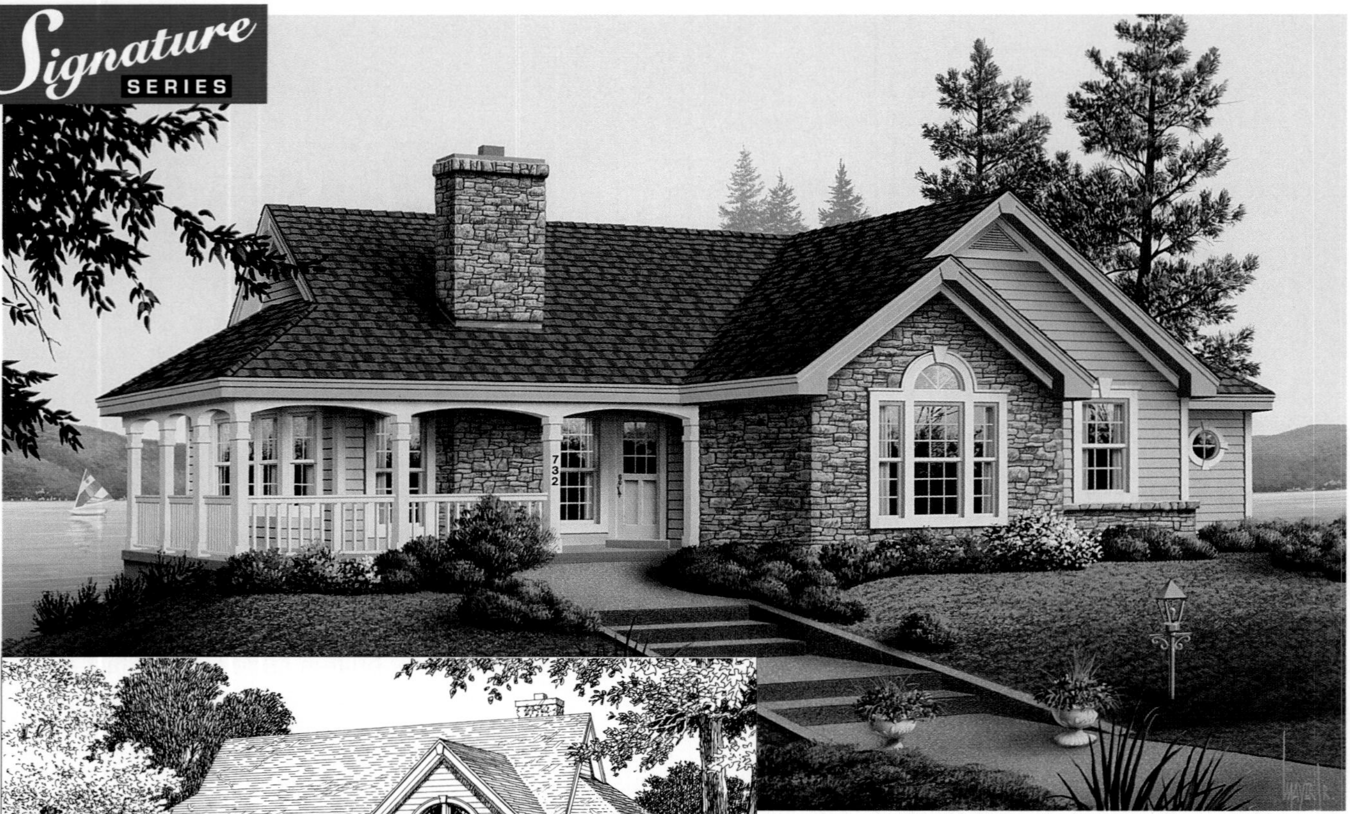

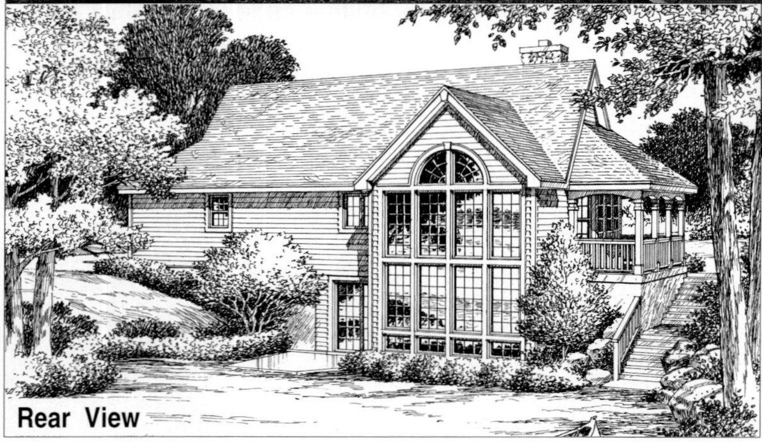

Rear View

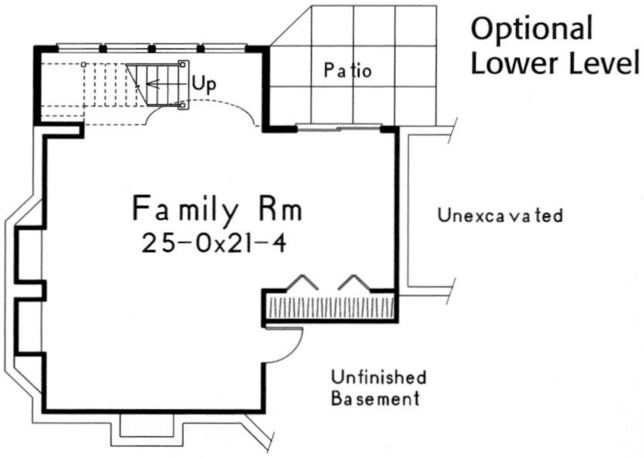

Optional Lower Level

Patio

Up

Family Rm 25-0x21-4

Unexcavated

Unfinished Basement

Plan #531-0732

Price Code A

Total Living Area: 1,384 Sq. Ft.

Home has 2 bedrooms, 2 baths, 1-car side entry garage and walk-out basement foundation.

Special features

- Wrap-around country porch for peaceful evenings
- Vaulted great room enjoys a large bay window, stone fireplace, pass-through kitchen and awesome rear views through atrium window wall
- Master suite features double entry doors, walk-in closet and a fabulous bath
- Atrium open to 611 square feet of optional living area below

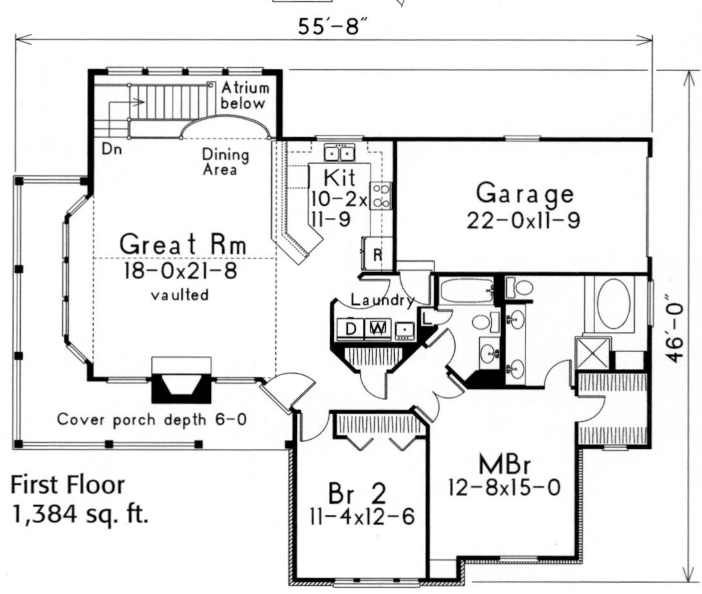
55'-8"
46'-0"
Atrium below
Dn
Dining Area
Kit 10-2x11-9
Garage 22-0x11-9
Great Rm 18-0x21-8 vaulted
R
Laundry
D W
L
Cover porch depth 6-0
Br 2 11-4x12-6
MBr 12-8x15-0

First Floor 1,384 sq. ft.

Classic Atrium Ranch With Rooms To Spare

LOWE'S

Signature
SERIES

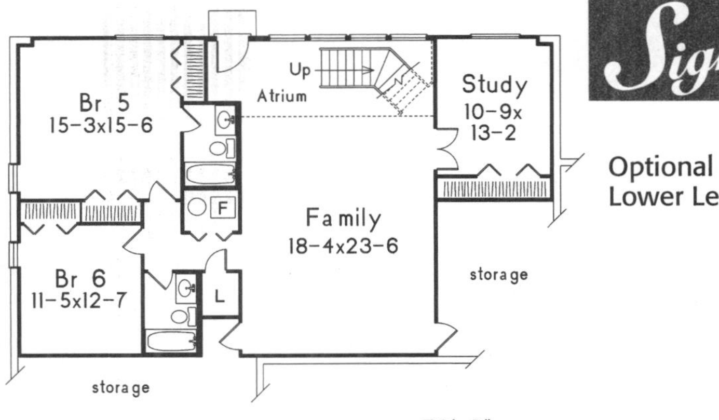
Br 5
15-3x15-6
Up
Atrium
Study
10-9x
13-2
F
Family
18-4x23-6
Br 6
11-5x12-7
L
storage
storage

Optional Lower Level

Plan #531-0747

Price Code C

Total Living Area: 1,977 Sq. Ft.

Home has 4 bedrooms, 2 1/2 baths, 3-car side entry garage and walk-out basement foundation.

Special features

- Classic traditional exterior always in style
- Spacious great room boasts a vaulted ceiling, dining area, atrium with elegant staircase and feature windows
- Atrium open to 1,416 square feet of optional living area below and consists of an optional family room, two bedrooms, two baths and a study

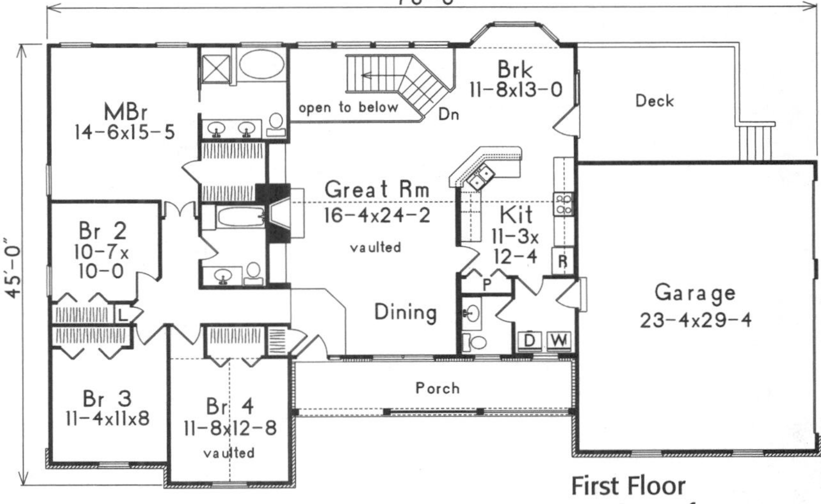
76'-0"
45'-0"
MBr
14-6x15-5
open to below
Dn
Brk
11-8x13-0
Deck
Great Rm
16-4x24-2
vaulted
Kit
11-3x
12-4
R
P
Br 2
10-7x
10-0
L
Dining
D
W
Garage
23-4x29-4
Porch
Br 3
11-4x11x8
Br 4
11-8x12-8
vaulted

First Floor
1,977 sq. ft.

LOWE'S

Charming Country Comfort

Plan #531-0247

Price Code E

Total Living Area: 2,988 Sq. Ft.

Home has 3 bedrooms, 3 1/2 baths, 2-car side entry garage and partial basement/crawl space foundation.

Special features

- Bedrooms #2 and #3 share a common bath
- Energy efficient home with 2" x 6" exterior walls
- Rear porch has direct access to master bedroom, living and dining rooms
- Spacious utility room located off garage entrance features a convenient bath with shower
- Large L-shaped kitchen has plenty of work space
- Oversized master suite complete with walk-in closet and master bath

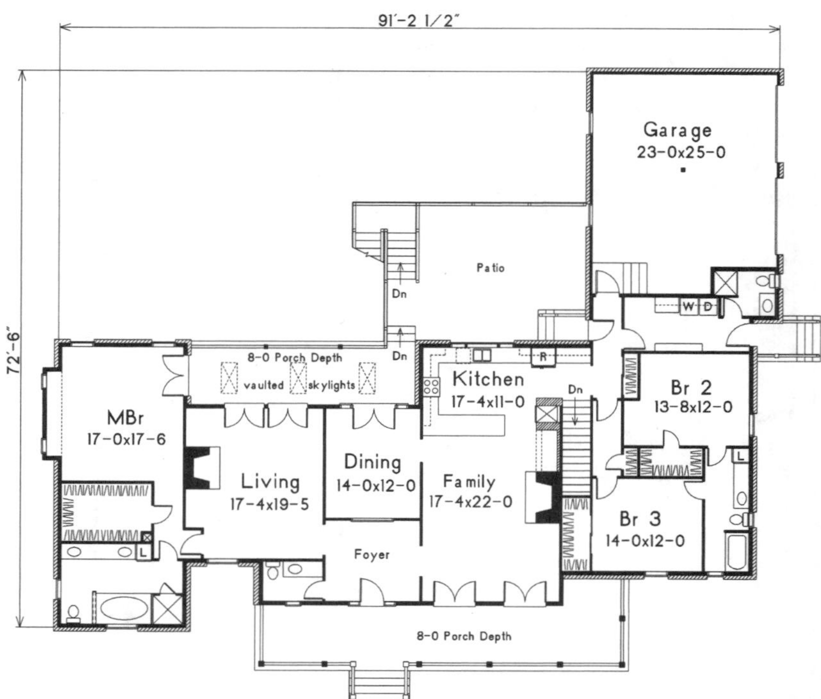
91'-2 1/2"
72'-6"
Garage
23-0x25-0
Patio
Dn
8-0 Porch Depth
vaulted skylights
MBr
17-0x17-6
Living
17-4x19-5
Dining
14-0x12-0
Kitchen
17-4x11-0
Family
17-4x22-0
Br 2
13-8x12-0
Br 3
14-0x12-0
Foyer
8-0 Porch Depth

 TO ORDER BLUEPRINTS USE THE FORM ON PAGE 290 OR CALL TOLL-FREE **1-800-DREAM HOME** (373-2646)

Country Home With Front Orientation

LOWE'S

Signature SERIES

Plan #531-0712

Price Code C

Total Living Area: 2,029 Sq. Ft.

Home has 4 bedrooms, 2 baths, 2-car side entry garage and basement foundation.

Special features

- Stonework, gables, roof dormer and double porches create a country flavor
- Kitchen enjoys extravagant cabinetry and counterspace in a bay, island snack bar, built-in pantry and cheery dining area with multiple tall windows
- Angled stair descends from large entry with wood columns and is open to vaulted great room with corner fireplace
- Master bedroom boasts his and hers walk-in closets, double-doors leading to an opulent master bath and private porch

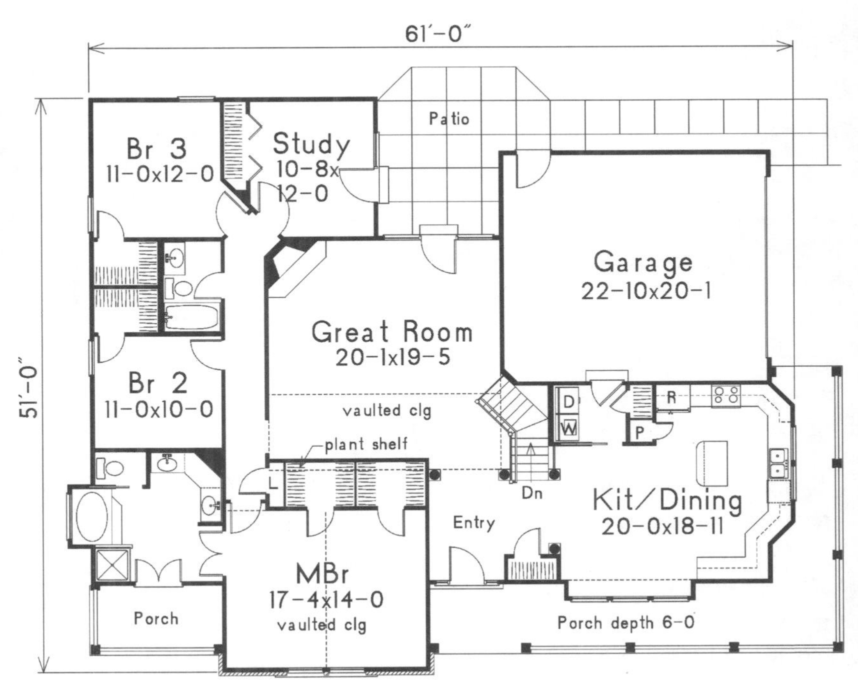
61'-0"
51'-0"
Patio
Br 3
11-0x12-0
Study
10-8x
12-0
Garage
22-10x20-1
Great Room
20-1x19-5
vaulted clg
plant shelf
Br 2
11-0x10-0
D
W
R
P
L
Dn
Entry
Kit/Dining
20-0x18-11
MBr
17-4x14-0
vaulted clg
Porch
Porch depth 6-0

LOWE'S

Rustic Design With Modern Features

Signature SERIES

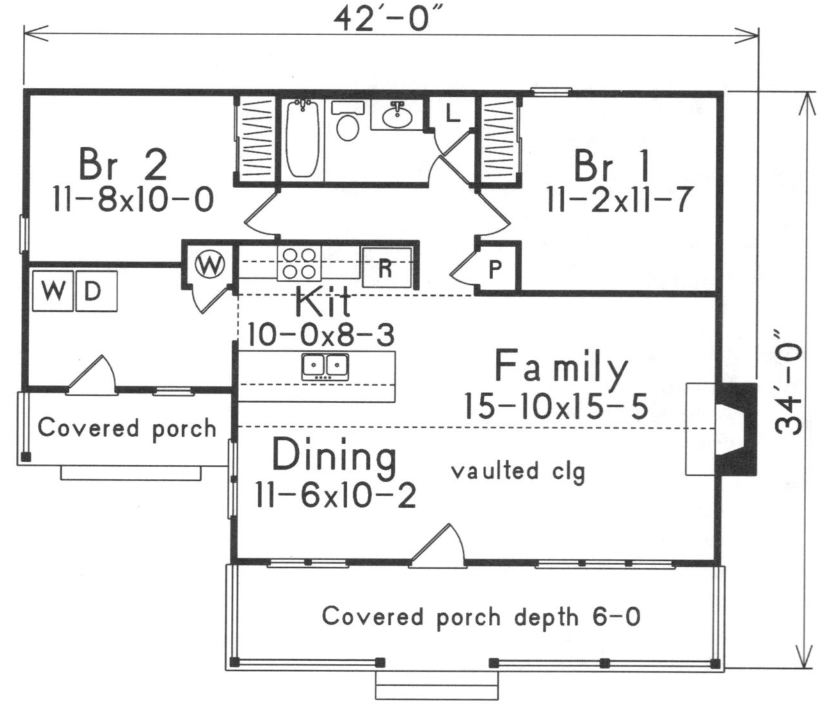
42′-0″
34′-0″
Br 2
11-8x10-0
Br 1
11-2x11-7
L
W
R
P
W D
Kit
10-0x8-3
Family
15-10x15-5
Covered porch
Dining
11-6x10-2
vaulted clg
Covered porch depth 6-0

Plan #531-0765

Price Code AA

Total Living Area: 1,000 Sq. Ft.

Home has 2 bedrooms, 1 bath and crawl space foundation.

Special features

- Large mud room with separate covered porch entrance
- Full-length covered front porch
- Bedrooms on opposite sides of the home for privacy
- Vaulted ceiling creates an open and spacious feeling

Covered Porch Highlights This Home

LOWE'S

Signature
SERIES
Study
Attic
Attic
Dn
Br 2
10-0x
13-2
Br 3
10-8x
13-2
Attic
Attic
open to
below

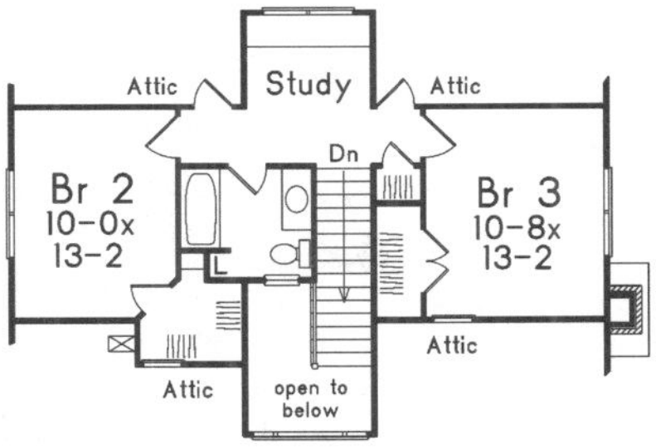

Second Floor
537 sq. ft.

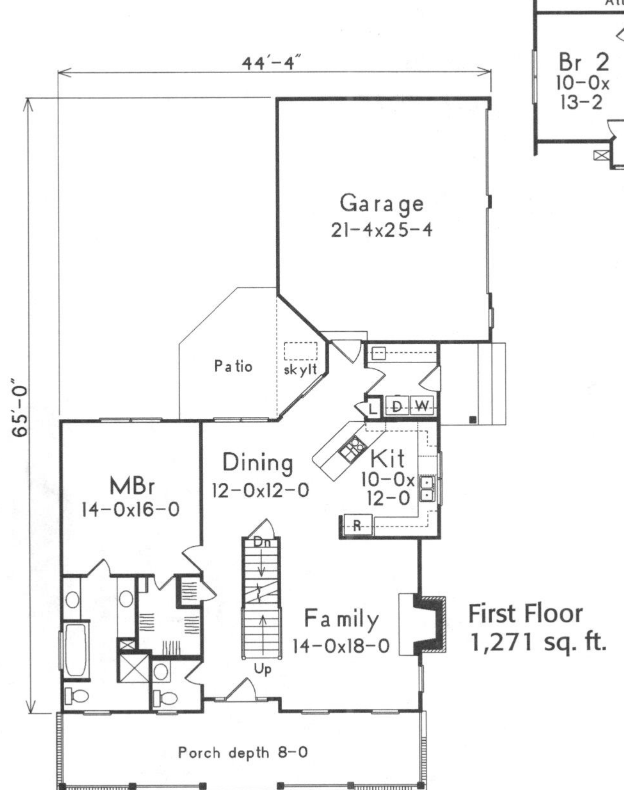
44'-4"
65'-0"
Garage
21-4x25-4
Patio
skylt
L
D
W
Dining
12-0x12-0
Kit
10-0x
12-0
R
MBr
14-0x16-0
Dn
Family
14-0x18-0
Up
Porch depth 8-0

First Floor
1,271 sq. ft.

Plan #531-0491

Price Code C

Total Living Area: 1,808 Sq. Ft.

Home has 3 bedrooms, 2 1/2 baths, 2-car side entry garage and basement foundation.

Special features

- Master bedroom has a walk-in closet, double vanities and separate tub and shower
- Two second floor bedrooms share a study area and full bath
- Partially covered patio is complete with a skylight
- Side entrance opens to utility room with convenient counter space and laundry sink

LOWE'S
Signature
SERIES

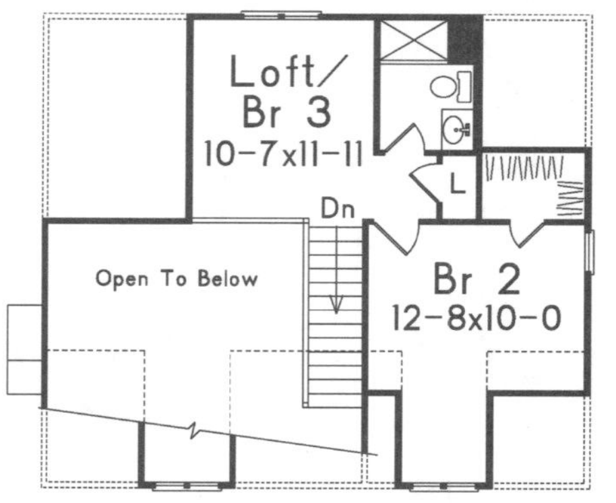
Loft/
Br 3
10-7x11-11
L
Dn
Open To Below
Br 2
12-8x10-0

Second Floor
415 sq. ft.

Plan #531-0726

Price Code A

Total Living Area: 1,428 Sq. Ft.

Home has 3 bedrooms, 2 baths and basement foundation.

Special features

- Large vaulted family room opens to dining and kitchen area with breakfast bar and access to surrounding porch
- First floor master suite offers large bath, walk-in closet and nearby laundry facilities
- A spacious loft/bedroom overlooking family room and an additional bedroom and bath conclude the second floor

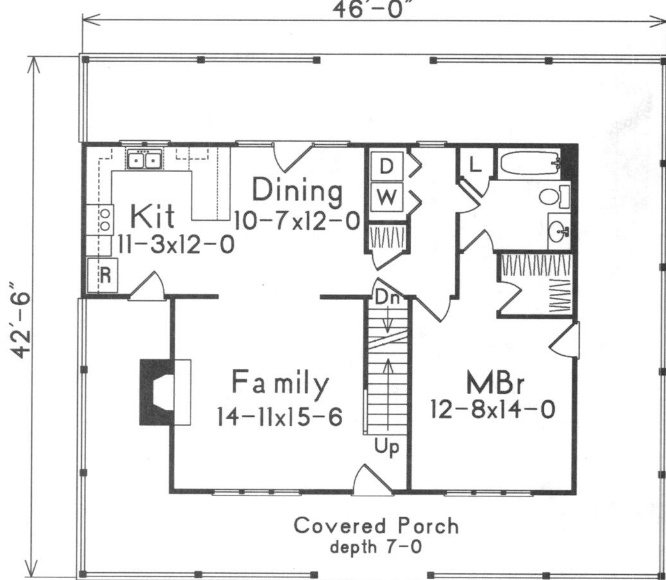
46′-0″
42′-6″
Kit
11-3x12-0
R
Dining
10-7x12-0
D
W
L
Dn
Family
14-11x15-6
Up
MBr
12-8x14-0
Covered Porch
depth 7-0

First Floor
1,013 sq. ft.

TO ORDER BLUEPRINTS USE THE FORM ON PAGE 290 OR CALL TOLL-FREE **1-800-DREAM HOME** (373-2646)

Traditional With Attention To Detail

LOWE'S

Signature SERIES

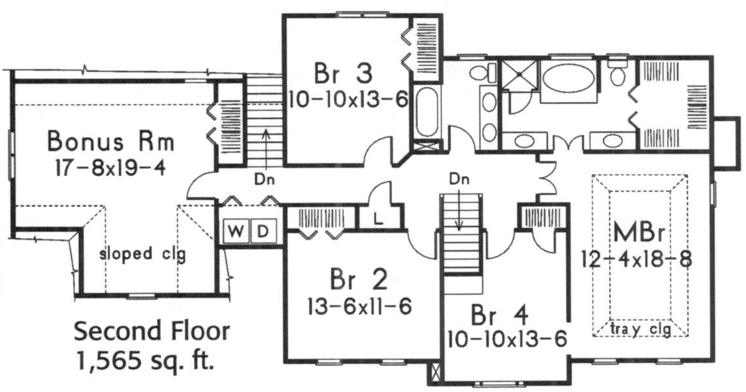
Br 3
10-10x13-6
Bonus Rm
17-8x19-4
Dn
Dn
sloped clg
W D
L
Br 2
13-6x11-6
MBr
12-4x18-8
Br 4
10-10x13-6
tray clg

Second Floor
1,565 sq. ft.

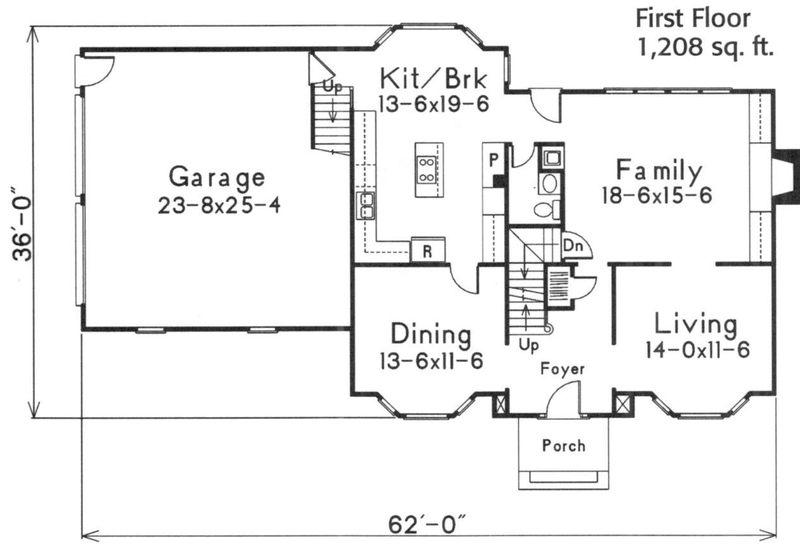
Kit/Brk
13-6x19-6
Up
Garage
23-8x25-4
P
R
Family
18-6x15-6
Dn
36'-0"
Dining
13-6x11-6
Up
Foyer
Living
14-0x11-6
Porch
62'-0"

First Floor
1,208 sq. ft.

Plan #531-0139

Price Code F

Total Living Area: 2,773 Sq. Ft.

Home has 4 bedrooms, 2 1/2 baths, 2-car side entry garage and basement foundation.

Special features

- Extensive use of bay and other large windows front and rear adds brightness and space
- Master bedroom suite features double-door entrance, oversized walk-in closet and coffered ceiling
- Rear stairway leads to bonus room, laundry and the second floor

Year-Round Or Weekend Getaway Home

Plan #531-0692

Price Code A

Total Living Area: 1,339 Sq. Ft.

Home has 3 bedrooms, 2 1/2 baths and crawl space foundation.

Special features

- Full-length covered porch enhances front facade
- Vaulted ceiling and stone fireplace add drama to family room
- Walk-in closets in bedrooms provide ample storage space
- Combined kitchen/dining area adjoins family room for perfect entertaining space

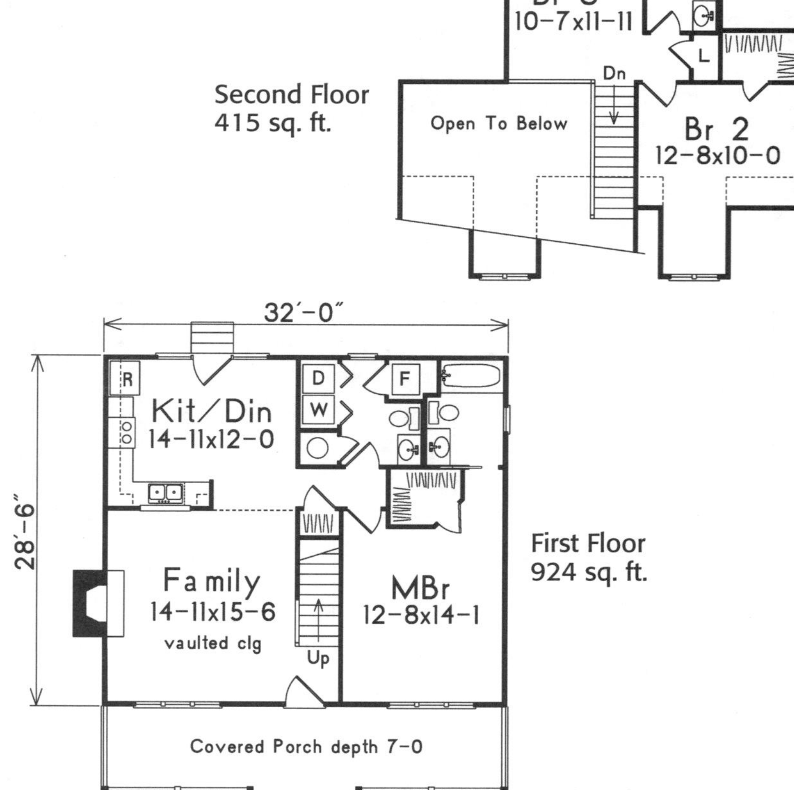
Loft/
Br 3
10-7x11-11
L
Dn
Second Floor
415 sq. ft.
Open To Below
Br 2
12-8x10-0
32'-0"
28'-6"
R
Kit/Din
14-11x12-0
D
W
F
Family
14-11x15-6
vaulted clg
Up
MBr
12-8x14-1
First Floor
924 sq. ft.
Covered Porch depth 7-0

TO ORDER BLUEPRINTS USE THE FORM ON PAGE 290 OR CALL TOLL-FREE **1-800-DREAM HOME** (373-2646)

Gabled, Covered Front Porch

LOWE'S

Signature SERIES

Plan #531-0297

Price Code A

Total Living Area: 1,320 Sq. Ft.

Home has 3 bedrooms, 2 baths and crawl space foundation.

Special features

- Functional U-shaped kitchen features pantry
- Large living and dining areas join to create open atmosphere
- Secluded master bedroom includes private full bath
- Covered front porch opens into large living area with convenient coat closet
- Utility/laundry room located near the kitchen

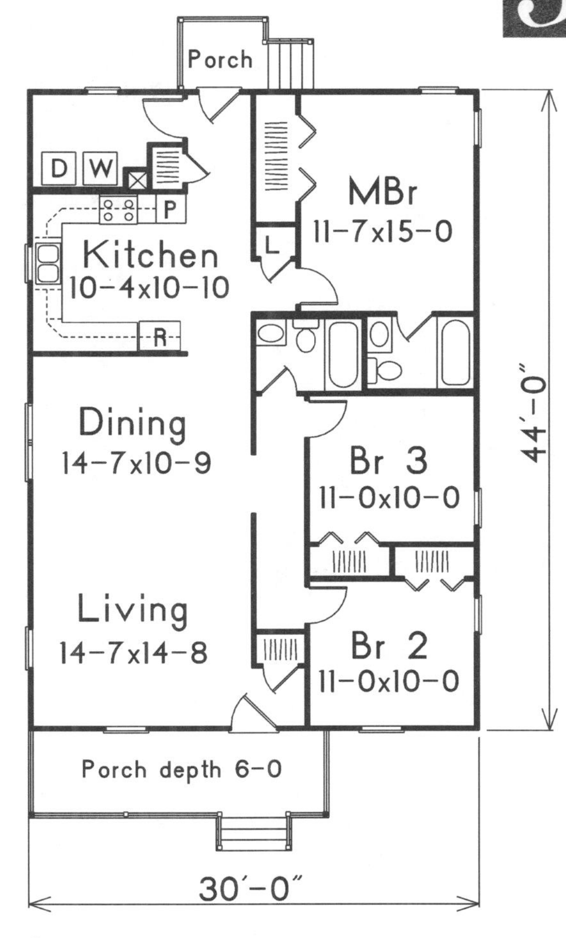
Porch
D
W
P
R
L
MBr
11-7x15-0
Kitchen
10-4x10-10
Dining
14-7x10-9
Br 3
11-0x10-0
Living
14-7x14-8
Br 2
11-0x10-0
Porch depth 6-0
44'-0"
30'-0"

Plan #531-0190

Price Code C

Total Living Area: 1,600 Sq. Ft.

Home has 3 bedrooms, 2 baths, 2-car side entry garage and slab foundation, drawings also include crawl space and basement foundations.

Special features

- Impressive sunken living room with massive stone fireplace and 16' vaulted ceilings
- Dining room conveniently located next to kitchen and divided for privacy
- Energy efficient home with 2" x 6" exterior walls
- Special amenities include sewing room, glass shelves in kitchen and master bath and a large utility area
- Sunken master bedroom features a distinctive sitting room

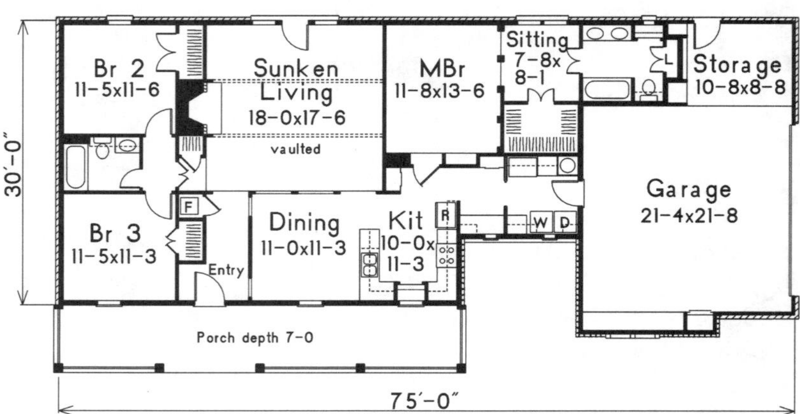
Br 2
11-5x11-6
Sunken
Living
18-0x17-6
vaulted
MBr
11-8x13-6
Sitting
7-8x
8-1
Storage
10-8x8-8
30'-0"
Garage
21-4x21-8
Br 3
11-5x11-3
Entry
Dining
11-0x11-3
Kit
10-0x
11-3
W D
Porch depth 7-0
75'-0"

Dormers Accent Country Home

LOWE'S

Signature SERIES

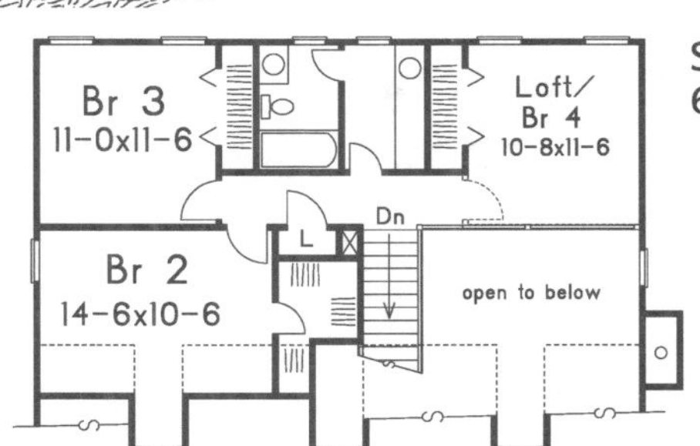
Br 3
11-0x11-6
Loft/
Br 4
10-8x11-6
Dn
Br 2
14-6x10-6
L
open to below

Second Floor
686 sq. ft.

Plan #531-0598

Price Code C

Total Living Area: 1,818 Sq. Ft.

Home has 4 bedrooms, 2 1/2 baths, 2-car drive under garage and basement foundation.

Special features

- Breakfast room is tucked behind the kitchen and has laundry closet and deck access
- Living/dining area combination share vaulted ceiling and fireplace
- Master bedroom has two closets, large double-bowl vanity and separate tub and shower
- Large front porch wraps around home

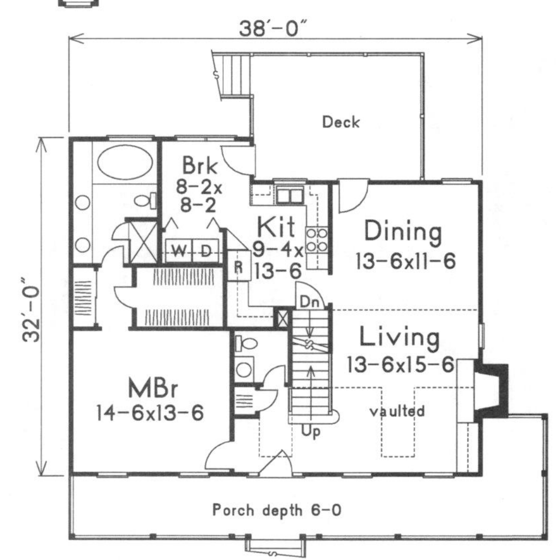
38'-0"
Deck
Brk
8-2x
8-2
W
D
Kit
9-4x
13-6
R
Dining
13-6x11-6
Dn
Living
13-6x15-6
vaulted
Up
MBr
14-6x13-6
32'-0"
Porch depth 6-0

First Floor
1,132 sq. ft.

Design Revolves Around Central Living Space

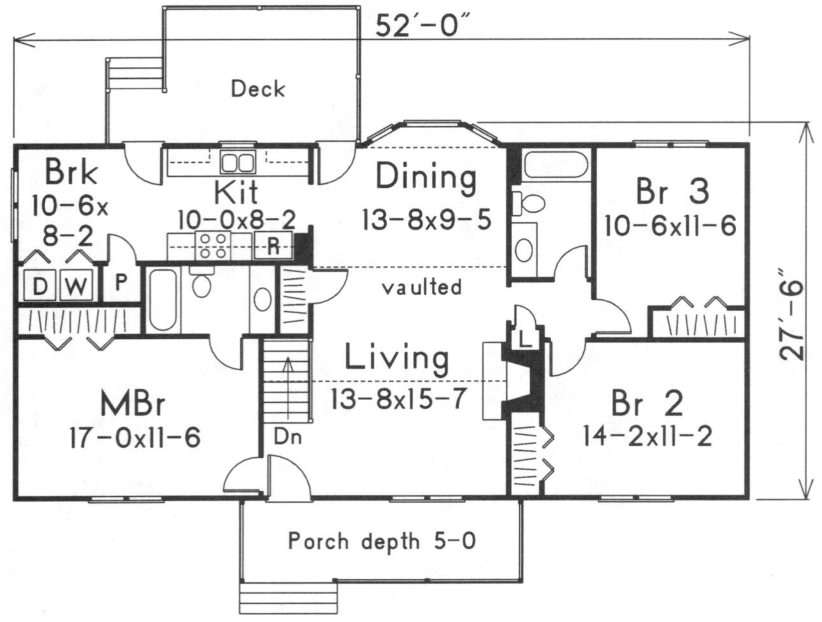
52'-0"
Deck
Brk
10-6x
8-2
Kit
10-0x8-2
Dining
13-8x9-5
Br 3
10-6x11-6
D W P
R
vaulted
Living
13-8x15-7
L
MBr
17-0x11-6
Dn
Br 2
14-2x11-2
27'-6"
Porch depth 5-0

Plan #531-0252

Price Code A

Total Living Area: 1,364 Sq. Ft.

Home has 3 bedrooms, 2 baths, 2-car drive under garage and basement foundation.

Special features

- Master bedroom includes full bath
- Pass-through kitchen opens into breakfast room with laundry closet and access to deck
- Adjoining dining and living rooms with vaulted ceilings and a fireplace create an open living area
- Dining room features large bay window

Double Bay Enhances Front Entry

LOWE'S

Signature SERIES

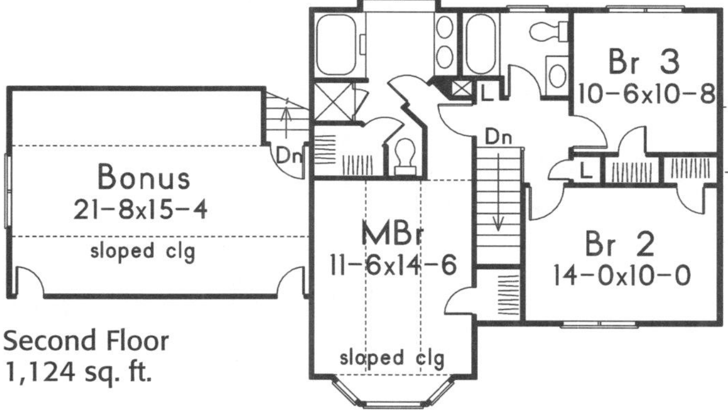

Br 3
10-6x10-8

Bonus
21-8x15-4
sloped clg

MBr
11-6x14-6
sloped clg

Br 2
14-0x10-0

Second Floor
1,124 sq. ft.

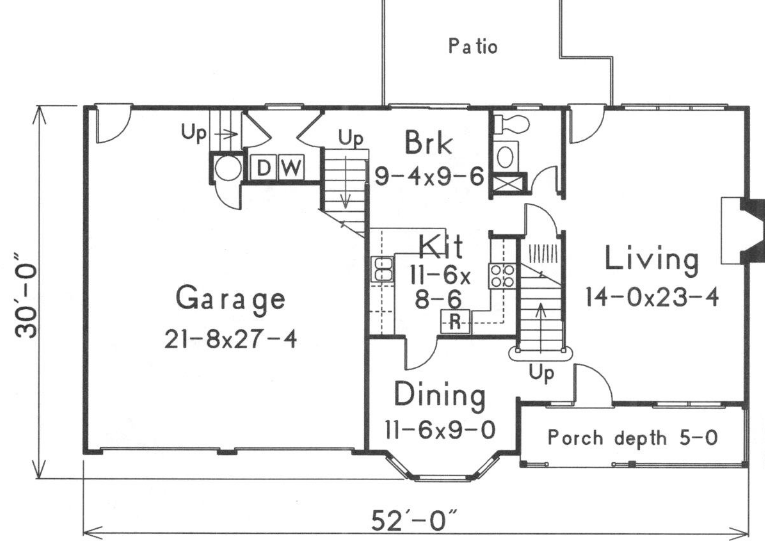

Patio
Up
D W
Up
Brk
9-4x9-6
Kit
11-6x
8-6
R
Living
14-0x23-4
Garage
21-8x27-4
Up
Dining
11-6x9-0
Porch depth 5-0
30'-0"
52'-0"

First Floor
868 sq. ft.

Plan #531-0113

Price Code C

Total Living Area: 1,992 Sq. Ft.

Home has 3 bedrooms, 2 1/2 baths, 2-car garage and crawl space foundation, drawings also include basement foundation.

Special features

- Distinct living, dining and breakfast areas
- Master bedroom boasts full end bay window and a cathedral ceiling
- Storage and laundry area located adjacent to the garage
- Bonus room over the garage for future office or playroom

Central Fireplace Brightens Family Living

Plan #531-0225

Price Code A

Total Living Area: 1,260 Sq. Ft.

Home has 3 bedrooms, 2 baths, 2-car garage and basement foundation, drawings also include crawl space and slab foundations.

Special features

- Spacious kitchen and dining area features large pantry, storage area, easy access to garage and laundry room
- Pleasant covered front porch adds a practical touch
- Master bedroom with a private bath adjoins two other bedrooms, all with plenty of closet space

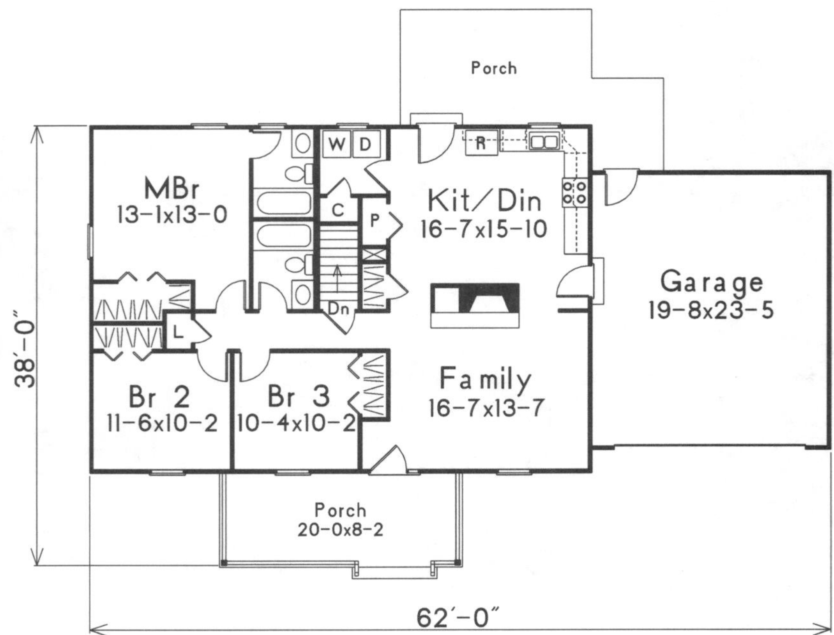
Porch
W D
R
MBr
13-1x13-0
C
P
Kit/Din
16-7x15-10
Dn
L
Garage
19-8x23-5
38'-0"
Br 2
11-6x10-2
Br 3
10-4x10-2
Family
16-7x13-7
Porch
20-0x8-2
62'-0"

TO ORDER BLUEPRINTS USE THE FORM ON PAGE 290 OR CALL TOLL-FREE **1-800-DREAM HOME** (373-2646)

Double French Doors Grace Living Room

LOWE'S

Signature SERIES

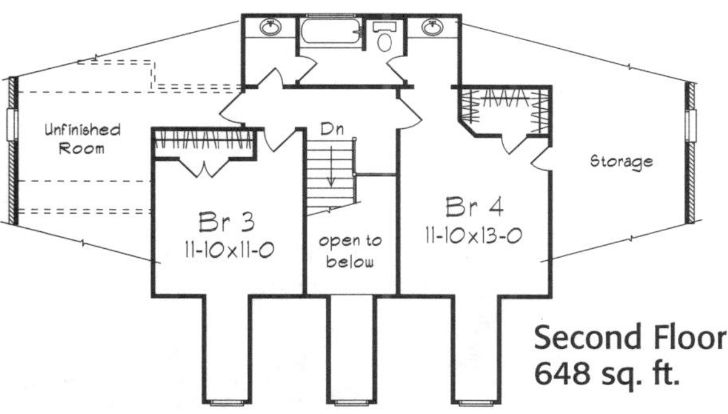
Unfinished Room
Dn
Br 3
11-10x11-0
open to below
Br 4
11-10x13-0
Storage

Second Floor
648 sq. ft.

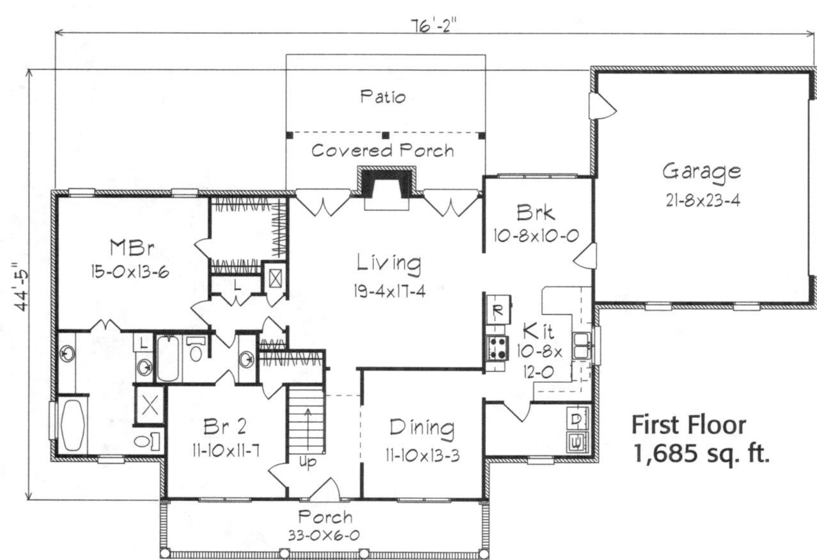
76'-2"
44'-5"
Patio
Covered Porch
Garage
21-8x23-4
Brk
10-8x10-0
MBr
15-0x13-6
Living
19-4x17-4
Kit
10-8x
12-0
Br 2
11-10x11-7
Up
Dining
11-10x13-3
Porch
33-0X6-0

First Floor
1,685 sq. ft.

Plan #531-0437

Price Code D

Total Living Area: 2,333 Sq. Ft.

Home has 4 bedrooms, 3 baths, 2-car side entry garage and slab foundation, drawings also include crawl space and partial crawl space/basement foundations.

Special features

- 9' ceilings on first floor
- Master bedroom features large walk-in closet and inviting double-door entry into spacious bath
- Convenient laundry room located near kitchen

TO ORDER BLUEPRINTS USE THE FORM ON PAGE 290 OR CALL TOLL-FREE **1-800-DREAM HOME** (373-2646)

LOWE'S

Signature SERIES

Bay Window Graces Luxury Master Bedroom

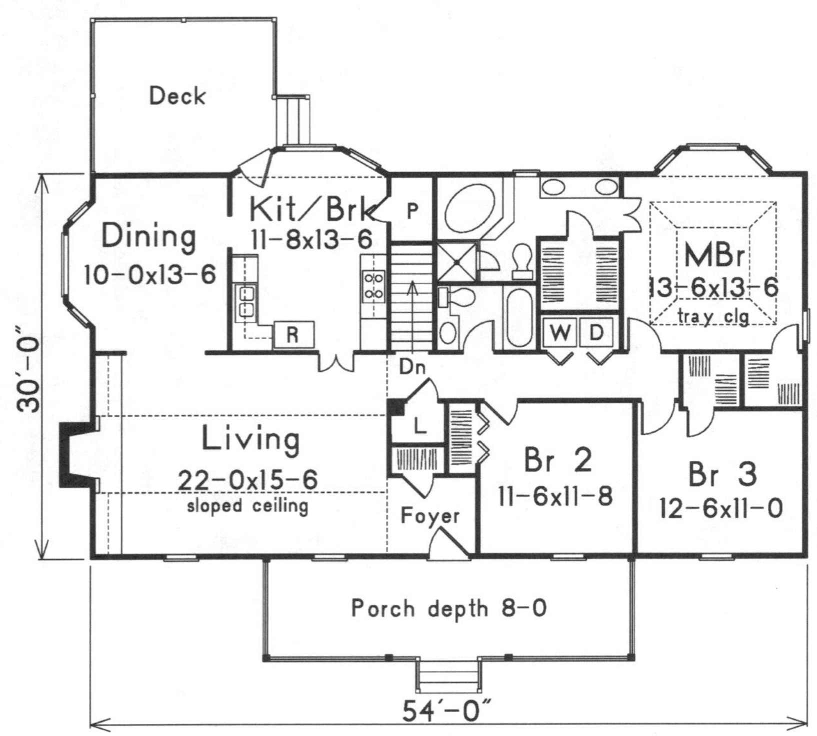
Deck
Kit/Brk
11-8x13-6
P
Dining
10-0x13-6
R
MBr
13-6x13-6
tray clg
W
D
Dn
30'-0"
L
Living
22-0x15-6
sloped ceiling
Br 2
11-6x11-8
Br 3
12-6x11-0
Foyer
Porch depth 8-0
54'-0"

Plan #531-0112

Price Code C

Total Living Area: 1,668 Sq. Ft.

Home has 3 bedrooms, 2 baths, 2-car drive under garage and basement foundation.

Special features

- Large bay windows in breakfast area, master bedroom and dining room
- Extensive walk-in closets and storage spaces throughout the home
- Handy entry covered porch
- Large living room has fireplace, built-in bookshelves and sloped ceiling

Country-Style Home With Large Front Porch

LOWE'S

Signature SERIES

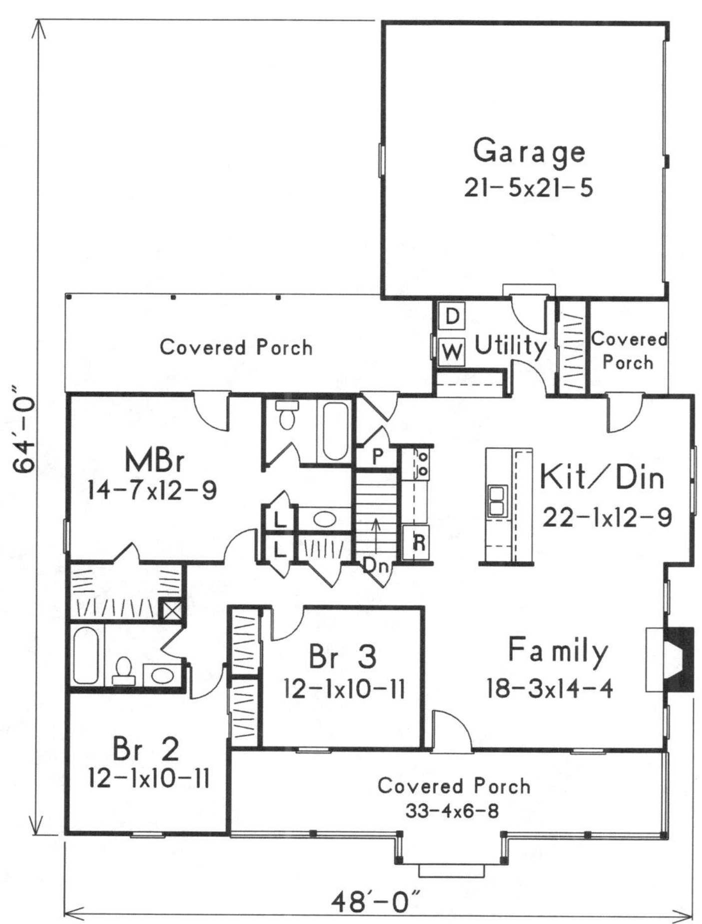

Garage
21-5x21-5
Covered Porch
D
W
Utility
Covered Porch
MBr
14-7x12-9
P
Kit/Din
22-1x12-9
L
L
R
Dn
Br 3
12-1x10-11
Family
18-3x14-4
Br 2
12-1x10-11
Covered Porch
33-4x6-8
64'-0"
48'-0"

Plan #531-0249

Price Code B

Total Living Area: 1,501 Sq. Ft.

Home has 3 bedrooms, 2 baths, 2-car side entry garage and basement foundation, drawings also include crawl space and slab foundations.

Special features

- Spacious kitchen with dining area open to the outdoors
- Convenient utility room adjacent to garage
- Master suite with private bath, dressing area and access to large covered porch
- Large family room creates openness

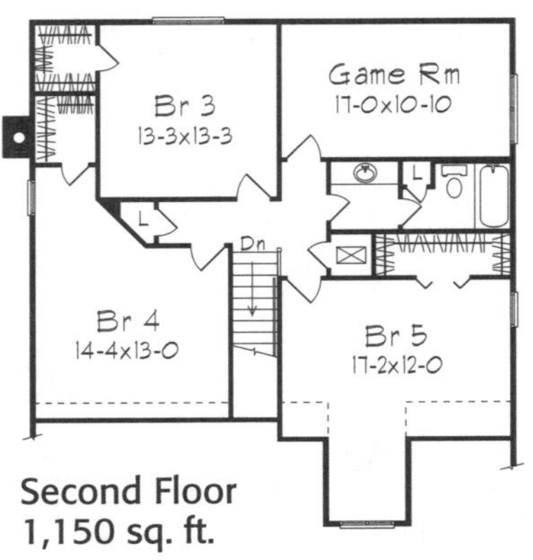
Game Rm
17-0x10-10
Br 3
13-3x13-3
Dn
Br 4
14-4x13-0
Br 5
17-2x12-0

Second Floor
1,150 sq. ft.

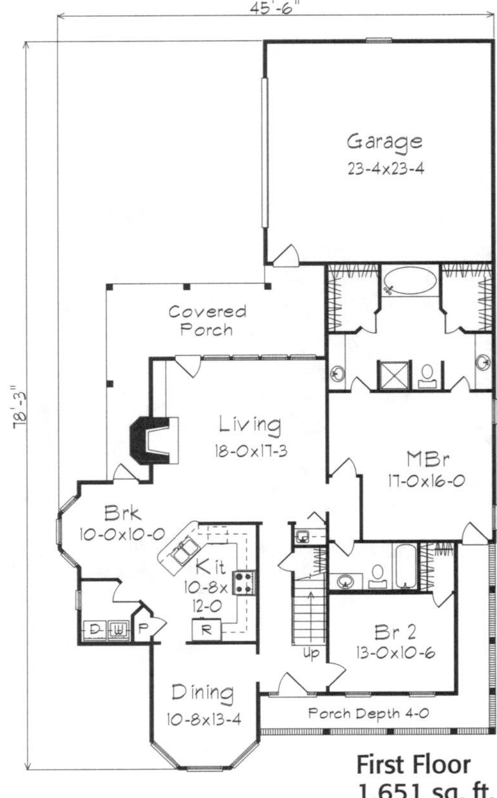
45'-6"
78'-3"
Garage
23-4x23-4
Covered
Porch
Living
18-0x17-3
MBr
17-0x16-0
Brk
10-0x10-0
Kit
10-8x
12-0
Br 2
13-0x10-6
Up
Dining
10-8x13-4
Porch Depth 4-0

First Floor
1,651 sq. ft.

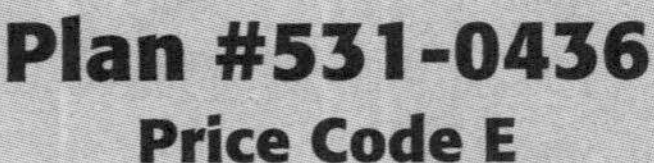

Plan #531-0436

Price Code E

Total Living Area: 2,801 Sq. Ft.

Home has 5 bedrooms, 3 baths, 2-car side entry garage and slab foundation.

Special features

- 9' ceilings on first floor
- Full view dining bay with elegant circle-top windows
- Wrap-around porches provide outdoor exposure in all directions
- Secluded master bedroom with double vanities and walk-in closets
- Convenient game room

TO ORDER BLUEPRINTS USE THE FORM ON PAGE 290 OR CALL TOLL-FREE **1-800-DREAM HOME** (373-2646)

Two-Story Foyer Adds To Country Charm

LOWE'S

Signature SERIES

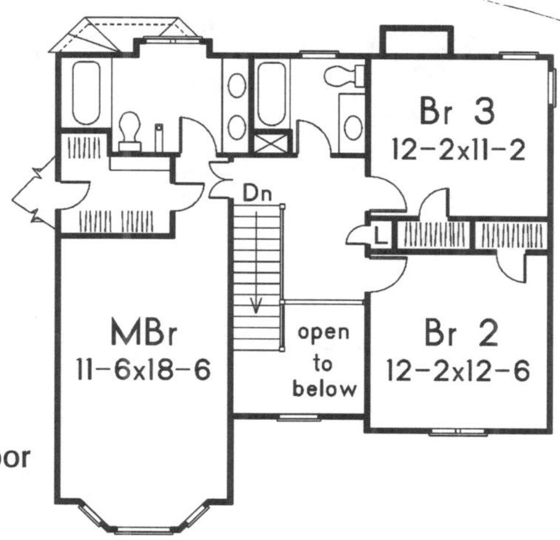

Br 3
12-2x11-2

Dn

L

MBr
11-6x18-6

open to below

Br 2
12-2x12-6

Second Floor
899 sq. ft.

Plan #531-0122

Price Code C

Total Living Area: 1,922 Sq. Ft.

Home has 3 bedrooms, 2 1/2 baths, 2-car garage and basement foundation.

Special features

- Varied front elevation features numerous accents
- Master bedroom suite well secluded with double-door entry and private bath
- Formal living and dining rooms located off the entry

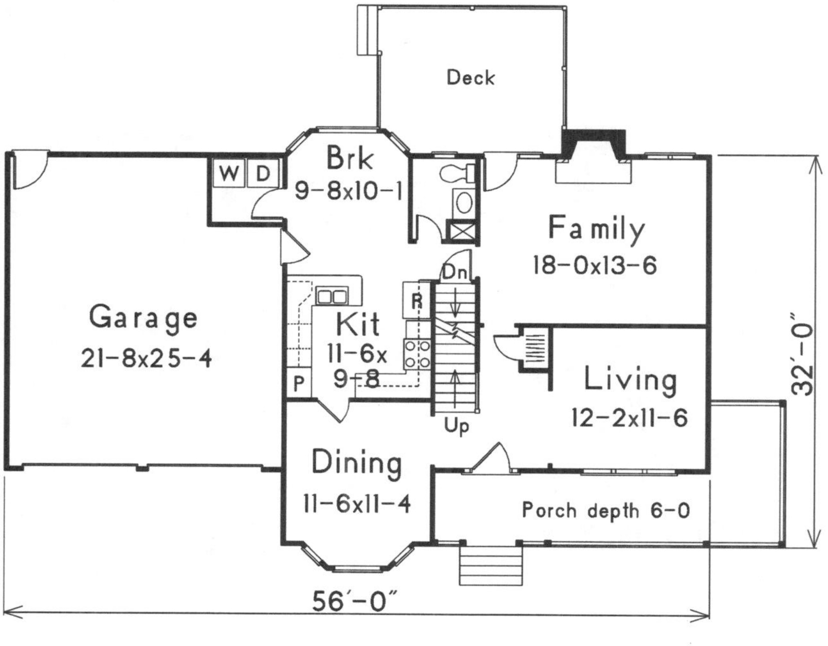

Deck

W D

Brk
9-8x10-1

Family
18-0x13-6

Dn

R

Garage
21-8x25-4

Kit
11-6x
9-8

P

Up

Living
12-2x11-6

32'-0"

Dining
11-6x11-4

Porch depth 6-0

56'-0"

First Floor
1,023 sq. ft.

LOWE'S

Signature
SERIES

Rambling Ranch With Country Charm

Plan #531-0748

Price Code D

Total Living Area: 2,514 Sq. Ft.

Home has 3 bedrooms, 2 baths, 3-car side entry garage and walk-out basement foundation.

Special features

- An expansive porch welcomes you to the foyer, spacious dining area with bay and a gallery-sized hall with plant shelf above
- A highly functional U-shaped kitchen is open to a bayed breakfast room, study and family room with a 46' vista
- The family will enjoy time spent in the vaulted rear sunroom with fireplace
- Oversized garage with workshop/ storage area

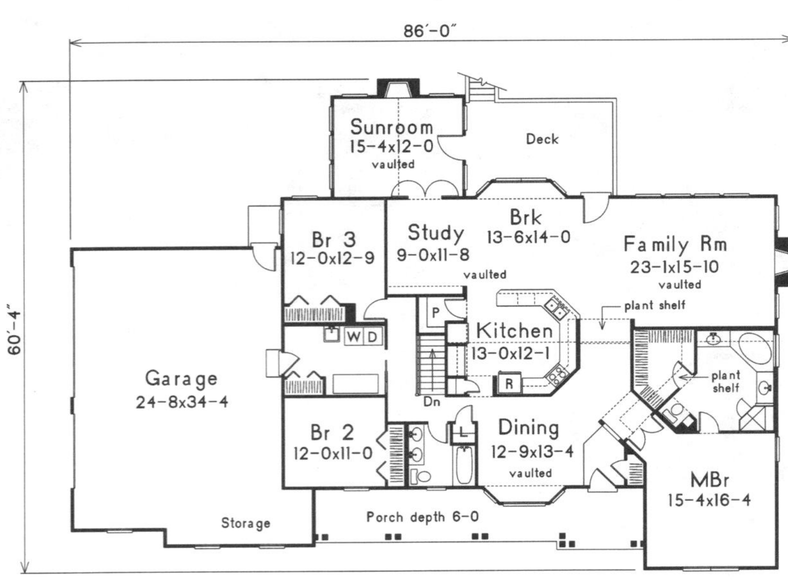
86'-0"
60'-4"
Sunroom
15-4x12-0
vaulted
Deck
Brk
13-6x14-0
Br 3
12-0x12-9
Study
9-0x11-8
vaulted
Family Rm
23-1x15-10
vaulted
plant shelf
W D
P
Kitchen
13-0x12-1
R
plant shelf
Garage
24-8x34-4
Dn
Br 2
12-0x11-0
L
Dining
12-9x13-4
vaulted
MBr
15-4x16-4
Storage
Porch depth 6-0

TO ORDER BLUEPRINTS USE THE FORM ON PAGE 290 OR CALL TOLL-FREE **1-800-DREAM HOME** (373-2646)

Wrap-Around Porch Adds Country Charm

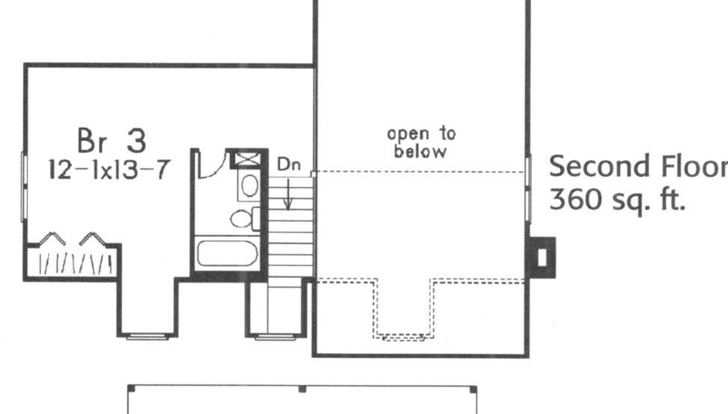
Br 3
12-1x13-7
Dn
open to below

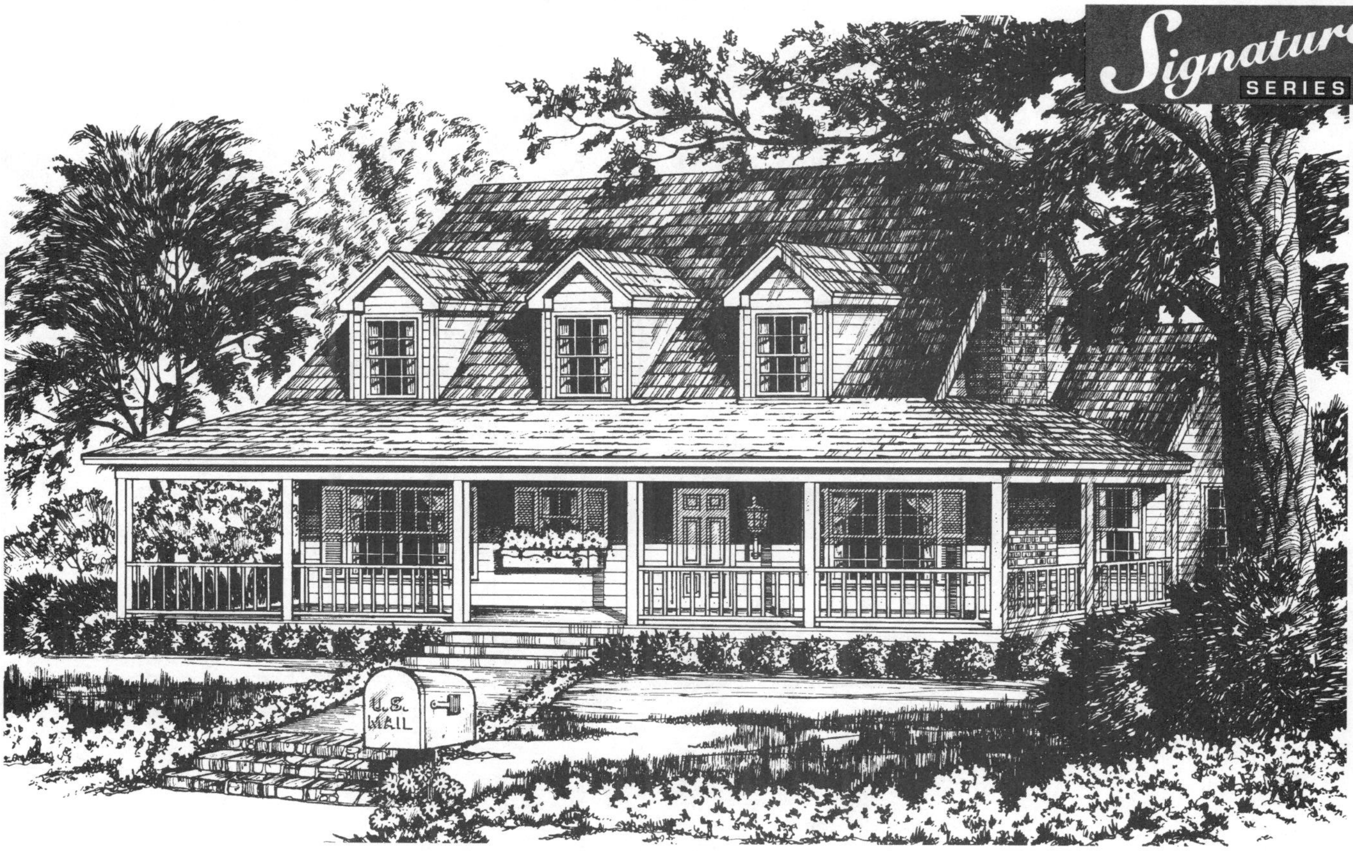

Second Floor
360 sq. ft.

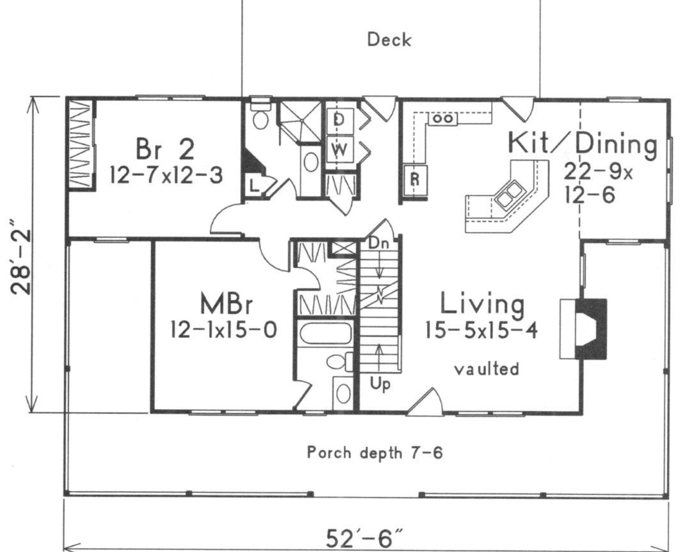
Deck
Br 2
12-7x12-3
L
D
W
R
Kit/Dining
22-9x
12-6
Dn
MBr
12-1x15-0
Living
15-5x15-4
vaulted
Up
Porch depth 7-6
28'-2"
52'-6"

First Floor
1,259 sq. ft.

Plan #531-0221

Price Code B

Total Living Area: 1,619 Sq. Ft.

Home has 3 bedrooms, 3 baths and basement foundation, drawings also include crawl space and slab foundations.

Special features

- Private second floor bedroom and bath
- Kitchen features a snack bar and adjacent dining area
- Master bedroom with private bath
- Centrally located washer and dryer

LOWE'S
Signature
SERIES

Compact Design Offers Privacy

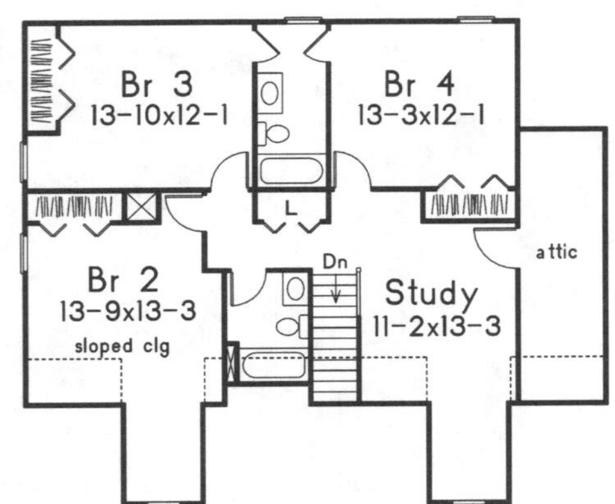
Br 3
13-10x12-1
Br 4
13-3x12-1
L
Dn
attic
Br 2
13-9x13-3
sloped clg
Study
11-2x13-3

Second Floor
1,102 sq. ft.

Plan #531-0183

Price Code E

Total Living Area: 2,847 Sq. Ft.

Home has 4 bedrooms, 3 1/2 baths, 2-car garage and basement foundation, drawings also include slab and crawl space foundations.

Special features

- Secluded first floor master bedroom includes an oversized window and a large walk-in closet
- Extensive attic storage and closet space
- Spacious second floor bedrooms, two of which share a private bath
- Great starter home with option to finish the second floor as needed

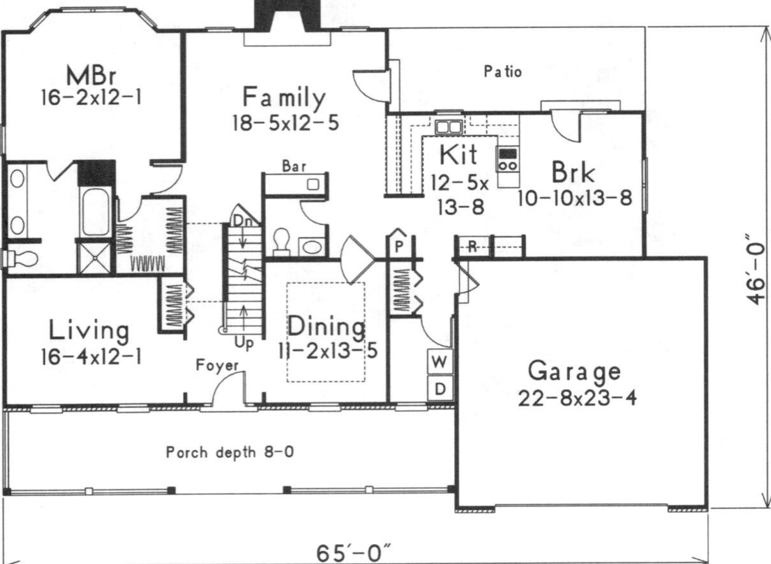
MBr
16-2x12-1
Family
18-5x12-5
Patio
Bar
Kit
12-5x
13-8
Brk
10-10x13-8
Dn
P
R
Living
16-4x12-1
Up
Dining
11-2x13-5
Foyer
W
D
Garage
22-8x23-4
Porch depth 8-0
46′-0″
65′-0″

First Floor
1,745 sq. ft.

Efficient Split-Level Design

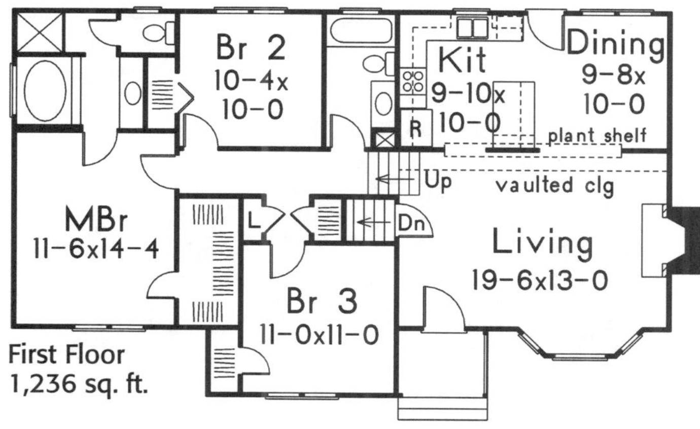
Br 2
10–4x
10–0
Kit
9–10x
10–0
Dining
9–8x
10–0
R
plant shelf
Up
vaulted clg
MBr
11–6x14–4
L
Dn
Living
19–6x13–0
Br 3
11–0x11–0
First Floor
1,236 sq. ft.

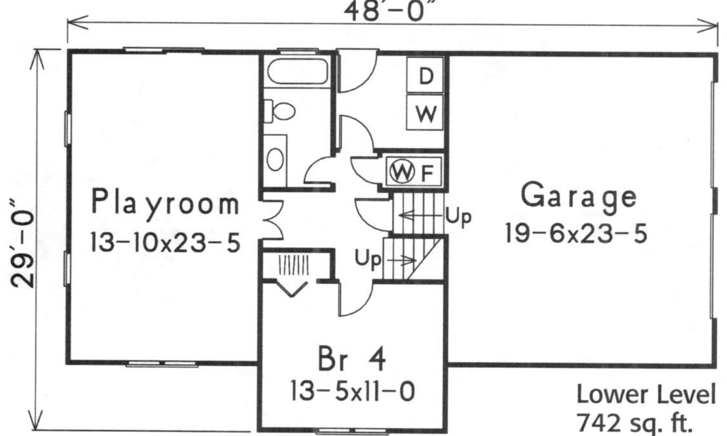
48′–0″
29′–0″
D
W
W
F
Playroom
13–10x23–5
Garage
19–6x23–5
Up
Up
Br 4
13–5x11–0
Lower Level
742 sq. ft.

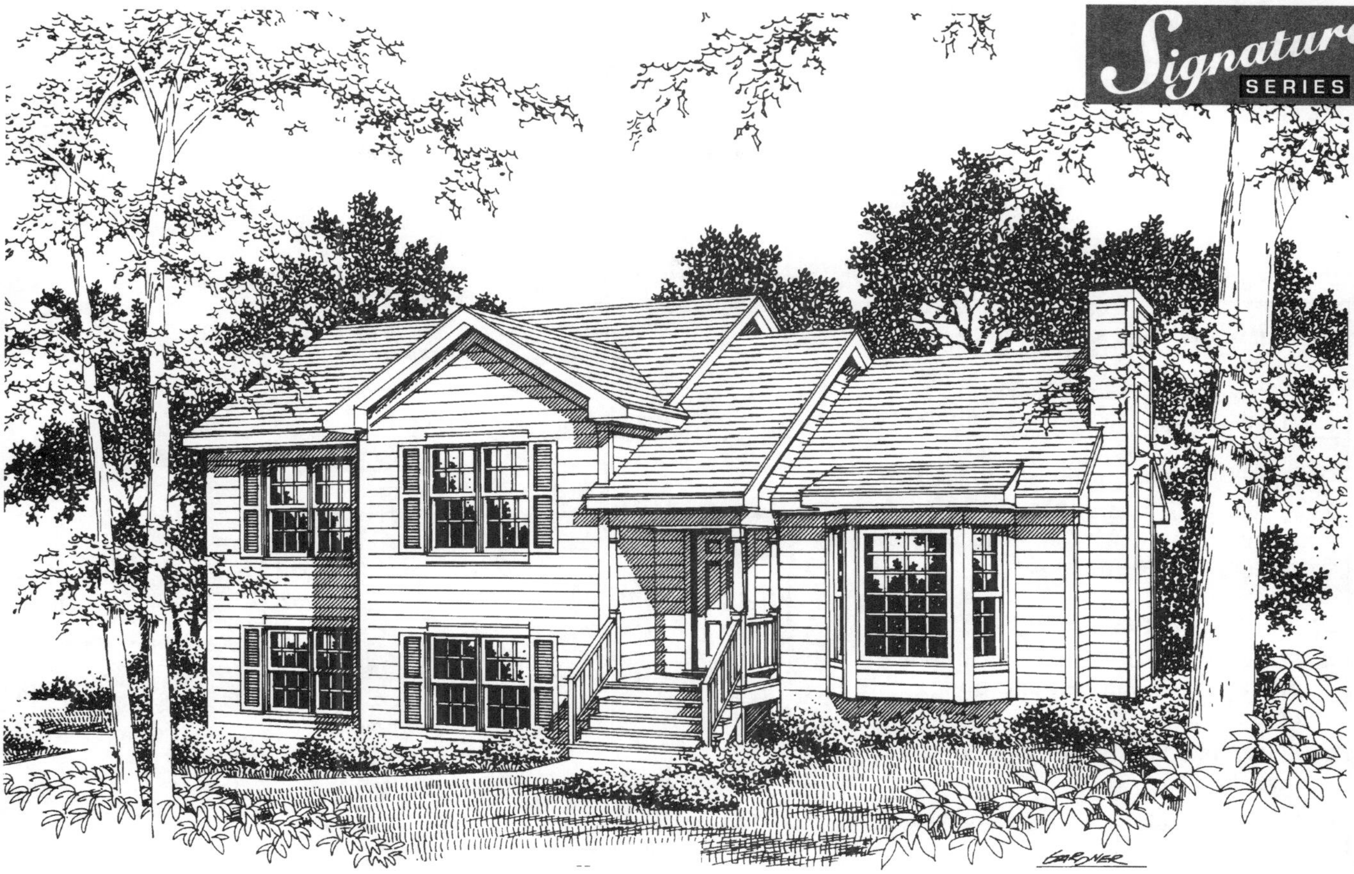

Plan #531-0248

Price Code C

Total Living Area: 1,978 Sq. Ft.

Home has 3 bedrooms, 2 baths, 2-car drive under garage and partial basement/ slab foundation.

Special features

- Master bedroom includes walk-in closet and private full bath
- Entry opens into large living area with bay window, fireplace and plant shelf
- Open kitchen/dining area includes bar and access to deck

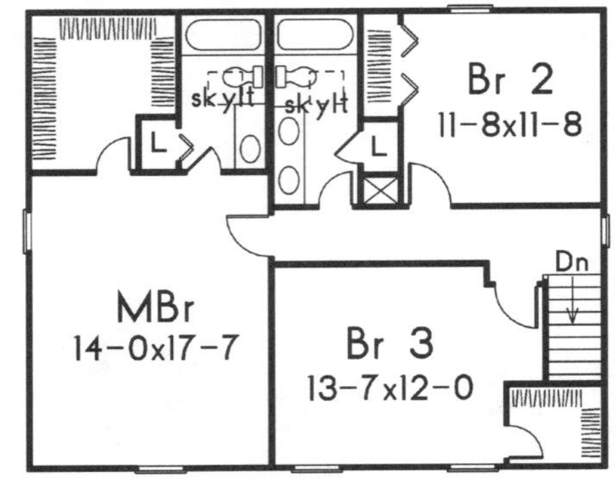
Br 2
11-8x11-8
skylt
skylt
L
L
MBr
14-0x17-7
Br 3
13-7x12-0
Dn

Second Floor
938 sq. ft.

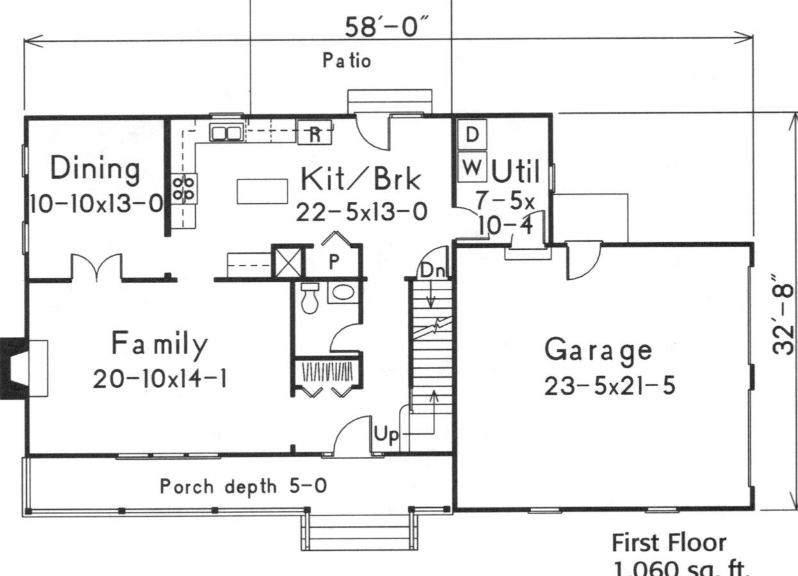
58′-0″
Patio
R
D
W
Util
7-5x
10-4
Dining
10-10x13-0
Kit/Brk
22-5x13-0
P
Dn
Family
20-10x14-1
Garage
23-5x21-5
32′-8″
Up
Porch depth 5-0

First Floor
1,060 sq. ft.

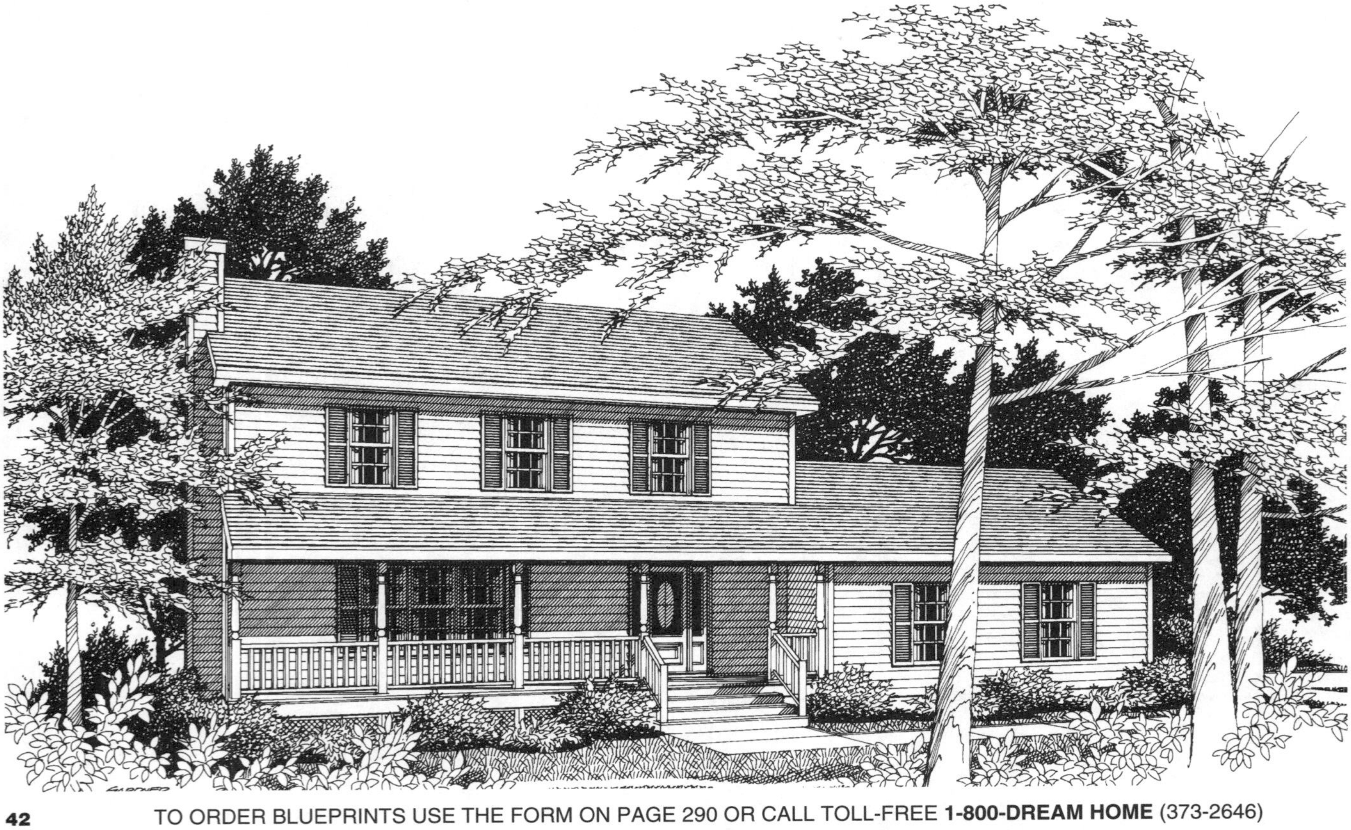

Plan #531-0218

Price Code D

Total Living Area: 1,998 Sq. Ft.

Home has 3 bedrooms, 2 1/2 baths, 2-car side entry garage and basement foundation, drawings also include crawl space and slab foundations.

Special features

- Large family room features fireplace and access to kitchen and dining area
- Skylights add daylight to second floor baths
- Utility room conveniently located near garage and kitchen
- Kitchen/breakfast area includes pantry, island work space and easy access to the patio

Distinctive Two-Level Porch

LOWE'S

Signature
SERIES

Br 2
11-4x14-4

Br 3
13-0x14-4

L

Dn

open to below

Br 4
13-0x11-4

Porch depth 6-0

Second Floor
855 sq. ft.

Plan #531-0305

Price Code E

Total Living Area: 2,605 Sq. Ft.

Home has 4 bedrooms, 2 1/2 baths, 2-car side entry garage and slab foundation, drawings also include crawl space and basement foundations.

Special features

- Master bedroom boasts vaulted ceiling and transom picture window which lights sitting area
- Country kitchen features appliances set in between brick dividers and beamed ceiling
- Living room features built-in bookcases, fireplace and raised tray ceiling

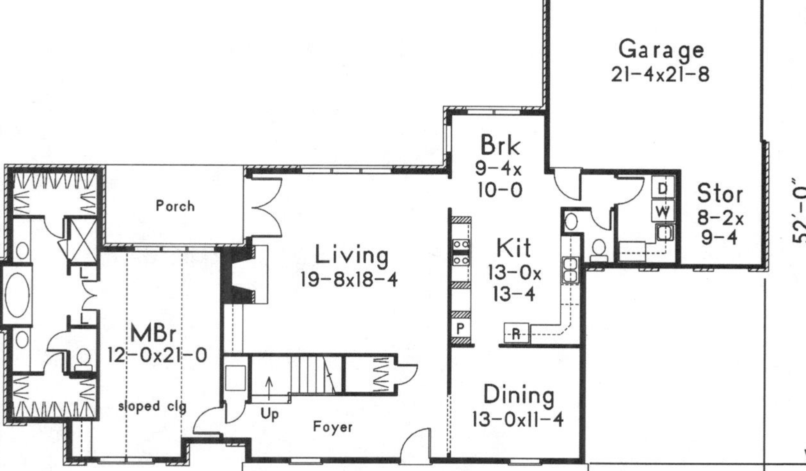

Garage
21-4x21-8
Brk
9-4x
10-0
Stor
8-2x
9-4
D
W
52'-0"
Porch
Living
19-8x18-4
Kit
13-0x
13-4
P
R
MBr
12-0x21-0
sloped clg
Up
Foyer
Dining
13-0x11-4
Porch depth 6-0
77'-0"

First Floor
1,750 sq. ft.

LOWE'S
Signature
SERIES

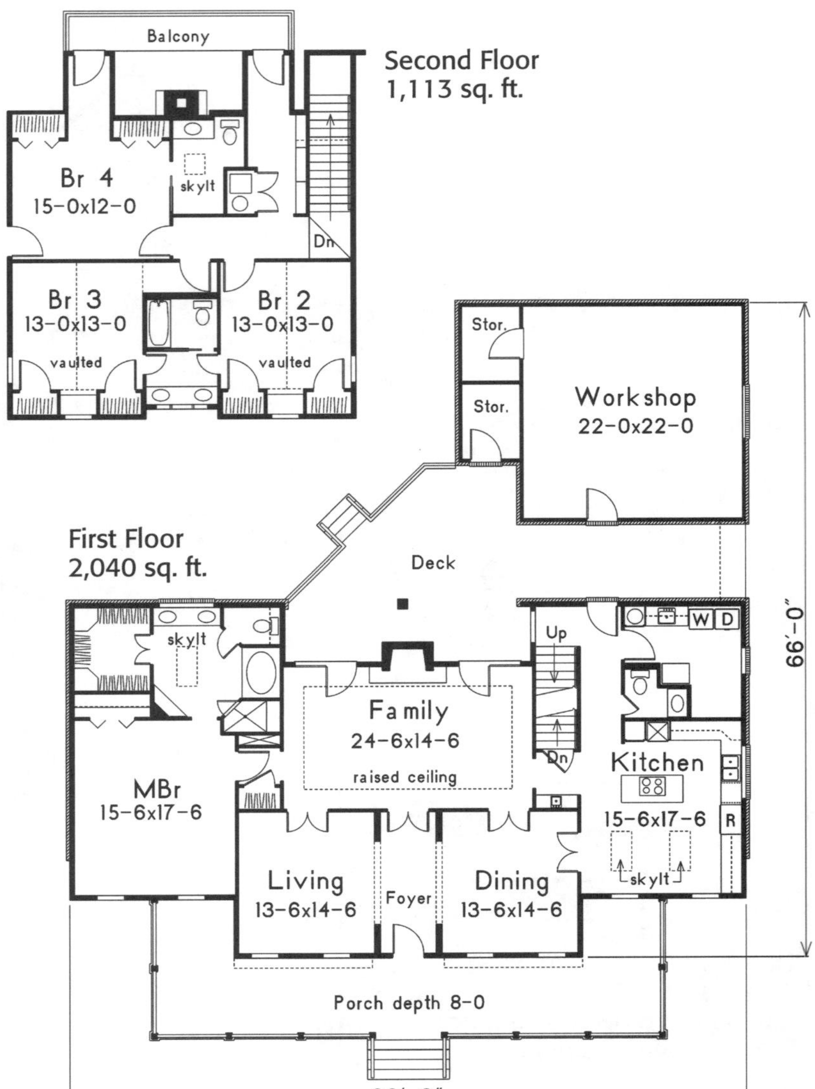
Balcony
Second Floor
1,113 sq. ft.
Br 4
15-0x12-0
skylt
Dn
Br 3
13-0x13-0
vaulted
Br 2
13-0x13-0
vaulted
Stor.
Stor.
Workshop
22-0x22-0
First Floor
2,040 sq. ft.
Deck
skylt
Up
W D
Family
24-6x14-6
raised ceiling
Dn
Kitchen
15-6x17-6
R
MBr
15-6x17-6
skylt
Living
13-6x14-6
Foyer
Dining
13-6x14-6
Porch depth 8-0
66'-0"
66'-0"

Plan #531-0307

Price Code E

Total Living Area: 3,153 Sq. Ft.

Home has 4 bedrooms, 3 1/2 baths, 2-car drive under garage and basement foundation, drawings also include crawl space and slab foundations.

Special features

- Master suite with full amenities
- Energy efficient design with 2" x 6" exterior walls
- Covered breezeway and front and rear porches
- Full-sized workshop and storage with garage below, a unique combination

TO ORDER BLUEPRINTS USE THE FORM ON PAGE 290 OR CALL TOLL-FREE **1-800-DREAM HOME** (373-2646)

Wrap-Around Veranda Softens Country Home

LOWE'S

Signature SERIES

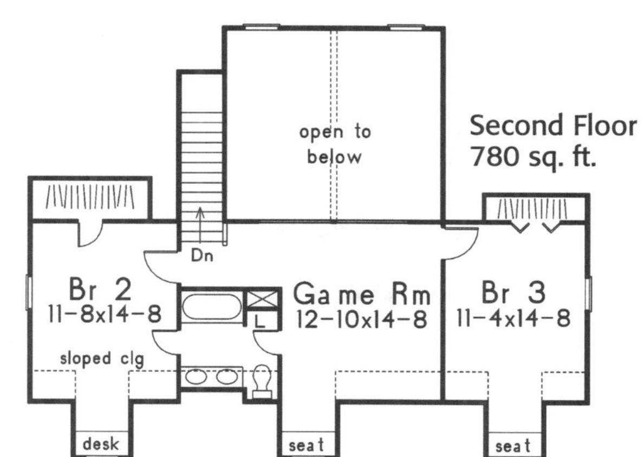
open to below
Dn
Br 2
11-8x14-8
sloped clg
Game Rm
12-10x14-8
L
Br 3
11-4x14-8
desk
seat
seat

Second Floor
780 sq. ft.

Plan #531-0143

Price Code E

Total Living Area: 2,449 Sq. Ft.

Home has 3 bedrooms, 2 1/2 baths, 2-car detached garage and slab foundation, drawings also include crawl space foundation.

Special features

- Striking living area features fireplace flanked with windows, cathedral ceiling and balcony
- First floor master bedroom with twin walk-in closets and large linen storage
- Dormers add space for desks or seats

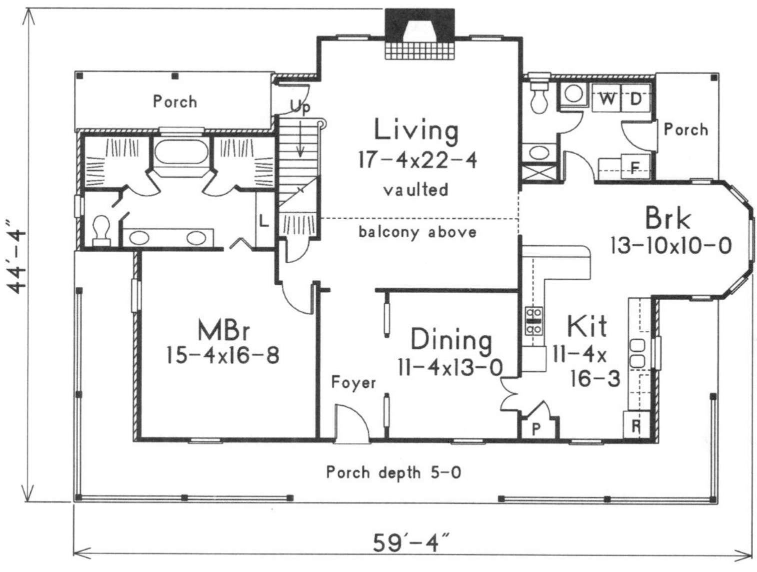
Porch
Up
Living
17-4x22-4
vaulted
balcony above
W D
Porch
F
L
Brk
13-10x10-0
MBr
15-4x16-8
Dining
11-4x13-0
Foyer
Kit
11-4x
16-3
P
R
Porch depth 5-0
44'-4"
59'-4"

First Floor
1,669 sq. ft.

LOWE'S

Signature
SERIES

Inviting Porch On All Sides

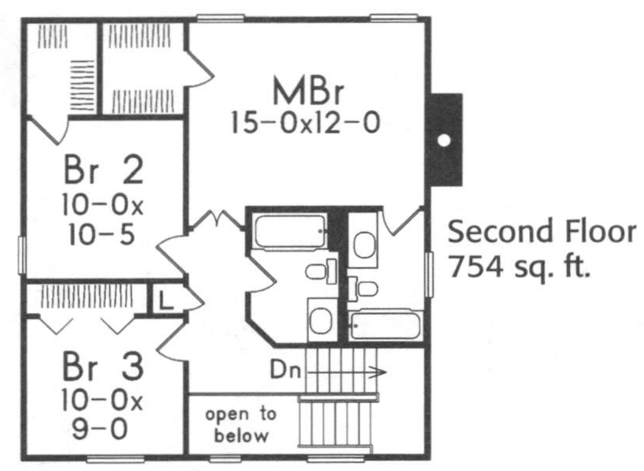
MBr
15-0x12-0
Br 2
10-0x
10-5
L
Br 3
10-0x
9-0
Dn
open to
below
Second Floor
754 sq. ft.

Plan #531-0480

Price Code B

Total Living Area: 1,618 Sq. Ft.

Home has 3 bedrooms, 2 1/2 baths, 1-car garage and basement foundation.

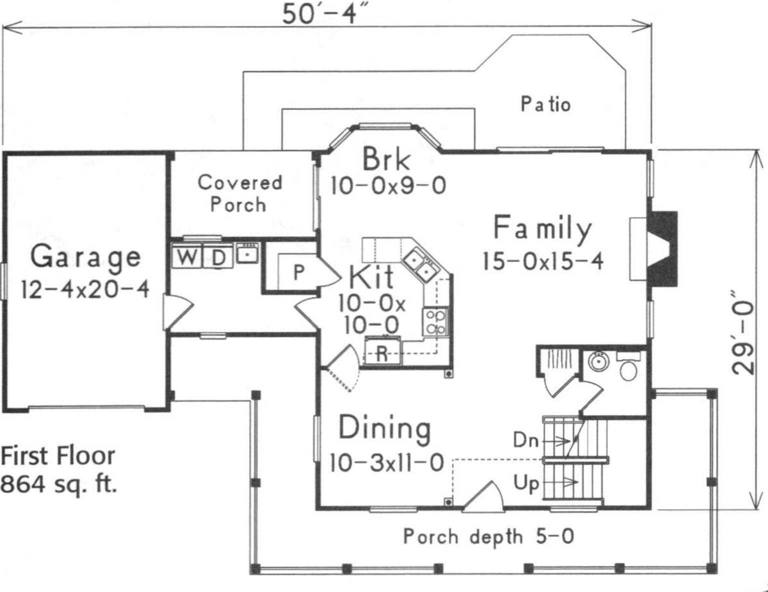
50'-4"
Patio
Brk
10-0x9-0
Covered
Porch
Family
15-0x15-4
Garage
12-4x20-4
W
D
P
Kit
10-0x
10-0
R
Dining
10-3x11-0
Dn
Up
29'-0"
Porch depth 5-0
First Floor
864 sq. ft.

Special features

- Wrap-around porch offers a covered passageway to the garage
- Dramatic two-story entry, with balcony above and staircase provide an expansive feel with an added decorative oval window
- Dazzling kitchen features walk-in pantry, convenient laundry and covered rear porch

TO ORDER BLUEPRINTS USE THE FORM ON PAGE 290 OR CALL TOLL-FREE **1-800-DREAM HOME** (373-2646)

Large Front Porch Adds Welcoming Appeal

LOWE'S

Signature SERIES

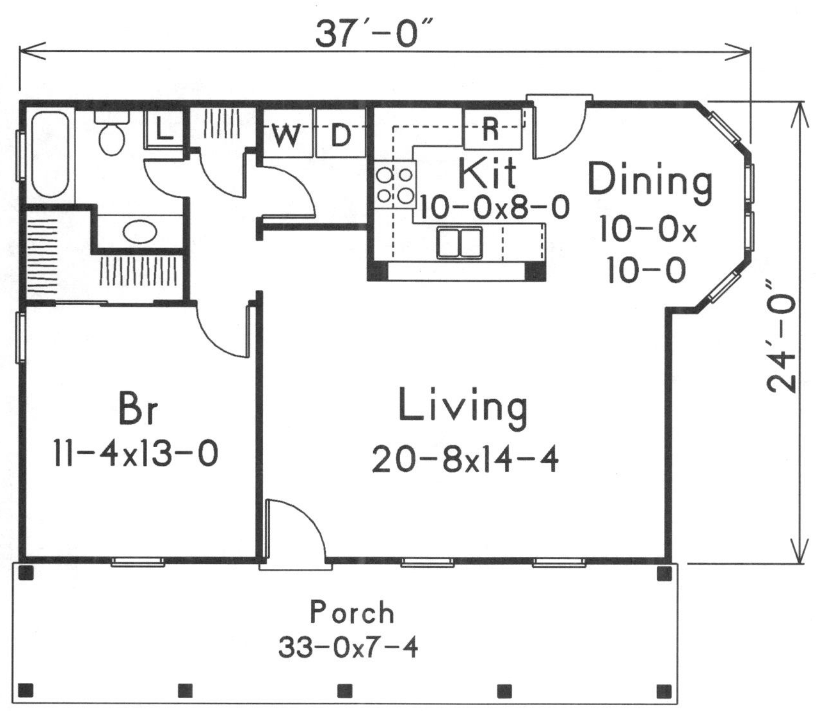
37′-0″
W
D
R
L
Kit
10-0x8-0
Dining
10-0x
10-0
24′-0″
Br
11-4x13-0
Living
20-8x14-4
Porch
33-0x7-4

Plan #531-0241

Price Code AAA

Total Living Area: 829 Sq. Ft.

Home has 1 bedroom, 1 bath and slab foundation.

Special features

- U-shaped kitchen opens into living area by a 42" high counter
- Oversized bay window and French door accent dining room
- Gathering space is created by the large living room
- Convenient utility room and linen closet

LOWE'S Signature SERIES

Stylish Ranch With Rustic Charm

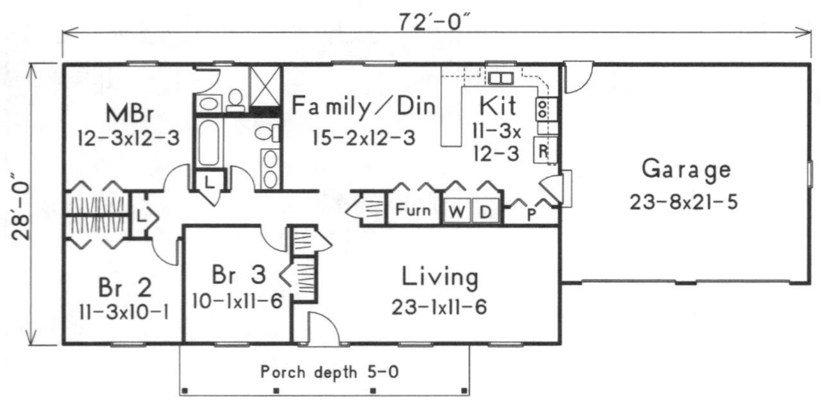
72'-0"
28'-0"
MBr
12-3x12-3
Family/Din
15-2x12-3
Kit
11-3x
12-3
R
L
L
Furn
W
D
P
Garage
23-8x21-5
Br 2
11-3x10-1
Br 3
10-1x11-6
Living
23-1x11-6
Porch depth 5-0

Plan #531-0515

Price Code A

Total Living Area: 1,344 Sq. Ft.

Home has 3 bedrooms, 2 baths, 2-car garage and crawl space foundation, drawings also include basement and slab foundations.

Special features

- Family/dining room with sliding door
- Master bedroom and private bath with shower
- Hall bath includes double vanity for added convenience
- Kitchen features U-shaped design, large pantry and laundry area

A Traditional For Lots Of Living

LOWE'S

Signature
SERIES

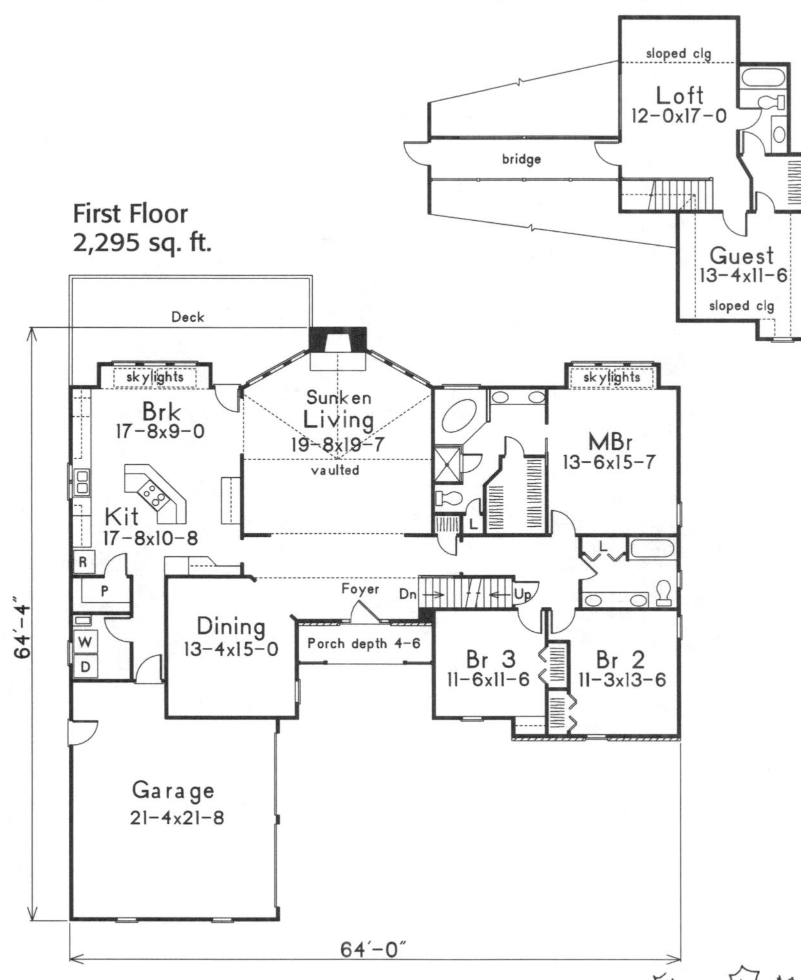
Second Floor
645 sq. ft.
sloped clg
Loft
12-0x17-0
bridge
Guest
13-4x11-6
sloped clg
First Floor
2,295 sq. ft.
Deck
skylights
Brk
17-8x9-0
Sunken
Living
19-8x19-7
vaulted
skylights
MBr
13-6x15-7
Kit
17-8x10-8
L
L
R
P
Foyer
Dn
Up
Dining
13-4x15-0
Porch depth 4-6
Br 3
11-6x11-6
Br 2
11-3x13-6
W
D
Garage
21-4x21-8
64'-4"
64'-0"

Plan #531-0168

Price Code E

Total Living Area: 2,940 Sq. Ft.

Home has 4 bedrooms, 3 baths, 2-car side entry garage and basement foundation.

Special features

- Two sets of twin dormers add outdoor charm while lighting the indoors
- Massive central foyer leads into sunken living room below and access to second floor attic
- Private master suite, complete with a luxurious corner tub and large walk-in closet
- A novel bridge provides view of living room below and access to second floor attic

Signature
SERIES

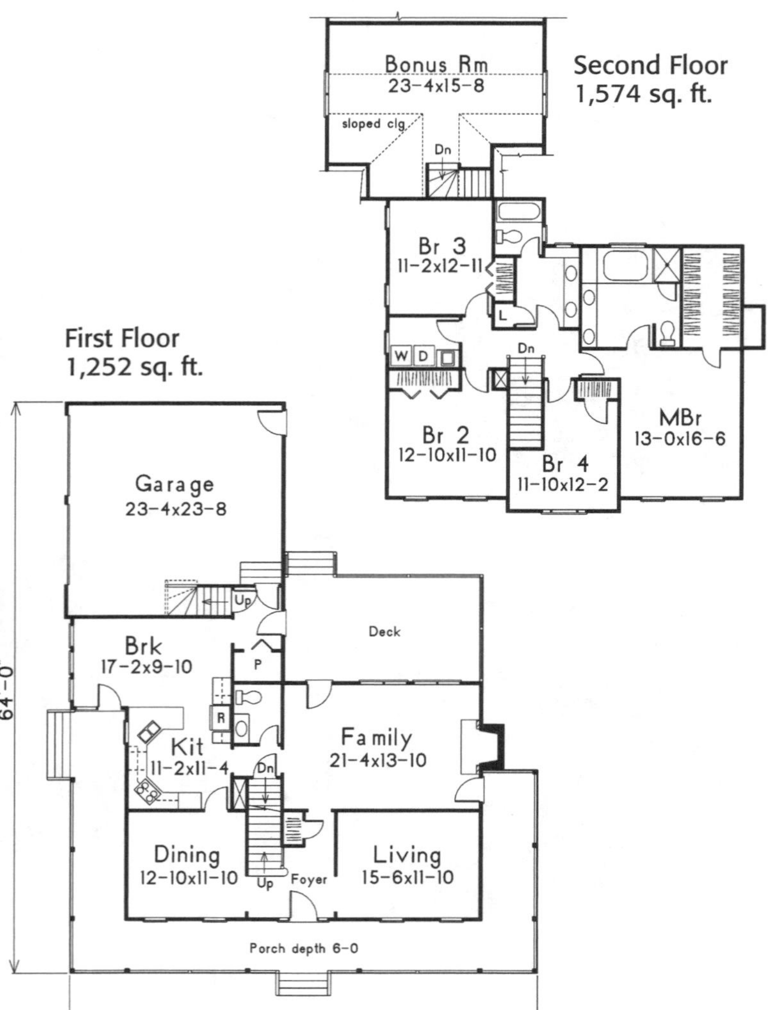
Bonus Rm
23-4x15-8
sloped clg.
Dn
Second Floor
1,574 sq. ft.
Br 3
11-2x12-11
L
W D
Dn
Br 2
12-10x11-10
Br 4
11-10x12-2
MBr
13-0x16-6
First Floor
1,252 sq. ft.
Garage
23-4x23-8
Up
Deck
Brk
17-2x9-10
P
R
Kit
11-2x11-4
Dn
Family
21-4x13-10
Dining
12-10x11-10
Up
Foyer
Living
15-6x11-10
Porch depth 6-0
64'-0"
51'-0"

Plan #531-0141

Price Code E

Total Living Area: 2,826 Sq. Ft.

Home has 4 bedrooms, 2 1/2 baths, 2-car side entry garage and basement foundation.

Special features

- Wrap-around covered porch is accessible from family and breakfast rooms in addition to front entrance
- Bonus room with separate entrance suitable for an office or private accommodations
- Large, full-windowed breakfast room

TO ORDER BLUEPRINTS USE THE FORM ON PAGE 290 OR CALL TOLL-FREE **1-800-DREAM HOME** (373-2646)

Master Bedroom Provides Retreat

LOWE'S

Signature SERIES

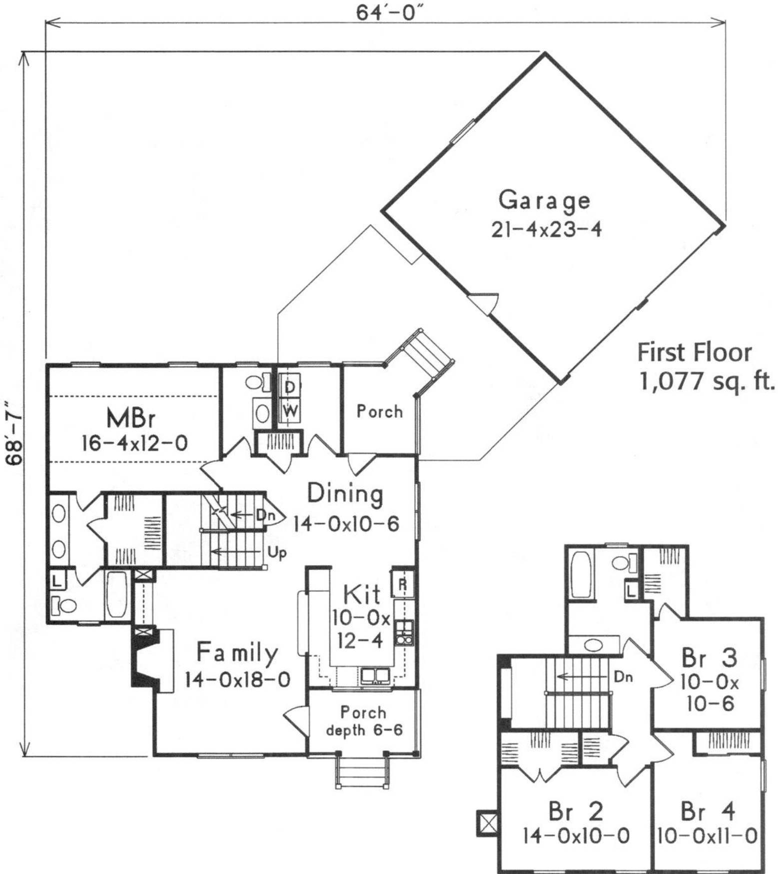
64'-0"
68'-7"
Garage
21-4x23-4
MBr
16-4x12-0
D
W
Porch
Dining
14-0x10-6
Dn
Up
Kit
10-0x
12-4
R
L
Family
14-0x18-0
Porch
depth 6-6
L
Br 3
10-0x
10-6
Dn
Br 2
14-0x10-0
Br 4
10-0x11-0

First Floor
1,077 sq. ft.

Second Floor
610 sq. ft.

Plan #531-0490

Price Code B

Total Living Area: 1,687 Sq. Ft.

Home has 4 bedrooms, 2 1/2 baths, 2-car detached garage and slab foundation.

Special features

- Family room with built-in cabinet and fireplace is focal point of this home
- U-shaped kitchen has bar that opens to the family room
- Back porch opens to dining room and leads to the garage via a walkway
- Convenient laundry room

Bright Entrance Enlarges Foyer

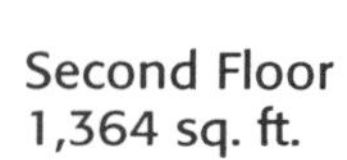
Second Floor
1,364 sq. ft.

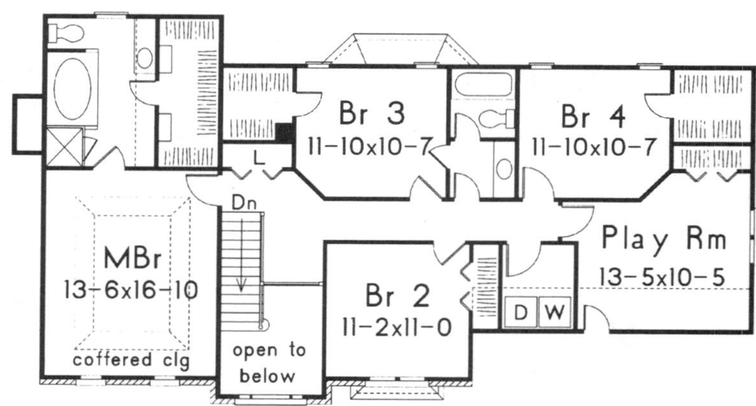
Br 3
11-10x10-7
Br 4
11-10x10-7
L
Dn
MBr
13-6x16-10
coffered clg
open to below
Br 2
11-2x11-0
Play Rm
13-5x10-5
D
W

Plan #531-0131

Price Code D

Total Living Area: 2,336 Sq. Ft.

Home has 4 bedrooms, 2 1/2 baths, 2-car garage and basement foundation.

Special features

- Two-story foyer with large second floor window creates a sunny, spacious entrance area
- Bonus area above the garage for a playroom or hobby area
- Laundry is conveniently located on second floor adjacent to bedrooms
- Master bath has a vaulted ceiling and luxurious appointments
- Coffered ceiling in master bedroom

First Floor
972 sq. ft.

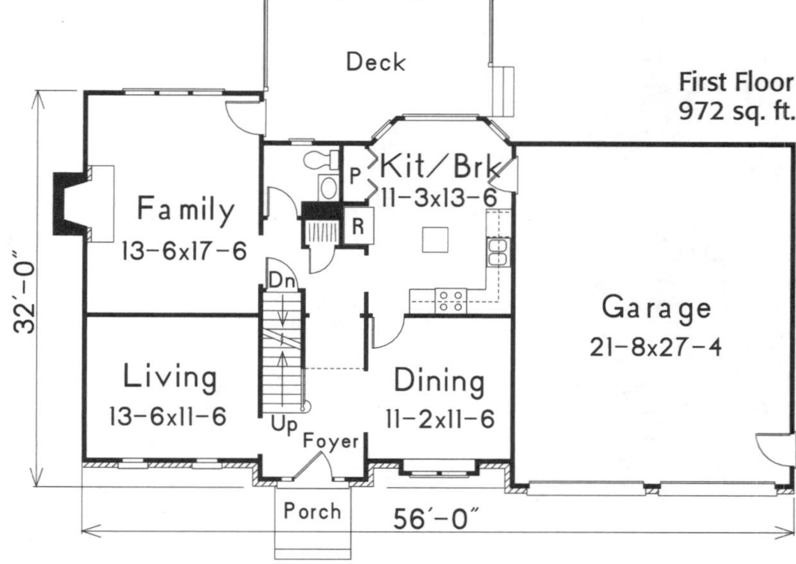
Deck
P
Kit/Brk
11-3x13-6
R
Family
13-6x17-6
Dn
Garage
21-8x27-4
32'-0"
Living
13-6x11-6
Up
Foyer
Dining
11-2x11-6
Porch
56'-0"

Atrium's Dramatic Ambiance

LOWE'S

Signature
SERIES

Plan #531-0370

Price Code C

Total Living Area: 1,721 Sq. Ft.

Home has 3 bedrooms, 2 baths, 3-car garage and walk-out basement foundation, drawings also include crawl space and slab foundations.

Special features

- Roof dormers add great curb appeal
- Vaulted great room and dining room immersed in light from atrium window wall
- Breakfast room opens onto covered porch
- Functionally designed kitchen

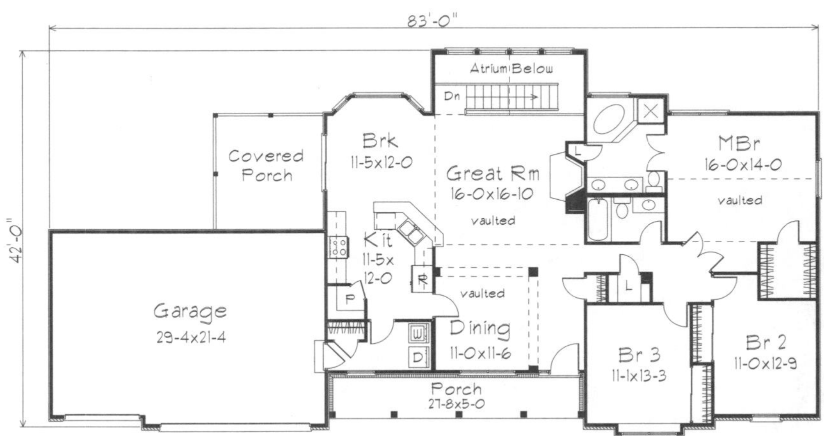
83'-0"
42'-0"
Atrium Below
Dn
Covered Porch
Brk 11-5x12-0
Great Rm 16-0x16-10 vaulted
MBr 16-0x14-0 vaulted
Kit 11-5x 12-0
Garage 29-4x21-4
vaulted
Dining 11-0x11-6
Porch 27-8x5-0
Br 3 11-1x13-3
Br 2 11-0x12-9

Rear View

LOWE'S
Signature
SERIES

Charming Extras Add Character To This Home

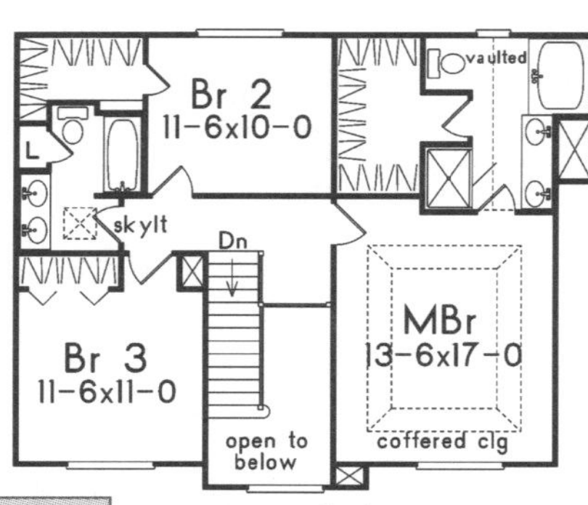
Br 2
11-6x10-0
vaulted
L
skylt
Dn
Br 3
11-6x11-0
MBr
13-6x17-0
open to
below
coffered clg

Second Floor
899 sq. ft.

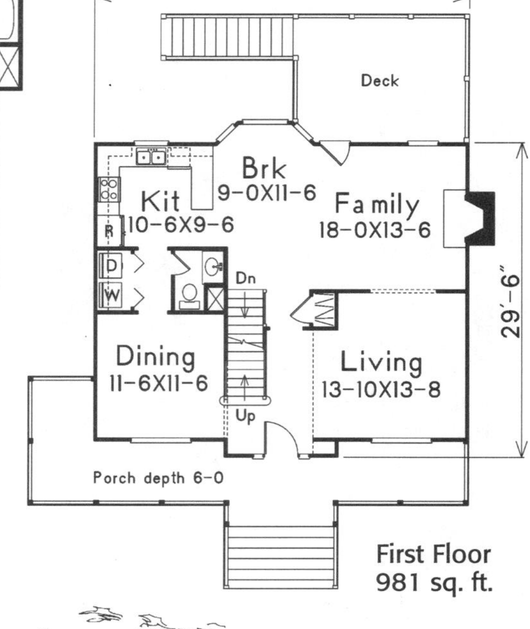
34'-0"
Deck
Brk
9-0X11-6
Kit
10-6X9-6
Family
18-0X13-6
R
D
W
Dn
29'-6"
Dining
11-6X11-6
Up
Living
13-10X13-8
Porch depth 6-0

First Floor
981 sq. ft.

Plan #531-0396

Price Code C

Total Living Area: 1,880 Sq. Ft.

Home has 3 bedrooms, 2 1/2 baths, 2-car drive under garage and basement foundation.

Special features

- Master suite enhanced with coffered ceiling
- Generous family and breakfast areas are modern and functional
- Front porch complements front facade

TO ORDER BLUEPRINTS USE THE FORM ON PAGE 290 OR CALL TOLL-FREE **1-800-DREAM HOME** (373-2646)

Stucco Finish And Southern Home Styling

LOWE'S
Signature
SERIES

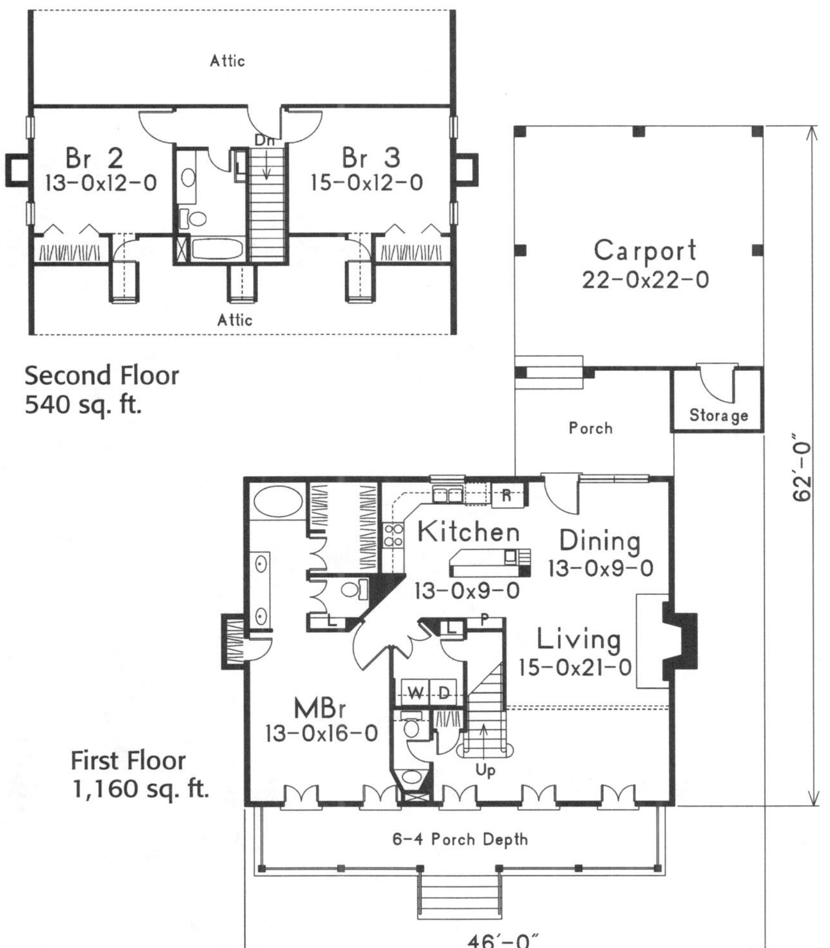
Attic
Br 2
13-0x12-0
Dn
Br 3
15-0x12-0
Attic
Second Floor
540 sq. ft.
Carport
22-0x22-0
Porch
Storage
Kitchen
13-0x9-0
Dining
13-0x9-0
R
P
Living
15-0x21-0
W D
MBr
13-0x16-0
Up
First Floor
1,160 sq. ft.
6-4 Porch Depth
62'-0"
46'-0"

Plan #531-0290

Price Code B

Total Living Area: 1,700 Sq. Ft.

Home has 3 bedrooms, 2 1/2 baths, 2-car attached carport and crawl space foundation, drawings also include basement and slab foundations.

Special features

- Fully appointed kitchen with wet bar
- Energy efficient home with 2" x 6" exterior walls
- Linen drop from the second floor bath to utility room
- Master bath includes raised marble tub and sloped ceiling

Cozy Front Porch Welcomes Guests

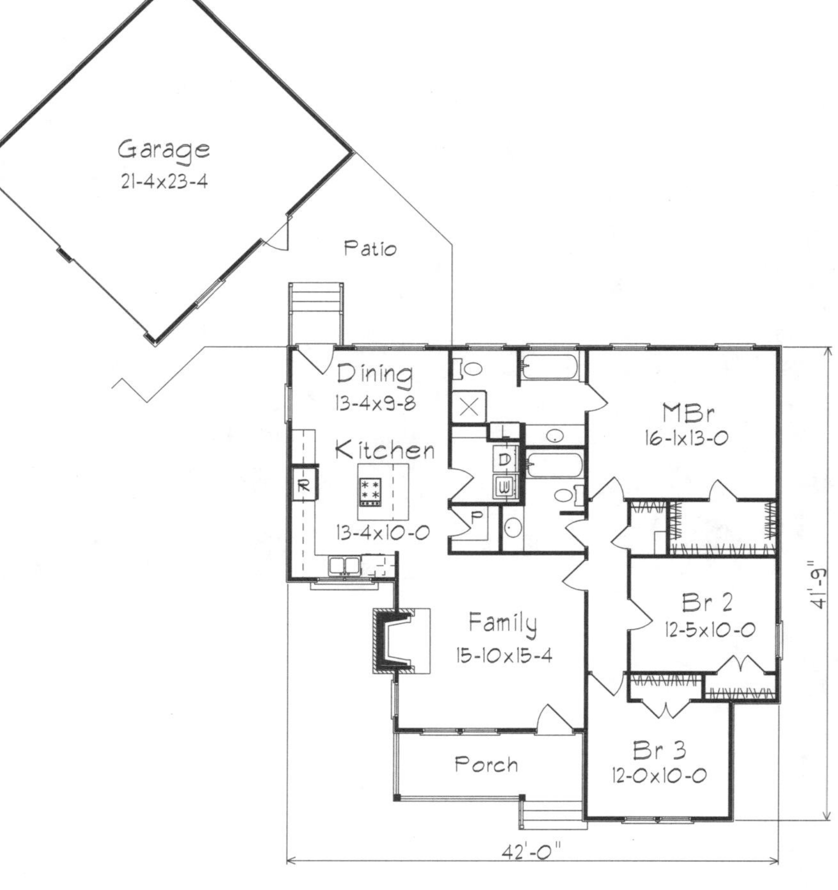
Garage
21-4x23-4
Patio
Dining
13-4x9-8
Kitchen
13-4x10-0
MBr
16-1x13-0
Family
15-10x15-4
Br 2
12-5x10-0
Br 3
12-0x10-0
Porch
42'-0"
41'-9"

Plan #531-0447

Price Code B

Total Living Area: 1,393 Sq. Ft.

Home has 3 bedrooms, 2 baths, 2-car detached garage and crawl space foundation, drawings also include slab foundation.

Special features

- L-shaped kitchen features walk-in pantry, island cooktop and is convenient to laundry room and dining area
- Master bedroom features large walk-in closet and private bath with separate tub and shower
- Convenient storage/coat closet in hall
- View to the patio and garage from dining area

Tall Windows And Sweeping Roof Lines

LOWE'S

Signature SERIES

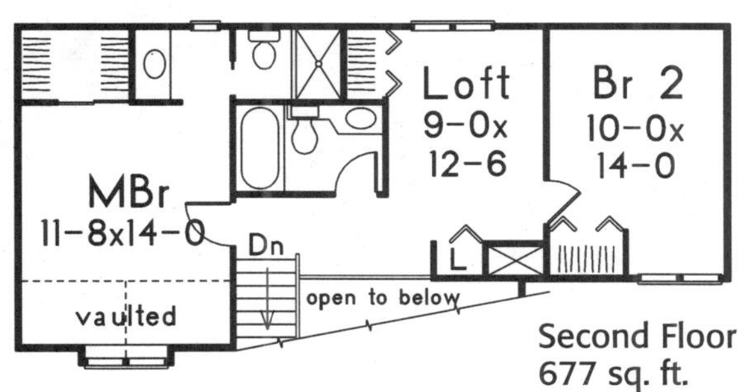
Loft
9-0x
12-6
Br 2
10-0x
14-0
MBr
11-8x14-0
Dn
L
vaulted
open to below

Second Floor
677 sq. ft.

Plan #531-0103

Price Code A

Total Living Area: 1,351 Sq. Ft.

Home has 3 bedrooms, 2 1/2 baths, 2-car garage and basement foundation.

Special features

- Roof lines and vaulted ceilings make this home look larger than its true size
- Central fireplace provides a focal point for dining and living areas
- Master bedroom suite is highlighted by a roomy window seat and a walk-in closet

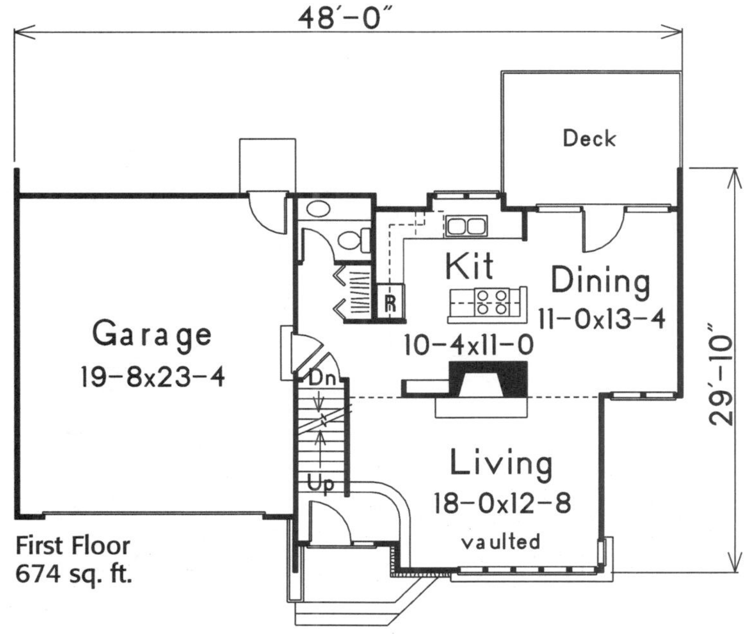
48'-0"
Deck
Kit
10-4x11-0
Dining
11-0x13-4
R
Garage
19-8x23-4
Dn
Up
Living
18-0x12-8
vaulted
29'-10"

First Floor
674 sq. ft.

Signature SERIES

Double Gables Frame Front Porch

Plan #531-0542

Price Code C

Total Living Area: 1,832 Sq. Ft.

Home has 3 bedrooms, 2 baths, 2-car detached garage and crawl space foundation, drawings also include basement and slab foundations.

Special features

- Distinctive master suite enhanced by skylights, garden tub, separate shower and walk-in closet
- U-shaped kitchen features convenient pantry, laundry area and full view to breakfast room
- Foyer opens into spacious living room
- Large front porch creates enjoyable outdoor living

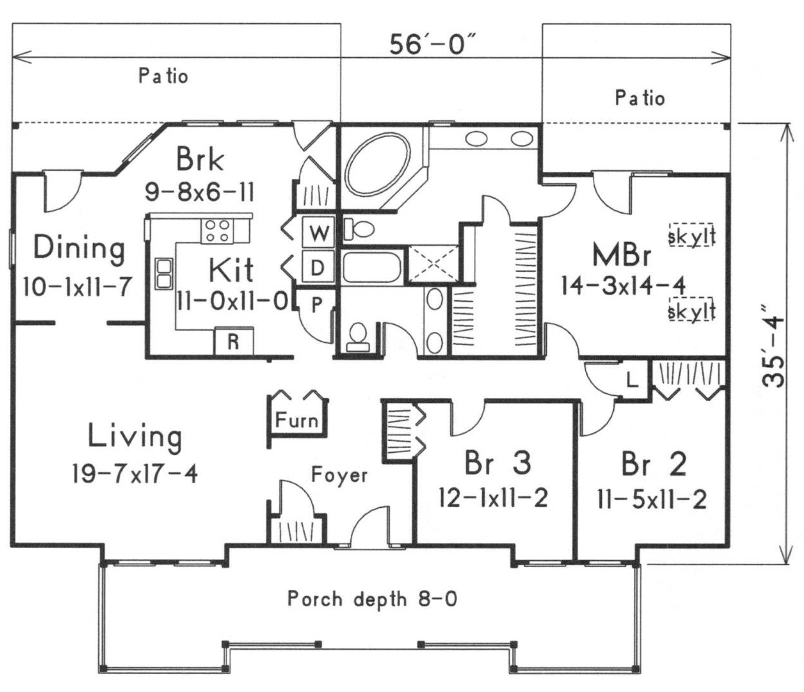
56′-0″
Patio
Patio
Brk
9-8x6-11
Dining
10-1x11-7
Kit
11-0x11-0
W
D
P
R
MBr
14-3x14-4
skylt
skylt
35′-4″
L
Furn
Living
19-7x17-4
Foyer
Br 3
12-1x11-2
Br 2
11-5x11-2
Porch depth 8-0

LOWE'S

Signature
SERIES

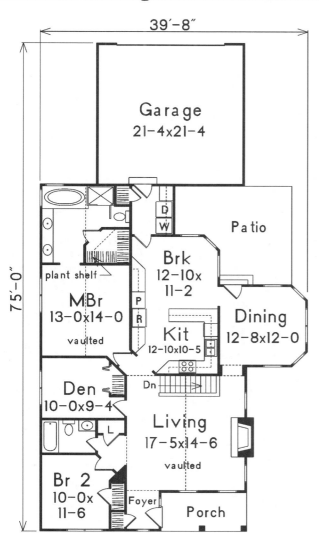

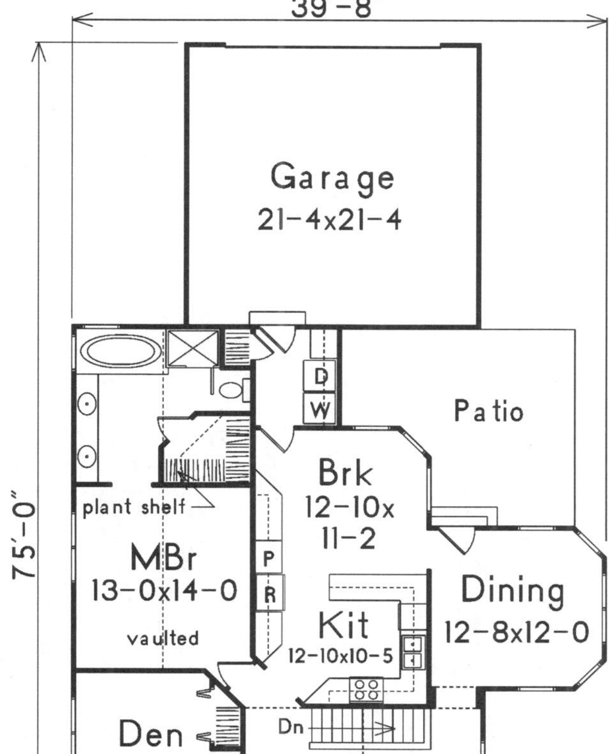
39'-8"
75'-0"
Garage
21-4x21-4
Patio
D
W
Brk
12-10x
11-2
plant shelf
MBr
13-0x14-0
vaulted
P
R
Kit
12-10x10-5
Dining
12-8x12-0
Den
10-0x9-4
Dn
Living
17-5x14-6
vaulted
L
Br 2
10-0x
11-6
Foyer
Porch

Plan #531-0394

Price Code B

Total Living Area: 1,558 Sq. Ft.

Home has 2 bedrooms, 2 baths, 2-car rear entry garage and basement foundation.

Special features

- Illuminated spaces created by visual access to outdoor living areas
- Vaulted master bedroom features private bath with whirlpool tub, separate shower and large walk-in closet
- Convenient first floor laundry has garage access
- Practical den or third bedroom
- U-shaped kitchen adjacent to sunny breakfast area

LOWE'S

Signature
SERIES

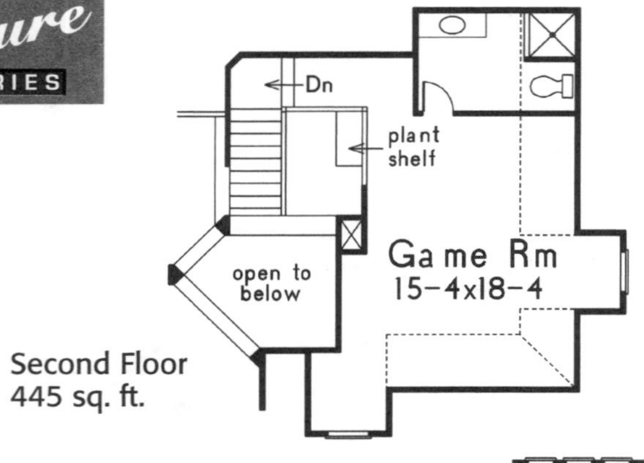
Dn
plant shelf
open to below
Game Rm
15-4x18-4
Second Floor
445 sq. ft.

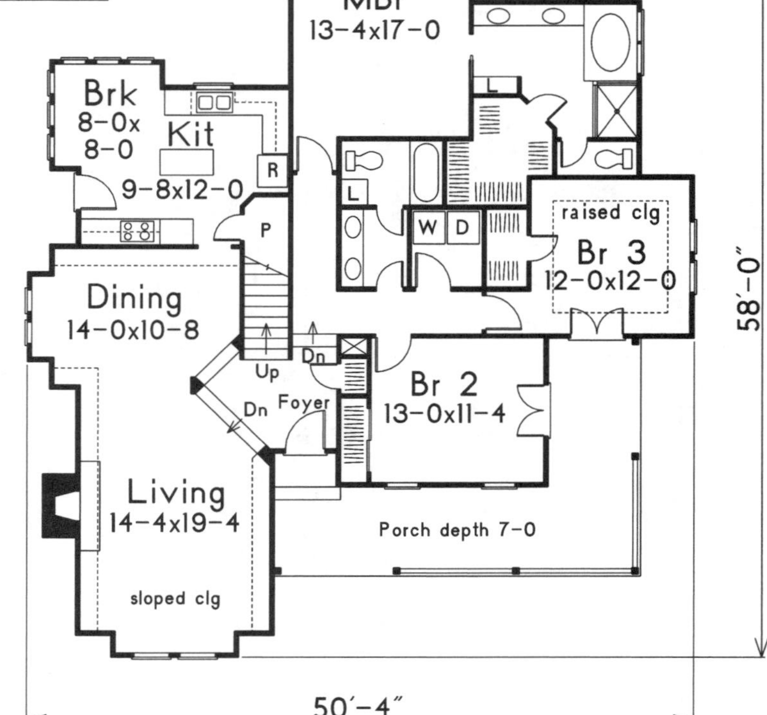
First Floor
1,837 sq. ft.
MBr
13-4x17-0
Brk
8-0x
8-0
Kit
9-8x12-0
R
P
W D
raised clg
Br 3
12-0x12-0
Dining
14-0x10-8
Up
Dn
Foyer
Dn
Br 2
13-0x11-4
Living
14-4x19-4
sloped clg
Porch depth 7-0
58'-0"
50'-4"

Plan #531-0167

Price Code D

Total Living Area: 2,282 Sq. Ft.

Home has 3 bedrooms, 3 baths, 2-car detached garage and slab foundation, drawings also include crawl space foundation.

Special features

- Living and dining rooms combine to create a large, convenient entertaining area that includes a fireplace
- Comfortable veranda allows access from secondary bedrooms
- Second floor game room overlooks foyer and includes a full bath
- Kitchen and breakfast areas are surrounded by mullioned windows

TO ORDER BLUEPRINTS USE THE FORM ON PAGE 290 OR CALL TOLL-FREE **1-800-DREAM HOME** (373-2646)

Gallery Opens Into Grand Living Room

LOWE'S

Signature SERIES

Plan #531-0285

Price Code E

Total Living Area: 2,648 Sq. Ft.

Home has 3 bedrooms, 2 baths, 2-car carport and crawl space foundation, drawings also include slab foundation.

Special features

- Private study with access to master bedroom and porch
- Grand-sized living room with sloped ceiling, fireplace and entry to porches
- Energy efficient home with 2" x 6" exterior walls
- Master suite boasts expansive bath with separate vanities, large walk-in closet and separate tub and shower units
- Large kitchen with eating area and breakfast bar
- Large utility room includes extra counter space and storage closet

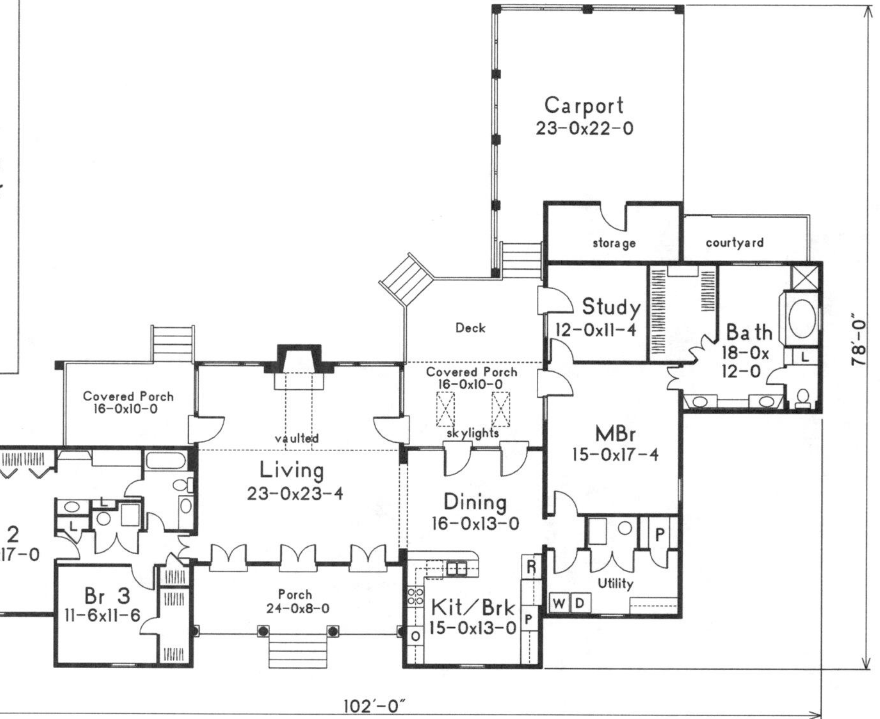

Carport
23-0x22-0
storage
courtyard
Study
12-0x11-4
Bath
18-0x
12-0
Deck
Covered Porch
16-0x10-0
skylights
MBr
15-0x17-4
Covered Porch
16-0x10-0
vaulted
Living
23-0x23-4
Dining
16-0x13-0
Br 2
13-6x17-0
Br 3
11-6x11-6
Porch
24-0x8-0
Kit/Brk
15-0x13-0
Utility
78'-0"
102'-0"

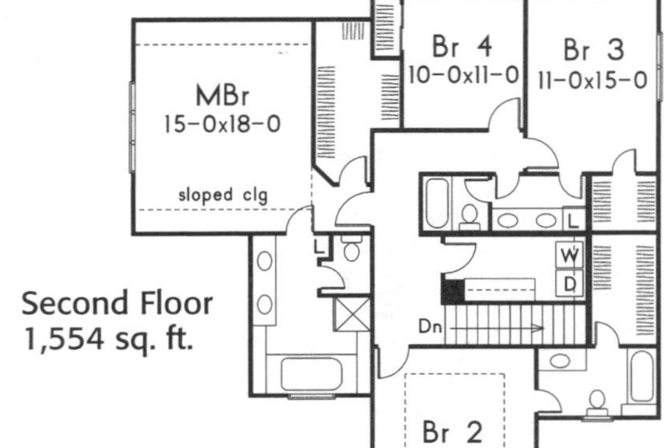
MBr
15-0x18-0
sloped clg
Br 4
10-0x11-0
Br 3
11-0x15-0
W
D
L
Dn
Br 2
14-0x16-0
raised clg
Second Floor
1,554 sq. ft.

First Floor
1,459 sq. ft.

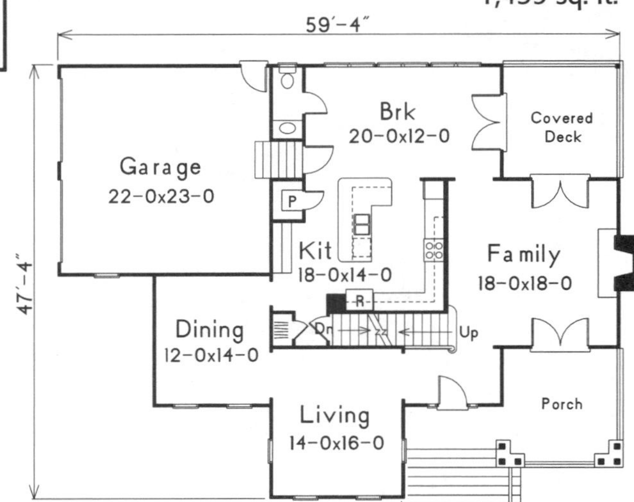
59'-4"
47'-4"
Garage
22-0x23-0
Brk
20-0x12-0
Covered
Deck
P
Kit
18-0x14-0
Family
18-0x18-0
R
Dining
12-0x14-0
Dn
Up
Living
14-0x16-0
Porch

Plan #531-0299

Price Code E

Total Living Area: 3,013 Sq. Ft.

Home has 4 bedrooms, 3 1/2 baths, 2-car side entry garage and basement foundation.

Special features

- Oversized rooms throughout
- Kitchen features island sink, large pantry and opens into sunroom/ breakfast room
- Large family room with fireplace accesses rear deck and front porch
- Master bedroom includes large walk-in closet and private deluxe bath

TO ORDER BLUEPRINTS USE THE FORM ON PAGE 290 OR CALL TOLL-FREE **1-800-DREAM HOME** (373-2646)

Separate Living Areas Lend Privacy

LOWE'S

Signature
SERIES

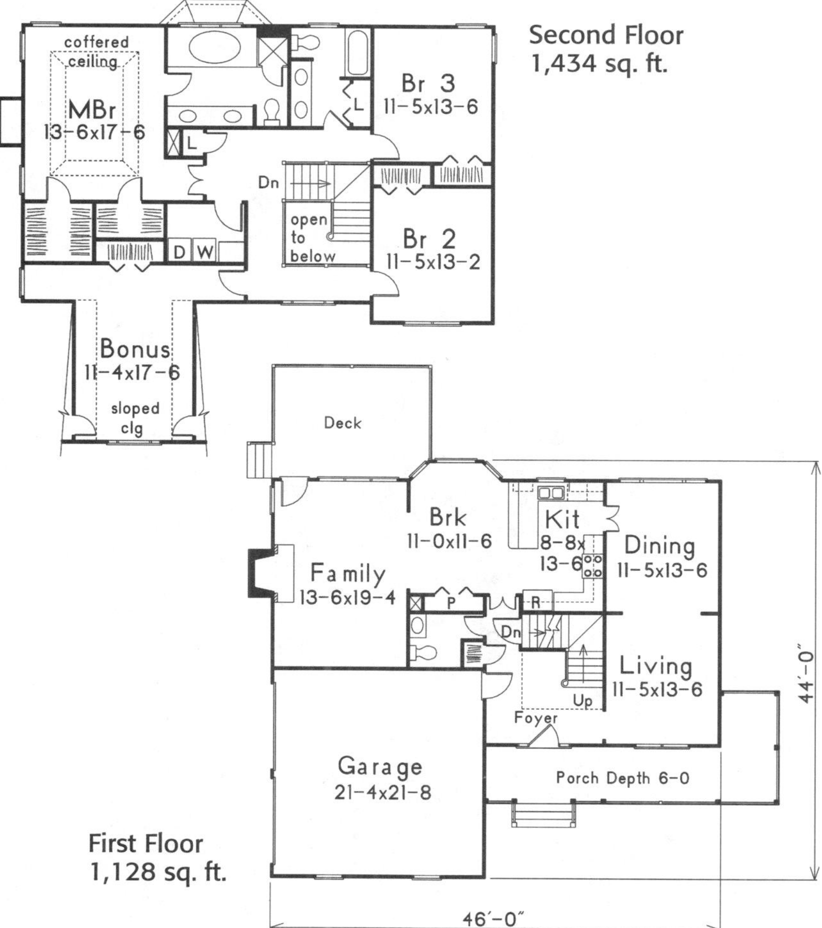
Second Floor
1,434 sq. ft.
coffered ceiling
MBr
13-6x17-6
L
Br 3
11-5x13-6
Dn
open to below
Br 2
11-5x13-2
D
W
Bonus
11-4x17-6
sloped clg
Deck
Brk
11-0x11-6
Kit
8-8x
13-6
Dining
11-5x13-6
Family
13-6x19-4
P
R
Dn
Living
11-5x13-6
Up
Foyer
Garage
21-4x21-8
Porch Depth 6-0
44'-0"
46'-0"
First Floor
1,128 sq. ft.

Plan #531-0177

Price Code D

Total Living Area: 2,562 Sq. Ft.

Home has 3 bedrooms, 2 1/2 baths, 2-car side entry garage and basement foundation, drawings also include slab and crawl space foundations.

Special features

- Large, open foyer creates a grand entrance
- Convenient open breakfast area includes peninsula counter, bay window and easy access to the sundeck
- Dining and living rooms flow together for expanded entertaining space

Trendsetting Appeal For A Narrow Lot

Second Floor
576 sq. ft.

MBr 16-2x11-6 vaulted
plant shelf
Dn
Studio/ Br 2 12-10x12-1
plant shelf
vaulted

Great Rm 19-8x15-0
Dining
Dn
Kit 8-0x9-6
R
P
Up
Garage 12-4x20-4
35'-8"
Entry
Porch depth 5-0
W
D
33'-0"

First Floor
718 sq. ft.

Plan #531-0479

Price Code A

Total Living Area: 1,294 Sq. Ft.

Home has 2 bedrooms, 1 full bath, 2 half baths, 1-car rear entry garage and basement foundation.

Special features

- Great room features fireplace and large bay with windows and patio doors
- Enjoy a laundry room immersed in light with large windows, arched transom and attractive planter box
- Vaulted master bedroom with bay window and walk-in closets
- Bedroom #2 boasts a vaulted ceiling, plant shelf and half bath, perfect for a studio

TO ORDER BLUEPRINTS USE THE FORM ON PAGE 290 OR CALL TOLL-FREE **1-800-DREAM HOME** (373-2646)

Front Entrance Framed By Triple Gables

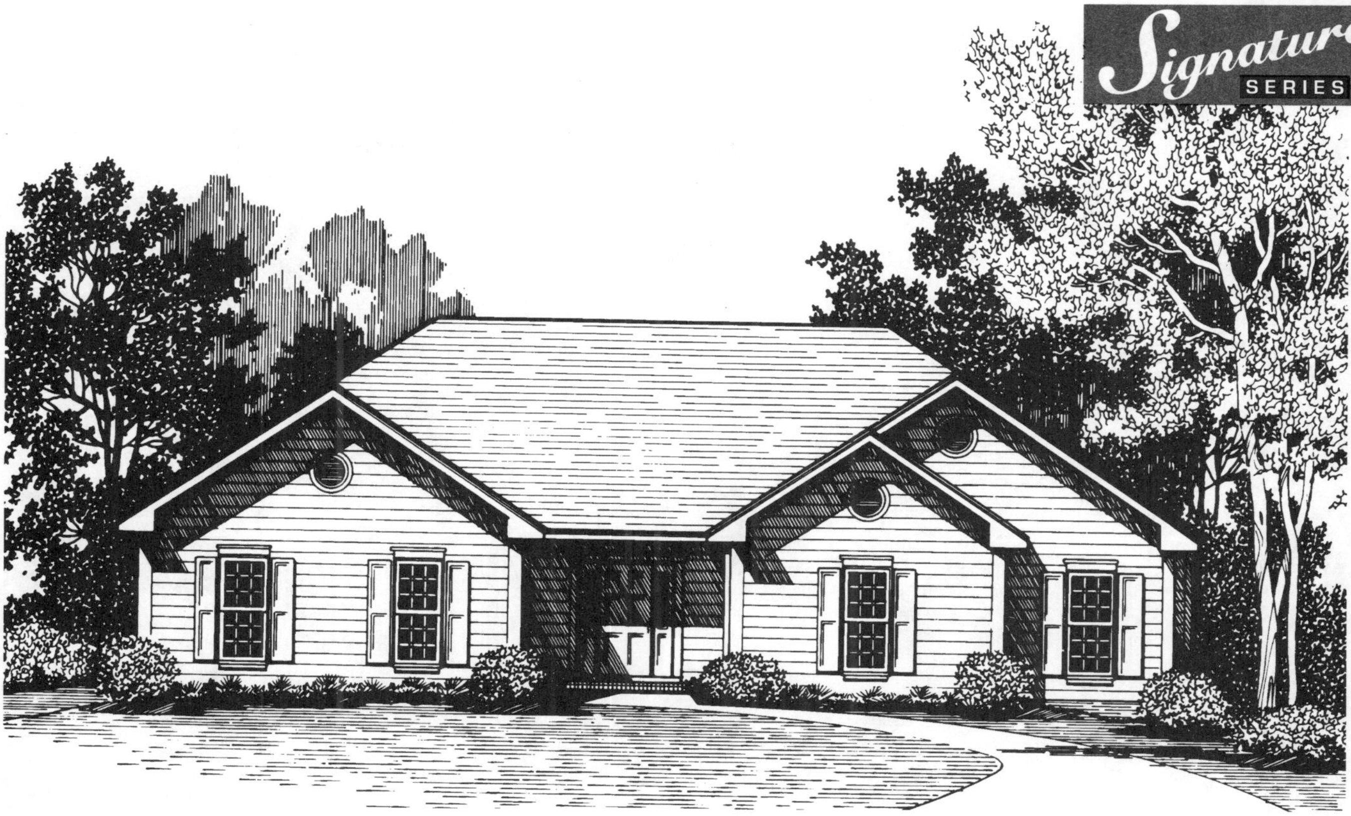

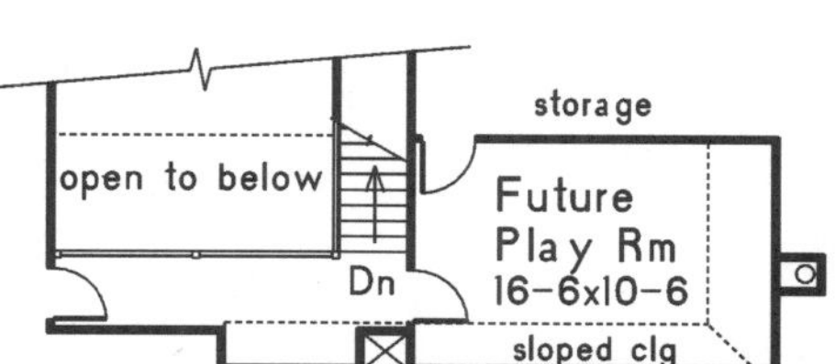
storage
open to below
Future
Play Rm
16-6x10-6
Dn
sloped clg

Second Floor
104 sq. ft.

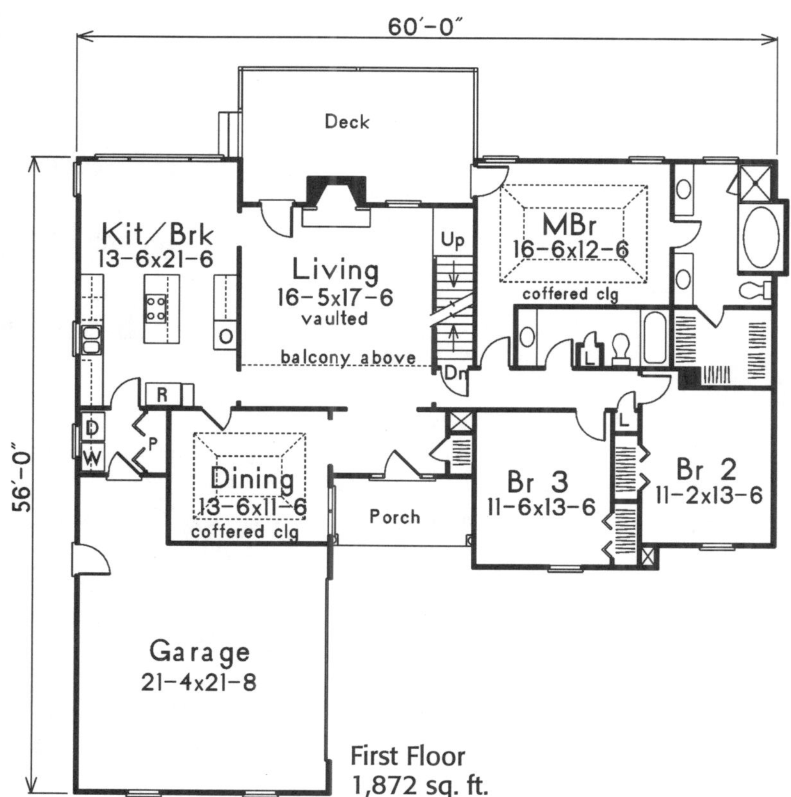
60'-0"
Deck
Kit/Brk
13-6x21-6
Living
16-5x17-6
vaulted
balcony above
Up
Dn
MBr
16-6x12-6
coffered clg
R
D
W
P
Dining
13-6x11-6
coffered clg
Porch
Br 3
11-6x13-6
Br 2
11-2x13-6
Garage
21-4x21-8
56'-0"

First Floor
1,872 sq. ft.

Plan #531-0121

Price Code C

Total Living Area: 1,976 Sq. Ft.

Home has 3 bedrooms, 2 baths, 2-car side entry garage and basement foundation.

Special features

- Compact ranch features garage entry near front door
- Vaulted living area has large balcony above
- Isolated master bedroom with coffered ceiling and luxurious bath
- Loft area has access to plenty of attic storage and future play room

LOWE'S Signature SERIES

Compact Layout, Amenity Full

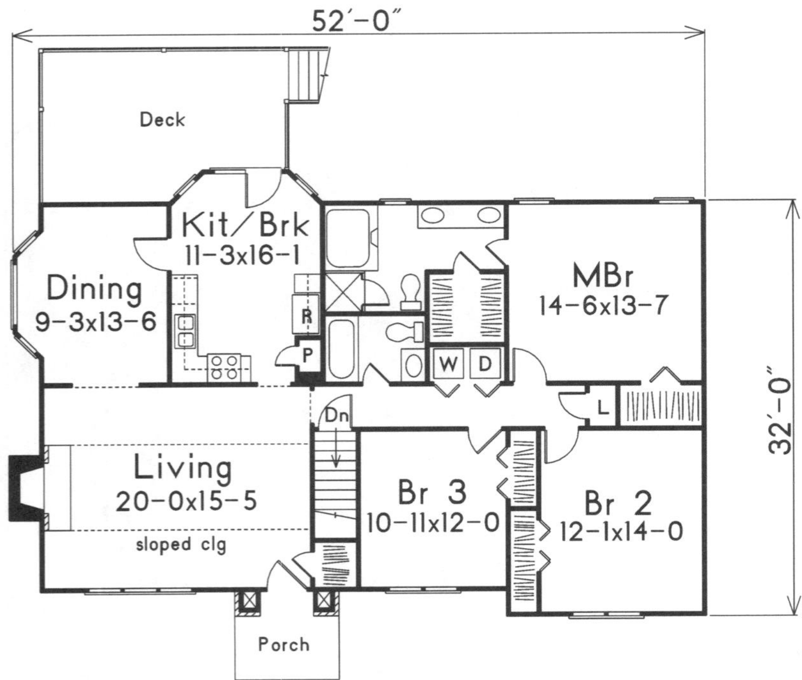

52′-0″
Deck
Kit/Brk
11-3x16-1
Dining
9-3x13-6
MBr
14-6x13-7
R
P
W
D
L
Dn
Living
20-0x15-5
sloped clg
Br 3
10-11x12-0
Br 2
12-1x14-0
32′-0″
Porch

Plan #531-0180

Price Code B

Total Living Area:	1,567 Sq. Ft.

Home has 3 bedrooms, 2 baths, 2-car drive under garage and basement foundation.

Special features

- Front gables and extended porch add charm to facade
- Large bay windows add brightness to breakfast and dining rooms
- The master bath boasts an oversized tub, separate shower, double sinks and large walk-in closet
- Living room features a vaulted ceiling and a prominent fireplace

TO ORDER BLUEPRINTS USE THE FORM ON PAGE 290 OR CALL TOLL-FREE **1-800-DREAM HOME** (373-2646)

Layout Creates Large Open Living Area

LOWE'S

Signature
SERIES

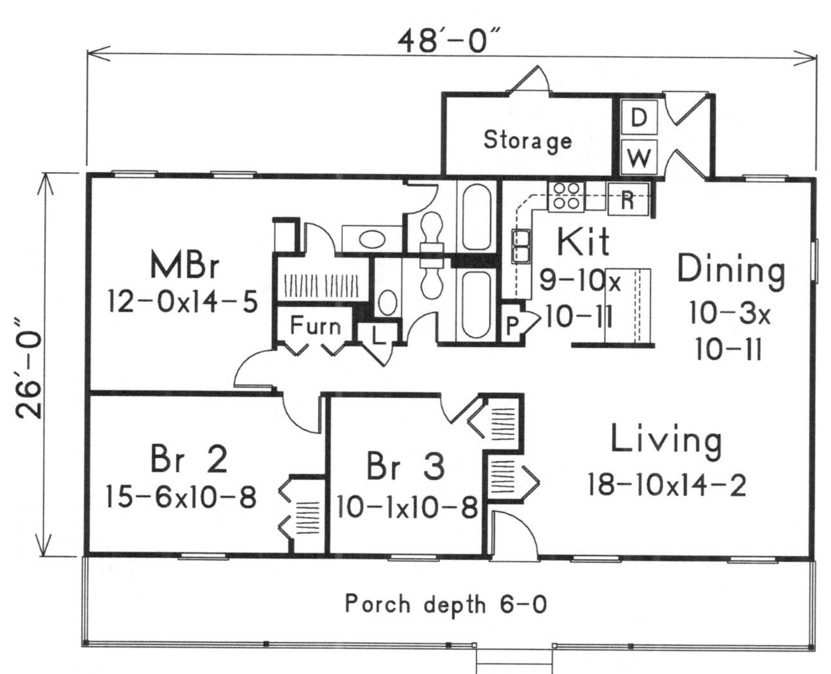
48′–0″
26′–0″
Storage
D
W
R
Kit
9–10x
10–11
P
Dining
10–3x
10–11
MBr
12–0x14–5
Furn
L
Br 2
15–6x10–8
Br 3
10–1x10–8
Living
18–10x14–2
Porch depth 6–0

Plan #531-0529

Price Code B

Total Living Area: 1,285 Sq. Ft.

Home has 3 bedrooms, 2 baths and crawl space foundation, drawings also include basement and slab foundations.

Special features

- Accommodating home with ranch-style porch
- Large storage area on back of home
- Master bedroom includes dressing area, private bath and built-in bookcase
- Kitchen features pantry, breakfast bar and complete view to dining room

Signature
SERIES

Quaint Exterior, Full Front Porch

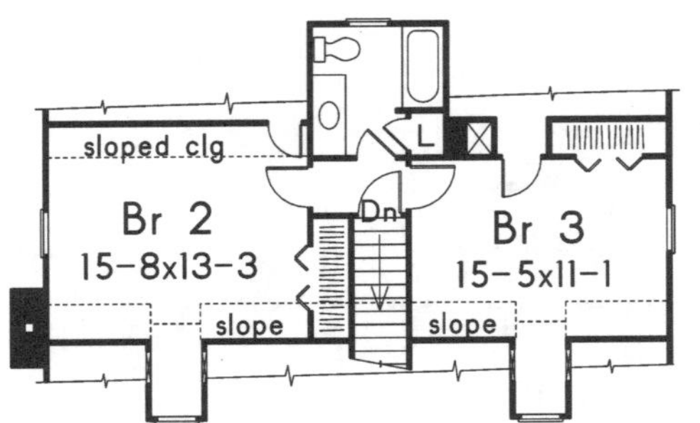
sloped clg
Br 2
15-8x13-3
L
Dn
Br 3
15-5x11-1
slope
slope

Second Floor
611 sq. ft.

Plan #531-0174

Price Code B

Total Living Area: 1,657 Sq. Ft.

Home has 3 bedrooms, 2 1/2 baths, 2-car drive under garage and basement foundation.

Special features

- Stylish pass-through between living and dining areas
- Master bedroom is secluded from living area for privacy
- Large windows in breakfast and dining areas

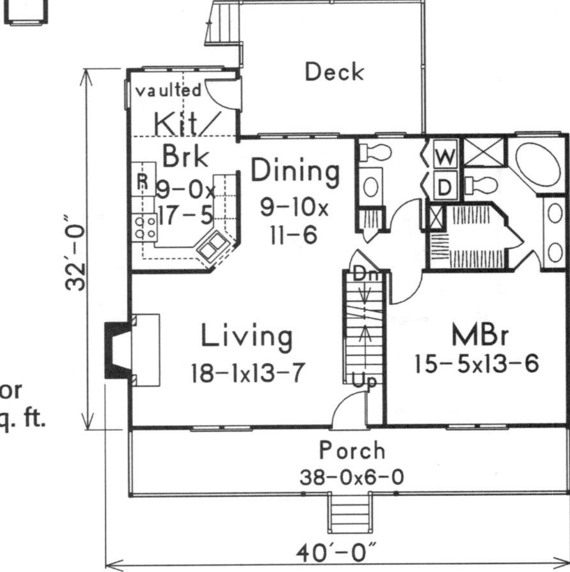
Deck
vaulted
Kit/
Brk
9-0x
17-5
R
Dining
9-10x
11-6
W
D
Dn
Living
18-1x13-7
Up
MBr
15-5x13-6
32'-0"
Porch
38-0x6-0
40'-0"

First Floor
1,046 sq. ft.

Wrap-Around Covered Porch

LOWE'S
Signature
SERIES

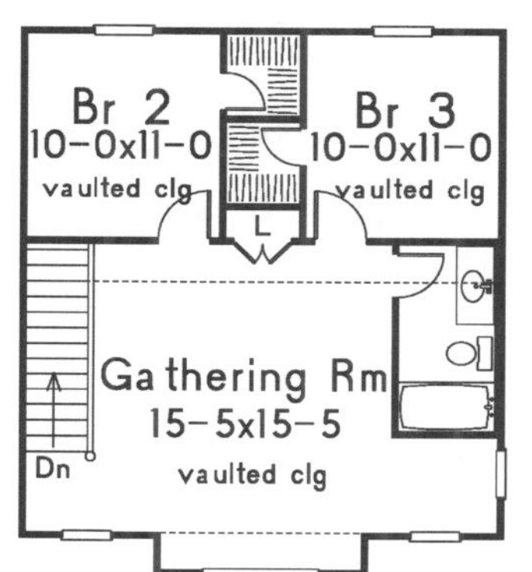

Br 2
10-0x11-0
vaulted clg
Br 3
10-0x11-0
vaulted clg
L
Gathering Rm
15-5x15-5
vaulted clg
Dn

Second Floor
672 sq. ft.

First Floor
1,112 sq. ft.

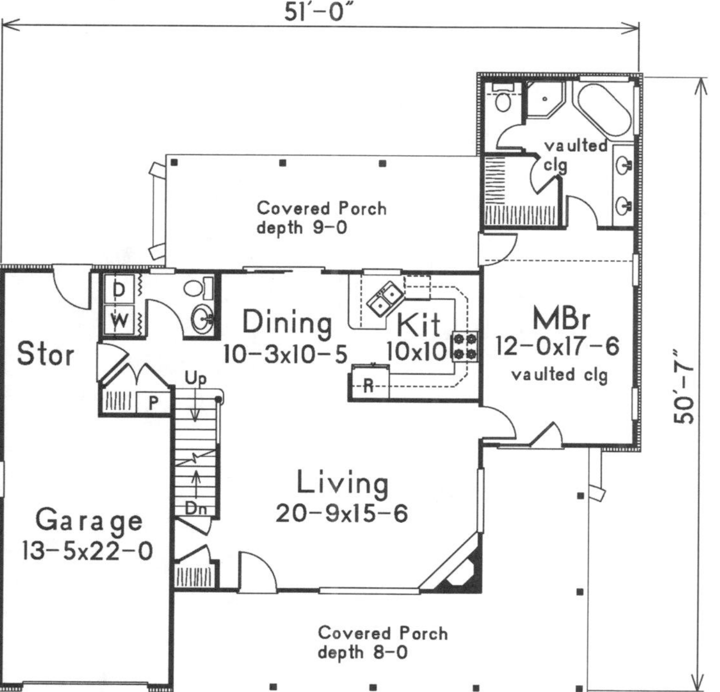

51'-0"
50'-7"
vaulted clg
Covered Porch
depth 9-0
D
W
Stor
Dining
10-3x10-5
Kit
10x10
MBr
12-0x17-6
vaulted clg
Up
P
R
Living
20-9x15-6
Dn
Garage
13-5x22-0
Covered Porch
depth 8-0

Plan #531-0723

Price Code B

Total Living Area: 1,784 Sq. Ft.

Home has 3 bedrooms, 2 1/2 baths, 1-car garage and basement foundation, drawings also include crawl space foundation.

Special features

- Spacious living area with corner fireplace offers a cheerful atmosphere with large windows
- Large second floor gathering room is great for kid's play area
- Secluded master suite has separate porch entrances and large master bath with walk-in closet

Appealing Ranch Has Attractive Front Dormers

Lowe's Signature Series

Plan #531-0282

Price Code B

Total Living Area: 1,642 Sq. Ft.

Home has 3 bedrooms, 2 baths, 2-car garage and basement foundation, drawings also include slab and crawl space foundations.

Special features

- Walk-through kitchen boasts vaulted ceiling and corner sink overlooking family room
- Vaulted family room features cozy fireplace and access to rear patio
- Master bedroom includes sloped ceiling, walk-in closet and private bath

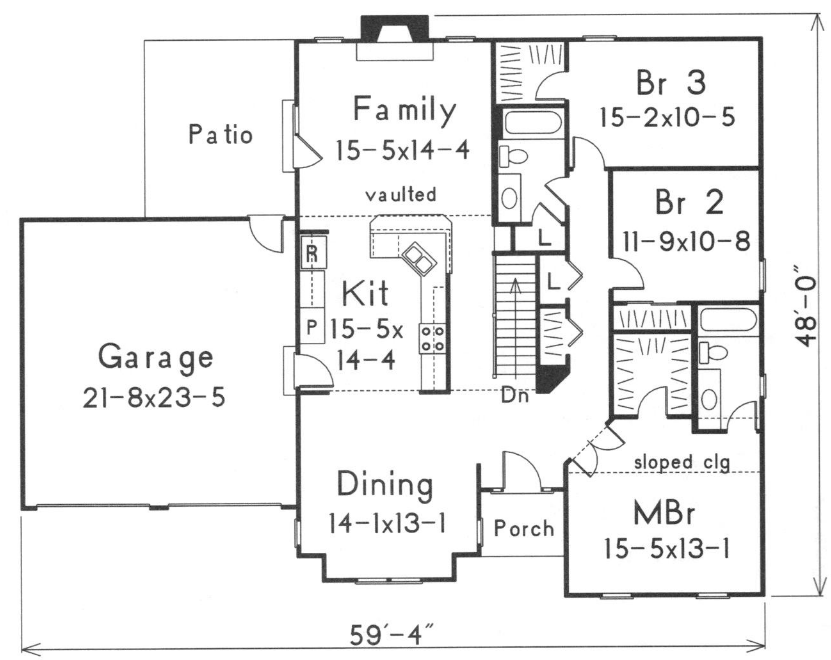

Patio
Family
15-5x14-4
vaulted
Br 3
15-2x10-5
Br 2
11-9x10-8
R
Kit
P
15-5x
14-4
L
L
Garage
21-8x23-5
Dn
48'-0"
sloped clg
Dining
14-1x13-1
Porch
MBr
15-5x13-1
59'-4"

TO ORDER BLUEPRINTS USE THE FORM ON PAGE 290 OR CALL TOLL-FREE **1-800-DREAM HOME** (373-2646)

Circular Stairway Adds To Front Entry

LOWE'S

Signature
SERIES

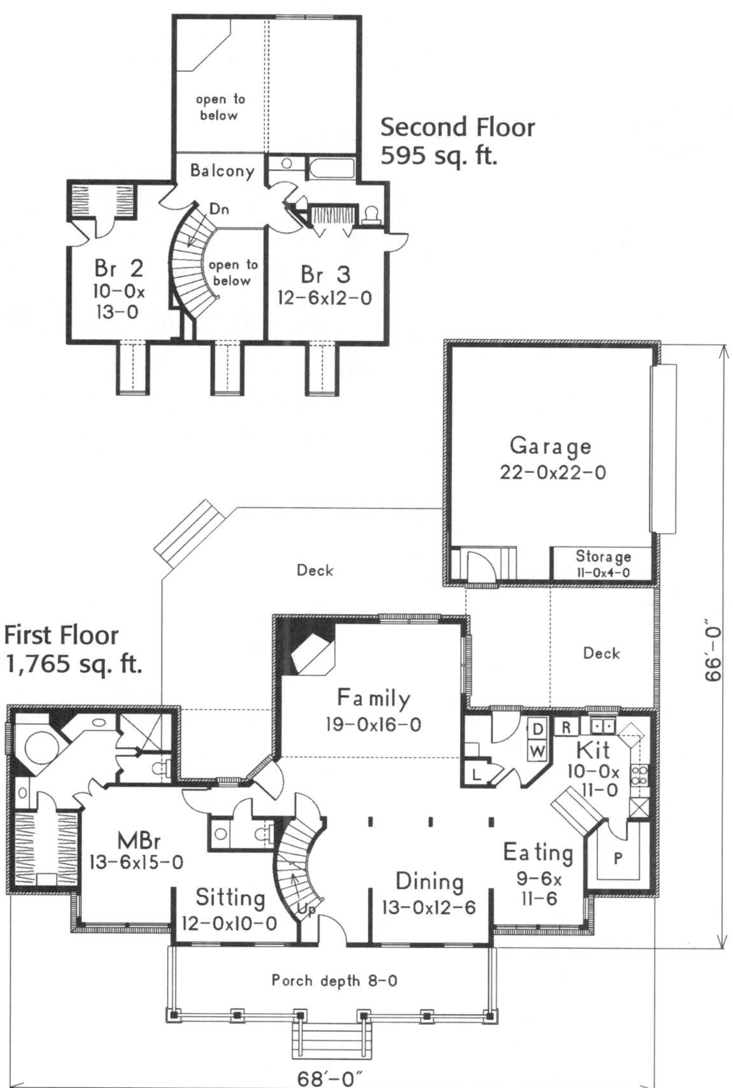
open to below
Second Floor
595 sq. ft.
Balcony
Dn
Br 2
10-0x
13-0
open to below
Br 3
12-6x12-0
Garage
22-0x22-0
Storage
11-0x4-0
Deck
First Floor
1,765 sq. ft.
Deck
Family
19-0x16-0
D
W
R
Kit
10-0x
11-0
L
MBr
13-6x15-0
Eating
9-6x
11-6
P
Sitting
12-0x10-0
Up
Dining
13-0x12-6
Porch depth 8-0
66'-0"
68'-0"

Plan #531-0306

Price Code D

Total Living Area: 2,360 Sq. Ft.

Home has 3 bedrooms, 2 1/2 baths, 2-car side entry garage and crawl space foundation, drawings also include slab and basement foundations.

Special features

- Master suite includes sitting area and large bath
- Sloped family room ceiling provides view from second floor balcony
- Kitchen features island bar and walk-in butler's pantry

Old-Fashioned Comfort And Privacy

Signature
SERIES

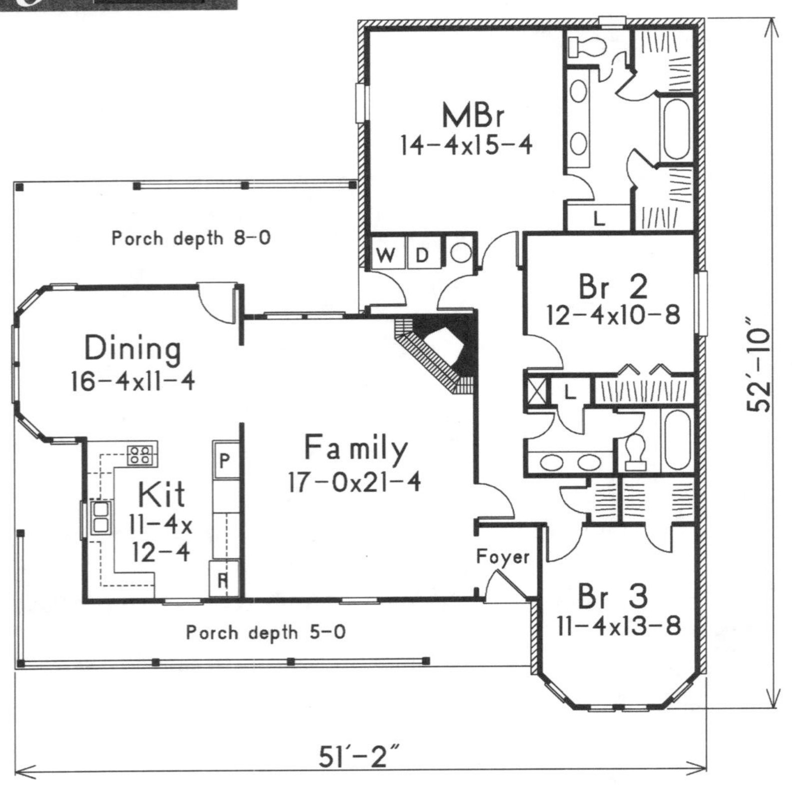
MBr
14-4x15-4
Porch depth 8-0
W D
L
Br 2
12-4x10-8
Dining
16-4x11-4
L
52'-10"
Family
17-0x21-4
P
Kit
11-4x
12-4
R
Foyer
Br 3
11-4x13-8
Porch depth 5-0
51'-2"

Plan #531-0163

Price Code C

Total Living Area: 1,772 Sq. Ft.

Home has 3 bedrooms, 2 baths, 2-car detached garage and slab foundation, drawings also include crawl space foundation.

Special features

- Extended porches in front and rear provide a charming touch
- Large bay windows lend distinction to dining room and bedroom #3
- Efficient U-shaped kitchen
- Master bedroom includes two walk-in closets
- Full corner fireplace in family room

TO ORDER BLUEPRINTS USE THE FORM ON PAGE 290 OR CALL TOLL-FREE **1-800-DREAM HOME** (373-2646)

Wrap-Around Porch Creates A Comfortable Feel

LOWE'S

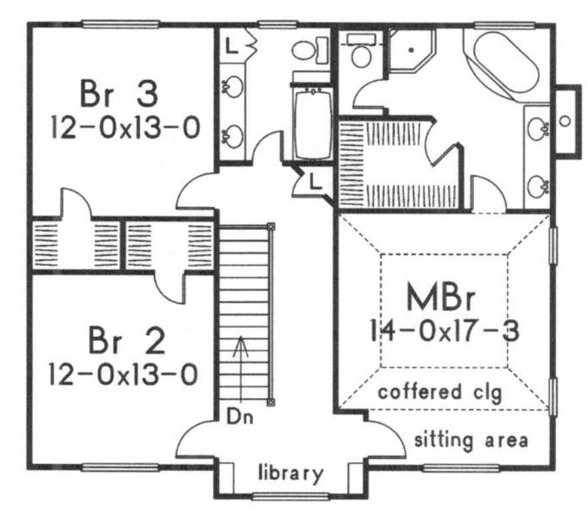
Br 3
12-0x13-0
L
L
Br 2
12-0x13-0
Dn
MBr
14-0x17-3
coffered clg
sitting area
library

Second Floor
1,050 sq. ft.

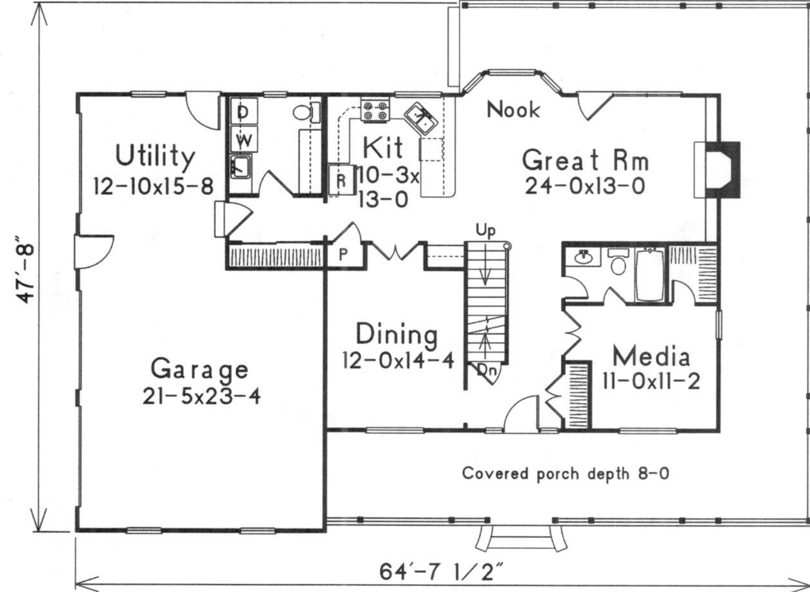
Utility
12-10x15-8
D
W
Kit
10-3x
13-0
R
Nook
Great Rm
24-0x13-0
P
Up
Dining
12-0x14-4
Dn
Media
11-0x11-2
Garage
21-5x23-4
Covered porch depth 8-0
47'-8"
64'-7 1/2"

First Floor
1,216 sq. ft.

Plan #531-0722

Price Code D

Total Living Area: 2,266 Sq. Ft.

Home has 3 bedrooms, 3 baths, 2-car side entry garage and basement foundation, drawings also include crawl space foundation.

Special features

- Great room includes fireplace flanked by built-in bookshelves and dining nook with bay window
- Unique media room includes double-door entrance, walk-in closet and access to full bath
- Master suite has lovely sitting area, walk-in closets and a private bath with step-up tub and double vanity

Plan #531-0205

Price Code E

Total Living Area: 2,665 Sq. Ft.

Home has 3 bedrooms, 2 1/2 baths, 2-car side entry garage and crawl space foundation.

Special features

- The fireplace provides a focus for family living by connecting the central living quarters
- The abundance of windows, combined with vaulted ceilings, give this plan a spacious feel
- Large sunroom opens to kitchen and breakfast areas
- Master suite features a huge walk-in closet, vaulted ceiling and luxurious bath facilities

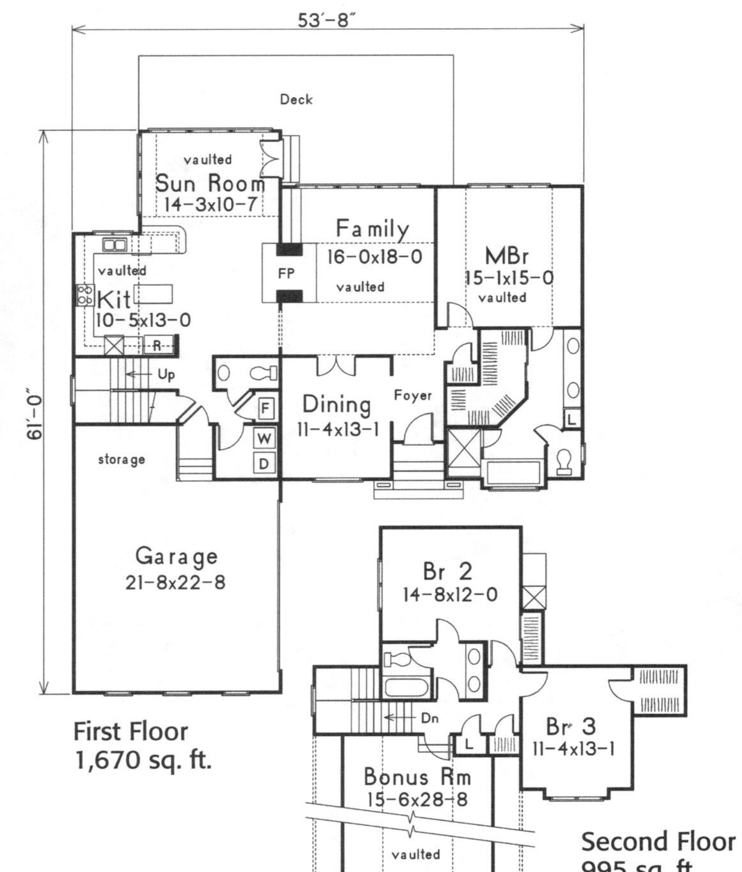
53'-8"
Deck
vaulted
Sun Room
14-3x10-7
Family
16-0x18-0
vaulted
FP
MBr
15-1x15-0
vaulted
vaulted
Kit
10-5x13-0
R
Up
Dining
11-4x13-1
Foyer
F
W
D
storage
61'-0"
Garage
21-8x22-8
Br 2
14-8x12-0
Dn
L
Br 3
11-4x13-1
Bonus Rm
15-6x28-8
vaulted

First Floor
1,670 sq. ft.

Second Floor
995 sq. ft.

TO ORDER BLUEPRINTS USE THE FORM ON PAGE 290 OR CALL TOLL-FREE **1-800-DREAM HOME** (373-2646)

Impressive Exterior, Spacious Interior

LOWE'S

Signature SERIES

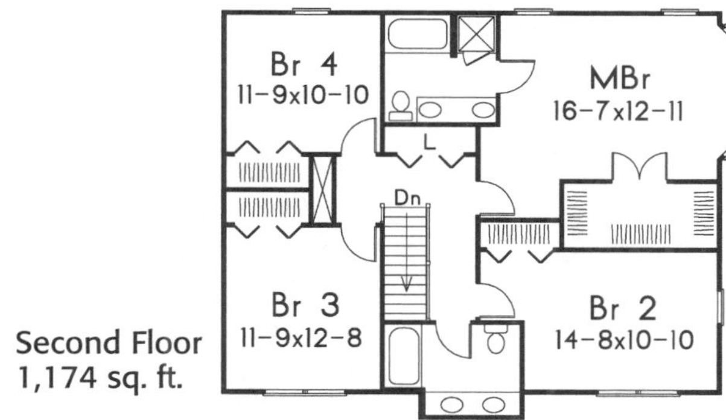

Br 4
11-9x10-10
MBr
16-7x12-11
L
Dn
Br 3
11-9x12-8
Br 2
14-8x10-10

Second Floor
1,174 sq. ft.

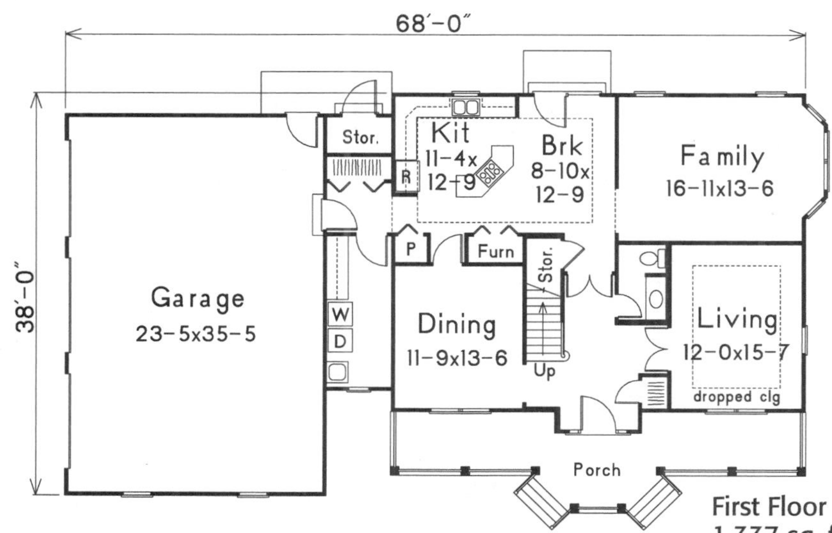

68'-0"
38'-0"
Stor.
Kit
11-4x
12-9
R
Brk
8-10x
12-9
Family
16-11x13-6
P
Furn
Stor.
Garage
23-5x35-5
W
D
Dining
11-9x13-6
Up
Living
12-0x15-7
dropped clg
Porch

First Floor
1,337 sq. ft.

Plan #531-0528

Price Code D

Total Living Area: 2,511 Sq. Ft.

Home has 4 bedrooms, 2 1/2 baths, 3-car side entry garage and basement foundation, drawings also include crawl space and slab foundations.

Special features

- Both kitchen/breakfast area and living room feature tray ceilings
- Various architectural elements combine to create impressive exterior
- Master bedroom includes large walk-in closet, oversized bay window and private bath with shower and tub
- Large utility room with convenient workspace

Well Sculptured Design, Inside And Out

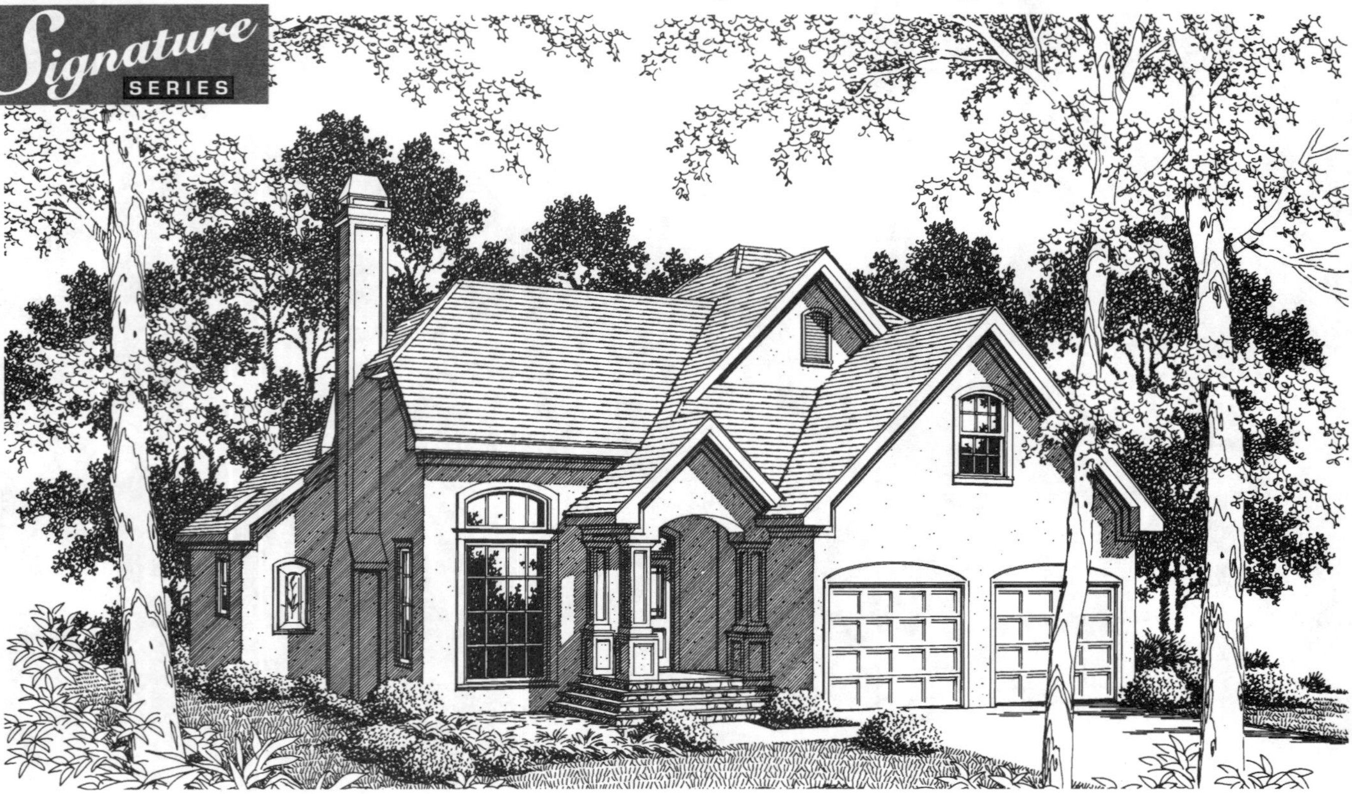

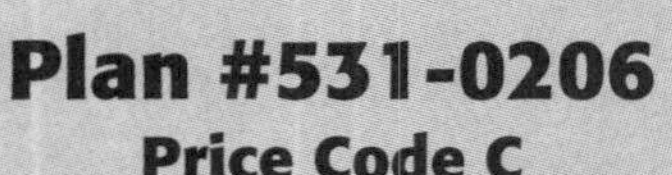

Plan #531-0206

Price Code C

Total Living Area: 1,889 Sq. Ft.

Home has 3 bedrooms, 2 1/2 baths, 2-car garage and basement foundation.

Special features

- The striking entry is created by a unique stair layout, an open high ceiling and a fireplace
- Garage bonus area converts to a fourth bedroom or activity center
- Second floor bedrooms share a private dressing area and bath

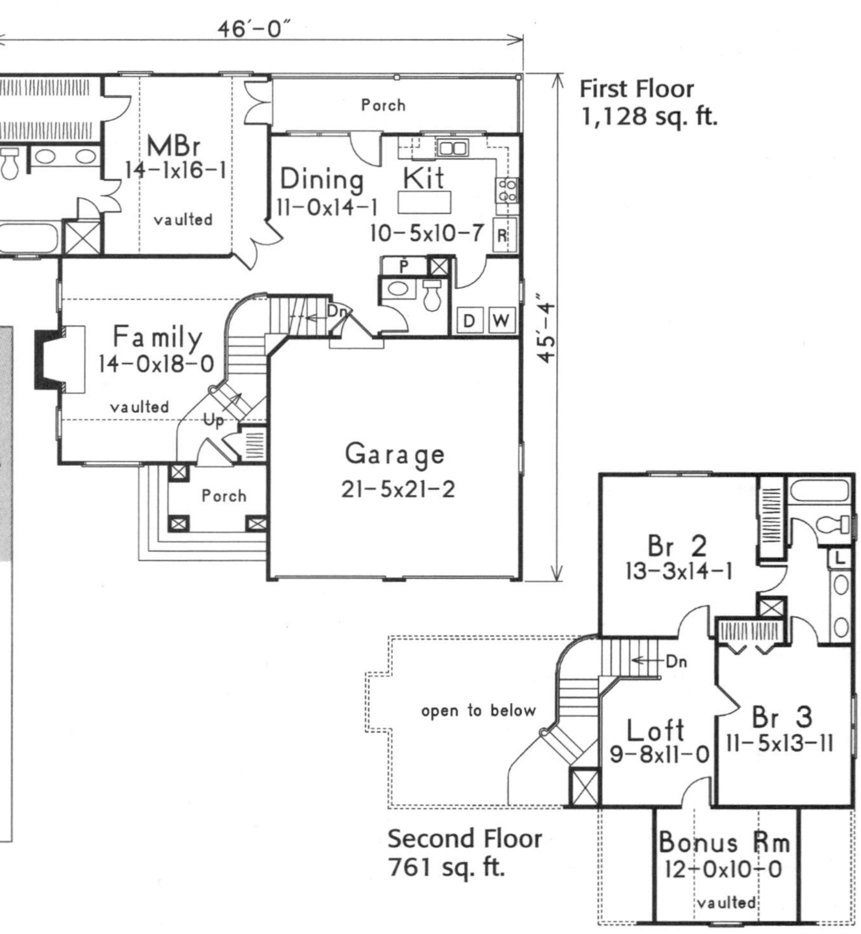
46'-0"
45'-4"
First Floor
1,128 sq. ft.
Porch
MBr
14-1x16-1
vaulted
Dining
11-0x14-1
Kit
10-5x10-7
R
P
Dn
D
W
Family
14-0x18-0
vaulted
Up
Porch
Garage
21-5x21-2
Br 2
13-3x14-1
L
Dn
open to below
Loft
9-8x11-0
Br 3
11-5x13-11
Bonus Rm
12-0x10-0
vaulted
Second Floor
761 sq. ft.

TO ORDER BLUEPRINTS USE THE FORM ON PAGE 290 OR CALL TOLL-FREE **1-800-DREAM HOME** (373-2646)

Trim Colonial For Practical Living

LOWE'S

Signature
SERIES

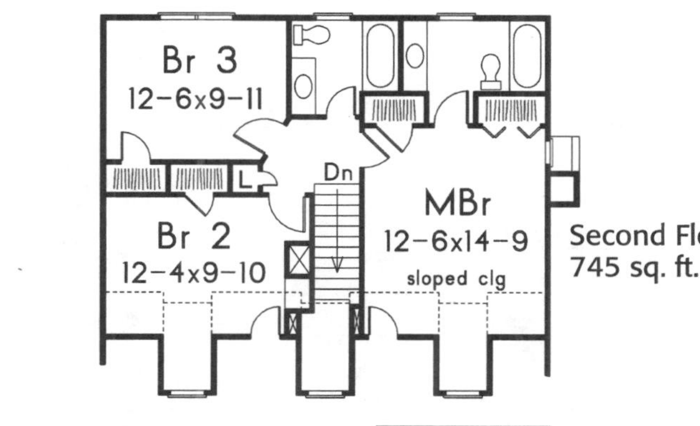
Br 3
12-6x9-11
L
Dn
MBr
12-6x14-9
sloped clg
Br 2
12-4x9-10

Second Floor
745 sq. ft.

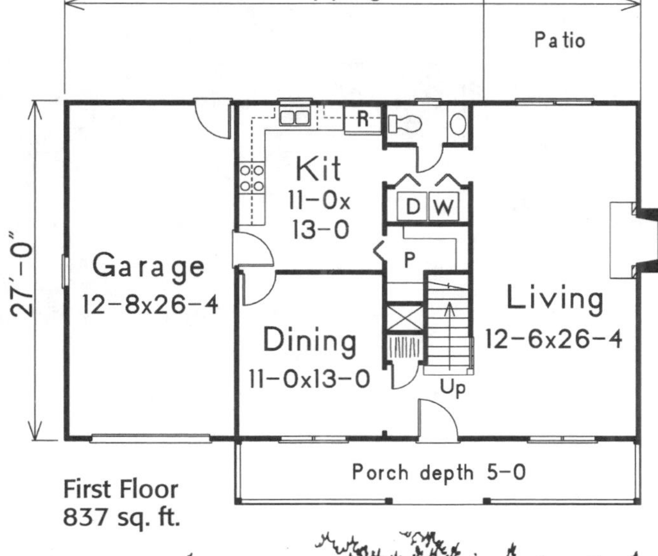
44'-0"
Patio
27'-0"
R
Kit
11-0x
13-0
D W
P
Garage
12-8x26-4
Living
12-6x26-4
Dining
11-0x13-0
Up
Porch depth 5-0

First Floor
837 sq. ft.

Plan #531-0111

Price Code B

Total Living Area: 1,582 Sq. Ft.

Home has 3 bedrooms, 2 1/2 baths, 1-car garage and slab foundation, drawings also include crawl space foundation.

Special features

- Conservative layout gives privacy to living and dining areas
- Large fireplace and windows enhance the living area
- Rear door in garage is convenient to the garden and kitchen
- Full front porch adds charm
- Dormers add light to the foyer and bedrooms

Central Fireplace Dominates Living Area

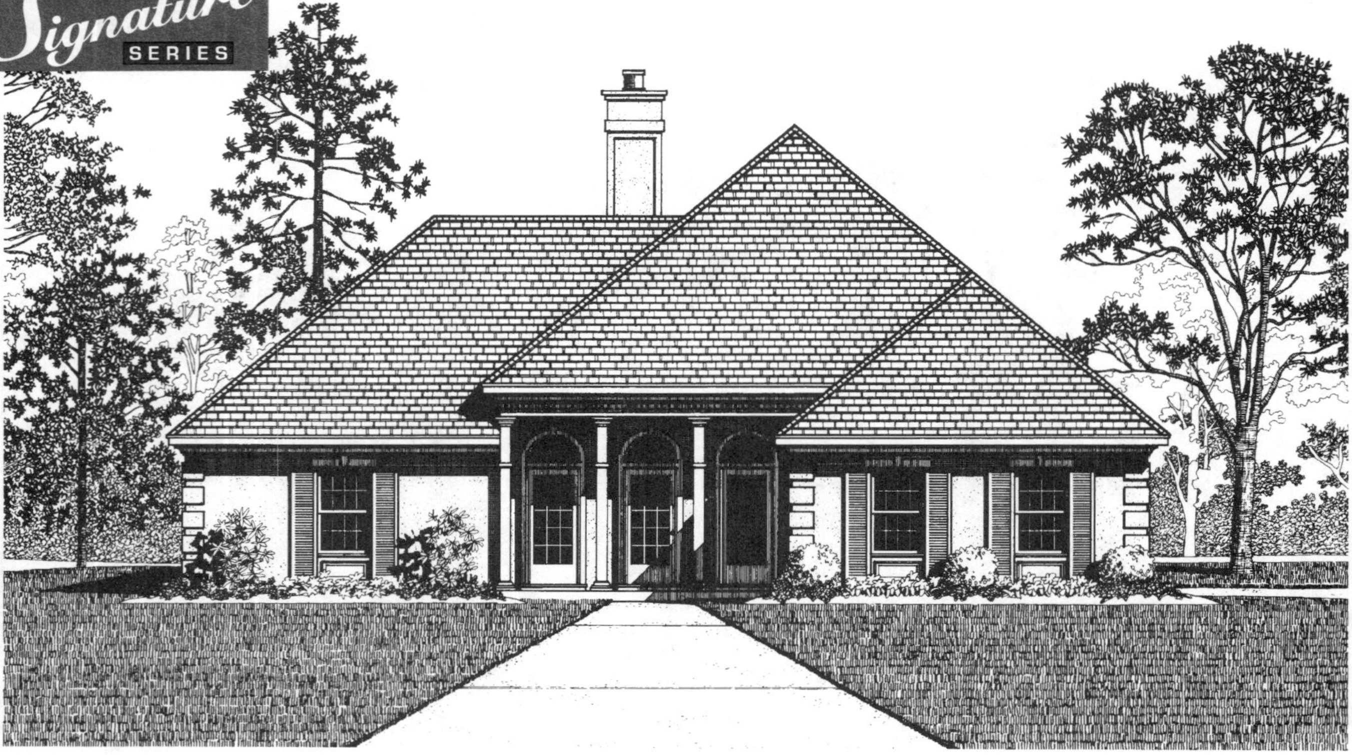

Plan #531-0194

Price Code A

Total Living Area: 1,444 Sq. Ft.

Home has 3 bedrooms, 2 baths, 2-car side entry garage and slab foundation, drawings also include crawl space foundation.

Special features

- High ceilings in living and dining rooms combine with a central fireplace to create large open living area
- Both secondary bedrooms have large walk-in closets
- Large storage area in garage suitable for a workshop or play area
- Front and rear covered porches add cozy touch
- U-shaped kitchen includes a laundry closet and serving bar

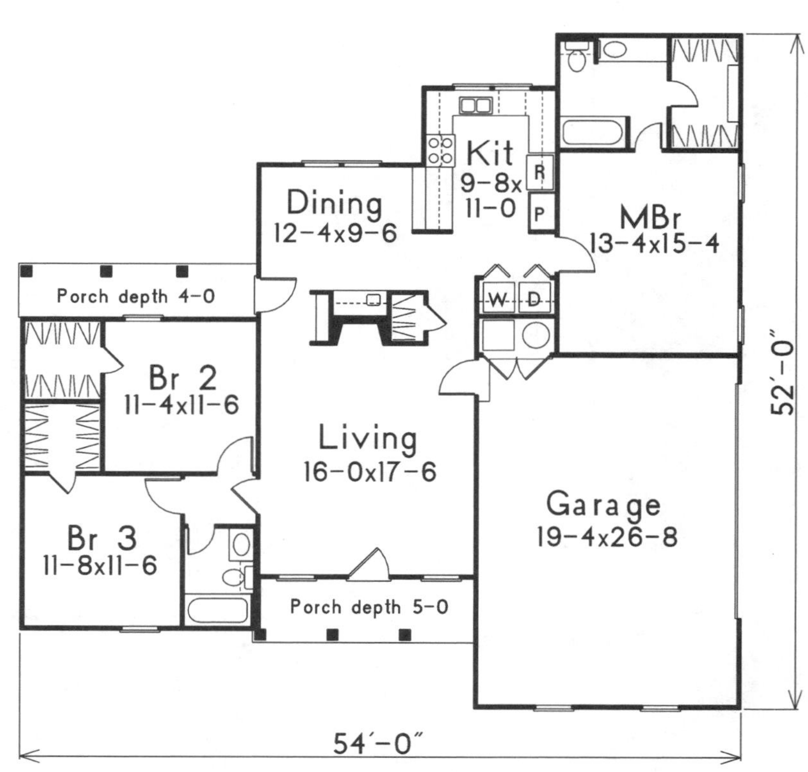
Kit
9-8x
11-0
R
P
Dining
12-4x9-6
MBr
13-4x15-4
Porch depth 4-0
W
D
Br 2
11-4x11-6
Living
16-0x17-6
Garage
19-4x26-8
Br 3
11-8x11-6
Porch depth 5-0
52′-0″
54′-0″

Gabled Front Entrance, Columned Porch

LOWE'S

Signature
SERIES

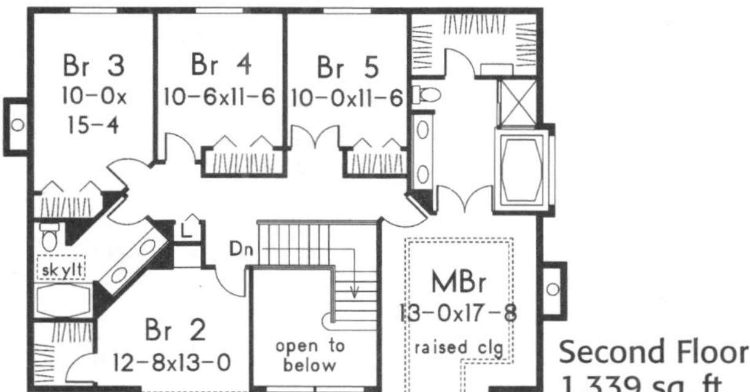
Br 3
10-0x
15-4
Br 4
10-6x11-6
Br 5
10-0x11-6
skylt
Dn
Br 2
12-8x13-0
open to below
MBr
13-0x17-8
raised clg
Second Floor
1,339 sq. ft.

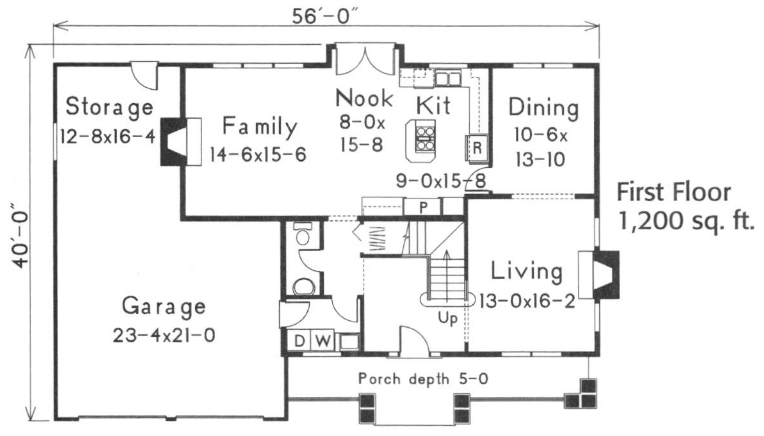
56'-0"
40'-0"
Storage
12-8x16-4
Family
14-6x15-6
Nook
8-0x
15-8
Kit
9-0x15-8
R
Dining
10-6x
13-10
P
Garage
23-4x21-0
D W
Up
Living
13-0x16-2
Porch depth 5-0
First Floor
1,200 sq. ft.

Plan #531-0326

Price Code D

Total Living Area: 2,539 Sq. Ft.

Home has 5 bedrooms, 2 1/2 baths, 2-car garage and crawl space foundation.

Special features

- Master bedroom features a tray ceiling and deluxe bath with walk-in closet
- Kitchen with island cooktop, desk and nook area access the outdoors
- Bedroom #2 includes walk-in closet and unique angled wall
- Living room includes a fireplace and opens to dining room

Signature SERIES

High-Styled Compact Plan

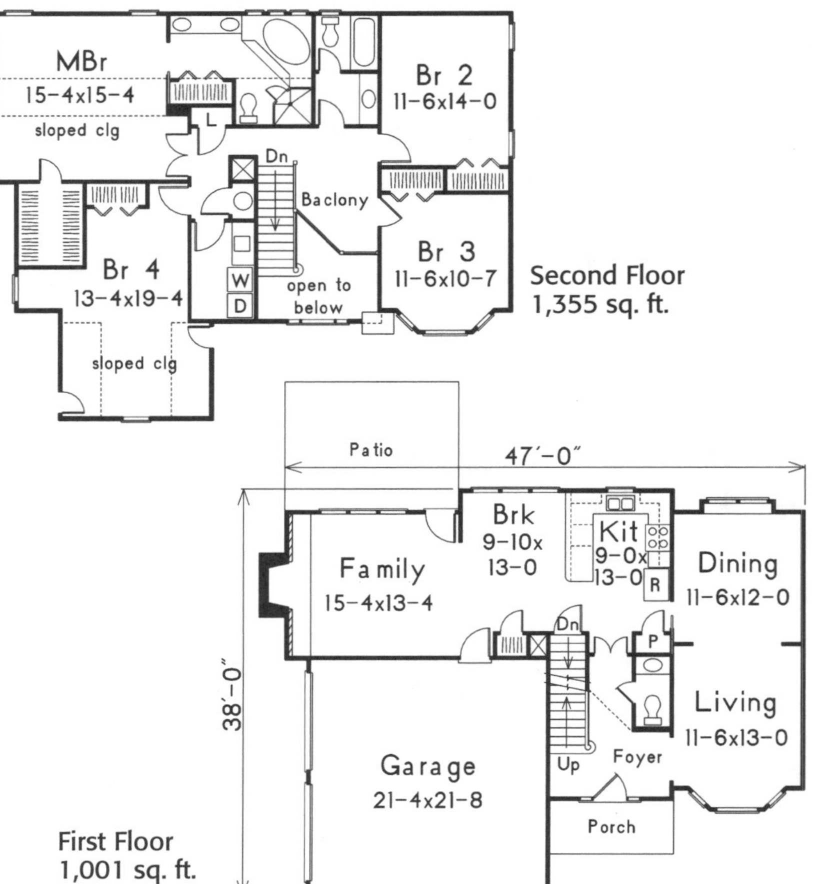

MBr
15-4x15-4
sloped clg
L
Br 2
11-6x14-0
Dn
Baclony
Br 3
11-6x10-7
Br 4
13-4x19-4
W
D
open to below
sloped clg
Second Floor
1,355 sq. ft.
Patio
47'-0"
Brk
9-10x
13-0
Kit
9-0x
13-0
R
Dining
11-6x12-0
Family
15-4x13-4
Dn
P
38'-0"
Living
11-6x13-0
Garage
21-4x21-8
Up
Foyer
Porch
First Floor
1,001 sq. ft.

Plan #531-0130

Price Code D

Total Living Area: 2,356 Sq. Ft.

Home has 4 bedrooms, 2 1/2 baths, 2-car side entry garage and basement foundation.

Special features

- Impressive arched and mullioned window treatment embellishes entrance and foyer
- Fourth bedroom located over the side entry garage has access to attic
- Full-size laundry facility
- Adjoining family room, breakfast area and kitchen form extensive living area

Spacious And Open Family Living Area

LOWE'S

Signature SERIES

Plan #531-0226

Price Code A

Total Living Area: 1,416 Sq. Ft.

Home has 3 bedrooms, 2 baths, 2-car garage and basement foundation, drawings also include crawl space and slab foundations.

Special features

- Family room includes fireplace, elevated plant shelf and vaulted ceiling
- Patio is accessible from dining area and garage
- Centrally located laundry area
- Oversized walk-in pantry

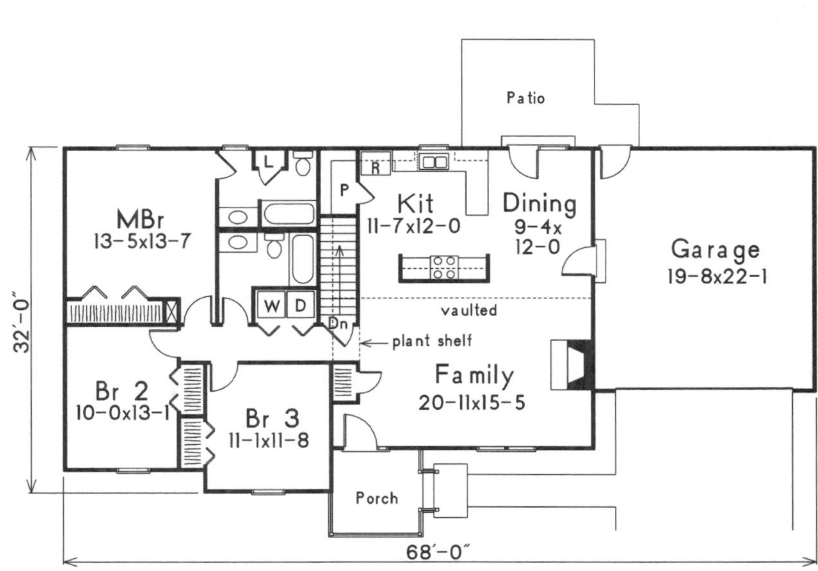

Patio
MBr
13-5x13-7
Kit
11-7x12-0
Dining
9-4x
12-0
Garage
19-8x22-1
vaulted
plant shelf
Family
20-11x15-5
Br 2
10-0x13-1
Br 3
11-1x11-8
Porch
32'-0"
68'-0"

Roomy Two-Story Has Screened-In Rear Porch

Plan #531-0291

Price Code B

Total Living Area: 1,600 Sq. Ft.

Home has 3 bedrooms, 2 baths, 2-car side entry garage and crawl space foundation, drawings also include slab foundation.

Special features

- Energy efficient home with 2" x 6" exterior walls
- First floor master suite accessible from two points of entry
- Master suite dressing area includes separate vanity and mirrored make-up counter
- Second floor bedrooms with generous storage, share a full bath

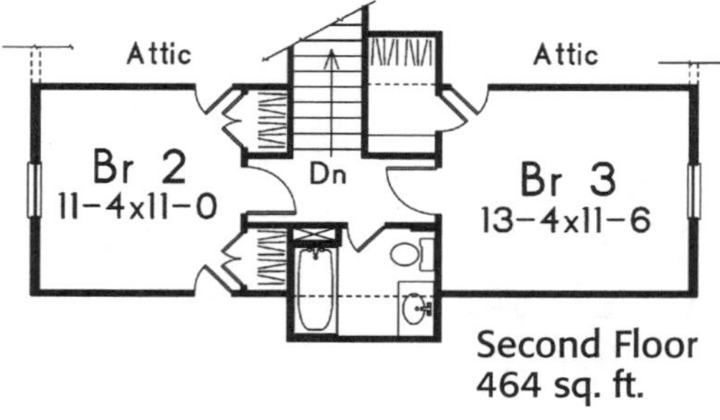

Attic
Attic
Br 2
11-4x11-0
Dn
Br 3
13-4x11-6

Second Floor
464 sq. ft.

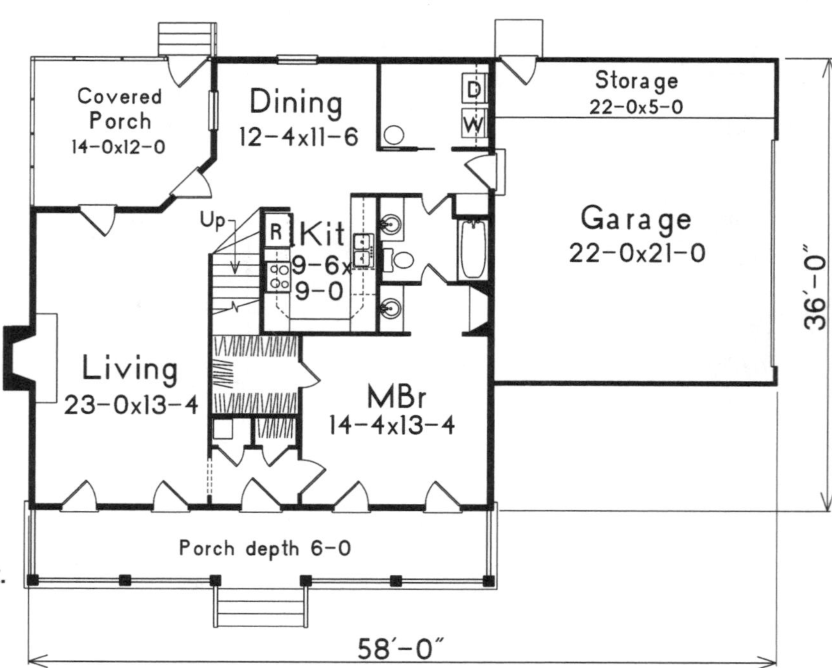

Covered Porch
14-0x12-0
Dining
12-4x11-6
D
W
Storage
22-0x5-0
Up
R
Kit
9-6x
9-0
Garage
22-0x21-0
36'-0"
Living
23-0x13-4
MBr
14-4x13-4
Porch depth 6-0
58'-0"

First Floor
1,136 sq. ft.

LOWE'S

Signature SERIES

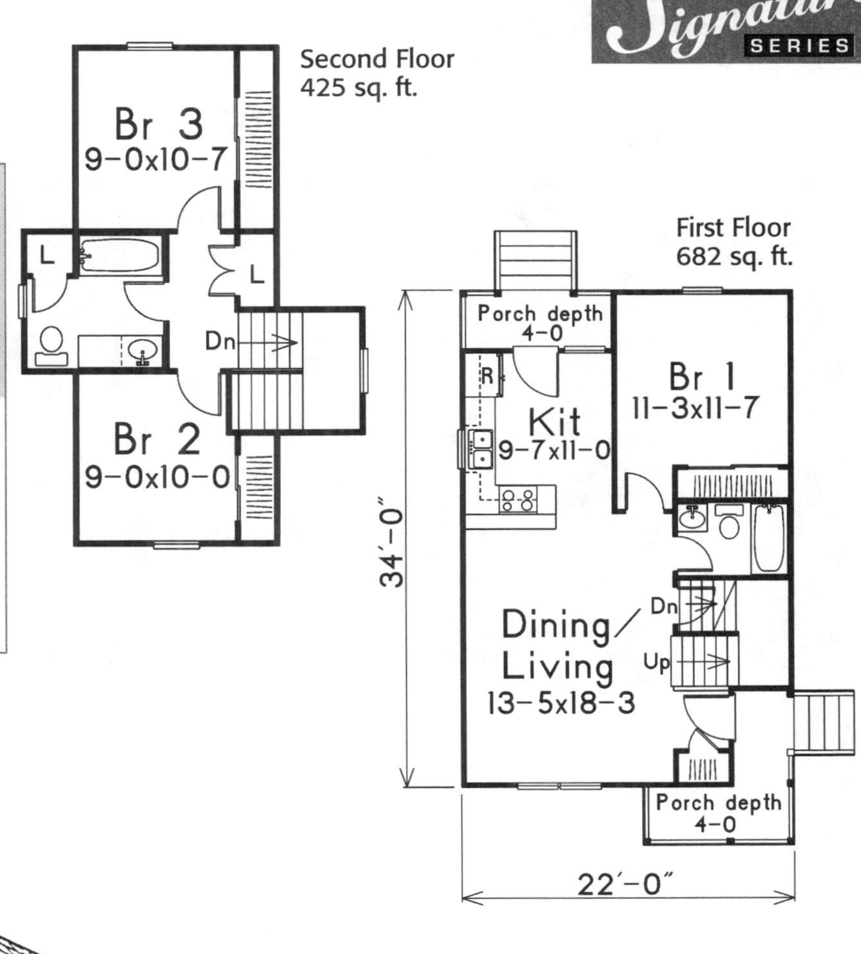

Second Floor
425 sq. ft.
Br 3
9-0x10-7
L
L
Dn
Br 2
9-0x10-0
First Floor
682 sq. ft.
Porch depth
4-0
R
Kit
9-7x11-0
Br 1
11-3x11-7
34'-0"
Dn
Dining/
Living
13-5x18-3
Up
Porch depth
4-0
22'-0"

Plan #531-0497

Price Code AA

Total Living Area: 1,107 Sq. Ft.

Home has 3 bedrooms, 2 baths and basement foundation.

Special features

- L-shaped kitchen has serving bar overlooking the dining/living room
- Second floor bedrooms share a bath with linen closet
- Front porch opens into foyer with convenient coat closet

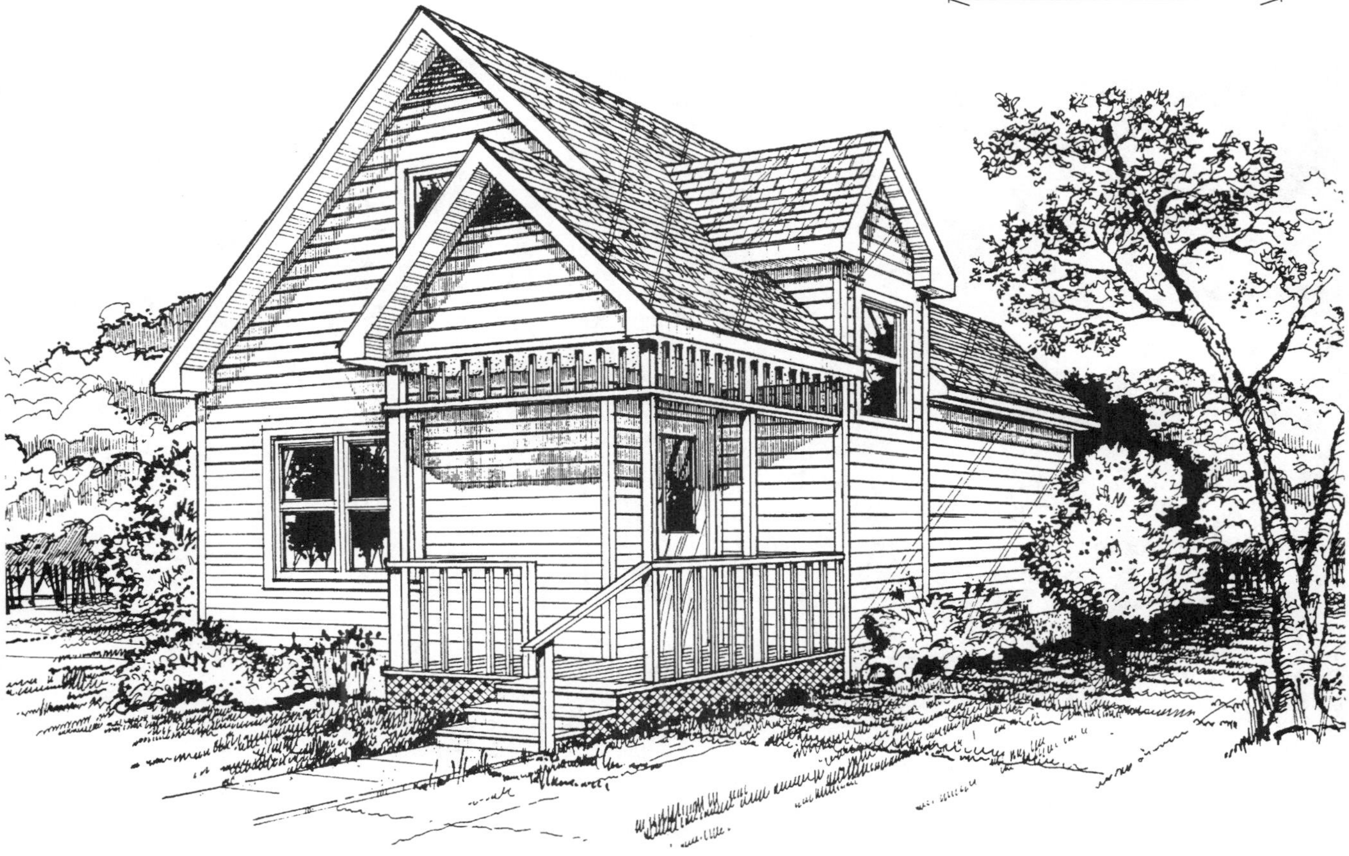

Charming With Many Gables

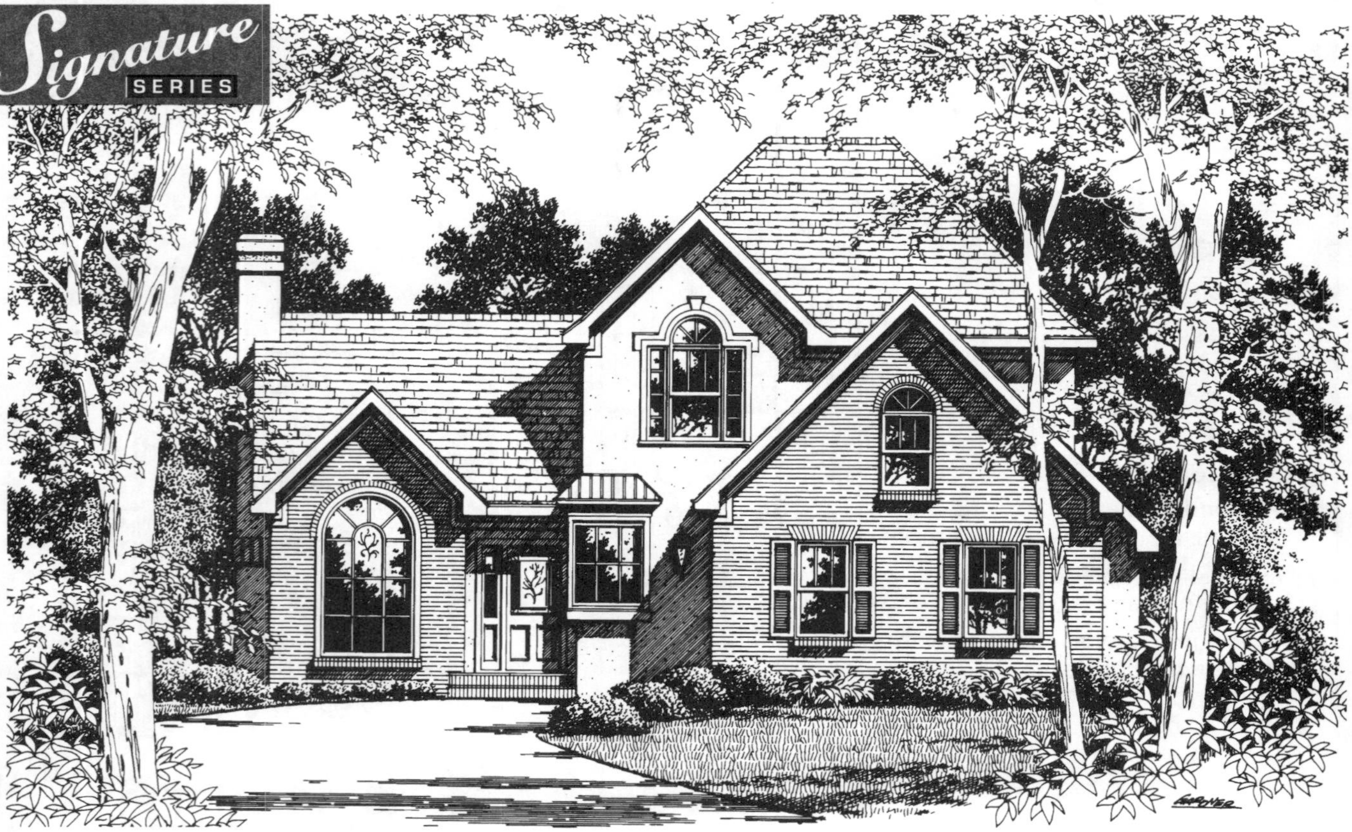

Plan #531-0204

Price Code C

Total Living Area: 2,128 Sq. Ft.

Home has 3 bedrooms, 2 1/2 baths, 2-car side entry garage and basement foundation.

Special features

- Large bonus area over garage converts to a fourth bedroom or activity center
- Family room fireplace and vaulted ceiling provide an attractive entry
- Master bedroom features bath with windowed tub, walk-in closet, separate shower and plenty of storage space

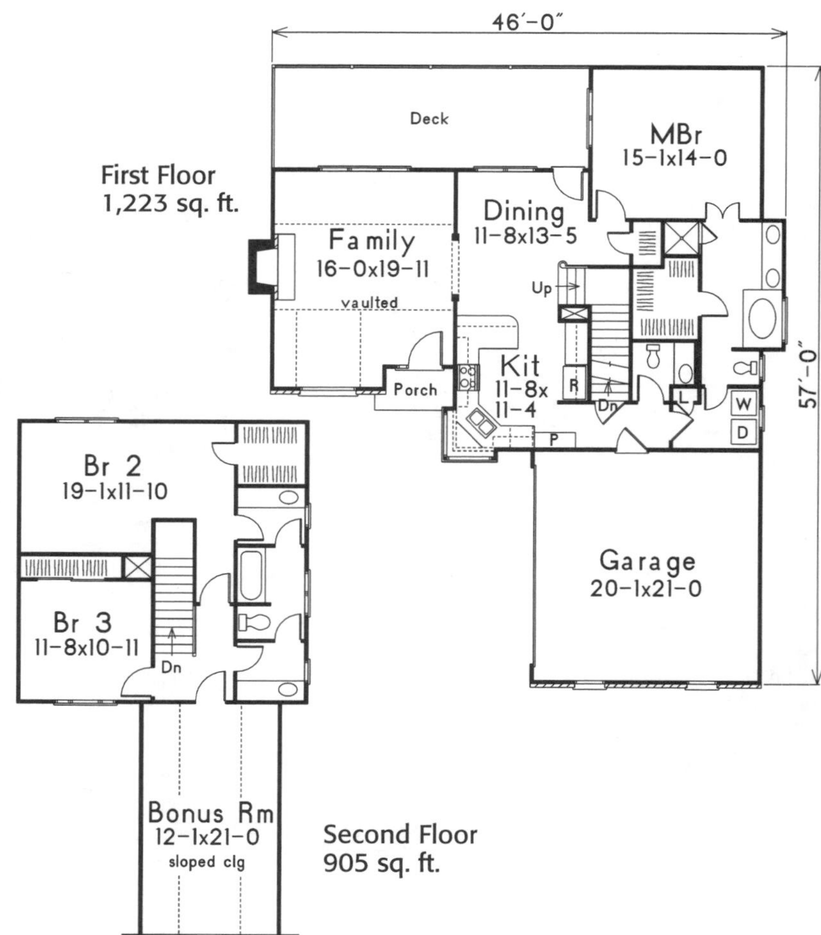
46'-0"
57'-0"
First Floor
1,223 sq. ft.
Deck
MBr
15-1x14-0
Dining
11-8x13-5
Family
16-0x19-11
vaulted
Up
Kit
11-8x
11-4
Porch
R
Dn
L
W
D
P
Garage
20-1x21-0
Br 2
19-1x11-10
Br 3
11-8x10-11
Dn
Bonus Rm
12-1x21-0
sloped clg
Second Floor
905 sq. ft.

Relax On The Covered Front Porch

LOWE'S

Signature SERIES

Plan #531-0489

Price Code B

Total Living Area: 1,543 Sq. Ft.

Home has 3 bedrooms, 2 1/2 baths, 2-car detached side entry garage and slab foundation, drawings also include crawl space foundation.

Special features

- Fireplace serves as the focal point of the large family room
- Efficient floor plan keeps hallways at a minimum
- Laundry room connects the kitchen to the garage
- Private first floor master bedroom has walk-in closet and bath

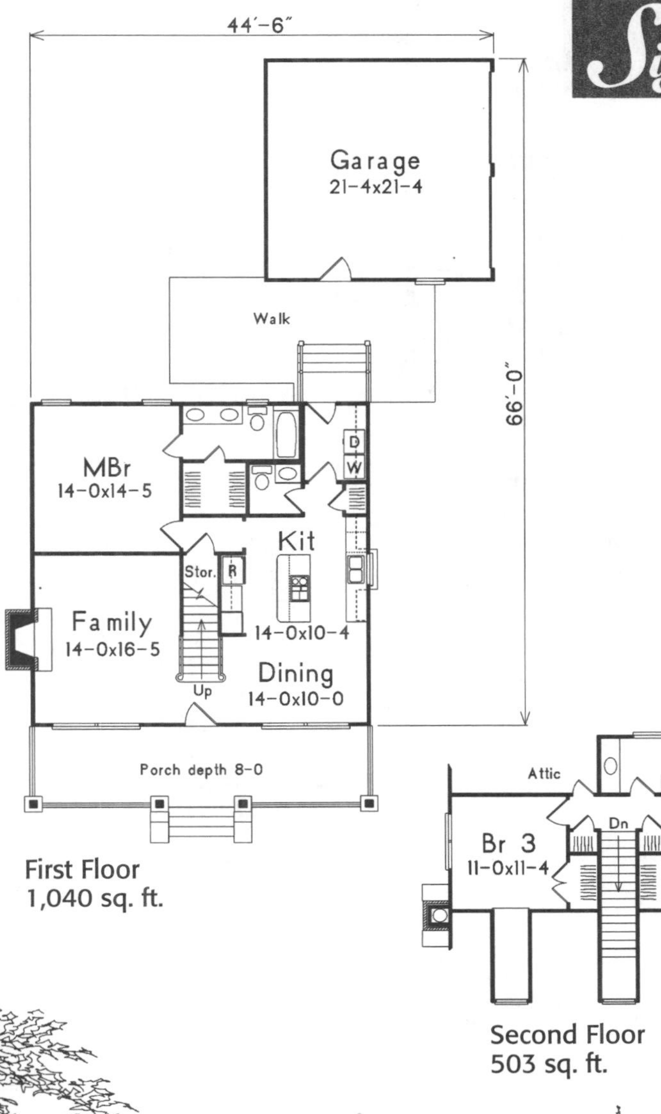
44'-6"
66'-0"
Garage
21-4x21-4
Walk
D
W
MBr
14-0x14-5
Kit
14-0x10-4
Stor.
R
Family
14-0x16-5
Up
Dining
14-0x10-0
Porch depth 8-0
Attic
Attic
Dn
Br 3
11-0x11-4
Br 2
11-0x11-4

First Floor
1,040 sq. ft.

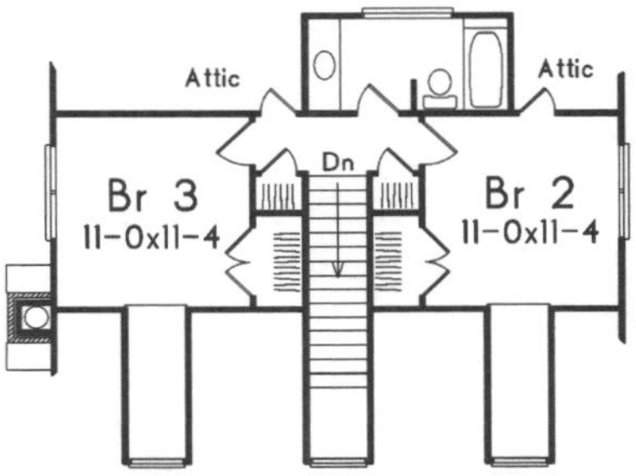

Second Floor
503 sq. ft.

LOWE'S

Signature SERIES

Practical Colonial Offers Great Value

Plan #531-0129

Price Code C

Total Living Area: 2,032 Sq. Ft.

Home has 4 bedrooms, 2 1/2 baths and crawl space foundation.

Special features

- Definite separation of living, dining and family rooms permits varied activities without disturbances
- Convenient side entrance directly to mud room, laundry and kitchen
- Breakfast room with charming bay window
- Handy outdoor storage room

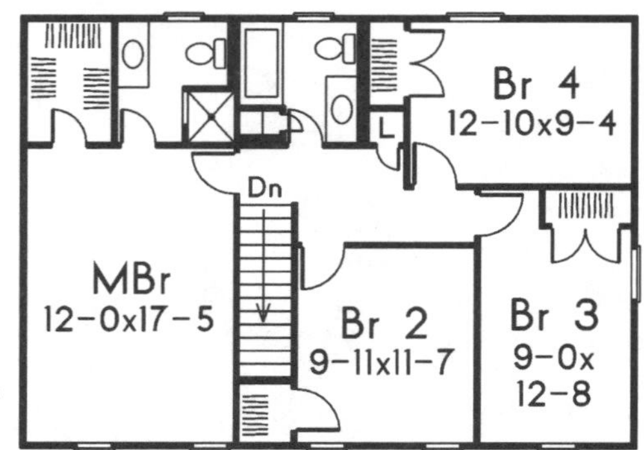
Br 4
12-10x9-4
L
Dn
MBr
12-0x17-5
Br 2
9-11x11-7
Br 3
9-0x
12-8

Second Floor
936 sq. ft.

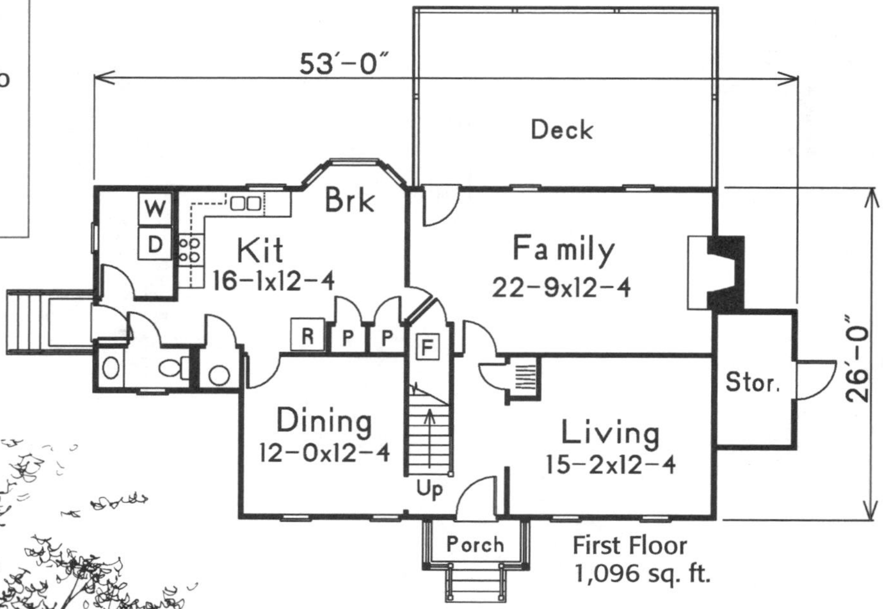

53′-0″
Deck
Brk
W
D
Kit
16-1x12-4
Family
22-9x12-4
R P P F
Stor.
26′-0″
Dining
12-0x12-4
Up
Living
15-2x12-4
Porch

First Floor
1,096 sq. ft.

RENDITIONS

TO ORDER BLUEPRINTS USE THE FORM ON PAGE 290 OR CALL TOLL-FREE **1-800-DREAM HOME** (373-2646)

Angled Walls Create Dramatic Layout

LOWE'S

Signature SERIES

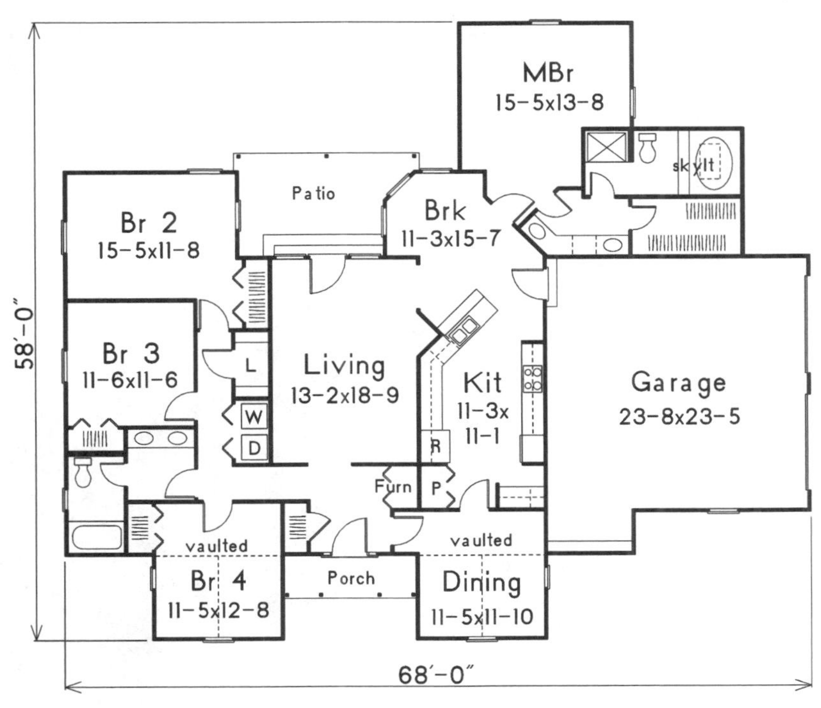
MBr
15-5x13-8
skylt
Patio
Brk
11-3x15-7
Br 2
15-5x11-8
Br 3
11-6x11-6
L
Living
13-2x18-9
Kit
11-3x
11-1
Garage
23-8x23-5
W
D
R
Furn
P
vaulted
Br 4
11-5x12-8
Porch
vaulted
Dining
11-5x11-10
58'-0"
68'-0"

Plan #531-0541

Price Code C

Total Living Area: 2,080 Sq. Ft.

Home has 4 bedrooms, 2 baths, 2-car side entry garage and crawl space foundation, drawings also include basement and slab foundations.

Special features

- Combined design elements create unique facade
- Foyer leads into large living room and direct view to patio
- Master bedroom includes spacious bath with garden tub, separate shower, walk-in closet and dressing area

LOWE'S
Signature
SERIES

Charming Two-Story With Dormers And Porch

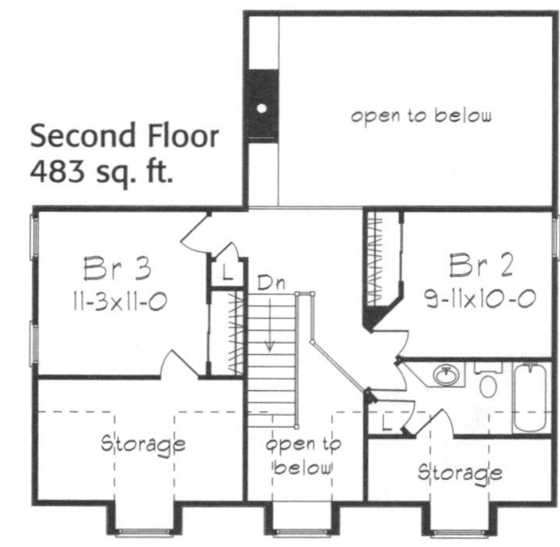
Second Floor
483 sq. ft.
open to below
Br 3
11-3x11-0
Dn
Br 2
9-11x10-0
Storage
open to below
Storage

Plan #531-0379

Price Code B

Total Living Area: 1,711 Sq. Ft.

Home has 3 bedrooms, 2 1/2 baths, 2-car garage and basement foundation.

Special features

- U-shaped kitchen joins breakfast and family rooms for open living atmosphere
- Master bedroom has secluded covered porch and private bath
- Balcony overlooks family room that features a fireplace and accesses deck

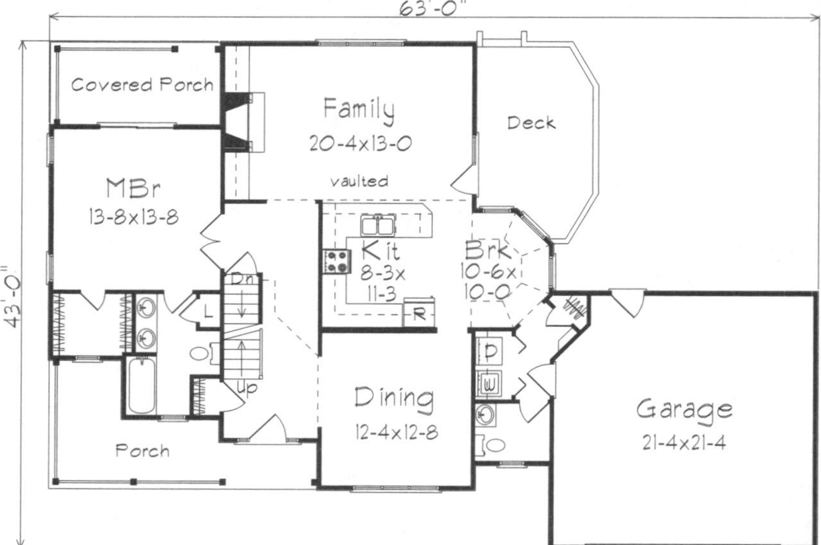
63'-0"
43'-0"
Covered Porch
Family
20-4x13-0
vaulted
Deck
MBr
13-8x13-8
Kit
8-3x
11-3
Brk
10-6x
10-0
Dn
Up
Dining
12-4x12-8
Garage
21-4x21-4
Porch

First Floor
1,228 sq. ft.

TO ORDER BLUEPRINTS USE THE FORM ON PAGE 290 OR CALL TOLL-FREE **1-800-DREAM HOME** (373-2646)

Compact Home For Functional Living

LOWE'S

Signature SERIES

Plan #531-0173

Price Code A

Total Living Area: 1,220 Sq. Ft.

Home has 3 bedrooms, 2 baths, 2-car drive under garage and basement foundation.

Special features

- Vaulted ceilings add luxury to living room and master suite
- Spacious living room accented with a large fireplace and hearth
- Gracious dining area is adjacent to the convenient wrap-around kitchen
- Washer and dryer handy to the bedrooms
- Covered porch entry adds appeal
- Rear sundeck adjoins dining area

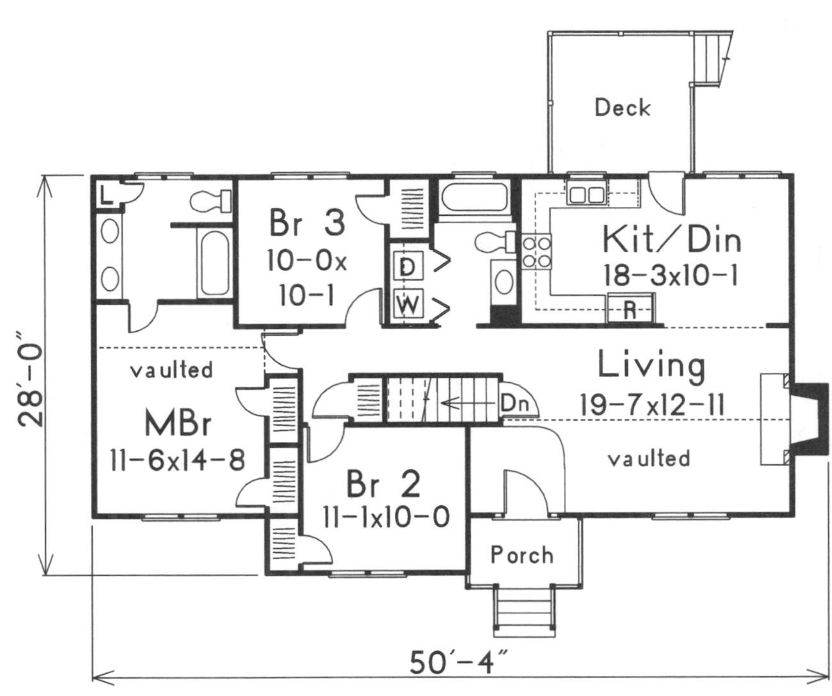
Deck
L
Br 3
10-0x
10-1
D
W
Kit/Din
18-3x10-1
R
vaulted
MBr
11-6x14-8
Living
19-7x12-11
Dn
vaulted
Br 2
11-1x10-0
Porch
28'-0"
50'-4"

Country Classic With Modern Floor Plan

Plan #531-0312

Price Code D

Total Living Area: 1,921 Sq. Ft.

Home has 3 bedrooms, 2 1/2 baths, 2-car garage and basement foundation.

Special features

- Sunken family room with built-in entertainment center and coffered ceiling
- Sunken formal living room with coffered ceiling
- Dressing area with double sinks, spa tub, shower and French door to private deck
- Large front porch adds to home's appeal
- Energy efficient home with 2" x 6" exterior walls

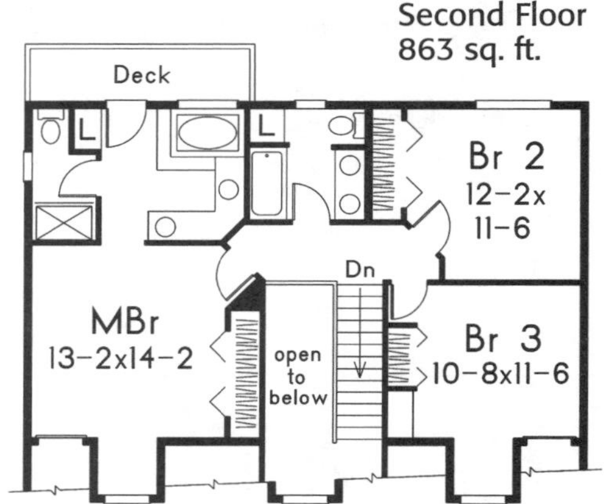
Second Floor
863 sq. ft.
Deck
L
L
Br 2
12-2x
11-6
Dn
MBr
13-2x14-2
open
to
below
Br 3
10-8x11-6

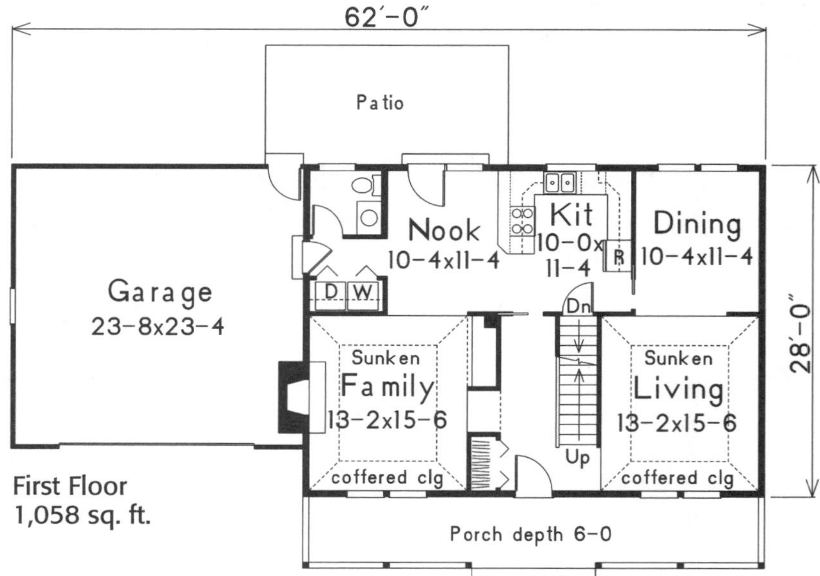
62'-0"
Patio
Nook
10-4x11-4
Kit
10-0x
11-4
B
Dining
10-4x11-4
Garage
23-8x23-4
D W
Dn
Sunken
Family
13-2x15-6
Sunken
Living
13-2x15-6
28'-0"
Up
coffered clg
coffered clg
First Floor
1,058 sq. ft.
Porch depth 6-0

 TO ORDER BLUEPRINTS USE THE FORM ON PAGE 290 OR CALL TOLL-FREE **1-800-DREAM HOME** (373-2646)

Small And Cozy Cabin

LOWE'S

Signature
SERIES

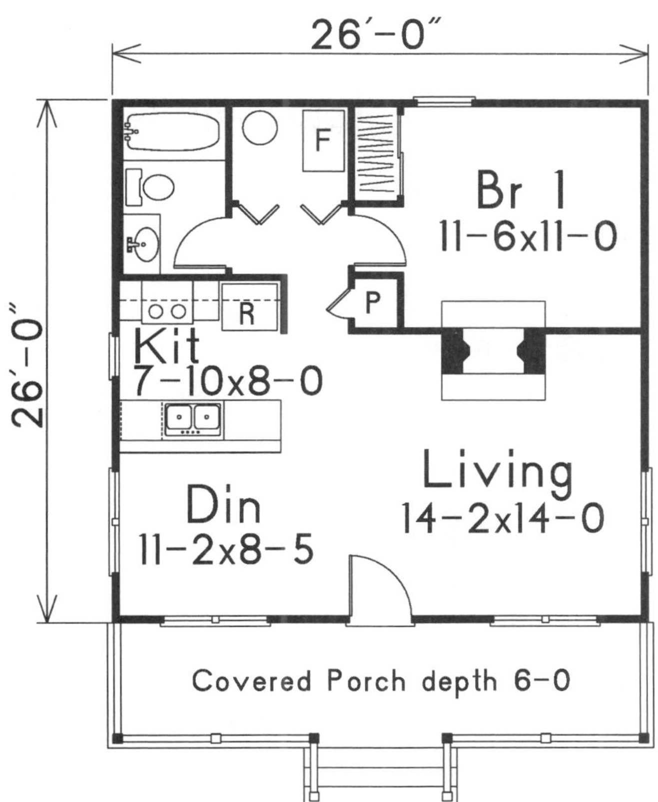
26′-0″
26′-0″
F
Br 1
11-6x11-0
R
P
Kit
7-10x8-0
Living
14-2x14-0
Din
11-2x8-5
Covered Porch depth 6-0

Plan #531-0696

Price Code AAA

Total Living Area: 676 Sq. Ft.

Home has 1 bedroom, 1 bath and crawl space foundation.

Special features

- See-through fireplace between bedroom and living area adds character
- Combined dining/living area creates open feeling
- Full-length front covered porch perfect for enjoying the outdoors
- Additional storage available in utility room

LOWE'S
Signature
SERIES

Plan #531-0374

Price Code D

Total Living Area: 2,213 Sq. Ft.

Home has 4 bedrooms, 2 1/2 baths, 2-car garage and basement foundation.

Special features

- Angled kitchen counter overlooks living room with large fireplace
- Hallway between family and living areas provides extra storage and convenient sink for entertaining
- Large master suite features vaulted ceiling and elegant master bath with walk-in closet
- Second floor open to foyer below and features distinctive plant shelf

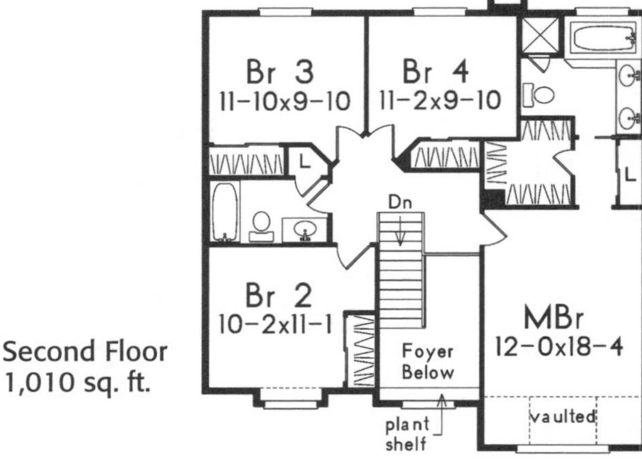
Br 3
11-10x9-10
Br 4
11-2x9-10
L
L
Dn
Br 2
10-2x11-1
Foyer
Below
MBr
12-0x18-4
vaulted
plant
shelf

Second Floor
1,010 sq. ft.

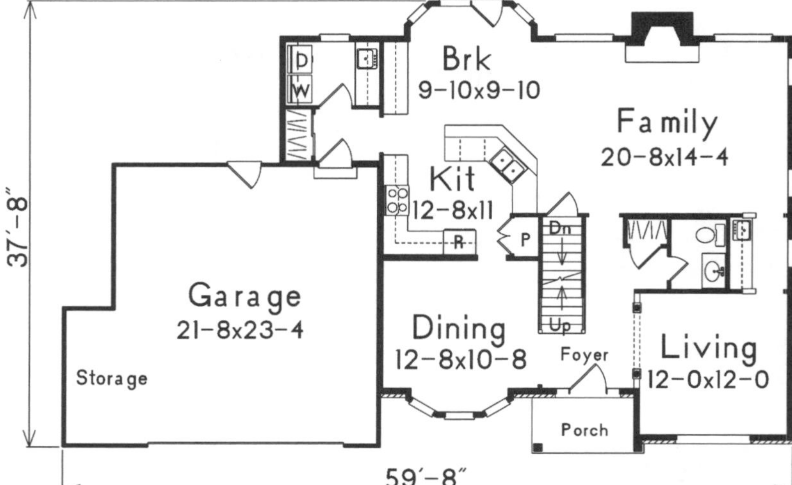
Brk
9-10x9-10
D
W
Family
20-8x14-4
Kit
12-8x11
R
P
Dn
Up
37'-8"
Garage
21-8x23-4
Storage
Dining
12-8x10-8
Foyer
Living
12-0x12-0
Porch
59'-8"

First Floor
1,203 sq. ft.

Colonial With Overhead Balcony

LOWE'S

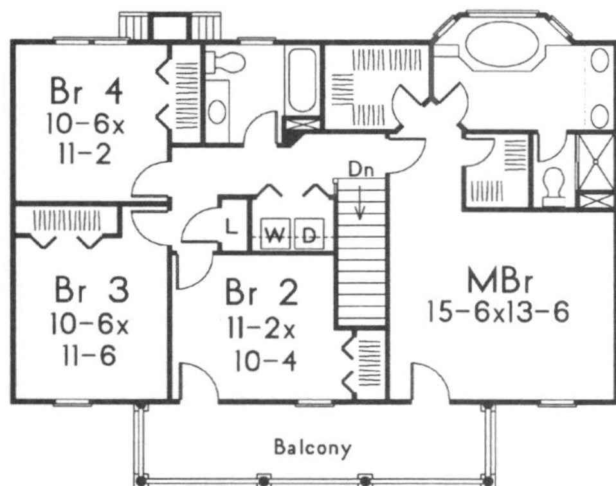
Br 4
10-6x
11-2
Dn
Br 3
10-6x
11-6
L
W
D
Br 2
11-2x
10-4
MBr
15-6x13-6
Balcony

Second Floor
1,108 sq. ft.

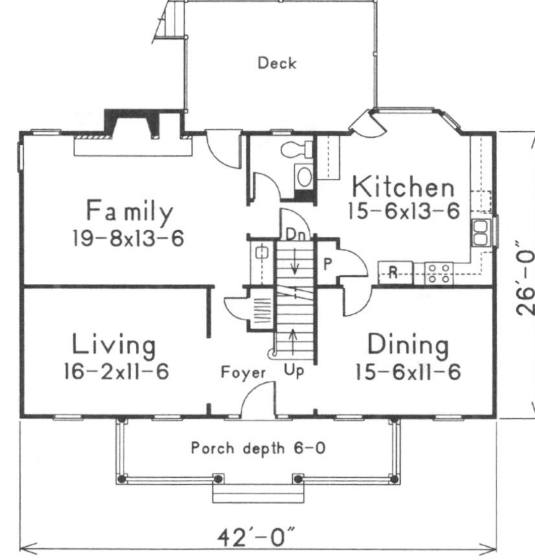
Deck
Family
19-8x13-6
Kitchen
15-6x13-6
Dn
P
R
Living
16-2x11-6
Foyer
Up
Dining
15-6x11-6
26'-0"
Porch depth 6-0
42'-0"

First Floor
1,108 sq. ft.

Plan #531-0134

Price Code D

Total Living Area: 2,216 Sq. Ft.

Home has 4 bedrooms, 2 1/2 baths, 2-car drive under garage and basement foundation.

Special features

- Luxury master bedroom suite features full-windowed bathtub bay, double walk-in closets and access to the front balcony
- Spacious kitchen/breakfast room combination
- Second floor laundry facility

LOWE'S
Signature
SERIES

Corner Fireplace Highlights The Living Area

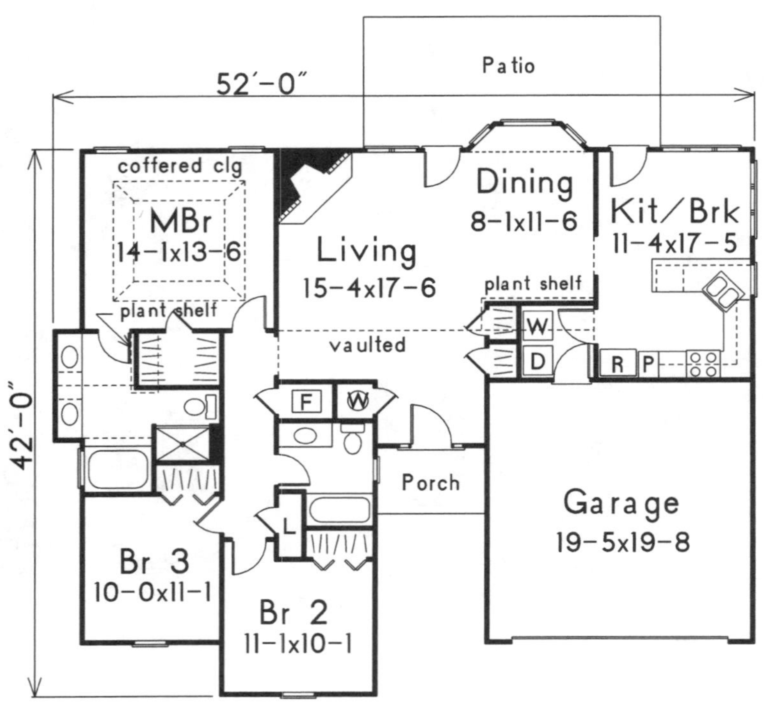
Patio
52'–0"
42'–0"
coffered clg
MBr
14–1x13–6
plant shelf
Living
15–4x17–6
vaulted
Dining
8–1x11–6
plant shelf
Kit/Brk
11–4x17–5
W
D
R
P
F
W
L
Porch
Garage
19–5x19–8
Br 3
10–0x11–1
Br 2
11–1x10–1

Plan #531-0253

Price Code A

Total Living Area: 1,458 Sq. Ft.

Home has 3 bedrooms, 2 baths, 2-car garage and crawl space foundation, drawings also include slab foundation.

Special features

- Convenient snack bar joins kitchen with breakfast room
- Large living/dining room with fireplace, plenty of windows, vaulted ceiling and plant shelves
- Master bedroom offers a private bath with vaulted ceiling, walk-in closet, plant shelf and coffered ceiling
- Corner windows provide abundant light in breakfast room

TO ORDER BLUEPRINTS USE THE FORM ON PAGE 290 OR CALL TOLL-FREE **1-800-DREAM HOME** (373-2646)

Old-Fashioned Porch Gives Welcoming Appeal

LOWE'S

Signature SERIES

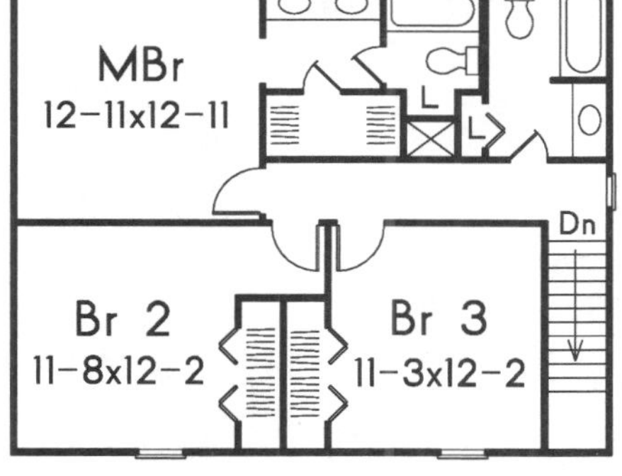
MBr
12–11x12–11
L
L
Dn
Br 2
11–8x12–2
Br 3
11–3x12–2

Second Floor
832 sq. ft.

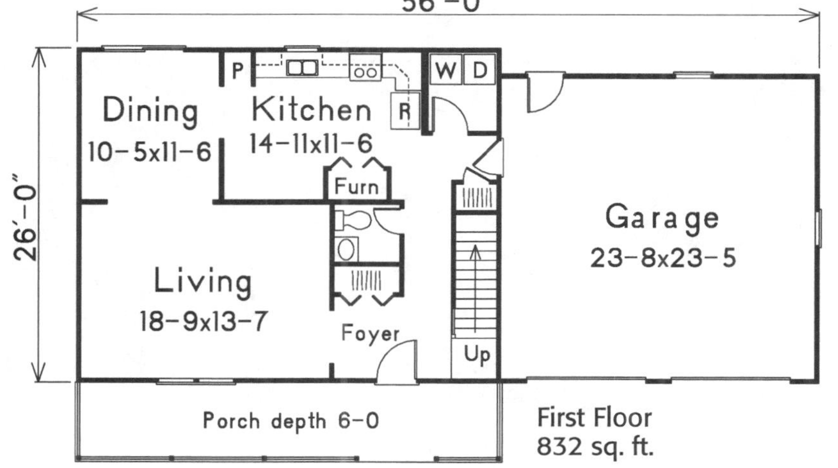
56'–0"
26'–0"
P
W
D
Dining
10–5x11–6
Kitchen
14–11x11–6
R
Furn
Garage
23–8x23–5
Living
18–9x13–7
Foyer
Up
Porch depth 6–0

First Floor
832 sq. ft.

Plan #531-0536

Price Code B

Total Living Area:	1,664 Sq. Ft.

Home has 3 bedrooms, 2 1/2 baths, 2-car garage and crawl space foundation, drawings also include basement and slab foundations.

Special features

- L-shaped country kitchen includes pantry and cozy breakfast area
- Bedrooms located on second floor for privacy
- Master bedroom includes walk-in closet, dressing area and bath

LOWE'S
Signature
SERIES

Breezeway Joins Living Space With Garage

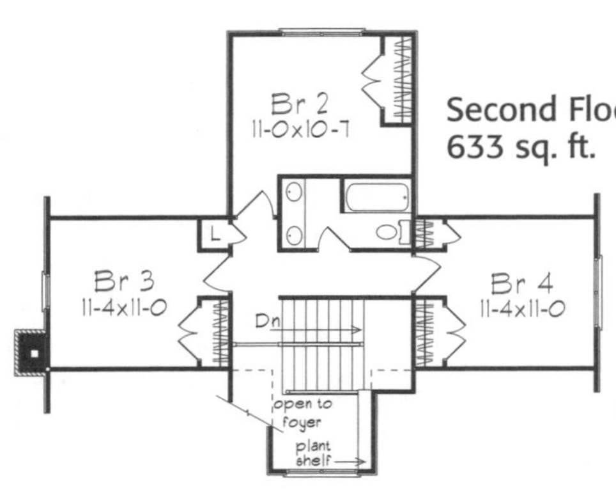

Br 2
11-0x10-7
L
Br 3
11-4x11-0
Dn
Br 4
11-4x11-0
open to foyer
plant shelf

Second Floor
633 sq. ft.

Plan #531-0362

Price Code C

Total Living Area: 1,874 Sq. Ft.

Home has 4 bedrooms, 2 1/2 baths, 2-car garage and basement foundation, drawings also include slab foundation.

Special features

- 9' ceilings throughout first floor
- Two-story foyer opens into large family room with fireplace
- First floor master suite includes private bath with tub and shower

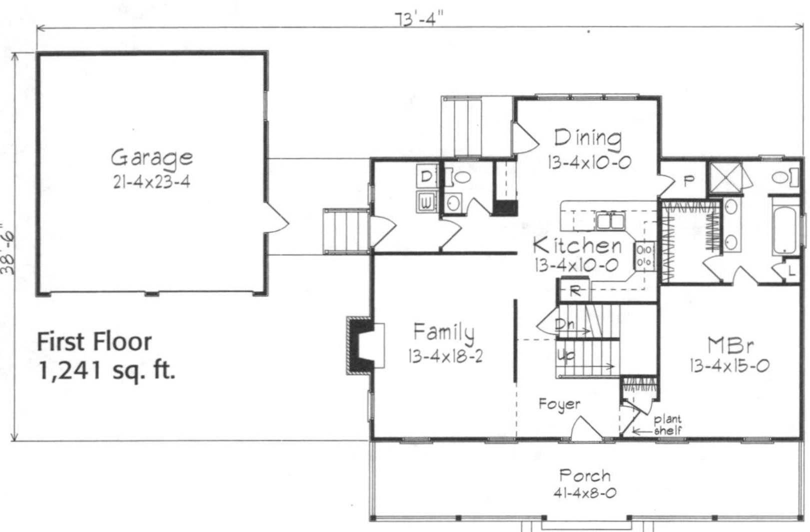

73'-4"
38'-6"
Garage
21-4x23-4
Dining
13-4x10-0
D
W
P
Kitchen
13-4x10-0
R
L
Family
13-4x18-2
Dn
Up
MBr
13-4x15-0
Foyer
plant shelf
Porch
41-4x8-0

First Floor
1,241 sq. ft.

Massive Ranch With Classy Features

LOWE'S

Signature SERIES

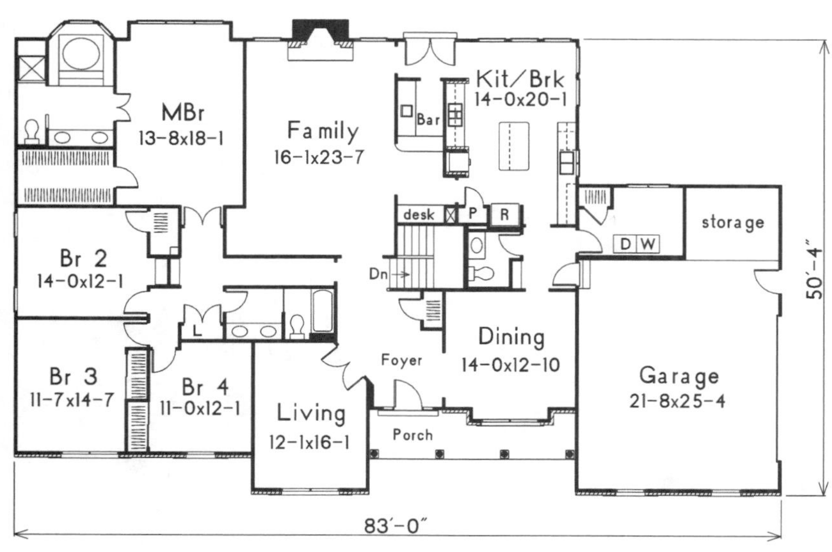

MBr
13-8x18-1
Family
16-1x23-7
Bar
Kit/Brk
14-0x20-1
desk
P
R
Dn
D W
storage
Br 2
14-0x12-1
L
Dining
14-0x12-10
Foyer
Garage
21-8x25-4
Br 3
11-7x14-7
Br 4
11-0x12-1
Living
12-1x16-1
Porch
50'-4"
83'-0"

Plan #531-0151

Price Code E

Total Living Area: 2,874 Sq. Ft.

Home has 4 bedrooms, 2 1/2 baths, 2-car side entry garage and basement foundation.

Special features

- Large family room with sloped ceiling and wood beams adjoins the kitchen and breakfast area with windows on two walls
- Large foyer opens to family room with massive stone fireplace and open stairs to the basement
- Private master bedroom with raised tub under the bay window, dramatic dressing area and a huge walk-in closet

LOWE'S

Signature
SERIES

Plan #531-0110

Price Code B

Total Living Area: 1,605 Sq. Ft.

Home has 3 bedrooms, 2 baths, 2-car garage and basement foundation, drawings also include slab and crawl space foundations.

Special features

- Vaulted ceilings in great room and kitchen/breakfast area
- Spacious great room features large bay window, fireplace, built-in bookshelves and a convenient wet bar
- Dine in formal dining room or breakfast room overlooking rear yard, perfect for entertaining or everyday living
- Master bedroom has a spacious master bath with oval tub and separate shower

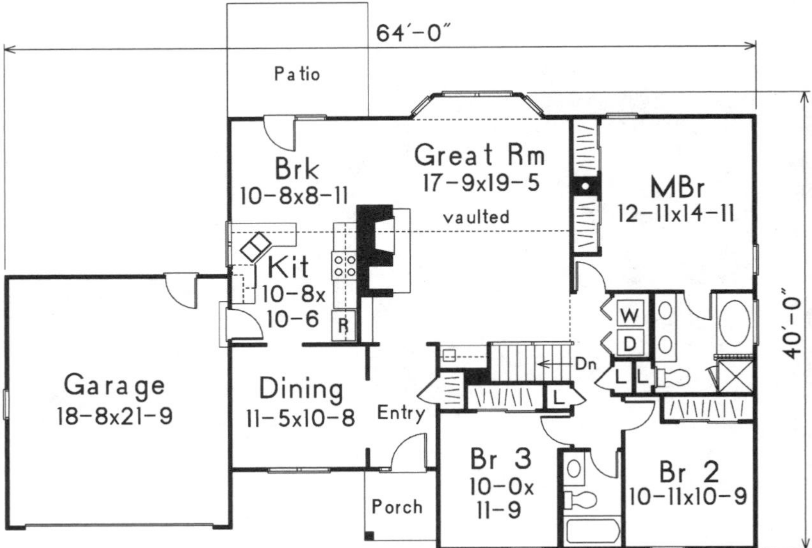
64'-0"
Patio
Brk
10-8x8-11
Great Rm
17-9x19-5
vaulted
MBr
12-11x14-11
Kit
10-8x
10-6
R
W
D
Dn
L
Garage
18-8x21-9
Dining
11-5x10-8
Entry
Br 3
10-0x
11-9
Br 2
10-11x10-9
Porch
40'-0"

 TO ORDER BLUEPRINTS USE THE FORM ON PAGE 290 OR CALL TOLL-FREE **1-800-DREAM HOME** (373-2646)

Quaint Country Home Is Ideal

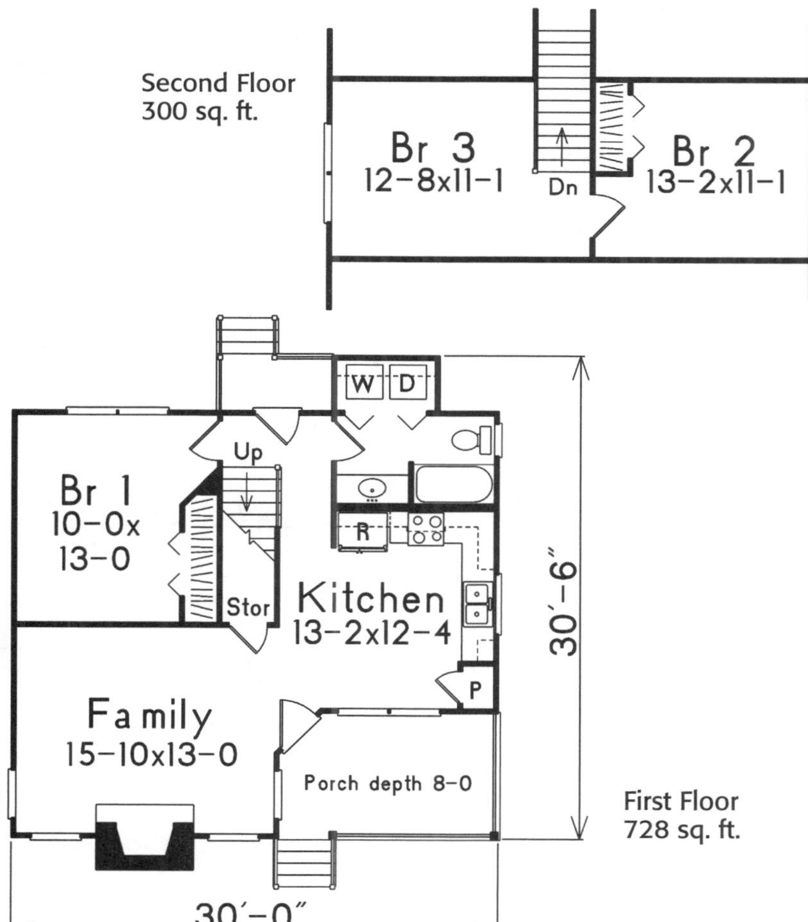
Second Floor
300 sq. ft.
Br 3
12-8x11-1
Dn
Br 2
13-2x11-1
W
D
Up
Br 1
10-0x
13-0
R
Stor
Kitchen
13-2x12-4
P
Family
15-10x13-0
Porch depth 8-0
30'-6"
30'-0"
First Floor
728 sq. ft.

Plan #531-0462

Price Code AA

Total Living Area: 1,028 Sq. Ft.

Home has 3 bedrooms, 1 bath and crawl space foundation.

Special features

- Master bedroom conveniently located on first floor
- Well-designed bath contains laundry facilities
- L-shaped kitchen with handy pantry
- Tall windows flank family room fireplace
- Cozy covered porch provides unique angled entry into home

TO ORDER BLUEPRINTS USE THE FORM ON PAGE 290 OR CALL TOLL-FREE **1-800-DREAM HOME** (373-2646)

LOWE'S Signature SERIES

Farmhouse Style Offers Great Privacy

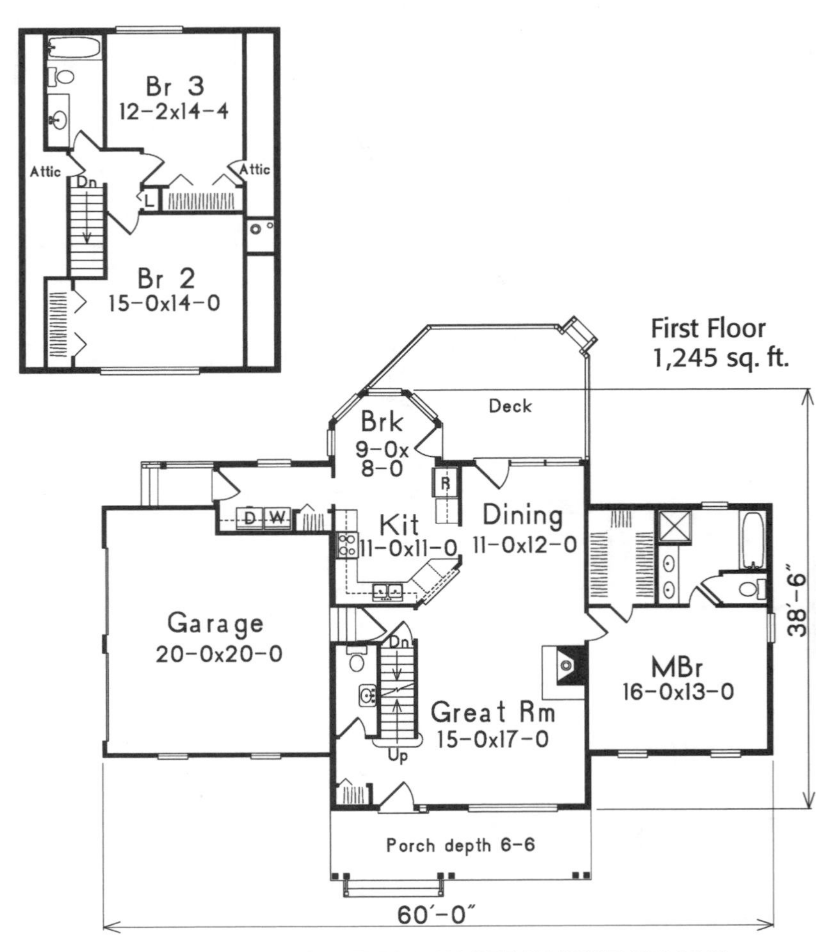

Second Floor
560 sq. ft.
Br 3
12-2x14-4
Attic
Dn
L
Attic
Br 2
15-0x14-0
First Floor
1,245 sq. ft.
Deck
Brk
9-0x
8-0
R
Dining
11-0x12-0
D W
Kit
11-0x11-0
Garage
20-0x20-0
Dn
MBr
16-0x13-0
Great Rm
15-0x17-0
Up
Porch depth 6-6
38'-6"
60'-0"

Plan #531-0673

Price Code C

Total Living Area: 1,805 Sq. Ft.

Home has 3 bedrooms, 2 1/2 baths, 2-car side entry garage and basement foundation, drawings also include slab foundation.

Special features

- Energy efficient home with 2" x 6" exterior walls
- Master suite forms its own wing
- Second floor bedrooms share a hall bath
- Large great room with fireplace spacially blends into a formal dining room

TO ORDER BLUEPRINTS USE THE FORM ON PAGE 290 OR CALL TOLL-FREE **1-800-DREAM HOME** (373-2646)

Charming Exterior And Cozy Interior

LOWE'S

Signature
SERIES

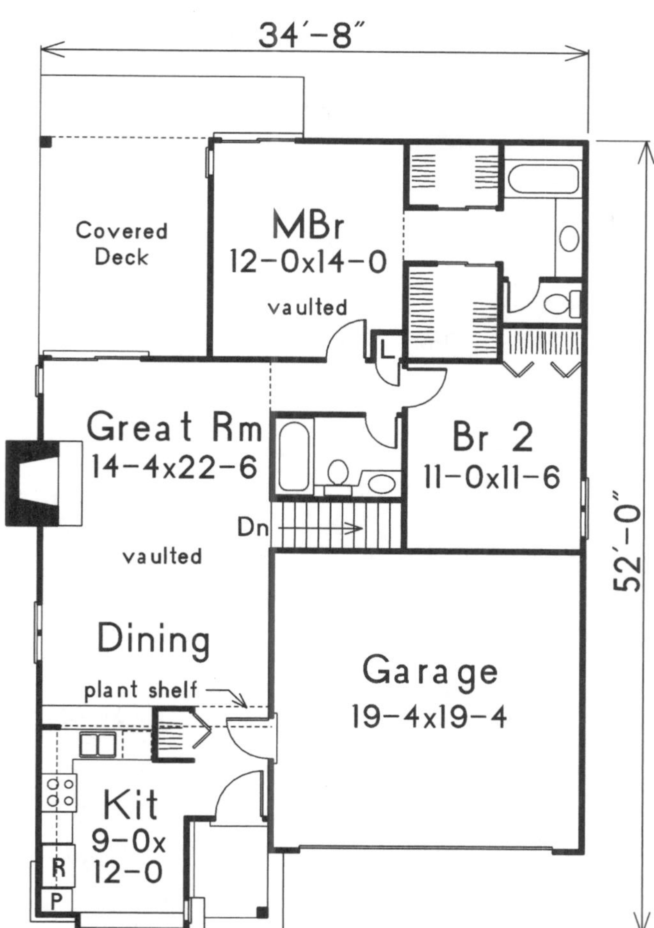
34'-8"
52'-0"
Covered Deck
MBr
12-0x14-0
vaulted
L
Great Rm
14-4x22-6
Br 2
11-0x11-6
Dn
vaulted
Dining
plant shelf
Garage
19-4x19-4
Kit
9-0x
12-0
R
P

Plan #531-0277

Price Code AA

Total Living Area: 1,127 Sq. Ft.

Home has 2 bedrooms, 2 baths, 2-car garage and basement foundation.

Special features

- Plant shelf joins kitchen and dining room
- Vaulted master suite with double walk-in closets, deck access and private bath
- Great room features vaulted ceiling, fireplace and sliding doors to covered deck
- Ideal home for a narrow lot

Formal Home, Enhanced By Huge Foyer

Plan #531-0158

Price Code F

Total Living Area: 3,200 Sq. Ft.

Home has 4 bedrooms, 2 1/2 baths, 2-car side entry garage and basement foundation.

Special features

- Two-story entry foyer and graceful curved stairway are flanked by separate living and dining rooms
- Master bedroom suite on the second floor has a double-door entry, fireplace and step-up tub built into the bay window

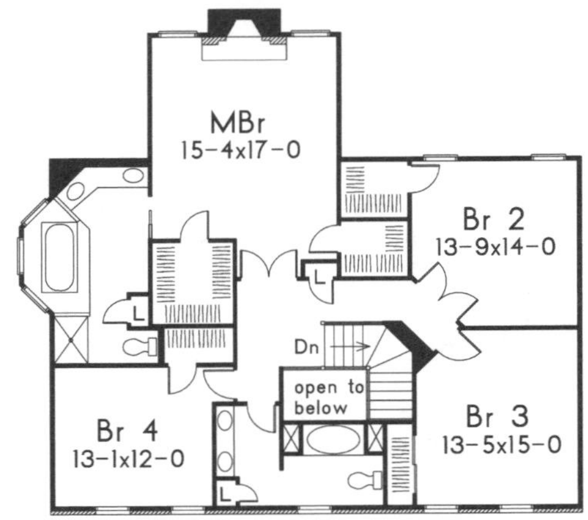
MBr
15-4x17-0
Br 2
13-9x14-0
Dn
open to below
Br 4
13-1x12-0
Br 3
13-5x15-0
L
L
L

Second Floor
1,514 sq. ft.

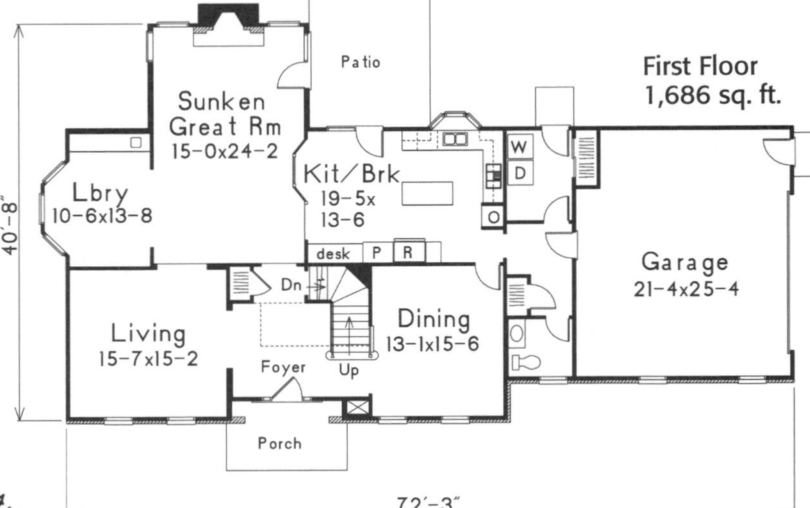
Patio
Sunken Great Rm
15-0x24-2
Lbry
10-6x13-8
Kit/Brk
19-5x
13-6
W
D
O
desk
P
R
Dn
Living
15-7x15-2
Foyer
Up
Dining
13-1x15-6
Garage
21-4x25-4
Porch
40'-8"
72'-3"

First Floor
1,686 sq. ft.

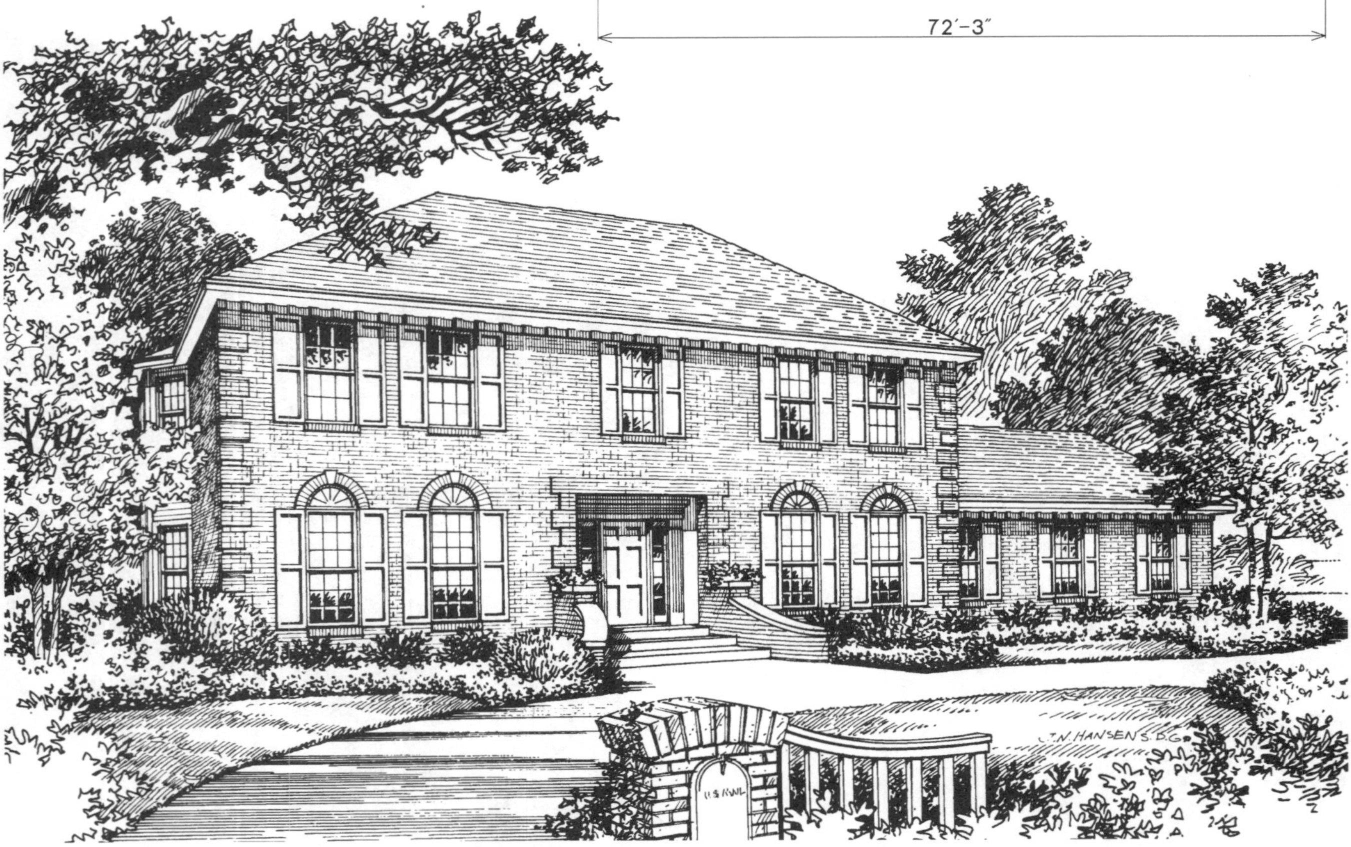

Gable Facade Adds Appeal To This Ranch

LOWE'S

Signature
SERIES

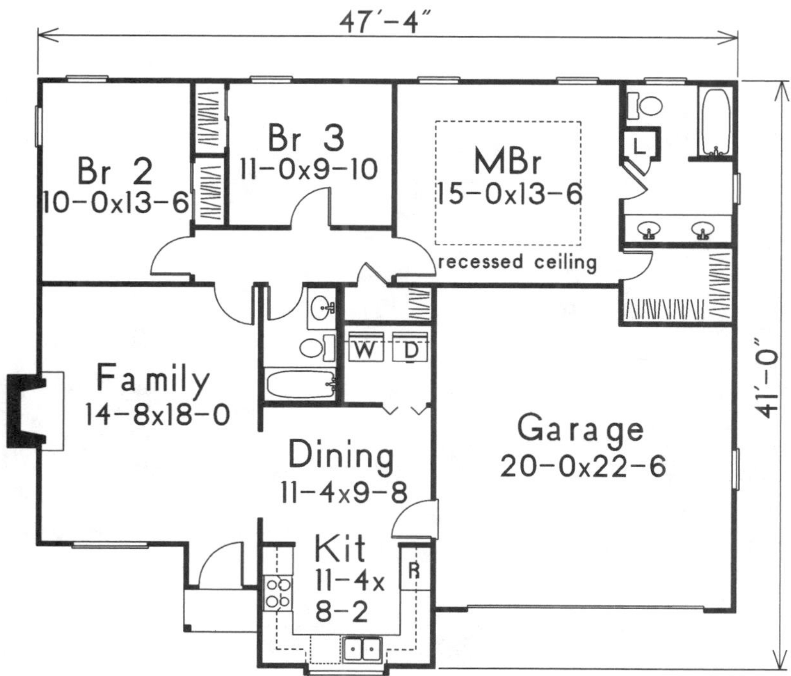
47'-4"
Br 2
10-0x13-6
Br 3
11-0x9-10
MBr
15-0x13-6
recessed ceiling
L
W
D
Family
14-8x18-0
Dining
11-4x9-8
Kit
11-4x
8-2
R
Garage
20-0x22-6
41'-0"

Plan #531-0292

Price Code A

Total Living Area: 1,304 Sq. Ft.

Home has 3 bedrooms, 2 baths, 2-car garage and slab foundation.

Special features

- Covered entrance leads into family room with 10' ceiling and fireplace
- 10' ceilings in kitchen, dining and family rooms
- Master bedroom features coffered ceiling, walk-in closet and private bath
- Efficient kitchen includes large window over the sink

LOWE'S
Signature
SERIES

Columns Accent The Living And Dining Rooms

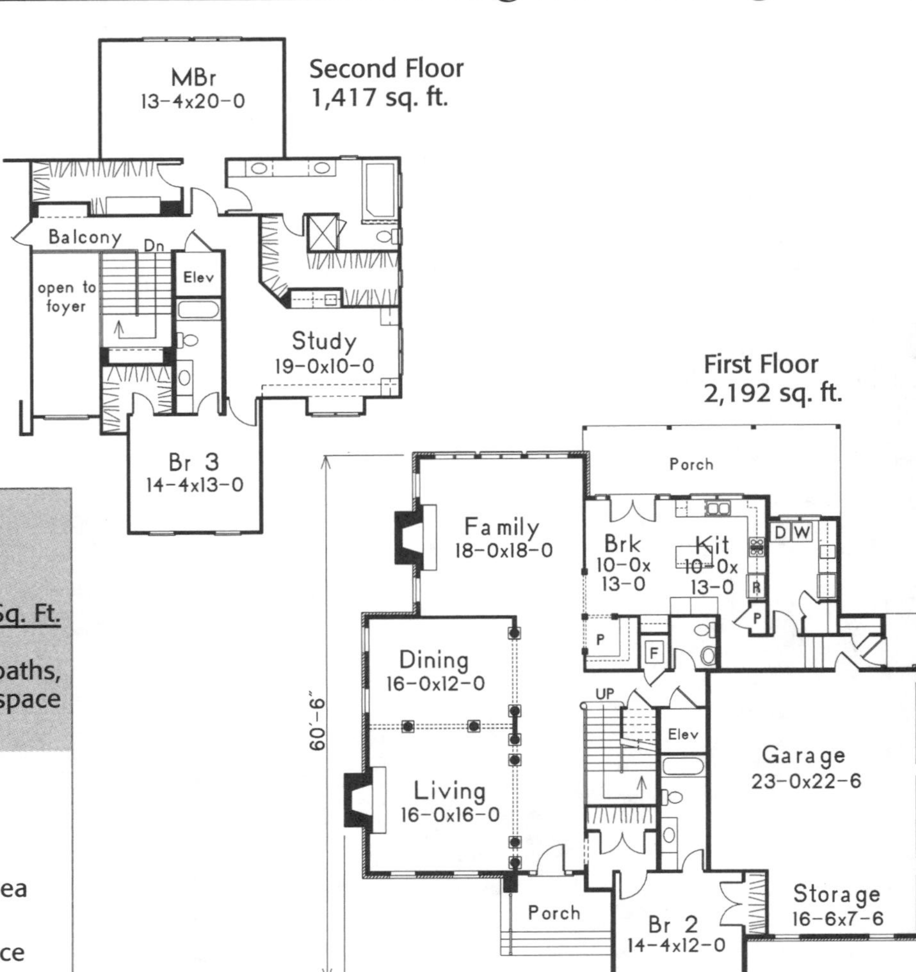
Second Floor
1,417 sq. ft.
MBr
13-4x20-0
Balcony
Dn
open to foyer
Elev
Study
19-0x10-0
Br 3
14-4x13-0
First Floor
2,192 sq. ft.
Porch
Family
18-0x18-0
Brk
10-0x
13-0
Kit
10-0x
13-0
DW
R
P
P
F
Dining
16-0x12-0
UP
Elev
Garage
23-0x22-6
60'-6"
Living
16-0x16-0
Storage
16-6x7-6
Porch
Br 2
14-4x12-0
64'-1"

Plan #531-0358

Price Code F

Total Living Area: 3,609 Sq. Ft.

Home has 3 bedrooms, 3 1/2 baths, 2-car side entry garage and crawl space foundation.

Special features

- 10' ceilings on first floor and 9' ceilings on second floor
- Butler's pantry and breakfast area add space to the kitchen
- Laundry room with storage space and work area
- Master bedroom features deluxe bath and separate walk-in closets

Large Sun Deck Creates Outdoor Living Area

LOWE'S

Signature
SERIES

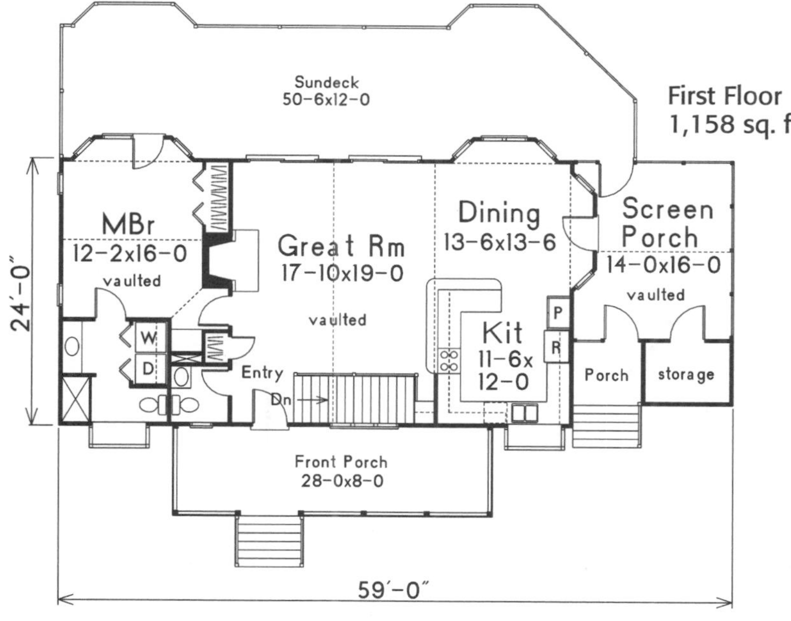
Sundeck
50-6x12-0
MBr
12-2x16-0
vaulted
Great Rm
17-10x19-0
vaulted
Dining
13-6x13-6
Kit
11-6x
12-0
Screen
Porch
14-0x16-0
vaulted
Porch
storage
Entry
Dn
W
D
P
R
Front Porch
28-0x8-0
24'-0"
59'-0"

First Floor
1,158 sq. ft.

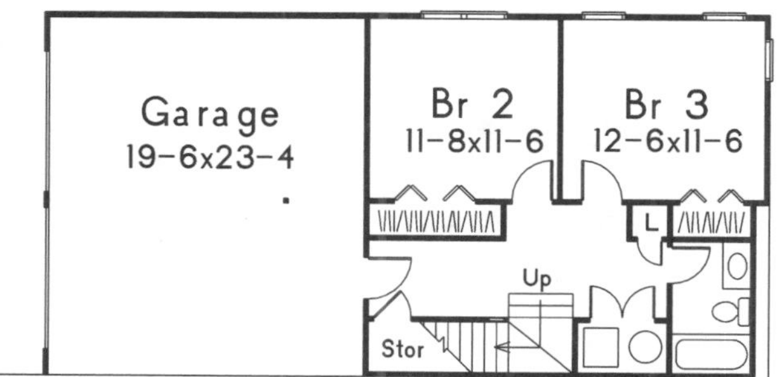
Garage
19-6x23-4
Br 2
11-8x11-6
Br 3
12-6x11-6
L
Up
Stor

Lower Level
574 sq. ft.

Plan #531-0254

Price Code B

Total Living Area: 1,732 Sq. Ft.

Home has 3 bedrooms, 2 1/2 baths, 2-car drive under garage and basement foundation.

Special features

- Spacious great room with vaulted ceiling and fireplace overlooks large sun deck
- Dramatic dining room boasts extensive windows and angled walls
- Vaulted master bedroom includes private bath with laundry area and accesses sun deck
- Convenient second entrance

Cottage-Style, Appealing And Cozy

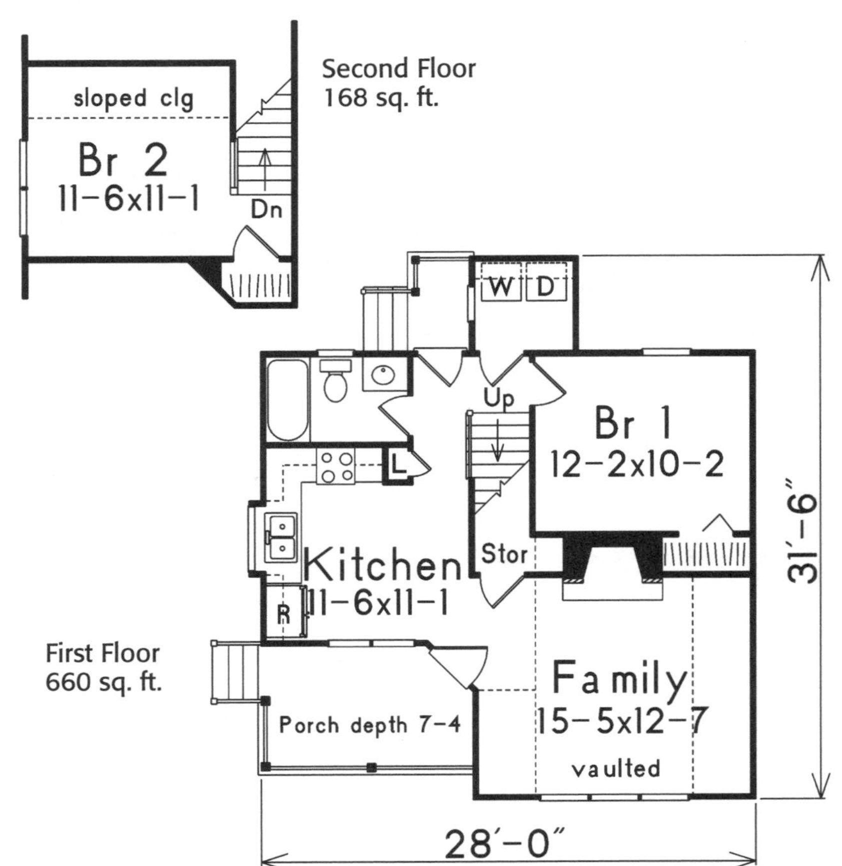
sloped clg
Br 2
11-6x11-1
Dn
Second Floor
168 sq. ft.
W
D
Up
Br 1
12-2x10-2
L
Kitchen
11-6x11-1
Stor
R
First Floor
660 sq. ft.
Porch depth 7-4
Family
15-5x12-7
vaulted
31′-6″
28′-0″

Plan #531-0461

Price Code AAA

Total Living Area: 828 Sq. Ft.

Home has 2 bedrooms, 1 bath and crawl space foundation.

Special features

- Vaulted ceiling in living area enhances space
- Convenient laundry room
- Sloped ceiling creates unique style in bedroom #2
- Efficient storage space under the stairs
- Covered entry porch provides cozy sitting area and plenty of shade

TO ORDER BLUEPRINTS USE THE FORM ON PAGE 290 OR CALL TOLL-FREE **1-800-DREAM HOME** (373-2646)

Exterior Accents Add Charm To This Cottage

LOWE'S

Signature SERIES

Second Floor
691 sq. ft.

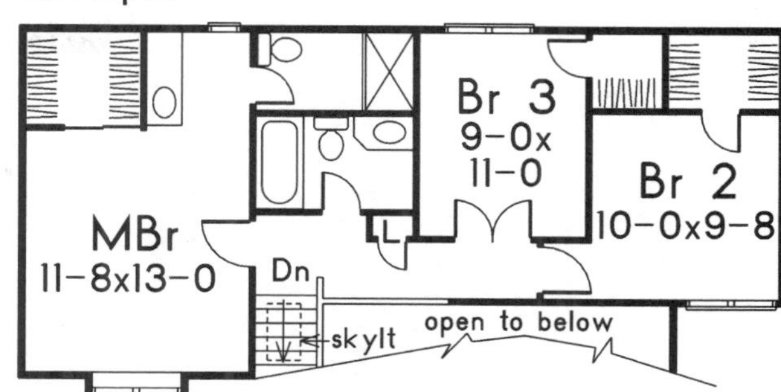
Br 3
9-0x
11-0
Br 2
10-0x9-8
MBr
11-8x13-0
Dn
L
skylt
open to below

Plan #531-0104

Price Code A

Total Living Area: 1,359 Sq. Ft.

Home has 3 bedrooms, 2 1/2 baths, 2-car garage and basement foundation.

Special features

- Lattice-trimmed porch, stone chimney and abundant windows lend outdoor appeal
- Spacious, bright breakfast area with pass-through to formal dining room
- Large walk-in closets in all bedrooms
- Extensive deck expands dining and entertaining area

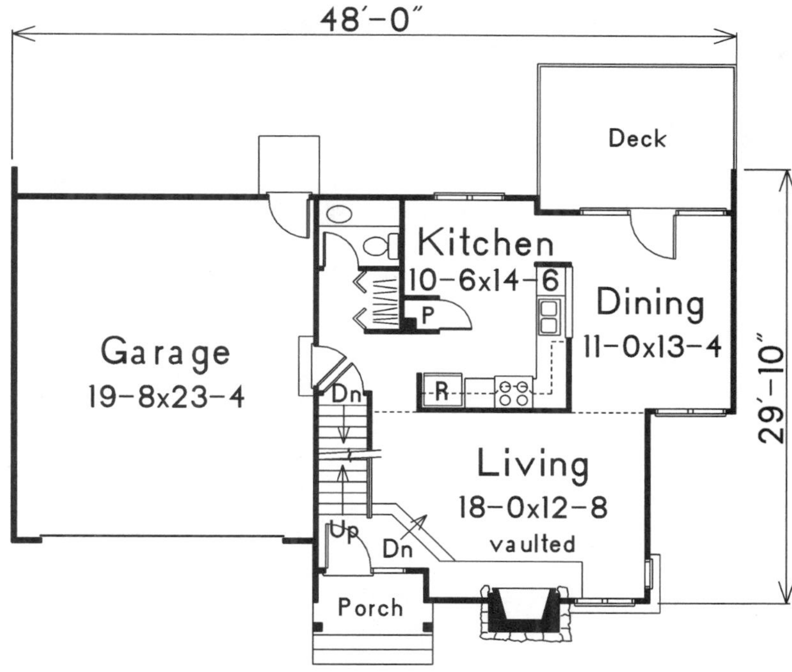
48'-0"
Deck
Kitchen
10-6x14-6
P
Dining
11-0x13-4
Garage
19-8x23-4
R
Dn
Living
18-0x12-8
vaulted
29'-10"
Up
Dn
Porch

First Floor
668 sq. ft.

Dramatic Appeal, Inside And Out

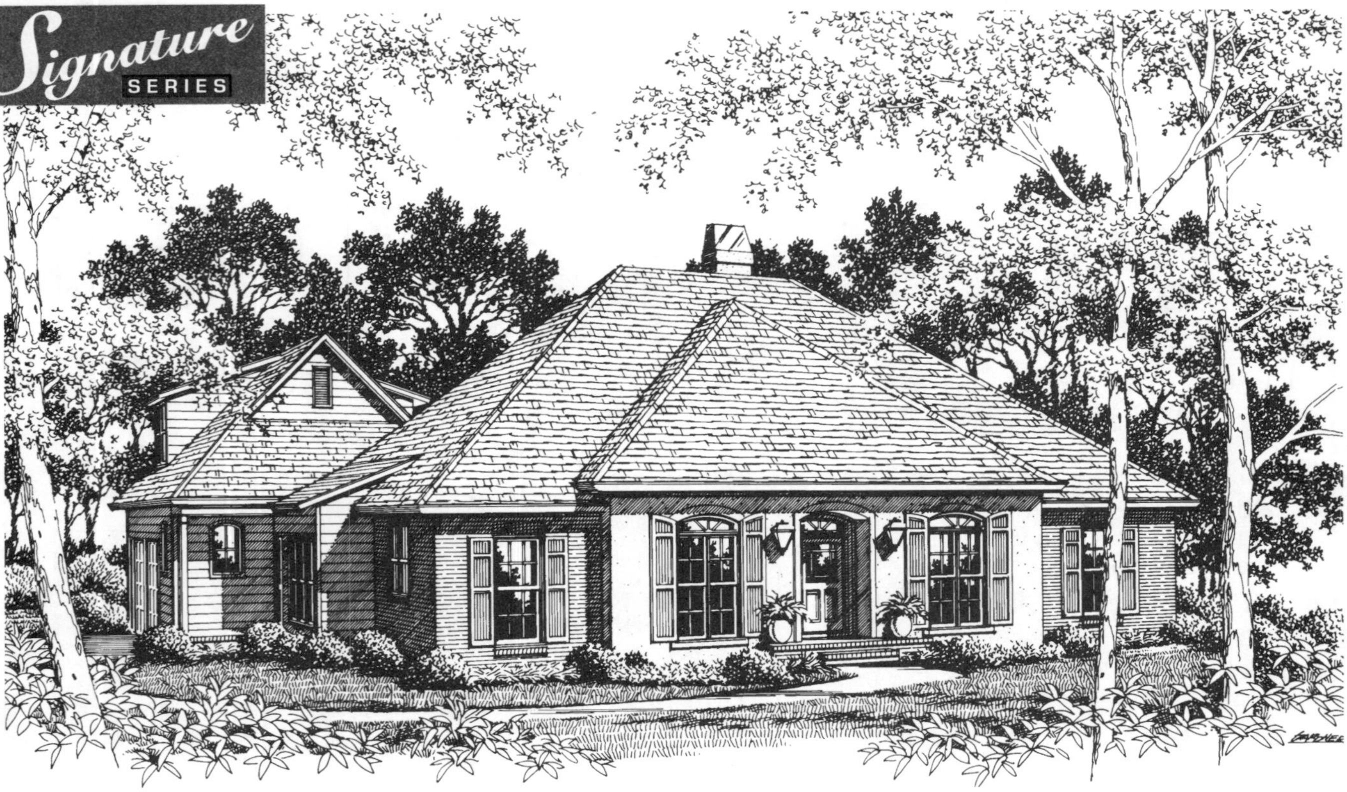

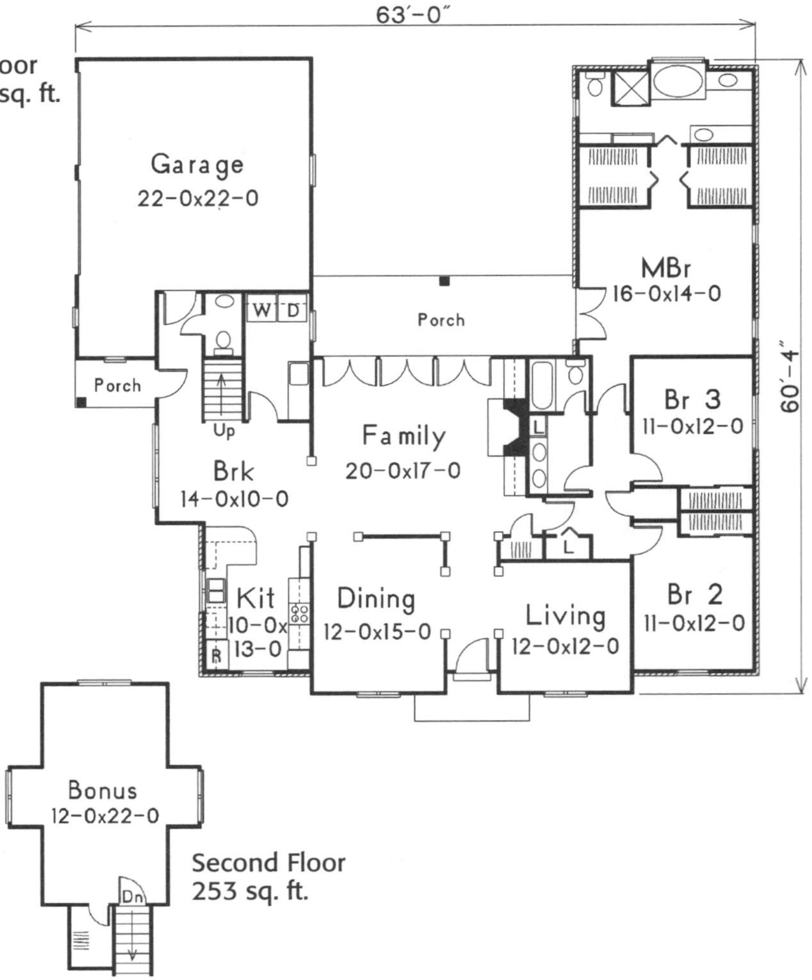
63'-0"
First Floor
2,215 sq. ft.
Garage
22-0x22-0
W D
Porch
Porch
MBr
16-0x14-0
Up
Family
20-0x17-0
Br 3
11-0x12-0
60'-4"
Brk
14-0x10-0
Kit
10-0x
13-0
Dining
12-0x15-0
Living
12-0x12-0
Br 2
11-0x12-0
Bonus
12-0x22-0
Dn
Second Floor
253 sq. ft.

Plan #531-0238

Price Code D

Total Living Area: 2,468 Sq. Ft.

Home has 3 bedrooms, 2 1/2 baths, 2-car side entry garage and slab foundation.

Special features

- Open floor plan in family room with columns, fireplace, triple French doors and 12' ceiling
- Master bath features double walk-in closets and vanities
- Bonus room above garage with private stairway
- Bedrooms separate from main living space for privacy

Welcoming Front Porch, A Country Touch

LOWE'S

Signature
SERIES

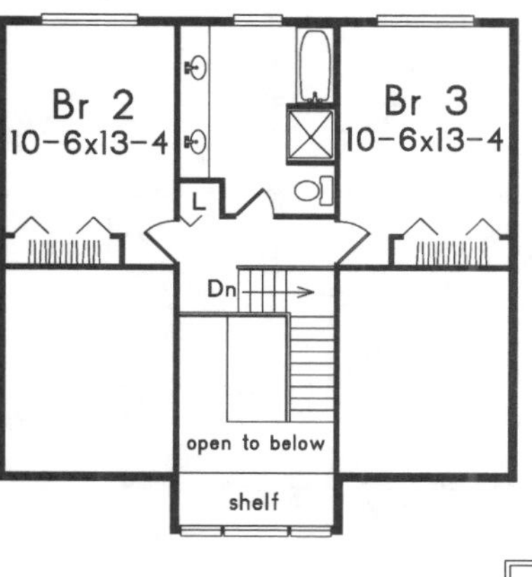
Br 2
10-6x13-4
Br 3
10-6x13-4
L
Dn
open to below
shelf

Second Floor
534 sq. ft.

Plan #531-0672

Price Code C

Total Living Area: 2,043 Sq. Ft.

Home has 3 bedrooms, 2 1/2 baths, 2-car side entry garage and basement foundation, drawings also include slab foundation.

Special features

- Energy efficient home with 2" x 6" exterior walls
- Two-story central foyer includes two coat closets
- Large combined space provided by the kitchen, family and breakfast rooms
- Breakfast nook for informal dining looks out to the deck and screened porch

First Floor
1,509 sq. ft.

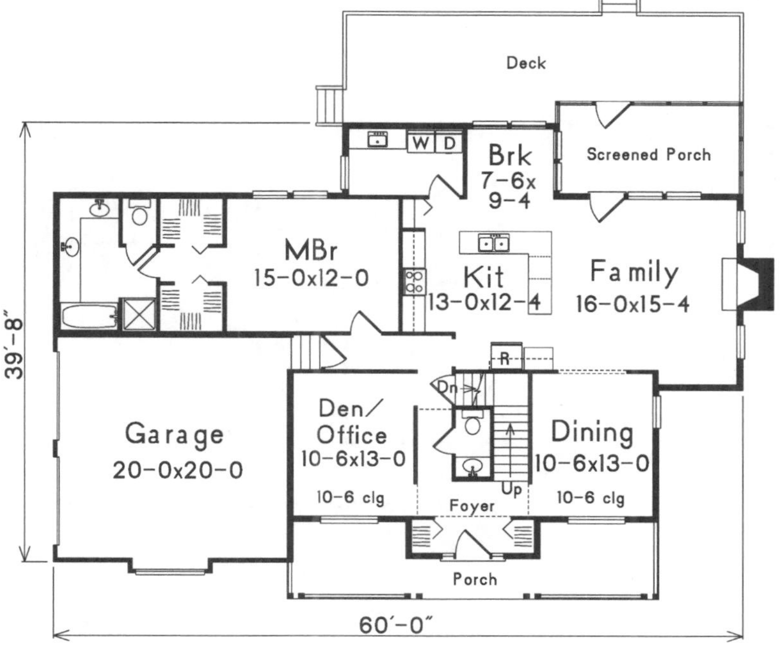
Deck
W D
Brk
7-6x
9-4
Screened Porch
MBr
15-0x12-0
Kit
13-0x12-4
Family
16-0x15-4
R
Garage
20-0x20-0
Den/
Office
10-6x13-0
10-6 clg
Dn
Up
Foyer
Dining
10-6x13-0
10-6 clg
Porch
39'-8"
60'-0"

Signature
SERIES

Charming Victorian Has Unexpected Pleasures

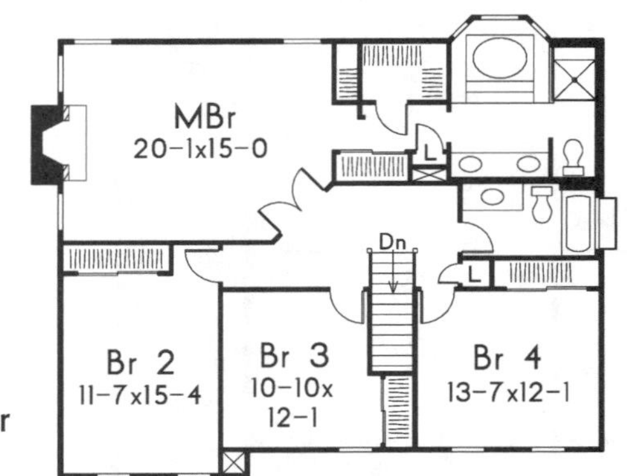
MBr
20-1x15-0
L
Dn
L
Br 2
11-7x15-4
Br 3
10-10x
12-1
Br 4
13-7x12-1

Second Floor
1,320 sq. ft.

Plan #531-0152

Price Code E

Total Living Area: 2,935 Sq. Ft.

Home has 4 bedrooms, 2 1/2 baths, 2-car side entry garage and basement foundation.

Special features

- Gracious entry foyer with handsome stairway opens to separate living and dining rooms
- Kitchen with vaulted ceiling and skylight, island worktop, breakfast area with bay window and two separate pantries
- Large second floor master bedroom suite with fireplace, raised tub, dressing area with vaulted ceiling and skylight

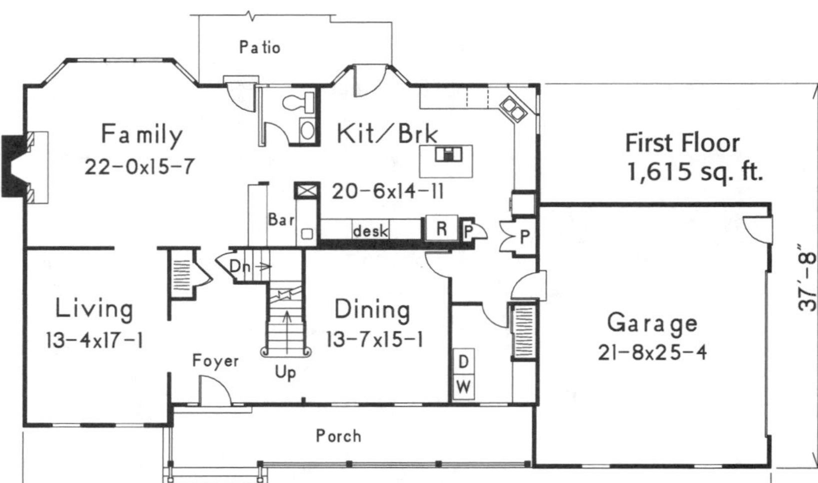
Patio
Family
22-0x15-7
Kit/Brk
20-6x14-11
Bar
desk
R
P
P
First Floor
1,615 sq. ft.
Dn
Living
13-4x17-1
Foyer
Up
Dining
13-7x15-1
D
W
Garage
21-8x25-4
Porch
37'-8"
71'-0"

 TO ORDER BLUEPRINTS USE THE FORM ON PAGE 290 OR CALL TOLL-FREE **1-800-DREAM HOME** (373-2646)

Economical Ranch For Easy Living

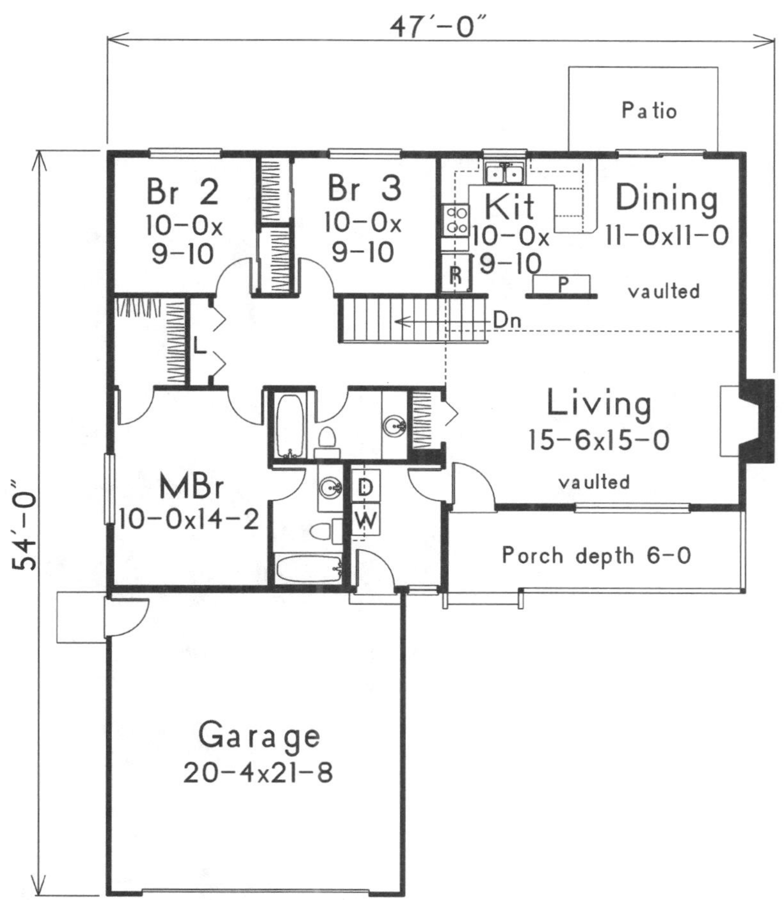

47'-0"
54'-0"
Patio
Br 2
10-0x
9-10
Br 3
10-0x
9-10
Kit
10-0x
9-10
Dining
11-0x11-0
vaulted
R
P
Dn
L
Living
15-6x15-0
vaulted
MBr
10-0x14-2
D
W
Porch depth 6-0
Garage
20-4x21-8

Plan #531-0265

Price Code A

Total Living Area: 1,314 Sq. Ft.

Home has 3 bedrooms, 2 baths, 2-car garage and basement foundation.

Special features

- Energy efficient home with 2" x 6" exterior walls
- Covered porch adds immediate appeal and welcoming charm
- Open floor plan combined with vaulted ceiling offers spacious living
- Functional kitchen complete with pantry and eating bar
- Cozy fireplace in the living room
- Private master bedroom features a large walk-in closet and bath

LOWE'S
Signature
SERIES

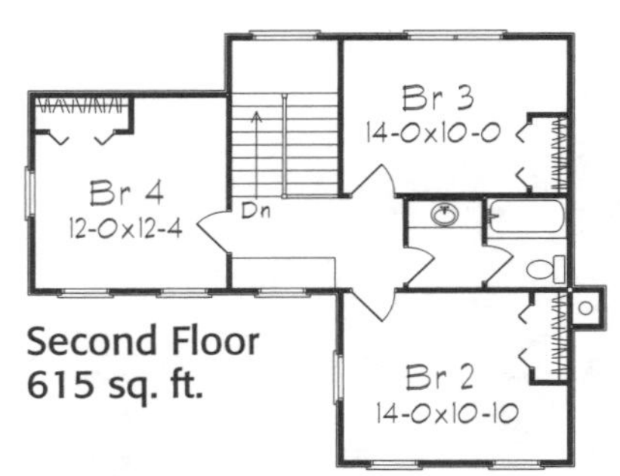
Br 3
14-0x10-0
Br 4
12-0x12-4
Dn
Br 2
14-0x10-10

Second Floor
615 sq. ft.

Plan #531-0448

Price Code C

Total Living Area: 1,597 Sq. Ft.

Home has 4 bedrooms, 2 1/2 baths, 2-car detached garage and basement foundation.

Special features

- Spacious family room includes fireplace and coat closet
- Open kitchen/dining room provides breakfast bar and access to the outdoors
- Convenient laundry area located near kitchen
- Secluded master suite with walk-in closet and private bath

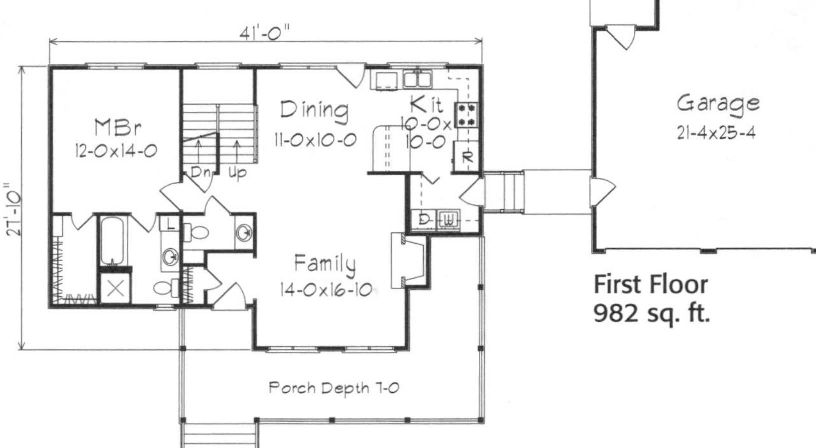
41'-0"
27'-10"
MBr
12-0x14-0
Dn
Up
Dining
11-0x10-0
Kit
10-0x
10-0
R
D
W
Family
14-0x16-10
Porch Depth 7-0
Garage
21-4x25-4

First Floor
982 sq. ft.

 TO ORDER BLUEPRINTS USE THE FORM ON PAGE 290 OR CALL TOLL-FREE **1-800-DREAM HOME** (373-2646)

Front Porch Adds Style To This Ranch

LOWE'S

Signature SERIES

46'-0"

36'-0"

Porch

Kit 11-0x 10-0

R

W

D

Dining 12-0x11-0

Dn

skylt

MBr 14-0x15-0

raised clg

L

L

Family 15-0x16-0

Br 3 10-0x 12-0

Br 2 10-0x 12-0

Porch depth 6-0

Plan #531-0239

Price Code A

Total Living Area: 1,496 Sq. Ft.

Home has 3 bedrooms, 2 baths, 2-car drive under garage and basement foundation.

Special features

- Master bedroom features coffered ceiling, walk-in closet and spacious bath
- Vaulted ceiling and fireplace grace family room
- Dining room adjacent to kitchen and features access to rear porch
- Convenient access to utility room from kitchen

Plan #531-0767

Price Code AA

Total Living Area: 990 Sq. Ft.

Home has 2 bedrooms, 1 bath and crawl space foundation.

Special features

- Covered front porch adds charming feel
- Vaulted ceilings in kitchen, family and dining rooms creates a spacious feel
- Large linen, pantry and storage closets throughout

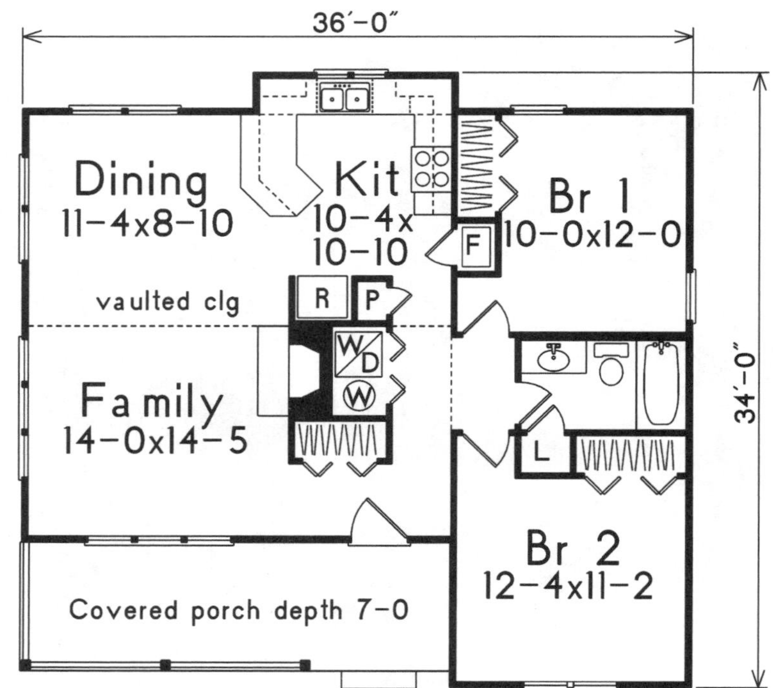
36′-0″
34′-0″
Dining
11-4x8-10
Kit
10-4x
10-10
Br 1
10-0x12-0
F
R
P
vaulted clg
W/D
W
Family
14-0x14-5
L
Br 2
12-4x11-2
Covered porch depth 7-0

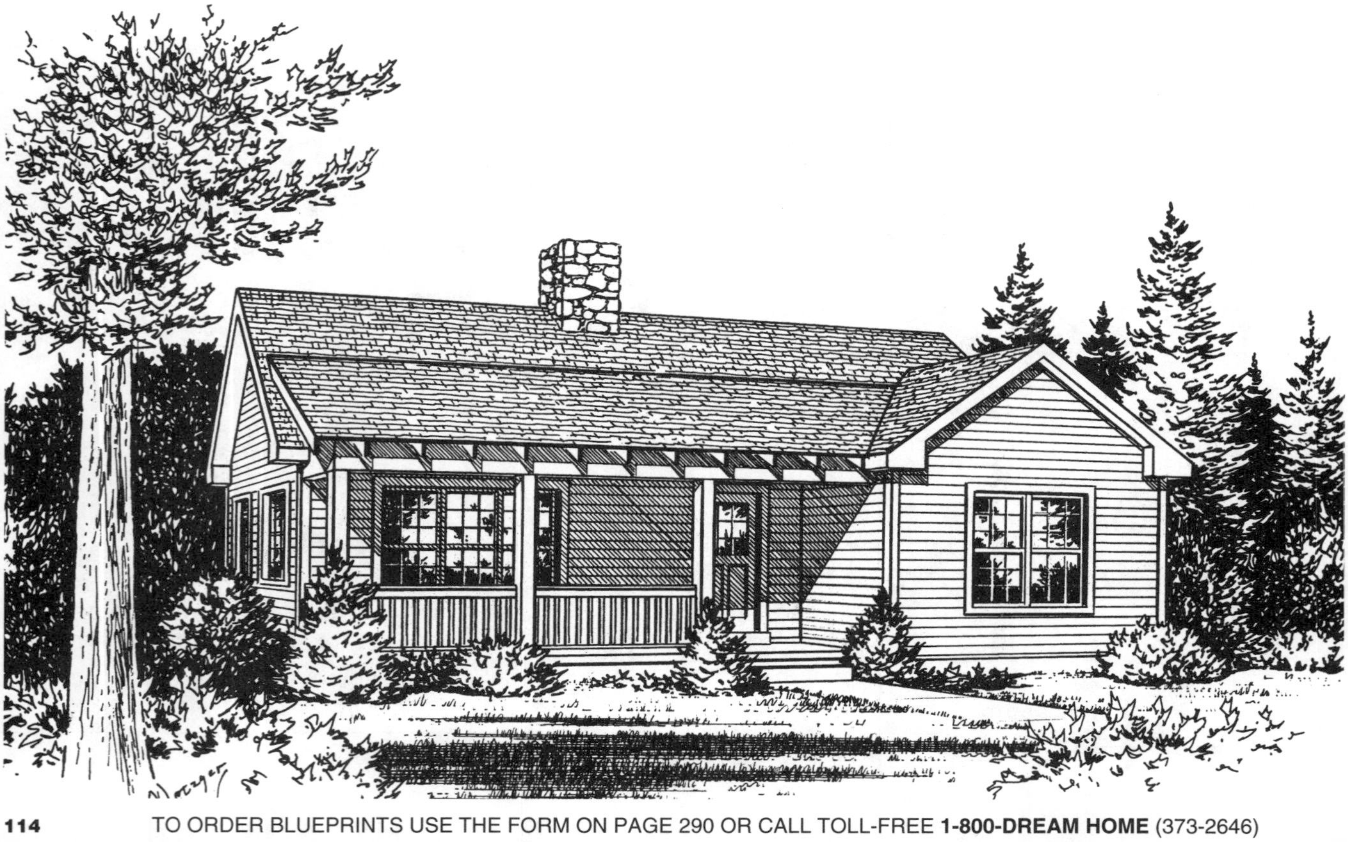

Tudor Influences Enhance This Duplex

LOWE'S

Signature SERIES

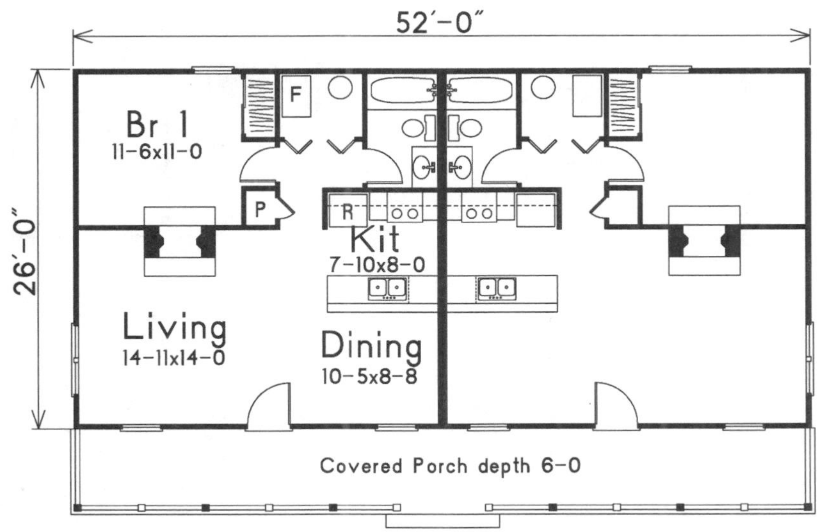
52'-0"
26'-0"
Br 1
11-6x11-0
F
P
R
Kit
7-10x8-0
Living
14-11x14-0
Dining
10-5x8-8
Covered Porch depth 6-0

Plan #531-0704

Price Code B

Total Living Area:	1,326 Sq. Ft.

Each unit has 1 bedroom, 1 bath and slab foundation.

Special features

- Duplex has 663 square feet of living space per unit
- See-through fireplace from living room into bedroom makes lasting impression
- Covered front porch perfect for relaxing evenings
- Galley-style kitchen is compact but well-organized for efficiency

Protected Entry Landscapes Well

Plan #531-0125

Price Code D

Total Living Area: 2,468 Sq. Ft.

Home has 3 bedrooms, 3 baths, 2-car garage and partial basement/crawl space foundation.

Special features

- Entry, flanked by gables, creates an interesting walkway
- Open entry foyer with access to the second floor future guest suite, work or play area
- Sunny breakfast room with full windows
- Bay window and garden tub add elegance to master bedroom suite
- Private loft area with bath and generous storage space

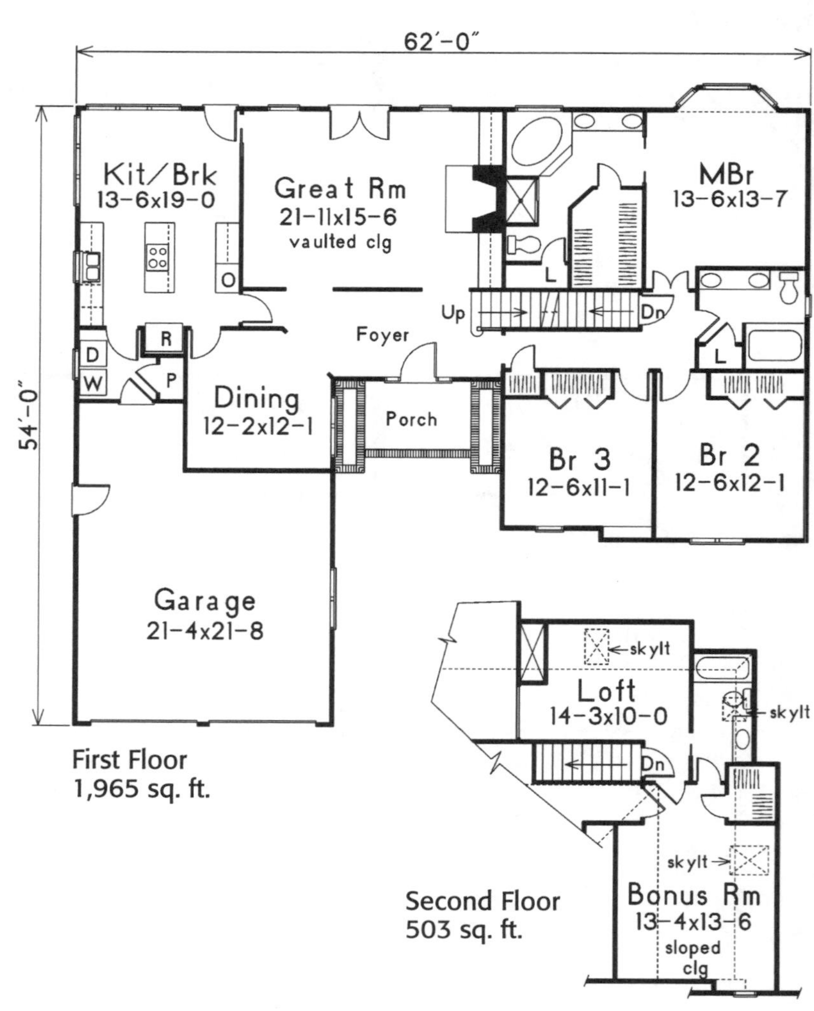

62'-0"
54'-0"
Kit/Brk
13-6x19-0
Great Rm
21-11x15-6
vaulted clg
MBr
13-6x13-7
Up
Dn
Foyer
R
D
W
P
L
Dining
12-2x12-1
Porch
Br 3
12-6x11-1
Br 2
12-6x12-1
Garage
21-4x21-8
skylt
Loft
14-3x10-0
skylt
Dn
skylt
Bonus Rm
13-4x13-6
sloped clg

First Floor
1,965 sq. ft.

Second Floor
503 sq. ft.

LOWE'S

Signature SERIES

Plan #531-0369

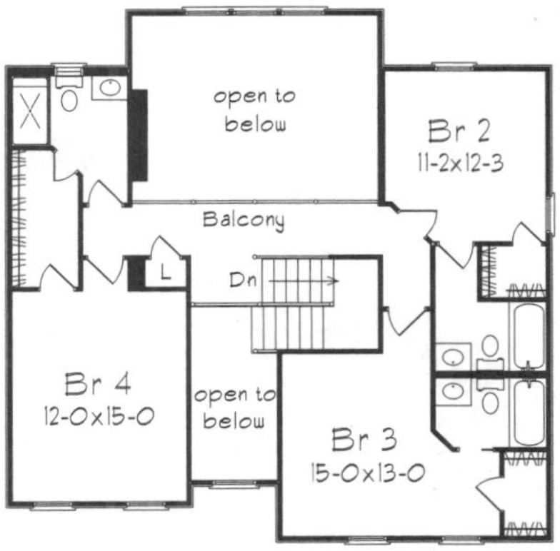

Price Code E

Total Living Area: 2,716 Sq. Ft.

Home has 4 bedrooms, 4 1/2 baths, 2-car side entry garage and basement foundation.

Special features

- 9' ceilings throughout first floor
- All bedrooms boast walk-in closets
- Great room and hearth room share see-through fireplace
- Balcony overlooks large great room

Second Floor
962 sq. ft.

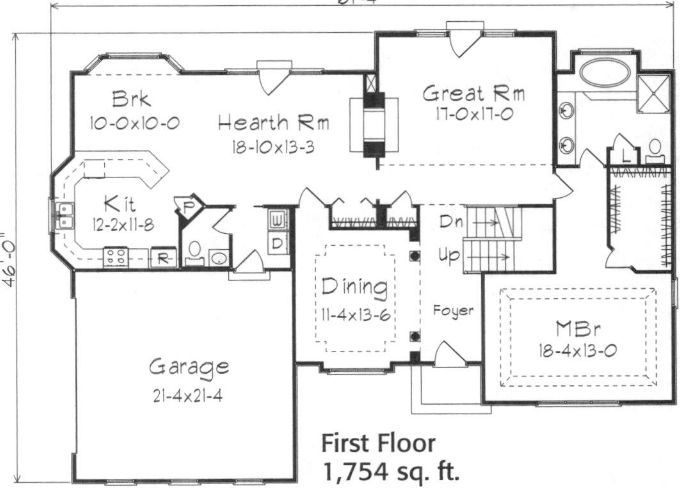

61'-4"
46'-0"
Brk
10-0x10-0
Hearth Rm
18-10x13-3
Great Rm
17-0x17-0
Kit
12-2x11-8
Dining
11-4x13-6
Foyer
MBr
18-4x13-0
Garage
21-4x21-4

First Floor
1,754 sq. ft.

Signature SERIES

Dining With A View

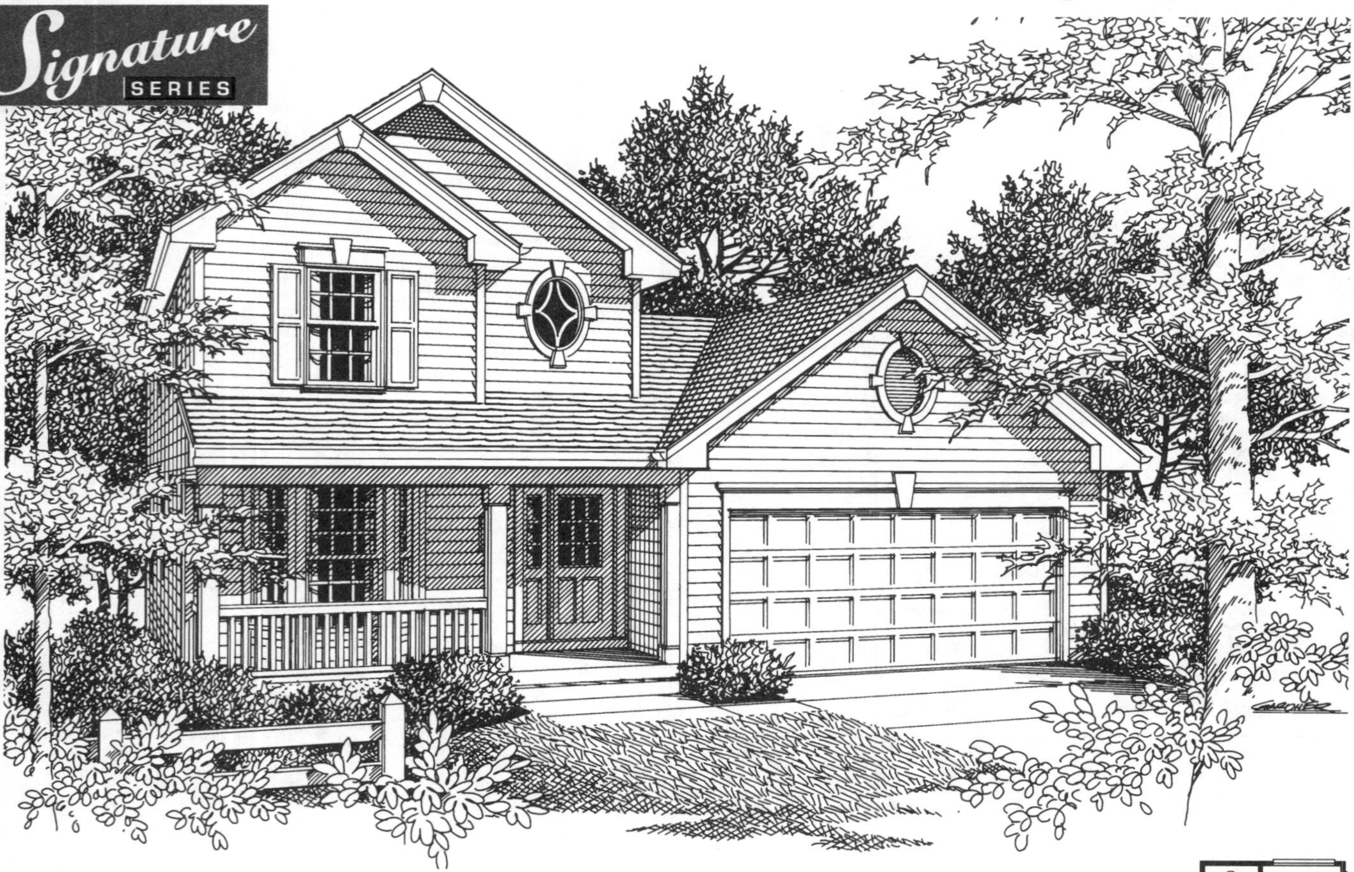

Plan #531-0652

Price Code B

Total Living Area: 1,524 Sq. Ft.

Home has 3 bedrooms, 2 1/2 baths, 2-car garage and basement foundation.

Special features

- Delightful balcony overlooks two-story entry illuminated by oval window
- Roomy first floor master suite offers quiet privacy
- All bedrooms feature one or more walk-in closets

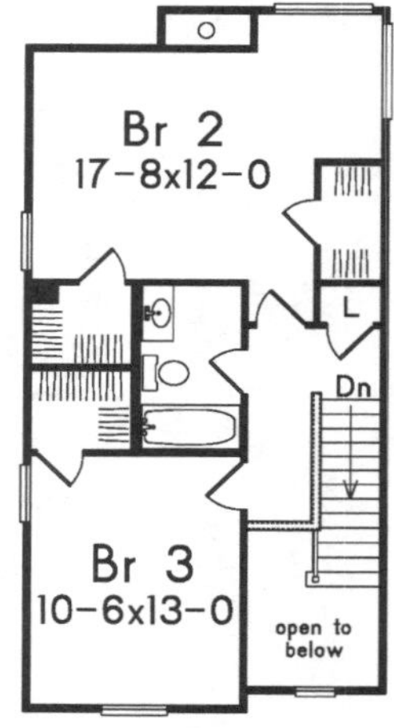

Br 2
17-8x12-0
L
Dn
Br 3
10-6x13-0
open to below

Second Floor
573 sq. ft.

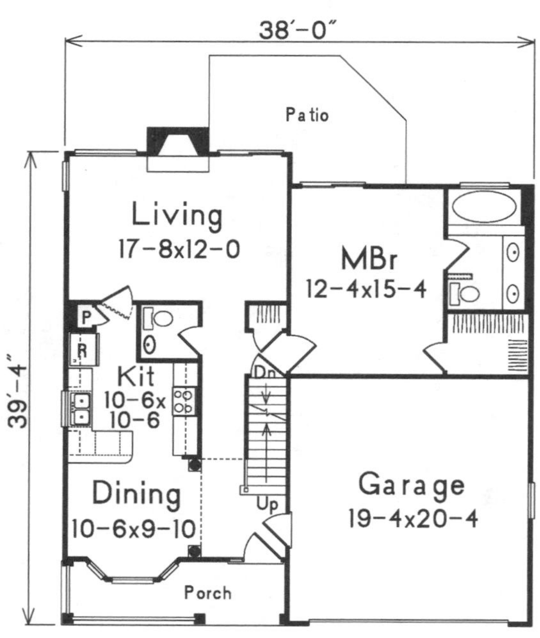

38′-0″
Patio
Living
17-8x12-0
MBr
12-4x15-4
P
R
Kit
10-6x
10-6
Dn
39′-4″
Dining
10-6x9-10
Up
Garage
19-4x20-4
Porch

First Floor
951 sq. ft.

Compact Home With Functional Design

LOWE'S

Signature
SERIES

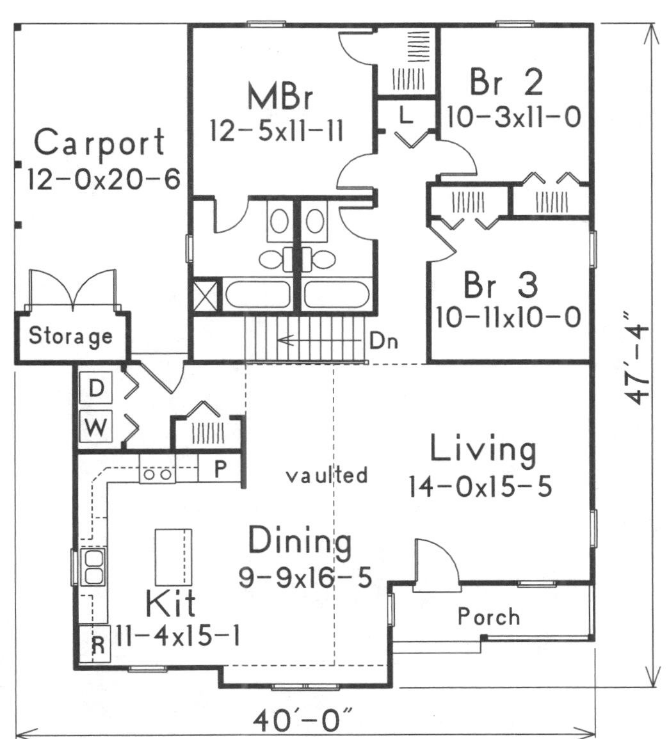
Carport
12-0x20-6
MBr
12-5x11-11
Br 2
10-3x11-0
L
Br 3
10-11x10-0
Storage
Dn
D
W
P
vaulted
Living
14-0x15-5
Dining
9-9x16-5
Kit
11-4x15-1
R
Porch
47'-4"
40'-0"

Plan #531-0296

Price Code A

Total Living Area: 1,396 Sq. Ft.

Home has 3 bedrooms, 2 baths, 1-car carport and basement foundation, drawings also include crawl space foundation.

Special features

- Gabled front adds interest to facade
- Living and dining rooms share a vaulted ceiling
- Master bedroom features a walk-in closet and private bath
- Functional kitchen with a center work island and convenient pantry

LOWE'S

Affordable Upscale, Amenity Full

Signature SERIES

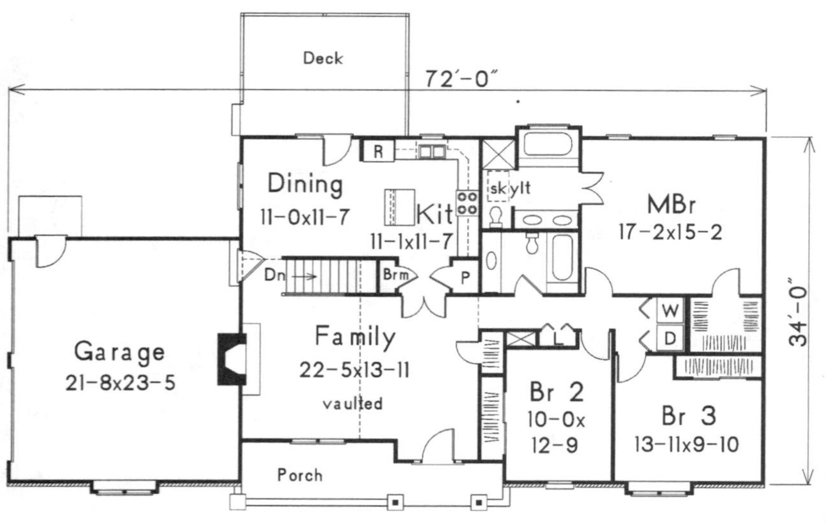
Deck
72'-0"
Dining
11-0x11-7
R
skylt
Kit
11-1x11-7
MBr
17-2x15-2
Garage
21-8x23-5
Dn
Brm
P
W
D
Family
22-5x13-11
vaulted
34'-0"
Br 2
10-0x
12-9
Br 3
13-11x9-10
Porch

Plan #531-0172

Price Code B

Total Living Area: 1,643 Sq. Ft.

Home has 3 bedrooms, 2 baths, 2-car side entry garage and basement foundation, drawings also include slab and crawl space foundations.

Special features

- Family room has vaulted ceiling, open staircase and arched windows allowing for plenty of light
- Kitchen captures full use of space, with pantry, storage, ample counter space and work island
- Large closets and storage areas throughout
- Roomy master bath has a skylight for natural lighting plus separate tub and shower
- Rear of house provides ideal location for future screened-in porch

 TO ORDER BLUEPRINTS USE THE FORM ON PAGE 290 OR CALL TOLL-FREE **1-800-DREAM HOME** (373-2646)

Living Room Has Balcony Overlook

LOWE'S

Signature
SERIES

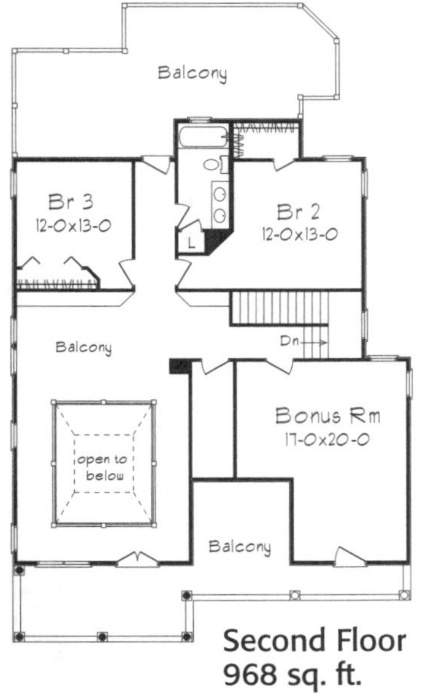
Balcony
Br 3
12-0x13-0
Br 2
12-0x13-0
Balcony
Dn
Bonus Rm
17-0x20-0
open to
below
Balcony

Second Floor
968 sq. ft.

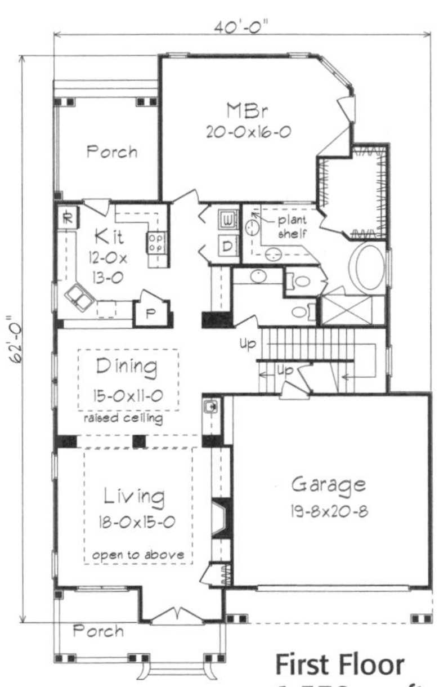
40'-0"
62'-0"
MBr
20-0x16-0
Porch
Kit
12-0x
13-0
plant
shelf
Dining
15-0x11-0
raised ceiling
Up
Up
Living
18-0x15-0
open to above
Garage
19-8x20-8
Porch

First Floor
1,530 sq. ft.

Plan #531-0408

Price Code D

Total Living Area: 2,498 Sq. Ft.

Home has 3 bedrooms, 2 1/2 baths, 2-car garage and crawl space foundation, drawings also include slab and basement foundations.

Special features

- 10' ceilings on first floor and 9' ceilings on second floor
- Dining room with raised ceiling and convenient wet bar
- Master suite features oversized walk-in closet and bath with garden tub

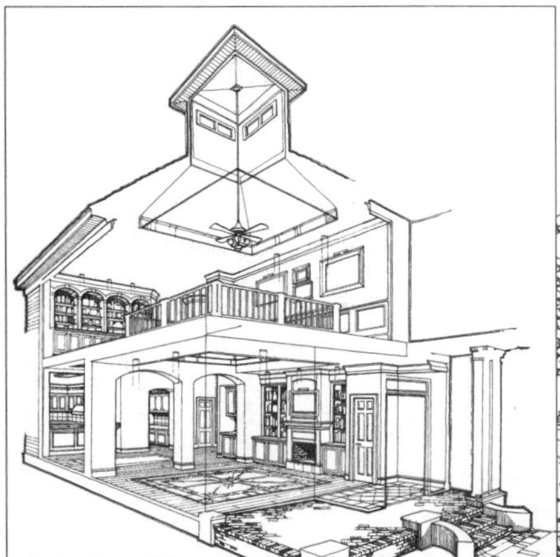

Interior View

LOWE'S
Signature
SERIES

Exterior Accents Complement Front Facade

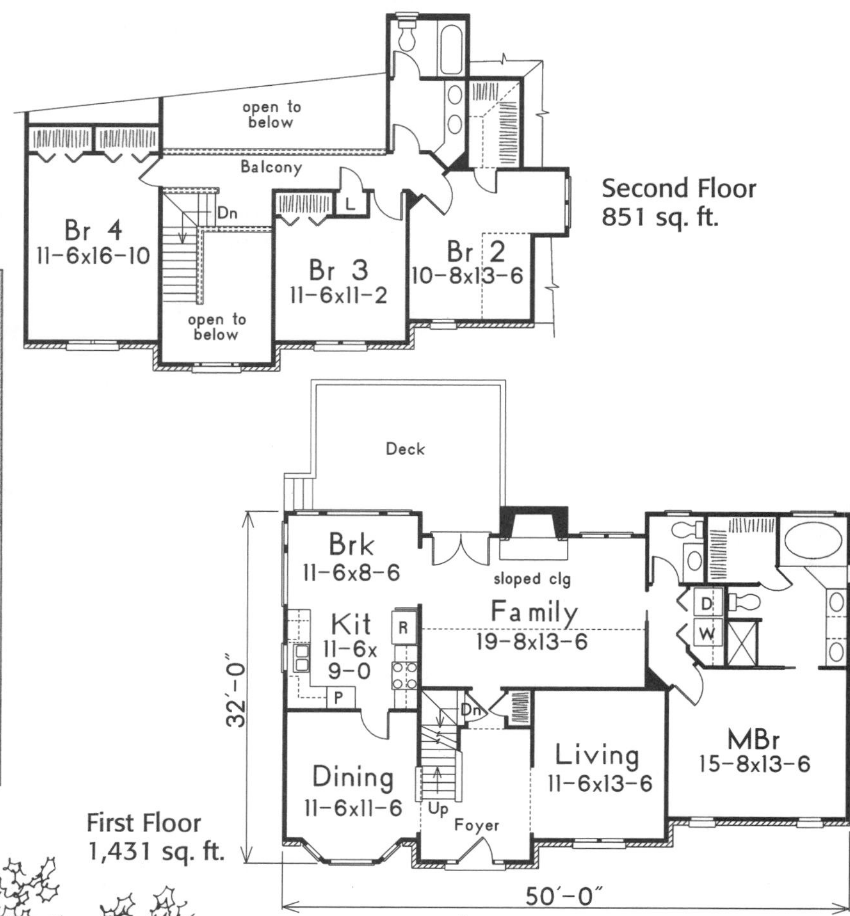
open to below
Balcony
Dn
L
Br 4
11-6x16-10
Br 3
11-6x11-2
Br 2
10-8x13-6
open to below
Second Floor
851 sq. ft.
Deck
Brk
11-6x8-6
sloped clg
Family
19-8x13-6
Kit
11-6x
9-0
R
P
D
W
Dn
Dining
11-6x11-6
Up
Foyer
Living
11-6x13-6
MBr
15-8x13-6
32'-0"
50'-0"
First Floor
1,431 sq. ft.

Plan #531-0137

Price Code E

Total Living Area: 2,282 Sq. Ft.

Home has 4 bedrooms, 2 1/2 baths, 2-car drive under garage and basement foundation.

Special features

- Balcony and two-story foyer add spaciousness to this compact plan
- First floor master suite has corner tub in large master bath
- Out-of-the-way kitchen is open to the full-windowed breakfast room

TO ORDER BLUEPRINTS USE THE FORM ON PAGE 290 OR CALL TOLL-FREE **1-800-DREAM HOME** (373-2646)

Timeless Country Facade

LOWE'S

Signature SERIES

Second Floor
1,000 sq. ft.

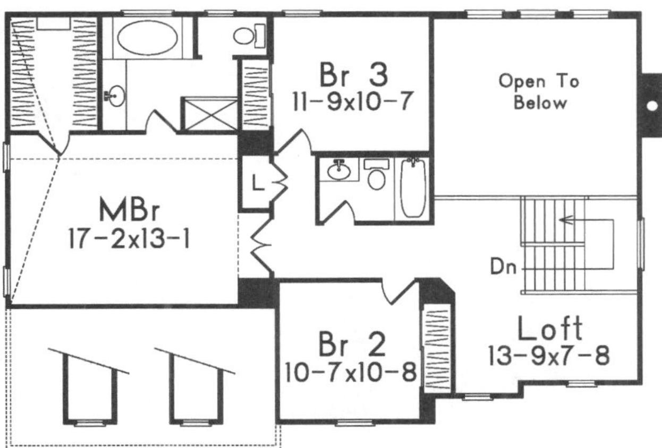
Br 3
11-9x10-7
Open To Below
MBr
17-2x13-1
L
Dn
Loft
13-9x7-8
Br 2
10-7x10-8

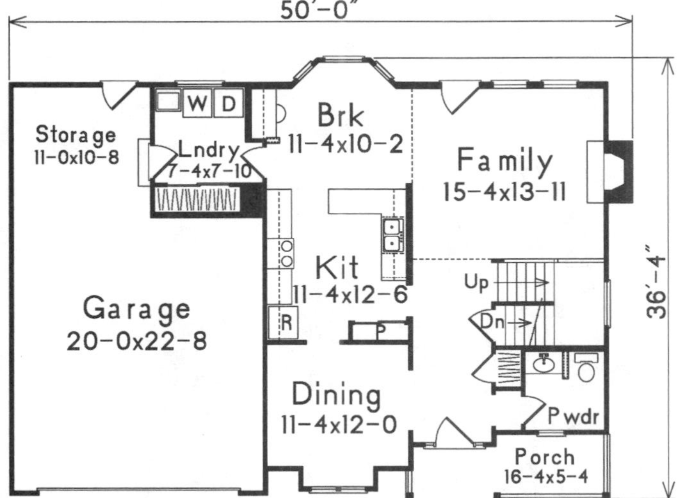
50'-0"
36'-4"
Storage
11-0x10-8
W
D
Lndry
7-4x7-10
Brk
11-4x10-2
Family
15-4x13-11
Kit
11-4x12-6
Up
Dn
R
P
Garage
20-0x22-8
Dining
11-4x12-0
Pwdr
Porch
16-4x5-4

First Floor
977 sq. ft.

Plan #531-0725

Price Code C

Total Living Area: 1,977 Sq. Ft.

Home has 3 bedrooms, 2 1/2 baths, 2-car garage and basement foundation.

Special features

- An enormous entry with adjacent dining area and powder room leads to a splendid two-story family room with fireplace
- Kitchen features an abundance of cabinets, built-in pantry and breakfast room with menu desk and bay window
- A spacious vaulted master suite, two secondary bedrooms with bath and loft area adorn the second floor
- Extra storage area in garage

Unique Features Create Style And Sophistication

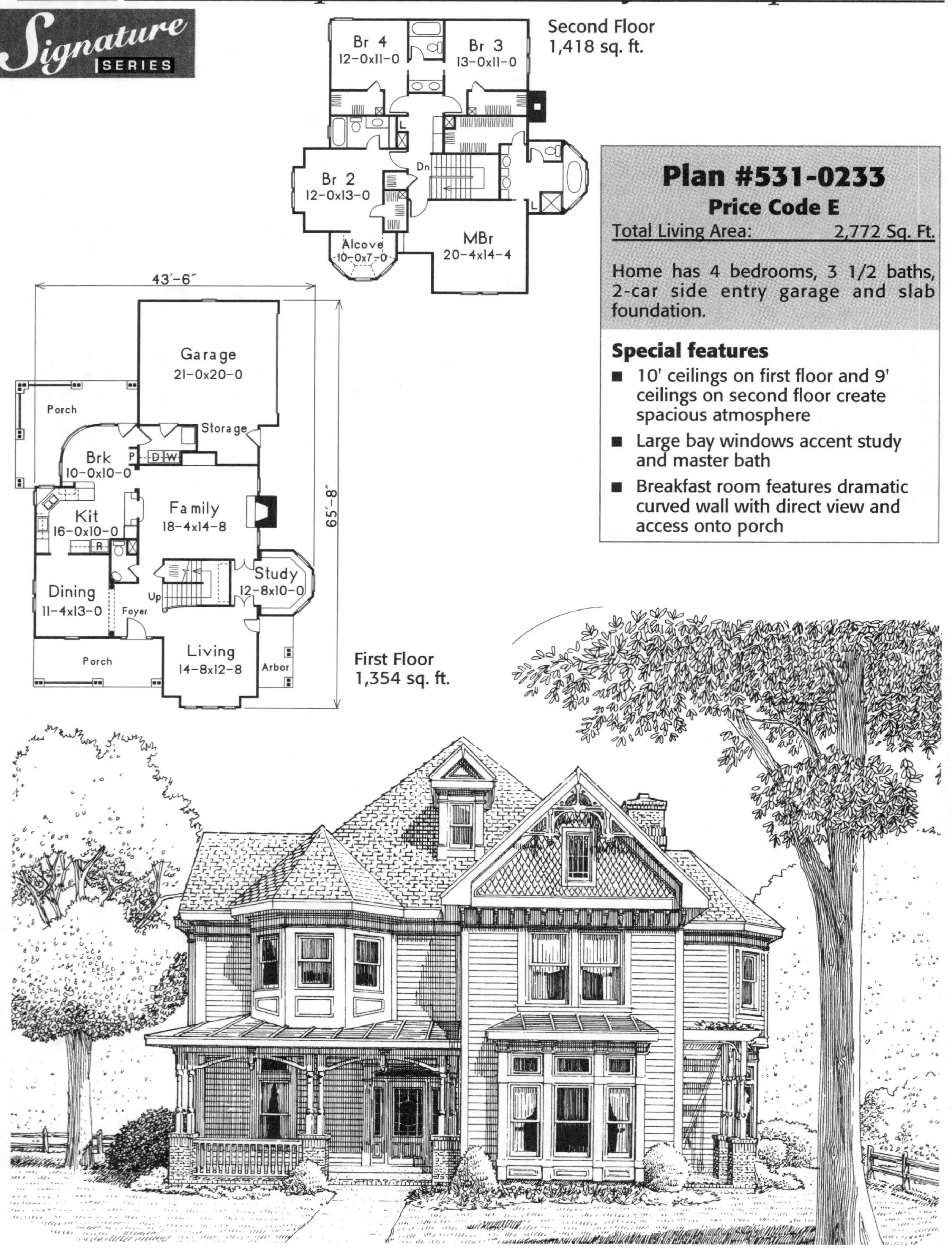
Second Floor
1,418 sq. ft.
Br 4
12-0x11-0
Br 3
13-0x11-0
Br 2
12-0x13-0
Dn
Alcove
10-0x7-0
MBr
20-4x14-4
43'-6"
65'-8"
Garage
21-0x20-0
Porch
Storage
Brk
10-0x10-0
Family
18-4x14-8
Kit
16-0x10-0
Dining
11-4x13-0
Up
Foyer
Study
12-8x10-0
Living
14-8x12-8
Porch
Arbor
First Floor
1,354 sq. ft.

Plan #531-0233

Price Code E

Total Living Area: 2,772 Sq. Ft.

Home has 4 bedrooms, 3 1/2 baths, 2-car side entry garage and slab foundation.

Special features

- 10' ceilings on first floor and 9' ceilings on second floor create spacious atmosphere
- Large bay windows accent study and master bath
- Breakfast room features dramatic curved wall with direct view and access onto porch

Country Home With Plenty Of Style

LOWE'S

Signature SERIES

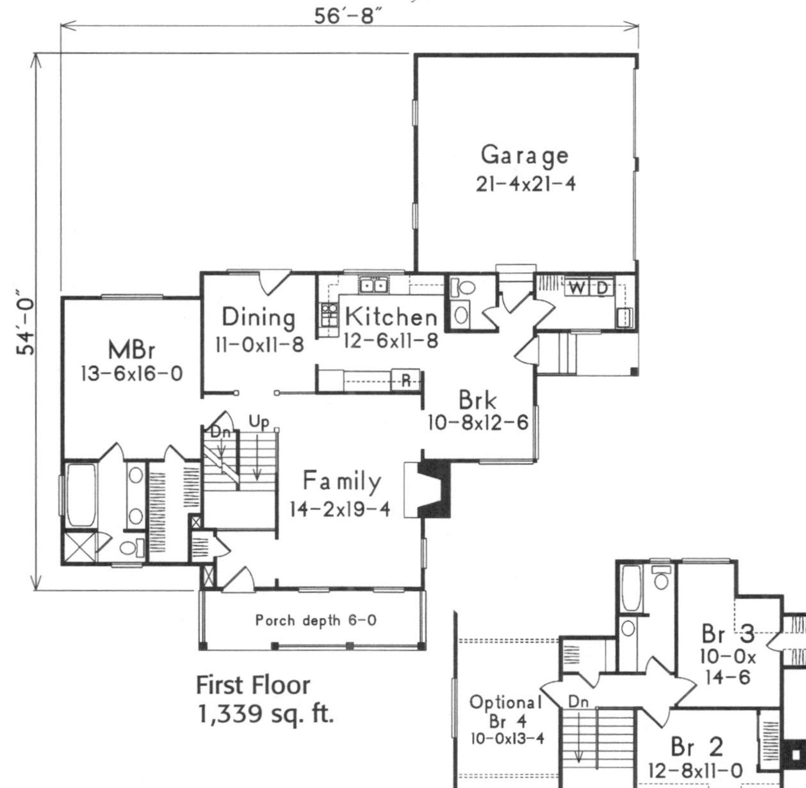
56'-8"
54'-0"
Garage
21-4x21-4
W D
Dining
11-0x11-8
Kitchen
12-6x11-8
MBr
13-6x16-0
R
Brk
10-8x12-6
Dn
Up
Family
14-2x19-4
Porch depth 6-0
Br 3
10-0x
14-6
Optional
Br 4
10-0x13-4
Dn
Br 2
12-8x11-0

First Floor
1,339 sq. ft.

Second Floor
490 sq. ft.

Plan #531-0492

Price Code C

Total Living Area: 1,829 Sq. Ft.

Home has 3 bedrooms, 2 1/2 baths, 2-car side entry garage and partial basement/crawl space foundation.

Special features

- Entry foyer with coat closet opens to large family room with fireplace
- Two second floor bedrooms share a full bath
- Optional second floor bedroom can be finished as your family grows
- Cozy porch provides convenient side entrance into home

Master Bath Has Elegant Features

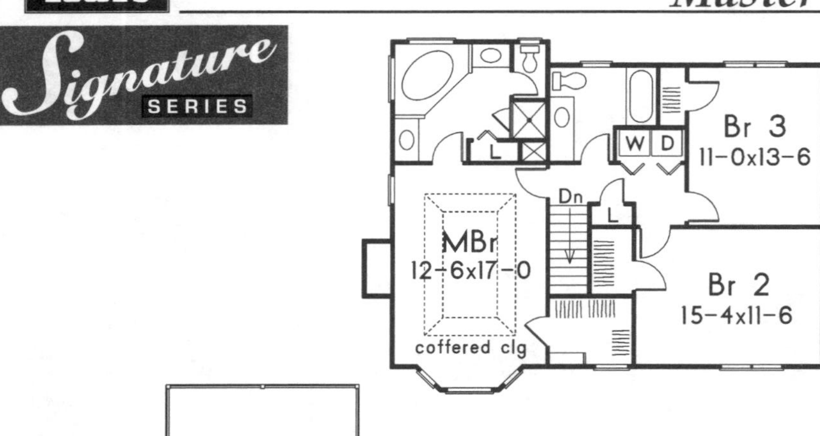
L
W D
Br 3
11-0x13-6
Dn
L
MBr
12-6x17-0
Br 2
15-4x11-6
coffered clg

Second Floor
976 sq. ft.

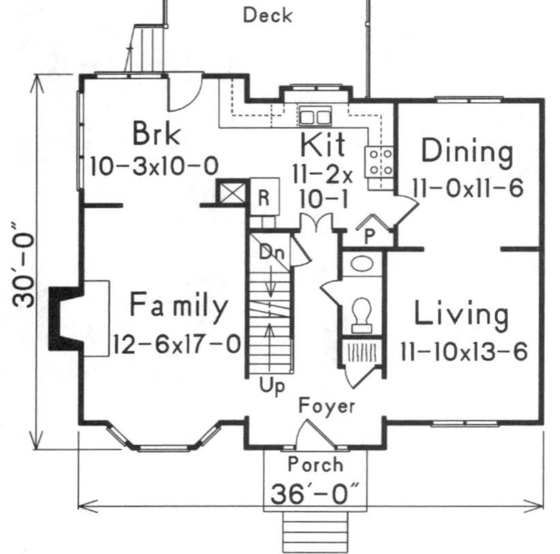
Deck
Brk
10-3x10-0
Kit
11-2x
10-1
Dining
11-0x11-6
R
P
Dn
30'-0"
Family
12-6x17-0
Living
11-10x13-6
Up
Foyer
Porch
36'-0"

First Floor
998 sq. ft.

Plan #531-0124

Price Code C

Total Living Area: 1,974 Sq. Ft.

Home has 3 bedrooms, 2 1/2 baths, 2-car drive under garage and basement foundation.

Special features

- Breakfast room with full windows blends into family room
- Second floor includes private master bedroom suite and easy access to laundry facility
- Elegant master bath has large corner tub with separate shower and vanities
- Traditional entrance framed by a covered porch and sidelights

TO ORDER BLUEPRINTS USE THE FORM ON PAGE 290 OR CALL TOLL-FREE **1-800-DREAM HOME** (373-2646)

Front Porch And Center Gable Add Style

LOWE'S

Signature SERIES

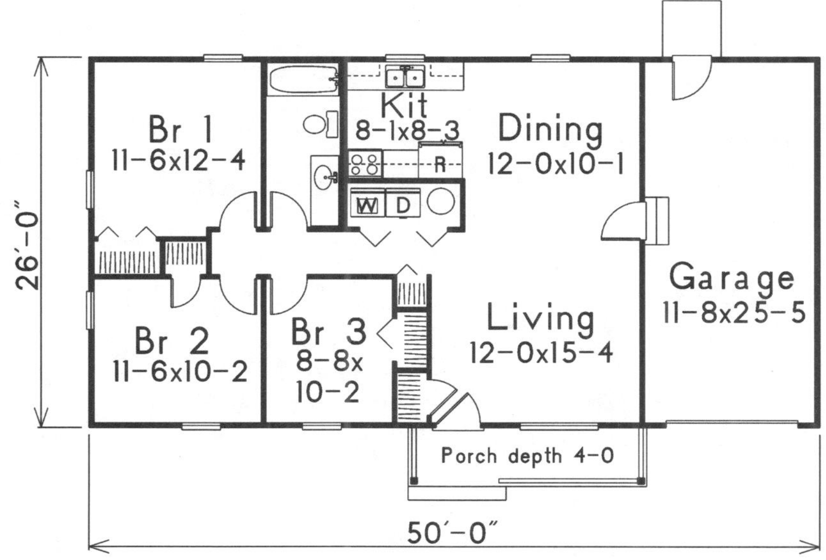
Br 1
11-6x12-4
Kit
8-1x8-3
R
W D
Dining
12-0x10-1
Garage
11-8x25-5
Br 2
11-6x10-2
Br 3
8-8x
10-2
Living
12-0x15-4
Porch depth 4-0
26'-0"
50'-0"

Plan #531-0195

Price Code AA

Total Living Area: 988 Sq. Ft.

Home has 3 bedrooms, 1 bath, 1-car garage and basement foundation, drawings also include crawl space foundation.

Special features

- Pleasant covered porch entry
- Living, dining and kitchen areas are combined to maximize space
- Entry has convenient coat closet
- Laundry closet is located adjacent to bedrooms

LOWE'S
Signature
SERIES

Compact Home, Perfect Fit For Narrow Lot

Br 3
8-8x9-2
L
L
Dn
Br 2
10-0x
9-2

Second Floor
400 sq. ft.

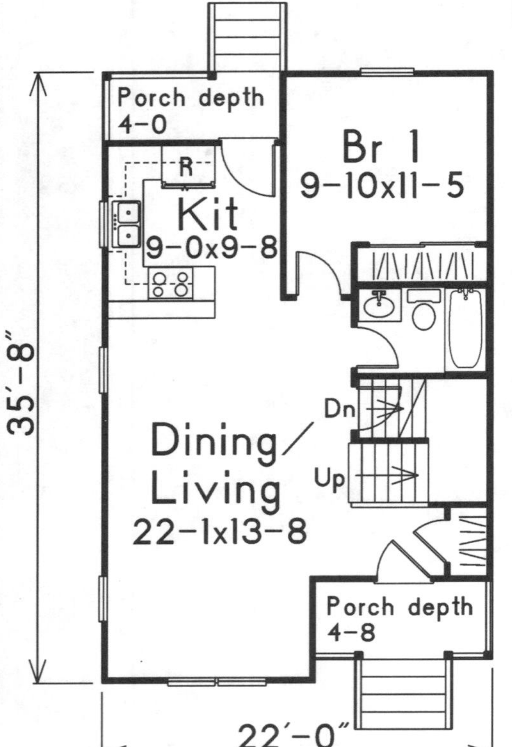
Porch depth
4-0
R
Kit
9-0x9-8
Br 1
9-10x11-5
Dn
Dining/
Living
22-1x13-8
Up
Porch depth
4-8
35'-8"
22'-0"

First Floor
685 sq. ft.

Plan #531-0494

Price Code AA

Total Living Area: 1,085 Sq. Ft.

Home has 3 bedrooms, 2 baths and basement foundation.

Special features

- Rear porch has a handy access through the kitchen
- Convenient hall linen closet located on the second floor
- Breakfast bar in kitchen offers additional counterspace
- Living and dining rooms combine for open living atmosphere

TO ORDER BLUEPRINTS USE THE FORM ON PAGE 290 OR CALL TOLL-FREE **1-800-DREAM HOME** (373-2646)

LOWE'S

Signature SERIES

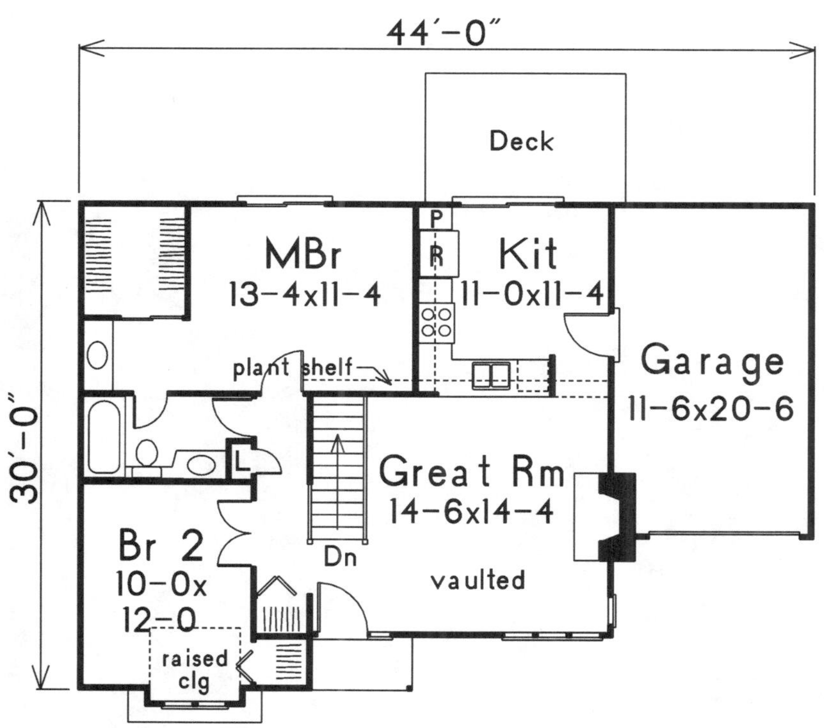
44'-0"
Deck
MBr
13-4x11-4
P
R
Kit
11-0x11-4
Garage
11-6x20-6
plant shelf
L
Great Rm
14-6x14-4
vaulted
Dn
Br 2
10-0x
12-0
raised
clg
30'-0"

Plan #531-0276

Price Code AA

Total Living Area: 950 Sq. Ft.

Home has 2 bedrooms, 1 bath, 1-car garage and basement foundation.

Special features

- Deck adjacent to kitchen/breakfast area for outdoor dining
- Vaulted ceiling, open stairway and fireplace complement great room
- Secondary bedroom with sloped ceiling and box bay window can convert to den
- Master bedroom with walk-in closet, plant shelf, separate dressing area and private access to bath
- Kitchen has garage access and opens to great room

Deluxe Master Suite Provides Ultimate Style

Plan #531-0376

Price Code E

Total Living Area: 3,019 Sq. Ft.

Home has 4 bedrooms, 2 1/2 baths, 3-car side entry garage and basement foundation.

Special features

- Master suite features double-doors, dramatic vaulted ceiling and spacious master bath with large bay window
- Bonus room accented by dormer windows and ceiling vaults
- Handy additional storage in secondary bath

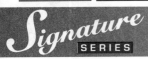

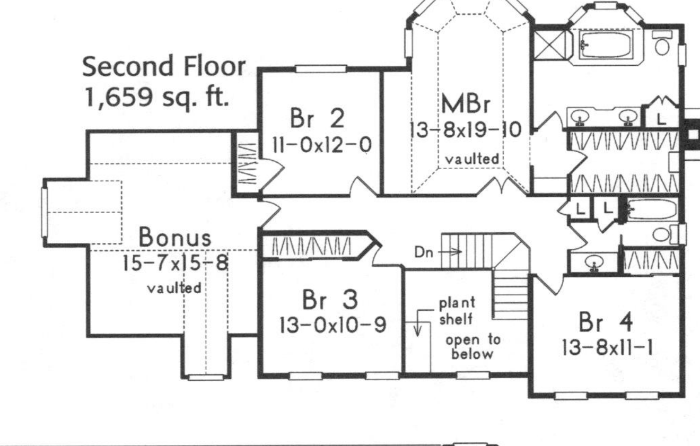
Second Floor
1,659 sq. ft.
Br 2
11-0x12-0
MBr
13-8x19-10
vaulted
Bonus
15-7x15-8
vaulted
Dn
Br 3
13-0x10-9
plant shelf
open to below
Br 4
13-8x11-1

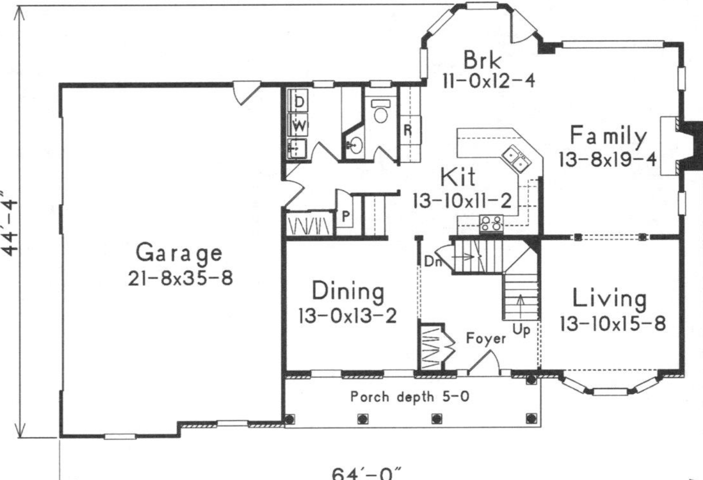
Brk
11-0x12-4
Family
13-8x19-4
Kit
13-10x11-2
Garage
21-8x35-8
Dining
13-0x13-2
Living
13-10x15-8
Foyer
Up
Dn
Porch depth 5-0
44'-4"
64'-0"

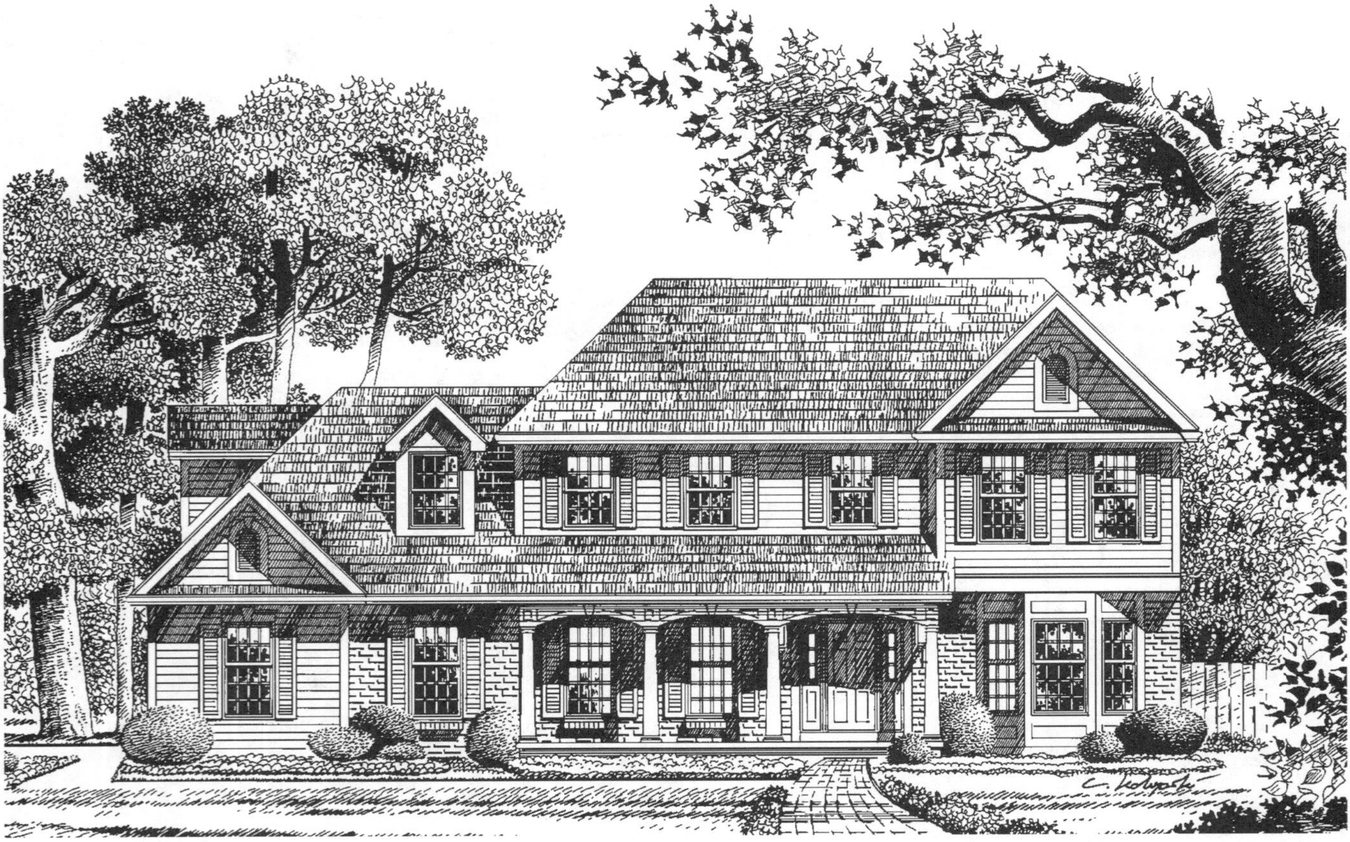

First Floor
1,360 sq. ft.

Family Room Fireplace Perfect For Gathering

LOWE'S

Signature SERIES

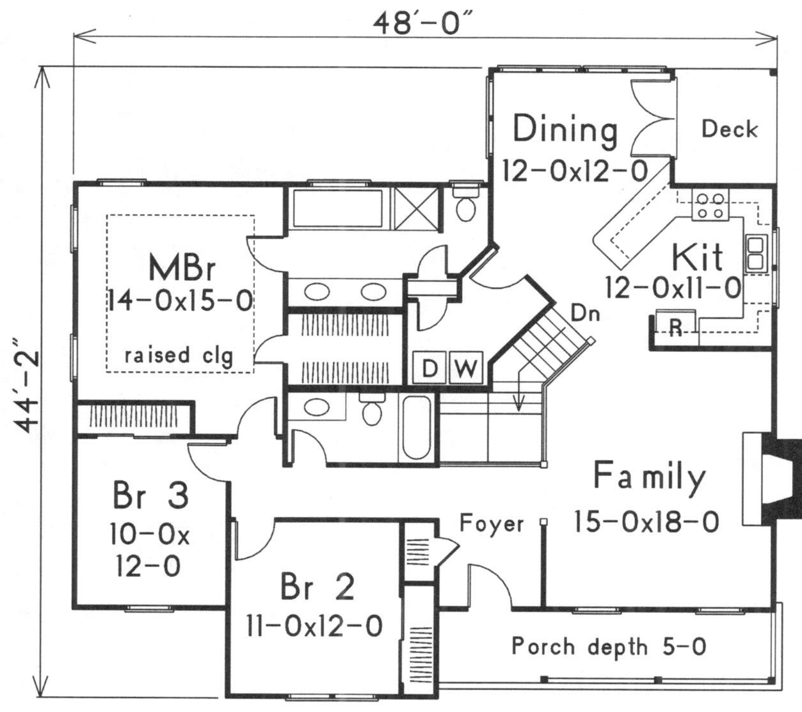
48'-0"
44'-2"
Dining
12-0x12-0
Deck
Kit
12-0x11-0
R
Dn
MBr
14-0x15-0
raised clg
D W
Family
15-0x18-0
Foyer
Br 3
10-0x
12-0
Br 2
11-0x12-0
Porch depth 5-0

Plan #531-0237

Price Code B

Total Living Area: 1,631 Sq. Ft.

Home has 3 bedrooms, 2 baths, 2-car drive under garage and basement foundation.

Special features

- 9' ceilings throughout this home
- Utility room conveniently located near kitchen
- Roomy kitchen and dining areas boast a breakfast bar and deck access
- Coffered ceiling accents master suite

LOWE'S

Signature SERIES

Handsome Traditional With Gabled Entrance

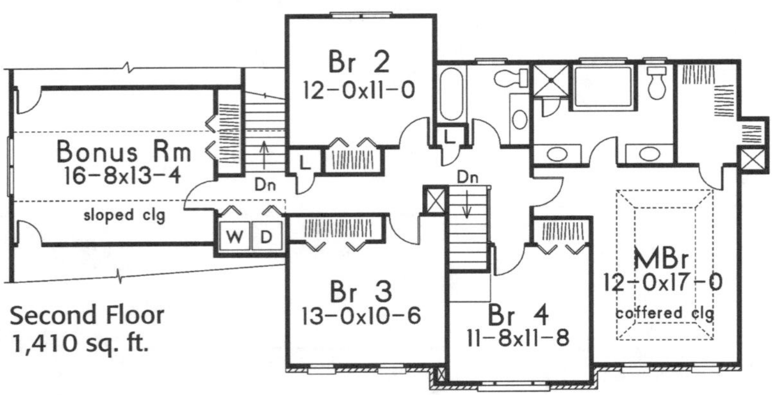

Br 2
12-0x11-0
Bonus Rm
16-8x13-4
sloped clg
Dn
W
D
L
L
Dn
Br 3
13-0x10-6
Br 4
11-8x11-8
MBr
12-0x17-0
coffered clg

Second Floor
1,410 sq. ft.

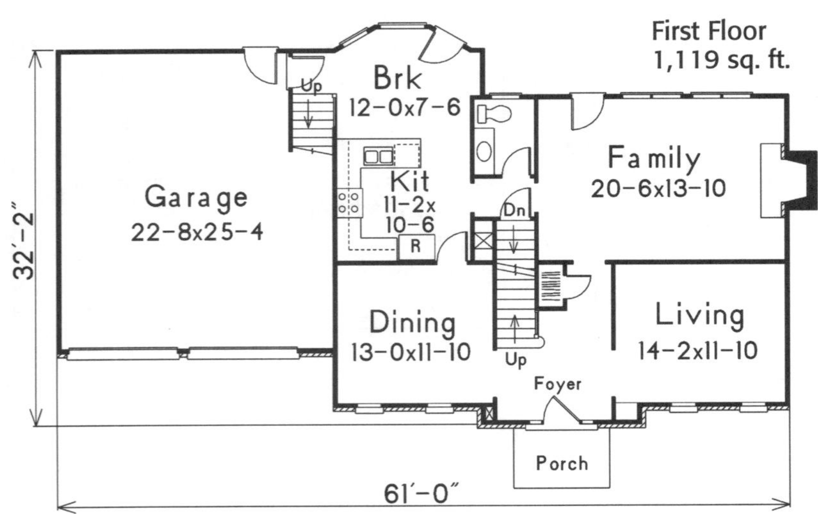

Brk
12-0x7-6
Up
Garage
22-8x25-4
Kit
11-2x
10-6
R
Dn
Family
20-6x13-10
Dining
13-0x11-10
Up
Foyer
Living
14-2x11-10
Porch
32'-2"
61'-0"

First Floor
1,119 sq. ft.

Plan #531-0135

Price Code E

Total Living Area: 2,529 Sq. Ft.

Home has 4 bedrooms, 2 1/2 baths, 2-car garage and basement foundation.

Special features

- Distinguished appearance enhances this home's classic interior arrangement
- Bonus room over the garage with direct access from the attic and the second floor hall
- Garden tub, walk-in closet and coffered ceiling in the master bedroom suite

TO ORDER BLUEPRINTS USE THE FORM ON PAGE 290 OR CALL TOLL-FREE **1-800-DREAM HOME** (373-2646)

Enchanting Country Cottage

LOWE'S

Signature
SERIES

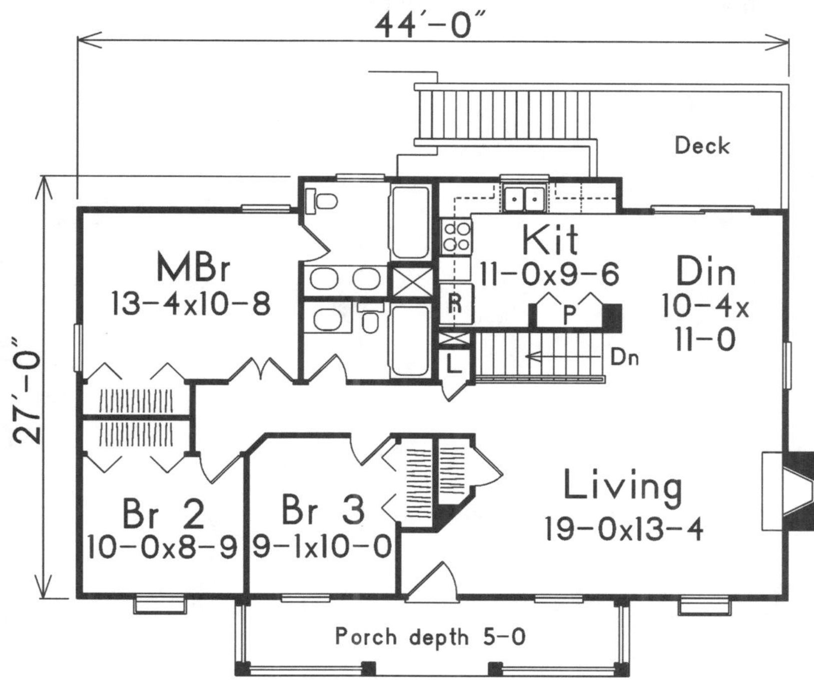
44'-0"
Deck
MBr
13-4x10-8
Kit
11-0x9-6
Din
10-4x
11-0
R
P
L
Dn
27'-0"
Living
19-0x13-4
Br 2
10-0x8-9
Br 3
9-1x10-0
Porch depth 5-0

Plan #531-0477

Price Code AA

Total Living Area: 1,140 Sq. Ft.

Home has 3 bedrooms, 2 baths, 2-car drive under garage and basement foundation.

Special features

- Open and spacious living and dining areas for family gatherings
- Well-organized kitchen with an abundance of cabinetry and a built-in pantry
- Roomy master bath features double-bowl vanity

LOWE'S

Signature SERIES

Second Floor
1,011 sq. ft.

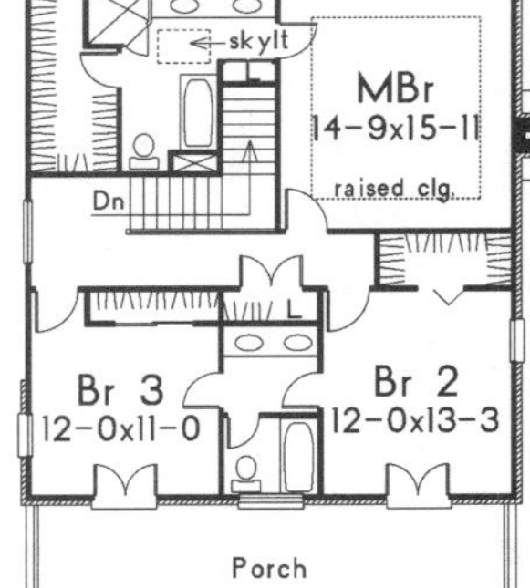
skylt
MBr
14-9x15-11
raised clg.
Dn
Br 3
12-0x11-0
Br 2
12-0x13-3
Porch

Plan #531-0360

Price Code D

Total Living Area: 2,327 Sq. Ft.

Home has 3 bedrooms, 2 1/2 baths, 2-car side entry garage and basement foundation.

Special features

- 9′ ceilings throughout
- Covered porches on both floors create an outdoor living area
- Secondary bedrooms share full bath
- L-shaped kitchen features island cooktop and convenient laundry room

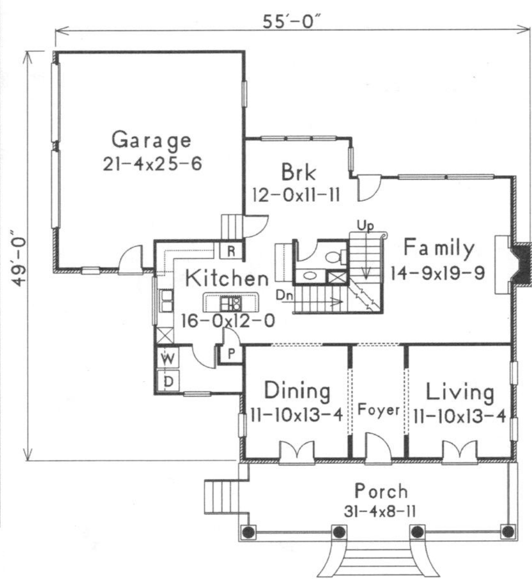
55′-0″
49′-0″
Garage
21-4x25-6
Brk
12-0x11-11
Up
Family
14-9x19-9
R
Kitchen
16-0x12-0
Dn
W
D
P
Dining
11-10x13-4
Foyer
Living
11-10x13-4
Porch
31-4x8-11

First Floor
1,316 sq. ft.

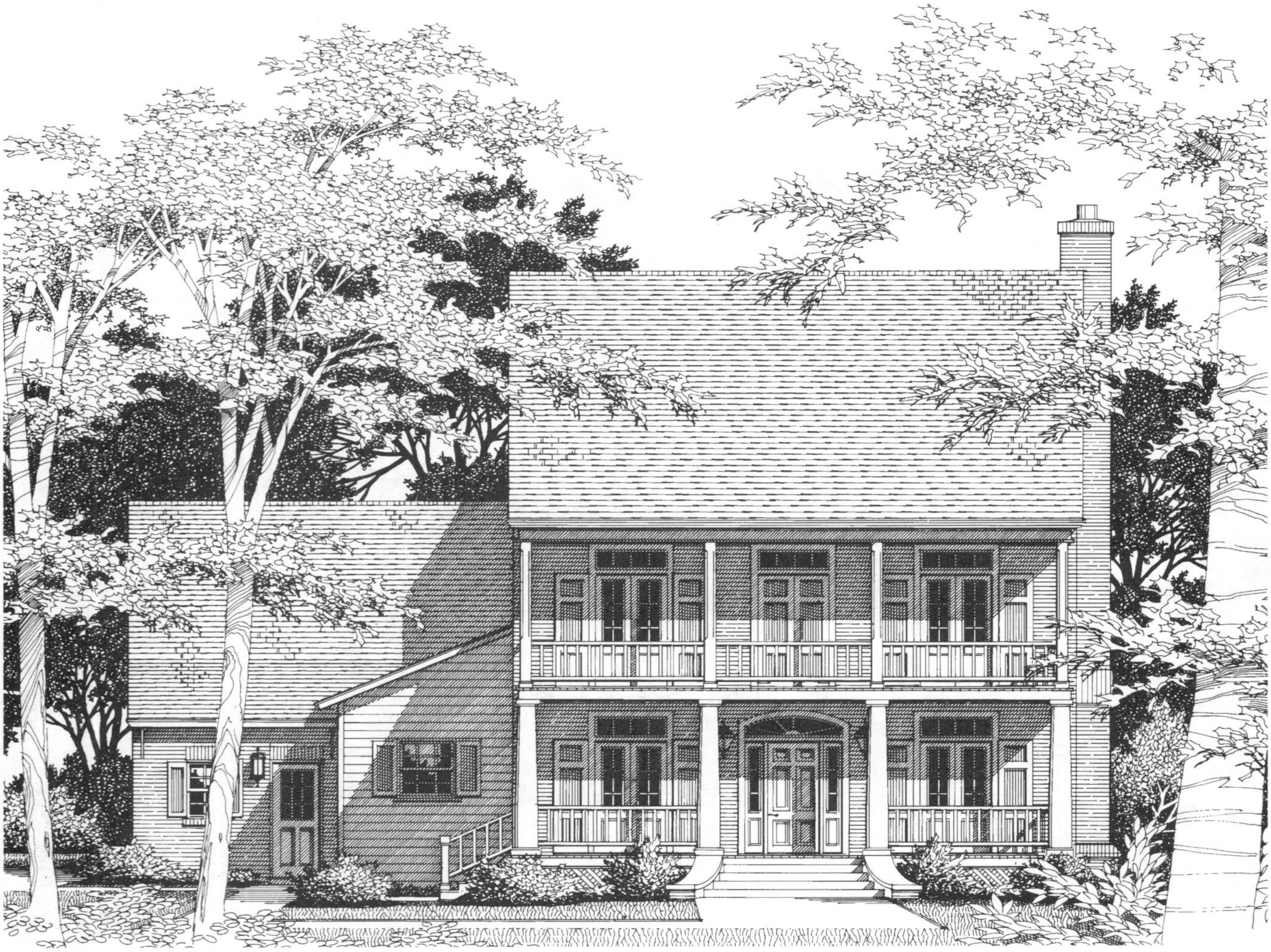

Victorian Turret Provides Dramatic Focus

LOWE'S

Signature SERIES

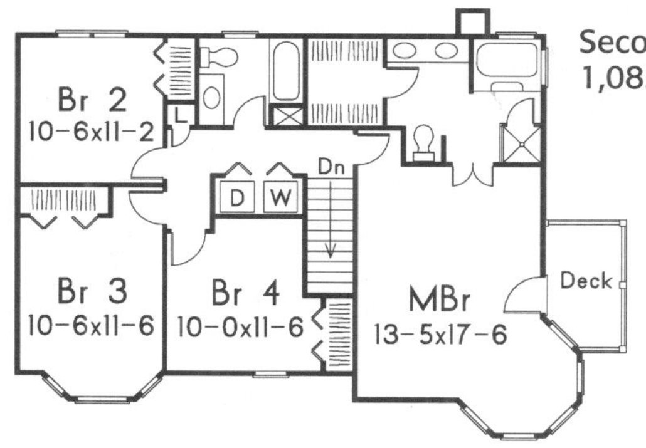

Br 2
10-6x11-2
Br 3
10-6x11-6
Br 4
10-0x11-6
D
W
Dn
MBr
13-5x17-6
Deck

Second Floor
1,085 sq. ft.

First Floor
1,129 sq. ft.

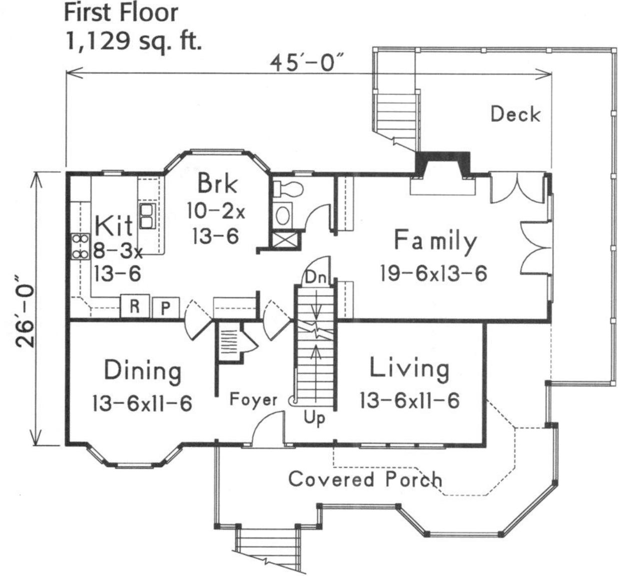

45'-0"
26'-0"
Deck
Brk
10-2x
13-6
Kit
8-3x
13-6
R
P
Family
19-6x13-6
Dn
Dining
13-6x11-6
Foyer
Up
Living
13-6x11-6
Covered Porch

Plan #531-0133

Price Code D

Total Living Area: 2,214 Sq. Ft.

Home has 4 bedrooms, 2 1/2 baths, 2-car drive under garage and basement foundation.

Special features

- Victorian accents dominate facade
- Covered porches and decks fan out to connect front and rear entries and add to outdoor living space
- Elegant master bedroom suite features a five-sided windowed alcove and private deck
- Corner kitchen with a sink-top peninsula

Three-Car Apartment Garage With Country Flair

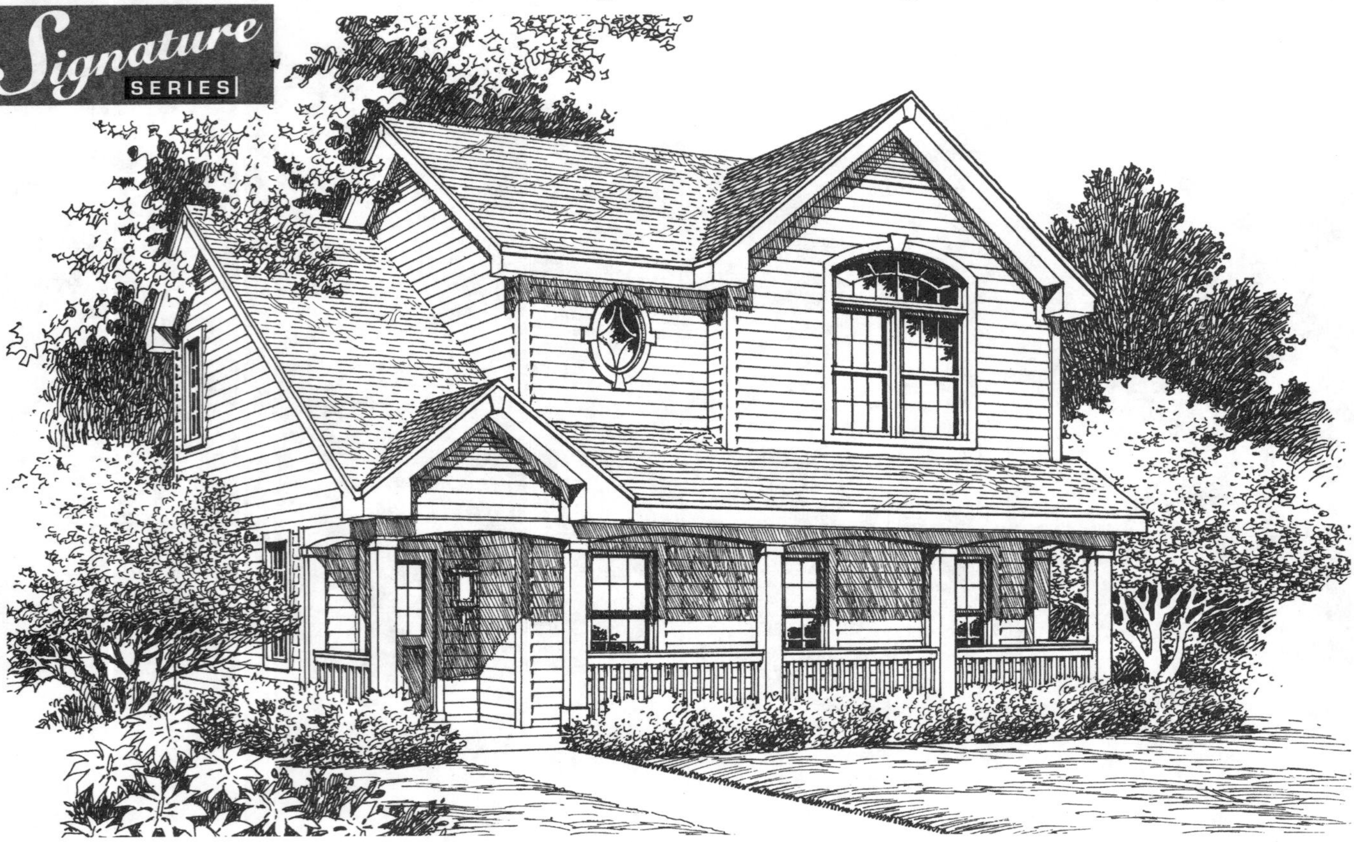

Plan #531-0734

Price Code AA

Total Living Area: 929 Sq. Ft.

Home has 2 bedrooms, 1 bath, 3-car side entry garage and slab foundation.

Special features

- Spacious living room with dining area has access to 8' x 12' deck through glass sliding doors
- Splendid U-shaped kitchen features a breakfast bar, oval window above sink and impressive cabinet storage
- Master bedroom enjoys a walk-in closet and large elliptical feature window
- Laundry, storage closet and mechanical space are located off first floor garage

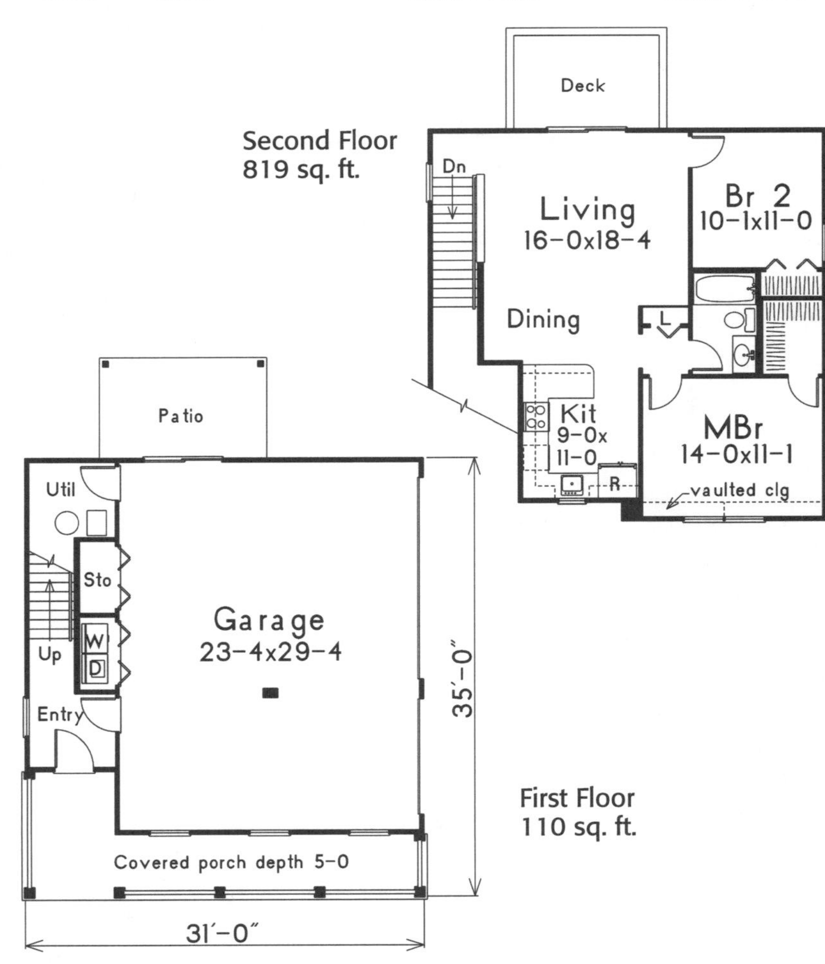
Deck
Second Floor
819 sq. ft.
Dn
Living
16-0x18-4
Br 2
10-1x11-0
Dining
L
Kit
9-0x
11-0
R
MBr
14-0x11-1
vaulted clg
Patio
Util
Sto
Up
W
D
Garage
23-4x29-4
Entry
35'-0"
Covered porch depth 5-0
31'-0"
First Floor
110 sq. ft.

LOWE'S

Signature
SERIES

Plan #531-0483

Price Code A

Total Living Area: 1,330 Sq. Ft.

Home has 4 bedrooms, 2 baths, 1-car garage and basement foundation.

Special features

- Vaulted living room is open to bayed dining room and kitchen creating ideal spaces for entertaining
- Two bedrooms, a bath and linen closet complete the first floor and are easily accessible
- The second floor offers two bedrooms with walk-in closets, a very large storage room and an opening with louvered doors which overlooks the living room

First Floor
884 sq. ft.

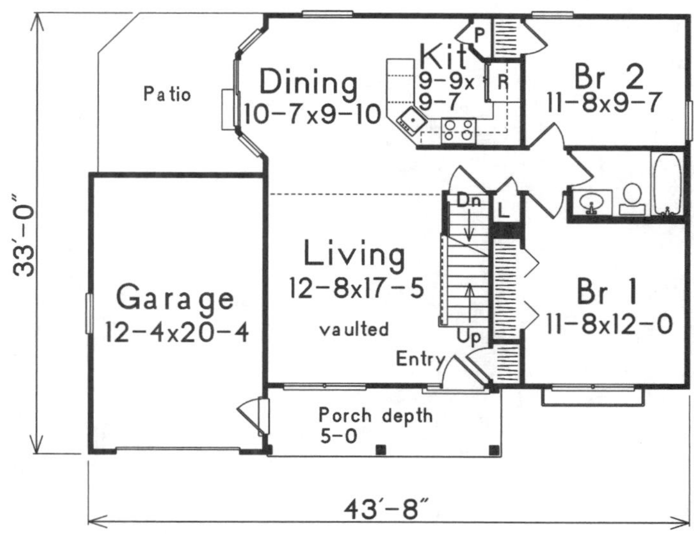
Patio
Dining
10-7x9-10
Kit
9-9x
9-7
P
R
Br 2
11-8x9-7
33'-0"
Dn
L
Living
12-8x17-5
vaulted
Garage
12-4x20-4
Br 1
11-8x12-0
Up
Entry
Porch depth
5-0
43'-8"

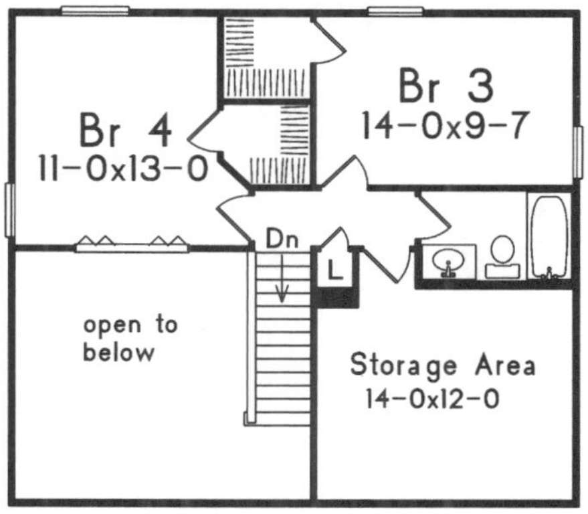

Br 4
11-0x13-0

Br 3
14-0x9-7

Dn

L

open to
below

Storage Area
14-0x12-0

Second Floor
446 sq. ft.

LOWE'S

Signature SERIES

Large Porch And Balcony Are Impressive

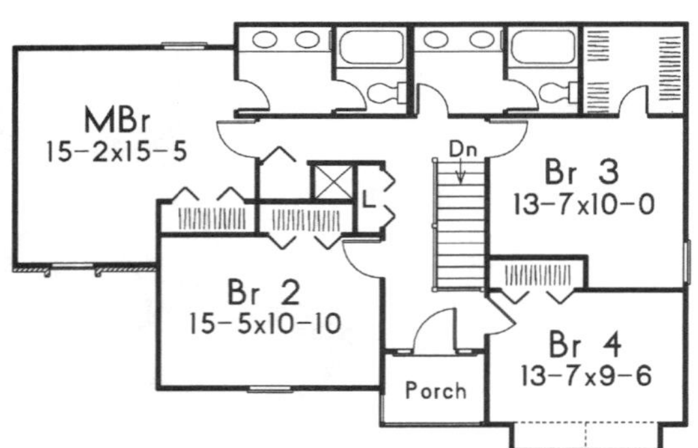

MBr
15-2x15-5
Dn
Br 3
13-7x10-0
L
Br 2
15-5x10-10
Br 4
13-7x9-6
Porch

Second Floor
1,182 sq. ft.

Plan #531-0540

Price Code D

Total Living Area: 2,352 Sq. Ft.

Home has 4 bedrooms, 2 1/2 baths, 2-car rear entry garage and crawl space foundation, drawings also include basement and slab foundations.

Special features

- Separate family and living rooms for casual and formal entertaining
- Master bedroom with private dressing area and bath
- Bedrooms located on second floor for privacy

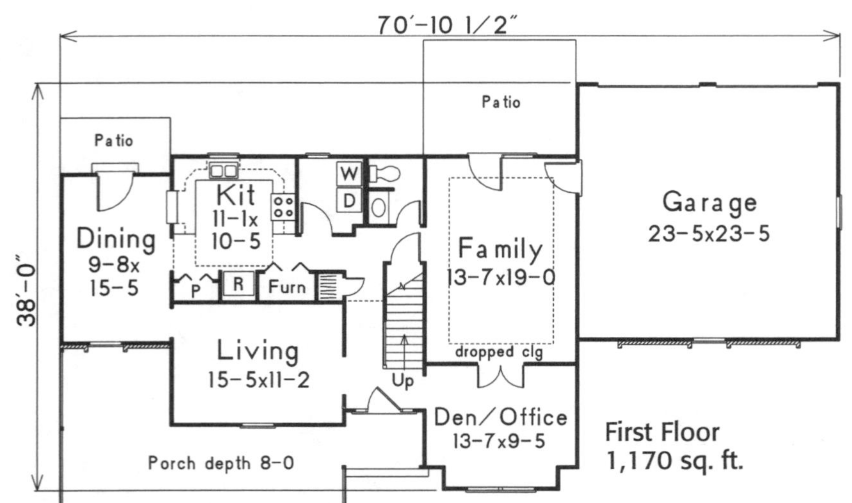

70'-10 1/2"
38'-0"
Patio
Patio
W
D
Kit
11-1x
10-5
Dining
9-8x
15-5
P
R
Furn
Family
13-7x19-0
dropped clg
Garage
23-5x23-5
Living
15-5x11-2
Up
Den/Office
13-7x9-5
Porch depth 8-0

First Floor
1,170 sq. ft.

TO ORDER BLUEPRINTS USE THE FORM ON PAGE 290 OR CALL TOLL-FREE **1-800-DREAM HOME** (373-2646)

Spacious Styling For Gracious Living

LOWE'S

Signature
SERIES

Br 4
12-4x14-8
Dn
Br 2
11-3x12-0
Br 3
11-4x12-0

Second Floor
787 sq. ft.

First Floor
2,263 sq. ft.

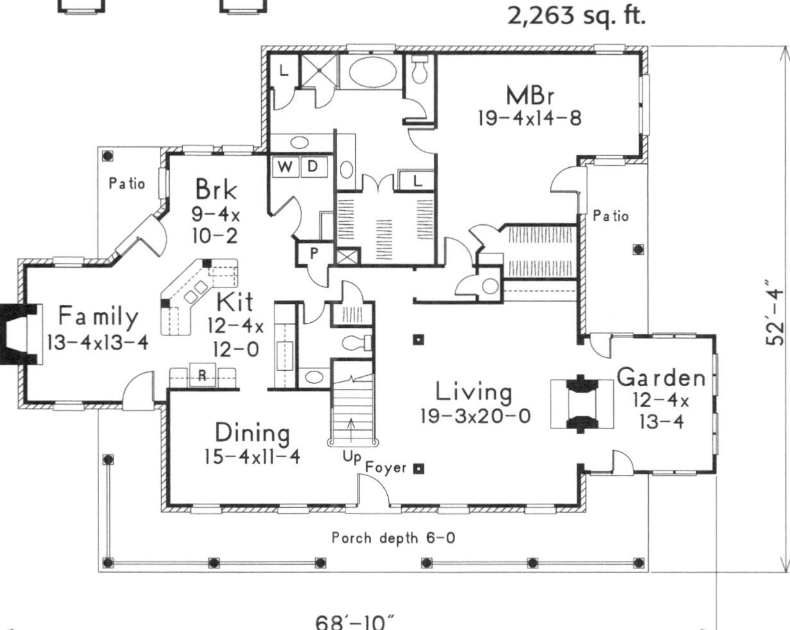
MBr
19-4x14-8
L
W D
L
Patio
Brk
9-4x
10-2
P
Patio
Family
13-4x13-4
Kit
12-4x
12-0
R
Living
19-3x20-0
Garden
12-4x
13-4
Dining
15-4x11-4
Up
Foyer
Porch depth 6-0
52'-4"
68'-10"

Plan #531-0156

Price Code E

Total Living Area: 3,050 Sq. Ft.

Home has 4 bedrooms, 3 1/2 baths, 2-car detached garage and slab foundation, drawings also include crawl space foundation.

Special features

- Sunny garden room and two-way fireplace create a bright, airy living room
- Front porch enhanced by arched transom windows and bold columns
- Sitting alcove, French door access to side patio, walk-in closets and abundant storage in master bedroom

Two-Story Offers Attractive Exterior

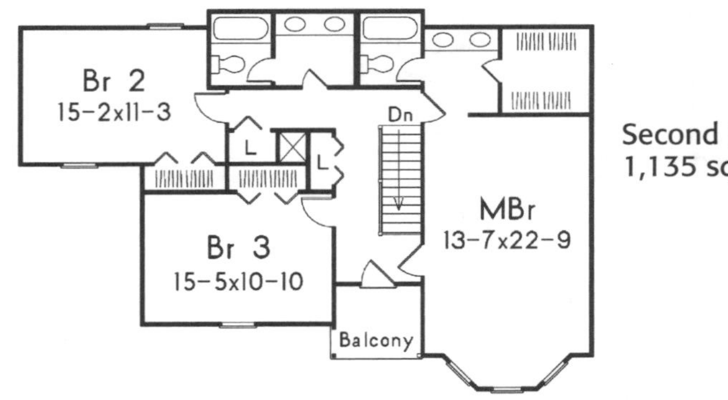
Br 2
15-2x11-3
Dn
L
L
MBr
13-7x22-9
Br 3
15-5x10-10
Balcony
Second Floor
1,135 sq. ft.

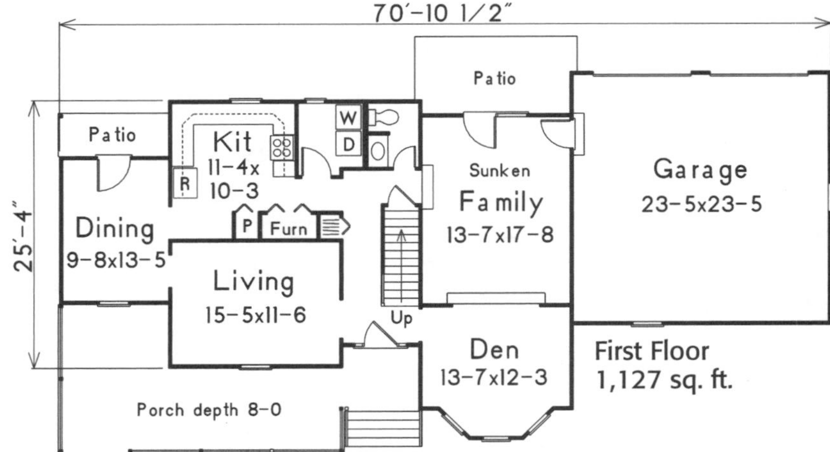
70'-10 1/2"
Patio
Patio
W
D
Kit
11-4x
10-3
R
Sunken
Family
13-7x17-8
Garage
23-5x23-5
P
Furn
Dining
9-8x13-5
25'-4"
Living
15-5x11-6
Up
Den
13-7x12-3
Porch depth 8-0
First Floor
1,127 sq. ft.

Plan #531-0526

Price Code D

Total Living Area: 2,262 Sq. Ft.

Home has 3 bedrooms, 2 1/2 baths, 2-car rear entry garage and crawl space foundation, drawings also include basement and slab foundations.

Special features

- Charming exterior features include large front porch, two patios, front balcony and double bay windows
- Den/office area provides impressive entry to sunken family room
- Conveniently located first floor laundry
- Large master bedroom with walk-in closet, dressing area and bath

TO ORDER BLUEPRINTS USE THE FORM ON PAGE 290 OR CALL TOLL-FREE **1-800-DREAM HOME** (373-2646)

Elegant Exterior

LOWE'S

Signature SERIES

Plan #531-0309

Price Code C

Total Living Area: 2,106 Sq. Ft.

Home has 3 bedrooms, 2 1/2 baths, 2-car garage and basement foundation.

Special features

- Large two-story foyer features open staircase and plant ledge
- Kitchen with centrally located eating bar offers double pantries for additional storage
- An arch with columns on either side separates dining and living rooms
- Master bath includes plush dressing area, double sinks, a spa tub, linen cabinet and a separate room with toilet and shower
- 9′ ceilings throughout home

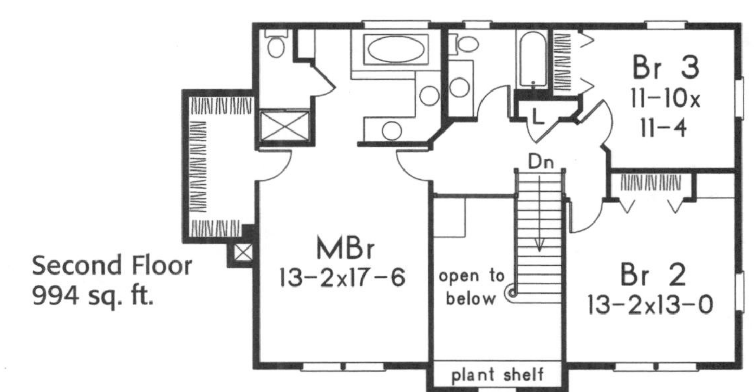
Br 3
11-10x
11-4
L
Dn
MBr
13-2x17-6
open to below
Br 2
13-2x13-0
plant shelf

Second Floor
994 sq. ft.

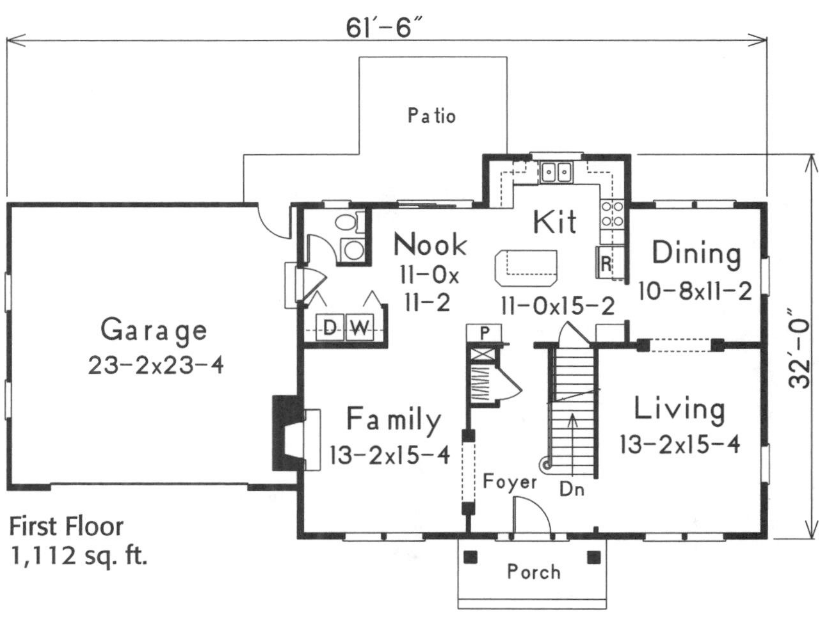
61′-6″
Patio
Kit
Nook
11-0x
11-2
11-0x15-2
Dining
10-8x11-2
R
D W
P
Garage
23-2x23-4
Family
13-2x15-4
Living
13-2x15-4
Foyer
Dn
32′-0″
Porch

First Floor
1,112 sq. ft.

Excellent Design For Comfortable Living

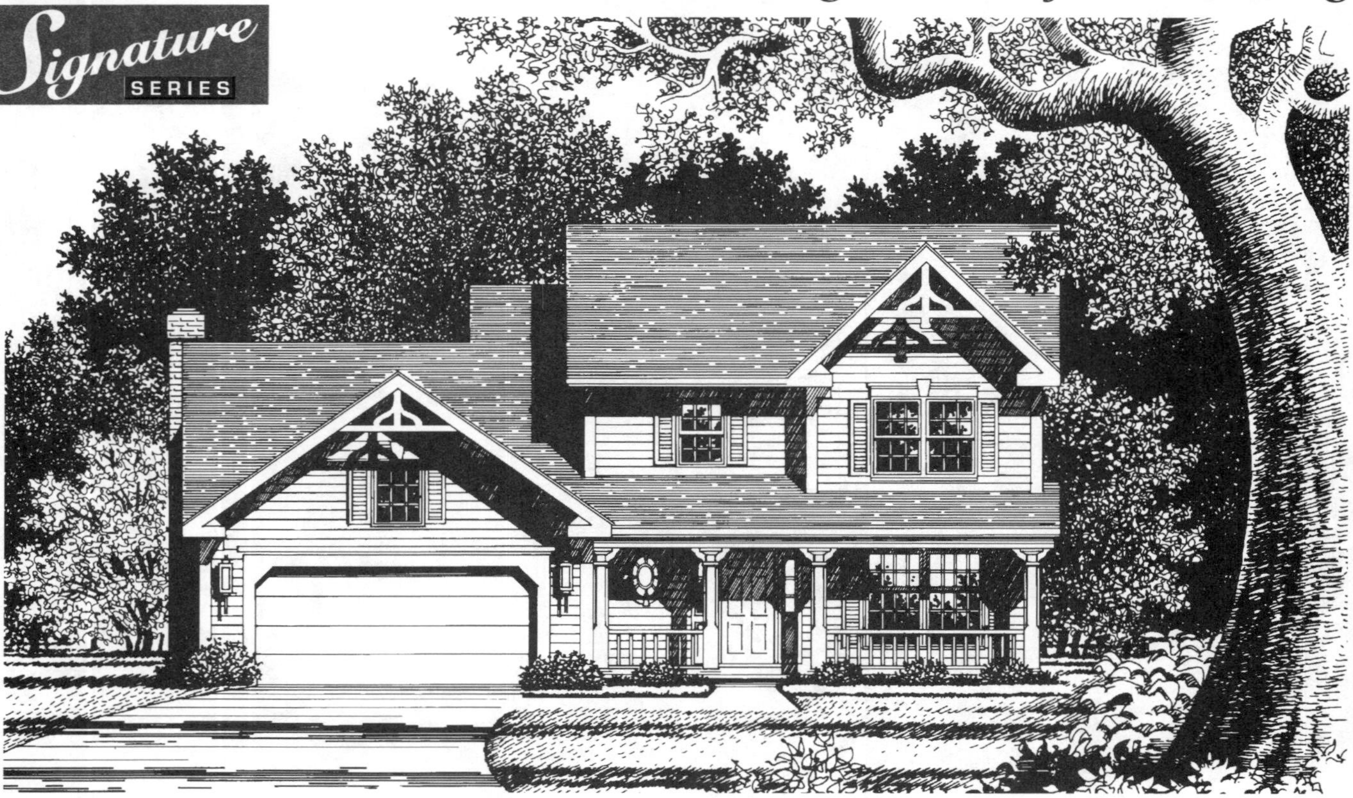

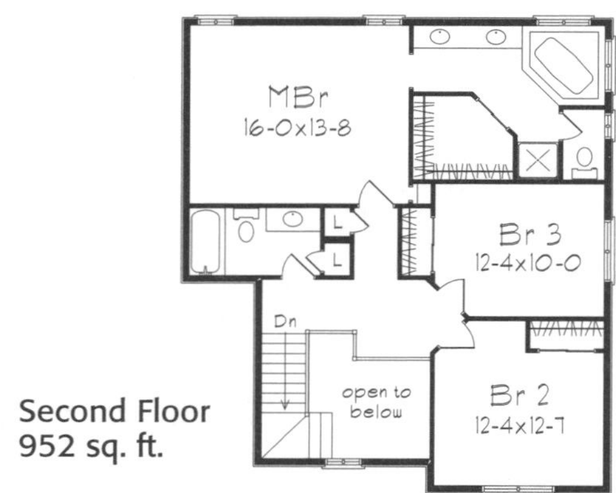

MBr
16-0x13-8
Br 3
12-4x10-0
Dn
open to below
Br 2
12-4x12-7
L
L

Second Floor
952 sq. ft.

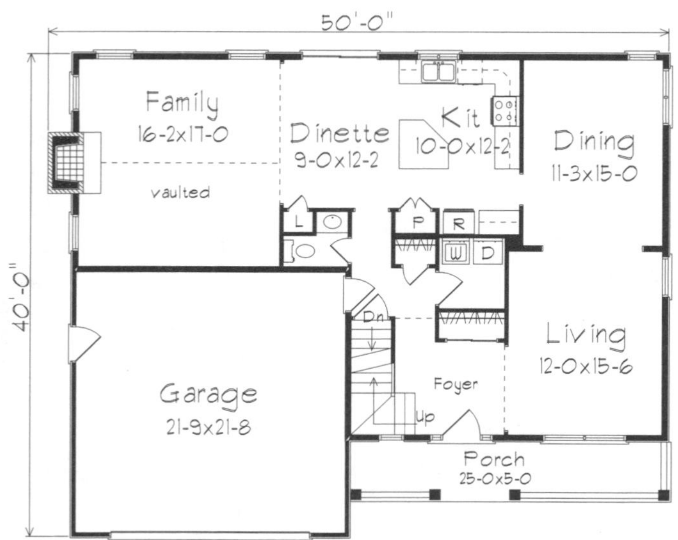

50'-0"
40'-0"
Family
16-2x17-0
vaulted
Dinette
9-0x12-2
Kit
10-0x12-2
Dining
11-3x15-0
L
P
R
W
D
Dn
Living
12-0x15-6
Foyer
Up
Garage
21-9x21-8
Porch
25-0x5-0

First Floor
1,228 sq. ft.

Plan #531-0378

Price Code C

Total Living Area: 2,180 Sq. Ft.

Home has 3 bedrooms, 2 1/2 baths, 2-car garage and basement foundation.

Special features

- Informal dinette and formal dining area flank kitchen
- Fireplace is focal point in vaulted family room
- Master bedroom includes bath with walk-in closet, shower and corner garden tub

LOWE'S

Signature
SERIES

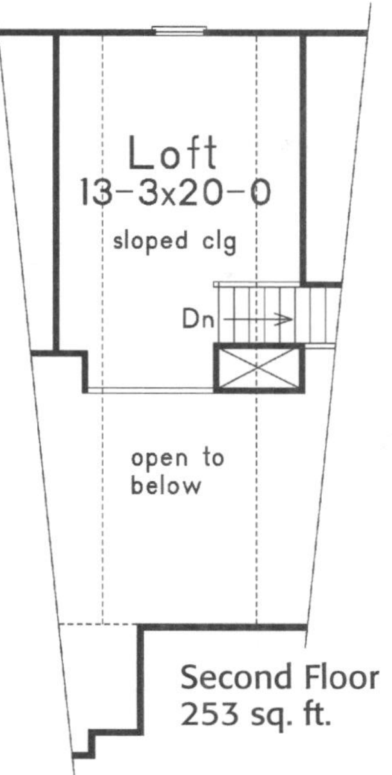
Loft
13-3x20-0
sloped clg
Dn
open to
below

Second Floor
253 sq. ft.

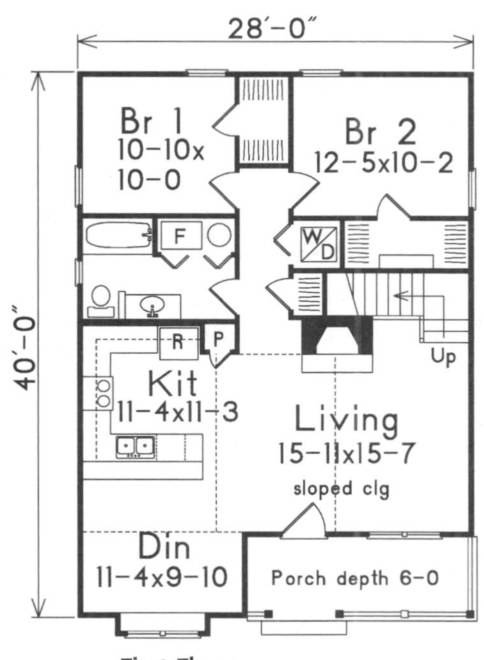
28'-0"
40'-0"
Br 1
10-10x
10-0
Br 2
12-5x10-2
F
W/D
R
P
Up
Kit
11-4x11-3
Living
15-11x15-7
sloped clg
Din
11-4x9-10
Porch depth 6-0

First Floor
1,032 sq. ft.

Plan #531-0694

Price Code A

Total Living Area: 1,285 Sq. Ft.

Home has 2 bedrooms, 1 bath and crawl space foundation.

Special features

- Dining nook creates warm feeling with sunny box bay window
- Second floor loft perfect for recreation space or office hideaway
- Bedrooms include walk-in closets allowing extra storage space
- Kitchen, dining and living areas combine making perfect gathering place

LOWE'S
Signature
SERIES

Columned Breakfast Room Adds Appeal

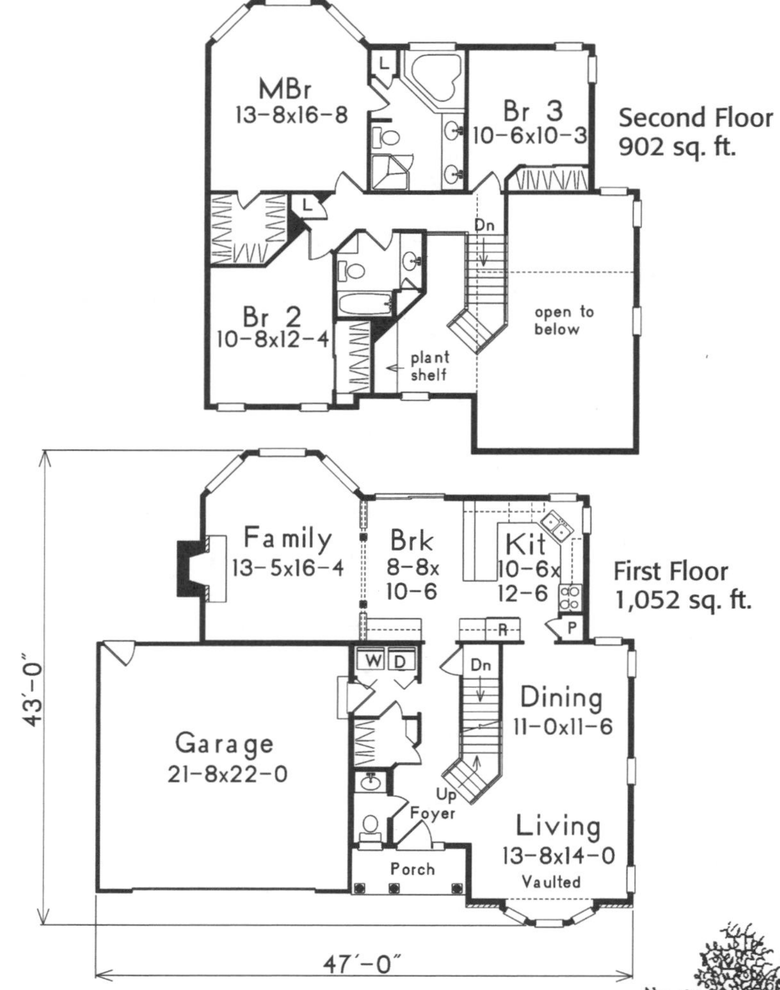

MBr
13-8x16-8
Br 3
10-6x10-3
Second Floor
902 sq. ft.
Dn
Br 2
10-8x12-4
open to below
plant shelf
Family
13-5x16-4
Brk
8-8x
10-6
Kit
10-6x
12-6
First Floor
1,052 sq. ft.
W D
Dn
Dining
11-0x11-6
Garage
21-8x22-0
Up
Foyer
Living
13-8x14-0
Vaulted
Porch
43'-0"
47'-0"

Plan #531-0375

Price Code C

Total Living Area: 1,954 Sq. Ft.

Home has 3 bedrooms, 2 1/2 baths, 2-car garage and basement foundation.

Special features

- Living and dining areas include vaulted ceilings and combine for added openness
- Convenient access to laundry room from garage
- Appealing bay window in family room attracts light
- Raised jacuzzi tub featured in master bath

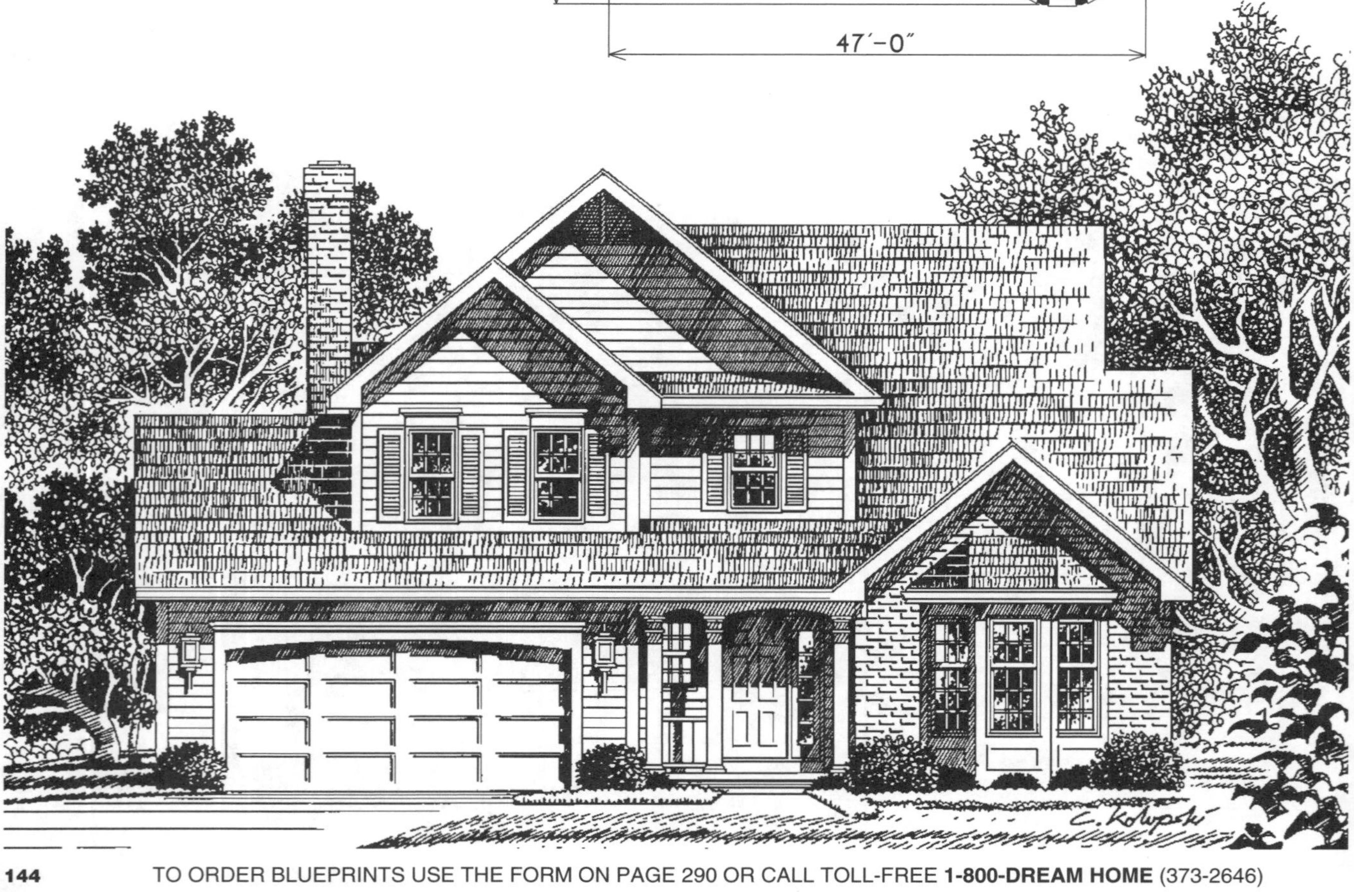

C. Kolupski

Rear Stairway Smooths Traffic Flow

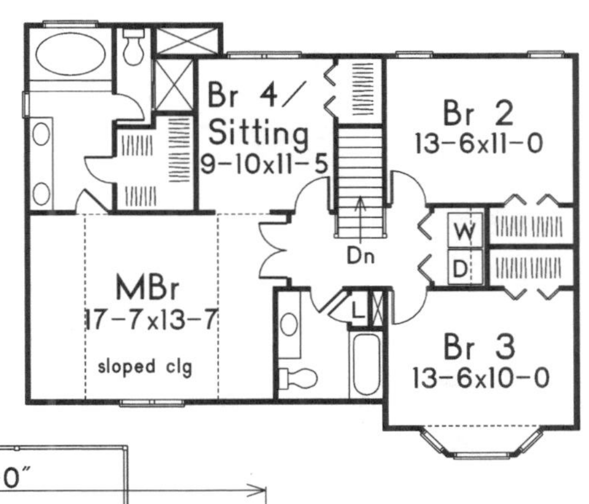
Br 4/
Sitting
9-10x11-5
Br 2
13-6x11-0
W
D
Dn
MBr
17-7x13-7
sloped clg
L
Br 3
13-6x10-0

Second Floor
1,059 sq. ft.

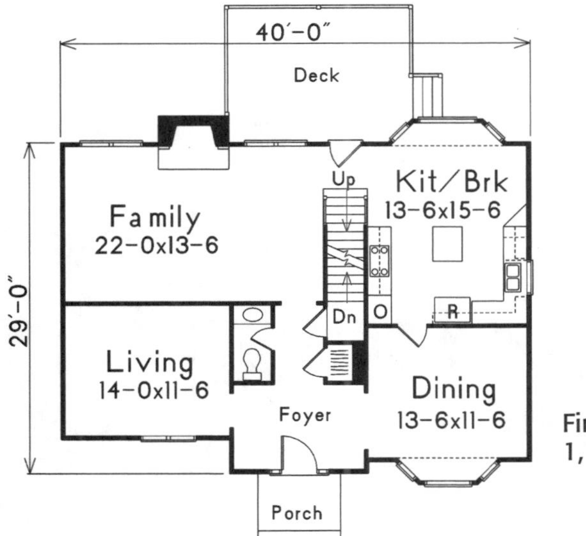
40'-0"
Deck
29'-0"
Up
Kit/Brk
13-6x15-6
Family
22-0x13-6
Dn
O
R
Living
14-0x11-6
Foyer
Dining
13-6x11-6
Porch

First Floor
1,136 sq. ft.

Plan #531-0132

Price Code C

Total Living Area: 2,195 Sq. Ft.

Home has 4 bedrooms, 2 1/2 baths, 2-car drive under garage and basement foundation.

Special features

- Striking facade provided by gracious two-story window treatment
- Bay windows add light and space
- Open family and breakfast areas exits onto the spacious rear deck

Outside Living Area Created By Veranda

Plan #531-0231
Price Code E

Total Living Area: 2,213 Sq. Ft.

Home has 4 bedrooms, 2 1/2 baths, 2-car side entry garage and slab foundation.

Special features

- Master bedroom features full bath with separate vanities, large walk-in closet and access to veranda
- Living room enhanced by a fireplace, bay window and columns framing the gallery
- 9' ceilings throughout home add to open feeling

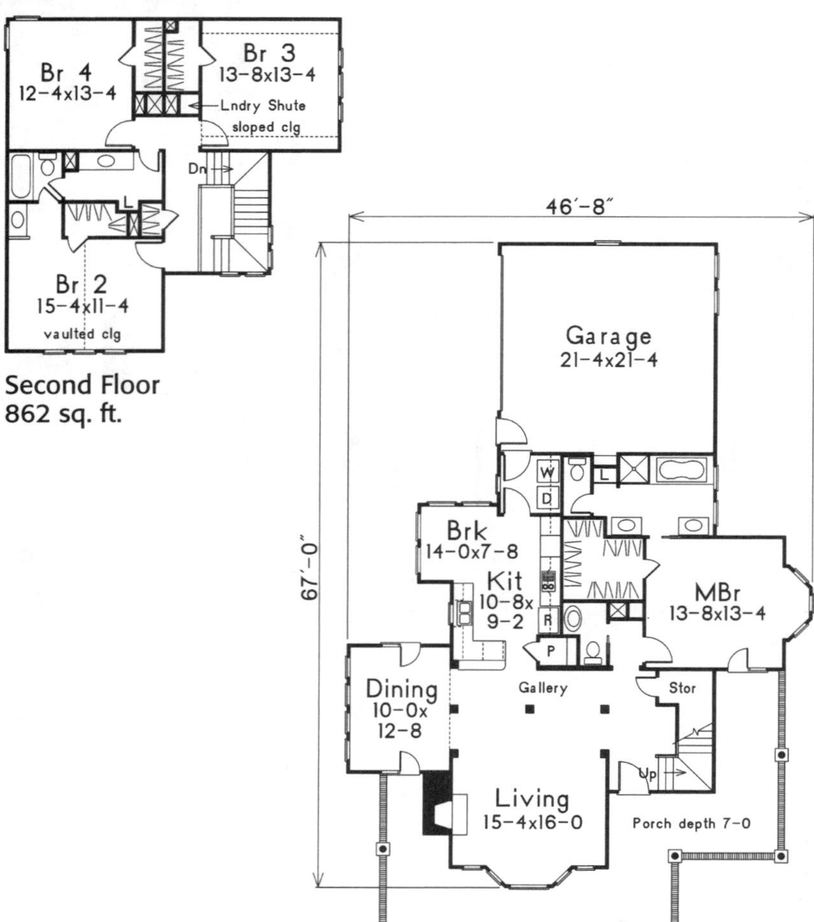
Br 4
12-4x13-4
Br 3
13-8x13-4
Lndry Shute
sloped clg
Dn
Br 2
15-4x11-4
vaulted clg
46'-8"
67'-0"
Garage
21-4x21-4
W
D
L
Brk
14-0x7-8
Kit
10-8x
9-2
R
P
MBr
13-8x13-4
Dining
10-0x
12-8
Gallery
Stor
Up
Living
15-4x16-0
Porch depth 7-0

Second Floor
862 sq. ft.

First Floor
1,351 sq. ft.

TO ORDER BLUEPRINTS USE THE FORM ON PAGE 290 OR CALL TOLL-FREE **1-800-DREAM HOME** (373-2646)

Grandscale Great Room In A Country Ranch

LOWE'S

Signature SERIES

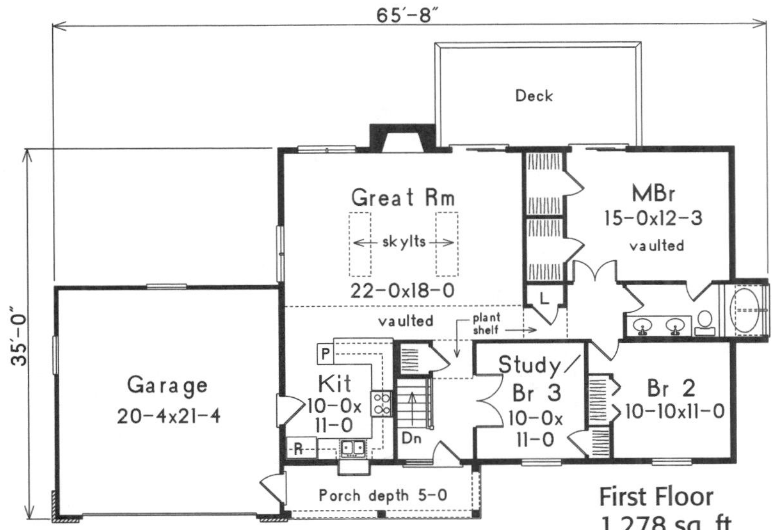
65'-8"
Deck
Great Rm
skylts
22-0x18-0
vaulted
MBr
15-0x12-3
vaulted
L
plant shelf
35'-0"
Garage
20-4x21-4
P
Kit
10-0x
11-0
R
Dn
Study/
Br 3
10-0x
11-0
Br 2
10-10x11-0
Porch depth 5-0

First Floor
1,278 sq. ft.

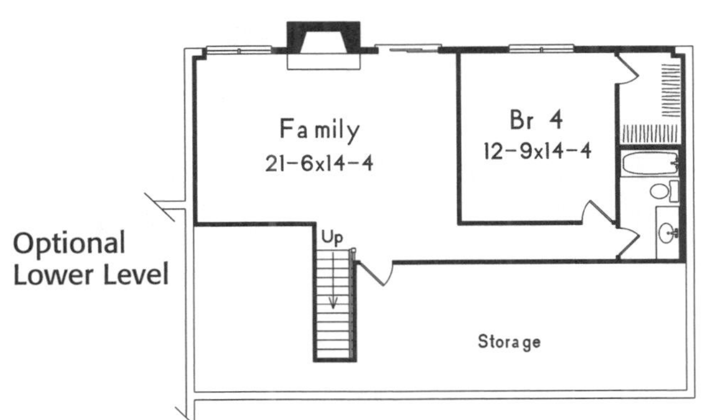
Family
21-6x14-4
Br 4
12-9x14-4
Up
Storage

Optional
Lower Level

Plan #531-0751

Price Code A

Total Living Area: 1,278 Sq. Ft.

Home has 3 bedrooms, 1 bath, 2-car garage and walk-out basement foundation.

Special features

- Excellent U-shaped kitchen with garden window opens to an enormous great room with vaulted ceiling, fireplace and two skylights
- Vaulted master bedroom offers double entry doors and two walk-in closets with access to deck and bath
- The bath has a double-bowl vanity and dramatic step-up garden tub with a lean-to greenhouse window
- 805 square feet of optional living area on lower level with family room, bedroom #4 and bath

Breakfast Bay Area Opens To Deck

Plan #531-0274

Price Code AA

Total Living Area: 1,020 Sq. Ft.

Home has 2 bedrooms, 1 bath, 2-car garage and basement foundation.

Special features

- Kitchen features open stairs, pass-through to great room, pantry and deck access
- Master bedroom features private entrance to bath, large walk-in closet and sliding doors to deck
- Informal entrance into home through the garage
- Great room with vaulted ceiling and fireplace

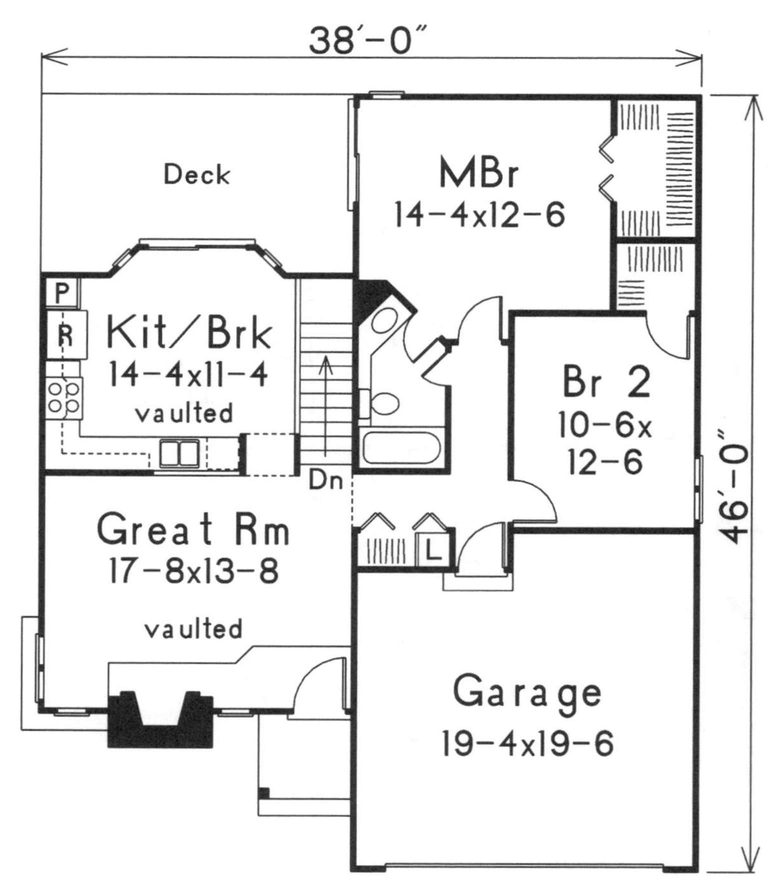

38'-0"
46'-0"
Deck
MBr
14-4x12-6
P
R
Kit/Brk
14-4x11-4
vaulted
Br 2
10-6x
12-6
Dn
Great Rm
17-8x13-8
vaulted
L
Garage
19-4x19-6

Practical Layout With Inviting Front Porch

LOWE'S

Signature
SERIES

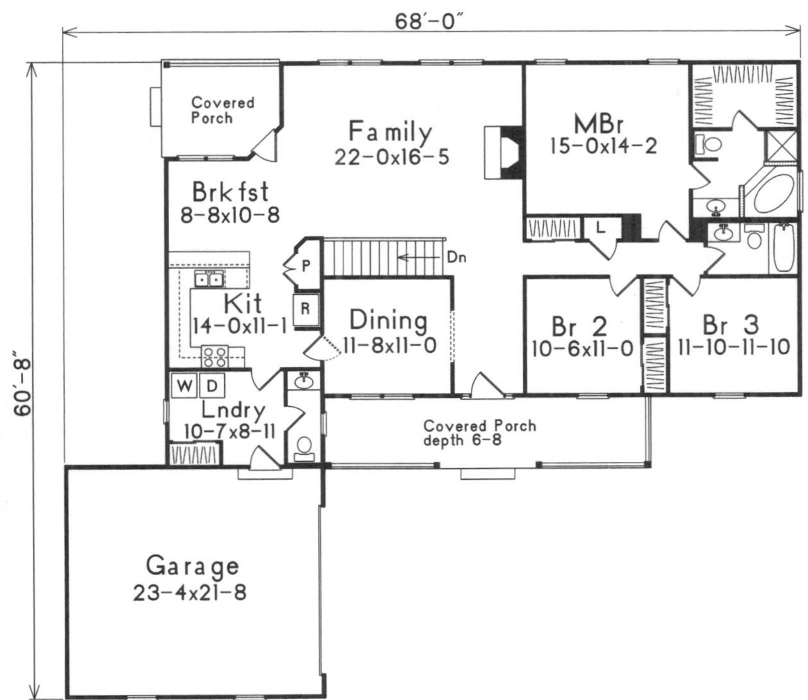
68'-0"
60'-8"
Covered Porch
Family 22-0x16-5
MBr 15-0x14-2
Brkfst 8-8x10-8
P
Dn
L
Kit 14-0x11-1
R
Dining 11-8x11-0
Br 2 10-6x11-0
Br 3 11-10-11-10
W D
Lndry 10-7x8-11
Covered Porch depth 6-8
Garage 23-4x21-8

Plan #531-0742

Price Code C

Total Living Area: 1,883 Sq. Ft.

Home has 3 bedrooms, 2 1/2 baths, 2-car side entry garage and basement foundation.

Special features

- Large laundry room located off the garage has coat closet and half bath
- Large family room with fireplace and access to covered porch is great central gathering room
- U-shaped kitchen has breakfast bar, large pantry and swing door to dining room for convenient serving

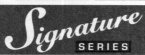

Second Floor
863 sq. ft.

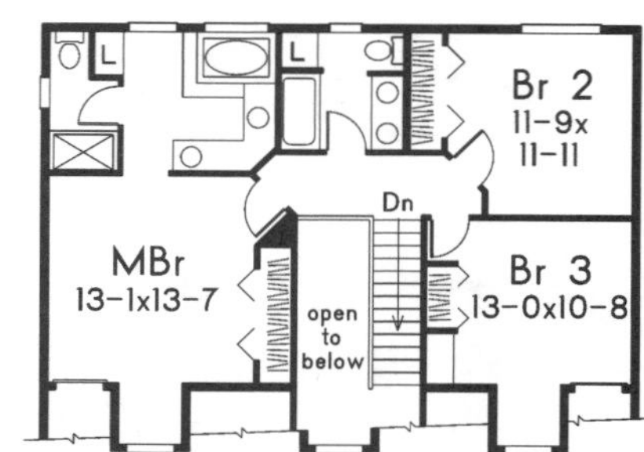
Br 2
11-9x
11-11
Dn
MBr
13-1x13-7
open
to
below
Br 3
13-0x10-8

Plan #531-0310

Price Code D

Total Living Area: 2,363 Sq. Ft.

Home has 3 bedrooms, 2 1/2 baths, 2-car garage and partial basement/crawl space foundation.

Special features

- Covered porches provide outdoor seating areas
- Corner fireplace becomes focal point of family room
- Kitchen features island cooktop and adjoining nook
- Energy efficient home with 2" x 6" exterior walls

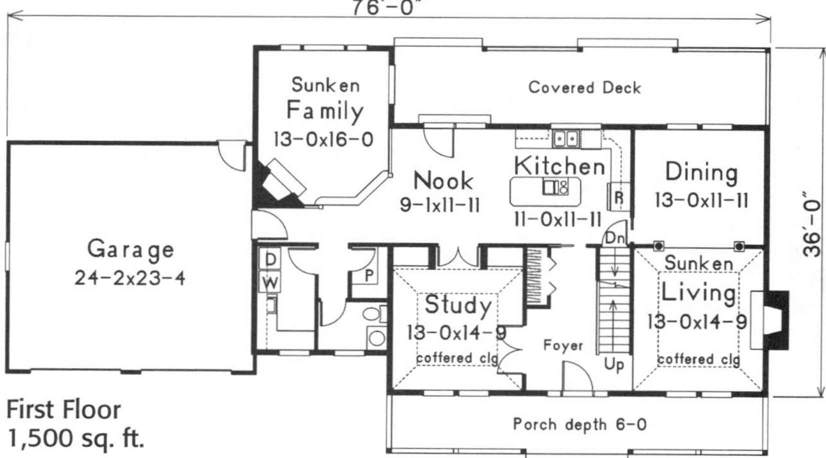
76'-0"
36'-0"
Sunken
Family
13-0x16-0
Covered Deck
Nook
9-1x11-11
Kitchen
11-0x11-11
Dining
13-0x11-11
Garage
24-2x23-4
Study
13-0x14-9
coffered clg
Foyer
Sunken
Living
13-0x14-9
coffered clg
Up
Dn
Porch depth 6-0

First Floor
1,500 sq. ft.

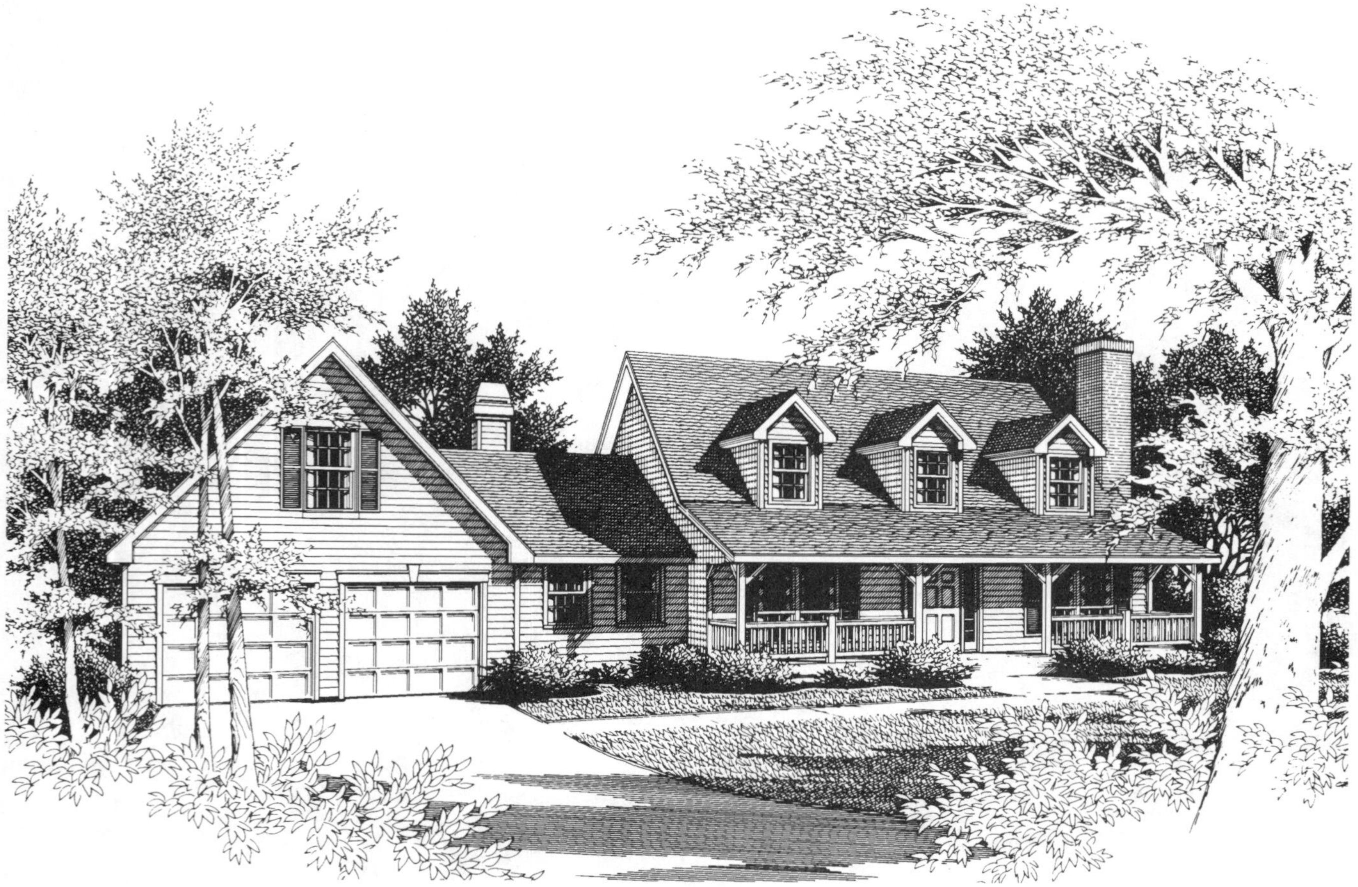

TO ORDER BLUEPRINTS USE THE FORM ON PAGE 290 OR CALL TOLL-FREE **1-800-DREAM HOME** (373-2646)

LOWE'S

Signature
SERIES

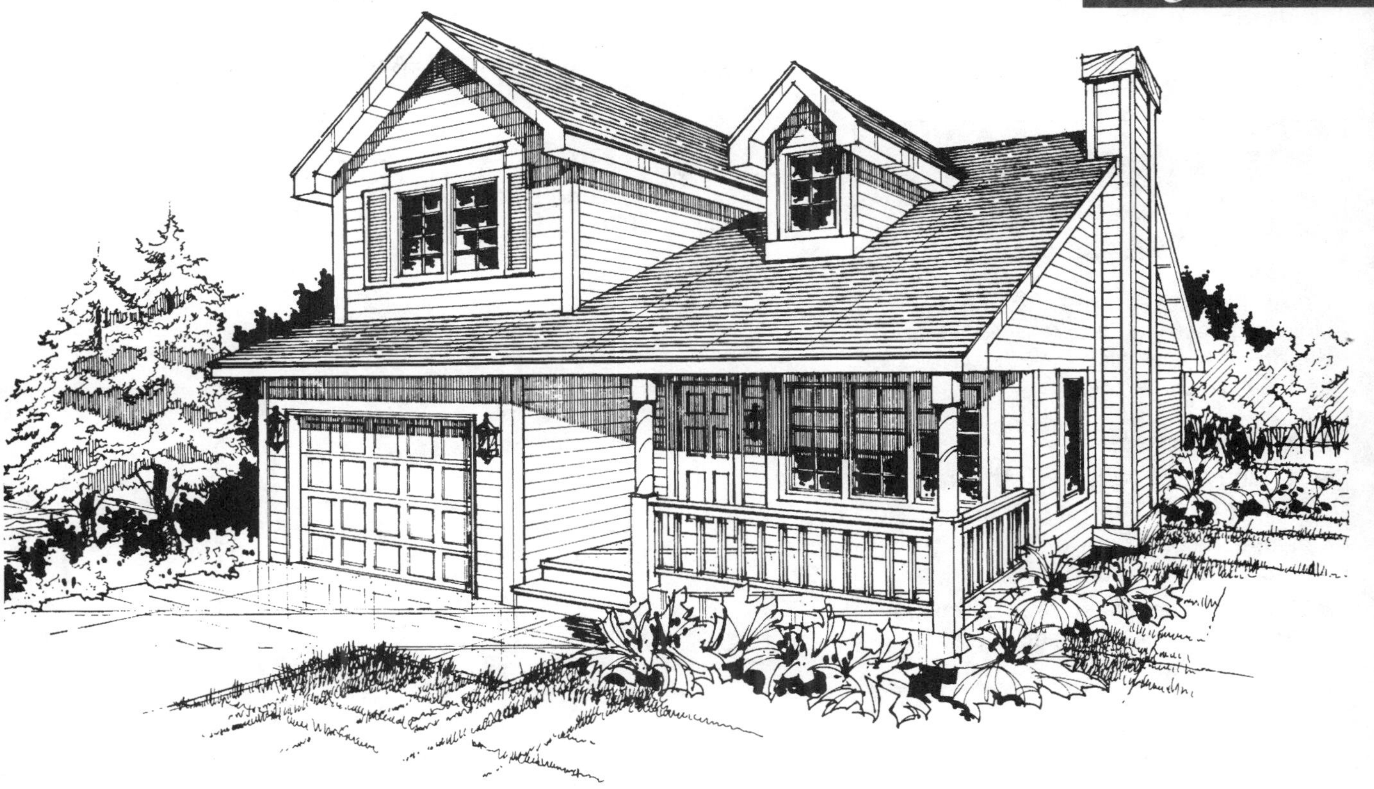

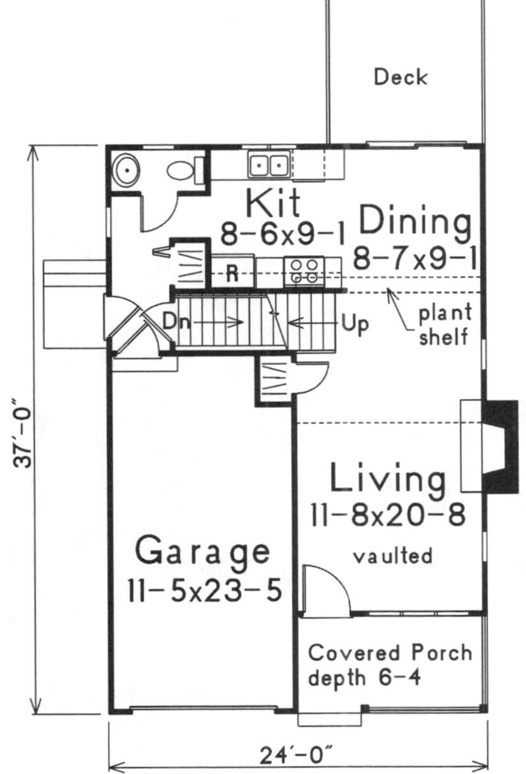
Deck
Kit
8-6x9-1
Dining
8-7x9-1
R
Dn
Up
plant shelf
Living
11-8x20-8
vaulted
Garage
11-5x23-5
Covered Porch
depth 6-4
37'-0"
24'-0"

First Floor
545 sq. ft.

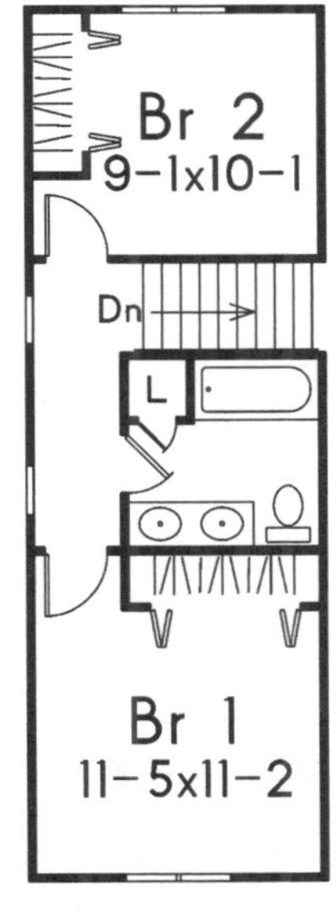
Br 2
9-1x10-1
Dn
L
Br 1
11-5x11-2

Second Floor
432 sq. ft.

Plan #531-0496

Price Code AA

Total Living Area: 977 Sq. Ft.

Home has 2 bedrooms, 1 1/2 baths, 1-car garage and basement foundation.

Special features

- Comfortable living room features a vaulted ceiling, fireplace, plant shelf and coat closet
- Both bedrooms are located on the second floor and share a bath with double-bowl vanity and linen closet
- Sliding glass doors in dining room provide access to the deck

LOWE'S

Signature
SERIES

Wrap-Around Country Porch

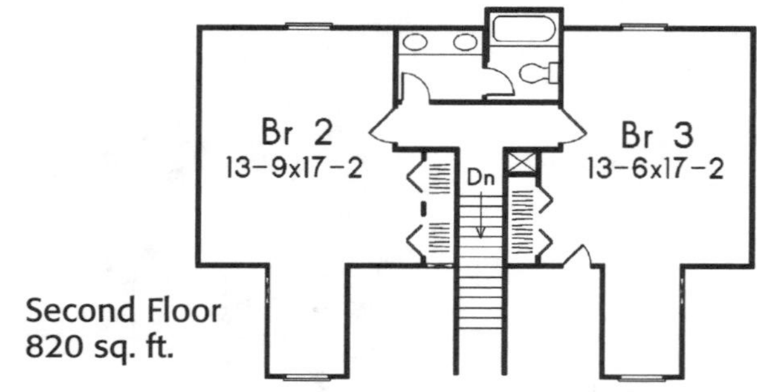
Br 2
13-9x17-2
Dn
Br 3
13-6x17-2

Second Floor
820 sq. ft.

Plan #531-0523

Price Code C

Total Living Area: 1,875 Sq. Ft.

Home has 3 bedrooms, 2 baths, 2-car side entry garage and crawl space foundation, drawings also include basement and slab foundations.

Special features

- Country-style exterior with wrap-around porch and dormers
- Large second floor bedrooms share a dressing area and bath
- Master bedroom suite includes bay window, walk-in closet, dressing area and bath

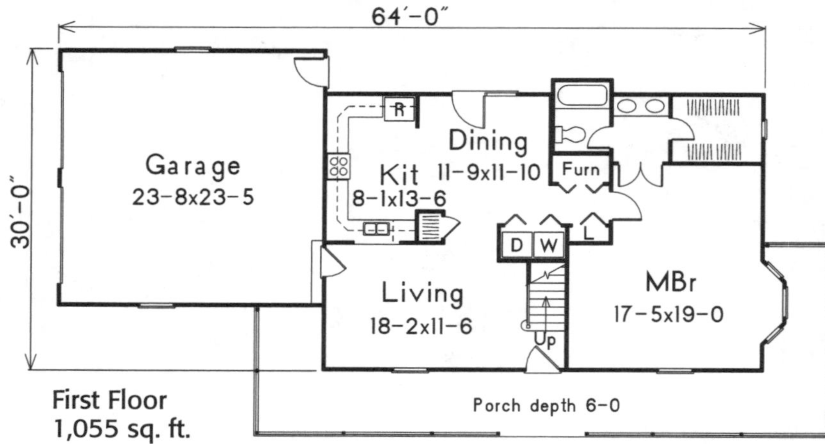
64'-0"
30'-0"
Garage
23-8x23-5
R
Dining
11-9x11-10
Kit
8-1x13-6
Furn
D
W
L
Living
18-2x11-6
Up
MBr
17-5x19-0
Porch depth 6-0

First Floor
1,055 sq. ft.

TO ORDER BLUEPRINTS USE THE FORM ON PAGE 290 OR CALL TOLL-FREE **1-800-DREAM HOME** (373-2646)

Gabled Front Porch Adds Charm And Value

LOWE'S

Signature SERIES

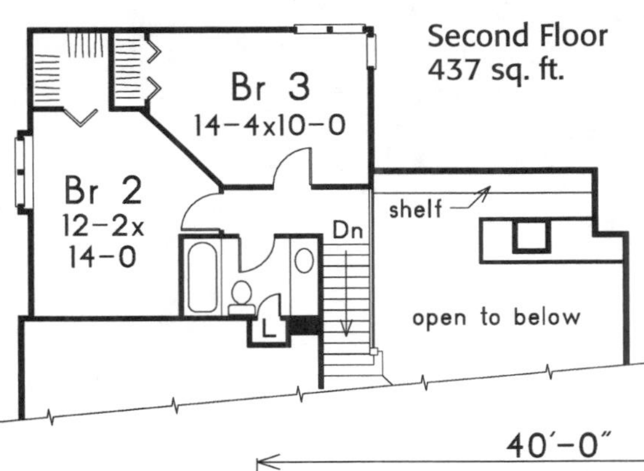
Br 3
14-4x10-0
Br 2
12-2x
14-0
shelf
Dn
L
open to below

Second Floor
437 sq. ft.

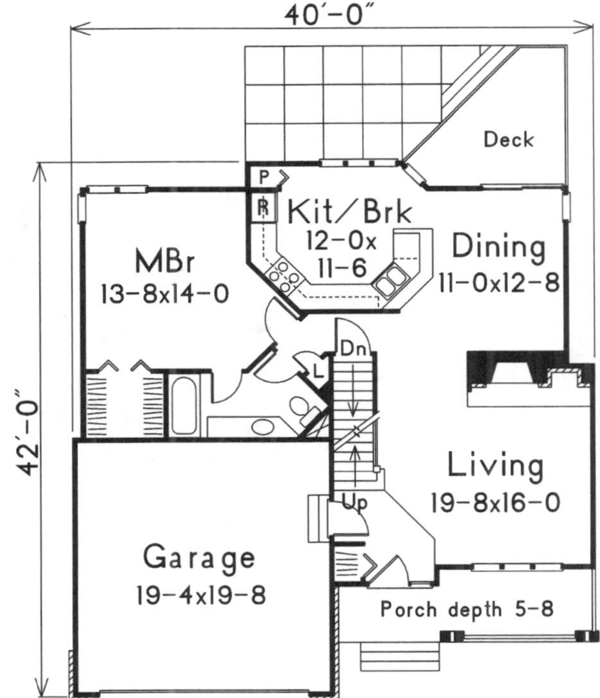
40'-0"
42'-0"
Deck
P
R
Kit/Brk
12-0x
11-6
Dining
11-0x12-8
MBr
13-8x14-0
Dn
L
Living
19-8x16-0
Up
Garage
19-4x19-8
Porch depth 5-8

First Floor
1,006 sq. ft.

Plan #531-0106

Price Code A

Total Living Area: 1,443 Sq. Ft.

Home has 3 bedrooms, 2 baths, 2-car garage and basement foundation.

Special features

- Raised foyer and cathedral ceiling in living room
- Impressive tall-wall fireplace between living and dining rooms
- Open U-shaped kitchen with breakfast bay
- Angular side deck accentuates patio and garden
- First floor master bedroom suite has a walk-in closet and a corner window

LOWE'S
Signature
SERIES

Covered Porch Is Focal Point Of Entry

Plan #531-0293

Price Code B

Total Living Area: 1,595 Sq. Ft.

Home has 3 bedrooms, 2 baths, 2-car side entry garage and slab foundation, drawings also include crawl space foundation.

Special features

- Dining room has convenient built-in desk and provides access to the outdoors
- L-shaped kitchen area features island cooktop
- Family room has high ceiling and a fireplace
- Private master suite includes large walk-in closet and bath with separate tub and shower units

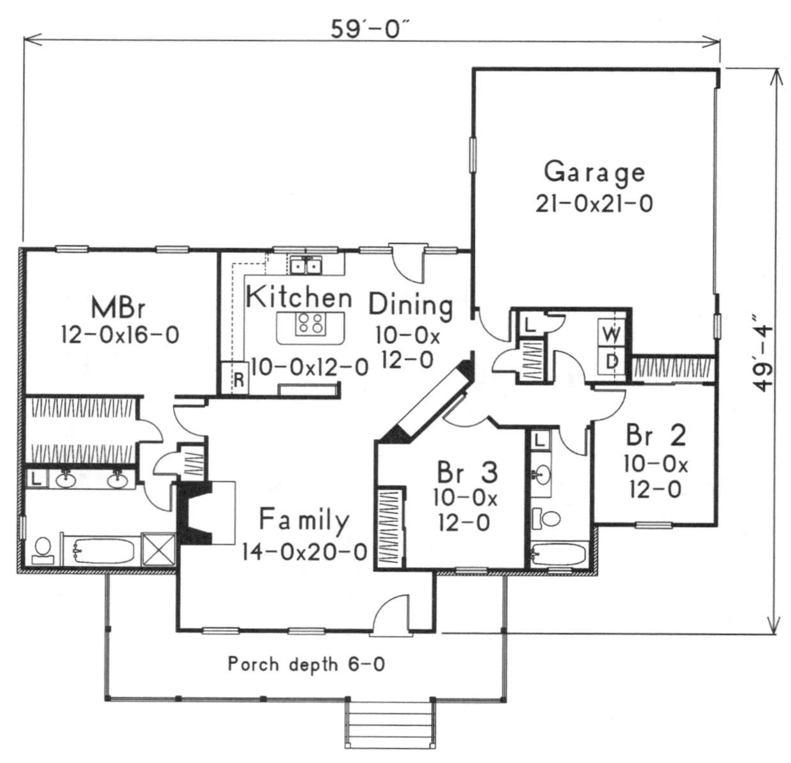
59'-0"
49'-4"
Garage
21-0x21-0
MBr
12-0x16-0
Kitchen
10-0x12-0
Dining
10-0x
12-0
W
D
L
R
Br 2
10-0x
12-0
Br 3
10-0x
12-0
Family
14-0x20-0
Porch depth 6-0

LOWE'S

Signature SERIES

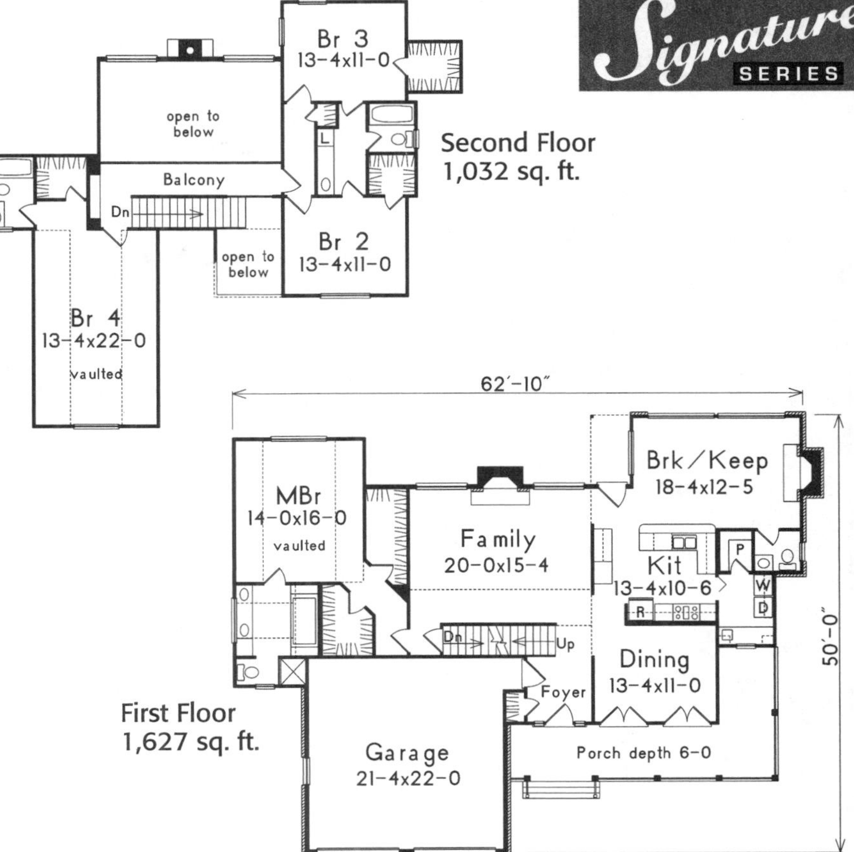
Br 3
13-4x11-0
open to below
Balcony
Dn
Br 2
13-4x11-0
open to below
Br 4
13-4x22-0
vaulted
Second Floor
1,032 sq. ft.
62'-10"
MBr
14-0x16-0
vaulted
Family
20-0x15-4
Brk/Keep
18-4x12-5
Kit
13-4x10-6
Dn
Up
Dining
13-4x11-0
Foyer
Garage
21-4x22-0
Porch depth 6-0
50'-0"
First Floor
1,627 sq. ft.

Plan #531-0359

Price Code E

Total Living Area: 2,659 Sq. Ft.

Home has 4 bedrooms, 3 1/2 baths, 2-car garage and basement foundation.

Special features

- 9' ceilings throughout first floor
- Balcony overlooks large family room
- Private first floor master suite features double walk-in closets, sloped ceilings and luxury bath
- Double French doors in dining room open onto porch

Signature SERIES

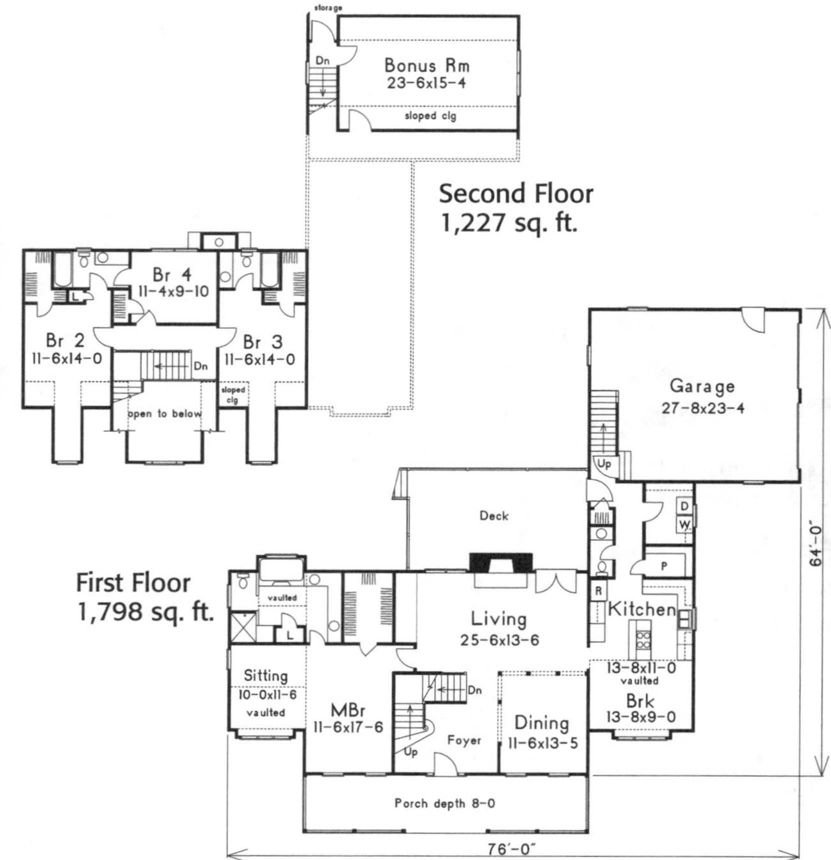
storage
Dn
Bonus Rm
23-6x15-4
sloped clg
Second Floor
1,227 sq. ft.
Br 4
11-4x9-10
Br 2
11-6x14-0
Br 3
11-6x14-0
Dn
sloped clg
open to below
Garage
27-8x23-4
Up
Deck
D
W
P
R
First Floor
1,798 sq. ft.
vaulted
L
Living
25-6x13-6
Kitchen
13-8x11-0
vaulted
Brk
13-8x9-0
Sitting
10-0x11-6
vaulted
MBr
11-6x17-6
Dn
Up
Foyer
Dining
11-6x13-5
Porch depth 8-0
64'-0"
76'-0"

Plan #531-0600

Price Code E

Total Living Area: 3,025 Sq. Ft.

Home has 4 bedrooms, 3 1/2 baths, 2-car side entry garage, 1-car drive under garage and basement foundation.

Special features

- Bonus room above garage has its own private entrance - great for home office, hobby or exercise room
- Master suite has generous walk-in closet, luxurious bath and a vaulted sitting area
- Spacious kitchen has an island cooktop and vaulted breakfast nook

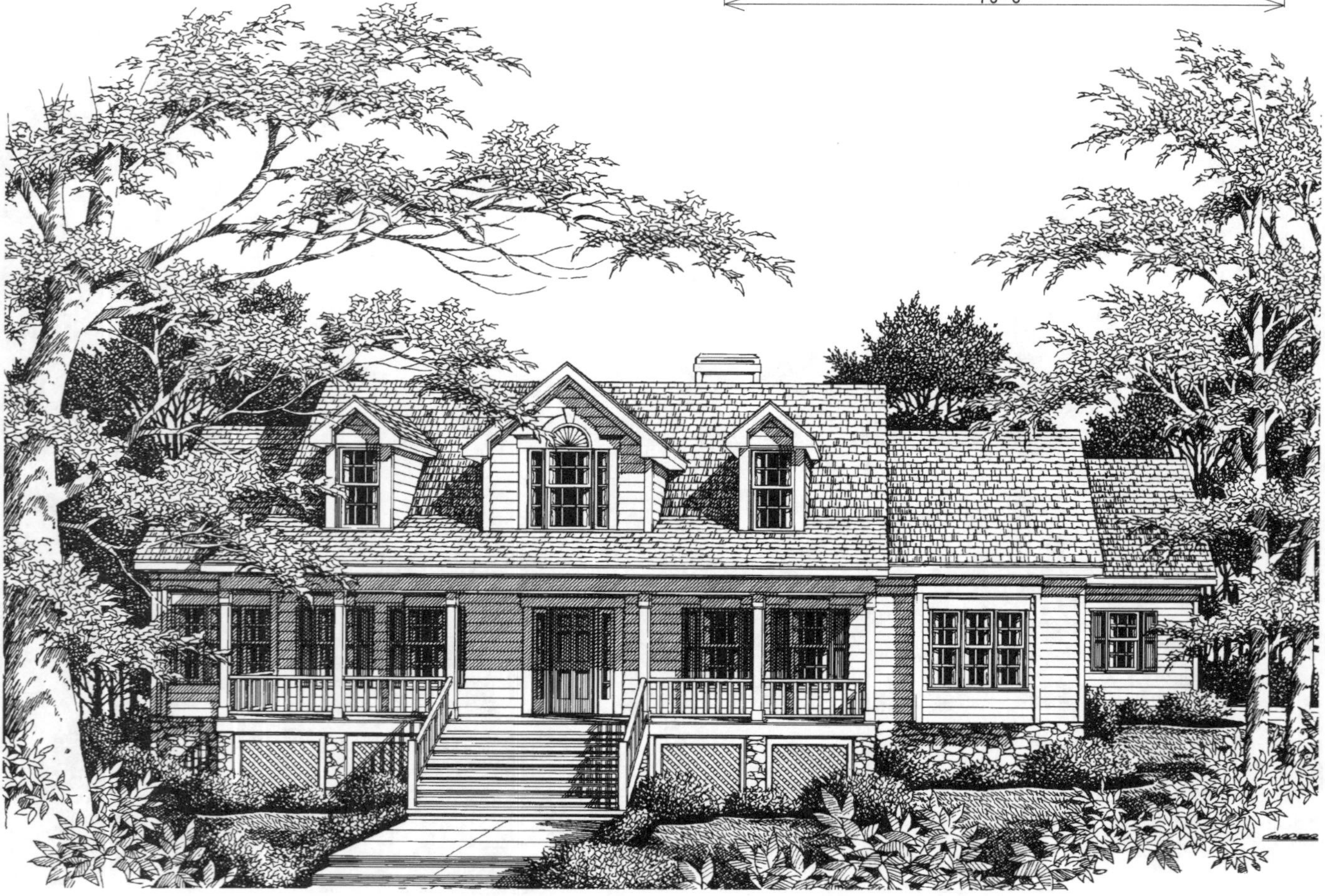

Sculptured Roof Line And Facade Add Charm

LOWE'S

Signature SERIES

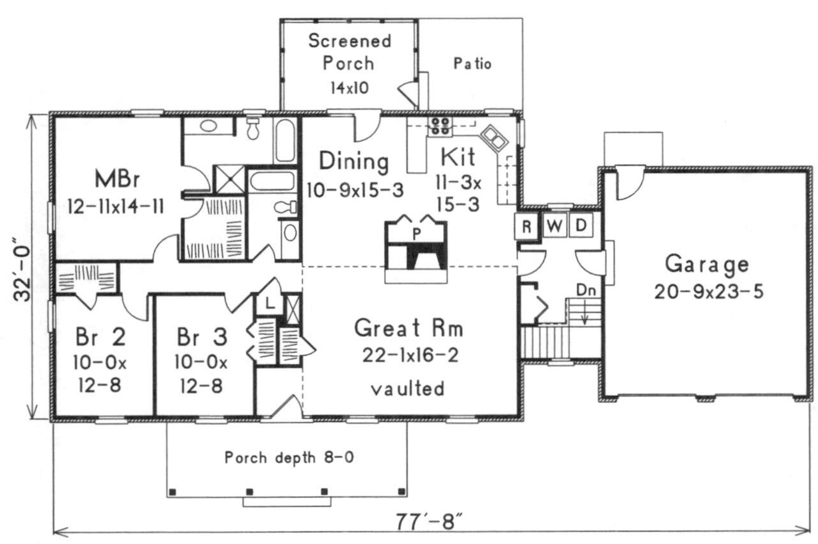
Screened Porch 14x10
Patio
MBr 12-11x14-11
Dining 10-9x15-3
Kit 11-3x 15-3
R W D
P
Garage 20-9x23-5
Dn
Br 2 10-0x 12-8
Br 3 10-0x 12-8
L
Great Rm 22-1x16-2 vaulted
Porch depth 8-0
32'-0"
77'-8"

Plan #531-0227

Price Code B

Total Living Area: 1,674 Sq. Ft.

Home has 3 bedrooms, 2 baths, 2-car garage and basement foundation, drawings also include crawl space and slab foundations.

Special features

- Great room, dining area and kitchen, surrounded with vaulted ceiling, central fireplace and log bin
- Convenient laundry/mud room located between garage and family area with handy stairs to basement
- Easily expandable screened porch and adjacent patio with access from dining area
- Master bedroom features full bath with tub, separate shower and walk-in closet

LOWE'S Signature SERIES

Covered Porch Adds Charm To Entrance

Plan #531-0294

Price Code B

Total Living Area: 1,655 Sq. Ft.

Home has 3 bedrooms, 2 baths, 2-car garage and crawl space foundation.

Special features

- Master bedroom features 9' ceiling, walk-in closet and bath with dressing area
- Oversized family room includes 10' ceiling and masonry see-through fireplace
- Island kitchen with convenient access to laundry room
- Handy covered walkway from garage to dining/kitchen area

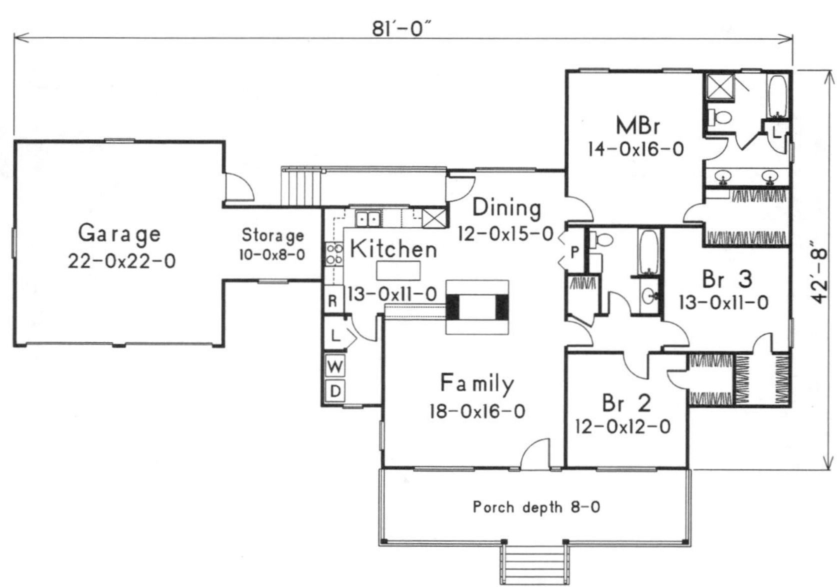

81'-0"
42'-8"
MBr
14-0x16-0
Dining
12-0x15-0
Garage
22-0x22-0
Storage
10-0x8-0
Kitchen
13-0x11-0
P
Br 3
13-0x11-0
R
L
W
D
Family
18-0x16-0
Br 2
12-0x12-0
Porch depth 8-0

Stylish Corner Entry Porch

LOWE'S

Signature SERIES

Plan #531-0404

Price Code C

Total Living Area: 2,195 Sq. Ft.

Home has 4 bedrooms, 2 1/2 baths, 2-car garage and basement foundation.

Special features

- Elegant parlor features attractive bay window
- Open floor plan in the family room, nook and kitchen
- Master bedroom with walk-in closet and private bath
- Energy efficient home with 2" x 6" exterior walls

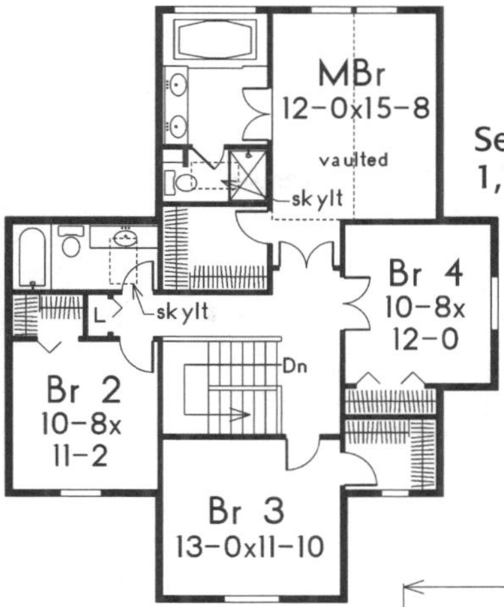

MBr
12-0x15-8
vaulted
skylt
Br 4
10-8x
12-0
skylt
L
Dn
Br 2
10-8x
11-2
Br 3
13-0x11-10

Second Floor
1,110 sq. ft.

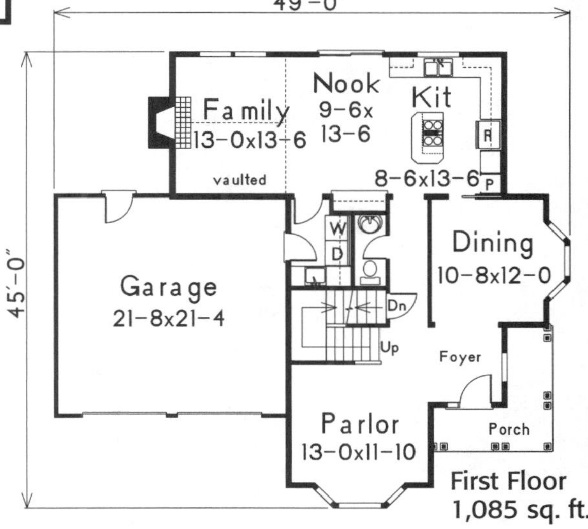

49'-0"
45'-0"
Nook
9-6x
13-6
Kit
8-6x13-6
P
Family
13-0x13-6
vaulted
W
D
Dining
10-8x12-0
Garage
21-8x21-4
Dn
Up
Foyer
Parlor
13-0x11-10
Porch

First Floor
1,085 sq. ft.

LOWE'S

Stately Country Home For The "Spacious Age"

Signature SERIES

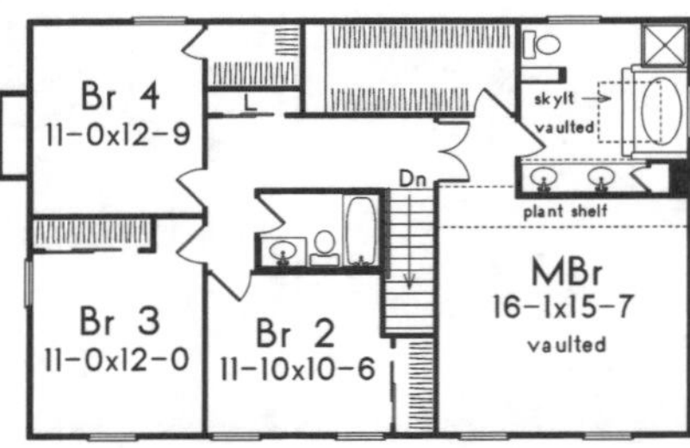

Br 4
11-0x12-9
skylt
vaulted
Dn
plant shelf
MBr
16-1x15-7
vaulted
Br 3
11-0x12-0
Br 2
11-10x10-6

Second Floor
1,204 sq. ft.

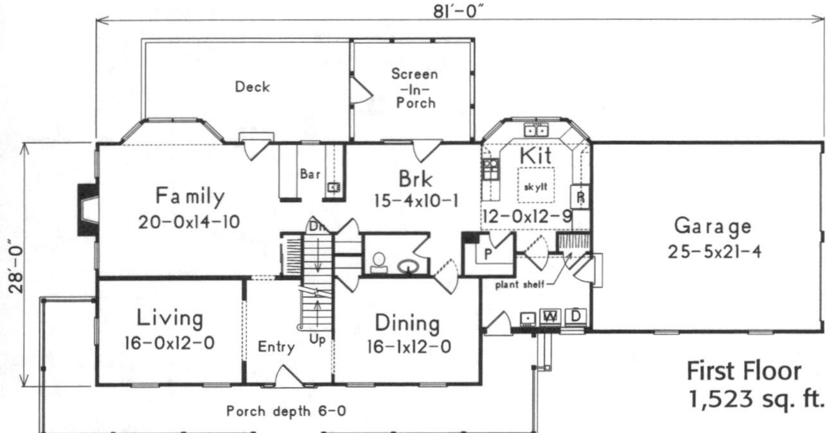

81'-0"
Deck
Screen -In- Porch
28'-0"
Family
20-0x14-10
Bar
Brk
15-4x10-1
Kit
skylt
12-0x12-9
R
Garage
25-5x21-4
Dn
P
plant shelf
W
D
Living
16-0x12-0
Entry
Up
Dining
16-1x12-0
Porch depth 6-0

First Floor
1,523 sq. ft.

Plan #531-0749

Price Code E

Total Living Area: 2,727 Sq. Ft.

Home has 4 bedrooms, 2 1/2 baths, 2-car side entry garage and walk-out basement foundation.

Special features

- Wrap-around porch and large foyer create impressive entrance
- A state-of-the-art vaulted kitchen features walk-in pantry and is open to a spacious breakfast room and adjoining screened-in porch
- A walk-in wet bar, fireplace bay window and deck access are many features of the perfect family room
- The vaulted master bedroom suite enjoys a luxurious bath with skylight and an enormous 13' deep walk-in closet

TO ORDER BLUEPRINTS USE THE FORM ON PAGE 290 OR CALL TOLL-FREE **1-800-DREAM HOME** (373-2646)

Compact Ranch An Ideal Starter Home

LOWE'S

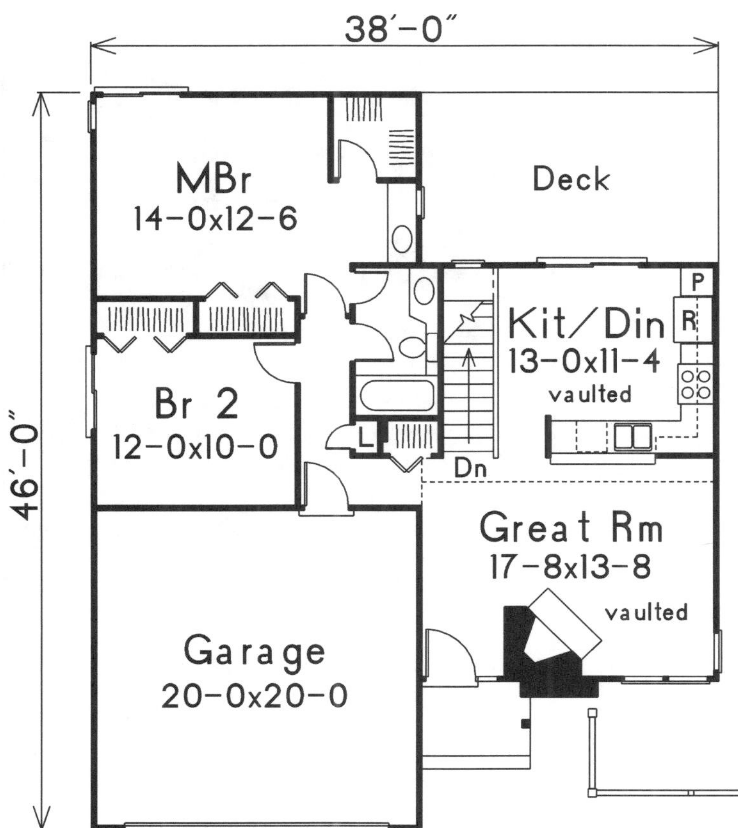
38'-0"
46'-0"
MBr
14-0x12-6
Deck
Kit/Din
13-0x11-4
vaulted
P
R
Br 2
12-0x10-0
L
Dn
Great Rm
17-8x13-8
vaulted
Garage
20-0x20-0

Plan #531-0273

Price Code AA

Total Living Area: 988 Sq. Ft.

Home has 2 bedrooms, 1 bath, 2-car garage and basement foundation.

Special features

- Great room features corner fireplace
- Vaulted ceiling and corner windows add space and light in great room
- Eat-in kitchen with vaulted ceiling accesses deck for outdoor living
- Master bedroom features separate vanity and private access to the bath

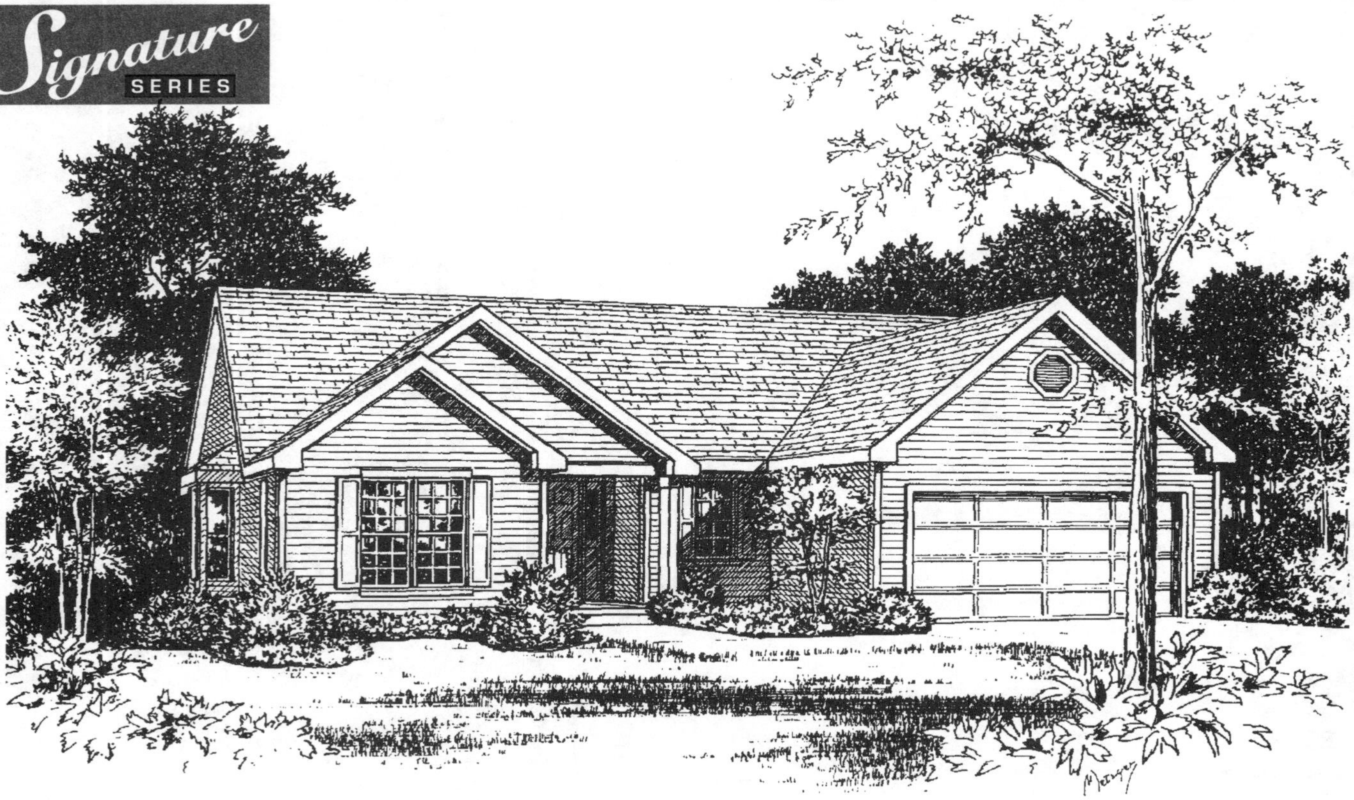

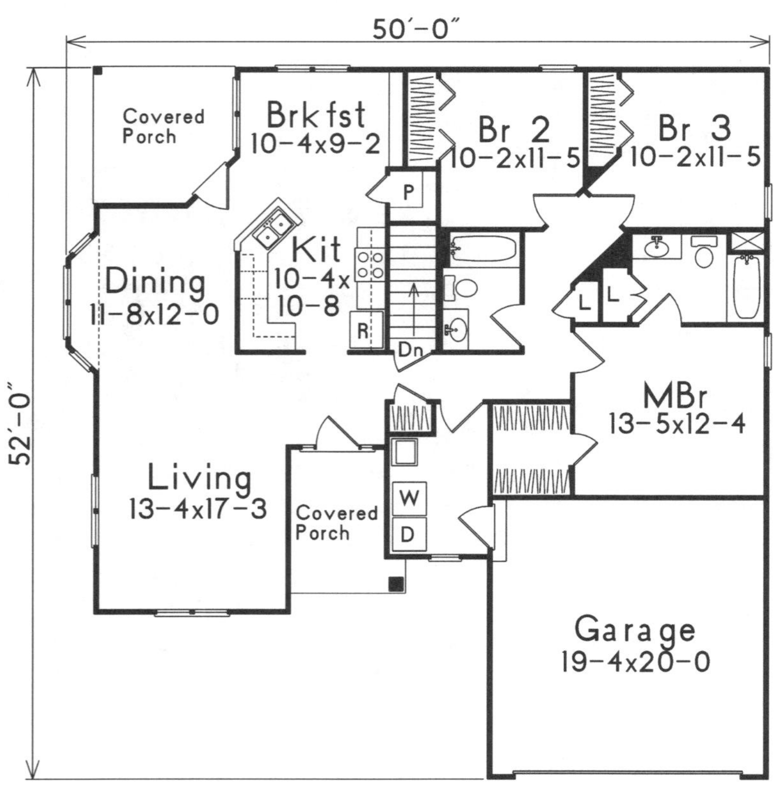
50'-0"
52'-0"
Covered Porch
Brkfst 10-4x9-2
Br 2 10-2x11-5
Br 3 10-2x11-5
P
Kit 10-4x 10-8
R
Dn
Dining 11-8x12-0
L
L
MBr 13-5x12-4
Living 13-4x17-3
Covered Porch
W
D
Garage 19-4x20-0

Plan #531-0741

Price Code B

Total Living Area: 1,578 Sq. Ft.

Home has 3 bedrooms, 2 baths, 2-car garage and basement foundation.

Special features

- Plenty of closet, linen and storage space
- Covered porches in the front and rear of home add charm to this design
- Open floor plan with unique angled layout

LOWE'S

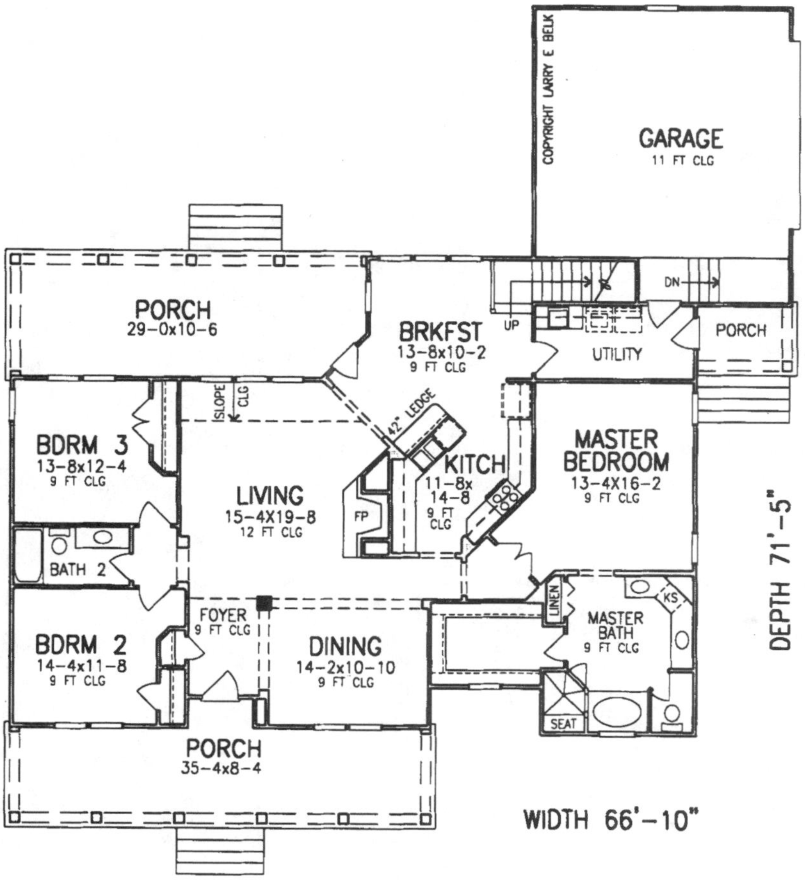

COPYRIGHT LARRY E. BELK
GARAGE
11 FT CLG
PORCH
29-0x10-6
BRKFST
13-8x10-2
9 FT CLG
UP
DN
UTILITY
PORCH
BDRM 3
13-8x12-4
9 FT CLG
SLOPE CLG
42" LEDGE
KITCH
11-8x
14-8
9 FT
CLG
MASTER
BEDROOM
13-4X16-2
9 FT CLG
LIVING
15-4X19-8
12 FT CLG
FP
BATH 2
LINEN
MASTER
BATH
9 FT CLG
KS
BDRM 2
14-4x11-8
9 FT CLG
FOYER
9 FT CLG
DINING
14-2x10-10
9 FT CLG
SEAT
PORCH
35-4x8-4
DEPTH 71'-5"
WIDTH 66'-10"

Plan #531-LBD-19-16A

Price Code C

Total Living Area: 1,993 Sq. Ft.

Home has 3 bedrooms, 2 baths, 2-car side entry garage and crawl space or slab foundation, please specify when ordering.

Special features

- Charming front and rear porches
- 12' ceiling in living room
- Exquisite master bath with large walk-in closet

Plan #531-FB-327

Price Code A

Total Living Area: 1,281 Sq. Ft.

Home has 3 bedrooms, 2 baths, 2-car drive under garage and crawl space, slab or walk-out basement foundation, please specify when ordering.

Special features

- Spacious master suite with tray ceiling, double closets and private bath
- Vaulted family room has lots of sunlight and a fireplace
- Plant shelf above kitchen and dining room is a nice decorative touch

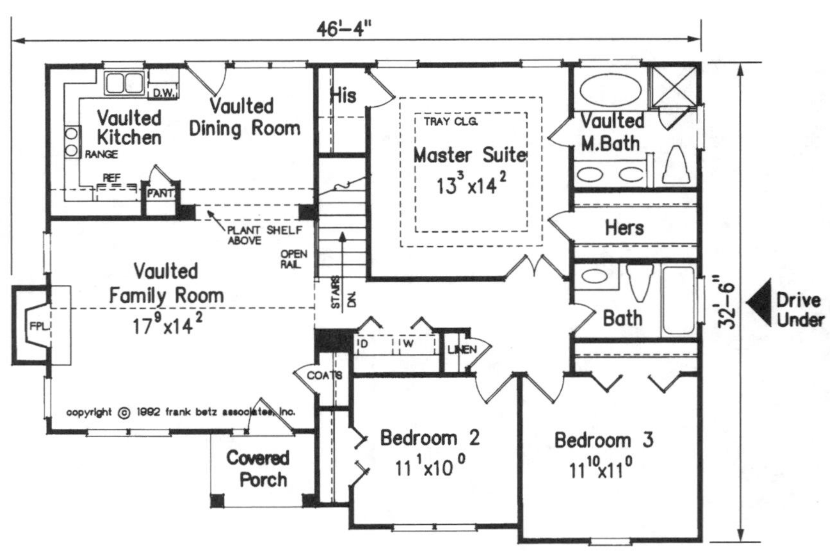
46'-4"
D.W.
Vaulted Kitchen
RANGE
REF
PANT
Vaulted Dining Room
His
TRAY CLG.
Master Suite
13³x14²
Vaulted M.Bath
Hers
PLANT SHELF ABOVE
OPEN RAIL
Vaulted Family Room
17⁹x14²
FPL
STAIRS DN
Bath
32'-6"
Drive Under
D
W
LINEN
COATS
copyright © 1992 frank betz associates, inc.
Bedroom 2
11¹x10⁰
Bedroom 3
11¹⁰x11⁰
Covered Porch

Attractive Gabled Roofline

LOWE'S

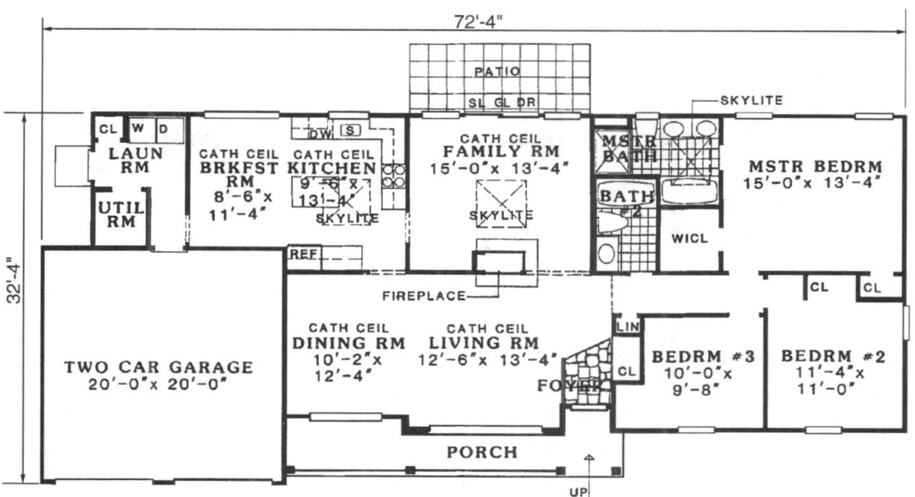

72'-4"
32'-4"
PATIO
SL GL DR
SKYLITE
CL
W
D
LAUN RM
UTIL RM
CATH CEIL BRKFST RM 8'-6"x 11'-4"
CATH CEIL KITCHEN 9'-6"x 13'-4"
DW
S
SKYLITE
REF
CATH CEIL FAMILY RM 15'-0"x 13'-4"
SKYLITE
MSTR BATH
BATH #2
MSTR BEDRM 15'-0"x 13'-4"
WICL
CL
CL
FIREPLACE
TWO CAR GARAGE 20'-0"x 20'-0"
CATH CEIL DINING RM 10'-2"x 12'-4"
CATH CEIL LIVING RM 12'-6"x 13'-4"
FOYER
LIN
CL
BEDRM #3 10'-0"x 9'-8"
BEDRM #2 11'-4"x 11'-0"
PORCH
UP

Plan #531-AX-90303

Price Code B

Total Living Area: 1,615 Sq. Ft.

Home has 3 bedrooms, 2 baths, 2-car garage and a basement, slab or crawl space foundation, please specify when ordering.

Special features

- Living and dining rooms are open to each other
- Family room has space for built-ins adjacent to the fireplace
- Master suite includes walk-in closet, spacious private bath with double vanity and a sloped ceiling with skylight

Inviting, Cheerful Home

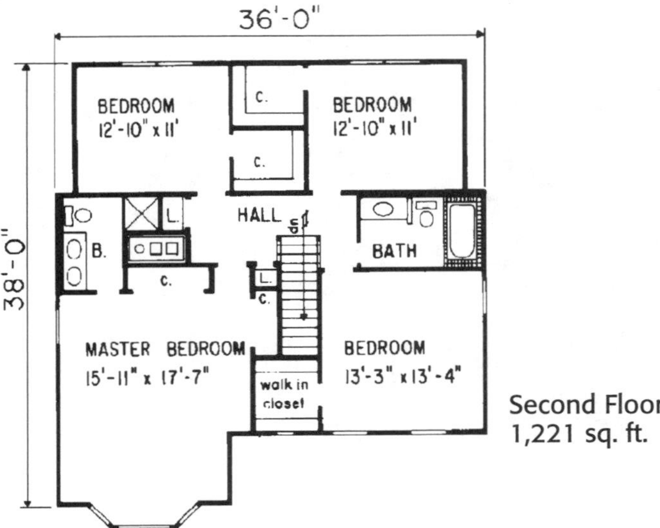
36'-0"
38'-0"
BEDROOM
12'-10" x 11'
C.
BEDROOM
12'-10" x 11'
C.
HALL
B.
L.
C.
BATH
L.
C.
MASTER BEDROOM
15'-11" x 17'-7"
walk in closet
BEDROOM
13'-3" x 13'-4"

Second Floor
1,221 sq. ft.

Plan #531-1213-1

basement

Plan #531-1213-2

crawl space & slab

Price Code D

Total Living Area: 2,554 Sq. Ft.

Home has 4 bedrooms, 2 1/2 baths, 2-car garage and basement, crawl space or slab foundation, please specify when ordering.

Special features

- Dual fireplaces enhance family and living rooms
- All three bedrooms include spacious walk-in closets
- Double-bowl vanity in master bath for convenience

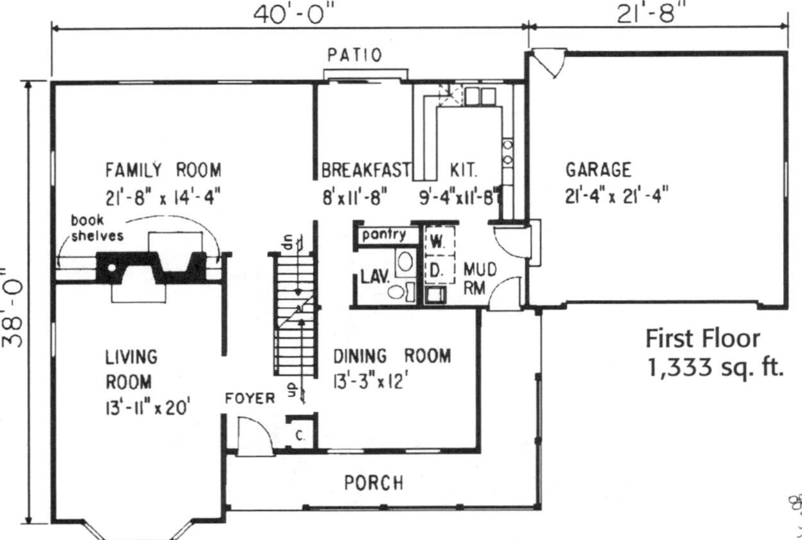
40'-0"
21'-8"
38'-0"
PATIO
FAMILY ROOM
21'-8" x 14'-4"
book shelves
BREAKFAST
8'x11'-8"
KIT.
9'-4"x11'-8"
GARAGE
21'-4" x 21'-4"
pantry
W.
D.
LAV.
MUD RM
LIVING ROOM
13'-11" x 20'
FOYER
C.
DINING ROOM
13'-3"x12'
PORCH

First Floor
1,333 sq. ft.

Handsome Ranch Design

LOWE'S

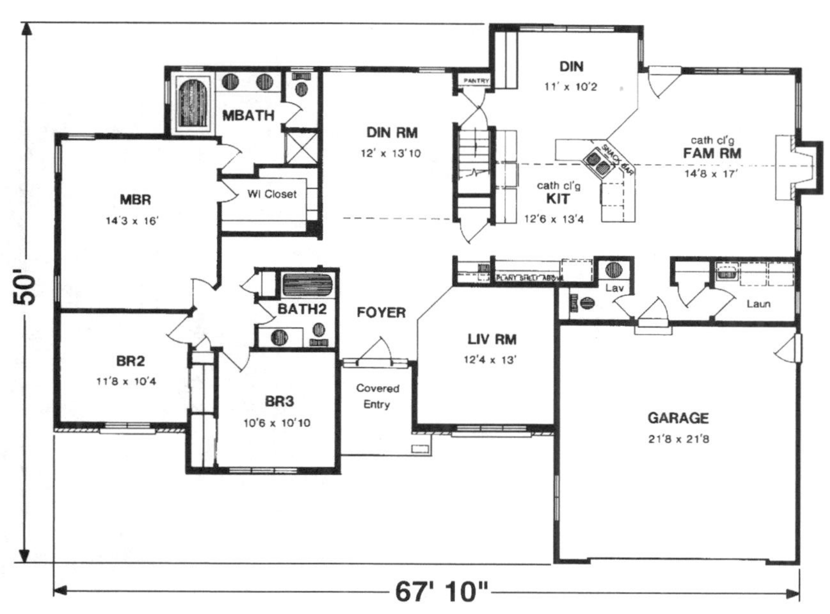

DIN
11' x 10'2
PANTRY
MBATH
DIN RM
12' x 13'10
cath cl'g
FAM RM
14'8 x 17'
SNACK BAR
MBR
14'3 x 16'
WI Closet
cath cl'g
KIT
12'6 x 13'4
50'
BATH2
FOYER
Lav
Laun
LIV RM
12'4 x 13'
BR2
11'8 x 10'4
BR3
10'6 x 10'10
Covered Entry
GARAGE
21'8 x 21'8
67' 10"

Plan #531-JFD-10-2096-2

Price Code C

Total Living Area: 2,096 Sq. Ft.

Home has 3 bedrooms, 2 1/2 baths, 2-car garage and basement foundation.

Special features

- Family room with cathedral ceiling and fireplace overlooks backyard
- Efficiently arranged kitchen has island with sink, dishwasher and eating area
- Secluded bedrooms maintain privacy
- 8' ceilings throughout this home

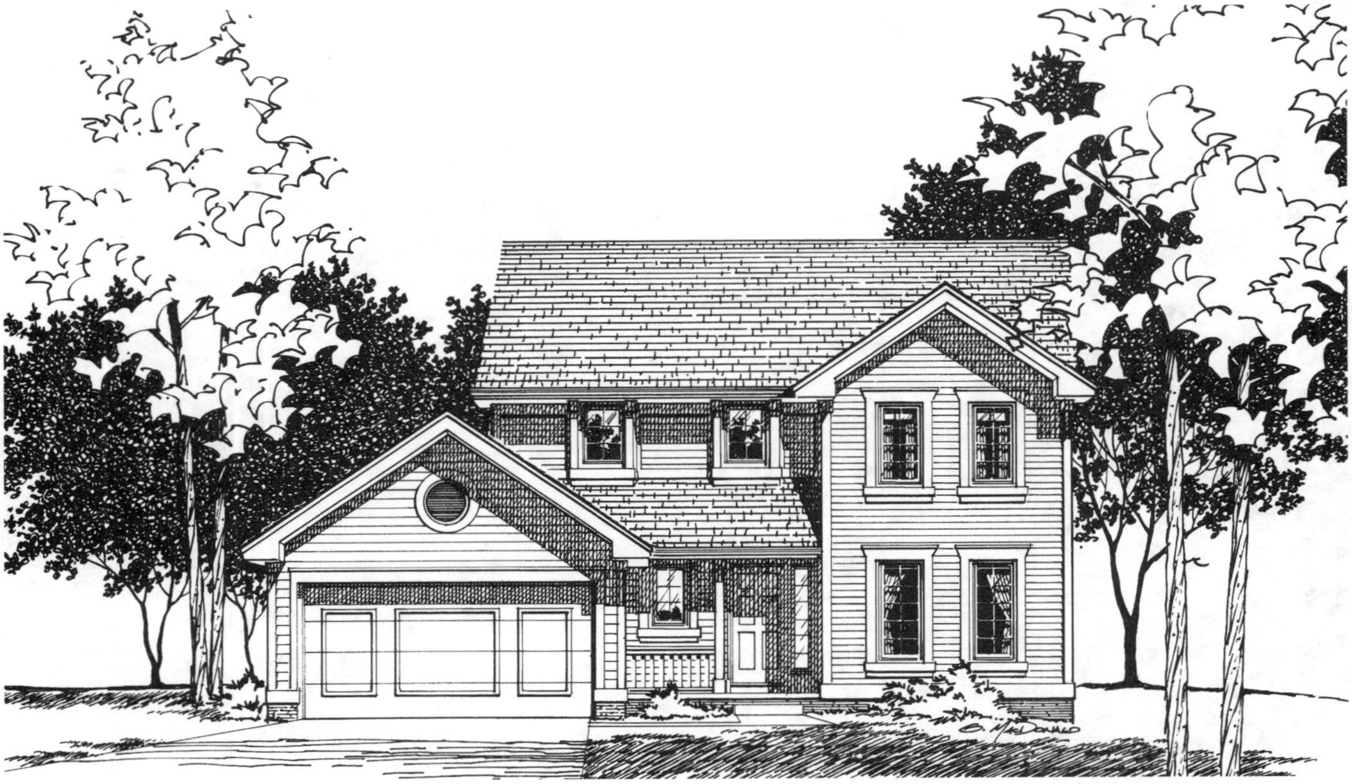

Second Floor
893 sq. ft.

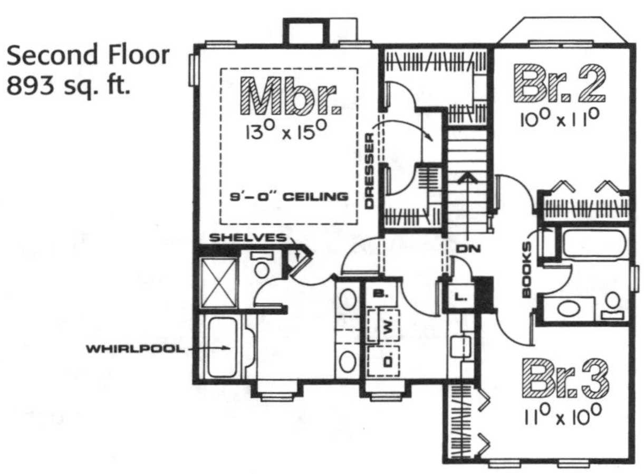
Mbr.
13^{0} x 15^{0}
9'–0" CEILING
DRESSER
SHELVES
WHIRLPOOL
B.
W.
D.
L.
DN
BOOKS
Br. 2
10^{0} x 11^{0}
Br. 3
11^{0} x 10^{0}

Plan #531-DB3097

Price Code B

Total Living Area: 1,745 Sq. Ft.

Home has 3 bedrooms, 2 1/2 baths, 2-car garage and basement foundation.

Special features

- Unique built-in dresser in master bedroom closet area is ideal for organization
- Plenty of closet space throughout
- Cozy fireplace in great room

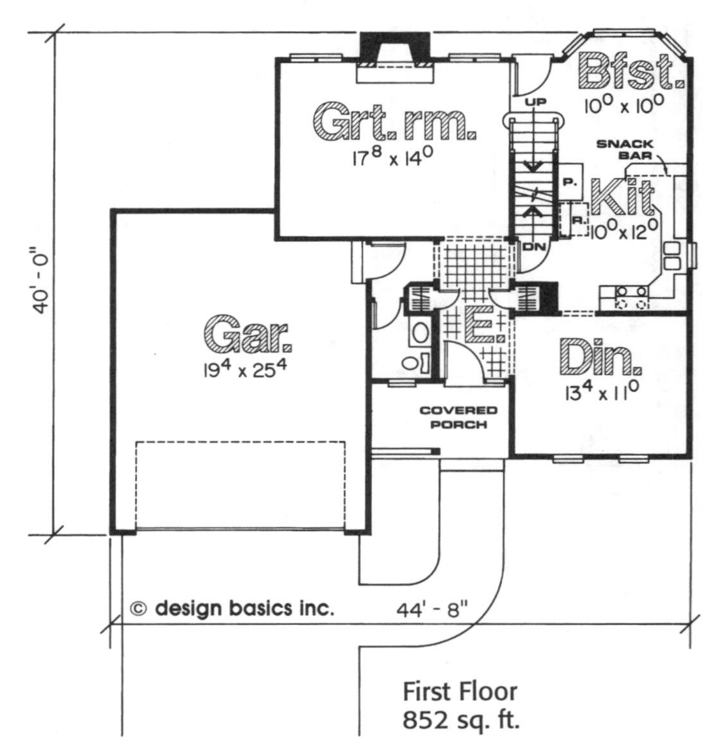
Bfst.
10^{0} x 10^{0}
UP
SNACK BAR
Grt. rm.
17^{8} x 14^{0}
P.
R.
Kit.
10^{0} x 12^{0}
DN
E.
Gar.
19^{4} x 25^{4}
Din.
13^{4} x 11^{0}
COVERED PORCH
40' - 0"
© design basics inc.
44' - 8"

First Floor
852 sq. ft.

Multi-Roof Levels Create Attractive Colonial Home

LOWE'S

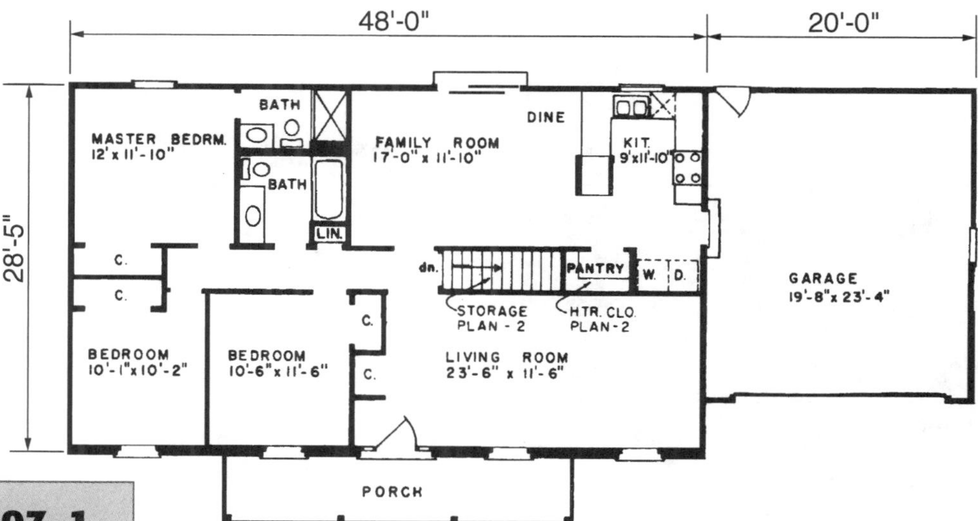
48'-0"
20'-0"
28'-5"
BATH
DINE
MASTER BEDRM.
12' x 11'-10"
FAMILY ROOM
17'-0" x 11'-10"
KIT.
9'x11'-10"
BATH
LIN.
C.
C.
dn.
PANTRY
W.
D.
GARAGE
19'-8" x 23'-4"
C.
STORAGE
PLAN - 2
HTR. CLO.
PLAN - 2
BEDROOM
10'-1" x 10'-2"
BEDROOM
10'-6" x 11'-6"
C.
LIVING ROOM
23'-6" x 11'-6"
PORCH

Plan #531-ES-103-1
basement
Plan #531-ES-103-2
crawl space & slab
Price Code A

Total Living Area: 1,364 Sq. Ft.

Home has 3 bedrooms, 2 baths, 2-car garage and basement, crawl space or slab foundation, please specify when ordering.

Special features

- Large porch and entry door with sidelights lead into the living room
- Well-planned U-shaped kitchen features a laundry closet, built-in pantry and open peninsula
- Master bedroom has its own bath with 4' shower
- Convenient to the kitchen is an oversized two-car garage with service door to rear

Plan #531-GSD-1748

Price Code A

Total Living Area: 1,496 Sq. Ft.

Home has 3 bedrooms, 2 baths, 2-car side entry garage and crawl space foundation.

Special features

- Large utility room with sink and extra counterspace
- Covered patio off breakfast nook extends dining to the outdoors
- Eating counter in kitchen overlooks vaulted family room

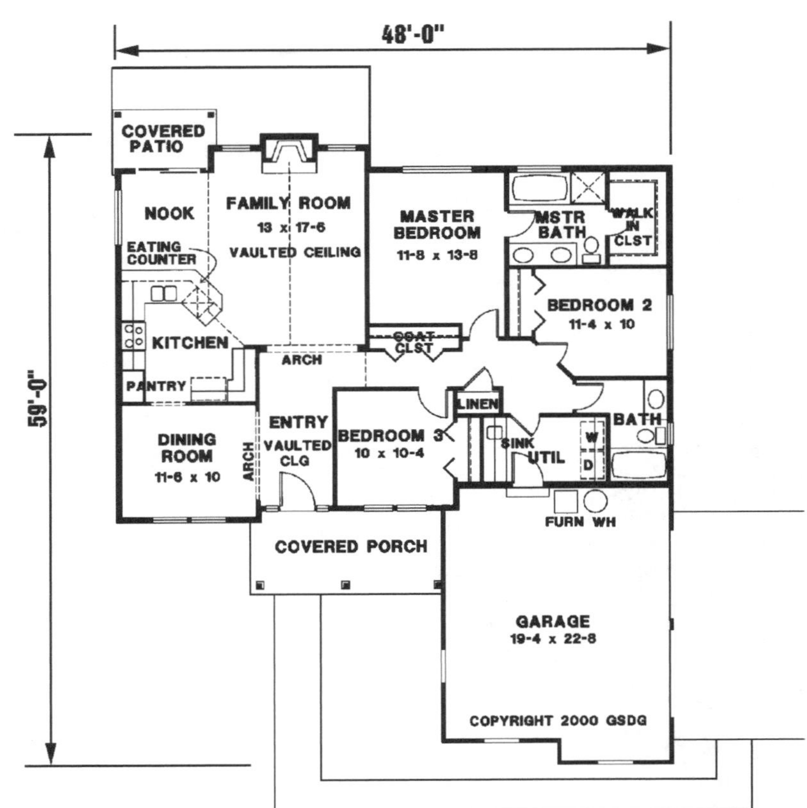
48'-0"
59'-0"
COVERED PATIO
NOOK
EATING COUNTER
FAMILY ROOM
13 x 17-6
VAULTED CEILING
MASTER BEDROOM
11-8 x 13-8
MSTR BATH
WALK IN CLST
BEDROOM 2
11-4 x 10
KITCHEN
COAT CLST
ARCH
PANTRY
LINEN
BATH
DINING ROOM
11-6 x 10
ARCH
ENTRY
VAULTED CLG
BEDROOM 3
10 x 10-4
SINK
UTIL
W
D
FURN WH
COVERED PORCH
GARAGE
19-4 x 22-8
COPYRIGHT 2000 GSDG

TO ORDER BLUEPRINTS USE THE FORM ON PAGE 290 OR CALL TOLL-FREE **1-800-DREAM HOME** (373-2646)

Wonderful Two-Story, Charming Yet Practical

LOWE'S

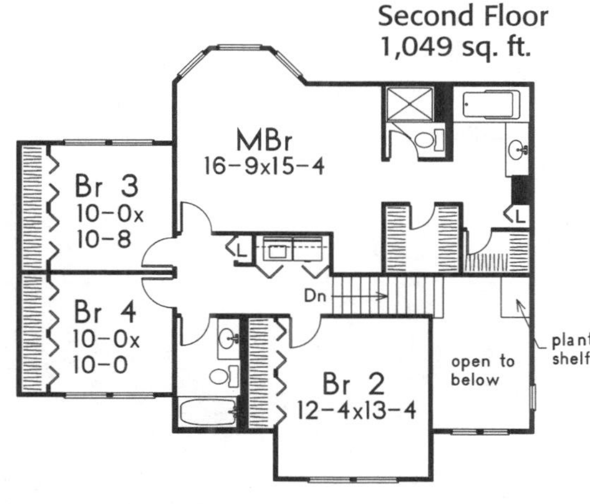
Second Floor
1,049 sq. ft.
MBr
16-9x15-4
Br 3
10-0x
10-8
Br 4
10-0x
10-0
Br 2
12-4x13-4
Dn
open to
below
plant
shelf
L

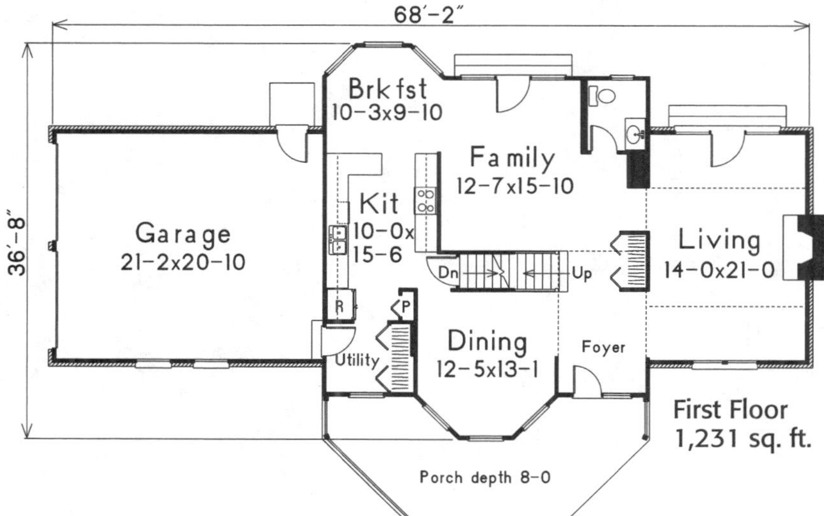
68′-2″
36′-8″
Brkfst
10-3x9-10
Family
12-7x15-10
Kit
10-0x
15-6
Garage
21-2x20-10
Living
14-0x21-0
Dining
12-5x13-1
Foyer
Utility
Dn
Up
R
P
Porch depth 8-0
First Floor
1,231 sq. ft.

Plan #531-1308

Price Code D

Total Living Area: 2,280 Sq. Ft.

Home has 4 bedrooms, 2 1/2 baths, 2-car side entry garage and basement foundation.

Special features

- Laundry area conveniently located on second floor
- Compact yet efficient kitchen
- Unique shaped dining room overlooks front porch
- Cozy living room enhanced with sloped ceilings and fireplace

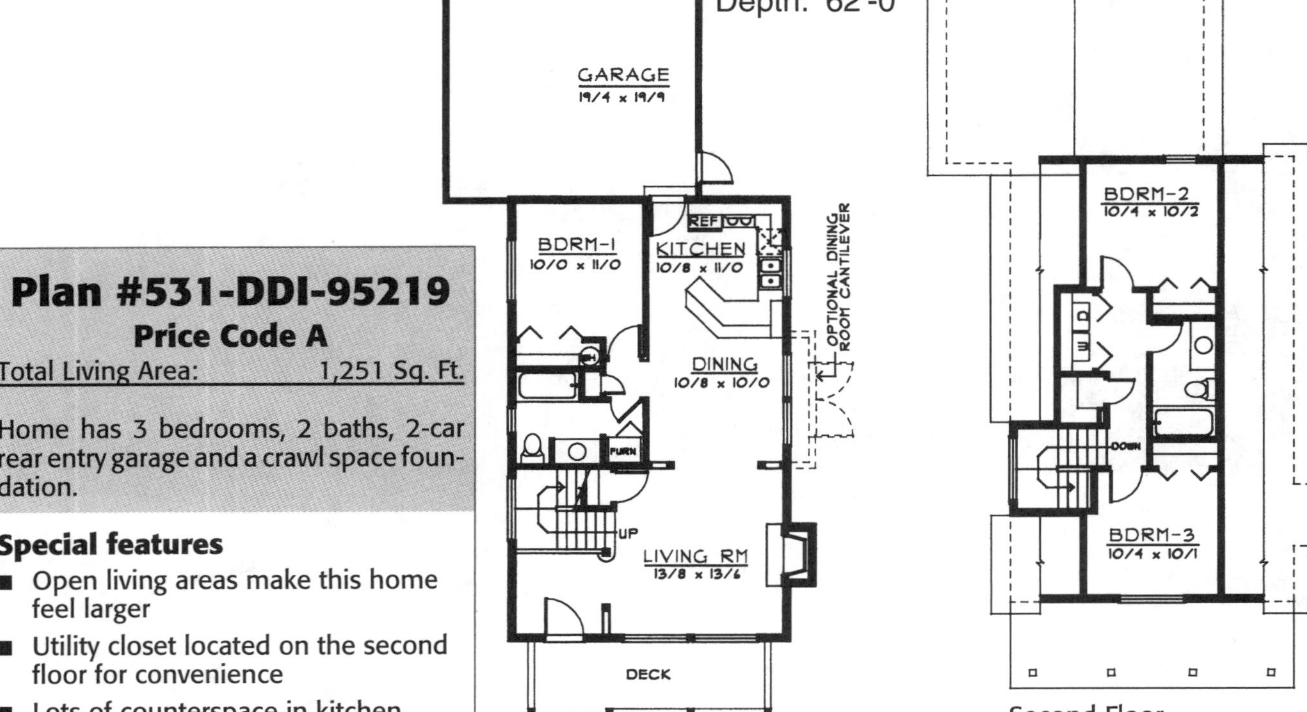
Width: 27'-0"
Depth: 62'-0"
GARAGE
19/4 x 19/9
BDRM-1
10/0 x 11/0
REF
KITCHEN
10/8 x 11/0
DINING
10/8 x 10/0
OPTIONAL DINING ROOM CANTILEVER
FURN
UP
LIVING RM
13/8 x 13/6
DECK
BDRM-2
10/4 x 10/2
W
D
DOWN
BDRM-3
10/4 x 10/1

First Floor
792 sq. ft.

Second Floor
459 sq. ft.

Plan #531-DDI-95219

Price Code A

Total Living Area: 1,251 Sq. Ft.

Home has 3 bedrooms, 2 baths, 2-car rear entry garage and a crawl space foundation.

Special features

- Open living areas make this home feel larger
- Utility closet located on the second floor for convenience
- Lots of counterspace in kitchen

Kitchen With Island Sink

LOWE'S

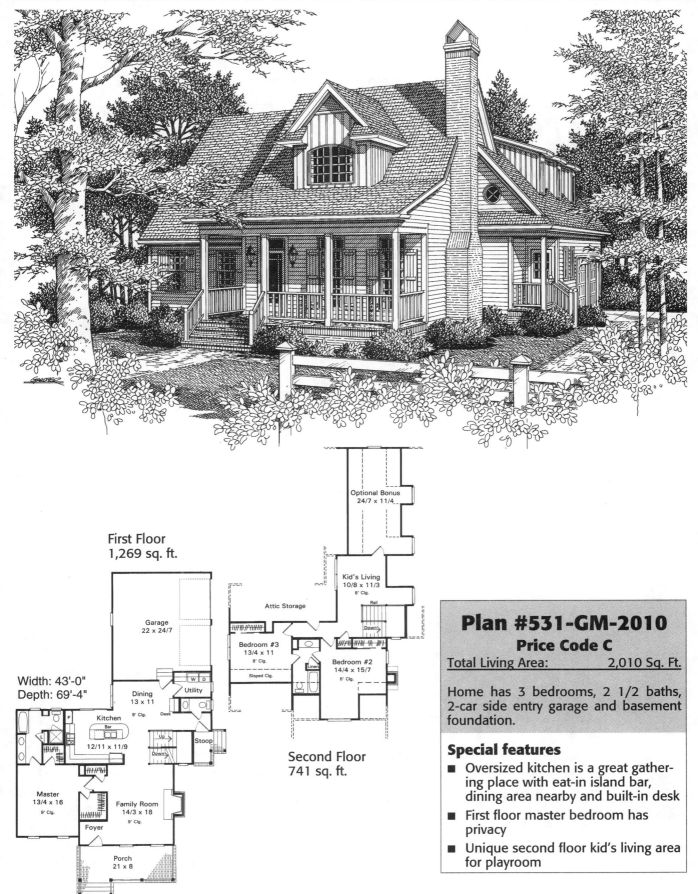

First Floor
1,269 sq. ft.

Width: 43'-0"
Depth: 69'-4"

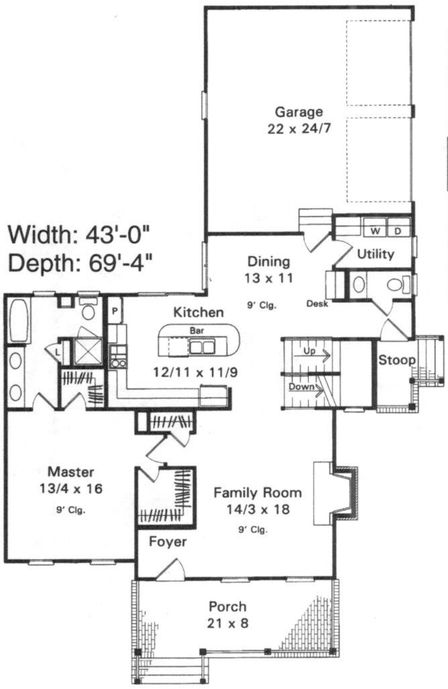

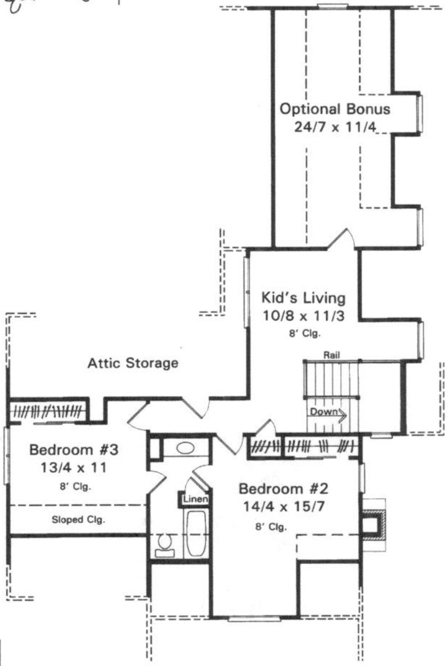

Garage
22 x 24/7
Dining
13 x 11
9' Clg.
Desk
W
D
Utility
Kitchen
Bar
12/11 x 11/9
Up
Down
Stoop
Master
13/4 x 16
9' Clg.
Family Room
14/3 x 18
9' Clg.
Foyer
Porch
21 x 8
Optional Bonus
24/7 x 11/4
Kid's Living
10/8 x 11/3
8' Clg.
Rail
Attic Storage
Down
Bedroom #3
13/4 x 11
8' Clg.
Sloped Clg.
Linen
Bedroom #2
14/4 x 15/7
8' Clg.

Second Floor
741 sq. ft.

Plan #531-GM-2010

Price Code C

Total Living Area: 2,010 Sq. Ft.

Home has 3 bedrooms, 2 1/2 baths, 2-car side entry garage and basement foundation.

Special features

- Oversized kitchen is a great gathering place with eat-in island bar, dining area nearby and built-in desk
- First floor master bedroom has privacy
- Unique second floor kid's living area for playroom

LOWE'S

European Styling Creates Elegant Facade

Plan #531-FD7507

Price Code F

Total Living Area: 3,239 Sq. Ft.

Home has 4 bedrooms, 3 1/2 baths, 3-car garage and basement, crawl space or slab foundation, please specify when ordering.

Special features

- Private study has a secluded reading area
- Casual family room has access to covered patio
- Gallery area is elegant and creates a formal atmosphere entering the living room
- 9' ceilings on the first floor

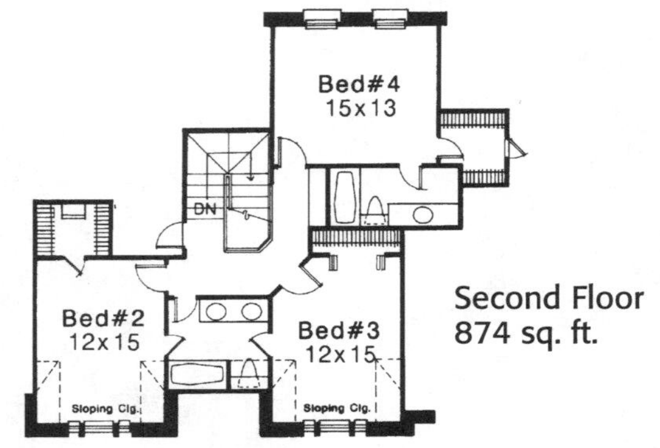
Bed#4
15x13
DN
Bed#2
12x15
Bed#3
12x15
Sloping Clg.
Sloping Clg.

Second Floor
874 sq. ft.

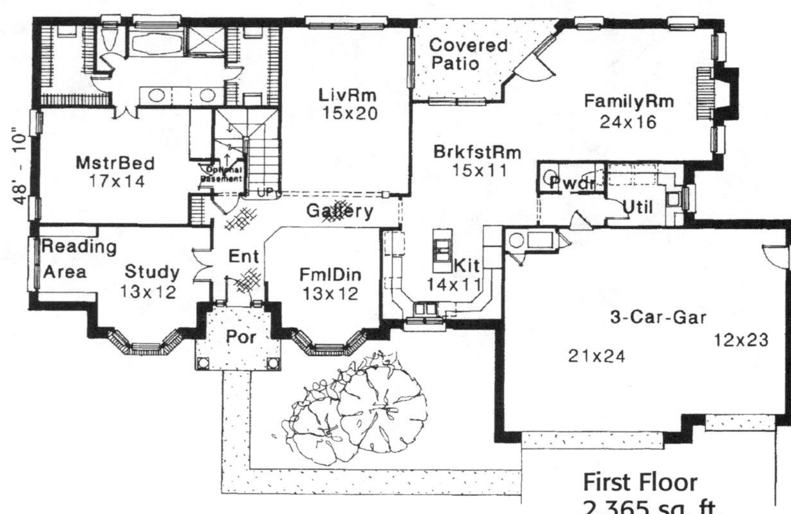
85' - 4"
48' - 10"
Covered Patio
LivRm
15x20
FamilyRm
24x16
BrkfstRm
15x11
MstrBed
17x14
Optional Basement
UP
Pwdr
Util
Gallery
Reading Area
Study
13x12
Ent
FmlDin
13x12
Kit
14x11
3-Car-Gar
21x24
12x23
Por

First Floor
2,365 sq. ft.

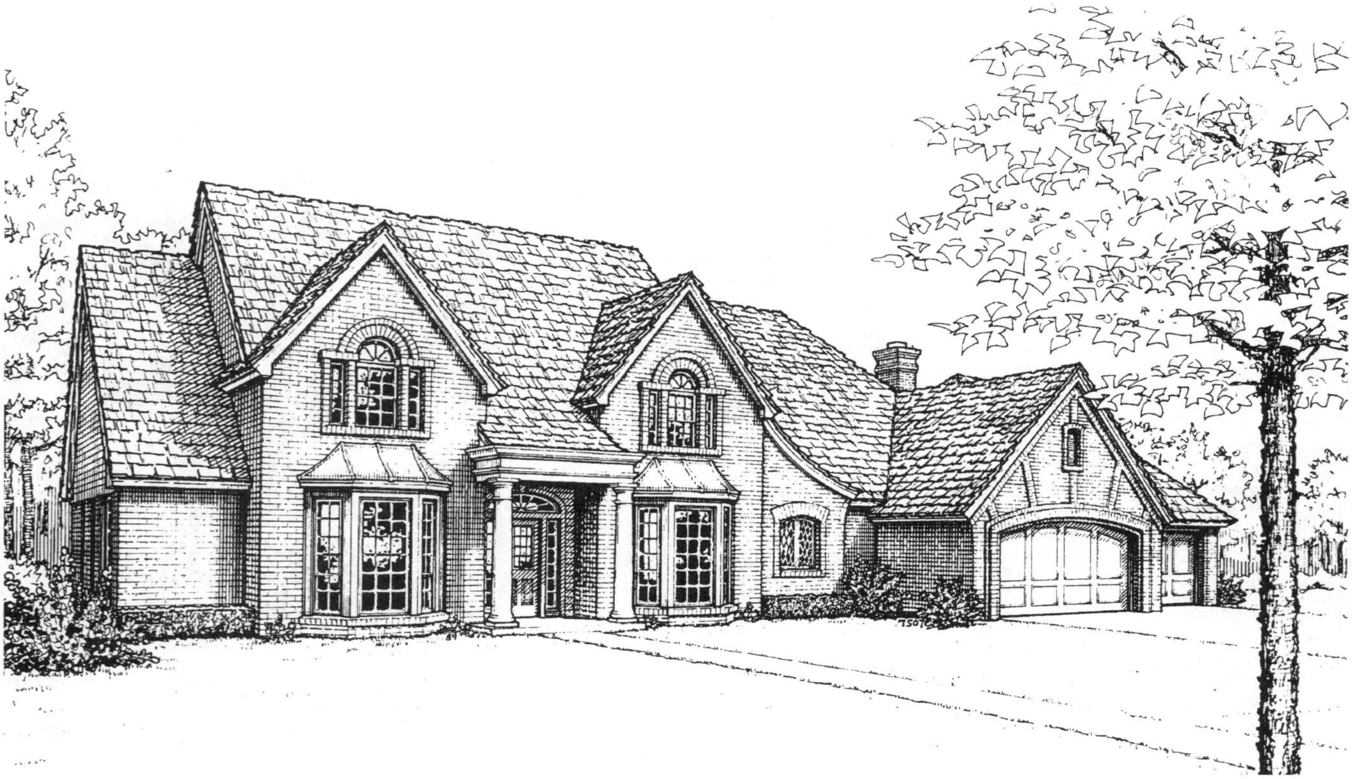

Perfect Country Haven

LOWE'S

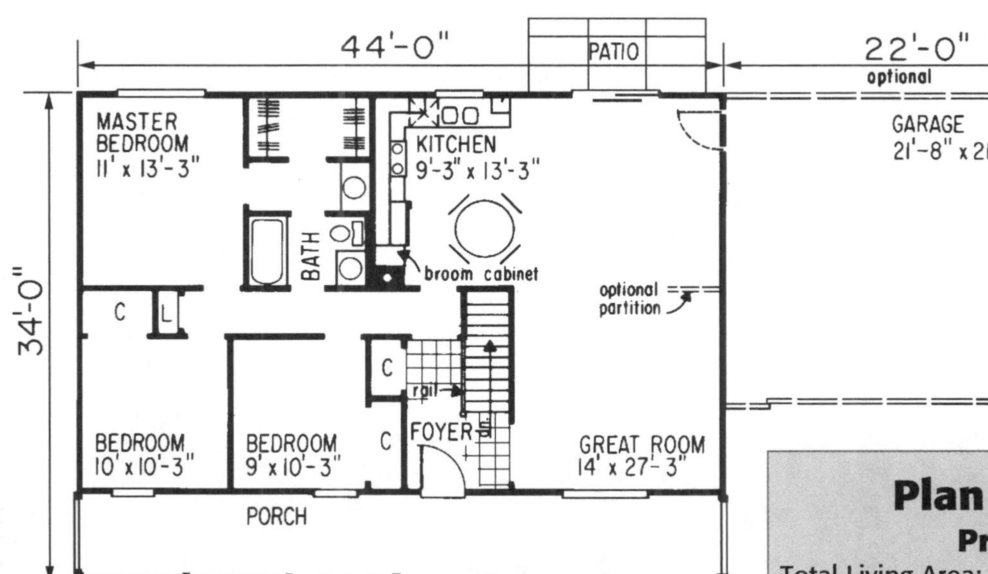
44'-0"
PATIO
22'-0"
optional
MASTER BEDROOM
11' x 13'-3"
KITCHEN
9'-3" x 13'-3"
GARAGE
21'-8" x 21'-4"
34'-0"
BATH
broom cabinet
optional partition
C
L
C
rail
C
FOYER
BEDROOM
10' x 10'-3"
BEDROOM
9' x 10'-3"
GREAT ROOM
14' x 27'-3"
PORCH

Plan #531-1120

Price Code A

Total Living Area: 1,232 Sq. Ft.

Home has 3 bedrooms, 1 bath, optional 2-car garage and basement foundation, drawings also include slab or crawl space foundations.

Special features

- Ideal porch for quiet quality evenings
- Great room opens to dining area for those large dinner gatherings
- Functional L-shaped kitchen includes broom cabinet
- Master bedroom contains large walk-in closet and compartmented bath

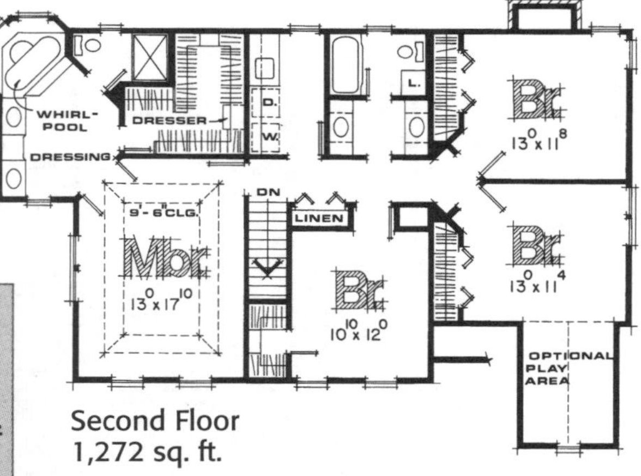
WHIRL-POOL
DRESSER
DRESSING
D.
W.
L.
9'-6" CLG.
Mbr.
13⁰ x 17¹⁰
DN
LINEN
Br.
10¹⁰ x 12⁰
Br.
13⁰ x 11⁸
Br.
13⁰ x 11⁴
OPTIONAL PLAY AREA

Second Floor
1,272 sq. ft.

Plan #531-DB1455

Price Code D

Total Living Area: 2,594 Sq. Ft.

Home has 4 bedrooms, 2 1/2 baths, 2-car side entry garage and basement foundation.

Special features

- Snack bar in kitchen creates an extra place for dining
- Master bath has interesting bayed whirlpool bath
- A wonderful sun room extends off the breakfast room creating a beautiful area for gathering

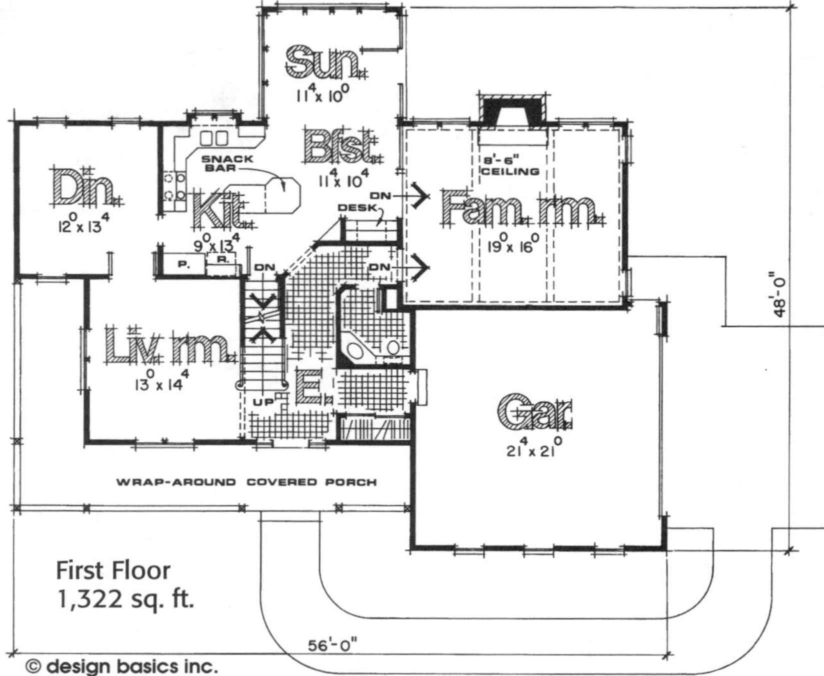
Sun.
11⁴ x 10⁰
Bfst.
11⁴ x 10⁴
SNACK BAR
Din.
12⁰ x 13⁴
Kit.
9⁰ x 13⁴
P.
R.
DN
DESK
DN
DN
8'-6" CEILING
Fam. rm.
19⁰ x 16⁰
Liv. rm.
13⁰ x 14⁴
UP
E.
Gar.
21⁴ x 21⁰
WRAP-AROUND COVERED PORCH
48'-0"
56'-0"

First Floor
1,322 sq. ft.

LOWE'S

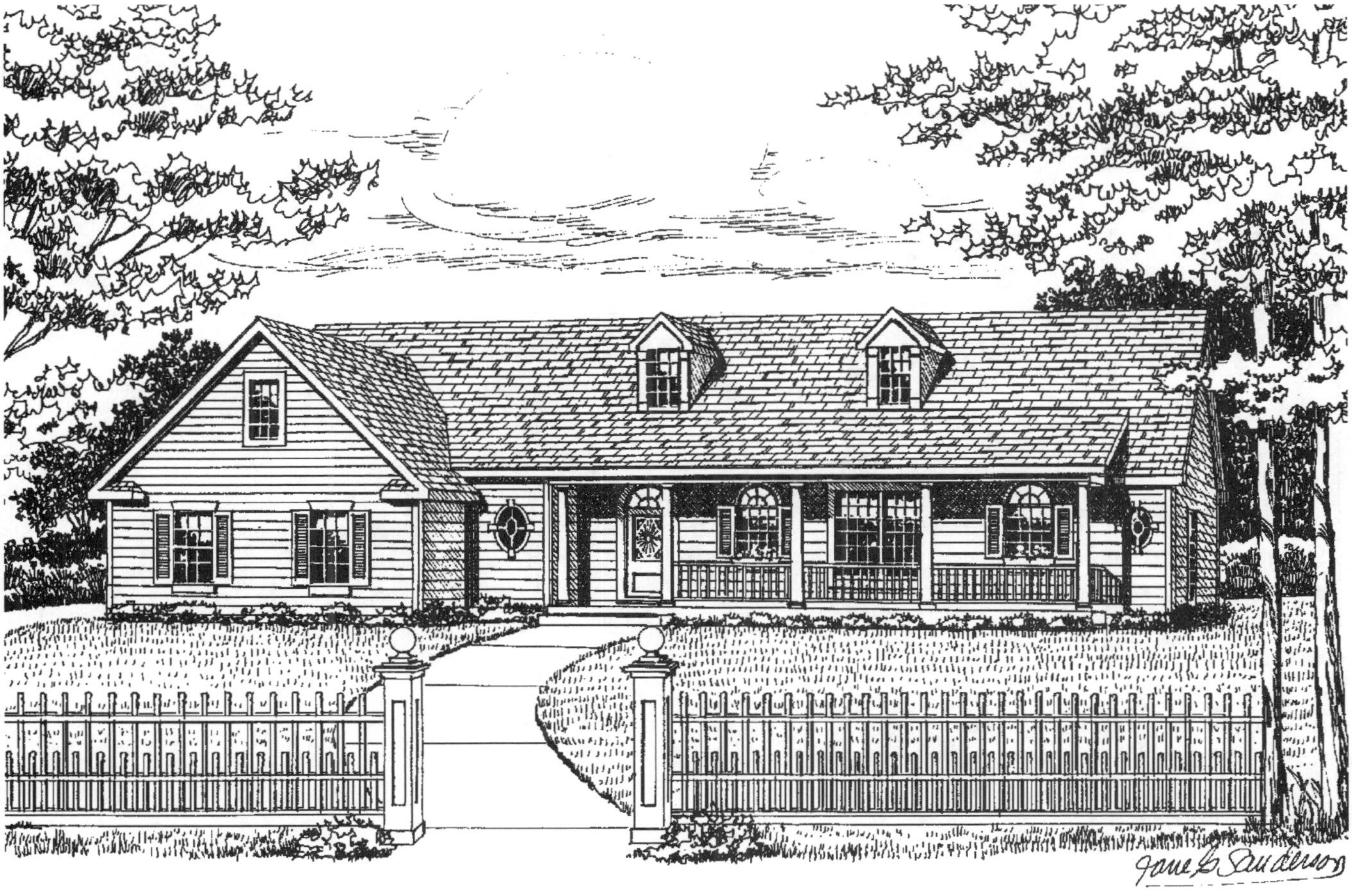

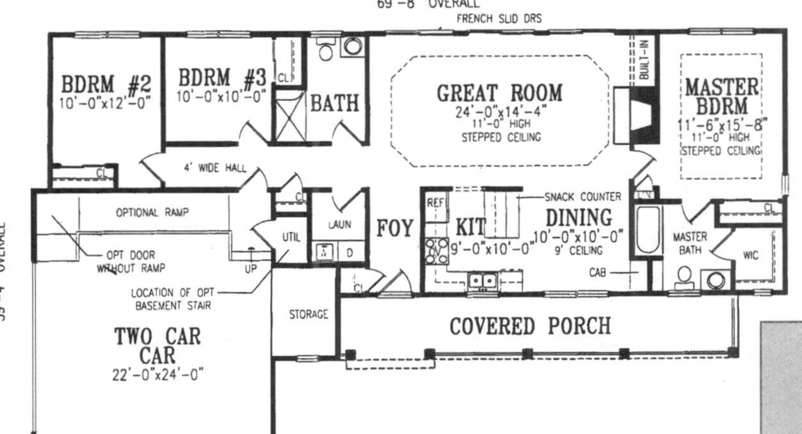
69'-8" OVERALL
FRENCH SLID DRS
BDRM #2
10'-0"x12'-0"
BDRM #3
10'-0"x10'-0"
CL
BATH
GREAT ROOM
24'-0"x14'-4"
11'-0" HIGH
STEPPED CEILING
BUILT-IN
MASTER
BDRM
11'-6"x15'-8"
11'-0" HIGH
STEPPED CEILING
4' WIDE HALL
CL
OPTIONAL RAMP
OPT DOOR
WITHOUT RAMP
LOCATION OF OPT
BASEMENT STAIR
UTIL
UP
LAUN
D
FOY
REF
KIT
9'-0"x10'-0"
SNACK COUNTER
DINING
10'-0"x10'-0"
9' CEILING
CAB
MASTER
BATH
WIC
CL
STORAGE
COVERED PORCH
TWO CAR
CAR
22'-0"x24'-0"
39'-4" OVERALL

Plan #531-AX-5380

Price Code A

Total Living Area: 1,480 Sq. Ft.

Home has 3 bedrooms, 2 baths, 2-car side entry garage and basement, crawl space or slab foundation, please specify when ordering.

Special features

- Split bedroom floor plan with private master suite includes large bath and walk-in closet
- Fabulous great room features 11′ high step ceiling, fireplace and media center
- Floor plan designed to be fully accessible for handicapped

Plan #531-1118-1
basement
Plan #531-1118-2
crawl space & slab

Price Code B

Total Living Area: 1,550 Sq. Ft.

Home has 3 bedrooms, 2 baths, 2-car side entry garage and basement, crawl space or slab foundation, please specify when ordering.

Special features

- Convenient mud room between garage and kitchen
- Oversized dining area allows plenty of space for entertaining
- Master bedroom has private bath and ample closet space
- Large patio off family room brings the outdoors in

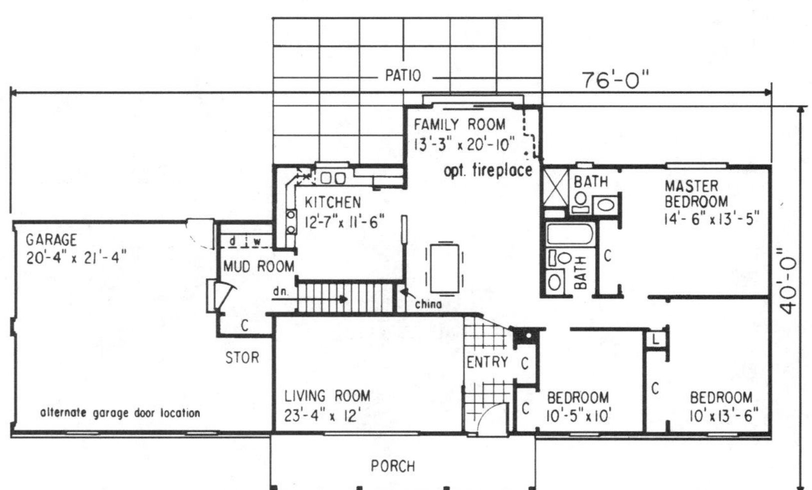
PATIO
76'-0"
FAMILY ROOM
13'-3" x 20'-10"
opt. fireplace
KITCHEN
12'-7" x 11'-6"
BATH
MASTER
BEDROOM
14'-6" x 13'-5"
GARAGE
20'-4" x 21'-4"
d w
MUD ROOM
dn.
china
BATH
C
40'-0"
STOR
ENTRY
C
L
LIVING ROOM
23'-4" x 12'
BEDROOM
10'-5" x 10'
BEDROOM
10' x 13'-6"
alternate garage door location
PORCH

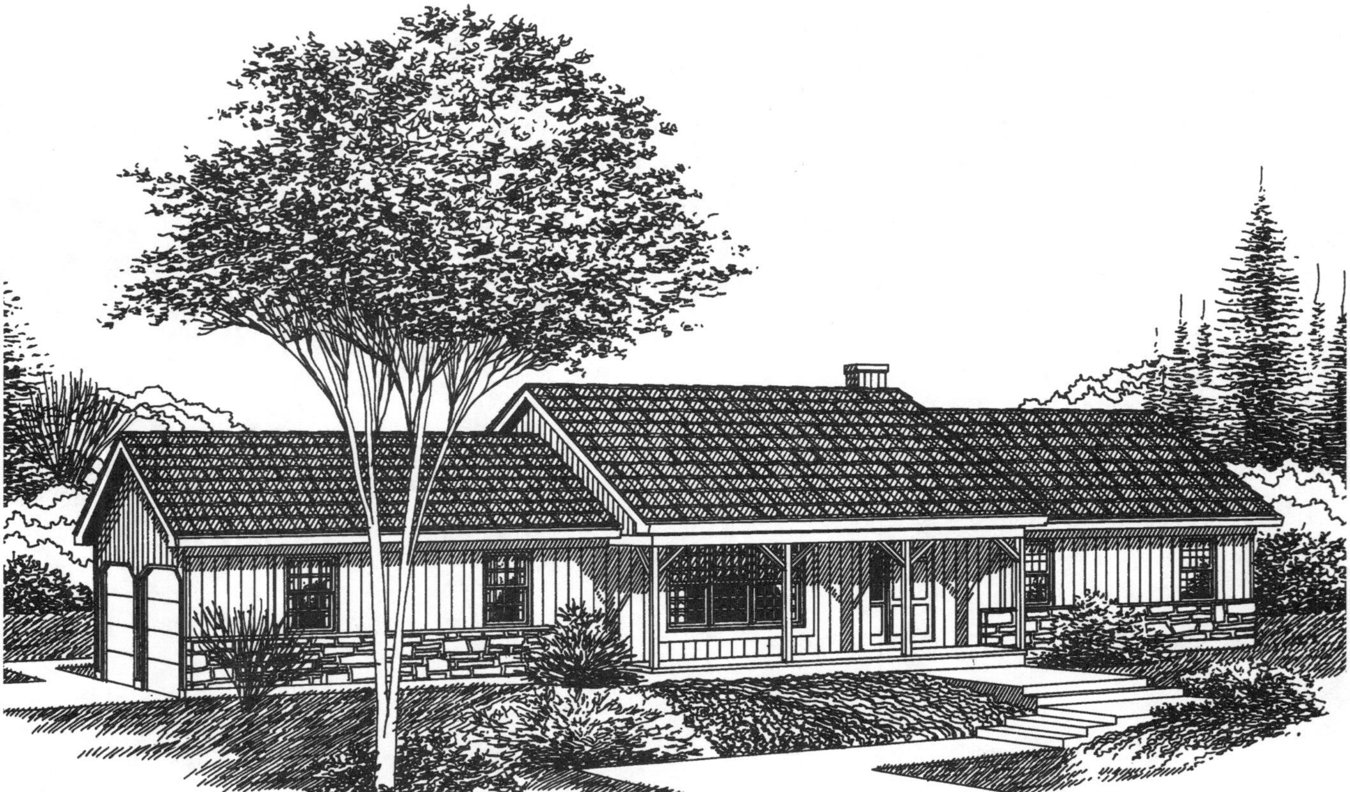

LOWE'S

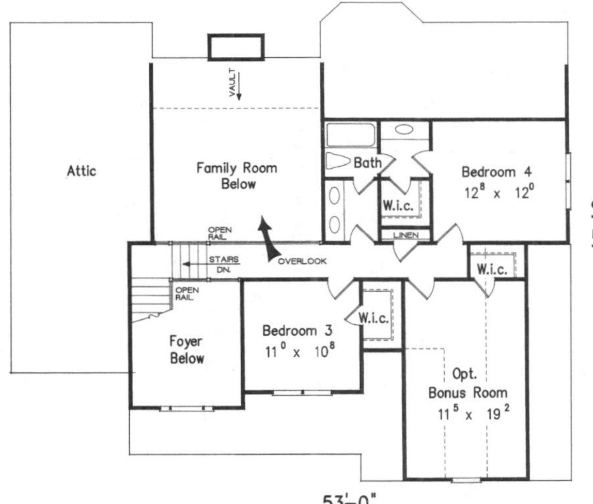
Attic
Family Room Below
VAULT
Bath
Bedroom 4
12⁸ x 12⁰
W.i.c.
LINEN
OPEN RAIL
STAIRS DN.
OVERLOOK
W.i.c.
OPEN RAIL
Foyer Below
Bedroom 3
11⁰ x 10⁸
W.i.c.
Opt. Bonus Room
11⁵ x 19²

Second Floor
543 sq. ft.

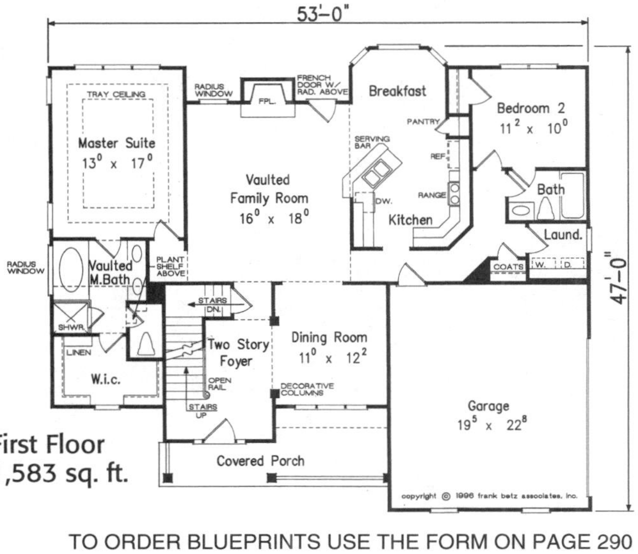

53'-0"
47'-0"
TRAY CEILING
Master Suite
13⁰ x 17⁰
RADIUS WINDOW
FPL.
FRENCH DOOR W/ RAD. ABOVE
Breakfast
PANTRY
Bedroom 2
11² x 10⁰
SERVING BAR
REF.
Vaulted Family Room
16⁰ x 18⁰
DW.
RANGE
Kitchen
Bath
Laund.
RADIUS WINDOW
Vaulted M.Bath
PLANT SHELF ABOVE
COATS
W. D.
SHWR.
STAIRS DN.
Two Story Foyer
Dining Room
11⁰ x 12²
LINEN
W.i.c.
OPEN RAIL
STAIRS UP
DECORATIVE COLUMNS
Garage
19⁵ x 22⁸
Covered Porch
copyright © 1996 frank betz associates, inc.

First Floor
1,583 sq. ft.

Plan #531-FB-963

Price Code C

Total Living Area: 2,126 Sq. Ft.

Home has 4 bedrooms, 3 baths, 2-car side entry garage and basement, crawl space or slab foundation, please specify when ordering.

Special features

- Two-story foyer creates airy feeling
- Kitchen overlooks vaulted family room with a handy serving bar
- Second floor includes an optional bonus room with an additional 251 square feet of living area

LOWE'S

Attic Storage
Stairs Down
Bedroom #3
14 x 12
8' Clg.
Linen
Bedroom #2
13/9 x 11/5
8' Clg.
Sloped Clg.

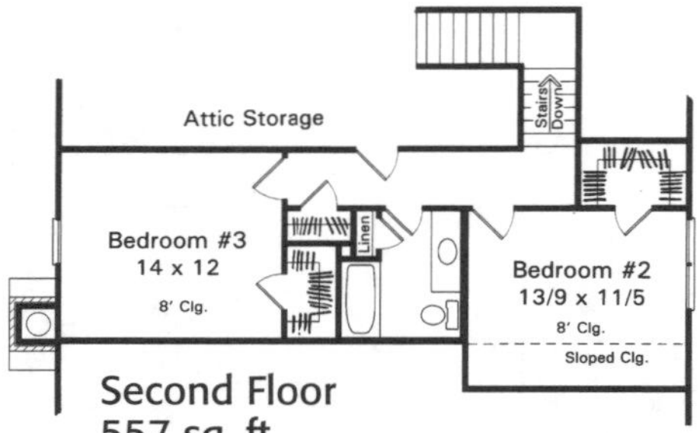

Second Floor
557 sq. ft.

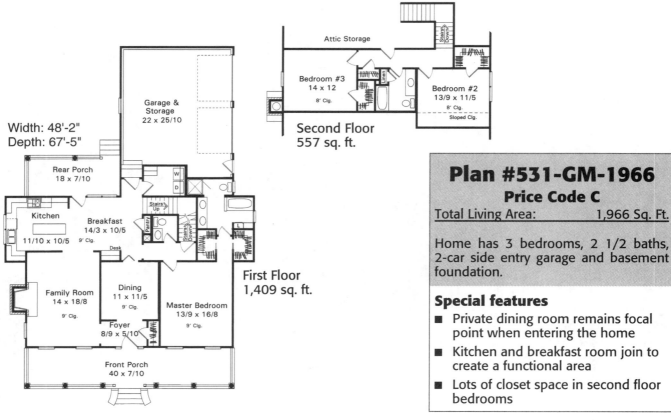

Width: 48'-2"
Depth: 67'-5"

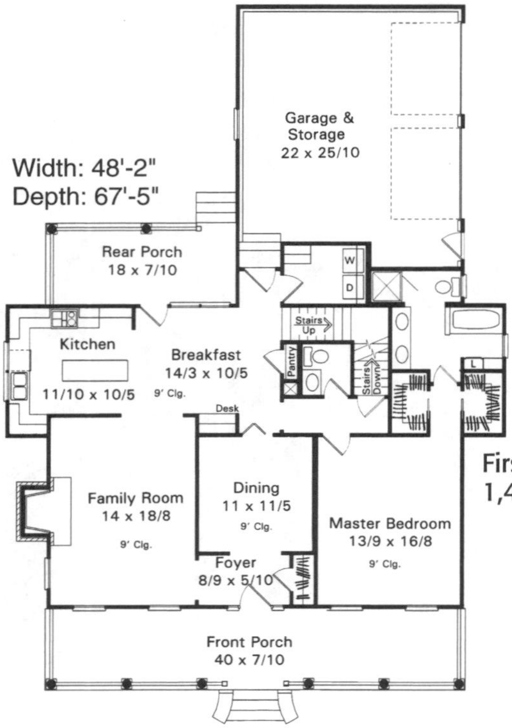

Garage &
Storage
22 x 25/10

Rear Porch
18 x 7/10

W
D

Kitchen
11/10 x 10/5

Breakfast
14/3 x 10/5
9' Clg.

Stairs Up
Pantry
Stairs Down
Desk
L

Family Room
14 x 18/8
9' Clg.

Dining
11 x 11/5
9' Clg.

Foyer
8/9 x 5/10

Master Bedroom
13/9 x 16/8
9' Clg.

Front Porch
40 x 7/10

First Floor
1,409 sq. ft.

Plan #531-GM-1966

Price Code C

Total Living Area: 1,966 Sq. Ft.

Home has 3 bedrooms, 2 1/2 baths, 2-car side entry garage and basement foundation.

Special features

- Private dining room remains focal point when entering the home
- Kitchen and breakfast room join to create a functional area
- Lots of closet space in second floor bedrooms

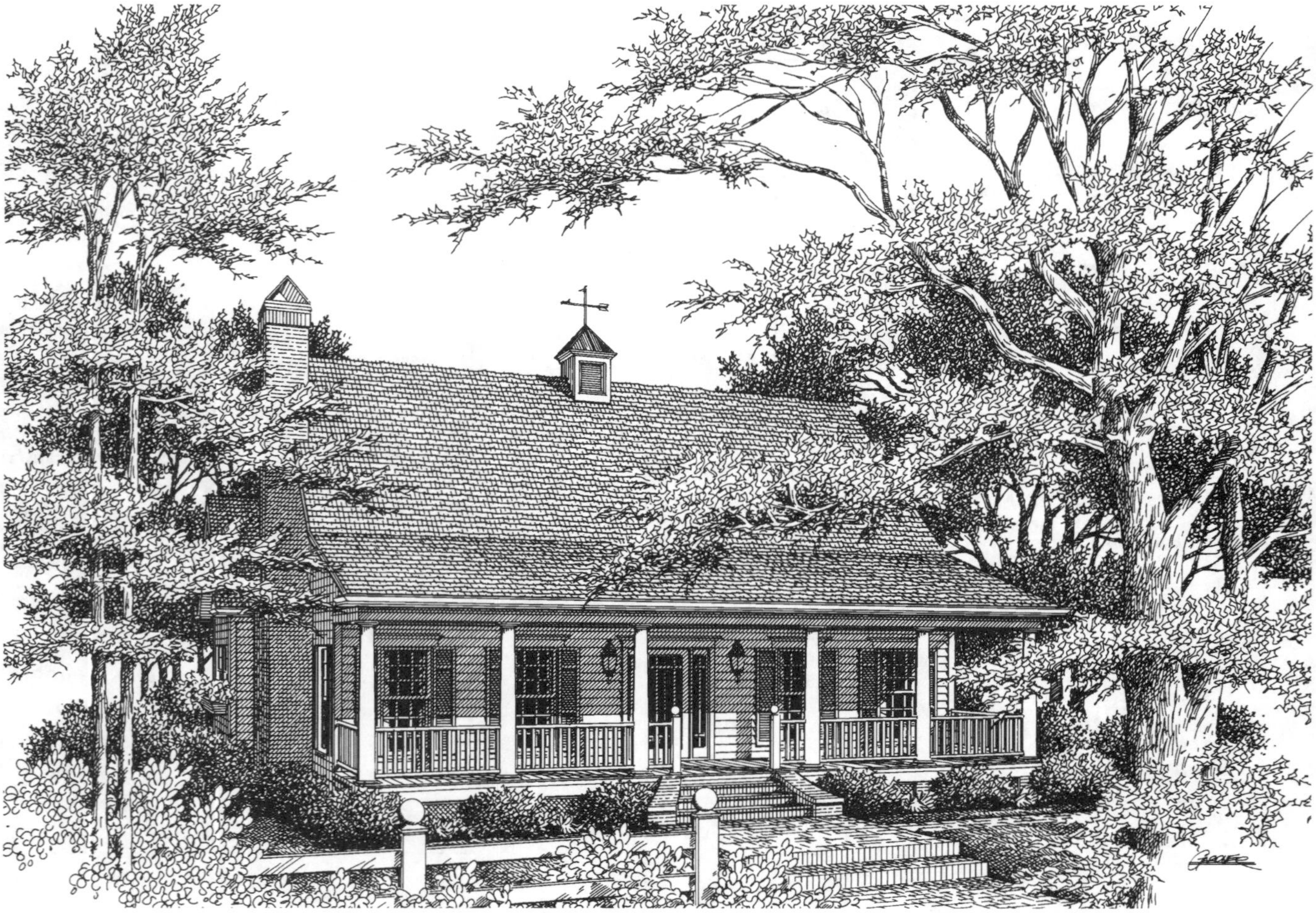

Dramatic U-Shaped Stairs

LOWE'S

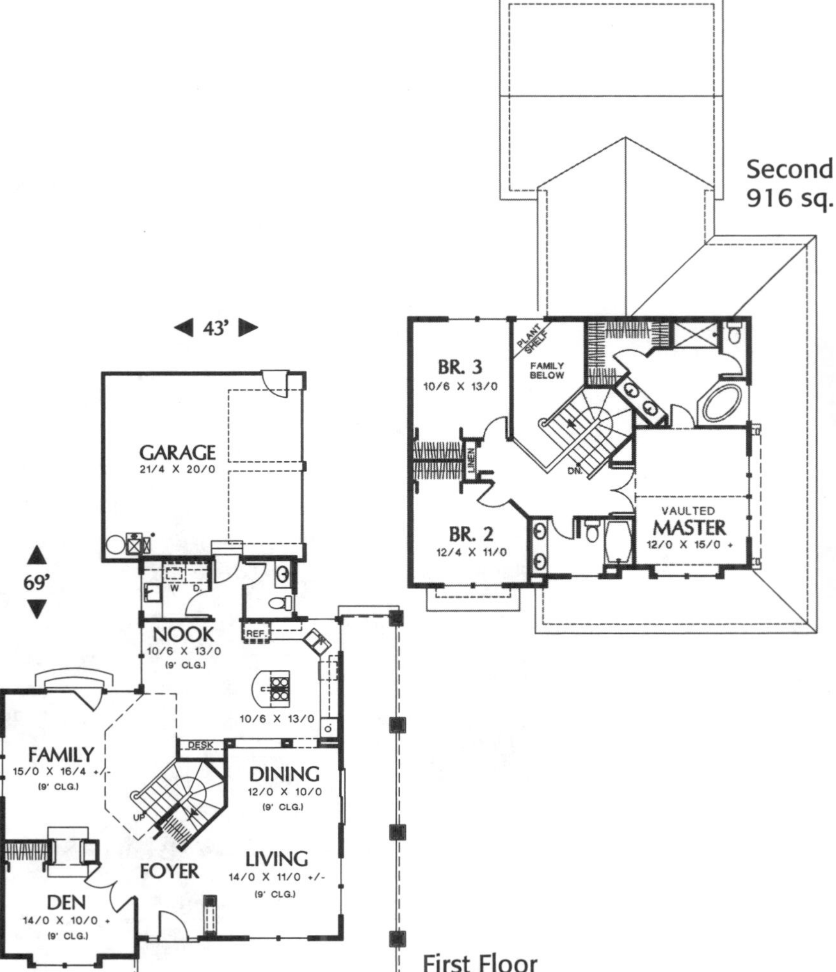
43'
69'
GARAGE
21/4 X 20/0
W
D
NOOK
10/6 X 13/0
(9' CLG.)
REF.
10/6 X 13/0
DESK
FAMILY
15/0 X 16/4 +/-
(9' CLG.)
DINING
12/0 X 10/0
(9' CLG.)
UP
FOYER
LIVING
14/0 X 11/0 +/-
(9' CLG.)
DEN
14/0 X 10/0 +
(9' CLG.)
BR. 3
10/6 X 13/0
PLANT SHELF
FAMILY BELOW
LINEN
DN.
BR. 2
12/4 X 11/0
VAULTED
MASTER
12/0 X 15/0 +

Second Floor
916 sq. ft.

First Floor
1,371 sq. ft.

Plan #531-AMD-2229

Price Code D

Total Living Area: 2,287 Sq. Ft.

Home has 4 bedrooms, 2 1/2 baths, 2-car side entry garage and crawl space foundation.

Special features

- Wrap-around porch creates inviting feeling
- First floor windows have transom windows above
- Den has see-through fireplace into the family area

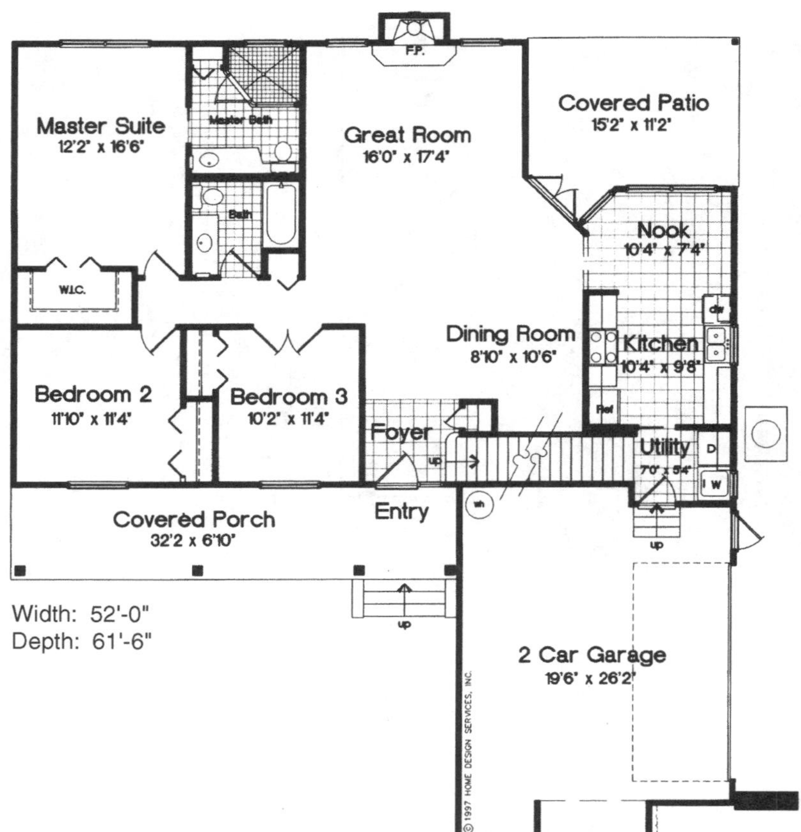
F.P.
Master Suite
12'2" x 16'6"
Master Bath
Great Room
16'0" x 17'4"
Covered Patio
15'2" x 11'2"
Bath
Nook
10'4" x 7'4"
W.I.C.
Dining Room
8'10" x 10'6"
Kitchen
10'4" x 9'8"
Bedroom 2
11'10" x 11'4"
Bedroom 3
10'2" x 11'4"
Foyer
Utility
7'0" x 5'4"
Covered Porch
32'2 x 6'10"
Entry
2 Car Garage
19'6" x 26'2"
© 1997 HOME DESIGN SERVICES, INC.

Width: 52'-0"
Depth: 61'-6"

Plan #531-HDS-1558-2

Price Code C

Total Living Area: 1,885 Sq. Ft.

Home has 3 bedrooms, 2 baths, 2-car side entry garage and basement foundation.

Special features

- Enormous covered patio
- Dining and great rooms combine to create one large and versatile living area
- Utility room directly off kitchen for convenience

TO ORDER BLUEPRINTS USE THE FORM ON PAGE 290 OR CALL TOLL-FREE **1-800-DREAM HOME** (373-2646)

LOWE'S

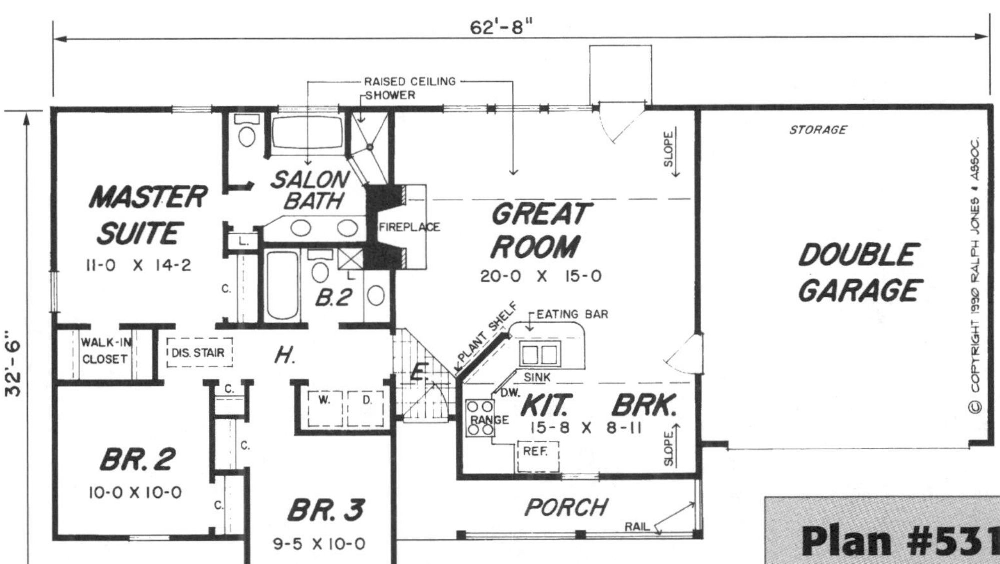
62'-8"
32'-6"
RAISED CEILING
SHOWER
MASTER SUITE
11-0 X 14-2
SALON BATH
FIREPLACE
GREAT ROOM
20-0 X 15-0
B.2
L.
C.
WALK-IN CLOSET
DIS. STAIR
H.
PLANT SHELF
EATING BAR
SINK
DW.
RANGE
KIT.
BRK.
15-8 X 8-11
REF.
W.
D.
E.
BR. 2
10-0 X 10-0
BR. 3
9-5 X 10-0
PORCH
RAIL
SLOPE
STORAGE
DOUBLE GARAGE
© COPYRIGHT 1990 RALPH JONES & ASSOC.

Plan #531-RJ-A1175

Price Code AA

Total Living Area: 1,192 Sq. Ft.

Home has 3 bedrooms, 2 baths, 2-car garage and slab or crawl space foundation, please specify when ordering.

Special features

- Kitchen eating bar overlooks well-designed great room
- Private bath in master suite
- Extra storage space in garage

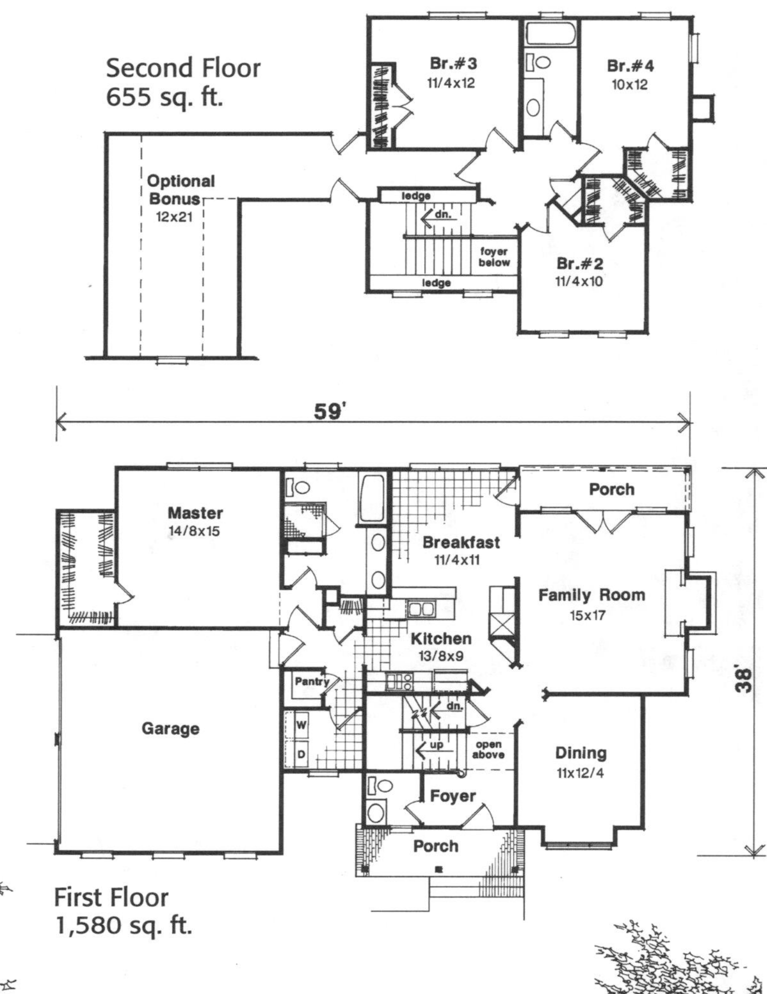
Second Floor
655 sq. ft.
Br.#3
11/4x12
Br.#4
10x12
Optional
Bonus
12x21
ledge
dn.
foyer
below
ledge
Br.#2
11/4x10
59'
Master
14/8x15
Porch
Breakfast
11/4x11
Family Room
15x17
Kitchen
13/8x9
Pantry
Garage
W
D
dn.
up
open
above
Dining
11x12/4
Foyer
Porch
38'
First Floor
1,580 sq. ft.

Plan #531-GM-2235

Price Code D

Total Living Area: 2,235 Sq. Ft.

Home has 4 bedrooms, 2 1/2 baths, 2-car side entry garage and basement foundation.

Special features

- Cheerful family room has double-doors leading to a covered porch
- Centrally located kitchen is convenient to all rooms on first floor
- Second floor bedrooms have large closets and lots of windows creating bright spaces

TO ORDER BLUEPRINTS USE THE FORM ON PAGE 290 OR CALL TOLL-FREE **1-800-DREAM HOME** (373-2646)

LOWE'S

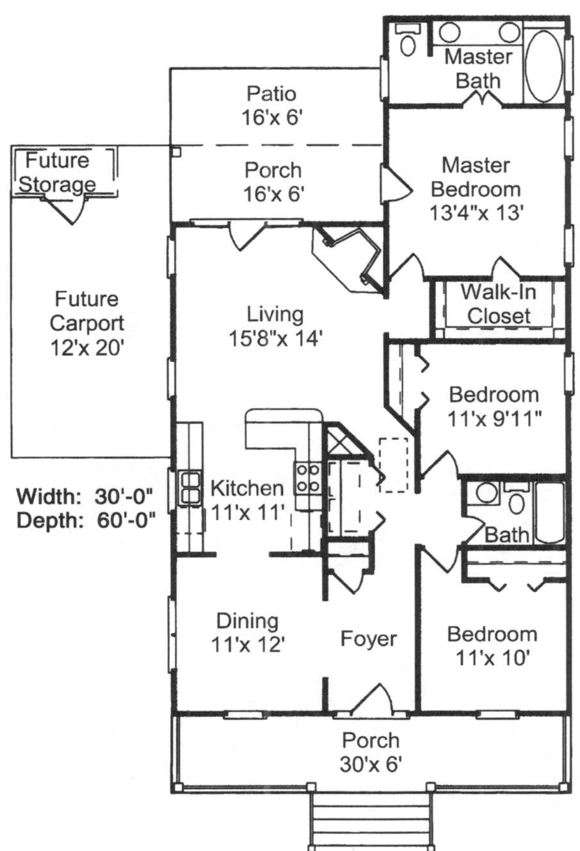
Master
Bath
Patio
16'x 6'
Future
Storage
Porch
16'x 6'
Master
Bedroom
13'4"x 13'
Walk-In
Closet
Living
15'8"x 14'
Future
Carport
12'x 20'
Bedroom
11'x 9'11"
Kitchen
11'x 11'
Bath
Width: 30'-0"
Depth: 60'-0"
Dining
11'x 12'
Foyer
Bedroom
11'x 10'
Porch
30'x 6'

Plan #531-CHP-1332A

Price Code A

Total Living Area: 1,363 Sq. Ft.

Home has 3 bedrooms, 2 baths, optional 1-car carport and slab foundation.

Special features

- Formal dining area conveniently located next to kitchen
- Master bedroom has private bath and walk-in closet
- Covered porch has patio which allows enough space for entertaining

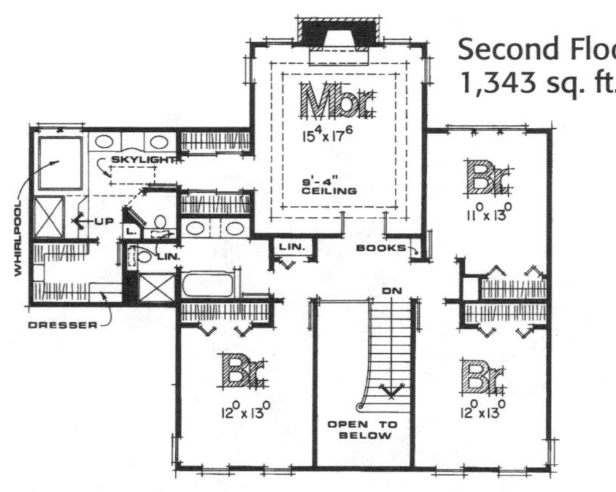
Mbr.
15⁴x17⁶
SKYLIGHT
9'-4" CEILING
Br.
11⁰x13⁰
WHIRLPOOL
UP
LIN.
LIN.
BOOKS
DN
DRESSER
Br.
12⁰x13⁰
OPEN TO BELOW
Br.
12⁰x13⁰

Second Floor
1,343 sq. ft.

Plan #531-DB1560

Price Code E

Total Living Area: 2,879 Sq. Ft.

Home has 4 bedrooms, 2 1/2 baths, 3-car side entry garage and basement foundation.

Special features

- Center island in kitchen makes a terrific work space
- Master bedroom has cozy fireplace and large private bath
- Great room features centered fireplace surrounded by cheerful windows

First Floor
1,536 sq. ft.

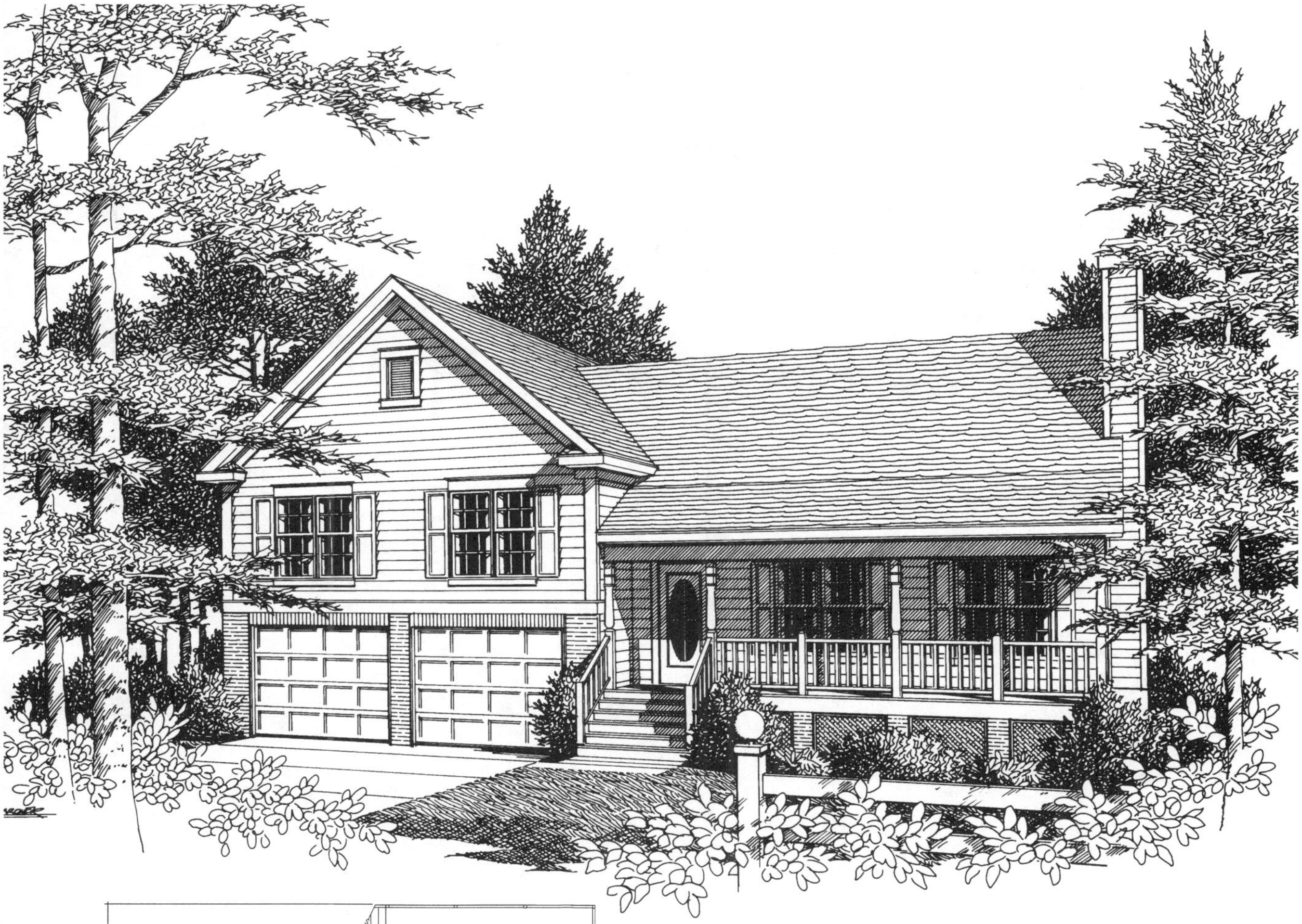

Space Saving Drive-Under Garage

LOWE'S

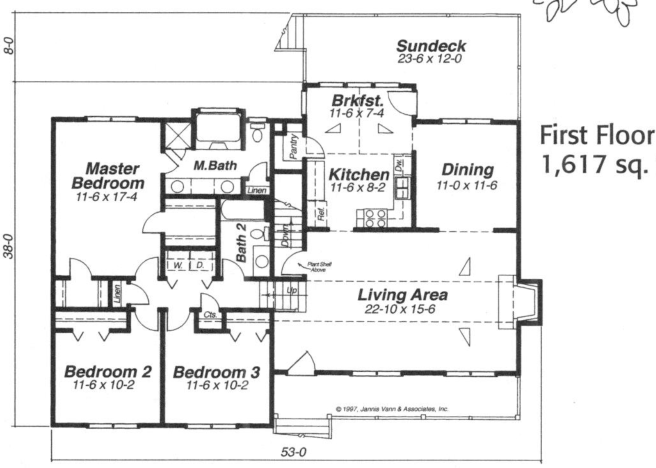
Sundeck
23-6 x 12-0
Brkfst.
11-6 x 7-4
Master Bedroom
11-6 x 17-4
M.Bath
Kitchen
11-6 x 8-2
Dining
11-0 x 11-6
Bath 2
Living Area
22-10 x 15-6
Bedroom 2
11-6 x 10-2
Bedroom 3
11-6 x 10-2
53-0
38-0
8-0

First Floor
1,617 sq. ft.

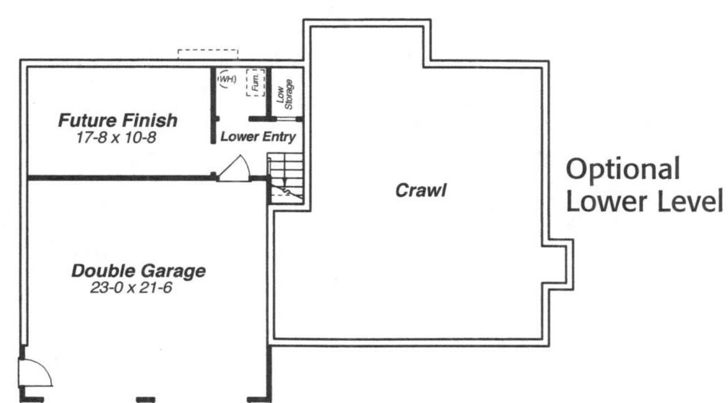
Future Finish
17-8 x 10-8
Lower Entry
Crawl
Double Garage
23-0 x 21-6

Optional
Lower Level

Plan #531-JV-1617-A-SJ

Price Code B

Total Living Area: 1,617 Sq. Ft.

Home has 3 bedrooms, 2 baths, 2-car drive under garage and basement or partial crawl space foundation, please specify when ordering.

Special features

- Vaulted ceilings in living and breakfast areas
- Formal dining room located off kitchen for convenience
- Beautiful split level design gives privacy to bedrooms

Dutch Colonial Design Has Outstanding Extras

Plan #531-1065

Price Code E

Total Living Area: 2,835 Sq. Ft.

Home has 4 bedrooms, 2 1/2 baths, 2-car garage and basement foundation.

Special features

- Studio loft above garage is ideal as an office space or children s playroom
- Double staircases to second floor provide easy access to any area of this home
- Handy U-shaped kitchen nestled between family and living rooms
- Unique sewing loft is conveniently located across from additional storage area on second floor

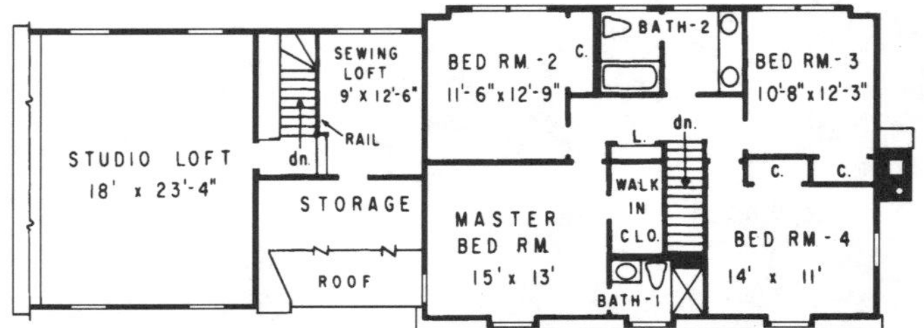
STUDIO LOFT
18' x 23'-4"
SEWING LOFT
9' x 12'-6"
RAIL
dn.
STORAGE
ROOF
BED RM - 2
11'-6" x 12'-9"
BATH - 2
BED RM - 3
10'-8" x 12'-3"
MASTER BED RM
15' x 13'
WALK IN CLO.
BATH - 1
BED RM - 4
14' x 11'

Second Floor - Four bedroom option
1,639 sq. ft.

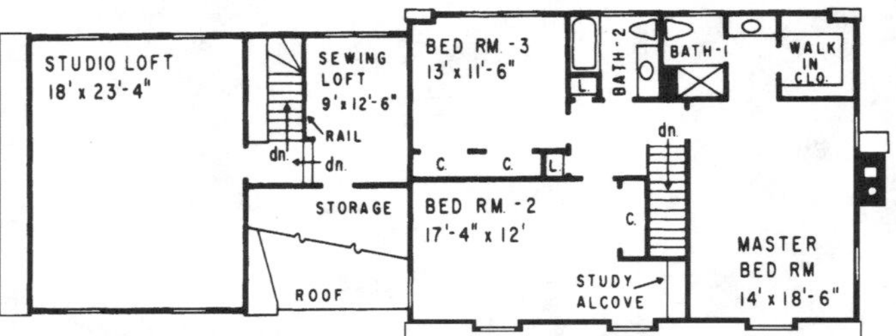
STUDIO LOFT
18' x 23'-4"
SEWING LOFT
9' x 12'-6"
RAIL
STORAGE
ROOF
BED RM - 3
13' x 11'-6"
BATH - 2
BATH - 1
WALK IN CLO.
BED RM - 2
17'-4" x 12'
STUDY ALCOVE
MASTER BED RM
14' x 18'-6"

Second Floor - Three bedroom option
1,639 sq. ft.

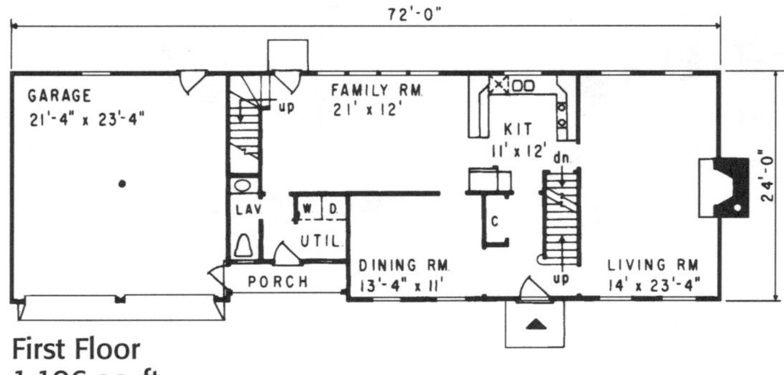
72'-0"
GARAGE
21'-4" x 23'-4"
FAMILY RM
21' x 12'
KIT
11' x 12'
LAV
UTIL
PORCH
DINING RM
13'-4" x 11'
LIVING RM
14' x 23'-4"
24'-0"

First Floor
1,196 sq. ft.

 TO ORDER BLUEPRINTS USE THE FORM ON PAGE 290 OR CALL TOLL-FREE **1-800-DREAM HOME** (373-2646)

Open Feeling In This Ranch

LOWE'S

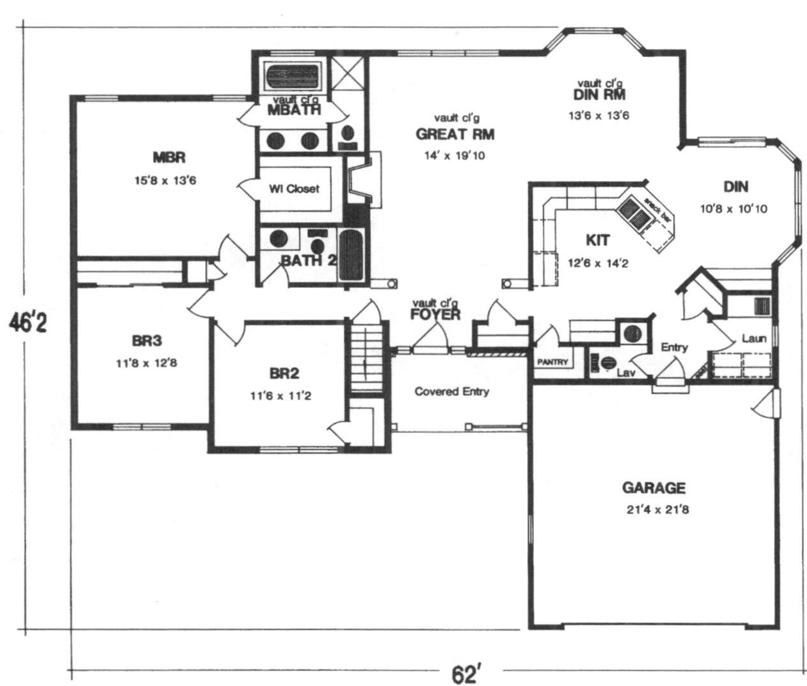

vault cl'g
MBATH
MBR
15'8 x 13'6
WI Closet
BATH 2
BR3
11'8 x 12'8
BR2
11'6 x 11'2
vault cl'g
GREAT RM
14' x 19'10
vault cl'g
DIN RM
13'6 x 13'6
DIN
10'8 x 10'10
KIT
12'6 x 14'2
snack bar
vault cl'g
FOYER
Covered Entry
PANTRY
Lav
Entry
Laun
GARAGE
21'4 x 21'8
46'2
62'

Plan #531-JFD-10-1875-1

Price Code C

Total Living Area: 1,875 Sq. Ft.

Home has 3 bedrooms, 2 1/2 baths, 2-car garage and basement foundation.

Special features

- Peninsula separating kitchen and dining room has sink, dishwasher and eating area
- Tall ceilings throughout living area create spaciousness
- Columned foyer adds style

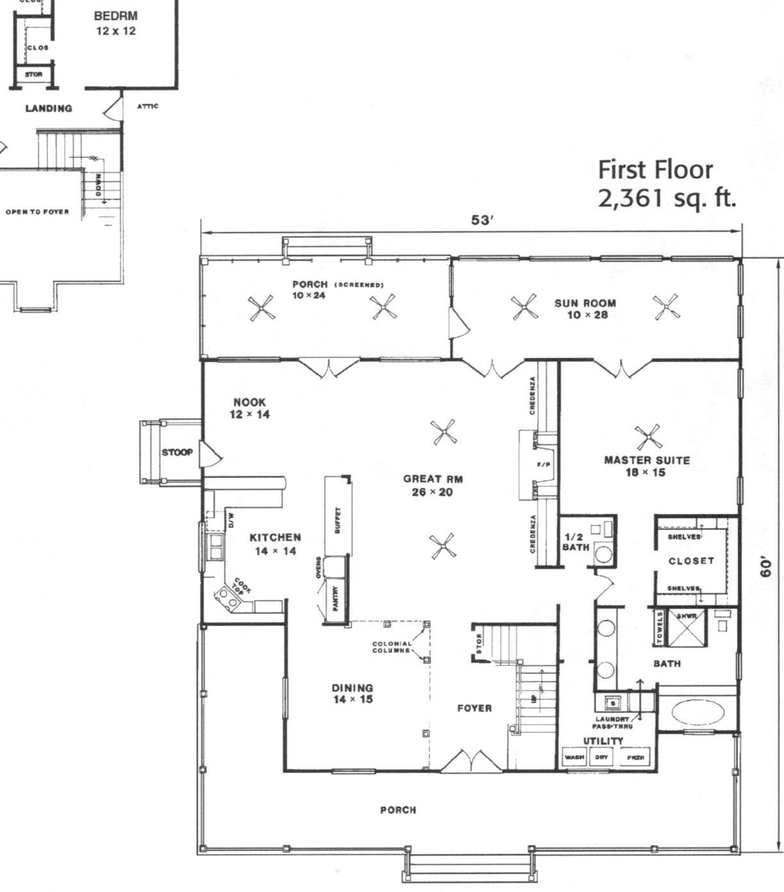
Second Floor
650 sq. ft.
BATH
DORMER
5 x 11
DRESSING
DRESSING
DORMER
5 x 11
CLOS
BEDRM
12 x 12
BEDRM
12 x 12
CLOS
STOR
LANDING
ATTIC
ATTIC
DOWN
OPEN TO FOYER
First Floor
2,361 sq. ft.
53'
PORCH (SCREENED)
10 × 24
SUN ROOM
10 × 28
NOOK
12 × 14
STOOP
CREDENZA
GREAT RM
26 × 20
F/P
CREDENZA
MASTER SUITE
18 × 15
KITCHEN
14 × 14
D/W
BUFFET
OVENS
PANTRY
COOK TOP
1/2
BATH
SHELVES
CLOSET
SHELVES
60'
TOWELS
SHWR
COLONIAL COLUMNS
STOR
DINING
14 × 15
FOYER
BATH
LAUNDRY PASS-THRU
UTILITY
WASH
DRY
FRZR
PORCH

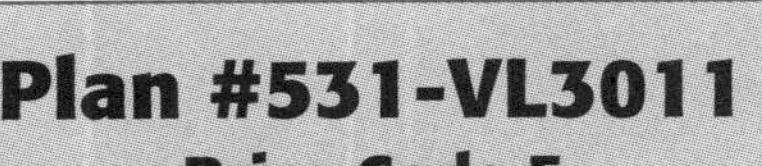

Plan #531-VL3011

Price Code E

Total Living Area: 3,011 Sq. Ft.

Home has 3 bedrooms, 2 1/2 baths and slab or crawl space foundation, please specify when ordering.

Special features

- Formal dining room has decorative columns separating it from foyer and great room
- Two secondary bedrooms share a full bath on the second floor
- Spacious master suite accesses sun room through double-doors and has spacious master bath
- 9′ ceilings on the first floor

TO ORDER BLUEPRINTS USE THE FORM ON PAGE 290 OR CALL TOLL-FREE **1-800-DREAM HOME** (373-2646)

Trio Of Dormers Enhance Facade

LOWE'S

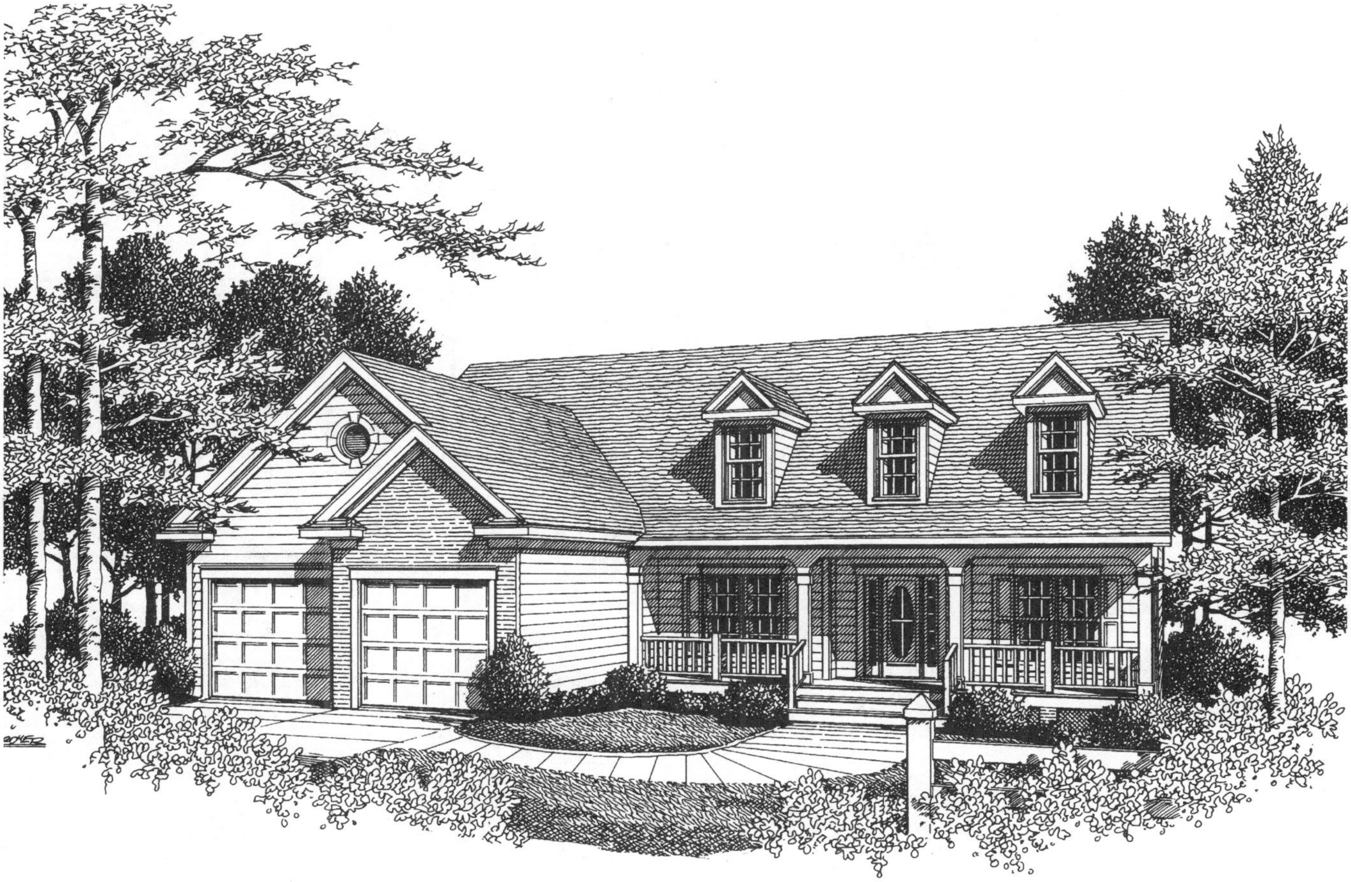

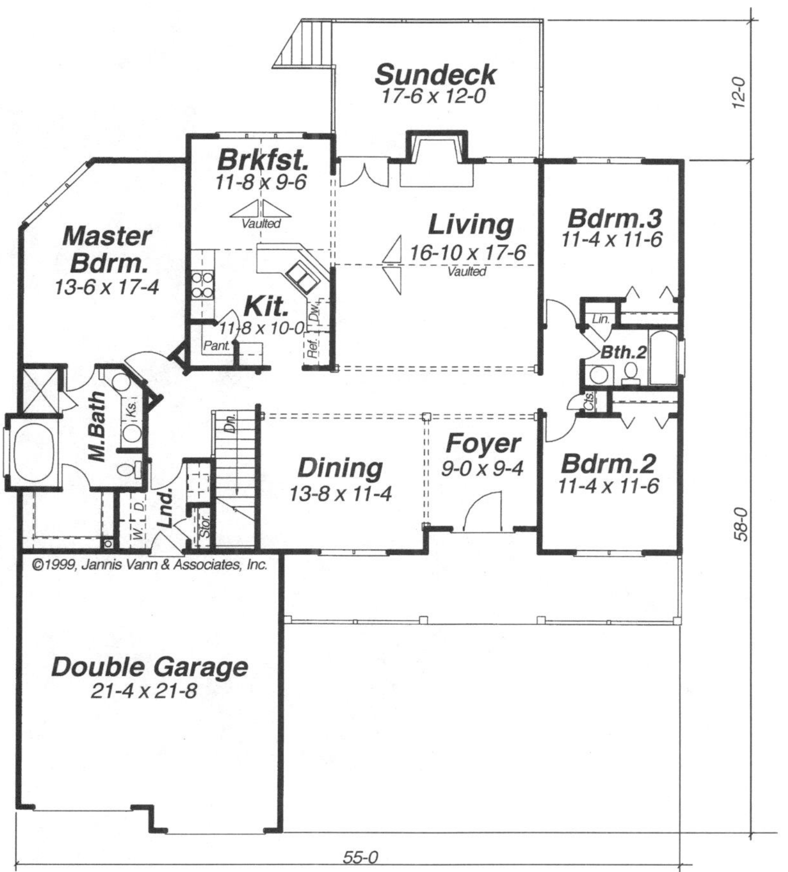
Sundeck
17-6 x 12-0
Brkfst.
11-8 x 9-6
Vaulted
Master
Bdrm.
13-6 x 17-4
Living
16-10 x 17-6
Vaulted
Bdrm.3
11-4 x 11-6
Kit.
11-8 x 10-0
Dw.
Pant.
Ref.
Lin.
Bth.2
Clo.
M.Bath
Ks.
W.I.C.
Lnd.
Stor.
Dn.
Dining
13-8 x 11-4
Foyer
9-0 x 9-4
Bdrm.2
11-4 x 11-6
Double Garage
21-4 x 21-8
12-0
58-0
55-0

Plan #531-JV-1865-A

Price Code C

Total Living Area: 1,865 Sq. Ft.

Home has 3 bedrooms, 2 baths, 2-car garage and basement foundation.

Special features

- French doors next to stately fireplace in living room lead to sun deck
- Open living and dining rooms create spacious feel
- Angled wall in master suite adds interest

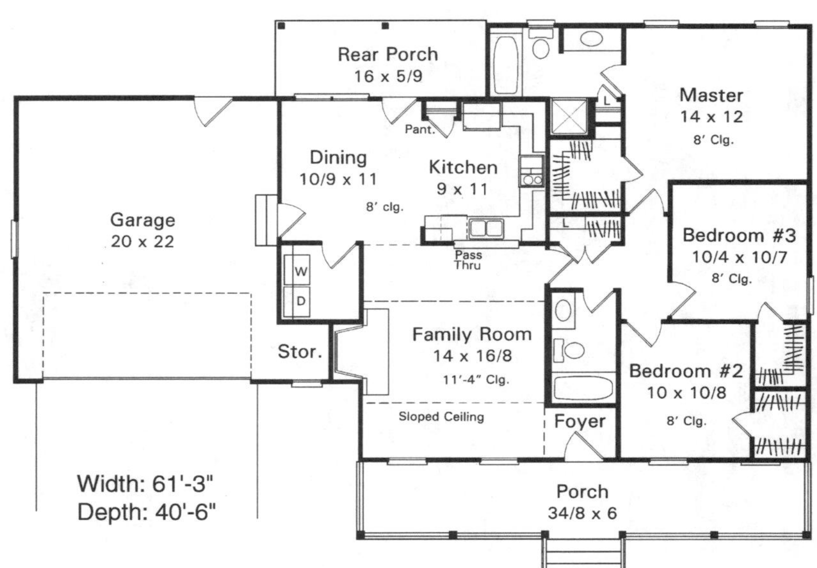
Rear Porch
16 x 5/9
Master
14 x 12
8' Clg.
Pant.
Dining
10/9 x 11
Kitchen
9 x 11
8' clg.
Garage
20 x 22
Bedroom #3
10/4 x 10/7
8' Clg.
Pass Thru
W
D
Family Room
14 x 16/8
11'-4" Clg.
Stor.
Bedroom #2
10 x 10/8
8' Clg.
Sloped Ceiling
Foyer
Width: 61'-3"
Depth: 40'-6"
Porch
34/8 x 6

Plan #531-GM-1253

Price Code A

Total Living Area: 1,253 Sq. Ft.

Home has 3 bedrooms, 2 baths, 2-car garage and crawl space or slab foundation, please specify when ordering.

Special features

- Sloped ceiling and fireplace in family room adds drama
- U-shaped kitchen efficiently designed
- Large walk-in closets are found in every bedroom

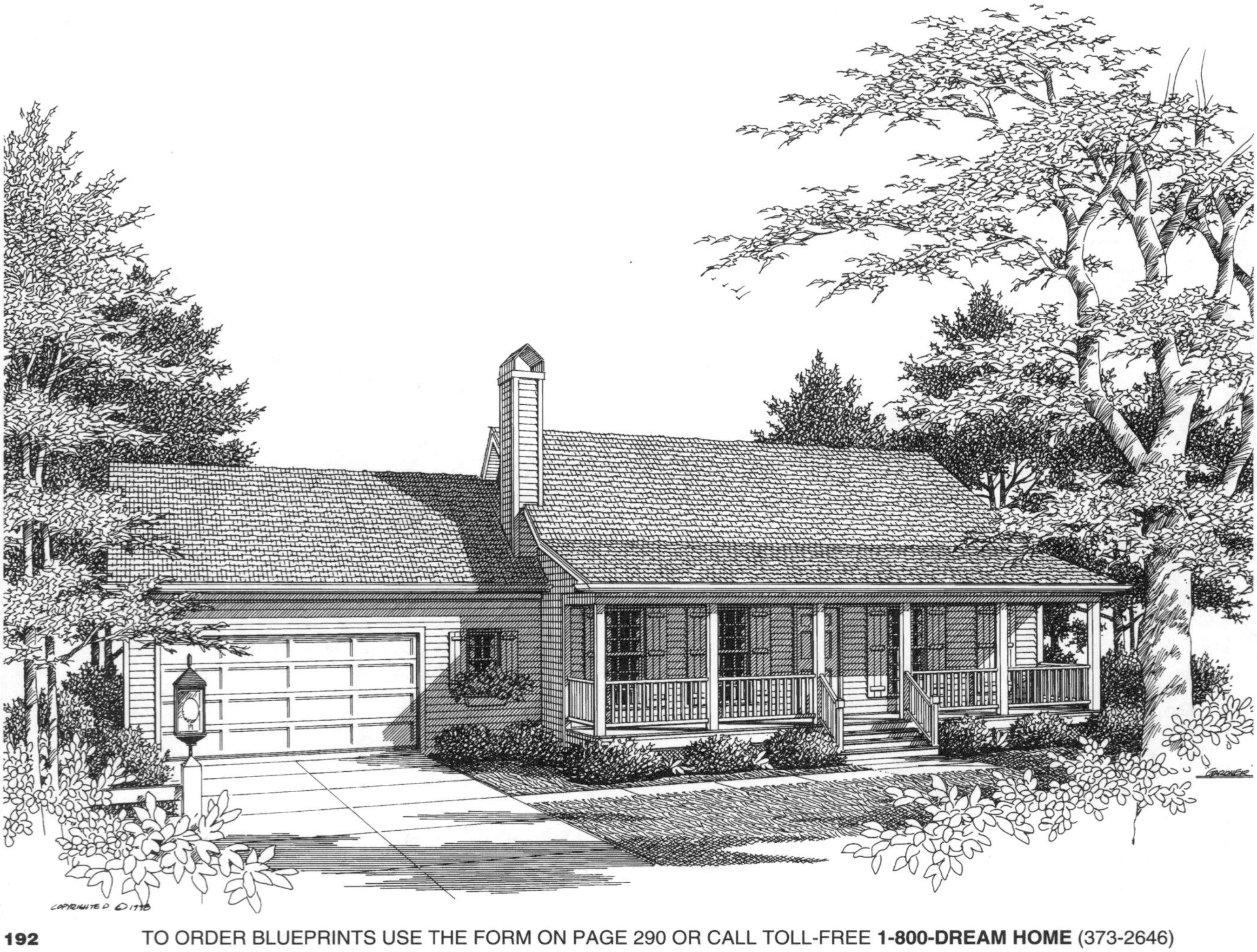

Charming Style With Traditional Accents

LOWE'S

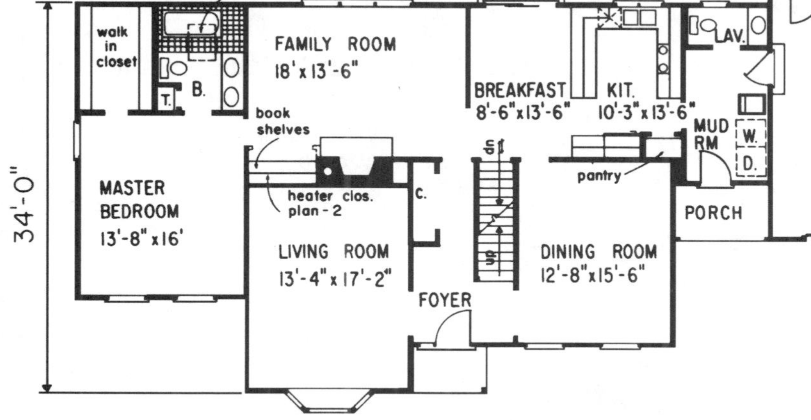
80'-0"
34'-0"
skylight
walk in closet
B.
T.
FAMILY ROOM
18' x 13'-6"
BREAKFAST
8'-6" x 13'-6"
KIT.
10'-3" x 13'-6"
LAV.
GARAGE
21'-4" x 21'-4"
book shelves
MUD RM
W.
D.
pantry
heater clos. plan - 2
C.
MASTER BEDROOM
13'-8" x 16'
PORCH
LIVING ROOM
13'-4" x 17'-2"
DINING ROOM
12'-8" x 15'-6"
FOYER

First Floor
1,633 sq. ft.

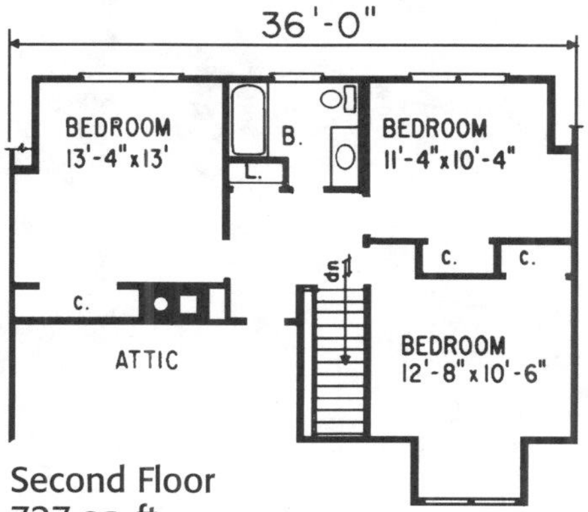

36'-0"

BEDROOM
13'-4" x 13'

B.

BEDROOM
11'-4" x 10'-4"

C.

C.

C.

ATTIC

BEDROOM
12'-8" x 10'-6"

Second Floor
727 sq. ft.

Plan #531-1207-1
partial basement/crawl space
Plan #531-1207-2
crawl space & slab
Price Code D

Total Living Area: 2,360 Sq. Ft.

Home has 4 bedrooms, 2 1/2 baths, 2-car garage and partial basement/crawl space, crawl space or slab foundation, please specify when ordering.

Special features

- Ample-sized living and dining rooms directly off foyer
- Family room enhanced with built-in bookshelves and cozy fireplace
- Master suite complemented with spacious walk-in closet and private bath with skylight

LOWE'S

Second Floor
1,021 sq. ft.

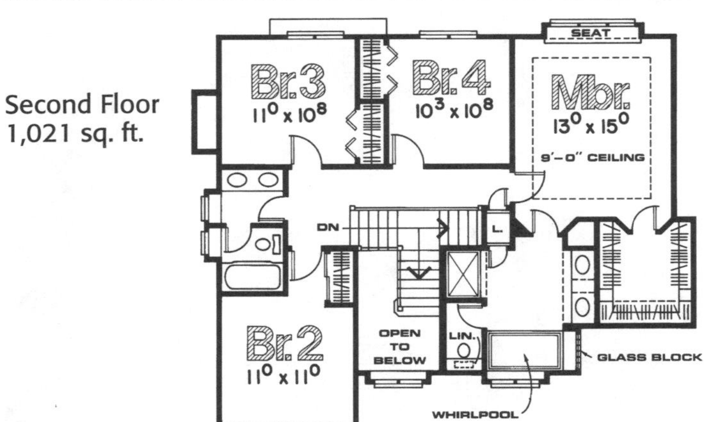
SEAT
Br.3
11⁰ x 10⁸
Br.4
10³ x 10⁸
Mbr.
13⁰ x 15⁰
9'-0" CEILING
DN
L
OPEN TO BELOW
LIN.
GLASS BLOCK
Br.2
11⁰ x 11⁰
WHIRLPOOL

First Floor
1,082 sq. ft.

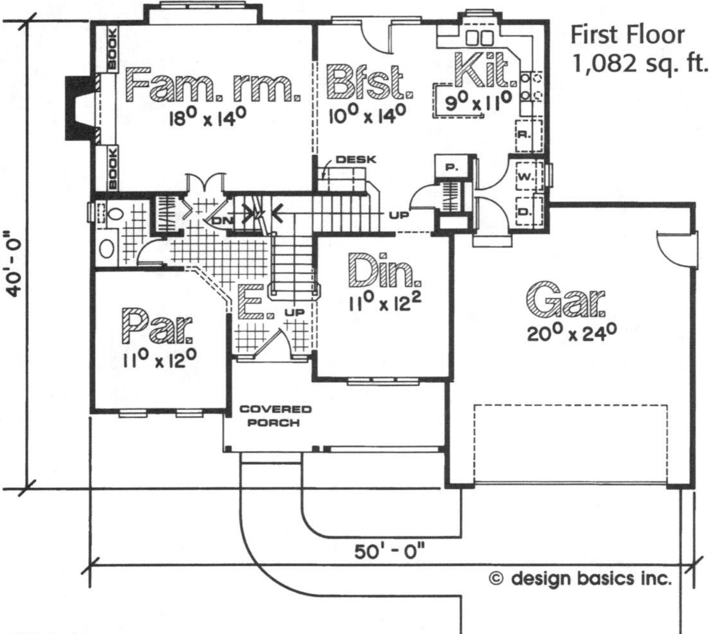
BOOK
Fam. rm.
18⁰ x 14⁰
Bfst.
10⁰ x 14⁰
Kit.
9⁰ x 11⁰
DESK
R.
P.
W.
D.
DN
UP
Din.
11⁰ x 12²
Gar.
20⁰ x 24⁰
Par.
11⁰ x 12⁰
E.
UP
COVERED PORCH
40'-0"
50'-0"
© design basics inc.

Plan #531-DB2638

Price Code C

Total Living Area: 2,103 Sq. Ft.

Home has 4 bedrooms, 2 1/2 baths, 2-car garage and basement foundation.

Special features

- Family room flows into breakfast room for optimal use of living space
- Secluded parlor is a perfect retreat
- Master bedroom has unique window seat and a glass block wall behind whirlpool tub in private bath

Attractive Combination Of Brick And Siding

LOWE'S

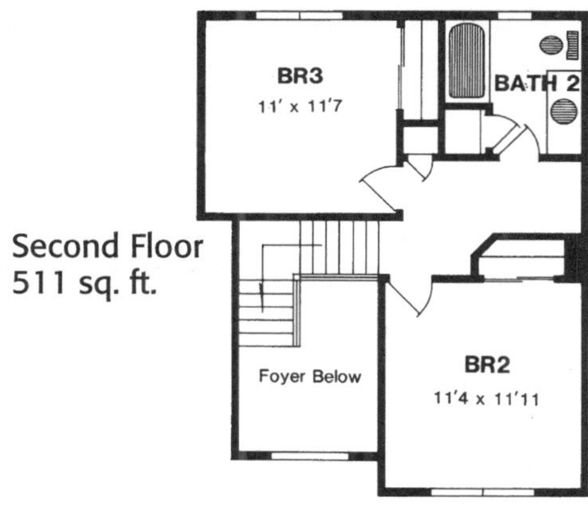
BR3
11' x 11'7
BATH 2
Foyer Below
BR2
11'4 x 11'11

Second Floor
511 sq. ft.

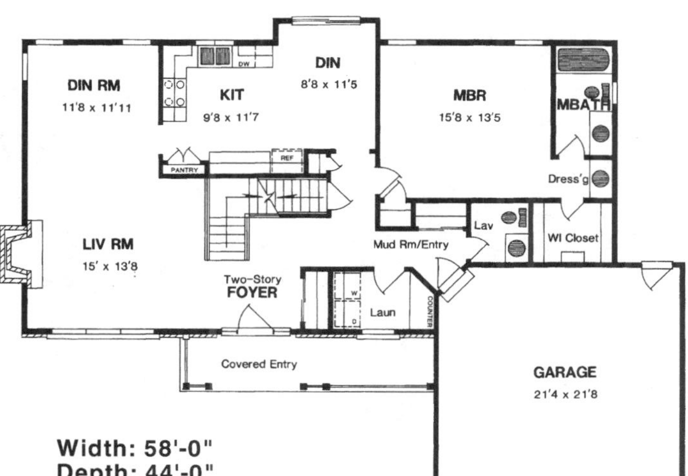
DIN RM
11'8 x 11'11
KIT
9'8 x 11'7
DIN
8'8 x 11'5
MBR
15'8 x 13'5
MBATH
Dress'g
PANTRY
REF
DW
LIV RM
15' x 13'8
Mud Rm/Entry
Lav
WI Closet
Two-Story
FOYER
Laun
COUNTER
Covered Entry
GARAGE
21'4 x 21'8

First Floor
1,281 sq. ft.

Width: 58'-0"
Depth: 44'-0"

Plan #531-JFD-20-17921

Price Code B

Total Living Area: 1,792 Sq. Ft.

Home has 3 bedrooms, 2 1/2 baths, 2-car garage and basement foundation.

Special features

- Traditional styling makes this a popular design
- First floor master bedroom maintains privacy
- Dining area has sliding glass doors leading to the outdoors
- Formal dining and living rooms combine for added gathering space

Distinct Country Look And Feel

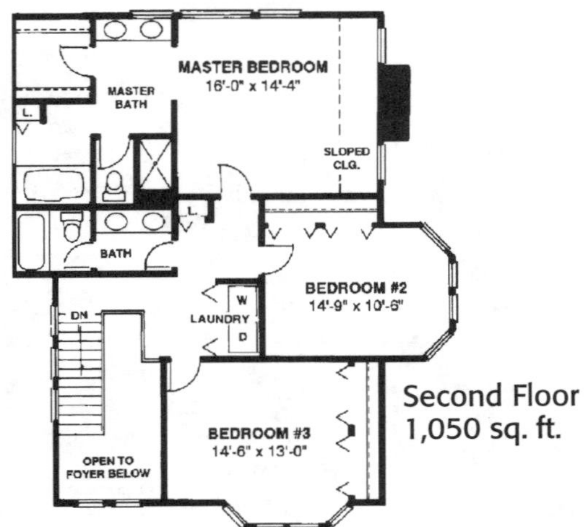
MASTER BEDROOM
16'-0" x 14'-4"
MASTER BATH
SLOPED CLG.
BATH
BEDROOM #2
14'-9" x 10'-6"
LAUNDRY
DN
BEDROOM #3
14'-6" x 13'-0"
OPEN TO FOYER BELOW

Second Floor
1,050 sq. ft.

Plan #531-1300

Price Code D

Total Living Area: 2,253 Sq. Ft.

Home has 3 bedrooms, 2 1/2 baths, 2-car garage and basement foundation.

Special features

- Great room joined by covered porch
- Secluded parlor provides area for peace and quiet or private office
- Sloped ceiling adds drama to master suite
- Great room and kitchen/breakfast area combine for large open living

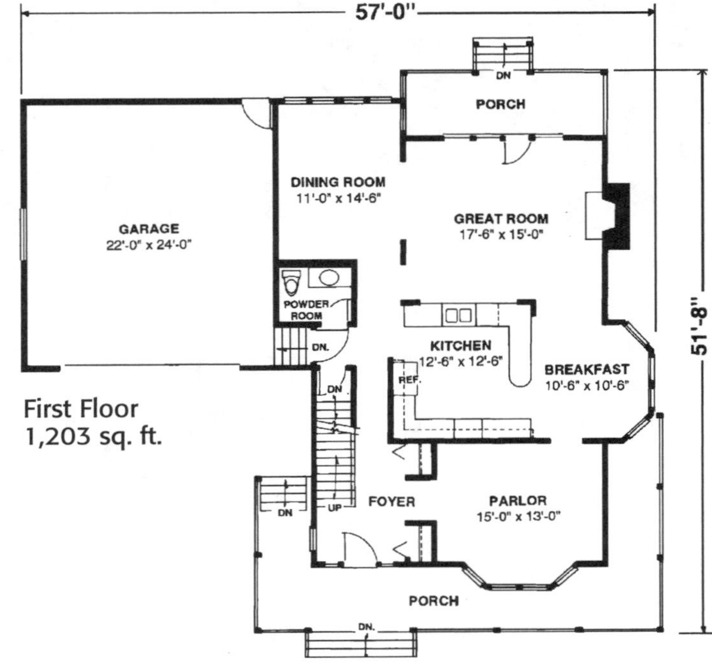
57'-0"
51'-8"
PORCH
DN
DINING ROOM
11'-0" x 14'-6"
GREAT ROOM
17'-6" x 15'-0"
GARAGE
22'-0" x 24'-0"
POWDER ROOM
KITCHEN
12'-6" x 12'-6"
REF.
BREAKFAST
10'-6" x 10'-6"
FOYER
UP
PARLOR
15'-0" x 13'-0"
PORCH

First Floor
1,203 sq. ft.

TO ORDER BLUEPRINTS USE THE FORM ON PAGE 290 OR CALL TOLL-FREE **1-800-DREAM HOME** (373-2646)

Covered Breezeway To Garage

LOWE'S

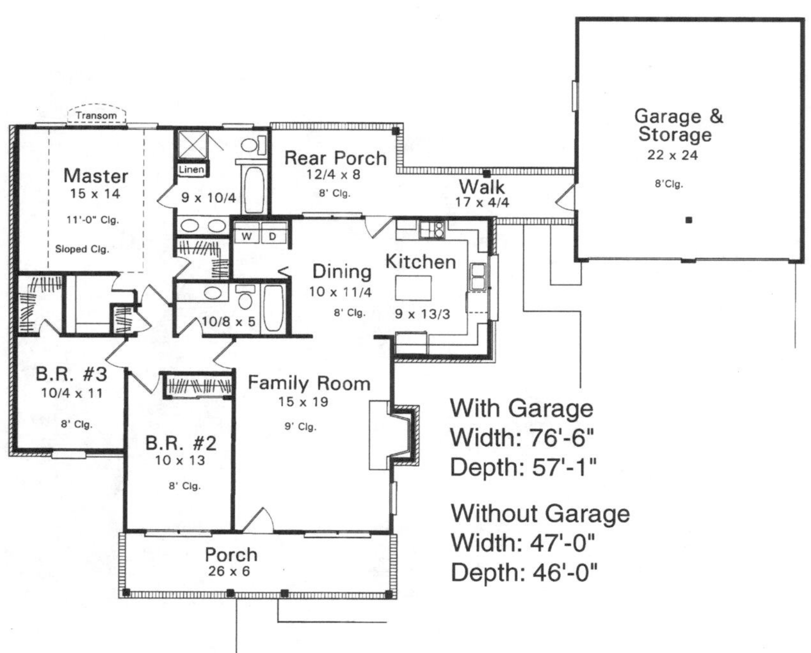
Transom
Master
15 x 14
11'-0" Clg.
Sloped Clg.
Linen
9 x 10/4
W D
Rear Porch
12/4 x 8
8' Clg.
Walk
17 x 4/4
Garage &
Storage
22 x 24
8'Clg.
Dining
10 x 11/4
8' Clg.
Kitchen
9 x 13/3
10/8 x 5
B.R. #3
10/4 x 11
8' Clg.
Family Room
15 x 19
9' Clg.
B.R. #2
10 x 13
8' Clg.
Porch
26 x 6
With Garage
Width: 76'-6"
Depth: 57'-1"
Without Garage
Width: 47'-0"
Depth: 46'-0"

Plan #531-GM-1406

Price Code A

Total Living Area: 1,406 Sq. Ft.

Home has 3 bedrooms, 2 baths, 2-car detached garage and slab or crawl space foundation, please specify when ordering.

Special features

- Enter family room from charming covered front porch and find fireplace and lots of windows
- Kitchen and dining areas merge becoming gathering place
- Master bedroom has sloped ceiling

Plan #531-BF-3007

Price Code E

Total Living Area: 3,012 Sq. Ft.

Home has 4 bedrooms, 3 1/2 baths, 2-car side entry garage and crawl space, slab or basement foundation, please specify when ordering.

Special features

- Master suite has sitting area with entertainment center/library
- Utility room has a sink and includes lots of storage and counterspace
- Future space above garage has its own stairway

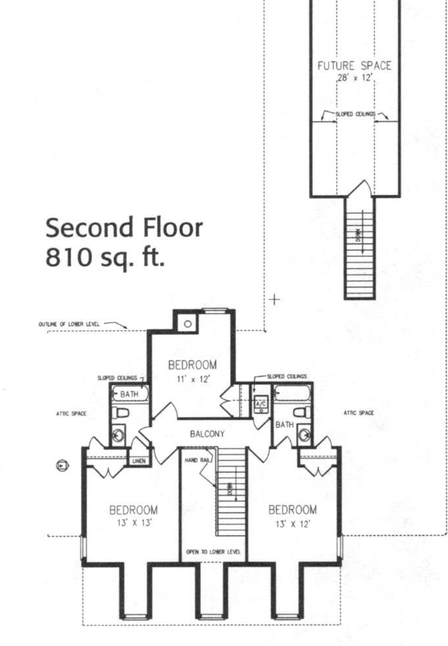
FUTURE SPACE
28' x 12'
BEDROOM
11' x 12'
BATH
BALCONY
BEDROOM
13' x 13'
BEDROOM
13' x 12'

Second Floor
810 sq. ft.

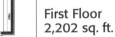

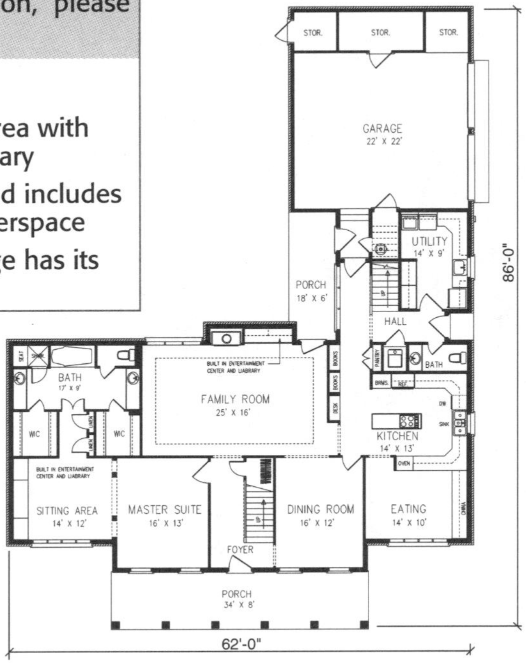

First Floor
2,202 sq. ft.

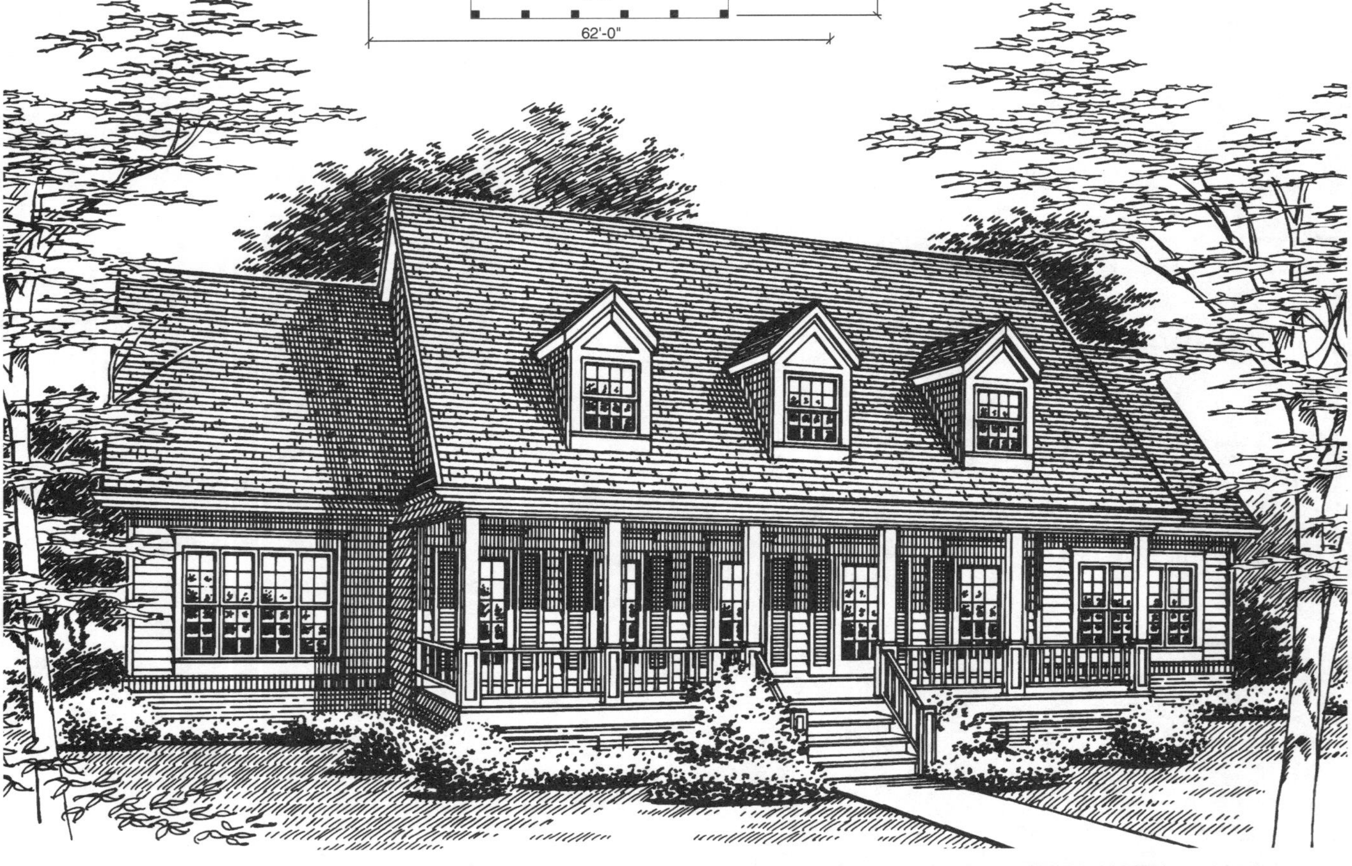

Cheerful And Bright Great Room

LOWE'S

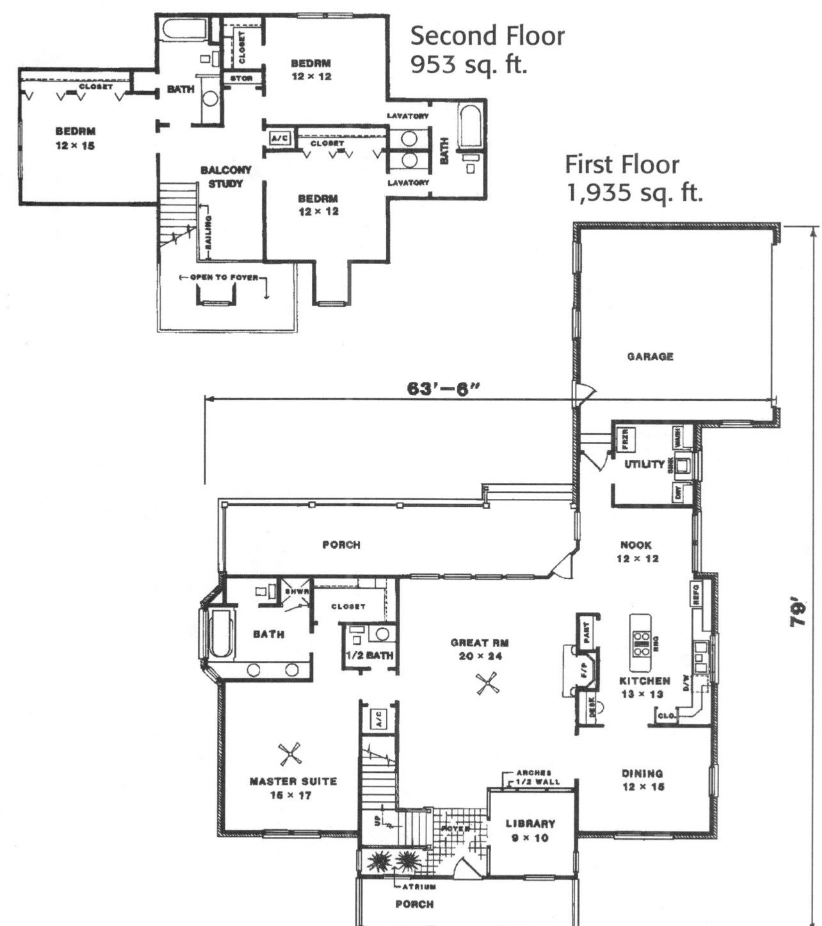
Second Floor
953 sq. ft.
BEDRM
12 × 12
CLOSET
BATH
STOR
BEDRM
12 × 15
A/C
CLOSET
LAVATORY
BATH
LAVATORY
BALCONY
STUDY
BEDRM
12 × 12
RAILING
OPEN TO FOYER
First Floor
1,935 sq. ft.
GARAGE
63'–6"
79'
FRZR
WASH
UTILITY
SINK
DRY
PORCH
NOOK
12 × 12
REFG
SHWR
CLOSET
BATH
1/2 BATH
GREAT RM
20 × 24
PANT
RNG
F/P
KITCHEN
13 × 13
DESK
D/W
CLO.
A/C
MASTER SUITE
15 × 17
ARCHES
1/2 WALL
DINING
12 × 15
UP
FOYER
LIBRARY
9 × 10
ATRIUM
PORCH

Plan #531-VL2888

Price Code E

Total Living Area: 2,888 Sq. Ft.

Home has 4 bedrooms, 3 1/2 baths, 2-car side entry garage and slab foundation.

Special features

- An arched half wall accents secluded library
- First floor master suite has a spacious bath with tub-in-a-bay
- Kitchen has center island with cooktop for convenience
- 9' ceilings on the first floor

Plan #531-1134-1

partial basement/crawl space

Plan #531-1134-2

crawl space

Price Code D

Total Living Area: 2,212 Sq. Ft.

Home has 3 bedrooms, 2 1/2 baths, 2-car garage and partial basement/crawl space or crawl space foundation, please specify when ordering.

Special features

- Louvered shutters, turned posts with railing and garage door detailing are a few inviting features
- Dining room is spacious and borders a well-planned U-shaped kitchen and breakfast room
- Colossal walk-in closet and oversized private bath are part of a gracious master suite

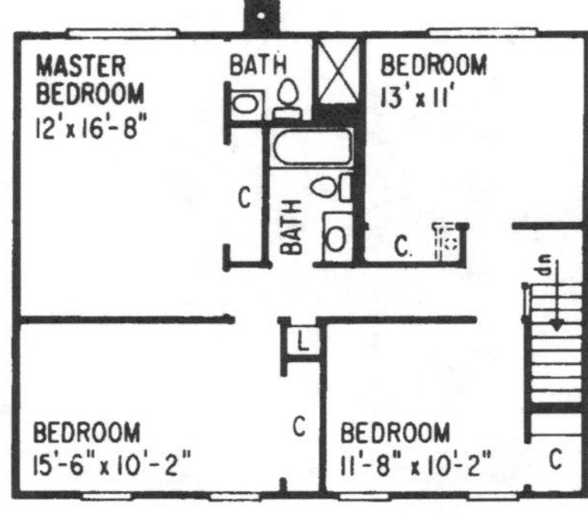
MASTER BEDROOM 12'x16'-8"
BATH
BEDROOM 13'x11'
C
BATH
C.
dn
L
BEDROOM 15'-6"x10'-2"
C
BEDROOM 11'-8"x10'-2"
C

Second Floor
Four bedroom option
952 sq. ft.

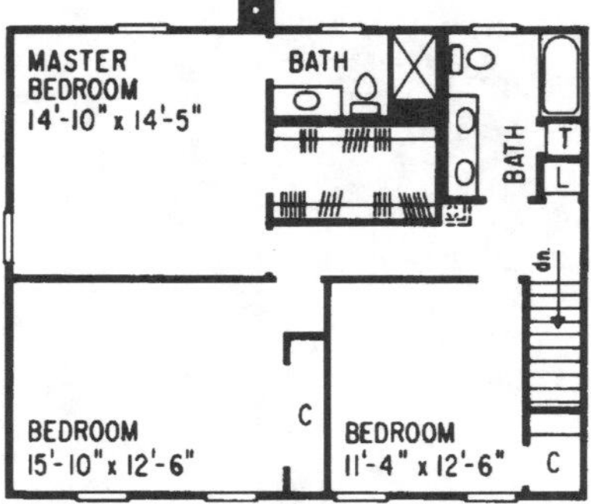
MASTER BEDROOM 14'-10"x14'-5"
BATH
BATH
T
L
dn
BEDROOM 15'-10"x12'-6"
C
BEDROOM 11'-4"x12'-6"
C

Second Floor
Three bedroom option
952 sq. ft.

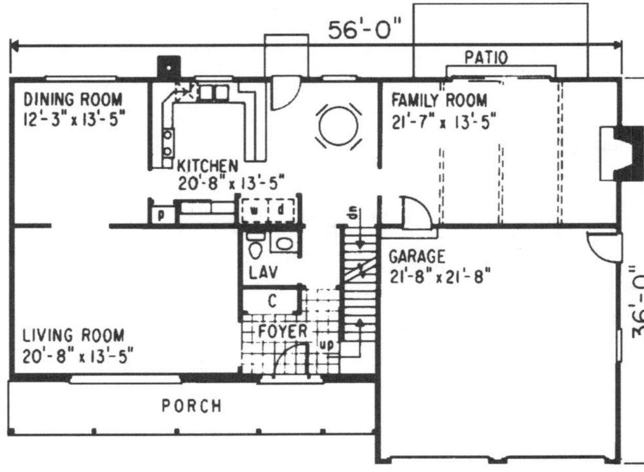
56'-0"
PATIO
DINING ROOM 12'-3"x13'-5"
KITCHEN 20'-8"x13'-5"
FAMILY ROOM 21'-7"x13'-5"
p
w d
dn
LAV
C
FOYER
up
GARAGE 21'-8"x21'-8"
LIVING ROOM 20'-8"x13'-5"
PORCH
36'-0"

First Floor
1,260 sq. ft.

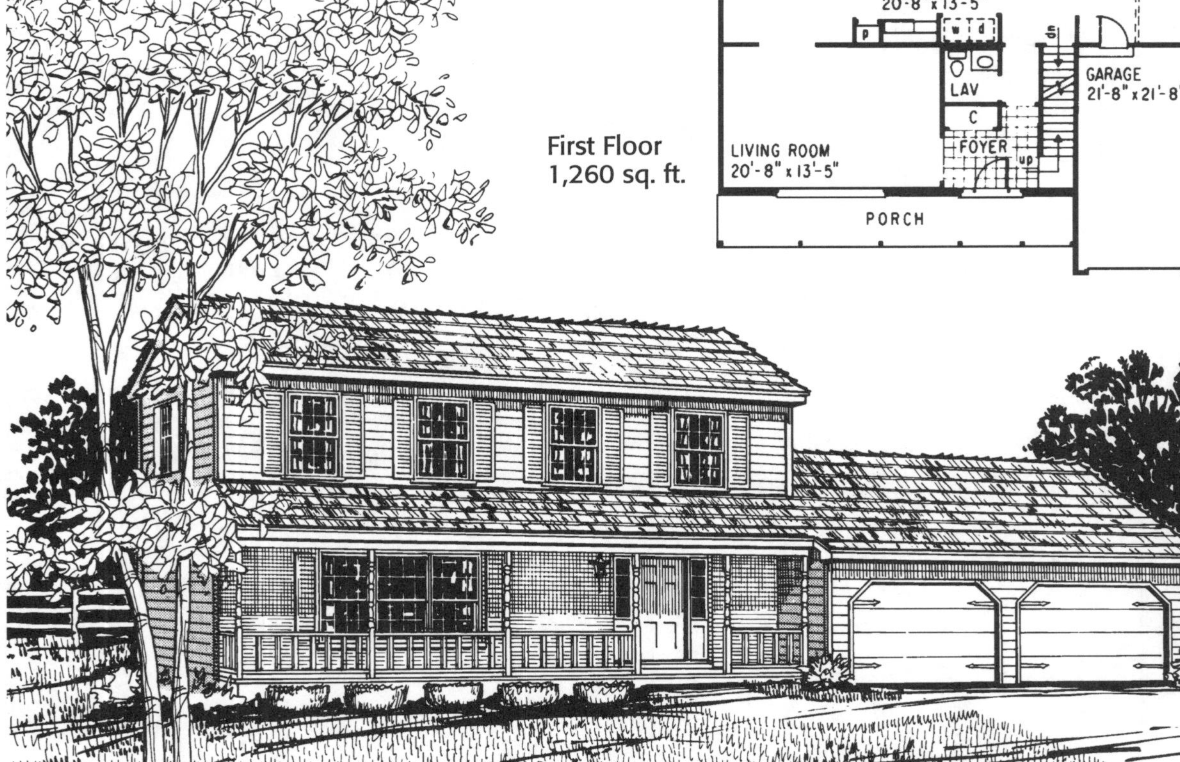

TO ORDER BLUEPRINTS USE THE FORM ON PAGE 290 OR CALL TOLL-FREE **1-800-DREAM HOME** (373-2646)

Kitchen Overlooks Living Area

LOWE'S

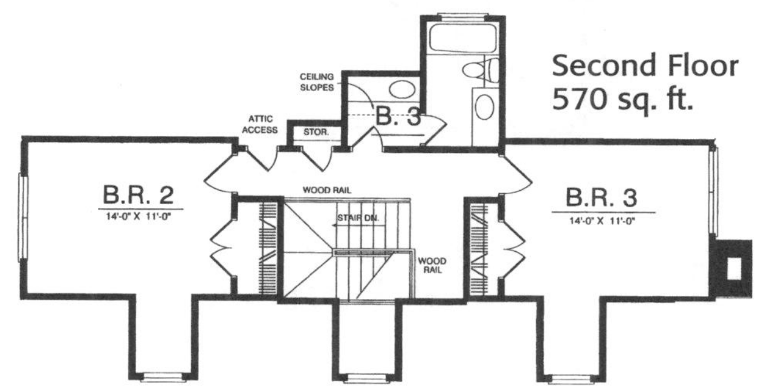
CEILING SLOPES
ATTIC ACCESS
STOR.
B. 3
B.R. 2
14'-0" X 11'-0"
WOOD RAIL
STAIR DN.
WOOD RAIL
B.R. 3
14'-0" X 11'-0"

Second Floor
570 sq. ft.

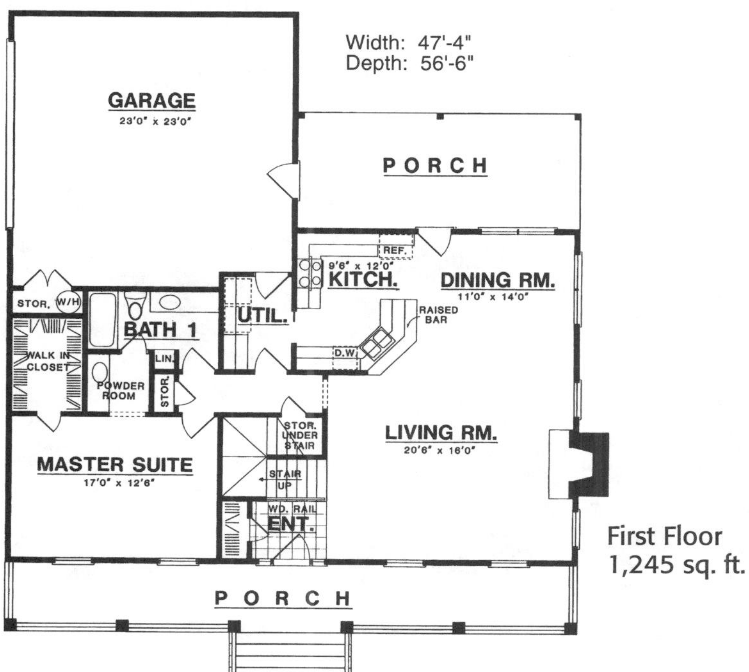
GARAGE
23'0" x 23'0"
PORCH
REF.
9'6" x 12'0"
KITCH.
DINING RM.
11'0" x 14'0"
RAISED BAR
STOR.
W/H
BATH 1
UTIL.
D.W.
WALK IN CLOSET
LIN.
POWDER ROOM
STOR.
STOR. UNDER STAIR
LIVING RM.
20'6" x 16'0"
MASTER SUITE
17'0" x 12'6"
STAIR UP
WD. RAIL
ENT.
PORCH

Width: 47'-4"
Depth: 56'-6"

First Floor
1,245 sq. ft.

Plan #531-RDD-1815-8

Price Code C

Total Living Area: 1,815 Sq. Ft.

Home has 3 bedrooms, 2 baths, 2-car side entry garage and basement, crawl space or slab foundation, please specify when ordering.

Special features

- Front and back porches unite this home with the outdoors
- First floor master suite with walk-in closet
- Well-designed kitchen opens to dining room and features raised breakfast bar

Plan #531-JA-53394

Price Code B

Total Living Area: 1,763 Sq. Ft.

Home has 3 bedrooms, 2 baths, 2-car garage and basement foundation.

Special features

- Master suite features a private master bath and bay-shaped sitting area with French doors
- Large foyer leads to a bright spacious living room
- Large open kitchen features a central work island with lots of extra storage space

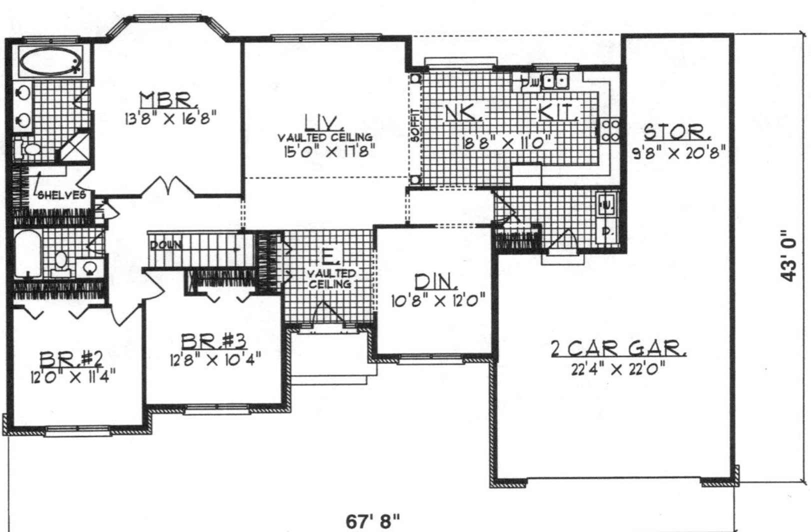
MBR.
13'8" X 16'8"
LIV.
VAULTED CEILING
15'0" X 17'8"
SOFFIT
NK.
KIT.
18'8" X 11'0"
DW
STOR.
9'8" X 20'8"
SHELVES
DOWN
E.
VAULTED CEILING
DIN.
10'8" X 12'0"
BR.#2
12'0" X 11'4"
BR.#3
12'8" X 10'4"
2 CAR GAR.
22'4" X 22'0"
43' 0"
67' 8"

Lovely Full-Width Column Porch

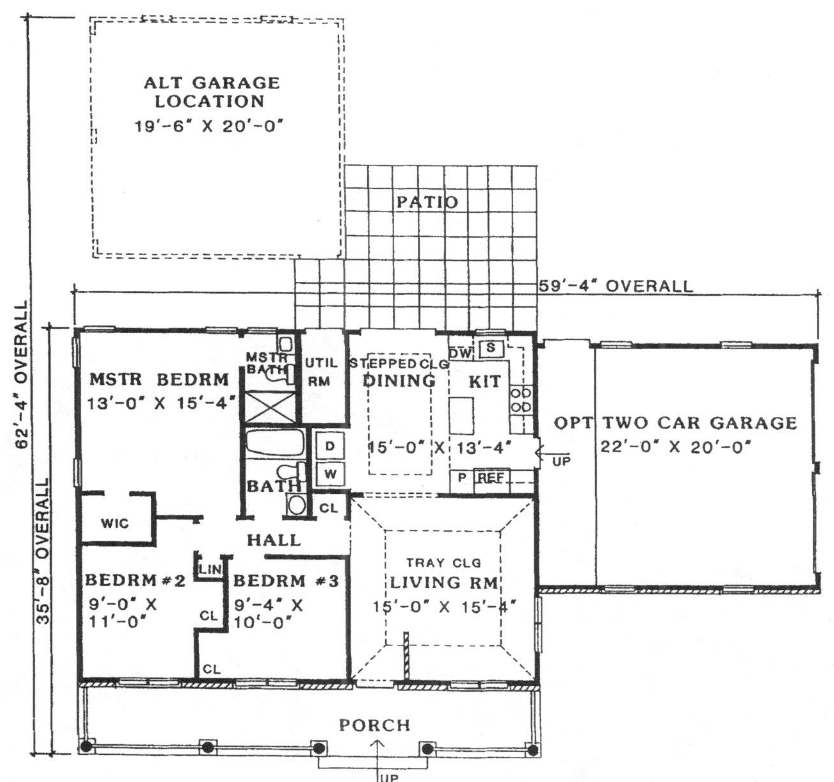
ALT GARAGE LOCATION
19'-6" X 20'-0"
PATIO
59'-4" OVERALL
62'-4" OVERALL
35'-8" OVERALL
MSTR BEDRM
13'-0" X 15'-4"
MSTR BATH
UTIL RM
STEPPED CLG DINING
15'-0" X 13'-4"
DW
S
KIT
OPT TWO CAR GARAGE
22'-0" X 20'-0"
UP
D
W
P
REF
BATH
CL
WIC
HALL
LIN
BEDRM #2
9'-0" X 11'-0"
BEDRM #3
9'-4" X 10'-0"
CL
CL
TRAY CLG
LIVING RM
15'-0" X 15'-4"
PORCH
UP

Plan #531-AX-91316

Price Code AA

Total Living Area: 1,097 Sq. Ft.

Home has 3 bedrooms, 2 baths, optional 2-car side entry garage and basement, crawl space or slab foundation, please specify when ordering.

Special features

- Living room provides expansive view to the rear
- Master suite includes its own private bath and walk-in closet
- U-shaped kitchen wraps around center island

Open Floor Plan With Plenty Of Light

Second Floor
729 sq. ft.

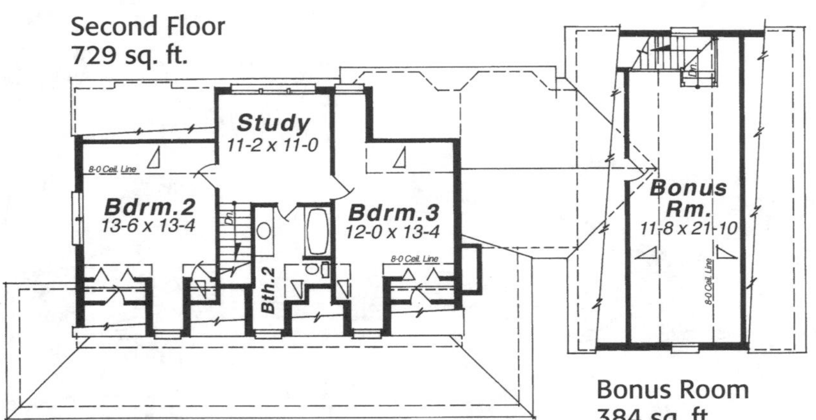
Study
11-2 x 11-0
Bdrm.2
13-6 x 13-4
Bdrm.3
12-0 x 13-4
Bth.2
8-0 Ceil. Line
Bonus
Rm.
11-8 x 21-10

Bonus Room
384 sq. ft.

Plan #531-JV-2091-A

Price Code D

Total Living Area: 2,475 Sq. Ft.

Home has 3 bedrooms, 2 1/2 baths, 2-car side entry garage and walk-out basement foundation.

Special features

- Country feeling with wrap-around porch and dormered front
- Open floor plan with living and dining areas combined has access to a sun deck
- First floor master bedroom with many luxuries

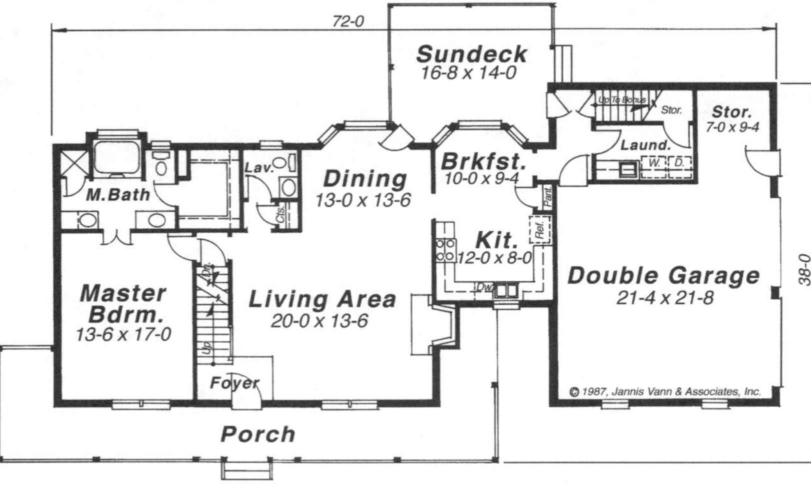
72-0
Sundeck
16-8 x 14-0
Stor.
7-0 x 9-4
Laund.
M.Bath
Lav.
Dining
13-0 x 13-6
Brkfst.
10-0 x 9-4
Kit.
12-0 x 8-0
Master
Bdrm.
13-6 x 17-0
Living Area
20-0 x 13-6
Double Garage
21-4 x 21-8
38-0
Foyer
Porch
© 1987, Jannis Vann & Associates, Inc.

First Floor
1,362 sq. ft.

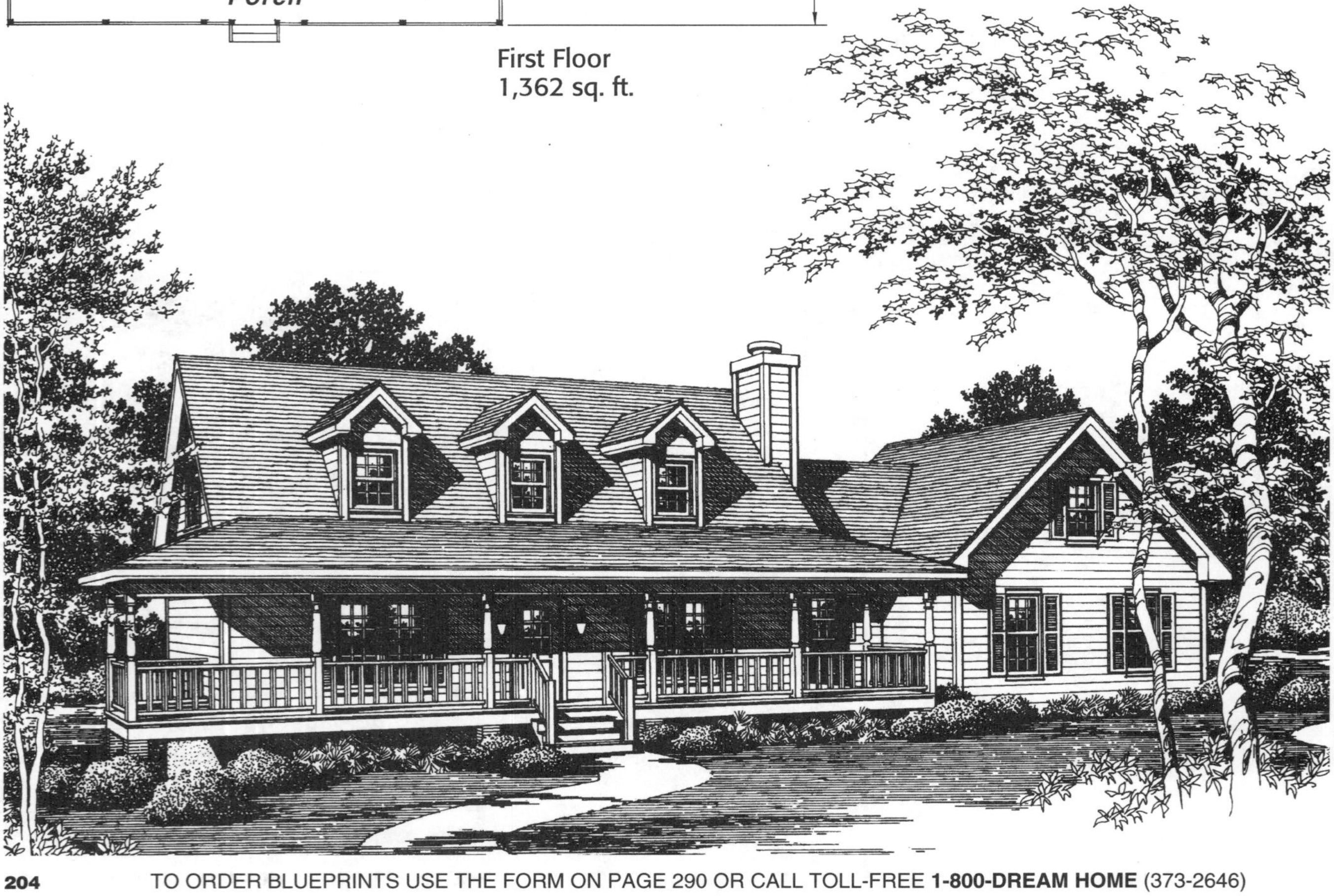

LOWE'S

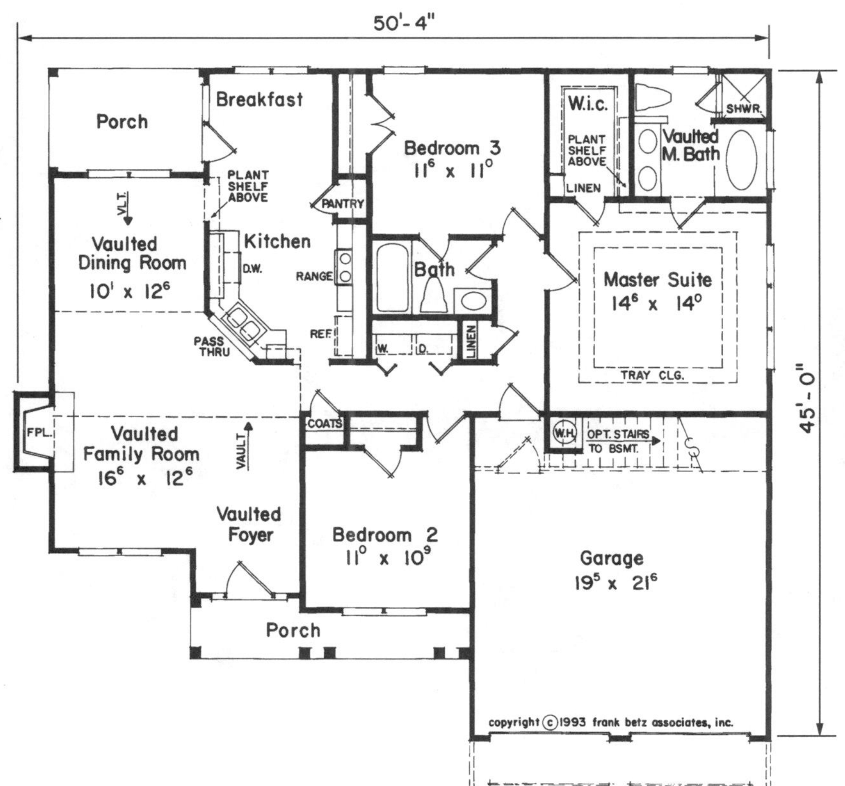
50'-4"
Porch
Breakfast
Bedroom 3
11⁶ x 11⁰
W.i.c.
PLANT SHELF ABOVE
LINEN
Vaulted M. Bath
SHWR.
PLANT SHELF ABOVE
PANTRY
VLT.
Vaulted Dining Room
10' x 12⁶
Kitchen
D.W.
RANGE
Bath
Master Suite
14⁶ x 14⁰
PASS THRU
REF.
W.
D.
LINEN
TRAY CLG.
FPL.
COATS
W.H.
OPT. STAIRS TO BSMT.
Vaulted Family Room
16⁶ x 12⁶
VAULT
45'-0"
Vaulted Foyer
Bedroom 2
11⁰ x 10⁹
Garage
19⁵ x 21⁶
Porch
copyright (c) 1993 frank betz associates, inc.

Plan #531-FB-676

Price Code A

Total Living Area: 1,373 Sq. Ft.

Home has 3 bedrooms, 2 baths, 2-car garage and crawl space or walk-out basement foundation, please specify when ordering.

Special features

- 9' ceilings throughout this home
- Sunny breakfast room is very accessible to kitchen
- Kitchen has pass-through to vaulted family room

Superb Home Accented With Victorian Details

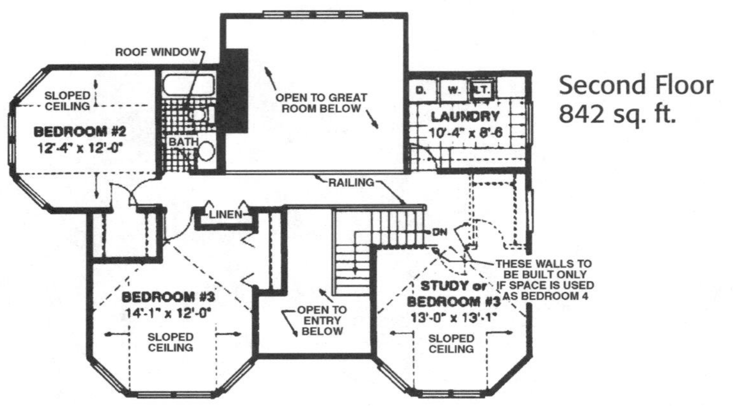
ROOF WINDOW
SLOPED CEILING
BEDROOM #2
12'-4" x 12'-0"
BATH
OPEN TO GREAT ROOM BELOW
D.
W.
LT.
LAUNDRY
10'-4" x 8'-6
RAILING
LINEN
DN
THESE WALLS TO BE BUILT ONLY IF SPACE IS USED AS BEDROOM 4
BEDROOM #3
14'-1" x 12'-0"
SLOPED CEILING
OPEN TO ENTRY BELOW
STUDY or BEDROOM #3
13'-0" x 13'-1"
SLOPED CEILING

Second Floor
842 sq. ft.

Plan #531-1307

Price Code D

Total Living Area: 2,370 Sq. Ft.

Home has 4 bedrooms, 2 1/2 baths, 2-car garage and basement foundation.

Special features

- Master suite filled with extras like unique master bath and lots of storage
- Extending off great room is a bright sun room with access to a deck
- Compact kitchen with nook creates useful breakfast area

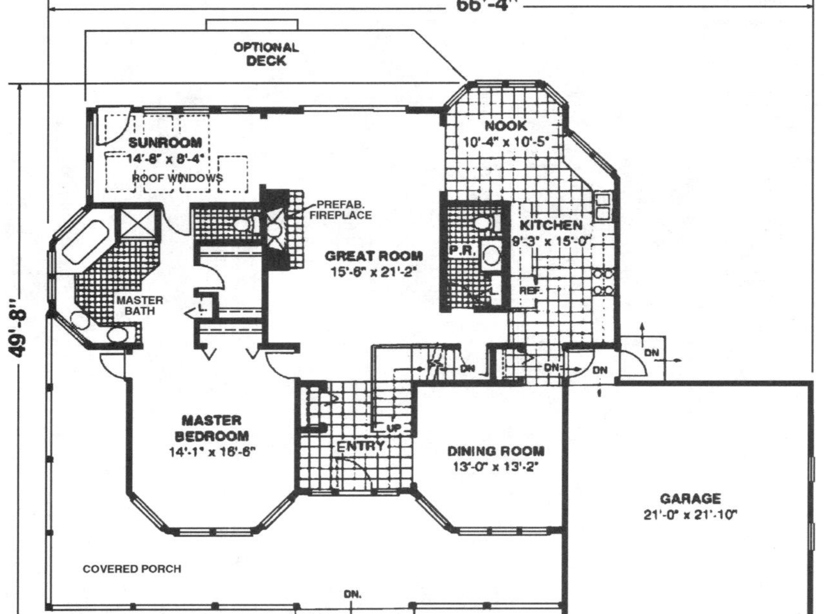
66'-4"
OPTIONAL DECK
NOOK
10'-4" x 10'-5"
SUNROOM
14'-8" x 8'-4"
ROOF WINDOWS
PREFAB. FIREPLACE
KITCHEN
9'-3" x 15'-0"
GREAT ROOM
15'-6" x 21'-2"
P.R.
REF.
MASTER BATH
49'-8"
DN
MASTER BEDROOM
14'-1" x 16'-6"
UP
ENTRY
DINING ROOM
13'-0" x 13'-2"
GARAGE
21'-0" x 21'-10"
COVERED PORCH
DN.

First Floor
1,578 sq. ft.

TO ORDER BLUEPRINTS USE THE FORM ON PAGE 290 OR CALL TOLL-FREE **1-800-DREAM HOME** (373-2646)

Traditional Ranch With Extras

LOWE'S

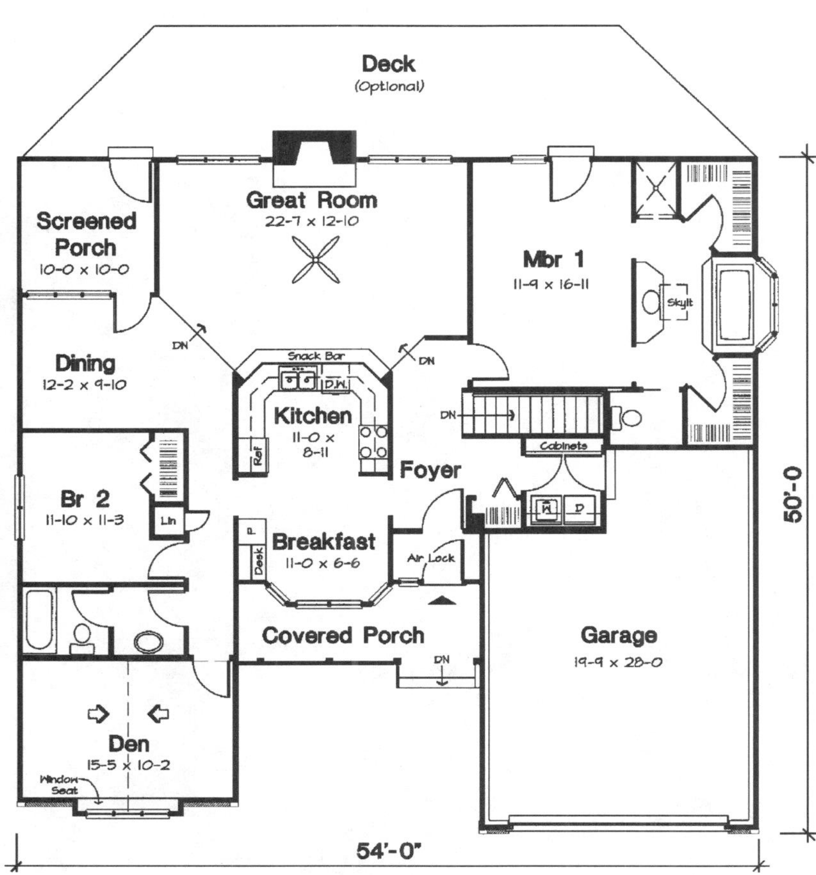
Deck
(Optional)
Screened Porch
10-0 x 10-0
Great Room
22-7 x 12-10
Mbr 1
11-9 x 16-11
Skylt
Dining
12-2 x 9-10
Snack Bar
D.W.
Kitchen
11-0 x 8-11
Ref
DN
Cabinets
Foyer
Br 2
11-10 x 11-3
Lin
Breakfast
11-0 x 6-6
Desk
Air Lock
Covered Porch
Garage
19-9 x 28-0
Den
15-5 x 10-2
Window Seat
50'-0
54'-0"

Plan #531-GH-24714

Price Code B

Total Living Area: 1,771 Sq. Ft.

Home has 2 bedrooms, 2 baths, 2-car garage and basement, crawl space or slab foundation, please specify when ordering.

Special features

- Den has sloped ceiling and charming window seat
- Private master bedroom has access outdoors
- Central kitchen allows for convenient access when entertaining

Plan #531-AM2155A

Price Code C

Total Living Area: 1,958 Sq. Ft.

Home has 3 bedrooms, 2 1/2 baths, 2-car garage and crawl space foundation.

Special features

- Cozy great room features fireplace and access to wrap-around porch
- Angled kitchen overlooks into breakfast nook
- All bedrooms located on second floor for privacy
- Bay window brightens den/parlor

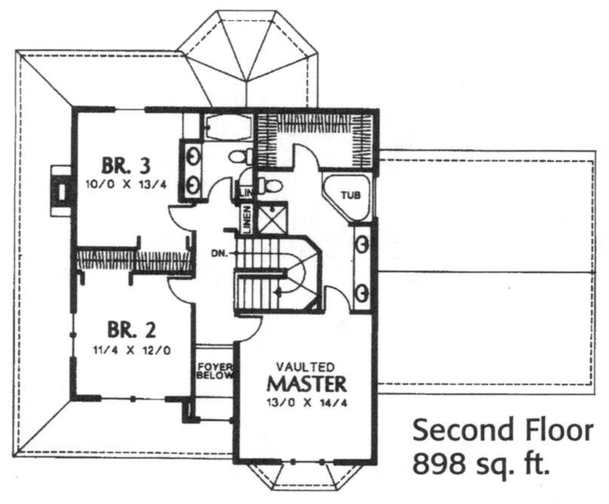
BR. 3
10/0 X 13/4
BR. 2
11/4 X 12/0
FOYER BELOW
VAULTED
MASTER
13/0 X 14/4
TUB
LINEN
DN.

Second Floor
898 sq. ft.

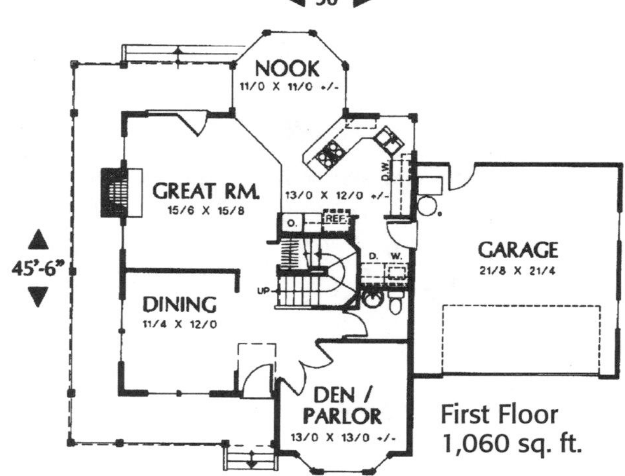
56'
NOOK
11/0 X 11/0 +/-
GREAT RM.
15/6 X 15/8
13/0 X 12/0 +/-
GARAGE
21/8 X 21/4
45'-6"
DINING
11/4 X 12/0
DEN / PARLOR
13/0 X 13/0 +/-
UP
D. W.

First Floor
1,060 sq. ft.

LOWE'S

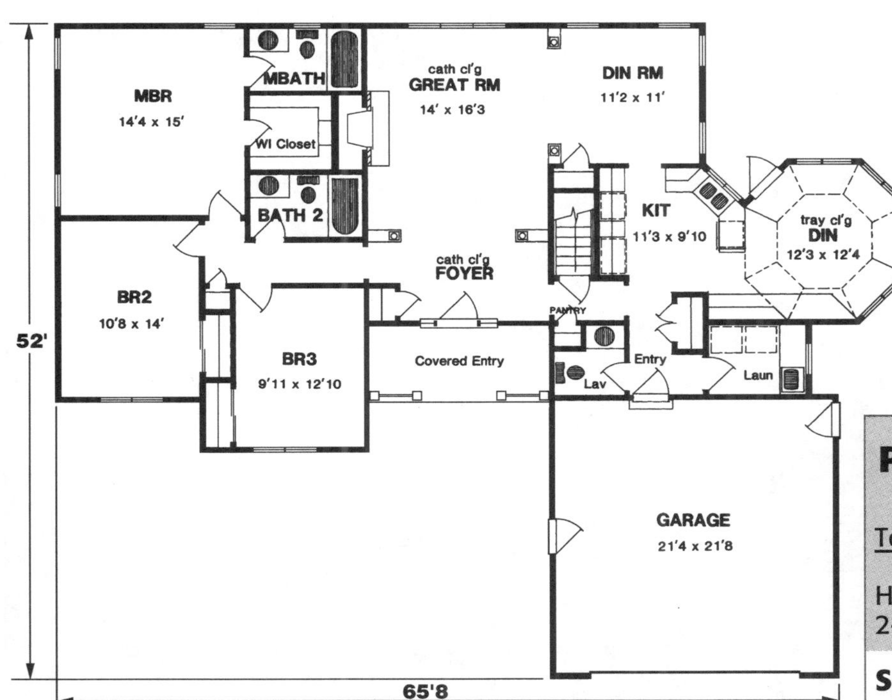
MBR
14'4 x 15'
MBATH
WI Closet
BATH 2
cath cl'g
GREAT RM
14' x 16'3
DIN RM
11'2 x 11'
KIT
11'3 x 9'10
tray cl'g
DIN
12'3 x 12'4
cath cl'g
FOYER
PANTRY
BR2
10'8 x 14'
BR3
9'11 x 12'10
Covered Entry
Entry
Lav
Laun
GARAGE
21'4 x 21'8
52'
65'8

Plan #531-JFD-10-1692-1

Price Code B

Total Living Area: 1,692 Sq. Ft.

Home has 3 bedrooms, 2 1/2 baths, 2-car garage and basement foundation.

Special features

- Dining area adds interest and a sunny atmosphere
- Great room is centrally located and includes an oversized fireplace
- Handy powder room located near kitchen and laundry area

TO ORDER BLUEPRINTS USE THE FORM ON PAGE 290 OR CALL TOLL-FREE **1-800-DREAM HOME** (373-2646)

Charming Country Facade

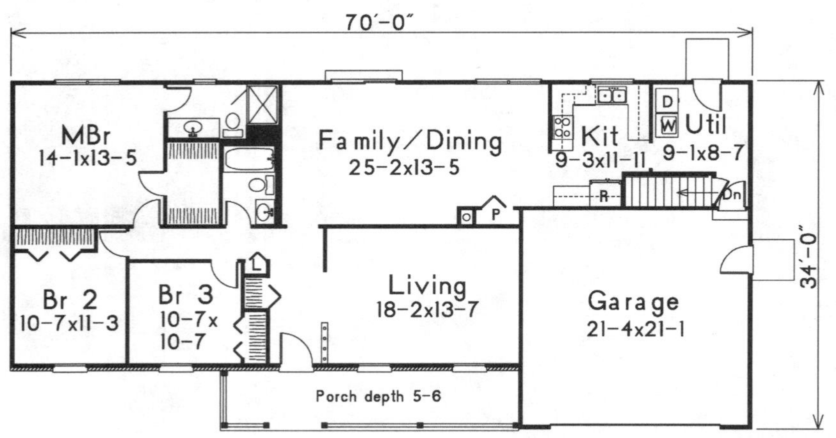
70'-0"
34'-0"
MBr
14-1x13-5
Family/Dining
25-2x13-5
Kit
9-3x11-11
Util
9-1x8-7
D
W
R
Dn
P
Br 2
10-7x11-3
Br 3
10-7x
10-7
Living
18-2x13-7
Garage
21-4x21-1
Porch depth 5-6

Plan #531-1101

Price Code B

Total Living Area: 1,643 Sq. Ft.

Home has 3 bedrooms, 2 baths, 2-car garage and basement foundation, drawings also include crawl space and slab foundations.

Special features

- Attractive front entry porch gives this ranch a country accent
- Spacious family room is the focal point of this design
- Kitchen and utility room are conveniently located near gathering areas
- Formal living room in the front of the home provides area for quiet and privacy
- Master suite has view to the rear of the home and a generous walk-in closet

Narrow Lot Home With Rear Entry Garage

LOWE'S

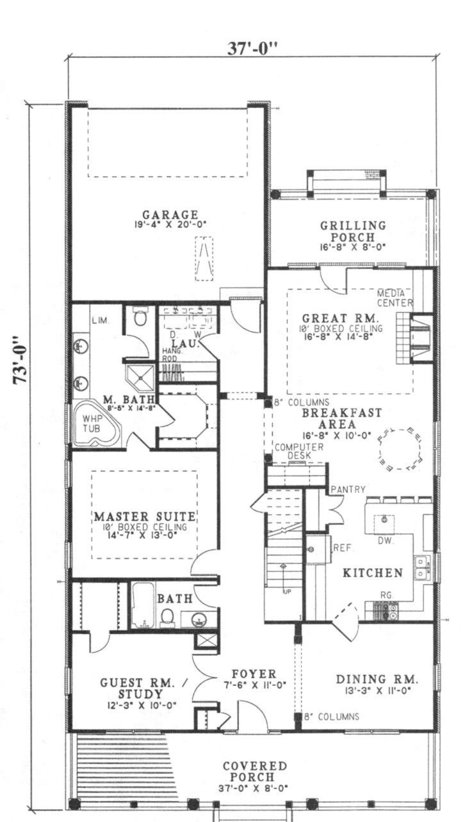

37'-0"
73'-0"
GARAGE
19'-4" X 20'-0"
GRILLING PORCH
16'-8" X 8'-0"
GREAT RM.
10' BOXED CEILING
16'-8" X 14'-8"
MEDIA CENTER
LIM
LAU.
M. BATH
8'-6" X 14'-8"
WHP TUB
8" COLUMNS
BREAKFAST AREA
16'-8" X 10'-0"
COMPUTER DESK
PANTRY
MASTER SUITE
10' BOXED CEILING
14'-7" X 13'-0"
REF
DW.
KITCHEN
RG
BATH
UP
GUEST RM. / STUDY
12'-3" X 10'-0"
FOYER
7'-6" X 11'-0"
DINING RM.
13'-3" X 11'-0"
8" COLUMNS
COVERED PORCH
37'-0" X 8'-0"

First Floor
1,713 sq. ft.

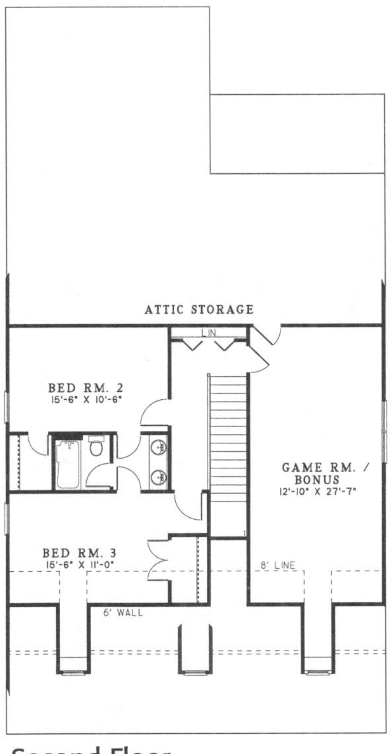

ATTIC STORAGE
LIN
BED RM. 2
15'-6" X 10'-6"
GAME RM. / BONUS
12'-10" X 27'-7"
BED RM. 3
15'-6" X 11'-0"
8' LINE
6' WALL

Second Floor
994 sq. ft.

Plan #531-NDG-307

Price Code E

Total Living Area: 2,707 Sq. Ft.

Home has 4 bedrooms, 3 baths, 2-car rear entry garage and crawl space or slab foundation, please specify when ordering.

Special features

- Double-doors lead into handsome study
- Kitchen and breakfast room flow into great room creating terrific gathering place
- Second floor includes bonus space perfect for game room

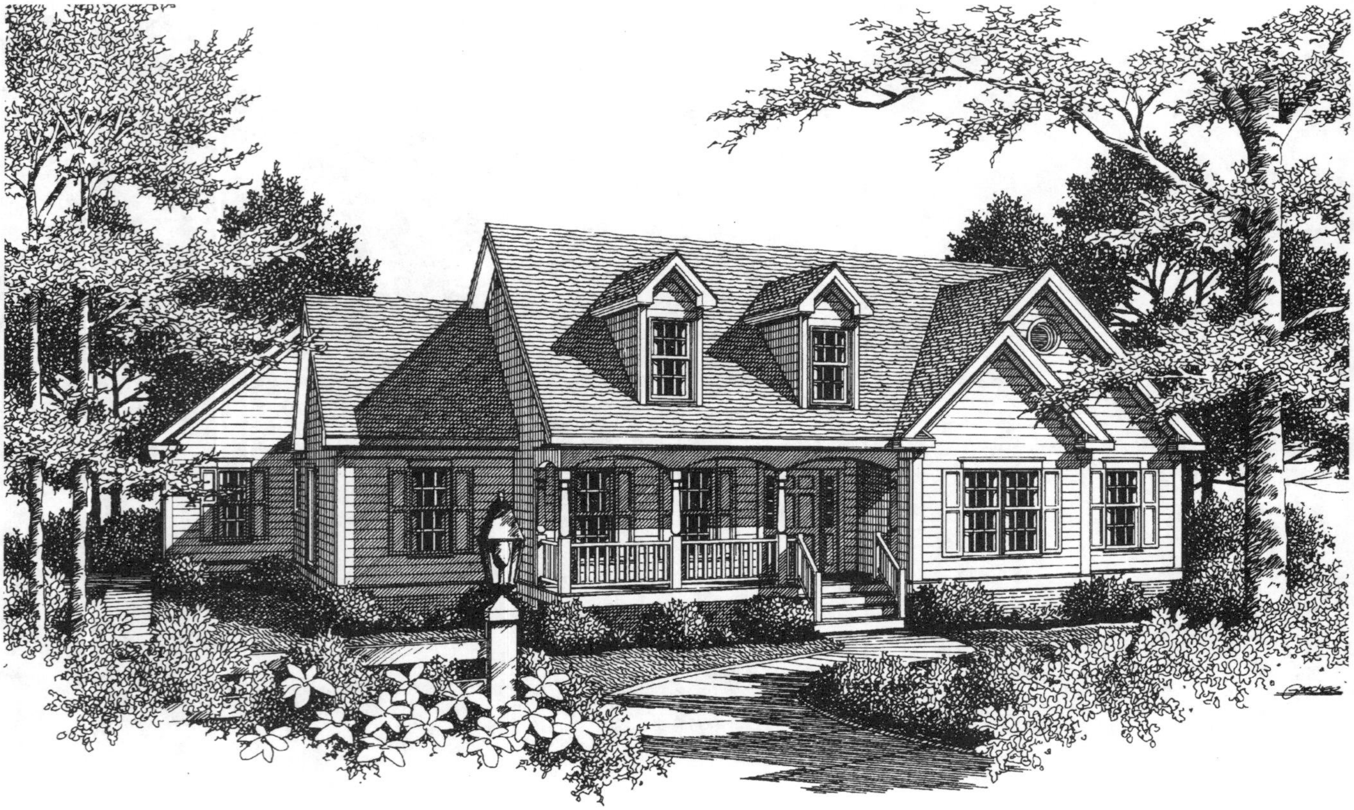

Classy Master Bedroom

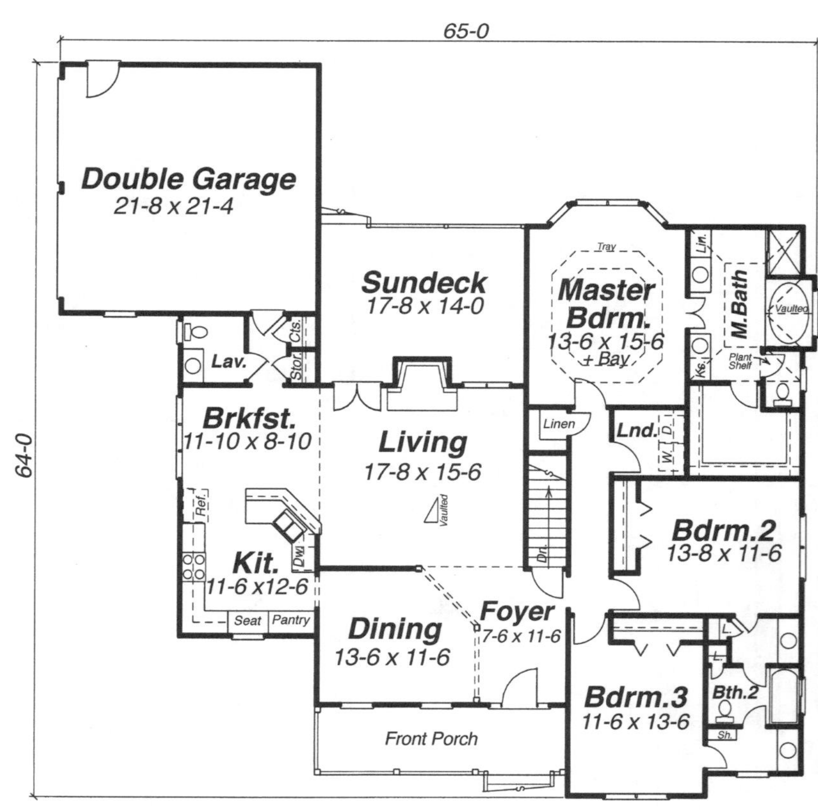
65-0
64-0
Double Garage
21-8 x 21-4
Sundeck
17-8 x 14-0
Tray
Master Bdrm.
13-6 x 15-6
+ Bay
Lin.
M.Bath
Vaulted
Plant Shelf
Lav.
Cts.
Stor.
Brkfst.
11-10 x 8-10
Living
17-8 x 15-6
Vaulted
Linen
Lnd.
W
D
Ref.
Kit.
11-6 x12-6
Dw
Seat
Pantry
Dn.
Bdrm.2
13-8 x 11-6
Foyer
7-6 x 11-6
Dining
13-6 x 11-6
Bdrm.3
11-6 x 13-6
Bth.2
Sh
Front Porch

Plan #531-JV-2012-A-SJ

Price Code C

Total Living Area: 2,012 Sq. Ft.

Home has 3 bedrooms, 2 1/2 baths, 2-car side entry garage and basement foundation.

Special features

- Kitchen with eat-in breakfast bar overlooks breakfast room
- Sunny living room is open and airy with vaulted ceiling
- Secondary bedrooms with convenient vanities skillfully share bath

LOWE'S

Plan #531-DBI-2332

Price Code F

Total Living Area: 3,775 Sq. Ft.

Home has 4 bedrooms, 3 1/2 baths, 3-car side entry garage and basement foundation.

Special features

- Screened porch off living and dining areas brings the outdoors in
- Bookshelves flank each side of the fireplace in the family room
- Built-in bookshelves in den
- Second floor master suite has bayed sitting area and a wonderful bath

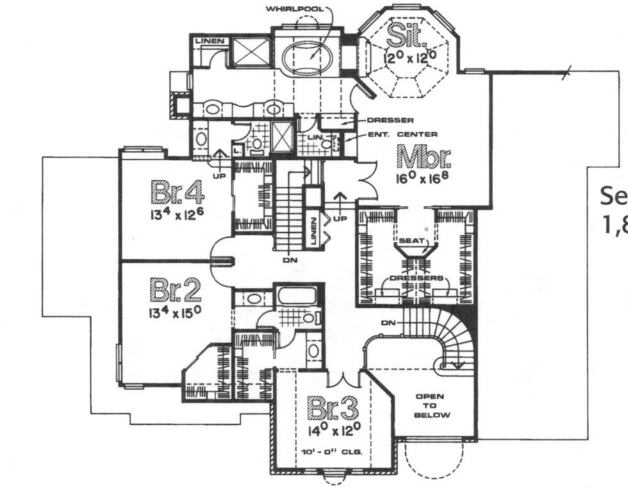
WHIRLPOOL
LINEN
Sit.
12⁰ x 12⁰
DRESSER
ENT. CENTER
Mbr.
16⁰ x 16⁸
Br.4
13⁴ x 12⁶
LINEN
UP
DN
SEAT
DRESSERS
Br.2
13⁴ x 15⁰
Br.3
14⁰ x 12⁰
10'-0" CLG.
OPEN TO BELOW

Second Floor
1,852 sq. ft.

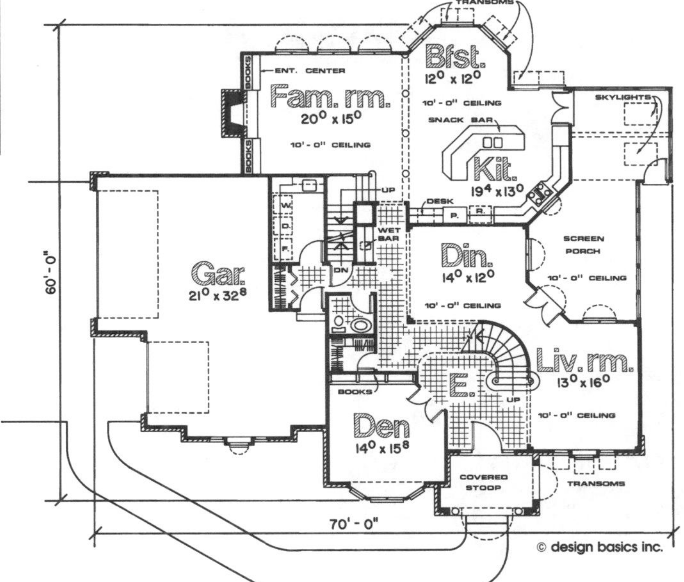
TRANSOMS
Bfst.
12⁰ x 12⁰
10'-0" CEILING
ENT. CENTER
BOOKS
Fam. rm.
20⁰ x 15⁰
10'-0" CEILING
SNACK BAR
Kit.
19⁴ x 13⁰
SKYLIGHTS
DESK
WET BAR
Din.
14⁰ x 12⁰
10'-0" CEILING
SCREEN PORCH
10'-0" CEILING
Gar.
21⁰ x 32⁸
60'-0"
Liv. rm.
13⁰ x 16⁰
10'-0" CEILING
E.
UP
BOOKS
Den
14⁰ x 15⁸
COVERED STOOP
TRANSOMS
70'-0"
© design basics inc.

First Floor
1,923 sq. ft.

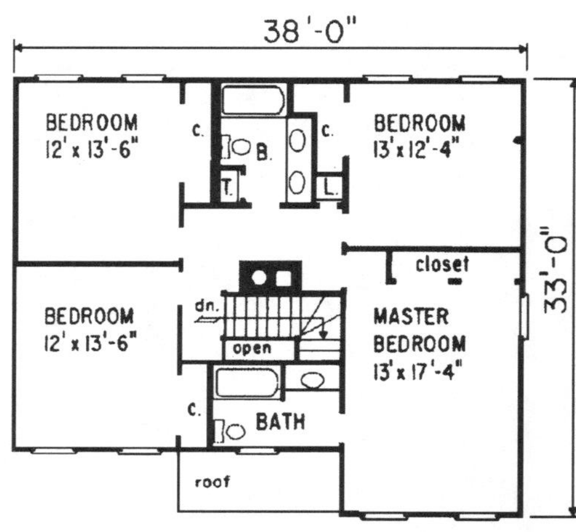
38'-0"
BEDROOM
12' x 13'-6"
c.
B.
T.
c.
BEDROOM
13' x 12'-4"
L.
closet
BEDROOM
12' x 13'-6"
dn.
open
MASTER
BEDROOM
13' x 17'-4"
c.
BATH
roof
33'-0"

Second Floor
1,132 sq. ft.

Plan #531-1211-1
partial basement/crawl space
Plan #531-1211-2
crawl space & slab
Price Code D

Total Living Area: 2,414 Sq. Ft.

Home has 4 bedrooms, 2 1/2 baths, 2-car garage and partial basement/crawl space, crawl space or slab foundation, please specify when ordering.

Special features

- Distinguished exterior reflects country living
- Partially open foyer creates impressive entry
- Informal great room features awesome size
- Spacious second floor bedrooms surround convenient hall bath with all the amenities

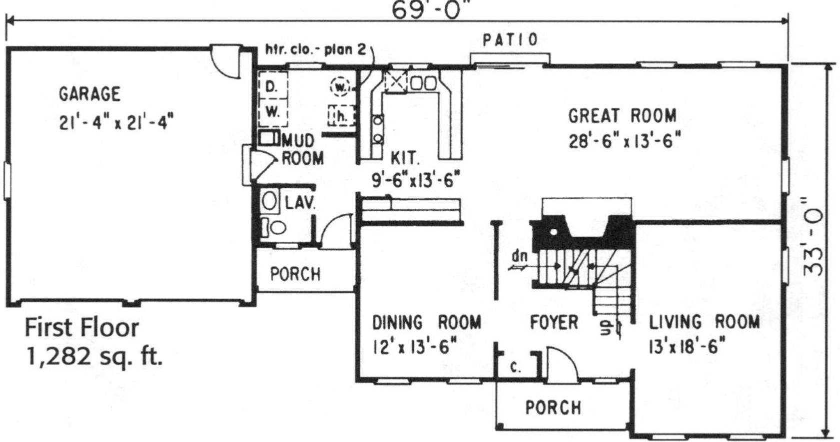
69'-0"
htr. clo. - plan 2
PATIO
GARAGE
21'-4" x 21'-4"
D.
W.
w.
h.
MUD
ROOM
KIT.
9'-6" x 13'-6"
GREAT ROOM
28'-6" x 13'-6"
LAV.
PORCH
dn
DINING ROOM
12' x 13'-6"
FOYER
up
LIVING ROOM
13' x 18'-6"
c.
PORCH
33'-0"

First Floor
1,282 sq. ft.

TO ORDER BLUEPRINTS USE THE FORM ON PAGE 290 OR CALL TOLL-FREE **1-800-DREAM HOME** (373-2646)

Corner Fireplace In Great Room

LOWE'S

Plan #531-GH-24717

Price Code B

Total Living Area: 1,642 Sq. Ft.

Home has 3 bedrooms, 2 baths, 2-car garage and basement, crawl space or slab foundation, please specify when ordering.

Special features

- Built-in cabinet in dining room adds a custom feel
- Secondary bedrooms share an oversized bath
- Master bedroom includes private bath with dressing table

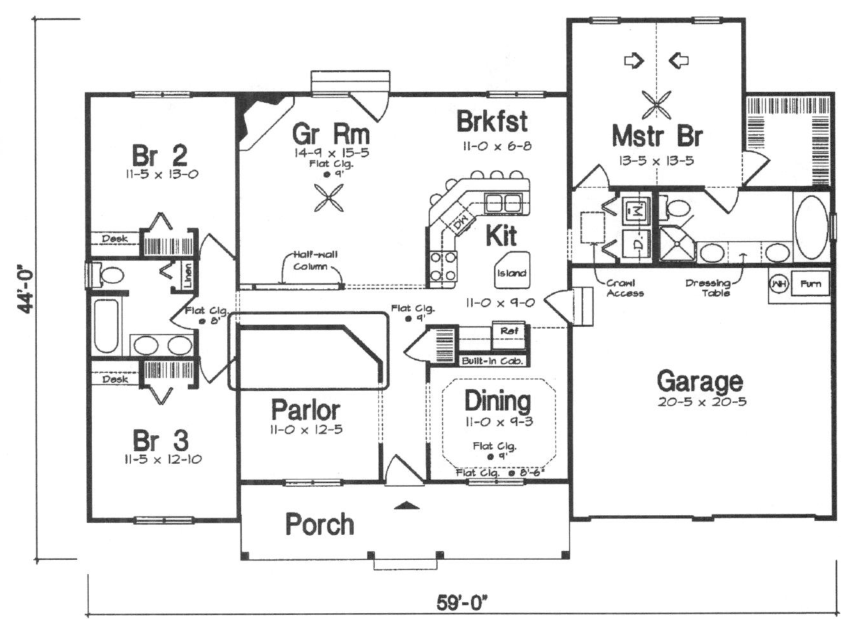
Gr Rm
14-9 x 15-5
Flat Clg.
9'
Brkfst
11-0 x 6-8
Mstr Br
13-5 x 13-5
Br 2
11-5 x 13-0
Desk
Linen
Half-wall
Column
Kit
Island
11-0 x 9-0
Flat Clg.
8'
Flat Clg.
9'
Crawl
Access
Dressing
Table
WH
Furn
Ref
Built-In Cab.
Garage
20-5 x 20-5
Dining
11-0 x 9-3
Flat Clg.
9'
Flat Clg. 8'-6"
Parlor
11-0 x 12-5
Br 3
11-5 x 12-10
Porch
44'-0"
59'-0"

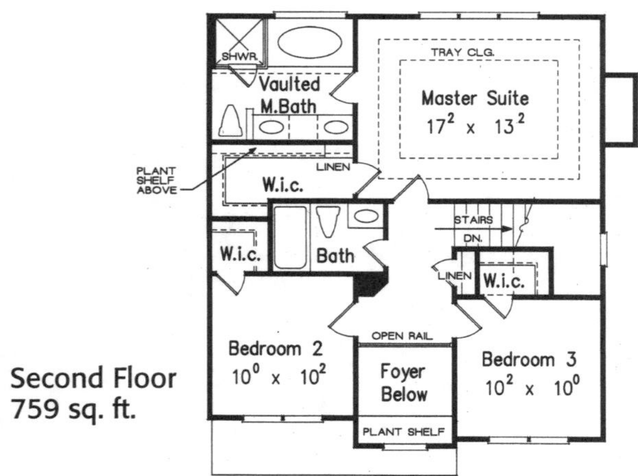
SHWR.
Vaulted M.Bath
TRAY CLG.
Master Suite
17^2 x 13^2
PLANT SHELF ABOVE
LINEN
W.i.c.
STAIRS DN.
W.i.c.
Bath
LINEN
W.i.c.
OPEN RAIL
Bedroom 2
10^0 x 10^2
Foyer Below
Bedroom 3
10^2 x 10^0
PLANT SHELF

Second Floor
759 sq. ft.

First Floor
1,103 sq. ft.

Plan #531-FB-959

Price Code C

Total Living Area: 1,862 Sq. Ft.

Home has 4 bedrooms, 3 baths, 2-car garage and basement or crawl space foundation, please specify when ordering.

Special features

- Dining and living rooms flank grand two-story foyer
- Open floor plan combines kitchen, breakfast and family rooms
- Study is tucked away on first floor for privacy
- Second floor bedrooms have walk-in closets

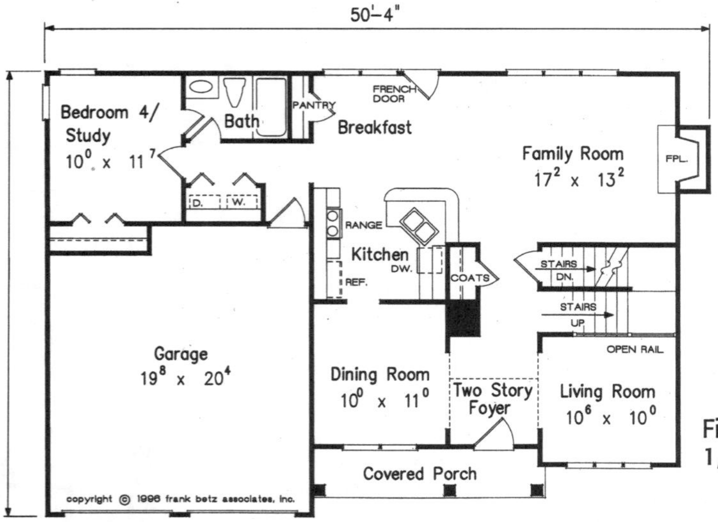

 TO ORDER BLUEPRINTS USE THE FORM ON PAGE 290 OR CALL TOLL-FREE **1-800-DREAM HOME** (373-2646)

Lovely Front Dormers

LOWE'S

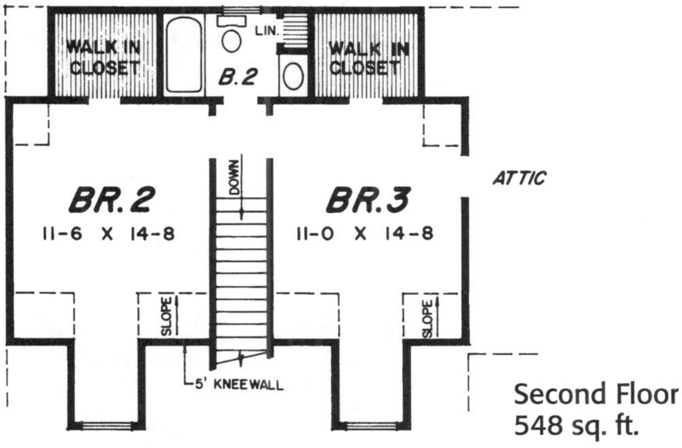
WALK IN CLOSET
LIN.
B.2
WALK IN CLOSET
ATTIC
BR.2
11-6 X 14-8
DOWN
BR.3
11-0 X 14-8
SLOPE
SLOPE
5' KNEEWALL

Second Floor
548 sq. ft.

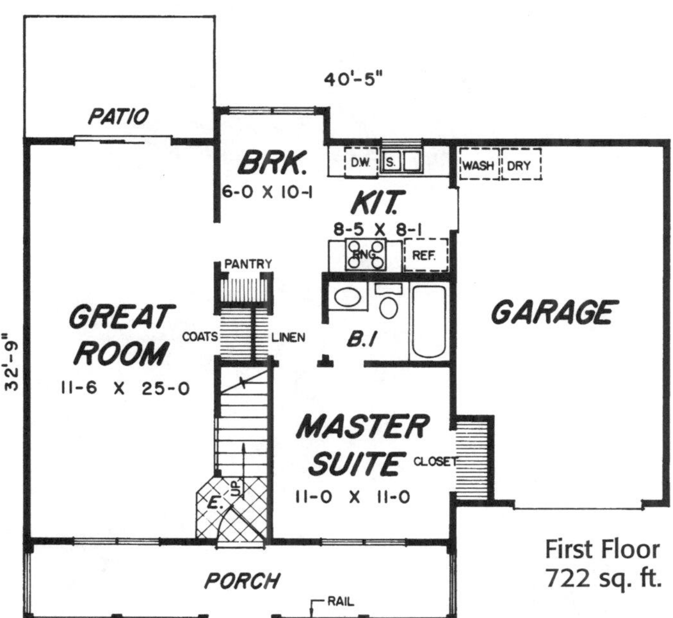
40'-5"
PATIO
BRK.
6-0 X 10-1
DW.
S.
WASH
DRY
KIT.
8-5 X 8-1
RNG.
REF.
PANTRY
GREAT ROOM
11-6 X 25-0
COATS
LINEN
B.1
GARAGE
32'-9"
MASTER SUITE
11-0 X 11-0
CLOSET
E.
UP
PORCH
RAIL

First Floor
722 sq. ft.

Plan #531-RJ-B123

Price Code A

Total Living Area: 1,270 Sq. Ft.

Home has 3 bedrooms, 2 baths, 1-car garage and slab or crawl space foundation, please specify when ordering.

Special features

- Convenient master suite on first floor
- Two secondary bedrooms on second floor each have a large walk-in closet and share a full bath
- Sunny breakfast room has lots of sunlight and easy access to great room and kitchen

LOWE'S

Perfect Home For Escaping To The Outdoors

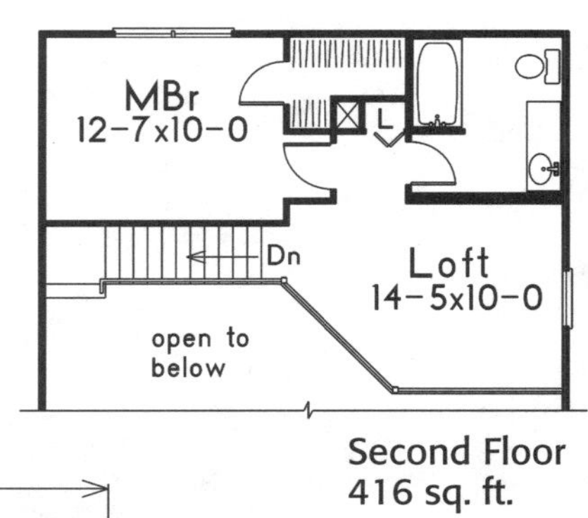
MBr
12-7x10-0
L
Dn
Loft
14-5x10-0
open to
below

Second Floor
416 sq. ft.

Plan #531-1293

Price Code A

Total Living Area: 1,200 Sq. Ft.

Home has 2 bedrooms, 2 baths and crawl space foundation.

Special features

- Enjoy lazy summer evenings on this magnificent porch
- Activity area has fireplace and ascending stair from cozy loft
- Kitchen features built-in pantry
- Master suite enjoys large bath, walk-in closet and cozy loft over-looking room below

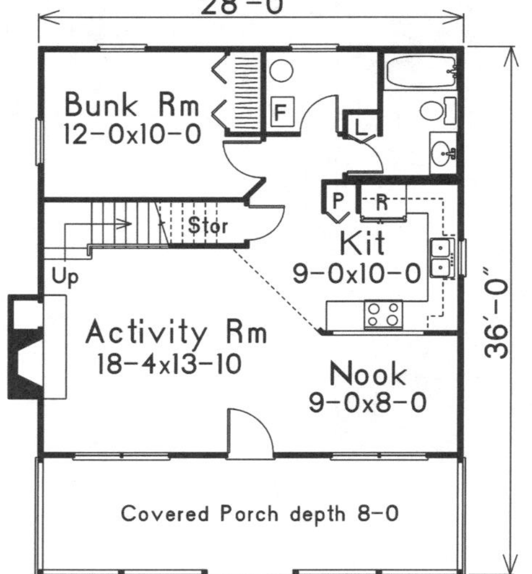
28′-0″
36′-0″
Bunk Rm
12-0x10-0
F
L
P
R
Stor
Up
Kit
9-0x10-0
Activity Rm
18-4x13-10
Nook
9-0x8-0
Covered Porch depth 8-0

First Floor
784 sq. ft.

LOWE'S

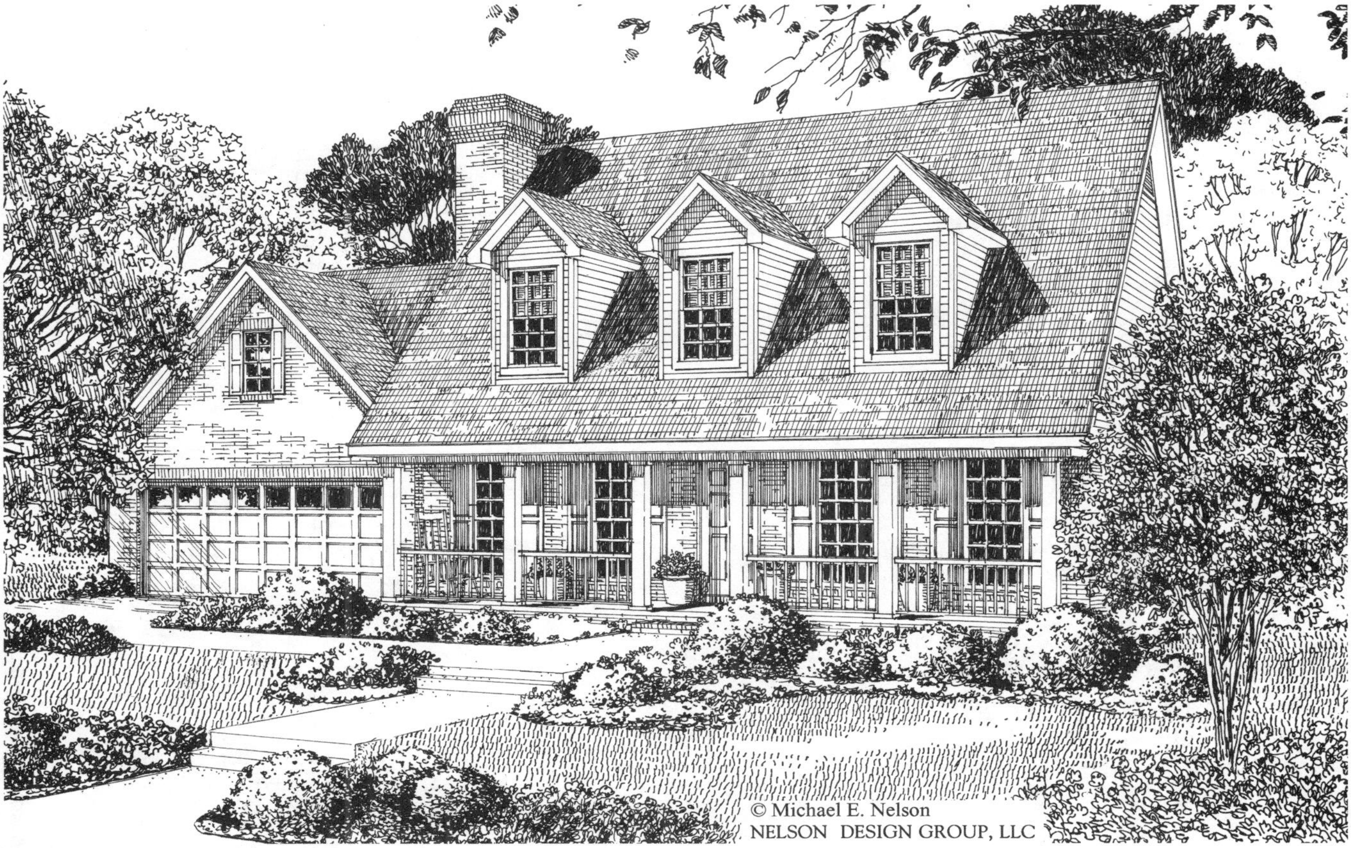

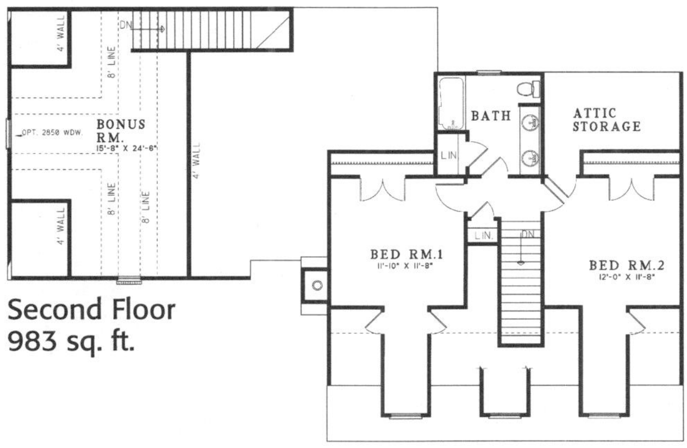
BONUS RM.
15'-8" X 24'-6"
OPT. 2650 WDW.
4' WALL
8' LINE
DN
BATH
LIN
ATTIC STORAGE
BED RM.1
11'-10" X 11'-8"
BED RM.2
12'-0" X 11'-8"

Second Floor
983 sq. ft.

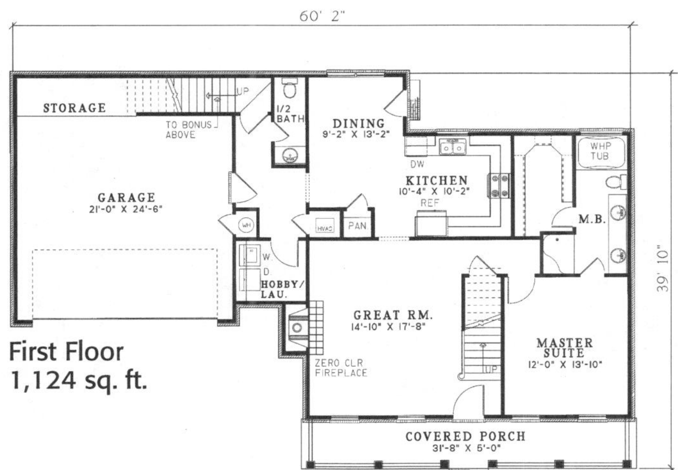
60' 2"
39' 10"
STORAGE
TO BONUS ABOVE
UP
1/2 BATH
DINING
9'-2" X 13'-2"
GARAGE
21'-0" X 24'-6"
KITCHEN
10'-4" X 10'-2"
DW
REF
PAN
HVAC
WHP TUB
M.B.
HOBBY/ LAU.
GREAT RM.
14'-10" X 17'-8"
ZERO CLR FIREPLACE
MASTER SUITE
12'-0" X 13'-10"
COVERED PORCH
31'-8" X 6'-0"

First Floor
1,124 sq. ft.

Plan #531-NDG-142

Price Code C

Total Living Area: 2,107 Sq. Ft.

Home has 3 bedrooms, 2 1/2 baths, 2-car garage and basement, crawl space or slab foundation, please specify when ordering.

Special features

- Kitchen has pantry and adjacent dining area
- Master bedroom with bath and large walk-in closet
- Second floor bedrooms have attic storage
- Rear stairs open into bonus room above garage

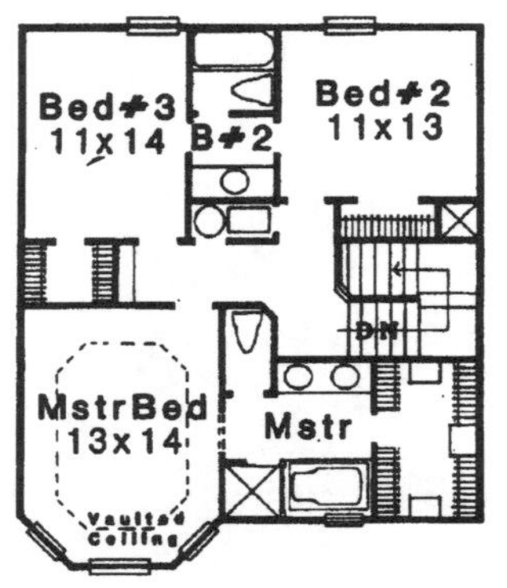
Bed#3
11x14
B#2
Bed#2
11x13
DN
MstrBed
13x14
Mstr
Vaulted
Ceiling

Second Floor
862 sq. ft.

Plan #531-FD7410

Price Code D

Total Living Area: 2,200 Sq. Ft.

Home has 3 bedrooms, 2 1/2 baths, 2-car garage and crawl space or slab foundation, please specify when ordering.

Special features

- Master bedroom has vaulted ceiling, spacious bath and enormous walk-in closet
- Spacious kitchen has efficient center island adding extra workspace
- Parlor/living room has gorgeous bay window looking out to covered front porch
- 9' ceiling on first floor

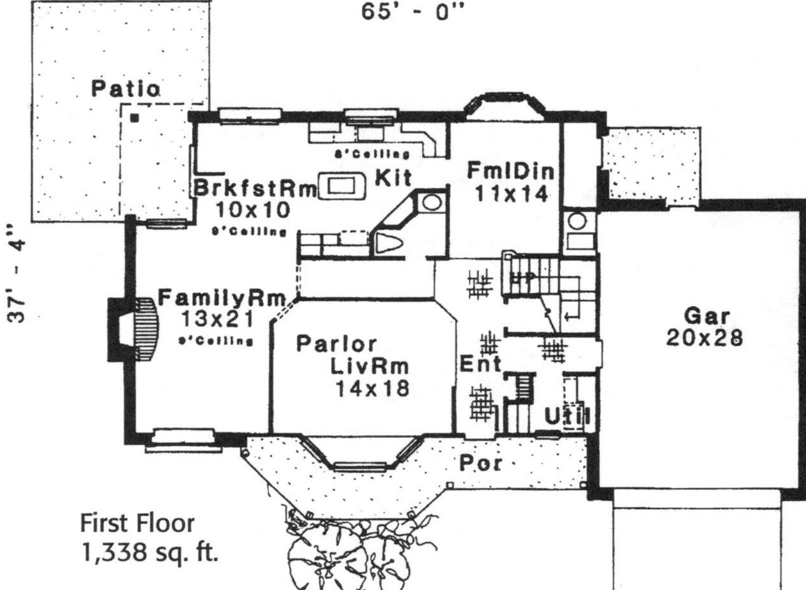
65' - 0"
37' - 4"
Patio
8'Ceiling
BrkfstRm
10x10
8'Ceiling
Kit
FmlDin
11x14
FamilyRm
13x21
8'Ceiling
Parlor
LivRm
14x18
UP
Ent
Util
Gar
20x28
Por

First Floor
1,338 sq. ft.

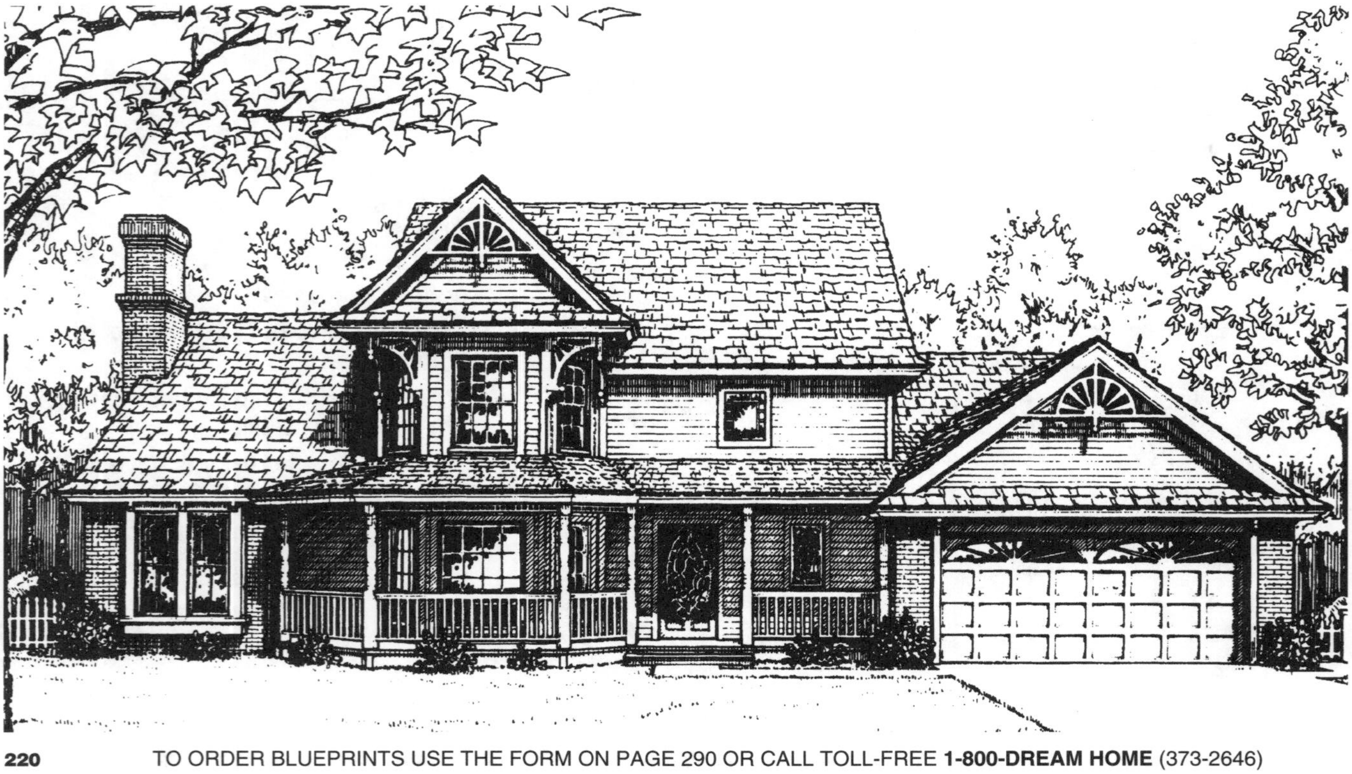

Two-Story Living Room

LOWE'S

Plan #531-BF-2108

Price Code C

Total Living Area: 2,194 Sq. Ft.

Home has 3 bedrooms, 3 1/2 baths, 2-car side entry garage and crawl space, slab or basement foundation, please specify when ordering.

Special features

- Energy efficient home with 2" x 6" exterior walls
- Utility room has laundry drop conveniently located next to kitchen
- Both second floor bedrooms have large closets and their own bath

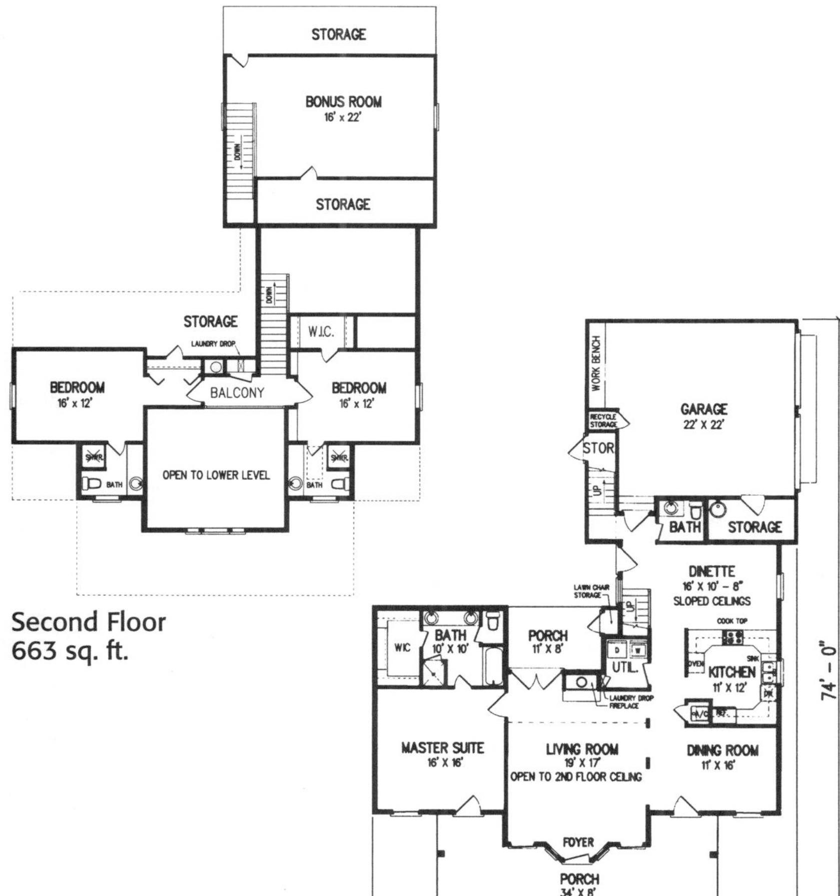
STORAGE
BONUS ROOM
16' x 22'
DOWN
STORAGE
STORAGE
LAUNDRY DROP
W.I.C.
BEDROOM
16' x 12'
BALCONY
BEDROOM
16' x 12'
BATH
OPEN TO LOWER LEVEL
BATH
WORK BENCH
GARAGE
22' X 22'
RECYCLE STORAGE
STOR
UP
BATH
STORAGE
DINETTE
16' X 10' - 8"
SLOPED CEILINGS
LAWN CHAIR STORAGE
UP
COOK TOP
WIC
BATH
10' X 10'
PORCH
11' X 8'
UTIL.
KITCHEN
11' X 12'
LAUNDRY DROP
FIREPLACE
MASTER SUITE
16' X 16'
LIVING ROOM
19' X 17'
OPEN TO 2ND FLOOR CEILING
DINING ROOM
11' X 16'
FOYER
PORCH
34' X 8'
52' – 0"
74' – 0"

Second Floor
663 sq. ft.

First Floor
1,531 sq. ft.

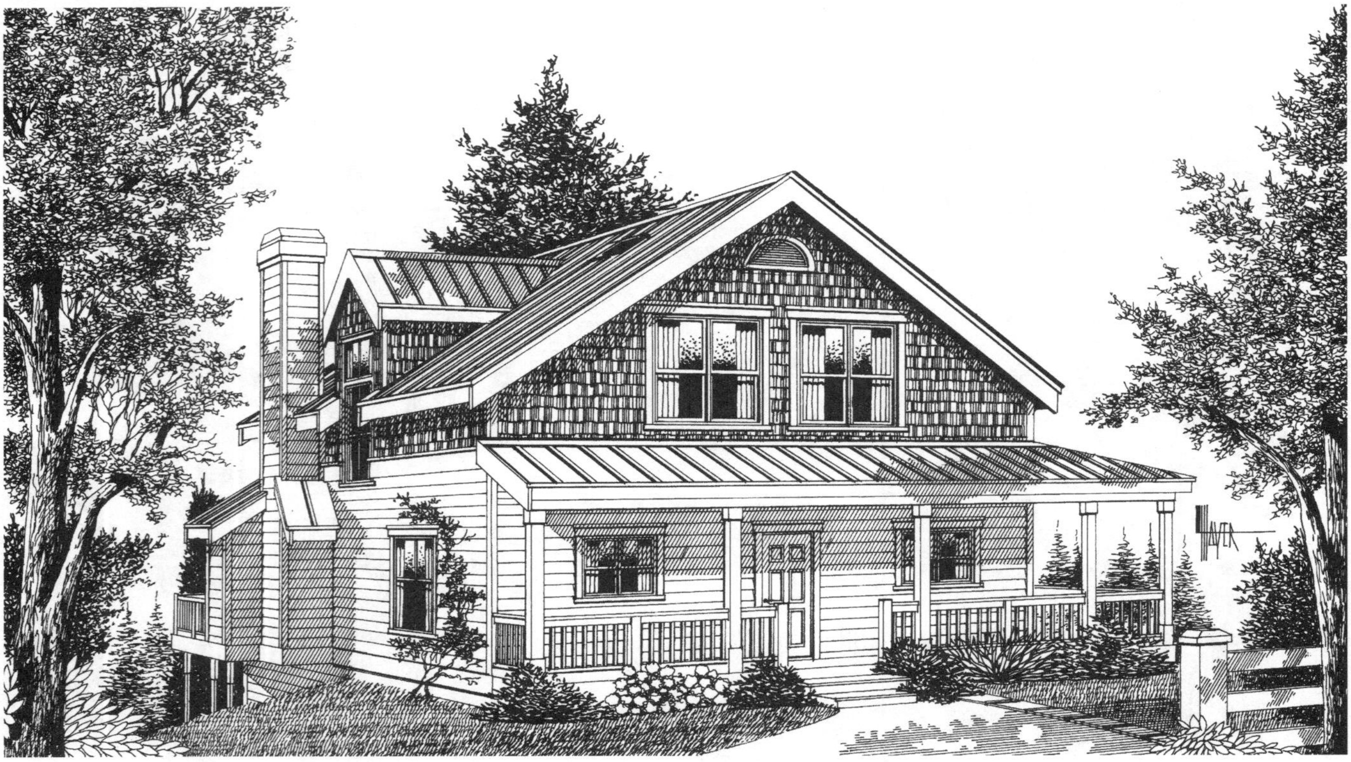

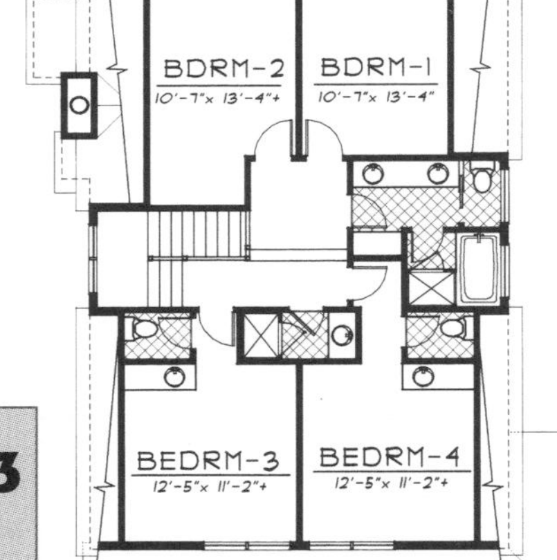
BDRM-2
10'-7"x 13'-4"+
BDRM-1
10'-7"x 13'-4"
BEDRM-3
12'-5"x 11'-2"+
BEDRM-4
12'-5"x 11'-2"+

Second Floor
1,028 sq. ft.

Plan #531-DDI-100213

Price Code D

Total Living Area: 2,202 Sq. Ft.

Home has 5 bedrooms, 4 full baths, 2 half baths, 2-car drive under garage and basement or walk-out basement foundation, please specify when ordering.

Special features

- 9' ceilings on first floor
- Guest bedroom located on the first floor for convenience could easily be converted to an office area
- Large kitchen with oversized island overlooks dining area

Width: 34'-0" Depth: 46'-0"

DECK
10'-0"+ x 38'-0"
STORAGE
LIVING RM
15'-0"x 15'-0"
DINING
14'-0"x 10'-0"
ISLAND
PANTRY
KITCHEN
11'-10"x 11'-2"
GUEST
10'-2"x 11'-0"
MUD ROOM
COVERED
PORCH

First Floor
1,174 sq. ft.

LOWE'S

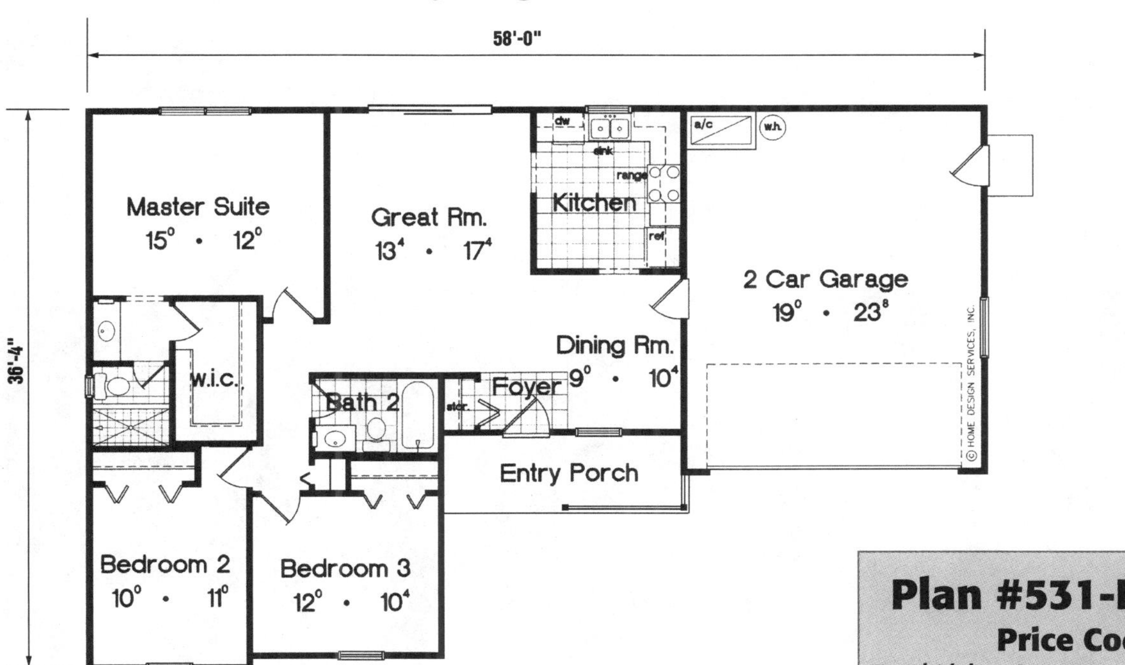
58'-0"
36'-4"
Master Suite
15^0 • 12^0
Great Rm.
13^4 • 17^4
Kitchen
dw
sink
range
ref.
a/c
w.h.
2 Car Garage
19^0 • 23^8
Dining Rm.
9^0 • 10^4
Foyer
Bath 2
stor.
w.i.c.
Entry Porch
Bedroom 2
10^0 • 11^0
Bedroom 3
12^0 • 10^4
© HOME DESIGN SERVICES, INC.

Plan #531-HDS-1167

Price Code AA

Total Living Area: 1,167 Sq. Ft.

Home has 3 bedrooms, 2 baths, 2-car garage and slab foundation.

Special features

- Master suite with private bath
- Handy coat closet in foyer
- Lots of storage space throughout

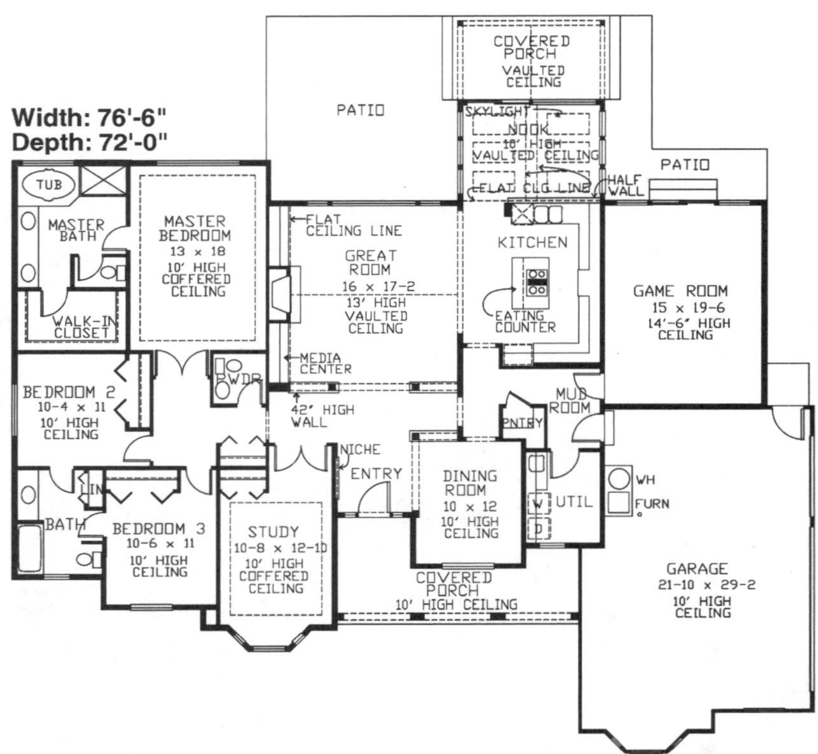
Width: 76'-6"
Depth: 72'-0"
COVERED PORCH
VAULTED CEILING
PATIO
SKYLIGHT
NOOK
10' HIGH VAULTED CEILING
FLAT CLG LINE
HALF WALL
PATIO
TUB
MASTER BATH
MASTER BEDROOM
13 x 18
10' HIGH COFFERED CEILING
FLAT CEILING LINE
GREAT ROOM
16 x 17-2
13' HIGH VAULTED CEILING
KITCHEN
EATING COUNTER
GAME ROOM
15 x 19-6
14'-6" HIGH CEILING
WALK-IN CLOSET
MEDIA CENTER
PWDR
BEDROOM 2
10-4 x 11
10' HIGH CEILING
42" HIGH WALL
PNTRY
MUD ROOM
NICHE
ENTRY
DINING ROOM
10 x 12
10' HIGH CEILING
UTIL
W
D
WH
FURN
LIN
BATH
BEDROOM 3
10-6 x 11
10' HIGH CEILING
STUDY
10-8 x 12-10
10' HIGH COFFERED CEILING
COVERED PORCH
10' HIGH CEILING
GARAGE
21-10 x 29-2
10' HIGH CEILING

Plan #531-GSD-1260

Price Code E

Total Living Area: 2,788 Sq. Ft.

Home has 3 bedrooms, 2 1/2 baths, 3-car side entry garage and crawl space foundation.

Special features

- Breakfast nook flooded with sunlight from skylights
- Fireplace in great room framed by media center and shelving
- Large game room is secluded for active children

Compact Ranch With Good Looks

Plan #531-ES-107-1

basement

Plan #531-ES-107-2

crawl space & slab

Price Code A

Total Living Area: 1,120 Sq. Ft.

Home has 3 bedrooms, 1 1/2 baths, 1-car carport and basement, crawl space or slab foundation, please specify when ordering.

Special features

- Porch and shuttered windows with lower accent panels add greatly to this home's appeal
- Kitchen offers snack counter and opens to family room
- All bedrooms provide excellent closet space
- Carport includes handy storage area

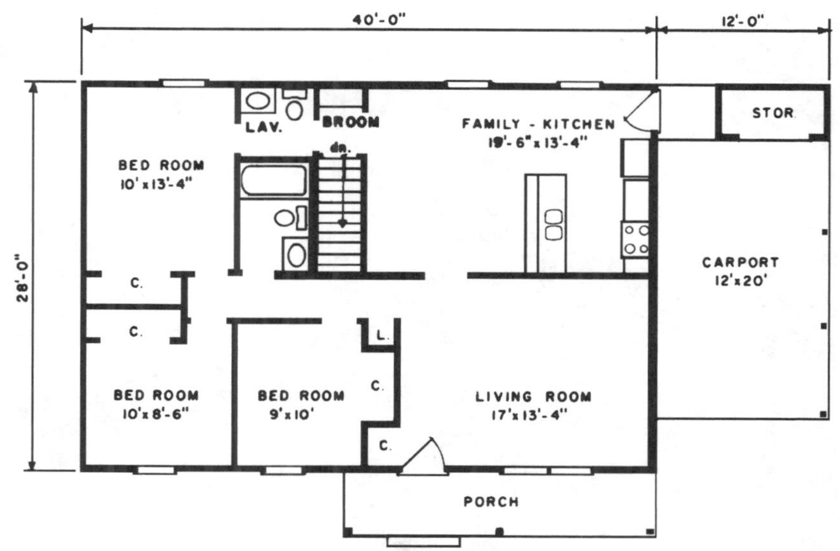
40'-0"
12'-0"
28'-0"
LAV.
BROOM
dn.
FAMILY - KITCHEN
19'-6"x13'-4"
STOR
BED ROOM
10'x13'-4"
C.
C.
CARPORT
12'x20'
L.
C.
BED ROOM
10'x8'-6"
BED ROOM
9'x10'
LIVING ROOM
17'x13'-4"
C.
PORCH

Open Living On First Floor

Plan #531-DDI-95220

Price Code B

Total Living Area: 1,584 Sq. Ft.

Home has 3 bedrooms, 2 1/2 baths, 2-car rear entry garage and crawl space foundation.

Special features

- Kitchen overlooks family room creating a natural gathering place
- Double vanity in master bath
- Dining room flows into living room

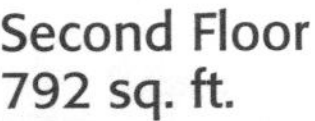
Second Floor
792 sq. ft.

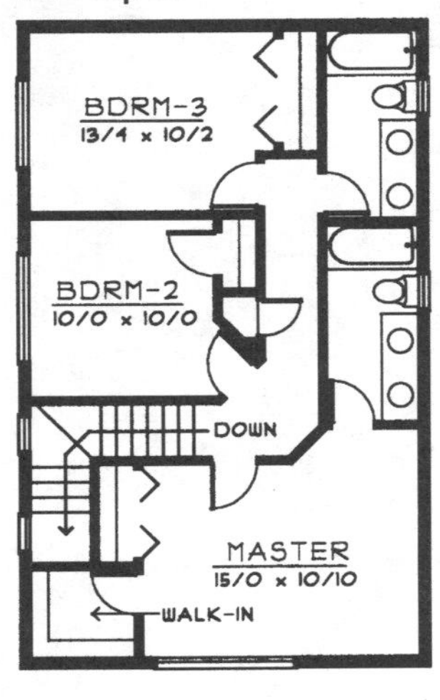
BDRM-3
13/4 x 10/2
BDRM-2
10/0 x 10/0
DOWN
MASTER
15/0 x 10/10
WALK-IN

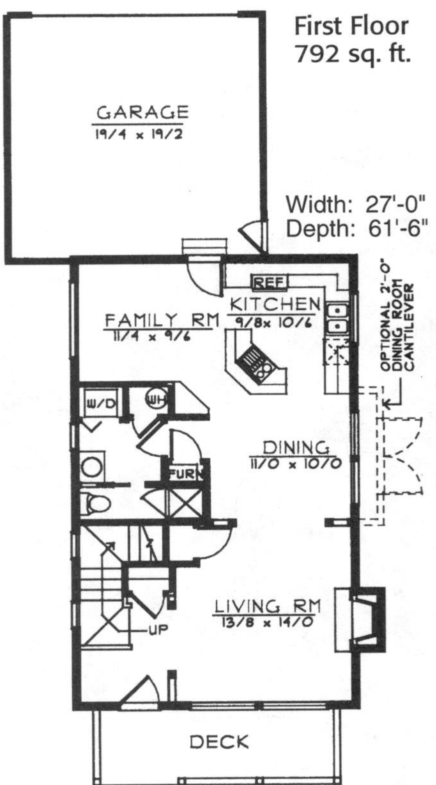
First Floor
792 sq. ft.
GARAGE
19/4 x 19/2
Width: 27'-0"
Depth: 61'-6"
REF
KITCHEN
9/8x 10/6
FAMILY RM
11/4 x 9/6
OPTIONAL 2'-0" DINING ROOM CANTILEVER
W/D
WH
FURN
DINING
11/0 x 10/0
LIVING RM
13/8 x 14/0
UP
DECK

TO ORDER BLUEPRINTS USE THE FORM ON PAGE 290 OR CALL TOLL-FREE **1-800-DREAM HOME** (373-2646)

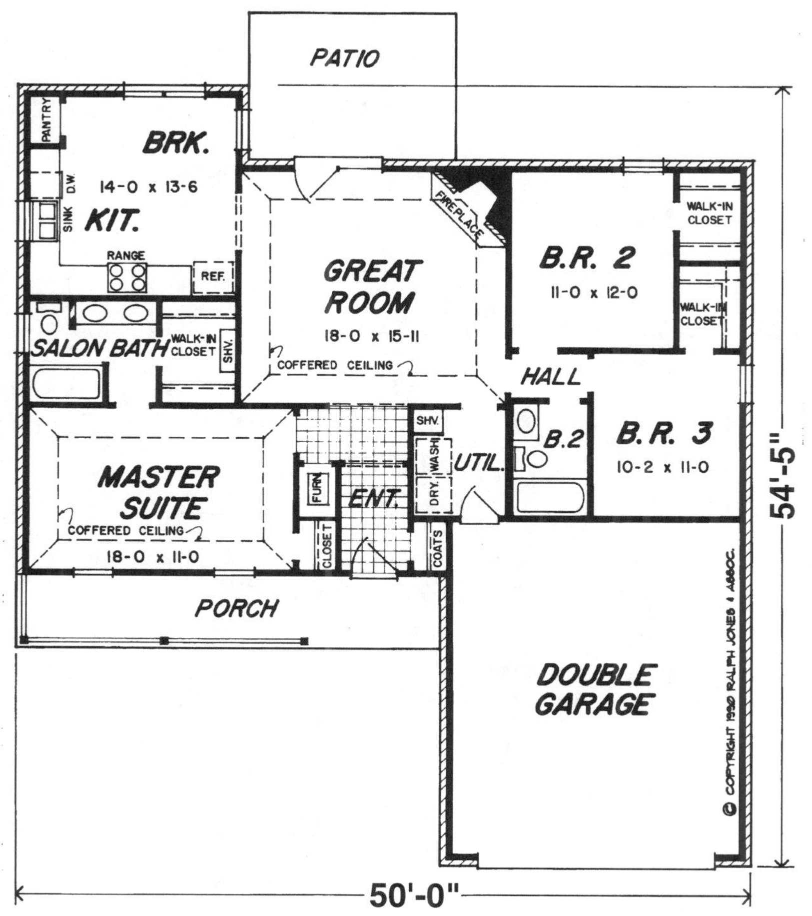
PATIO
PANTRY
BRK.
14-0 x 13-6
D.W.
SINK
KIT.
RANGE
REF.
GREAT ROOM
18-0 x 15-11
COFFERED CEILING
FIREPLACE
B.R. 2
11-0 x 12-0
WALK-IN CLOSET
WALK-IN CLOSET
SALON BATH
WALK-IN CLOSET
SHV.
HALL
MASTER SUITE
COFFERED CEILING
18-0 x 11-0
SHV.
WASH
DRY.
UTIL.
FURN
ENT.
CLOSET
COATS
B.2
B.R. 3
10-2 x 11-0
54'-5"
PORCH
DOUBLE GARAGE
© COPYRIGHT 1990 RALPH JONES & ASSOC.
50'-0"

Plan #531-RJ-A1485

Price Code A

Total Living Area: 1,436 Sq. Ft.

Home has 3 bedrooms, 2 baths, 2-car garage and slab foundation.

Special features

- Corner fireplace in great room warms home
- Kitchen and breakfast room combine for convenience
- Centrally located utility room

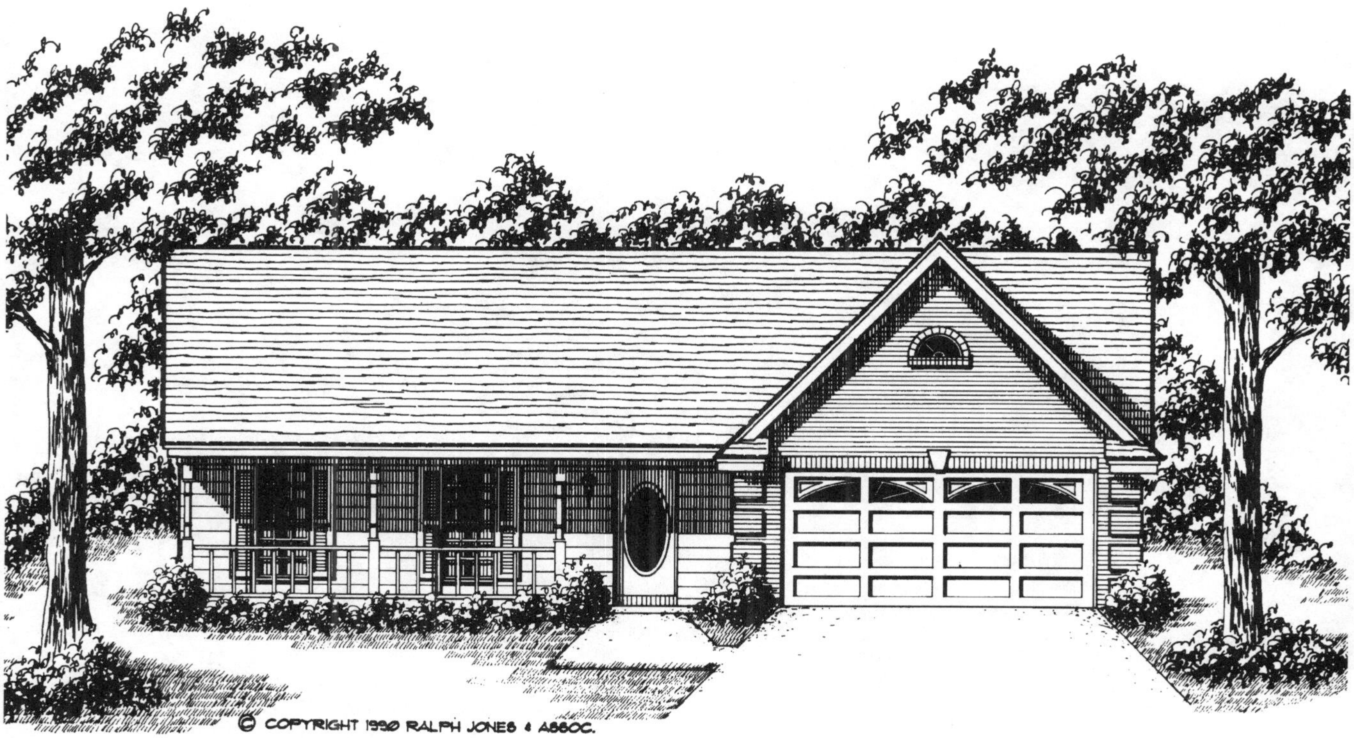

Plan #531-BF-1718

Price Code E

Total Living Area: 2,665 Sq. Ft.

Home has 3 bedrooms, 2 baths, 2-car side entry garage and slab or crawl space foundation, please specify when ordering.

Special features

- Open floor plan makes this home feel spacious
- 12' ceilings in living, breakfast/kitchen and dining areas
- Kitchen is the center of activity with views into all gathering places

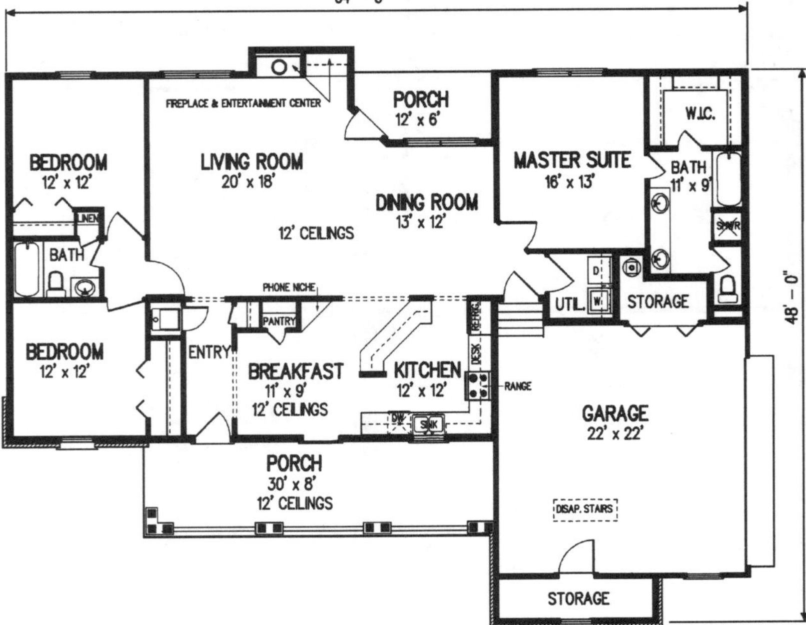
64' – 0"
48' – 0"
FIREPLACE & ENTERTAINMENT CENTER
PORCH
12' x 6'
BEDROOM
12' x 12'
LIVING ROOM
20' x 18'
MASTER SUITE
16' x 13'
W.I.C.
BATH
11' x 9'
DINING ROOM
13' x 12'
12' CEILINGS
LINEN
BATH
SHWR
PHONE NICHE
UTIL.
D
W
STORAGE
PANTRY
REFRIG.
BEDROOM
12' x 12'
ENTRY
BREAKFAST
11' x 9'
12' CEILINGS
DESK
KITCHEN
12' x 12'
RANGE
GARAGE
22' x 22'
DW
SINK
PORCH
30' x 8'
12' CEILINGS
DISAP. STAIRS
STORAGE

TO ORDER BLUEPRINTS USE THE FORM ON PAGE 290 OR CALL TOLL-FREE **1-800-DREAM HOME** (373-2646)

Inviting Victorian Details

LOWE'S

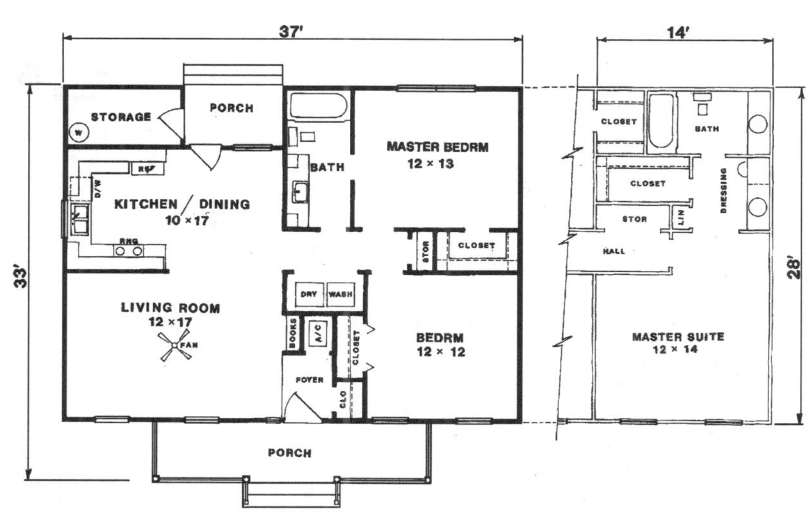
37'
14'
33'
28'
STORAGE
W
PORCH
MASTER BEDRM
12 × 13
BATH
REF
D/W
KITCHEN / DINING
10 × 17
RNG
STOR
CLOSET
DRY
WASH
LIVING ROOM
12 × 17
FAN
BOOKS
A/C
CLOSET
BEDRM
12 × 12
FOYER
CLO
PORCH
CLOSET
BATH
CLOSET
DRESSING
STOR
LIN
HALL
MASTER SUITE
12 × 14

Plan #531-VL947

Price Code AA

Total Living Area: 947 Sq. Ft.

Home has 2 bedrooms, 1 bath and crawl space or slab foundation, please specify when ordering.

Special features

- Future expansion plans included which allow the home to become 392 square feet larger with 3 bedrooms and 2 baths
- Compact and efficient kitchen adjacent to dining area
- Plenty of closet space throughout

Covered Porch Adds Charm

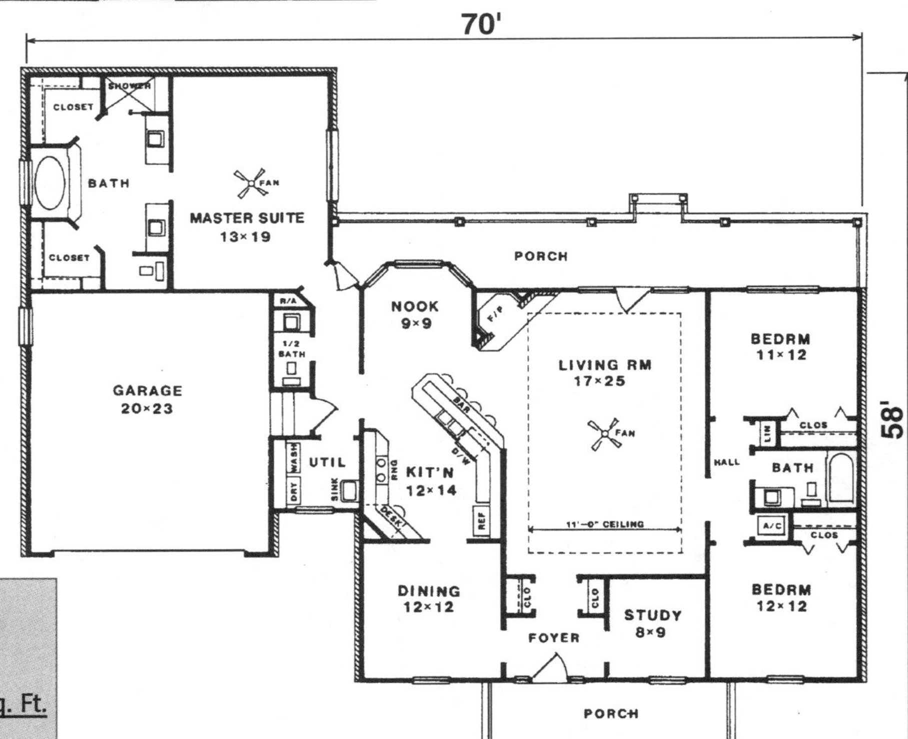

70'
58'
SHOWER
CLOSET
BATH
CLOSET
FAN
MASTER SUITE
13×19
PORCH
R/A
1/2 BATH
NOOK
9×9
F/P
LIVING RM
17×25
FAN
11'-0" CEILING
BEDRM
11×12
CLOS
LIN
HALL
BATH
A/C
CLOS
GARAGE
20×23
WASH
DRY
UTIL
SINK
RNG
BAR
D/W
KIT'N
12×14
DESK
REF
DINING
12×12
CLO
CLO
FOYER
STUDY
8×9
BEDRM
12×12
PORCH

Plan #531-VL2069

Price Code C

Total Living Area: 2,069 Sq. Ft.

Home has 3 bedrooms, 2 1/2 baths, 2-car garage and slab or crawl space foundation, please specify when ordering.

Special features

- Kitchen has many amenities including a snack bar
- 9' ceilings throughout this home
- Large front and rear porches

 TO ORDER BLUEPRINTS USE THE FORM ON PAGE 290 OR CALL TOLL-FREE **1-800-DREAM HOME** (373-2646)

Southern Styling With Covered Porch

LOWE'S

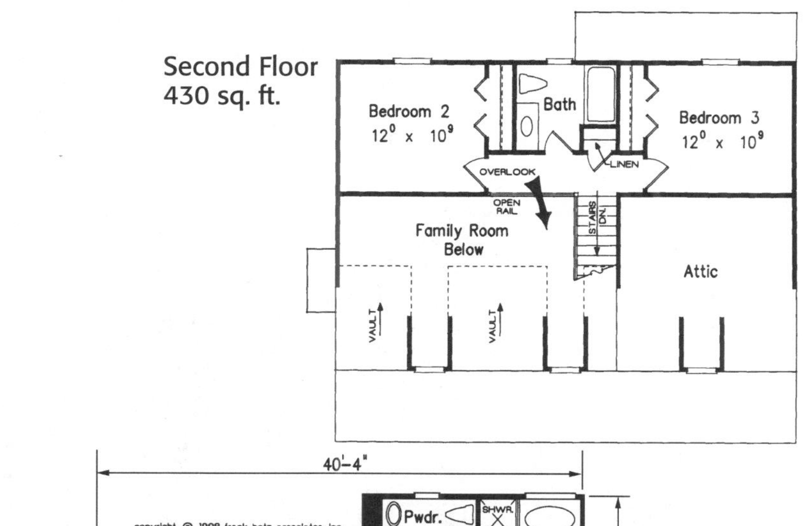
Second Floor
430 sq. ft.
Bedroom 2
12⁰ x 10⁹
Bath
Bedroom 3
12⁰ x 10⁹
OVERLOOK
LINEN
OPEN RAIL
STAIRS DN.
Family Room Below
Attic
VAULT
VAULT

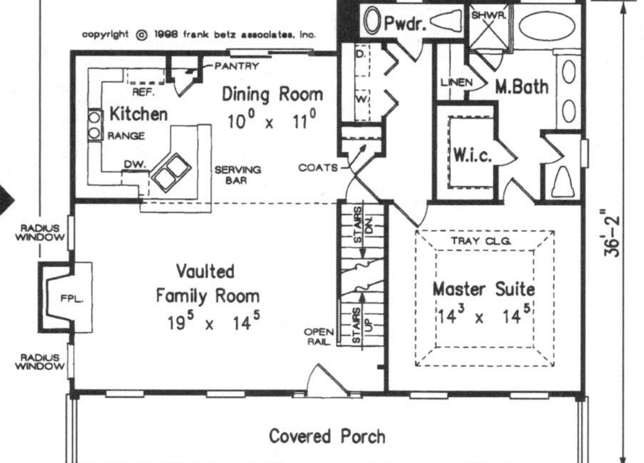
40'-4"
copyright © 1998 frank betz associates, inc.
Pwdr.
SHWR.
PANTRY
REF.
Dining Room
10⁰ x 11⁰
Kitchen
RANGE
DW.
SERVING BAR
D.
W.
LINEN
M.Bath
W.i.c.
COATS
DRIVE UNDER
RADIUS WINDOW
STAIRS DN.
TRAY CLG.
36'-2"
Vaulted
Family Room
19⁵ x 14⁵
FPL.
Master Suite
14³ x 14⁵
OPEN RAIL
STAIRS UP
RADIUS WINDOW
Covered Porch

First Floor
1,061 sq. ft.

Plan #531-FB-1148

Price Code A

Total Living Area: 1,491 Sq. Ft.

Home has 3 bedrooms, 2 1/2 baths, 2-car drive under garage and walk-out basement foundation.

Special features

- Two-story family room has vaulted ceiling
- Well-organized kitchen has serving bar which overlooks family and dining rooms
- First floor master suite has tray ceiling, walk-in closet and master bath

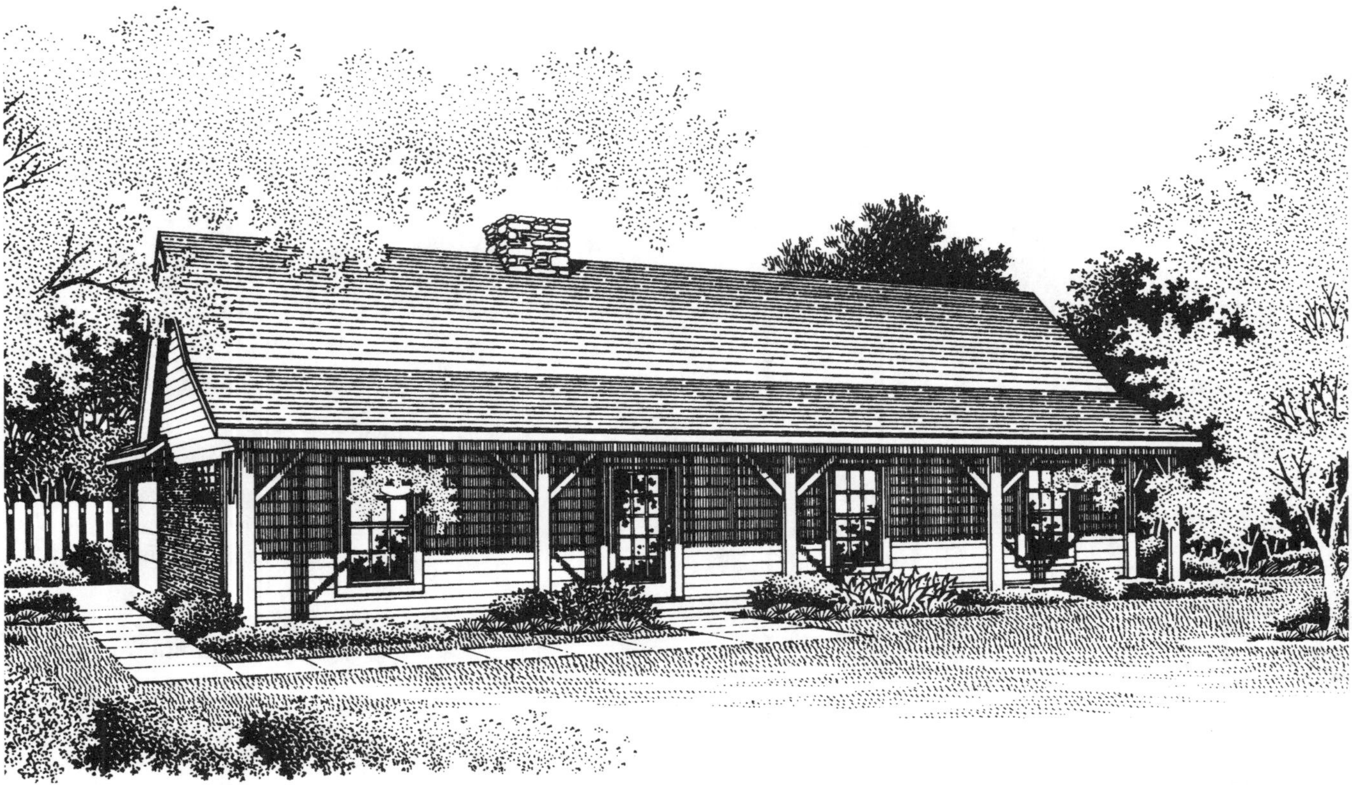

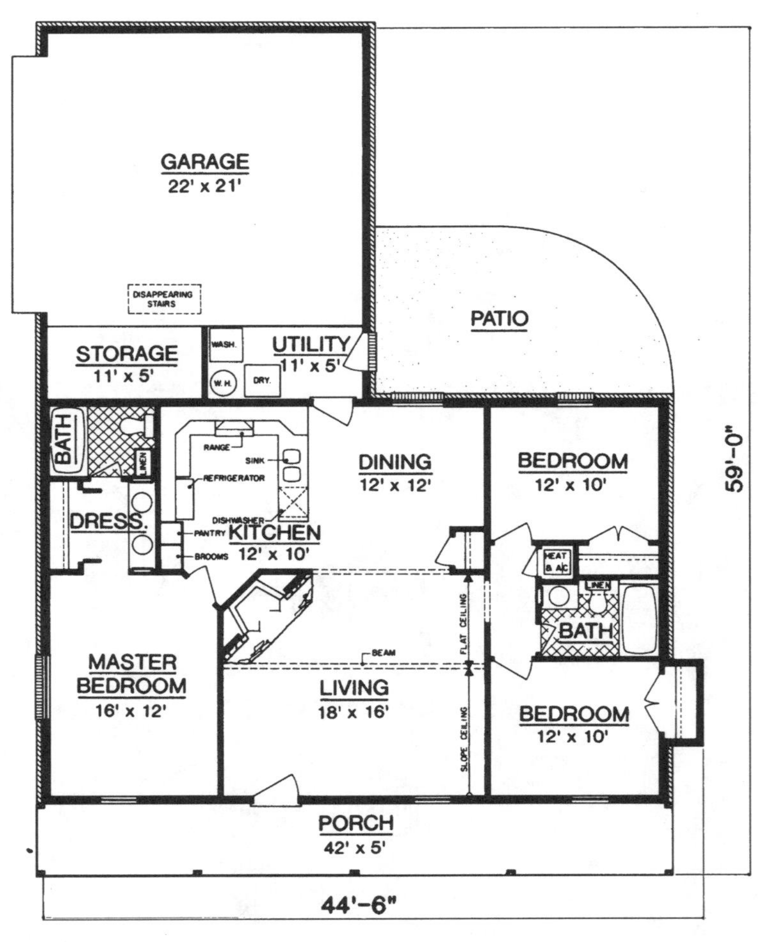
GARAGE
22' x 21'
DISAPPEARING STAIRS
PATIO
STORAGE
11' x 5'
WASH.
W.H.
DRY.
UTILITY
11' x 5'
BATH
LINEN
RANGE
SINK
REFRIGERATOR
DISHWASHER
PANTRY
BROOMS
KITCHEN
12' x 10'
DINING
12' x 12'
BEDROOM
12' x 10'
DRESS.
HEAT & A/C
LINEN
BATH
BEAM
FLAT CEILING
SLOPE CEILING
MASTER BEDROOM
16' x 12'
LIVING
18' x 16'
BEDROOM
12' x 10'
PORCH
42' x 5'
44'-6"
59'-0"

Plan #531-BF-DR1109

Price Code AA

Total Living Area: 1,191 Sq. Ft.

Home has 3 bedrooms, 2 baths, 2-car side entry garage and slab or crawl space foundation, please specify when ordering.

Special features

- Energy efficient 2" x 6" exterior walls
- Master bedroom located near living areas for maximum convenience
- Living room has cathedral ceiling and stone fireplace

LOWE'S

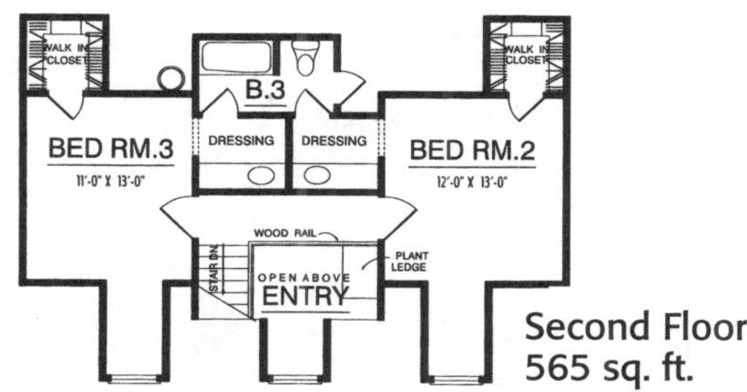
WALK IN CLOSET
WALK IN CLOSET
B.3
BED RM.3
11'-0" X 13'-0"
DRESSING
DRESSING
BED RM.2
12'-0" X 13'-0"
WOOD RAIL
PLANT LEDGE
STAIR DN
OPEN ABOVE
ENTRY

Second Floor
565 sq. ft.

Plan #531-RDD-1895-9

Price Code C

Total Living Area: 1,895 Sq. Ft.

Home has 3 bedrooms, 2 1/2 baths, 2-car garage and basement, crawl space or slab foundation, please specify when ordering.

Special features

- Master suite has private bath and access to covered rear porch
- Living area has built-in bookshelves flanking fireplace
- Kitchen overlooks both the breakfast nook and living room for an open floor plan

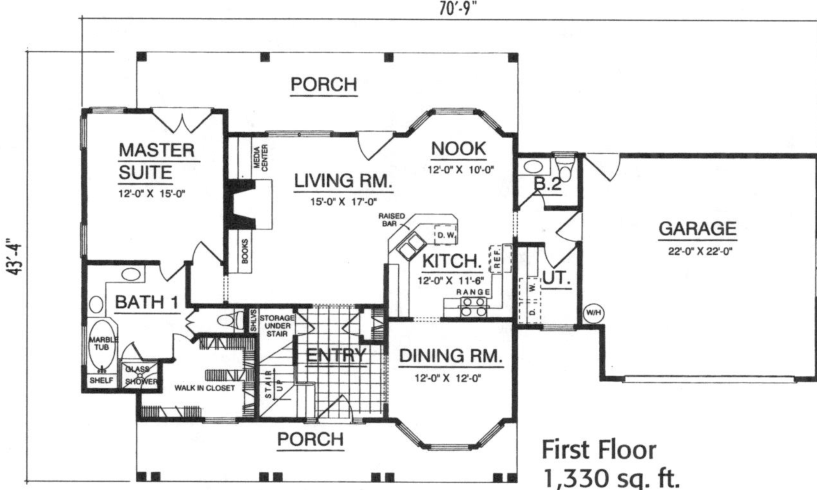
70'-9"
43'-4"
PORCH
MASTER SUITE
12'-0" X 15'-0"
MEDIA CENTER
LIVING RM.
15'-0" X 17'-0"
NOOK
12'-0" X 10'-0"
B.2
GARAGE
22'-0" X 22'-0"
BOOKS
RAISED BAR
D.W.
KITCH.
12'-0" X 11'-6"
REF.
RANGE
UT.
W/H
BATH 1
MARBLE TUB
SHELF
GLASS SHOWER
WALK IN CLOSET
SHLVS
STORAGE UNDER STAIR
STAIR UP
ENTRY
DINING RM.
12'-0" X 12'-0"
PORCH

First Floor
1,330 sq. ft.

Quaint Porch Adds Charm

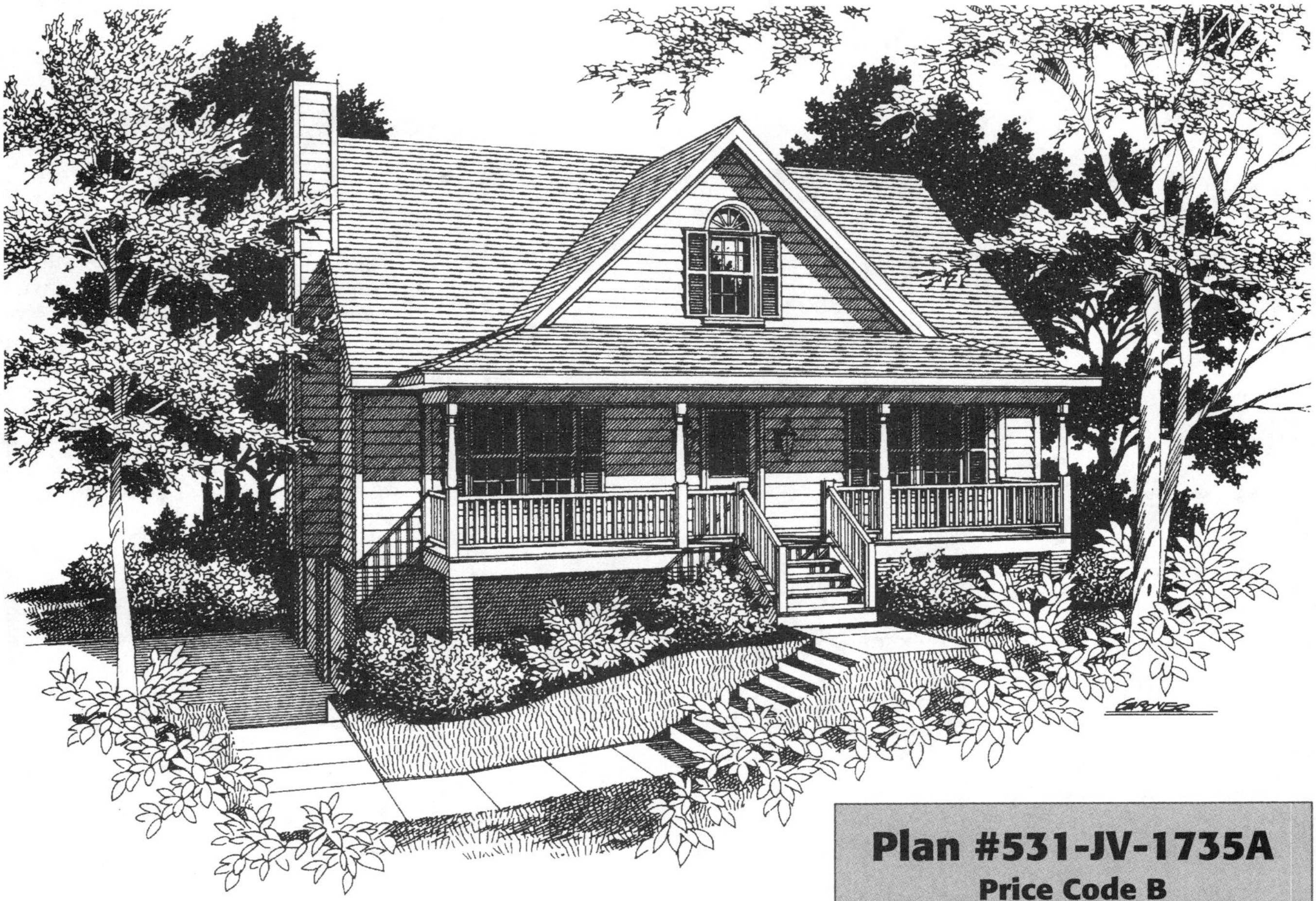

Plan #531-JV-1735A

Price Code B

Total Living Area: 1,735 Sq. Ft.

Home has 3 bedrooms, 2 1/2 baths, 2-car side entry garage and basement foundation.

Special features

- Angled kitchen wall expands space into the dining room
- Second floor has cozy sitting area with cheerful window
- Two spacious bedrooms on second floor share a bath

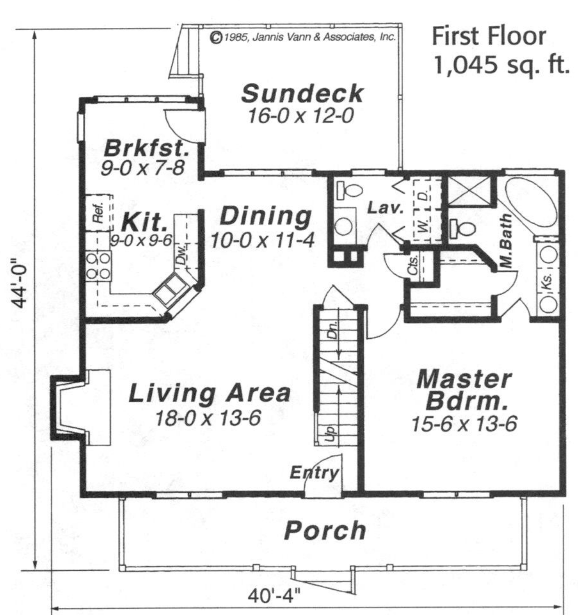

©1985, Jannis Vann & Associates, Inc.
Sundeck
16-0 x 12-0
Brkfst.
9-0 x 7-8
Kit.
9-0 x 9-6
Ref.
Dw.
Dining
10-0 x 11-4
Lav.
W
D
Cls.
M.Bath
Ks.
Dn.
Living Area
18-0 x 13-6
Master
Bdrm.
15-6 x 13-6
Up
Entry
Porch
44'-0"
40'-4"

First Floor
1,045 sq. ft.

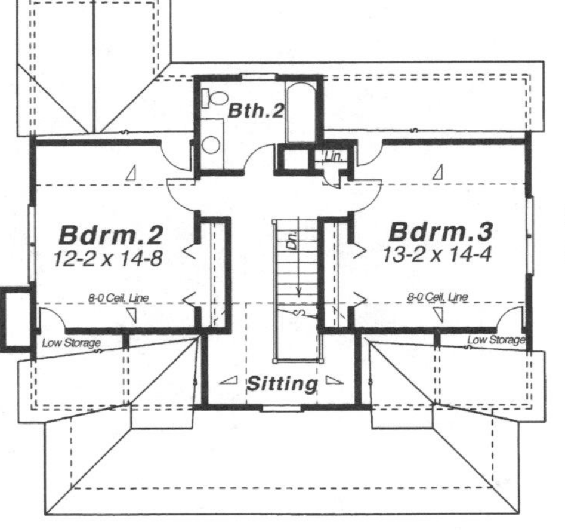

Bth.2
Lin.
Bdrm.2
12-2 x 14-8
Bdrm.3
13-2 x 14-4
Dn
8-0 Ceil. Line
8-0 Ceil. Line
Low Storage
Low Storage
Sitting

Second Floor
690 sq. ft.

Cozy Covered Front Porch

LOWE'S

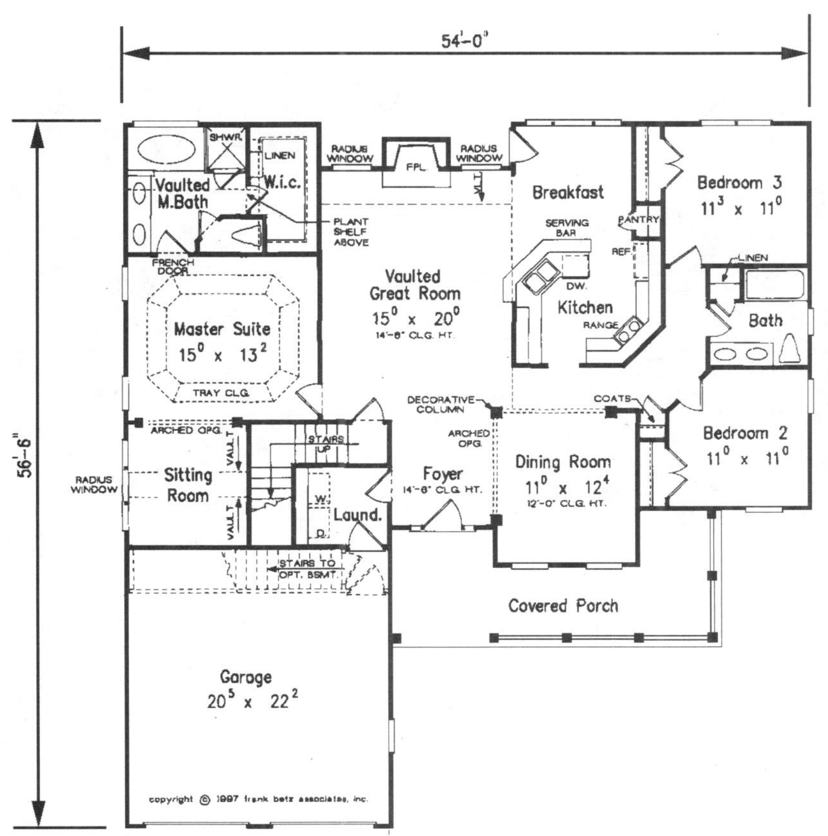
54'-0"
56'-6"
SHWR.
LINEN
Vaulted M.Bath
W.i.c.
RADIUS WINDOW
FPL.
RADIUS WINDOW
PLANT SHELF ABOVE
Breakfast
SERVING BAR
PANTRY
REF.
Bedroom 3
11³ x 11⁰
LINEN
FRENCH DOOR
Vaulted Great Room
15⁰ x 20⁰
14'-6" CLG. HT.
DW.
Kitchen
RANGE
Bath
Master Suite
15⁰ x 13²
TRAY CLG.
DECORATIVE COLUMN
COATS
ARCHED OPG.
STAIRS UP
ARCHED OPG.
Bedroom 2
11⁰ x 11⁰
RADIUS WINDOW
Sitting Room
VAULT
Foyer
14'-6" CLG. HT.
Dining Room
11⁰ x 12⁴
12'-0" CLG. HT.
Laund.
STAIRS TO OPT. BSMT.
Covered Porch
Garage
20⁵ x 22²
copyright © 1997 frank betz associates, inc.

Plan #531-FB-1043

Price Code B

Total Living Area: 1,692 Sq. Ft.

Home has 3 bedrooms, 2 baths, 2-car garage and basement, walk-out basement or crawl space foundation, please specify when ordering.

Special features

- Tray ceiling in master bedroom
- Breakfast bar overlooks vaulted great room
- Additional bedrooms are located away from master bedroom for privacy

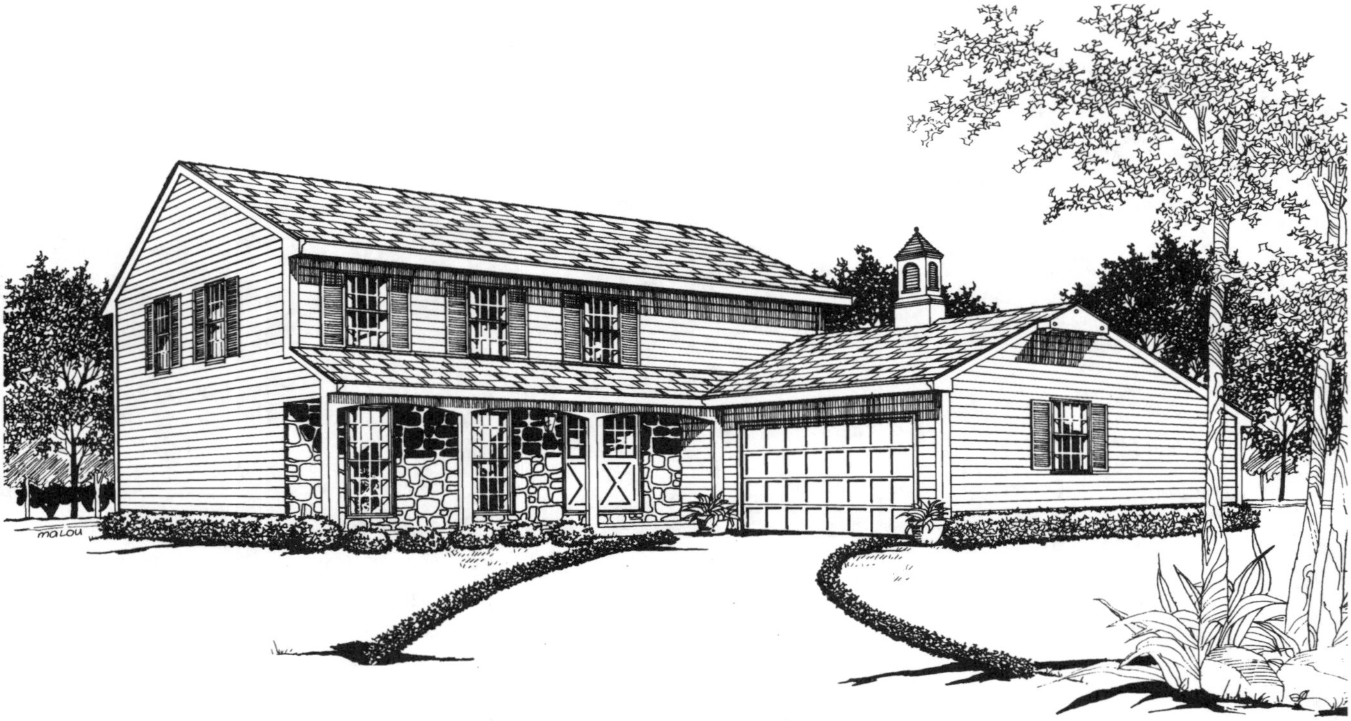

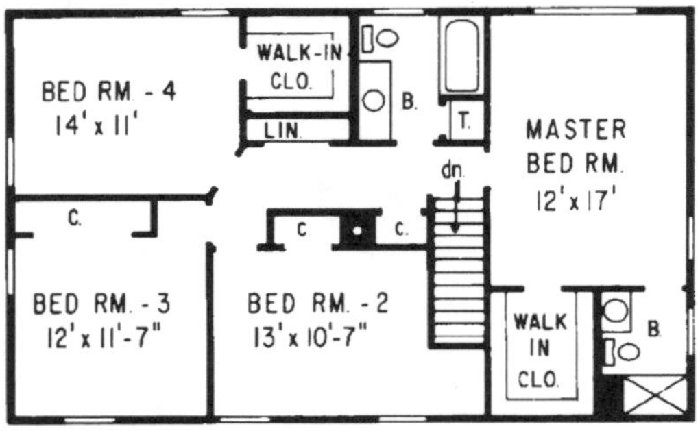

Second Floor
1,092 sq. ft.

Plan #531-1077-1
basement
Plan #531-1077-2
crawl space & slab
Price Code C

Total Living Area: 2,196 Sq. Ft.

Home has 4 bedrooms, 2 1/2 baths, 2-car side entry garage and basement, crawl space or slab foundation, please specify when ordering.

Special features

- Ideal formal and informal areas
- Well-designed kitchen for your cooking pleasure
- Garage features convenient storage areas
- Master bedroom offers huge walk-in closet

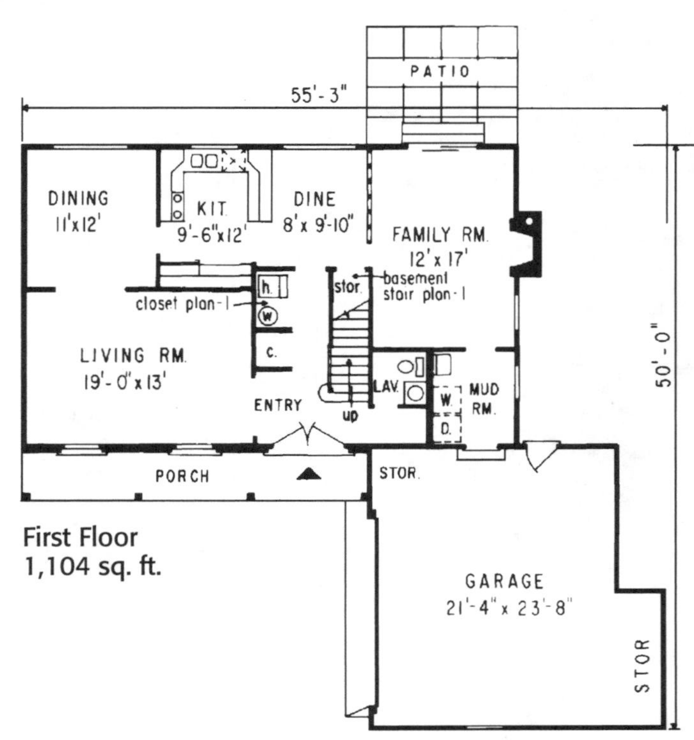
PATIO
55'-3"
DINING
11'x12'
KIT.
9'-6"x12'
DINE
8'x 9'-10"
FAMILY RM.
12' x 17'
stor.
basement stair plan-1
closet plan-1
h.
w
c.
LIVING RM.
19'-0"x 13'
ENTRY
up
LAV.
W.
D.
MUD RM.
50'-0"
PORCH
STOR.
GARAGE
21'-4" x 23'-8"
STOR

First Floor
1,104 sq. ft.

A Ranch With A Rustic Feel

LOWE'S

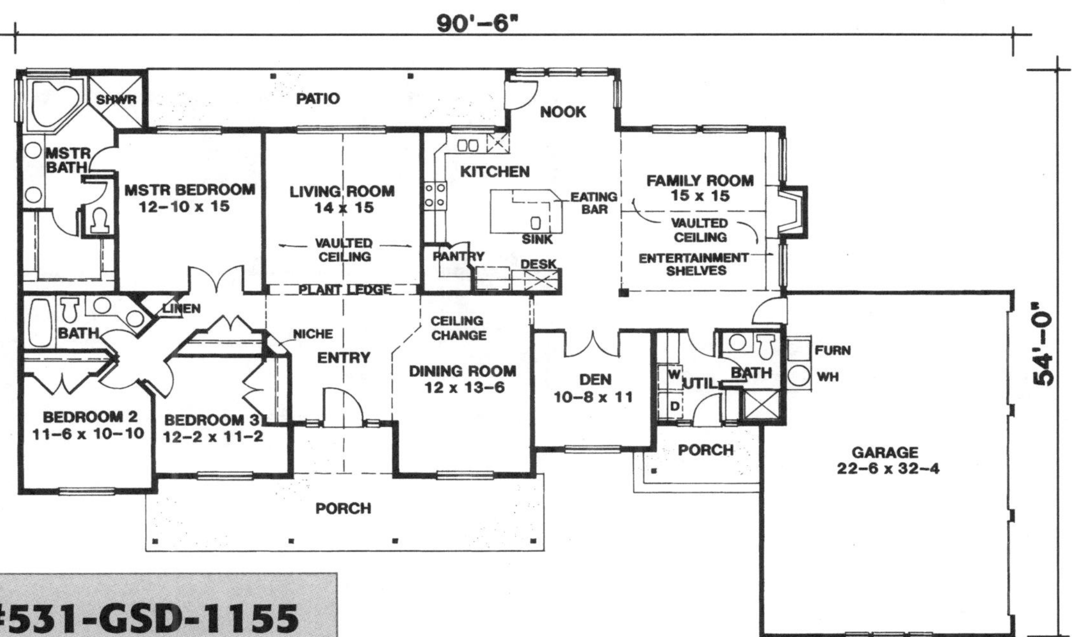
90'-6"
54'-0"
PATIO
NOOK
SHWR
MSTR BATH
MSTR BEDROOM
12-10 x 15
LIVING ROOM
14 x 15
VAULTED CEILING
KITCHEN
EATING BAR
SINK
PANTRY
DESK
FAMILY ROOM
15 x 15
VAULTED CEILING
ENTERTAINMENT SHELVES
PLANT LEDGE
LINEN
BATH
NICHE
ENTRY
CEILING CHANGE
DINING ROOM
12 x 13-6
DEN
10-8 x 11
UTIL
BATH
FURN
WH
BEDROOM 2
11-6 x 10-10
BEDROOM 3
12-2 x 11-2
PORCH
PORCH
GARAGE
22-6 x 32-4

Plan #531-GSD-1155

Price Code D

Total Living Area: 2,355 Sq. Ft.

Home has 3 bedrooms, 3 baths, 3-car side entry garage and crawl space foundation.

Special features

- Double-doors lead into a private den perfect for a home office
- Vaulted ceilings and a fireplace make the family room a terrific gathering spot
- Cheerful nook off kitchen makes an ideal breakfast area
- 9′ ceilings throughout home

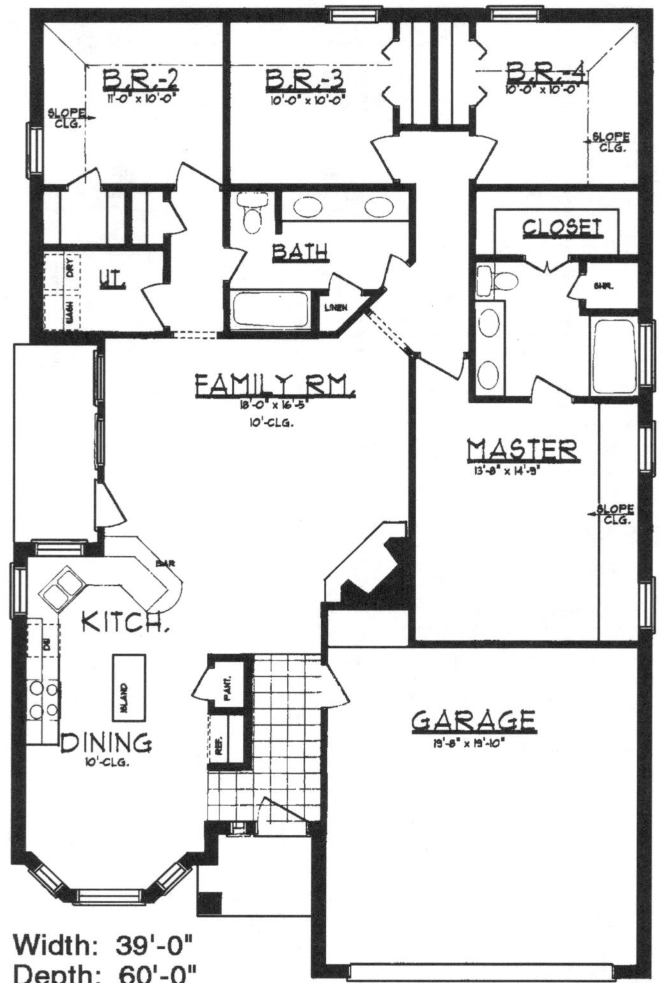
B.R.-2
11'-0" x 10'-0"
SLOPE CLG.
B.R.-3
10'-0" x 10'-0"
B.R.-4
10'-0" x 10'-0"
SLOPE CLG.
CLOSET
BATH
UT.
LINEN
FAMILY RM.
18'-0" x 16'-5"
10'-CLG.
MASTER
13'-8" x 14'-9"
SLOPE CLG.
BAR
KITCH.
ISLAND
PANT.
REF.
DINING
10'-CLG.
GARAGE
19'-8" x 19'-10"
Width: 39'-0"
Depth: 60'-0"

Plan #531-DL-17104L1

Price Code B

Total Living Area: 1,710 Sq. Ft.

Home has 4 bedrooms, 2 baths, 2-car garage and slab foundation.

Special features

- Bedrooms have plenty of closet space
- Laundry area located near bedrooms for efficiency
- Corner fireplace warms large family room with 10' ceiling

Luxurious Ranch

LOWE'S

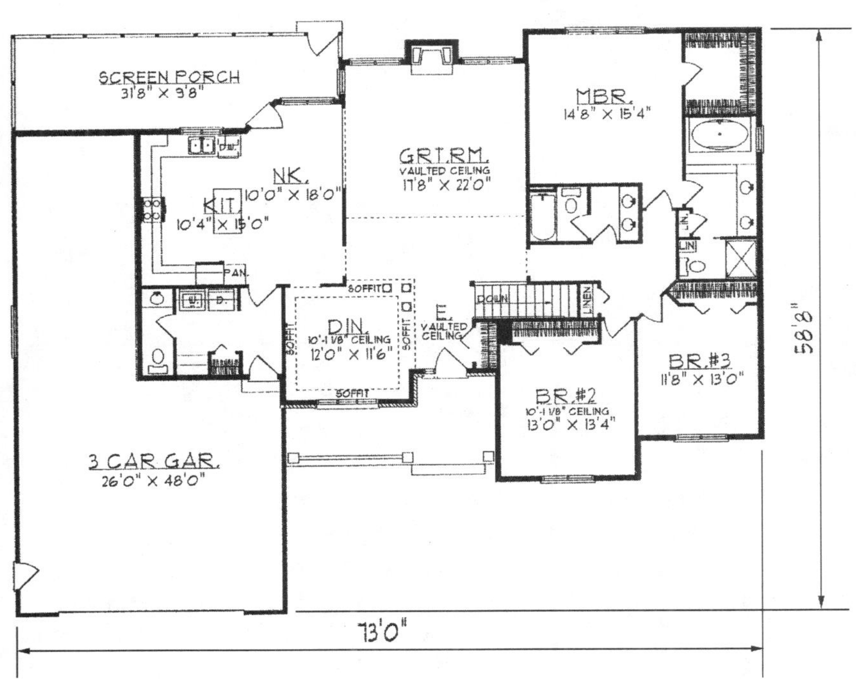
SCREEN PORCH
31'8" X 9'8"
NK.
10'0" X 18'0"
KIT.
10'4" X 15'0"
PAN.
GRT.RM.
VAULTED CEILING
17'8" X 22'0"
MBR.
14'8" X 15'4"
LIN
DIN.
10'-1 1/8" CEILING
12'0" X 11'6"
SOFFIT
E.
VAULTED CEILING
DOWN
LINEN
BR.#2
10'-1 1/8" CEILING
13'0" X 13'4"
BR.#3
11'8" X 13'0"
3 CAR GAR.
26'0" X 48'0"
73'0"
58'8"

Plan #531-JA-64396

Price Code C

Total Living Area: 2,196 Sq. Ft.

Home has 3 bedrooms, 2 1/2 baths, 3-car garage and basement foundation.

Special features

- Covered front porch leads to the vaulted foyer which invites guests into the great room
- Master bedroom features walk-in closet, private bath with double vanity, spa tub and linen closet
- Large open kitchen

LOWE'S

Formal Country Charm

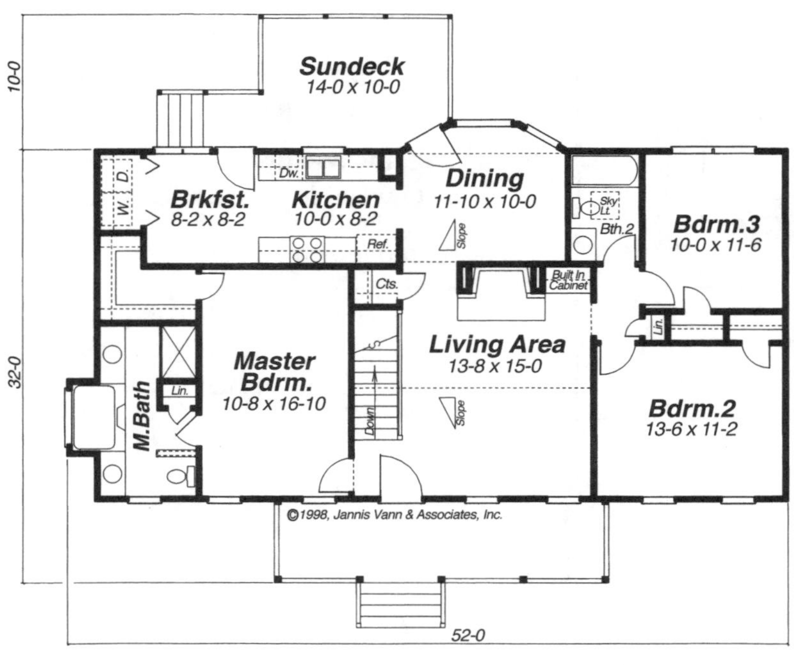
Sundeck
14-0 x 10-0
Dining
11-10 x 10-0
Brkfst.
8-2 x 8-2
Kitchen
10-0 x 8-2
Dw.
Ref.
W.
D.
Slope
Sky Lt.
Bth.2
Bdrm.3
10-0 x 11-6
Cts.
Built In Cabinet
Living Area
13-8 x 15-0
Lin.
Master Bdrm.
10-8 x 16-10
M.Bath
Lin.
Down
Slope
Bdrm.2
13-6 x 11-2
©1998, Jannis Vann & Associates, Inc.
10-0
32-0
52-0

Plan #531-JV-1325-B

Price Code A

Total Living Area: 1,325 Sq. Ft.

Home has 3 bedrooms, 2 baths, 2-car drive under garage and basement foundation.

Special features

- Sloped ceiling and a fireplace in living area create a cozy feeling
- Formal dining and breakfast areas have an efficiently designed kitchen between them
- Master bedroom has walk-in closet with luxurious private bath

TO ORDER BLUEPRINTS USE THE FORM ON PAGE 290 OR CALL TOLL-FREE **1-800-DREAM HOME** (373-2646)

Bright Spacious And Appealing

LOWE'S

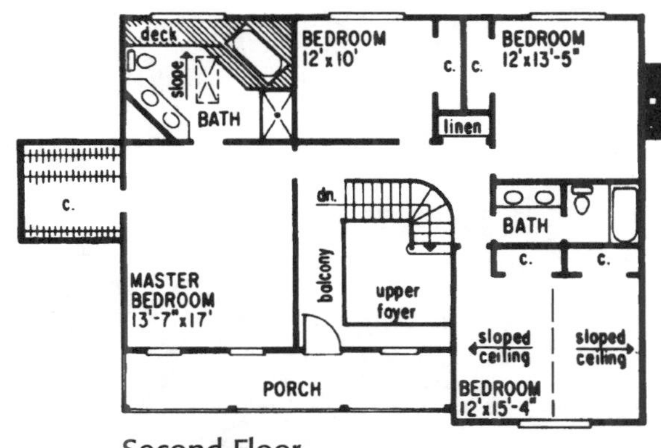
deck
slope
BATH
BEDROOM
12'x10'
c.
c.
BEDROOM
12'x13'-5"
linen
c.
dn.
BATH
c.
c.
MASTER
BEDROOM
13'-7"x17'
balcony
upper
foyer
sloped
ceiling
sloped
ceiling
PORCH
BEDROOM
12'x15'-4"

Second Floor
1,369 sq. ft.

Plan #531-1219-1

partial basement

Plan #531-1219-2

crawl space

Price Code E

Total Living Area: 2,797 Sq. Ft.

Home has 4 bedrooms, 2 1/2 baths, 3-car garage and partial basement or crawl space foundation, please specify when ordering.

Special features

- U-shaped kitchen with lots of counterspace and storage
- Built-in bookshelves flank the family room fireplace
- Luxurious master bath accented by skylight, sloped ceiling and built-in garden tub

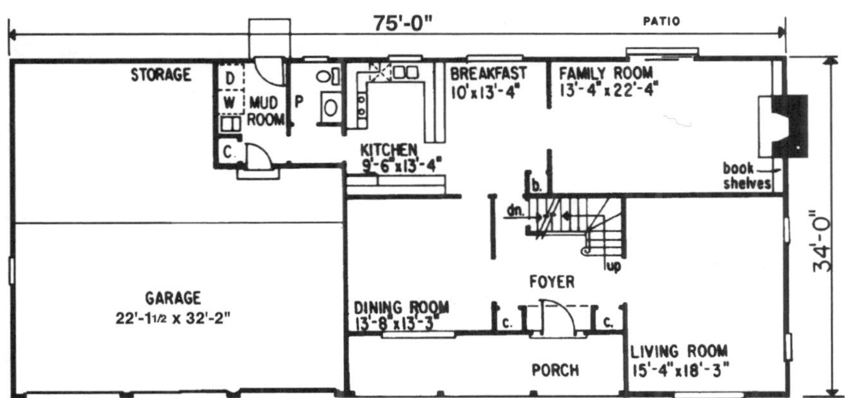
75'-0"
PATIO
STORAGE
D
W
MUD
ROOM
P
C.
BREAKFAST
10'x13'-4"
FAMILY ROOM
13'-4"x22'-4"
KITCHEN
9'-6"x13'-4"
b.
dn.
book
shelves
up
34'-0"
GARAGE
22'-1 1/2 x 32'-2"
FOYER
DINING ROOM
13'-8"x13'-3"
c.
c.
PORCH
LIVING ROOM
15'-4"x18'-3"

First Floor
1,428 sq. ft.

Well-Designed Ranch With Plenty Of Space

Plan #531-1396

Price Code C

Total Living Area: 1,820 Sq. Ft.

Home has 3 bedrooms, 2 baths, 2-car garage and basement foundation.

Special features

- Living room has stunning cathedral ceiling
- Spacious laundry room with easy access to kitchen, garage and the outdoors
- Plenty of closet space throughout
- Covered front porch enhances outdoor living

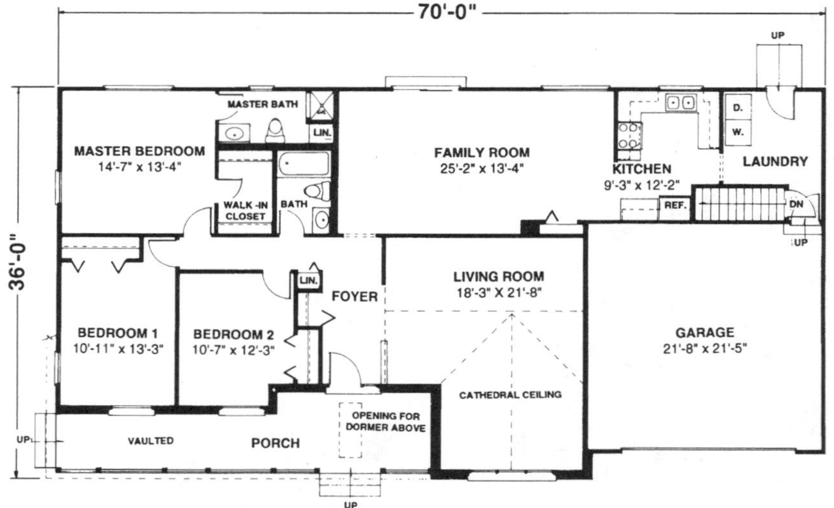
70'-0"
36'-0"
MASTER BEDROOM
14'-7" x 13'-4"
MASTER BATH
LIN.
WALK-IN CLOSET
BATH
FAMILY ROOM
25'-2" x 13'-4"
KITCHEN
9'-3" x 12'-2"
REF.
D.
W.
LAUNDRY
UP
DN
BEDROOM 1
10'-11" x 13'-3"
BEDROOM 2
10'-7" x 12'-3"
LIN.
FOYER
LIVING ROOM
18'-3" X 21'-8"
CATHEDRAL CEILING
GARAGE
21'-8" x 21'-5"
OPENING FOR DORMER ABOVE
VAULTED
PORCH
UP

 TO ORDER BLUEPRINTS USE THE FORM ON PAGE 290 OR CALL TOLL-FREE **1-800-DREAM HOME** (373-2646)

LOWE'S

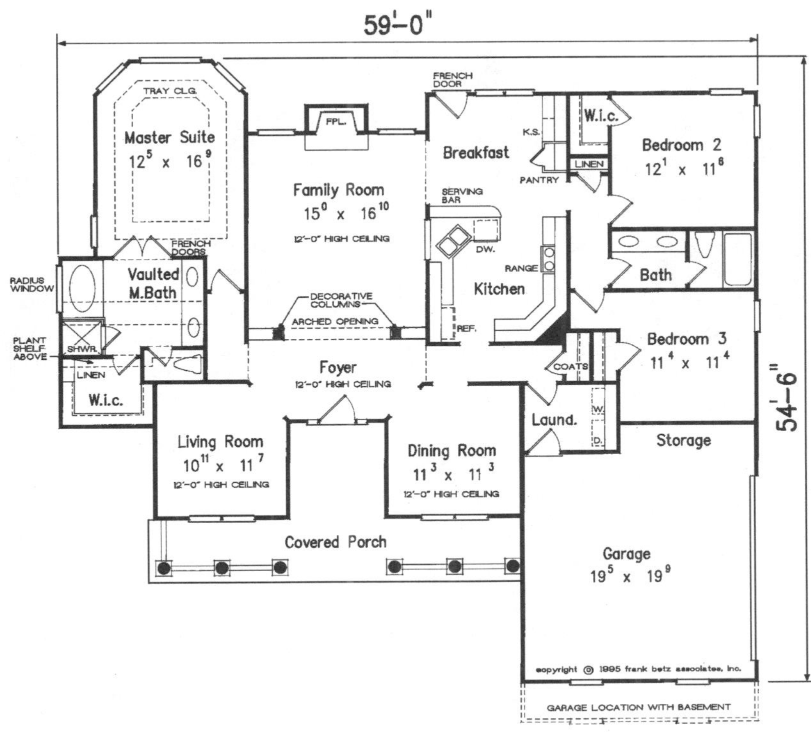
59'-0"
54'-6"
TRAY CLG.
Master Suite
12⁵ x 16⁹
FPL.
Family Room
15⁰ x 16¹⁰
12'-0" HIGH CEILING
FRENCH DOOR
Breakfast
K.S.
PANTRY
SERVING BAR
W.i.c.
LINEN
Bedroom 2
12¹ x 11⁶
FRENCH DOORS
RADIUS WINDOW
Vaulted M.Bath
PLANT SHELF ABOVE
SHWR.
LINEN
W.i.c.
DECORATIVE COLUMNS
ARCHED OPENING
DW.
RANGE
Kitchen
REF.
Bath
Foyer
12'-0" HIGH CEILING
COATS
Bedroom 3
11⁴ x 11⁴
Living Room
10¹¹ x 11⁷
12'-0" HIGH CEILING
Dining Room
11³ x 11³
12'-0" HIGH CEILING
Laund.
W.
D.
Storage
Covered Porch
Garage
19⁵ x 19⁹
copyright © 1995 frank betz associates, inc.
GARAGE LOCATION WITH BASEMENT

Plan #531-FB-902

Price Code C

Total Living Area: 1,856 Sq. Ft.

Home has 3 bedrooms, 2 baths, 2-car side entry garage and basement, crawl space or slab foundation, please specify when ordering.

Special features

- Beautiful covered porch creates a Southern accent
- Kitchen has an organized feel with lots of cabinetry
- Large foyer has a grand entrance and leads into family room through columns and arched opening

© HOME DESIGN SERVICES, INC.

Family Room Interior View

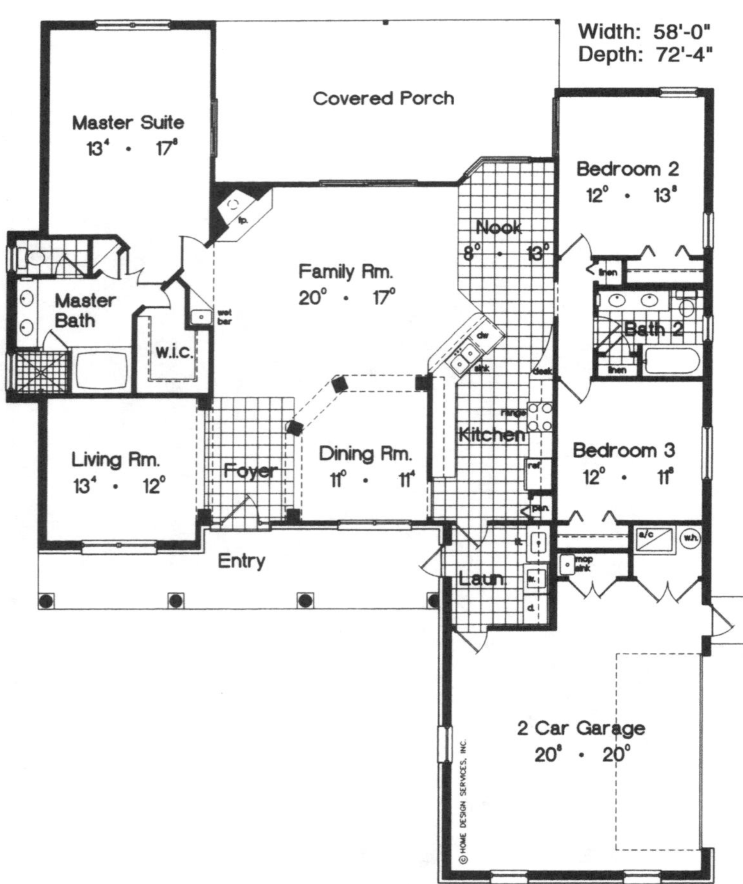
Width: 58'-0"
Depth: 72'-4"
Covered Porch
Master Suite
13^{4} · 17^{8}
Bedroom 2
12^{0} · 13^{8}
Nook
8^{0} · 13^{0}
Family Rm.
20^{0} · 17^{0}
Master Bath
w.i.c.
Bath 2
Living Rm.
13^{4} · 12^{0}
Foyer
Dining Rm.
11^{0} · 11^{4}
Kitchen
Bedroom 3
12^{0} · 11^{8}
Entry
Laun
2 Car Garage
20^{8} · 20^{0}
© HOME DESIGN SERVICES, INC.

Plan #531-HDS-1993

Price Code C

Total Living Area: 1,993 Sq. Ft.

Home has 3 bedrooms, 2 baths, 2-car side entry garage and slab foundation.

Special features

- Kitchen and nook share open view to the outdoors
- Ample-sized secondary bedrooms
- Well-designed master bath

TO ORDER BLUEPRINTS USE THE FORM ON PAGE 290 OR CALL TOLL-FREE **1-800-DREAM HOME** (373-2646)

Quaint Country-Style Home

LOWE'S

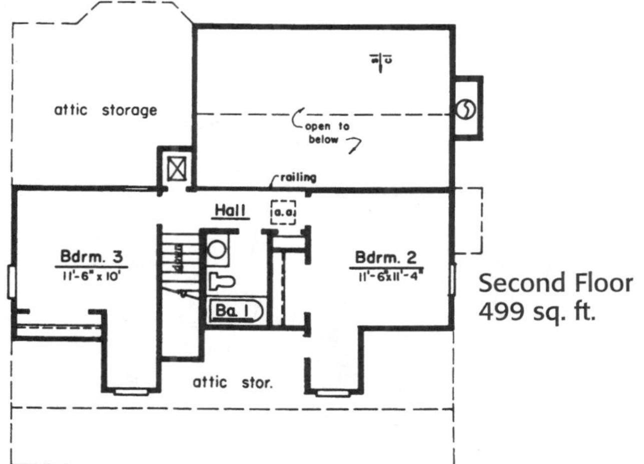
attic storage
open to below
railing
Hall
a.a.
Bdrm. 3
11'-6" x 10'
Ba. 1
Bdrm. 2
11'-6"x11'-4"
attic stor.

Second Floor
499 sq. ft.

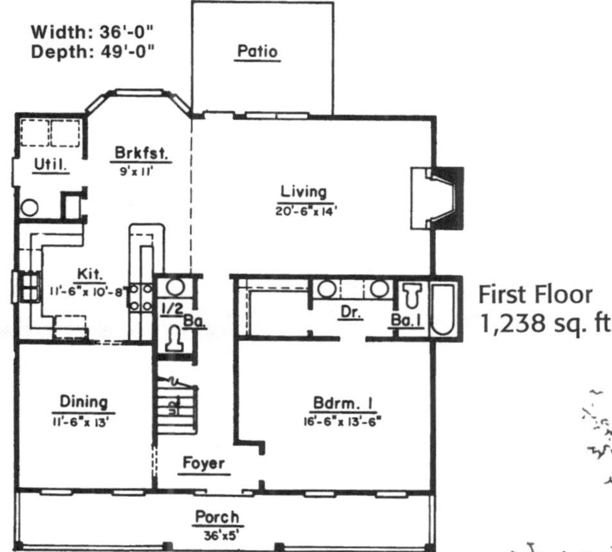
Width: 36'-0"
Depth: 49'-0"
Patio
Util.
Brkfst.
9' x 11'
Living
20'-6" x 14'
Kit.
11'-6" x 10'-8"
1/2 Ba.
Dr.
Ba. 1
Dining
11'-6" x 13'
Bdrm. 1
16'-6" x 13'-6"
Foyer
Porch
36' x 5'

First Floor
1,238 sq. ft.

Plan #531-CHP-1733-A-7

Price Code B

Total Living Area: 1,737 Sq. Ft.

Home has 3 bedrooms, 2 1/2 baths and slab or crawl space foundation, please specify when ordering.

Special features

- U-shaped kitchen, sunny bayed breakfast room and living area become one large gathering area
- Living area has sloped ceilings and a balcony overlook from second floor
- Second floor includes lots of storage area

Plan #531-DL-17353L1

Price Code B

Total Living Area: 1,735 Sq. Ft.

Home has 3 bedrooms, 2 baths, 2-car garage and basement foundation.

Special features

- Luxurious master bath has spa tub, shower, double vanity and large walk-in closet
- Peninsula in kitchen has sink and dishwasher
- Massive master bedroom has step up ceiling and private location

PATIO
LINEN
BATH
MASTER
13'-0" x 17'-8"
SHR.
DINING
10'-0" x 13'-0"
FAMILY RM.
18'-0" x 20'-8"
10'-CLG.
KNEE SPACE
STEP UP CLG.
CLOSET
NOOK
PLANT LEDGE ABOVE
BAR
10'-CLG.
DW
ENTRY
B.R.-2
10'-0" x 11'-0"
10'-CLG.
BATH
KITCH.
10'-6" x 11'-0"
UTIL.
P.
REF.
POR.
B.R.-3
11'-6" x 11'-0"
BARN CLG.
GARAGE
19'-6" x 20'-0"

Width: 50'-0"
Depth: 55'-0"

 TO ORDER BLUEPRINTS USE THE FORM ON PAGE 290 OR CALL TOLL-FREE **1-800-DREAM HOME** (373-2646)

LOWE'S

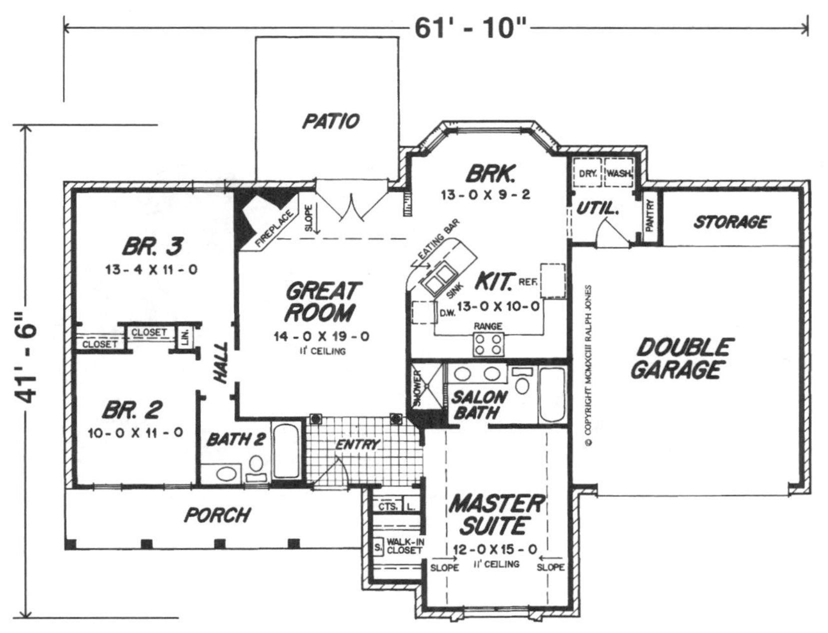
61' - 10"
41' - 6"
PATIO
BRK.
13-0 X 9-2
DRY.
WASH.
UTIL.
PANTRY
STORAGE
BR. 3
13-4 X 11-0
FIREPLACE
SLOPE
EATING BAR
GREAT ROOM
14-0 X 19-0
11' CEILING
KIT.
REF.
SINK
D.W.
13-0 X 10-0
RANGE
CLOSET
CLOSET
LIN.
HALL
BR. 2
10-0 X 11-0
BATH 2
ENTRY
SHOWER
SALON BATH
DOUBLE GARAGE
© COPYRIGHT MCMXCIII RALPH JONES
CTS.
L.
PORCH
MASTER SUITE
12-0 X 15-0
11' CEILING
SLOPE
SLOPE
S.
WALK-IN CLOSET

Plan #531-RJ-A1390

Price Code A

Total Living Area: 1,389 Sq. Ft.

Home has 3 bedrooms, 2 baths, 2-car garage and slab or crawl space foundation, please specify when ordering.

Special features

- Great open space for entertaining with eating bar in kitchen overlooking breakfast and great rooms
- Private master suite has sloped ceiling and secluded bath
- Handy extra storage space in garage

© COPYRIGHT MCMXCIII RALPH JONES
BENJAMIN GRADWELL

Plan #531-1127-1

partial basement/crawl space

Plan #531-1127-2

crawl space & slab

Price Code D

Total Living Area: 2,331 Sq. Ft.

Home has 3 bedrooms, 2 baths, 2-car garage and partial basement/crawl space, crawl space or slab foundation, please specify when ordering.

Special features

- Double staircases in front and back of home ideal for convenience
- Gathering room, dining room and kitchen combine creating a multi-purpose room perfect for entire family
- Studio loft above garage provides bonus space for office or hobby area

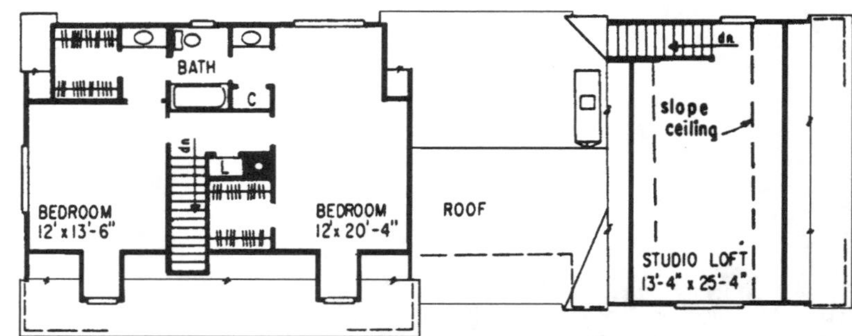

BATH
C
dn
L
BEDROOM 12' x 13'-6"
BEDROOM 12' x 20'-4"
ROOF
dn
slope ceiling
STUDIO LOFT 13'-4" x 25'-4"

Second Floor
717 sq. ft.

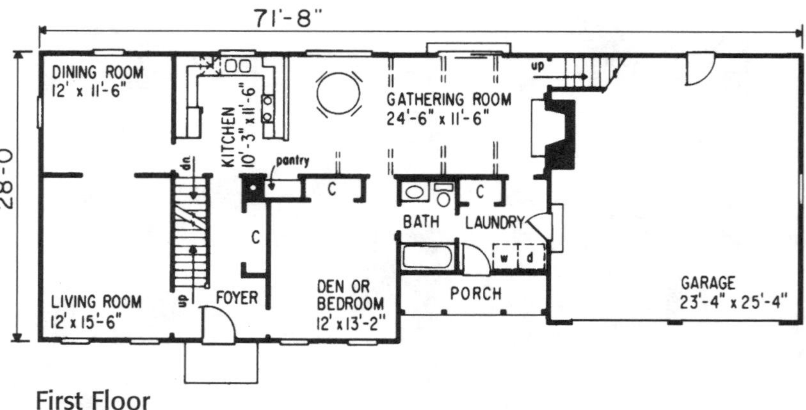

71'-8"
28'-0"
DINING ROOM 12' x 11'-6"
KITCHEN 10'-3" x 11'-6"
GATHERING ROOM 24'-6" x 11'-6"
up
dn
pantry
C
C
BATH
LAUNDRY
C
w
d
LIVING ROOM 12' x 15'-6"
up
FOYER
DEN OR BEDROOM 12' x 13'-2"
PORCH
GARAGE 23'-4" x 25'-4"

First Floor
1,250 sq. ft.

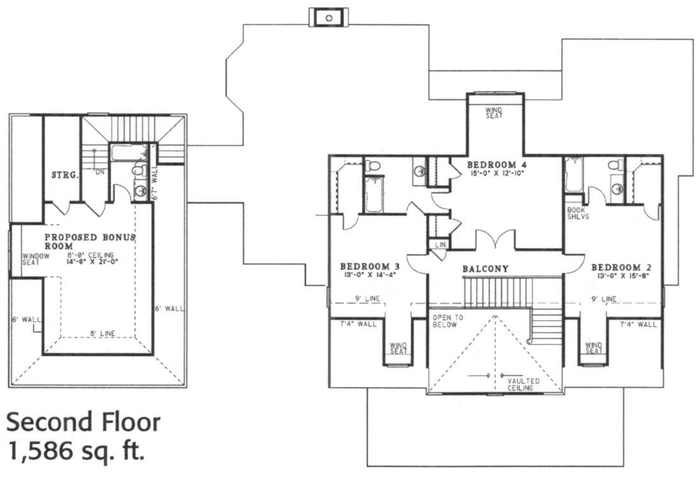

Second Floor
1,586 sq. ft.

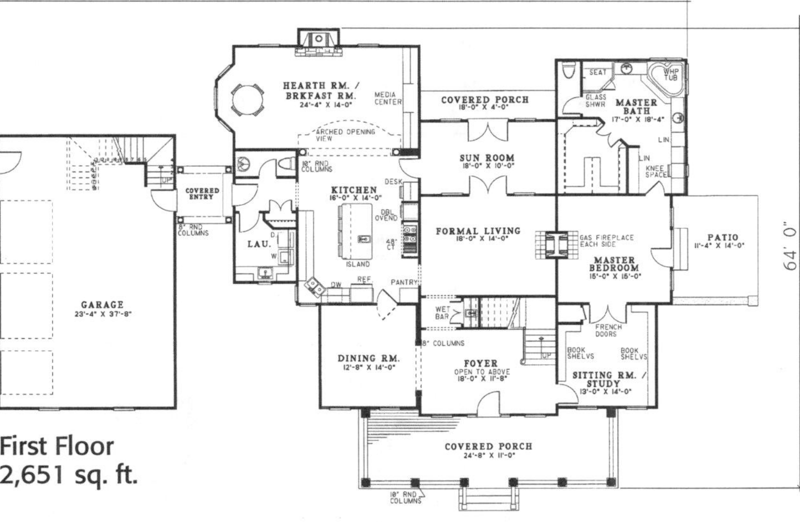

First Floor
2,651 sq. ft.

Plan #531-NDG-143

Price Code G

Total Living Area: 4,237 Sq. Ft.

Home has 4 bedrooms, 3 1/2 baths, 3-car side entry garage and basement, crawl space or slab foundation, please specify when ordering.

Special features

- Grand entrance has vaulted two-story foyer
- Fireplaces in formal living room and master bedroom
- Second floor bedrooms have their own window seats

Gabled Front Porch Gives A Country Flair

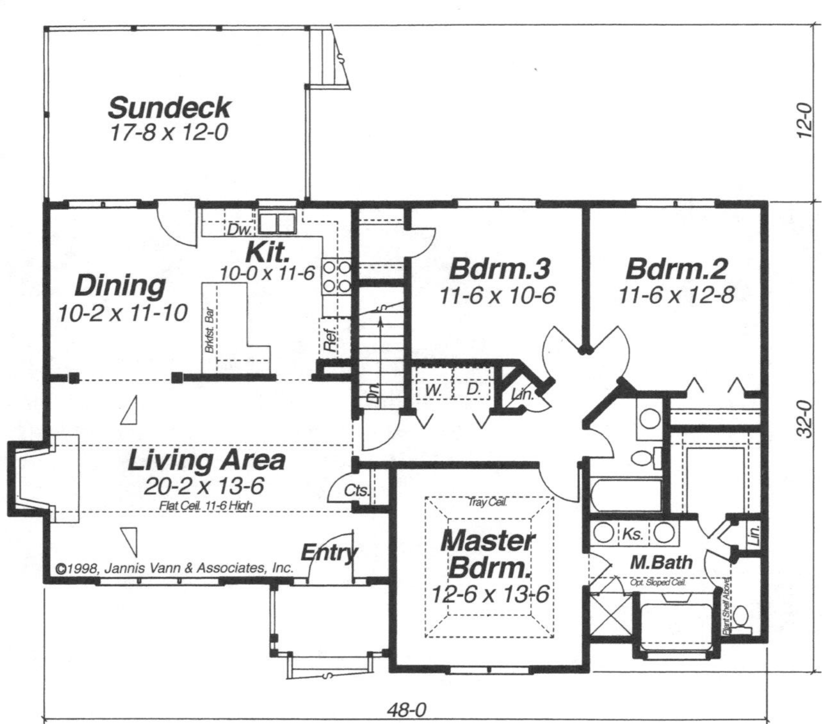
Sundeck
17-8 x 12-0
12-0
Dw.
Kit.
10-0 x 11-6
Dining
10-2 x 11-10
Brkfst. Bar
Ref.
Bdrm.3
11-6 x 10-6
Bdrm.2
11-6 x 12-8
Dn.
W.
D.
Lin.
32-0
Living Area
20-2 x 13-6
Flat Ceil. 11-6 High
Cts.
Tray Ceil.
Master
Bdrm.
12-6 x 13-6
Ks.
Lin.
M.Bath
Opt. Sloped Ceil.
Entry
©1998, Jannis Vann & Associates, Inc.
48-0

Plan #531-JV-1379

Price Code A

Total Living Area: 1,379 Sq. Ft.

Home has 3 bedrooms, 2 baths, 2-car drive under garage and basement foundation.

Special features

- Living area has spacious feel with 11'-6" ceiling
- Kitchen has eat-in breakfast bar open to dining area
- Laundry located near bedrooms
- Large cased opening with columns opens the living/dining area

 TO ORDER BLUEPRINTS USE THE FORM ON PAGE 290 OR CALL TOLL-FREE **1-800-DREAM HOME** (373-2646)

Inviting Home With Country Flavor

LOWE'S

malou

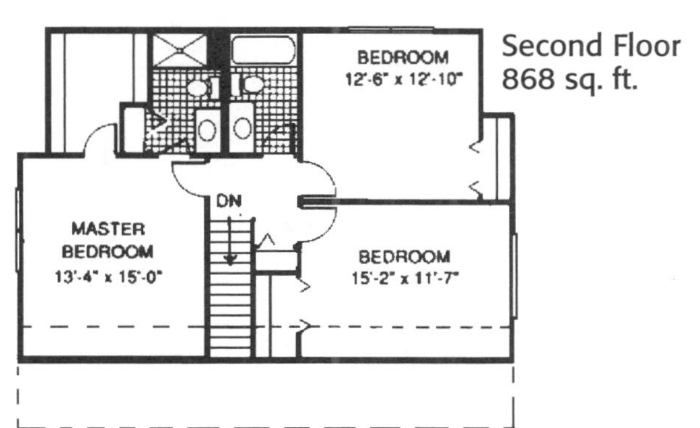
BEDROOM
12'-6" x 12'-10"
DN
MASTER BEDROOM
13'-4" x 15'-0"
BEDROOM
15'-2" x 11'-7"

Second Floor
868 sq. ft.

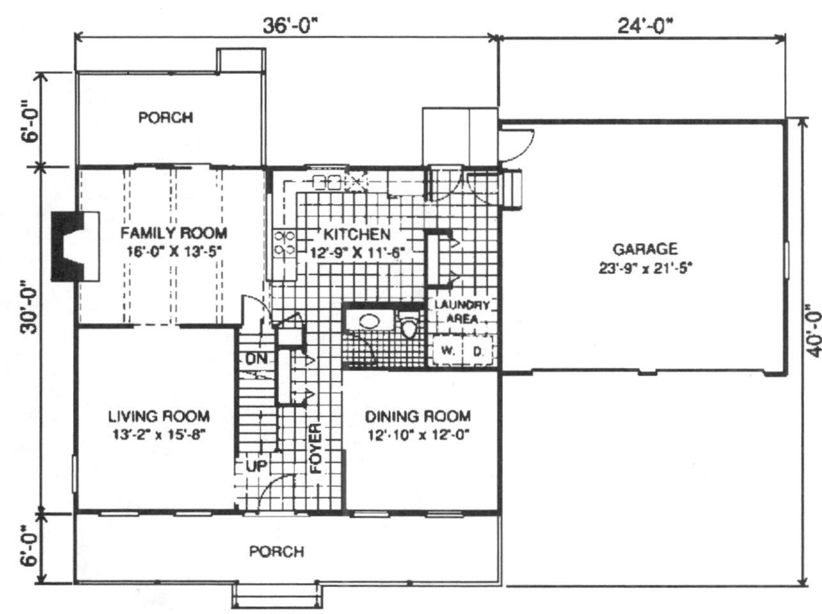
36'-0"
24'-0"
6'-0"
PORCH
FAMILY ROOM
16'-0" X 13'-5"
KITCHEN
12'-9" X 11'-6"
GARAGE
23'-9" x 21'-5"
30'-0"
LAUNDRY AREA
W. D.
40'-0"
DN
LIVING ROOM
13'-2" x 15'-8"
FOYER
DINING ROOM
12'-10" x 12'-0"
UP
6'-0"
PORCH

First Floor
1,080 sq. ft.

Plan #531-1347-1

basement

Plan #531-1347-2

crawl space

Price Code C

Total Living Area: 1,948 Sq. Ft.

Home has 3 bedrooms, 2 1/2 baths, 2-car garage and basement or crawl space foundation, please specify when ordering.

Special features

- Large elongated porch for moonlit evenings
- Stylish family room features beamed ceiling
- Skillfully designed kitchen convenient to an oversized laundry area
- Second floor bedrooms all generously sized

Plan #531-DDI-100214

Price Code C

Total Living Area: 2,104 Sq. Ft.

Home has 3 bedrooms, 2 baths, 2-car garage and crawl space foundation.

Special features

- 9' ceilings on the first floor
- Living room opens onto deck through double French doors
- Second floor includes large storage room

BDRM-3
13'-4"x 10'-5"
OPEN TO BELOW
STORAGE
10'-8"x 13'-2"
LOFT
BDRM-2
13'-4"x 10'-5"

Second Floor
669 sq. ft.

Width: 44'-0"
Depth: 65'-0"

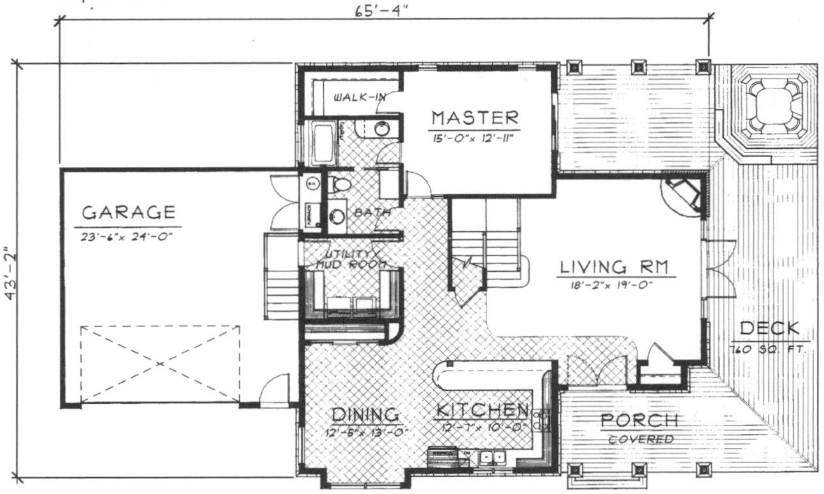

65'-4"
43'-2"
WALK-IN
MASTER
15'-0"x 12'-11"
GARAGE
23'-6"x 24'-0"
BATH
UTILITY/MUD ROOM
LIVING RM
18'-2"x 19'-0"
DECK
760 SQ. FT.
DINING
12'-5"x 13'-0"
KITCHEN
12'-1"x 10'-0"
PORCH
COVERED

First Floor
1,435 sq. ft.

Dramatic Angled Kitchen

LOWE'S

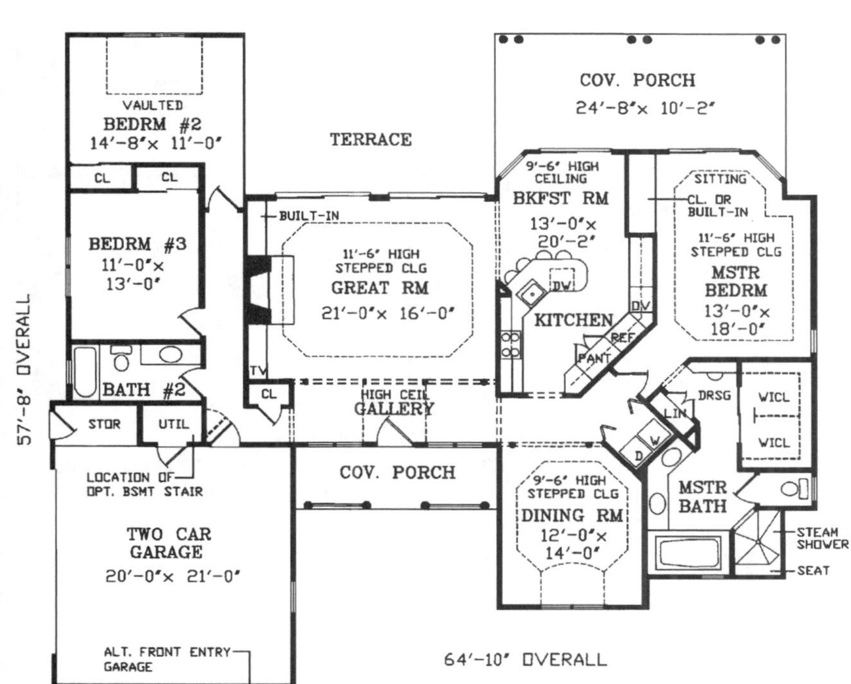
VAULTED
BEDRM #2
14'-8"× 11'-0"
TERRACE
COV. PORCH
24'-8"× 10'-2"
CL
CL
BUILT-IN
BEDRM #3
11'-0"×
13'-0"
11'-6" HIGH
STEPPED CLG
GREAT RM
21'-0"× 16'-0"
9'-6" HIGH
CEILING
BKFST RM
13'-0"×
20'-2"
DW
KITCHEN
REF
PANT
DW
SITTING
CL. OR
BUILT-IN
11'-6" HIGH
STEPPED CLG
MSTR
BEDRM
13'-0"×
18'-0"
57'-8" OVERALL
BATH #2
TV
CL
HIGH CEIL
GALLERY
DRSG
WICL
WICL
LIN
W
D
STOR
UTIL
LOCATION OF
OPT. BSMT STAIR
COV. PORCH
9'-6" HIGH
STEPPED CLG
DINING RM
12'-0"×
14'-0"
MSTR
BATH
STEAM
SHOWER
SEAT
TWO CAR
GARAGE
20'-0"× 21'-0"
ALT. FRONT ENTRY
GARAGE
64'-10" OVERALL

Plan #531-AX-4315

Price Code C

Total Living Area: 2,018 Sq. Ft.

Home has 3 bedrooms, 2 baths, 2-car side entry garage and basement, slab or crawl space foundation, please specify when ordering.

Special features

- Large expanses of elegant curved transomed windows flank the beautiful entrance
- Great room includes French doors to a large covered rear porch
- Luxurious master suite has fabulous master bath, double closets and accesses rear porch

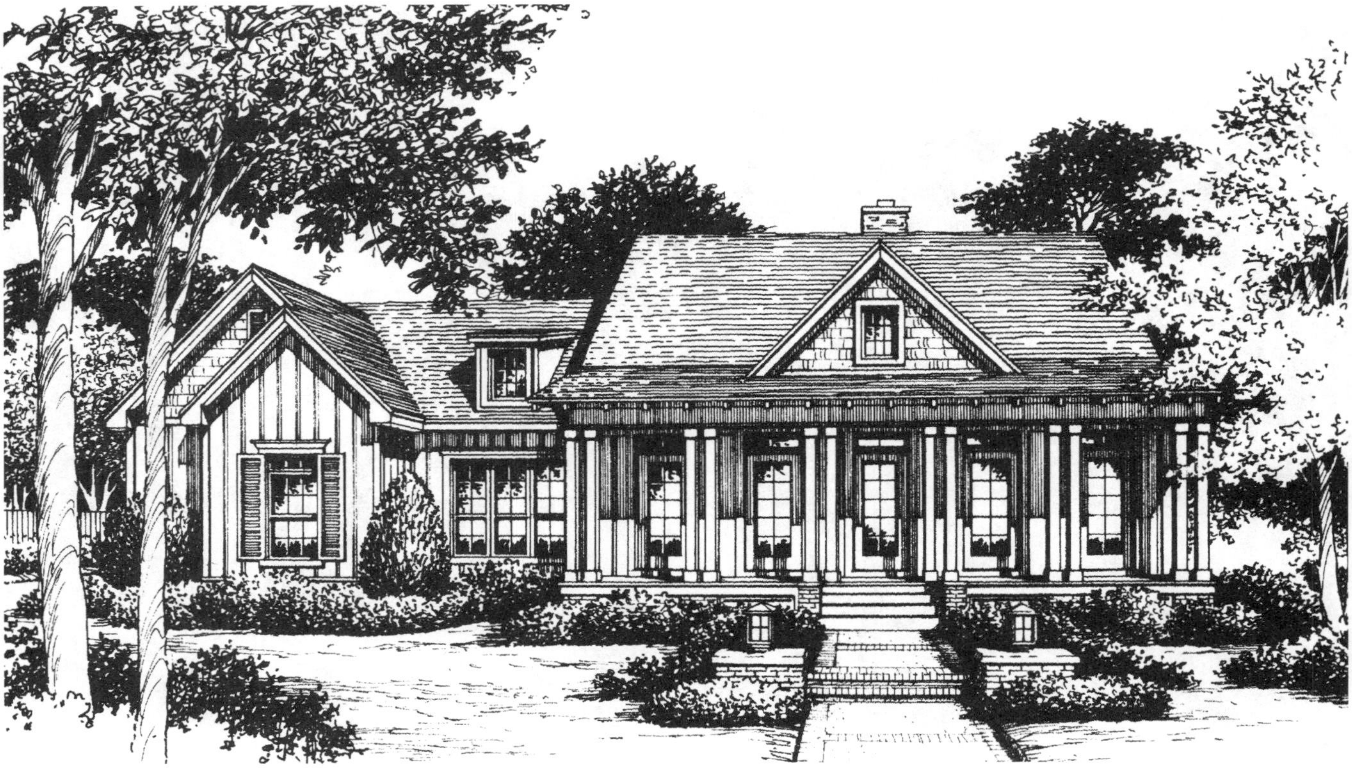

Charming Covered Porch

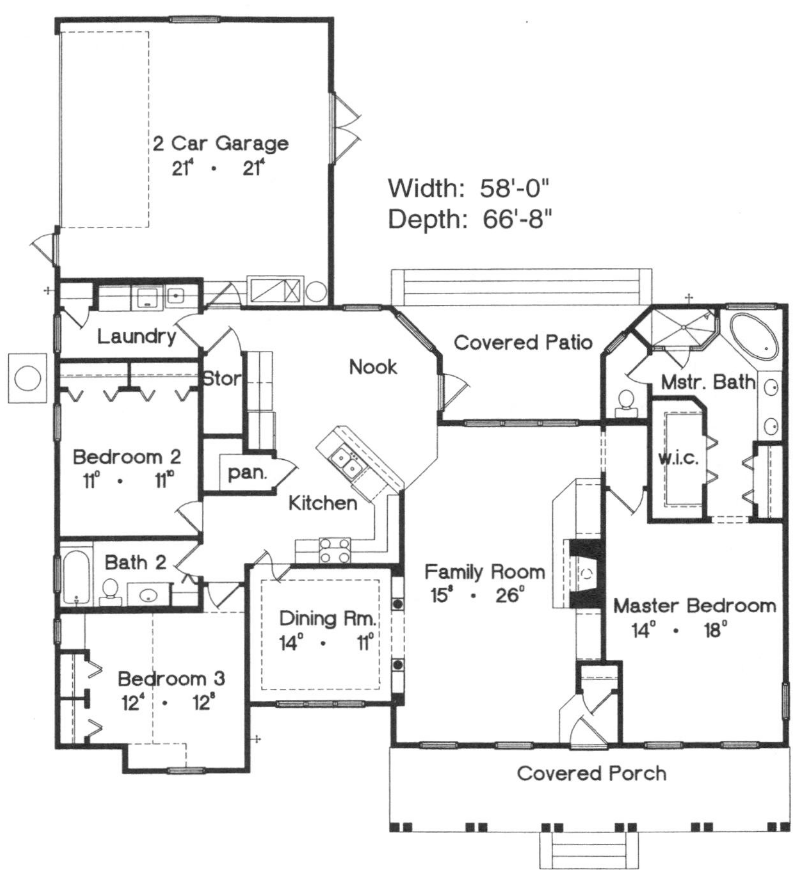
2 Car Garage
$21^{4} \cdot 21^{4}$
Width: 58'-0"
Depth: 66'-8"
Laundry
Stor
Nook
Covered Patio
Mstr. Bath
Bedroom 2
$11^{0} \cdot 11^{10}$
pan.
Kitchen
w.i.c.
Bath 2
Family Room
$15^{8} \cdot 26^{0}$
Master Bedroom
$14^{0} \cdot 18^{0}$
Dining Rm.
$14^{0} \cdot 11^{0}$
Bedroom 3
$12^{4} \cdot 12^{8}$
Covered Porch

Plan #531-HDS-1963

Price Code C

Total Living Area: 1,963 Sq. Ft.

Home has 3 bedrooms, 2 baths, 2-car side entry garage and basement, slab or crawl space foundation, please specify when ordering.

Special features

- Spacious breakfast nook is a great gathering place
- Master bedroom has its own wing with private bath and lots of closet space
- Large laundry room with closet and sink

LOWE'S

Width: 43'-0"
Depth: 74'-0"

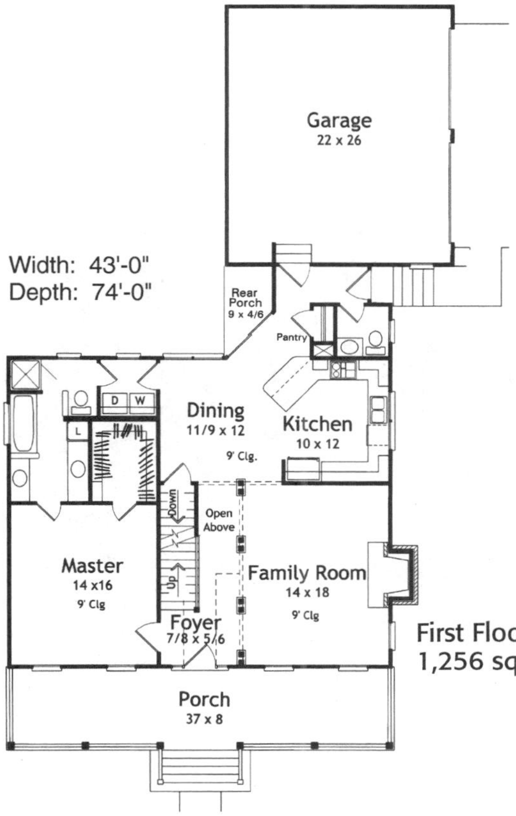

Garage 22 x 26
Rear Porch 9 x 4/6
Pantry
Dining 11/9 x 12 9' Clg.
Kitchen 10 x 12
D W
Master 14 x 16 9' Clg
Open Above
Family Room 14 x 18 9' Clg
Foyer 7/8 x 5/6
Porch 37 x 8

First Floor
1,256 sq. ft.

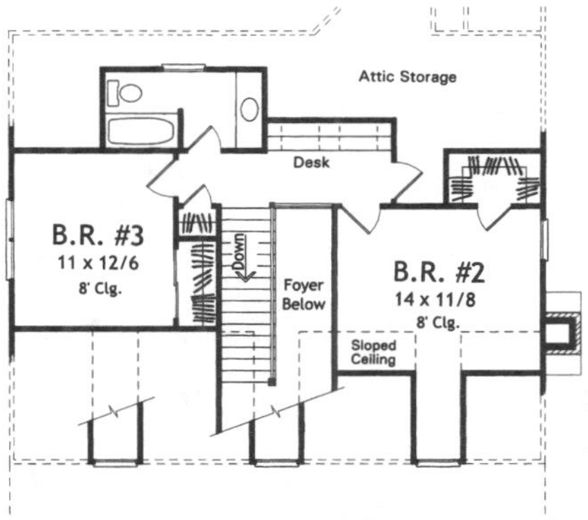

Attic Storage
Desk
B.R. #3 11 x 12/6 8' Clg.
Foyer Below
B.R. #2 14 x 11/8 8' Clg.
Sloped Ceiling

Second Floor
559 sq. ft.

Plan #531-GM-1815

Price Code C

Total Living Area: 1,815 Sq. Ft.

Home has 3 bedrooms, 2 1/2 baths, 2-car side entry garage and basement foundation.

Special features

- Inviting covered porch
- Lots of counterspace and cabinetry in kitchen
- Two doors into laundry area make it handy from master bedroom and the rest of the home
- Second floor has built-in desk in hall; ideal as a computer work station or mini office area

LOWE'S

ARTLINE
GSDG 2107

Second Floor
927 sq. ft.

VAULTED CEILING LINE
ATTIC STOR.
OPEN TO BELOW
OPEN RAILING
PLANT LEDGE
STOR
DN
BEDROOM 2
11-6 x 11-2
BATH
OPEN RAILING
PLAYROOM
13-2 x 19-2
STOR/ LINEN
OPEN TO BELOW
SLOPED CLG
BEDROOM 3
11-6 x 12

WIDTH 40'-0"
DEPTH 66'-6"

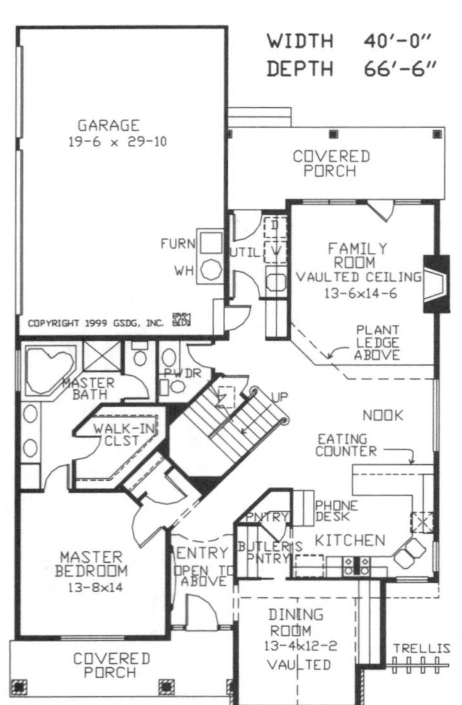
GARAGE
19-6 x 29-10
COVERED PORCH
FURN
WH
UTIL
FAMILY ROOM
VAULTED CEILING
13-6x14-6
COPYRIGHT 1999 GSDG, INC.
PLANT LEDGE ABOVE
PWDR
MASTER BATH
UP
NOOK
WALK-IN CLST
EATING COUNTER
PNTRY
PHONE DESK
KITCHEN
MASTER BEDROOM
13-8x14
ENTRY
OPEN TO ABOVE
BUTLER'S PNTRY
DINING ROOM
13-4x12-2
VAULTED
TRELLIS
COVERED PORCH

First Floor
1,495 sq. ft.

Plan #531-GSD-2107

Price Code D

Total Living Area: 2,422 Sq. Ft.

Home has 3 bedrooms, 2 1/2 baths, 3-car side entry garage and crawl space foundation.

Special features

- Covered porches invite guests into home
- Convenient and private first floor master suite
- Family room has vaulted ceiling
- 10' ceiling in dining room has formal feel
- Kitchen has walk-in pantry and eating bar

Attractive Dormers Enhance Facade

LOWE'S

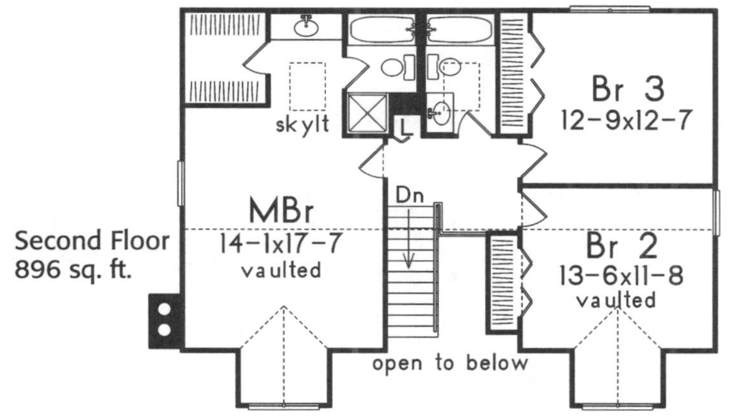
skylt
MBr
14-1x17-7
vaulted
Dn
Br 3
12-9x12-7
Br 2
13-6x11-8
vaulted
open to below

Second Floor
896 sq. ft.

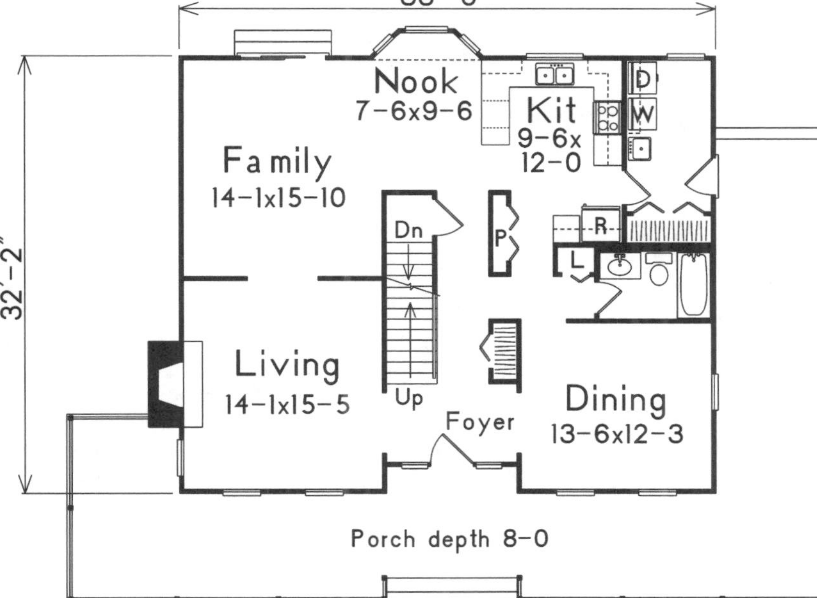
38'-0"
32'-2"
Nook
7-6x9-6
Kit
9-6x
12-0
D
W
Family
14-1x15-10
Dn
P
R
L
Living
14-1x15-5
Up
Foyer
Dining
13-6x12-3
Porch depth 8-0

First Floor
1,216 sq. ft.

Plan #531-1311

Price Code C

Total Living Area: 2,112 Sq. Ft.

Home has 3 bedrooms, 2 1/2 baths and basement foundation, drawings also include crawl space foundation.

Special features

- Double-door entrance from kitchen to dining area
- Both baths on second floor feature skylights
- Nook located between family room and kitchen makes an ideal breakfast area

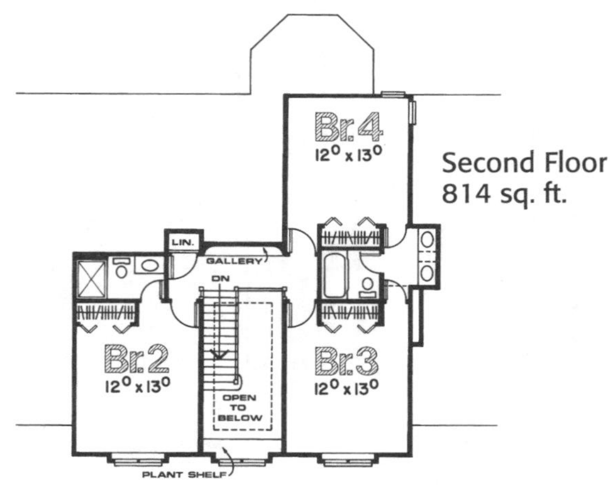
Br. 4
12⁰ x 13⁰
LIN.
GALLERY
DN
Br. 2
12⁰ x 13⁰
Br. 3
12⁰ x 13⁰
OPEN TO BELOW
PLANT SHELF

Second Floor
814 sq. ft.

Plan #531-DB2460

Price Code E

Total Living Area: 2,695 Sq. Ft.

Home has 4 bedrooms, 3 1/2 baths, 3-car side entry garage and basement foundation.

Special features

- Formal living room includes built-in bookshelves making this a perfect private retreat or study
- Master bedroom has dramatic cathedral ceiling, double closets and a luxurious bath with corner whirlpool tub
- Octagon-shaped breakfast room has cheerful atmosphere

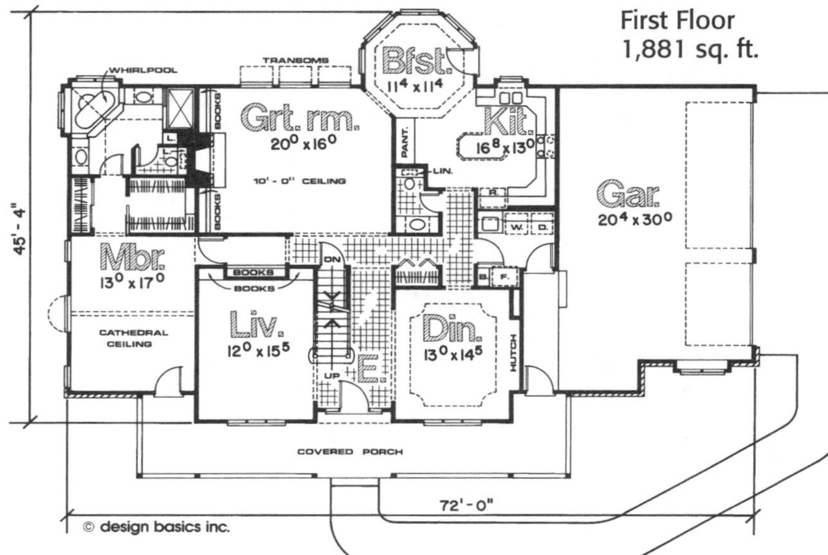
WHIRLPOOL
TRANSOMS
Bfst.
11⁴ x 11⁴
Grt. rm.
20⁰ x 16⁰
10' - 0" CEILING
BOOKS
PANT.
LIN.
Kit.
16⁸ x 13⁰
Gar.
20⁴ x 30⁰
W. D.
45' - 4"
Mbr.
13⁰ x 17⁰
CATHEDRAL CEILING
BOOKS
Liv.
12⁰ x 15⁵
DN
UP
E.
Din.
13⁰ x 14⁵
HUTCH
B. F.
COVERED PORCH
72' - 0"
© design basics inc.

First Floor
1,881 sq. ft.

Unique Octagon-Shaped Porch

LOWE'S

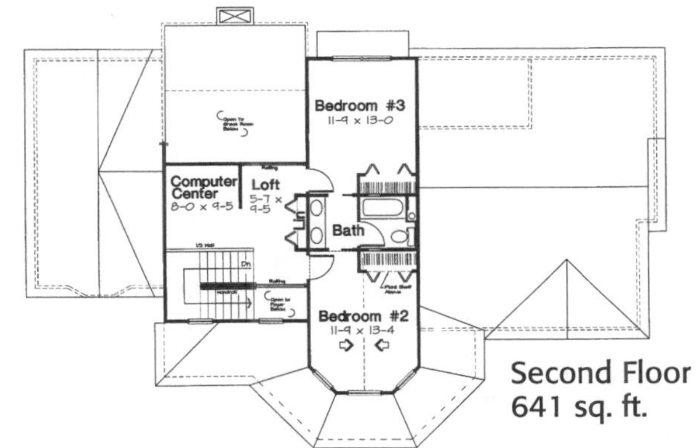

Bedroom #3
11-9 x 13-0
Computer Center
8-0 x 9-5
Loft
5-7 x 9-5
Bath
Bedroom #2
11-9 x 13-4

Second Floor
641 sq. ft.

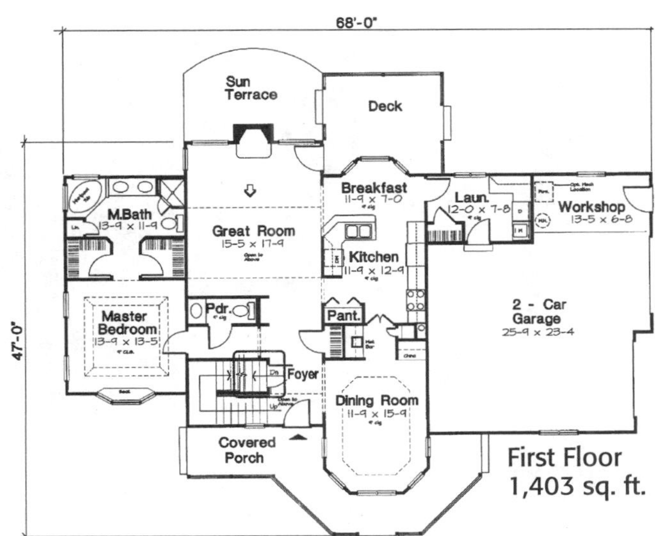

68'-0"
47'-0"
Sun Terrace
Deck
M.Bath
13-9 x 11-9
Great Room
15-5 x 17-9
Breakfast
11-9 x 7-0
Laun.
12-0 x 7-8
Workshop
13-5 x 6-8
Kitchen
11-9 x 12-9
Master Bedroom
13-9 x 13-5
Pdr.
Pant.
2 - Car Garage
25-9 x 23-4
Foyer
Dining Room
11-9 x 15-9
Covered Porch

First Floor
1,403 sq. ft.

Plan #531-GH-24736

Price Code C

Total Living Area: 2,044 Sq. Ft.

Home has 3 bedrooms, 2 1/2 baths, 2-car side entry garage and basement, crawl space or slab foundation, please specify when ordering.

Special features

- Formal dining area easily accesses kitchen through double-doors
- Two-car garage features a workshop area for projects or extra storage
- Second floor includes loft space ideal for office area and a handy computer center
- Colossal master bedroom with double walk-in closets, private bath bay window seat

Plan #531-AM2281

Price Code E

Total Living Area: 2,730 Sq. Ft.

Home has 3 bedrooms, 2 1/2 baths, 2-car garage and crawl space foundation.

Special features

- Enormous double-door bonus room on second floor can easily convert to children's play area or home office
- Nook makes ideal breakfast room adjacent to kitchen
- Spacious parlor creates a place for quiet
- 9' ceilings on first floor

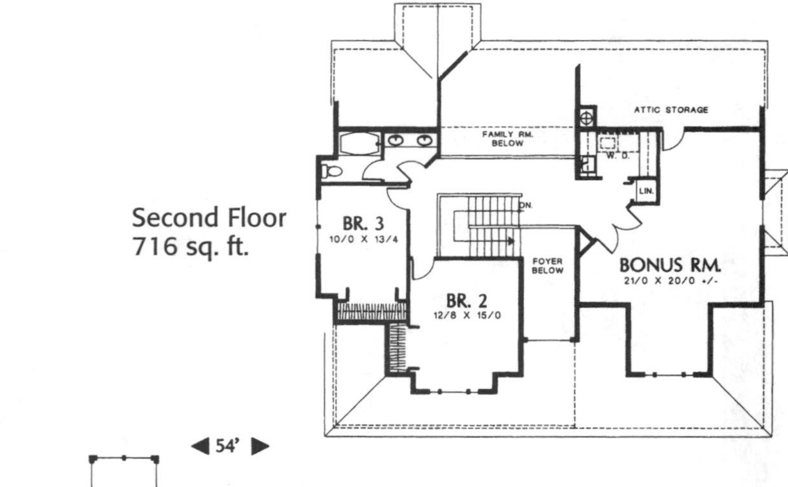
ATTIC STORAGE
FAMILY RM. BELOW
W. D.
LIN.
BR. 3
10/0 X 13/4
DN.
FOYER BELOW
BONUS RM.
21/0 X 20/0 +/-
BR. 2
12/8 X 15/0

Second Floor
716 sq. ft.

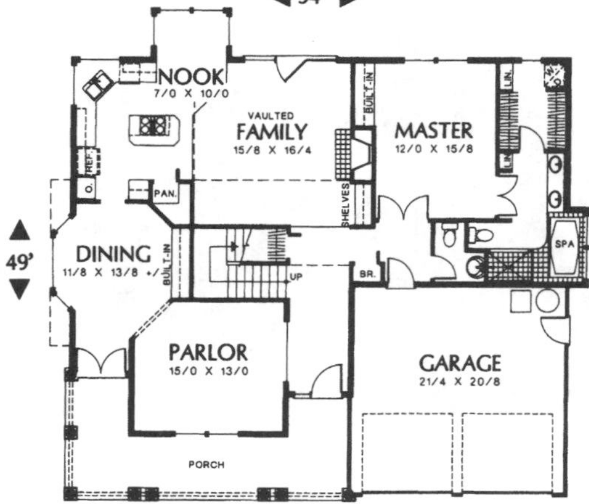
54'
49'
NOOK
7/0 X 10/0
VAULTED
FAMILY
15/8 X 16/4
MASTER
12/0 X 15/8
BUILT-IN
LIN.
REF.
O.
PAN.
SHELVES
DINING
11/8 X 13/8 +/-
BUILT-IN
UP
BR.
SPA
PARLOR
15/0 X 13/0
GARAGE
21/4 X 20/8
PORCH

First Floor
1,587 sq. ft.

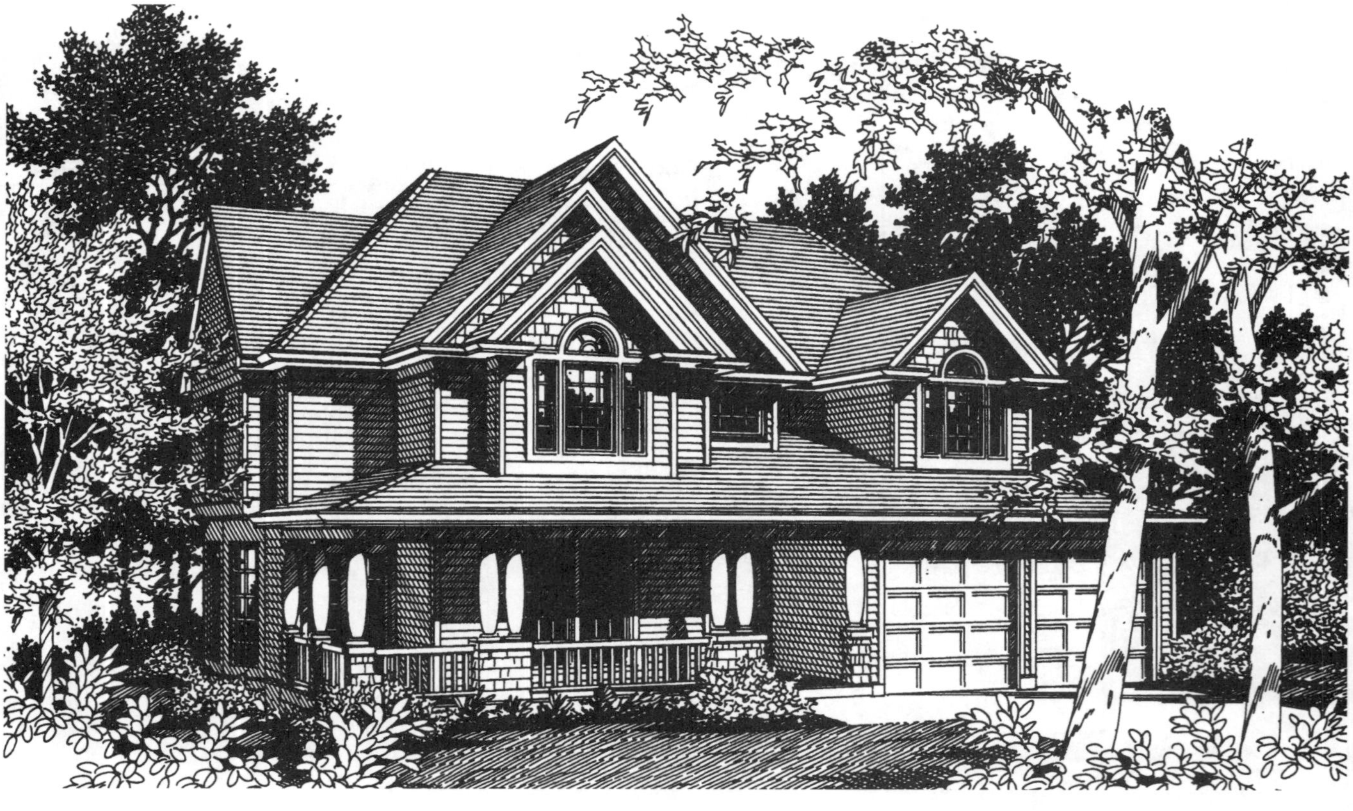

Country Styling With Splendid Floor Plan

LOWE'S

Plan #531-1112

Price Code C

Total Living Area: 2,137 Sq. Ft.

Home has 4 bedrooms, 2 1/2 baths, 2-car garage and partial basement/crawl space foundation.

Special features

- Spacious porch for plants, chairs and family gatherings
- Huge living room includes front and rear views
- U-shaped kitchen features abundant storage
- Laundry with large closet has its own porch

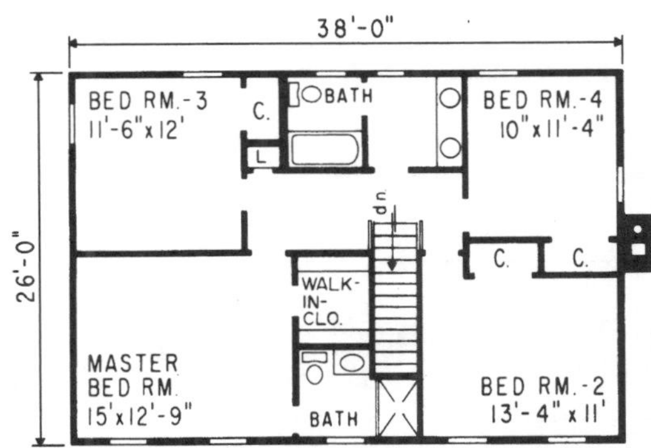
38'-0"
26'-0"
BED RM.-3
11'-6"x12'
C.
BATH
L
BED RM.-4
10"x11'-4"
dn
C.
C.
WALK-IN-CLO.
MASTER BED RM.
15'x12'-9"
BATH
BED RM.-2
13'-4"x11'

Second Floor
988 sq. ft.

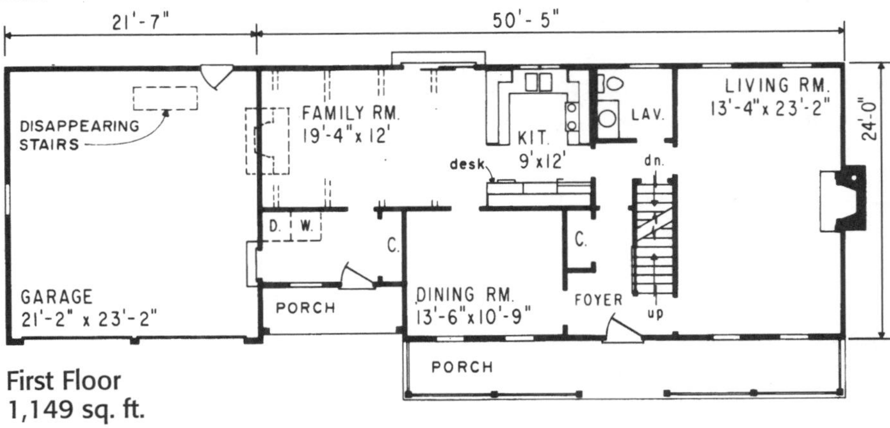
21'-7"
50'-5"
24'-0"
DISAPPEARING STAIRS
FAMILY RM.
19'-4"x12'
KIT.
9'x12'
desk
LAV.
LIVING RM.
13'-4"x23'-2"
dn.
D. W.
C.
C.
GARAGE
21'-2" x 23'-2"
PORCH
DINING RM.
13'-6"x10'-9"
FOYER
up
PORCH

First Floor
1,149 sq. ft.

LOWE'S

High Ceilings Create Open Atmosphere

Plan #531-JA-70797

Price Code B

Total Living Area: 1,633 Sq. Ft.

Home has 3 bedrooms, 2 baths, 2-car garage and basement foundation.

Special features

- Large open kitchen has ample counterspace
- Laundry room conveniently located
- Cathedral ceilings in master bedroom

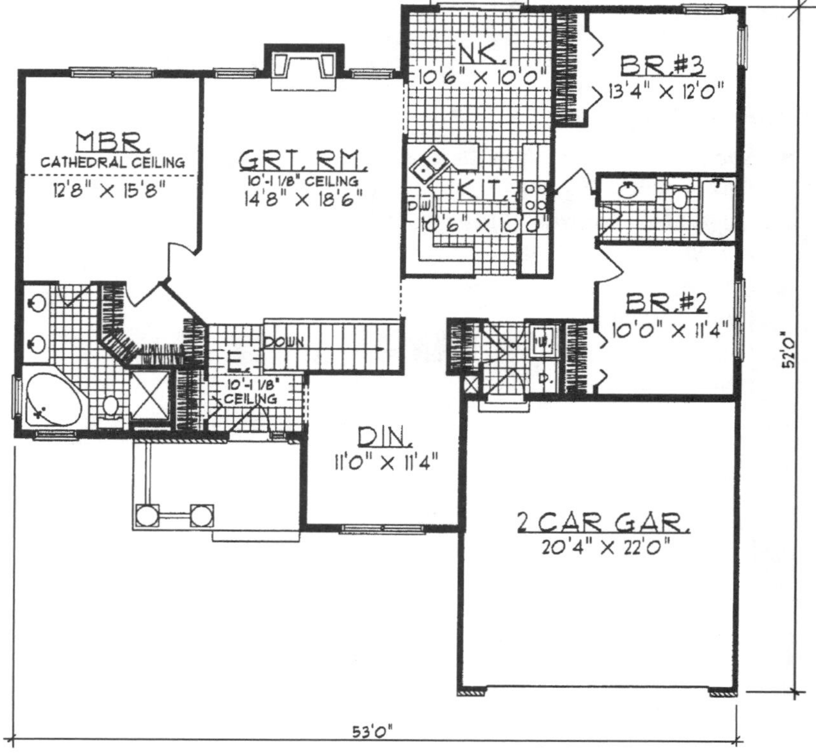
NK.
10'6" X 10'0"
BR.#3
13'4" X 12'0"
MBR.
CATHEDRAL CEILING
12'8" X 15'8"
GRT. RM.
10'-1 1/8" CEILING
14'8" X 18'6"
KIT.
10'6" X 10'0"
BR.#2
10'0" X 11'4"
DOWN
E.
10'-1 1/8" CEILING
DIN.
11'0" X 11'4"
2 CAR GAR.
20'4" X 22'0"
52'0"
53'0"

LOWE'S

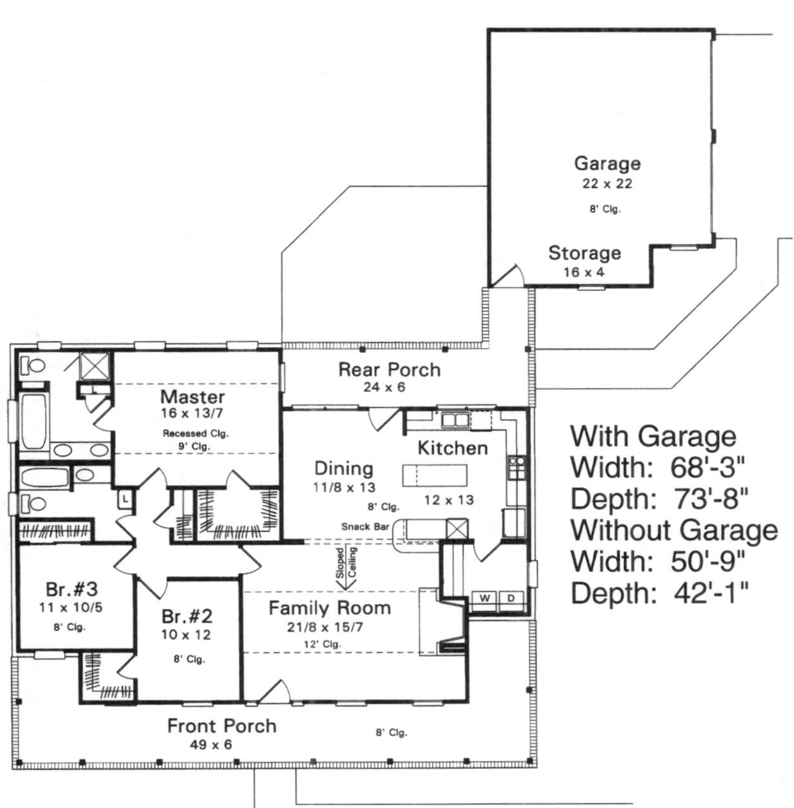
Garage
22 x 22
8' Clg.
Storage
16 x 4
Rear Porch
24 x 6
Master
16 x 13/7
Recessed Clg.
9' Clg.
Dining
11/8 x 13
8' Clg.
Kitchen
12 x 13
Snack Bar
Sloped Ceiling
Br.#3
11 x 10/5
8' Clg.
Br.#2
10 x 12
8' Clg.
Family Room
21/8 x 15/7
12' Clg.
W
D
L
Front Porch
49 x 6
8' Clg.
With Garage
Width: 68'-3"
Depth: 73'-8"
Without Garage
Width: 50'-9"
Depth: 42'-1"

Plan #531-GM-1550

Price Code B

Total Living Area: 1,550 Sq. Ft.

Home has 3 bedrooms, 2 baths, 2-car detached garage and slab or crawl space foundation, please specify when ordering.

Special features

- Wrap-around front porch is an ideal gathering place
- Handy snack bar is positioned so kitchen flows into family room
- Master bedroom has many amenities

WIDTH: 66'-0"
DEPTH: 44'-0'

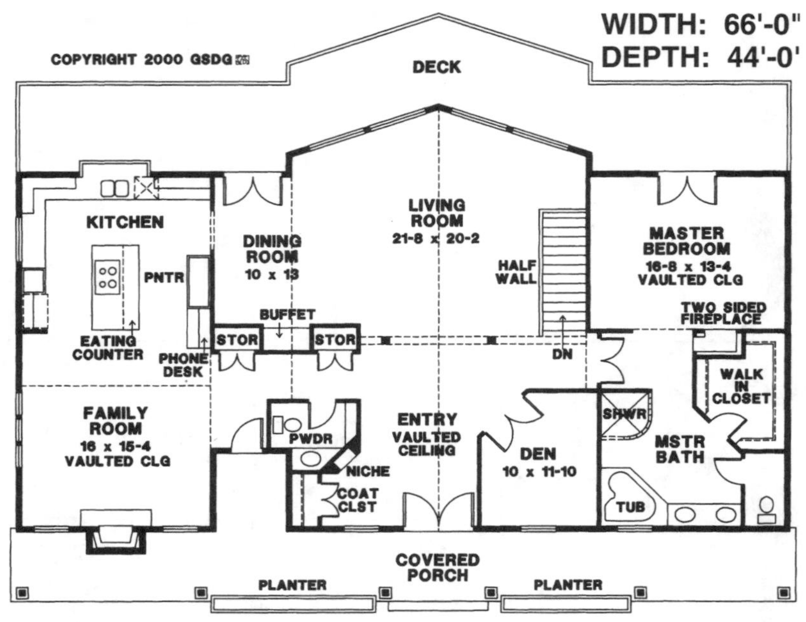
COPYRIGHT 2000 GSDG
DECK
KITCHEN
DINING ROOM 10 x 13
LIVING ROOM 21-8 x 20-2
MASTER BEDROOM 16-8 x 13-4 VAULTED CLG
PNTR
HALF WALL
BUFFET
TWO SIDED FIREPLACE
EATING COUNTER
PHONE DESK
STOR
STOR
DN
WALK IN CLOSET
FAMILY ROOM 16 x 15-4 VAULTED CLG
PWDR
ENTRY VAULTED CEILING
SHWR
MSTR BATH
DEN 10 x 11-10
NICHE
COAT CLST
TUB
COVERED PORCH
PLANTER
PLANTER

First Floor
2,169 sq. ft.

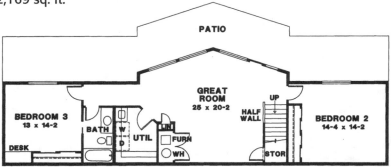

Plan #531-GSD-2825

Price Code F

Total Living Area: 3,230 Sq. Ft.

Home has 3 bedrooms, 2 1/2 baths and walk-out basement foundation.

Special features

- Efficiently designed eating counter in kitchen for added dining
- Enormous deck surrounds the rear of this home making it perfect for entertaining
- Interesting two-sided fireplace in master bedroom
- Open living areas create a feeling of spaciousness

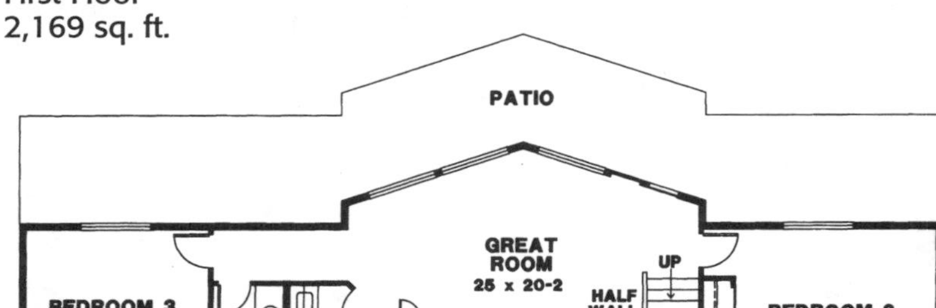
PATIO
GREAT ROOM 25 x 20-2
UP
HALF WALL
BEDROOM 3 13 x 14-2
BEDROOM 2 14-4 x 14-2
BATH
W
D
UTIL
LIN
FURN
WH
DESK
STOR

Lower Level
1,061 sq. ft.

GSDG 2825

TO ORDER BLUEPRINTS USE THE FORM ON PAGE 290 OR CALL TOLL-FREE **1-800-DREAM HOME** (373-2646)

LOWE'S

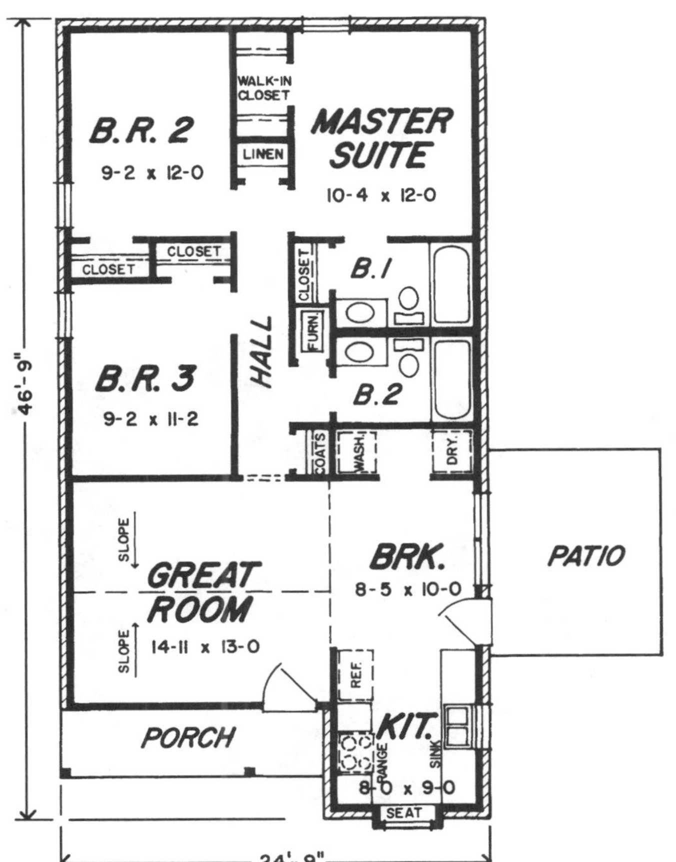
WALK-IN CLOSET
B.R. 2
9-2 x 12-0
LINEN
MASTER SUITE
10-4 x 12-0
CLOSET
CLOSET
CLOSET
B.1
FURN.
HALL
B.R. 3
9-2 x 11-2
B.2
COATS
WASH.
DRY.
SLOPE
GREAT ROOM
14-11 x 13-0
SLOPE
BRK.
8-5 x 10-0
PATIO
REF.
KIT.
RANGE
SINK
8-0 x 9-0
SEAT
PORCH
46'-9"
24'-9"

Plan #531-RJ-A1068V

Price Code AA

Total Living Area: 1,053 Sq. Ft.

Home has 3 bedrooms, 2 baths and slab or crawl space foundation, please specify when ordering.

Special features

- Handy utility closet off breakfast room
- Organized kitchen has everything close by for easy preparation
- Sloped ceiling in great room adds a dramatic touch

Plan #531-DB2384

Price Code C

Total Living Area: 1,948 Sq. Ft.

Home has 3 bedrooms, 2 1/2 baths, 2-car garage and basement foundation.

Special features

- Bayed breakast room connects to kitchen for convenience
- Master bath has impressive corner whirlpool tub and is covered in sunlight
- Transom windows in dining and great rooms flood the area with sunlight

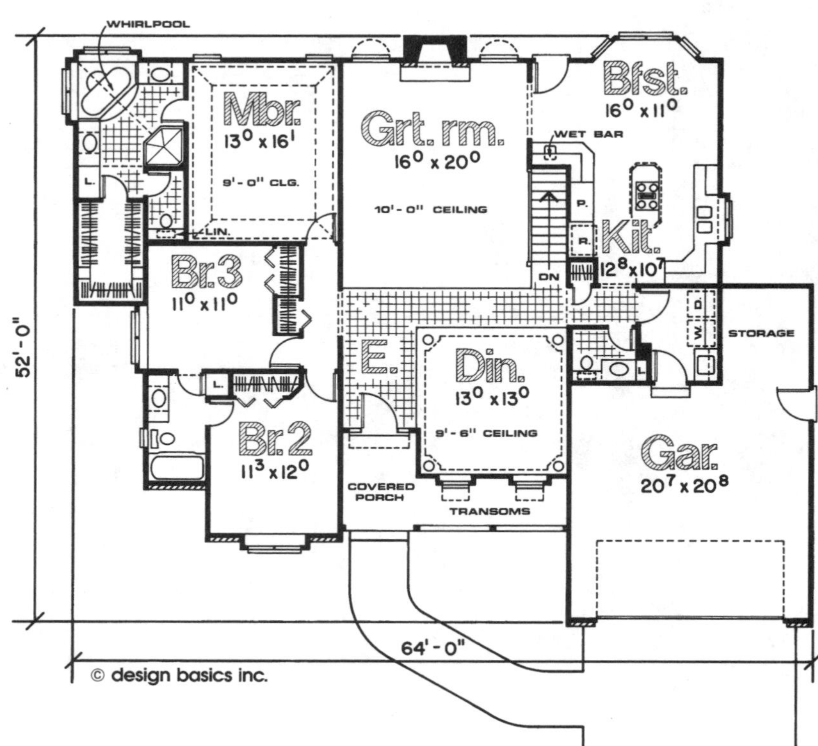
WHIRLPOOL
Mbr.
13^{0} x 16^{1}
9'-0" CLG.
Grt. rm.
16^{0} x 20^{0}
10'-0" CEILING
Bfst.
16^{0} x 11^{0}
WET BAR
Kit.
12^{8} x 10^{7}
LIN.
Br.3
11^{0} x 11^{0}
DN
STORAGE
E.
Din.
13^{0} x 13^{0}
9'-6" CEILING
Br.2
11^{3} x 12^{0}
COVERED PORCH
TRANSOMS
Gar.
20^{7} x 20^{8}
52'-0"
64'-0"
© design basics inc.

Stucco With Brick Accents

LOWE'S

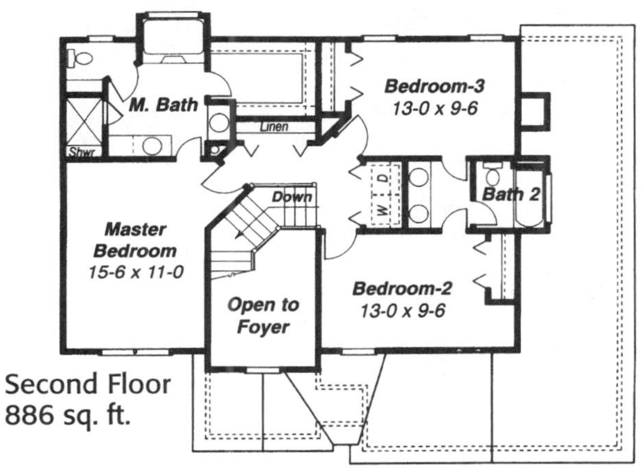
M. Bath
Shwr
Linen
Bedroom-3
13-0 x 9-6
Down
W D
Bath 2
Master
Bedroom
15-6 x 11-0
Open to
Foyer
Bedroom-2
13-0 x 9-6

Second Floor
886 sq. ft.

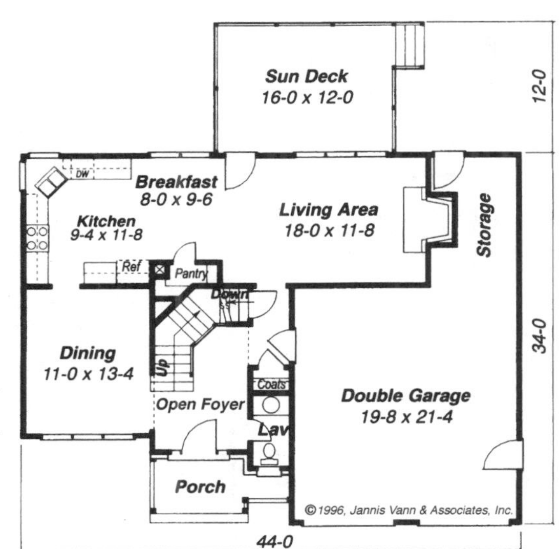
Sun Deck
16-0 x 12-0
12-0
DW
Breakfast
8-0 x 9-6
Living Area
18-0 x 11-8
Kitchen
9-4 x 11-8
Storage
Ref
Pantry
Down
Dining
11-0 x 13-4
Up
Coats
Open Foyer
Double Garage
19-8 x 21-4
34-0
Lav
Porch
©1996, Jannis Vann & Associates, Inc.
44-0

First Floor
797 sq. ft.

Plan #531-JV-1683-B

Price Code B

Total Living Area: 1,683 Sq. Ft.

Home has 3 bedrooms, 2 1/2 baths, 2-car garage and walk-out basement foundation.

Special features

- Open foyer and angled stairs add drama to entry
- Rear living areas are open and spacious
- Master bath features garden tub, double vanities and private toilet area

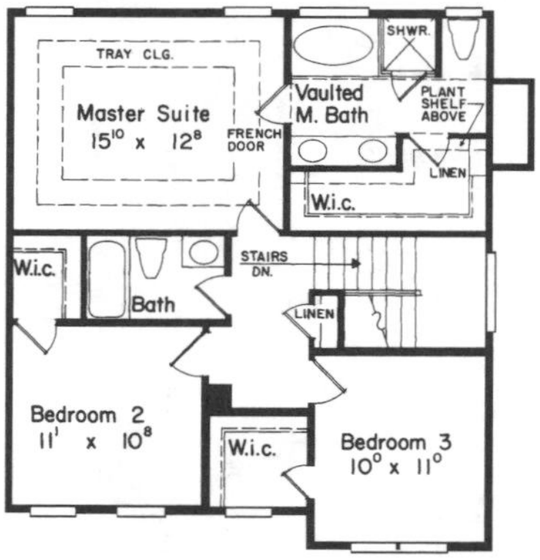

Plan #531-FB-766

Price Code B

Total Living Area: 1,671 Sq. Ft.

Home has 3 bedrooms, 2 1/2 baths, 2-car garage and crawl space or walk-out basement foundation, please specify when ordering.

Special features

- 9' ceilings throughout the first floor
- Master suite has spacious bath with enormous walk-in closet, oversized tub and double vanity
- Handsome formal living and dining rooms in the front of the home

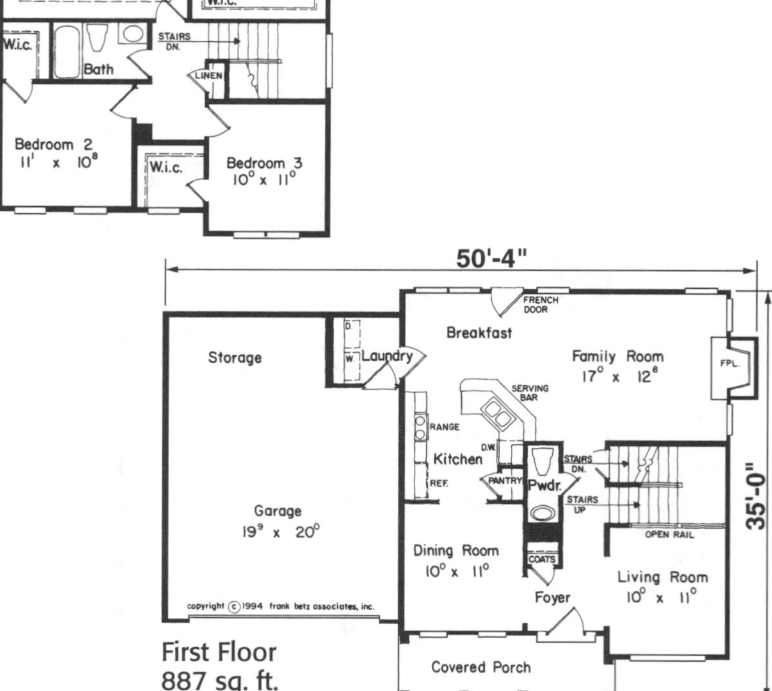
TRAY CLG.
Master Suite
15¹⁰ x 12⁸
FRENCH DOOR
Vaulted M. Bath
SHWR.
PLANT SHELF ABOVE
LINEN
W.i.c.
STAIRS DN.
W.i.c.
Bath
LINEN
Bedroom 2
11¹ x 10⁸
W.i.c.
Bedroom 3
10⁰ x 11⁰
Second Floor
784 sq. ft.
50'-4"
35'-0"
FRENCH DOOR
Breakfast
Storage
Laundry
Family Room
17⁰ x 12⁸
FPL.
SERVING BAR
RANGE
D.W.
Kitchen
REF.
PANTRY
Pwdr.
STAIRS DN.
STAIRS UP
Garage
19⁹ x 20⁰
OPEN RAIL
Dining Room
10⁰ x 11⁰
COATS
Living Room
10⁰ x 11⁰
Foyer
copyright (c) 1994 frank betz associates, inc.
Covered Porch
First Floor
887 sq. ft.

TO ORDER BLUEPRINTS USE THE FORM ON PAGE 290 OR CALL TOLL-FREE **1-800-DREAM HOME** (373-2646)

LOWE'S

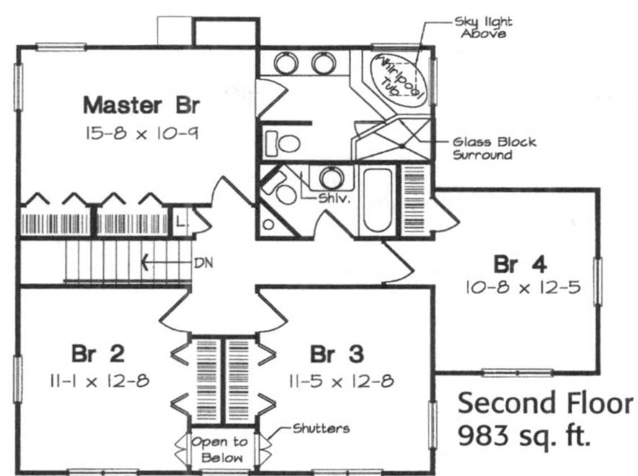
Sky light
Above
Whirlpool
Tub
Master Br
15-8 x 10-9
Glass Block
Surround
Shlv.
DN
Br 4
10-8 x 12-5
Br 2
11-1 x 12-8
Br 3
11-5 x 12-8
Shutters
Open to
Below

Second Floor
983 sq. ft.

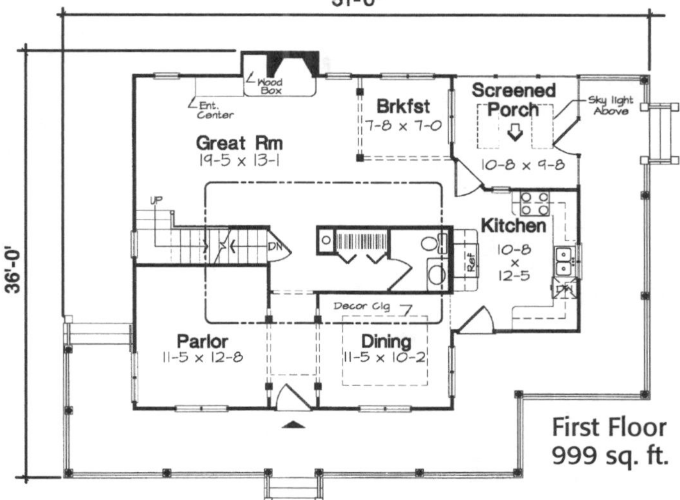
51'-0"
36'-0'
Wood
Box
Ent.
Center
Brkfst
7-8 x 7-0
Screened
Porch
10-8 x 9-8
Sky light
Above
Great Rm
19-5 x 13-1
UP
DN
Kitchen
10-8
x
12-5
Ref
DW
Decor Clg
Parlor
11-5 x 12-8
Dining
11-5 x 10-2

First Floor
999 sq. ft.

Plan #531-GH-24724

Price Code C

Total Living Area:	1,982 Sq. Ft.

Home has 4 bedrooms, 2 1/2 baths and crawl space or slab foundation, please specify when ordering.

Special features

- Spacious master bedroom has bath with corner whirlpool tub and sunny skylight above
- Breakfast area overlooks into great room
- Screened porch with skylight above extends the home outdoors and allows for entertainment area

Plan #531-1102

Price Code D

Total Living Area: 2,298 Sq. Ft.

Home has 3 bedrooms, 2 1/2 baths, 2-car garage and basement foundation, drawings also include crawl space or slab foundations.

Special features

- Great room features spectacular sloped ceiling adding drama
- Laundry and hobby room connects to garage for easy access
- Second floor loft area creates an ideal children's play area or secluded home office

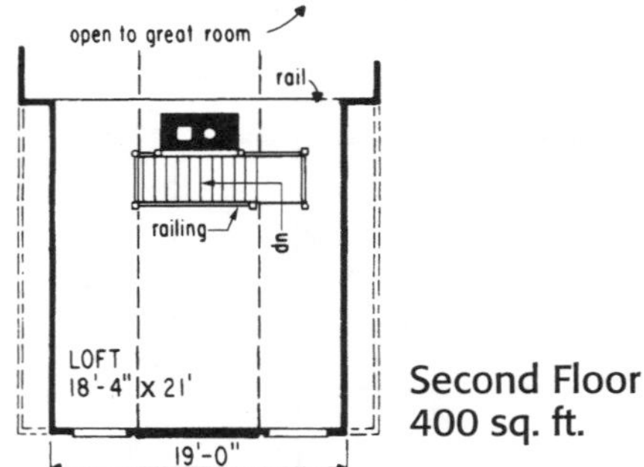
open to great room
rail
railing
dn
LOFT
18'-4" x 21'
19'-0"

Second Floor
400 sq. ft.

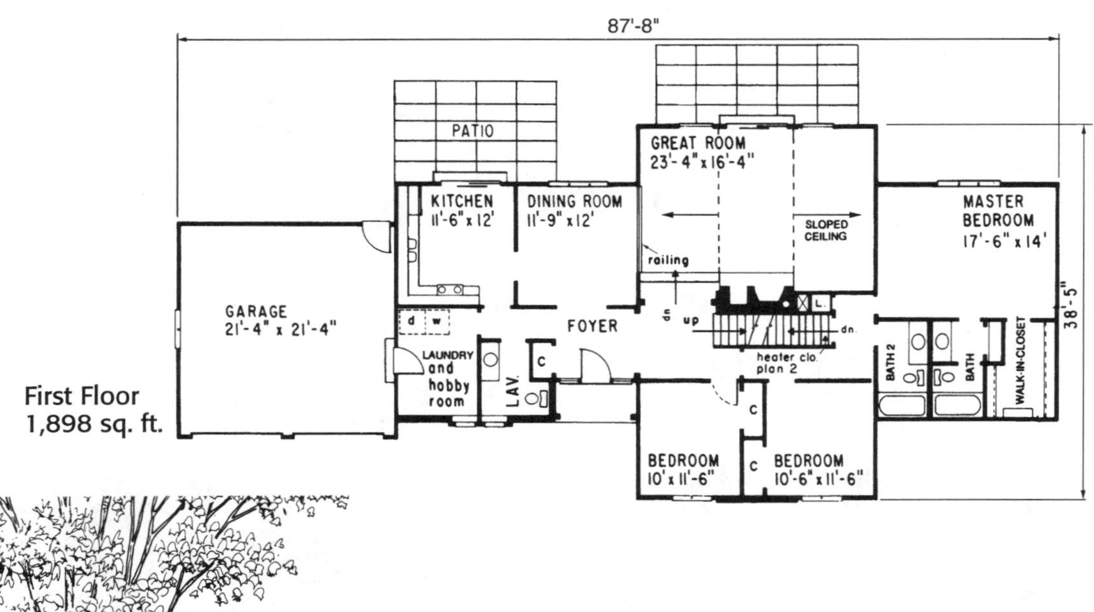
87'-8"
PATIO
GREAT ROOM
23'-4" x 16'-4"
SLOPED CEILING
railing
KITCHEN
11'-6" x 12'
DINING ROOM
11'-9" x 12'
MASTER BEDROOM
17'-6" x 14'
GARAGE
21'-4" x 21'-4"
FOYER
dn
up
dn
LAUNDRY and hobby room
LAV.
heater clo. plan 2
BATH 2
BATH
WALK-IN-CLOSET
38'-5"
BEDROOM
10' x 11'-6"
BEDROOM
10'-6" x 11'-6"

First Floor
1,898 sq. ft.

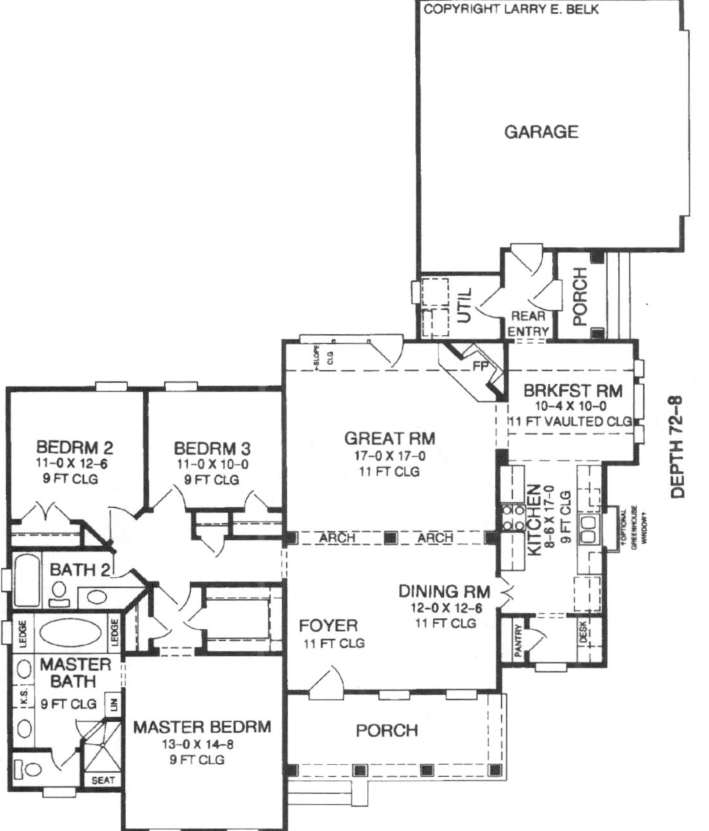
COPYRIGHT LARRY E. BELK
GARAGE
UTIL
REAR ENTRY
PORCH
FP
BRKFST RM
10–4 X 10–0
11 FT VAULTED CLG
GREAT RM
17–0 X 17–0
11 FT CLG
BEDRM 2
11–0 X 12–6
9 FT CLG
BEDRM 3
11–0 X 10–0
9 FT CLG
ARCH
ARCH
KITCHEN
8–6 X 17–0
9 FT CLG
BATH 2
DINING RM
12–0 X 12–6
11 FT CLG
FOYER
11 FT CLG
PANTRY
DESK
LEDGE
LEDGE
MASTER BATH
9 FT CLG
MASTER BEDRM
13–0 X 14–8
9 FT CLG
PORCH
SEAT
DEPTH 72–8
WIDTH 56–4

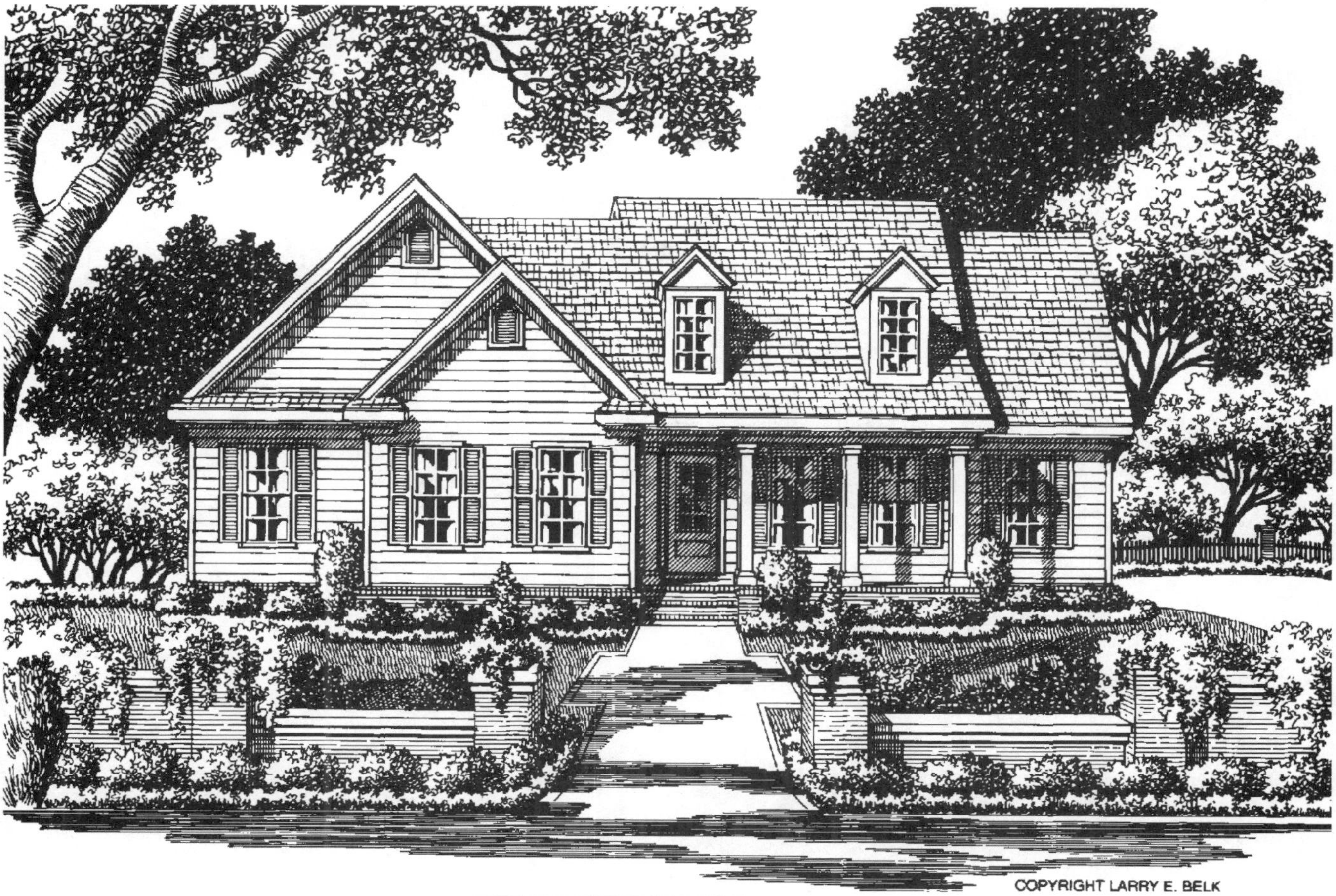

Plan #531-LBD-17-14A

Price Code B

Total Living Area: 1,725 Sq. Ft.

Home has 3 bedrooms, 2 baths, 2-car side entry garage and slab or crawl space foundation, please specify when ordering.

Special features

- Spectacular arches when entering foyer
- Dining room has double-doors leading to kitchen
- Unique built-in desk

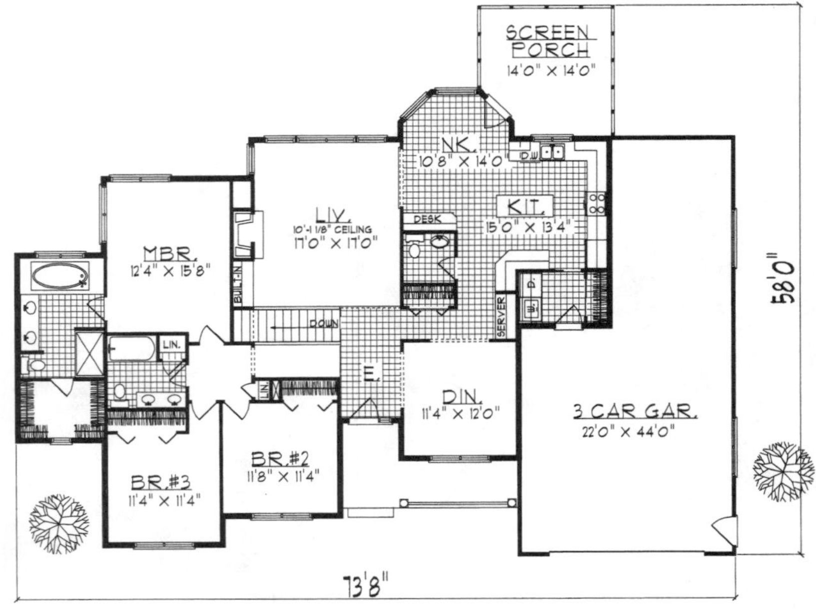
SCREEN PORCH
14'0" X 14'0"
NK.
10'8" X 14'0"
KIT.
15'0" X 13'4"
DESK
LIV.
10'-1 1/8" CEILING
17'0" X 17'0"
MBR.
12'4" X 15'8"
BUILT-IN
DOWN
SERVER
LIN.
E.
DIN.
11'4" X 12'0"
3 CAR GAR.
22'0" X 44'0"
BR.#2
11'8" X 11'4"
BR.#3
11'4" X 11'4"
58'0"
73'8"

Plan #531-JA-65996

Price Code C

Total Living Area: 1,962 Sq. Ft.

Home has 3 bedrooms, 2 1/2 baths, 3-car garage and basement foundation.

Special features

- Kitchen has work island and planning desk
- Open living room offers a fireplace, built-in cabinetry and exceptional views to the outdoors
- Formal dining room has a butler's pantry for entertaining

FREILING

Wrap-Around Porch Adds To Farmhouse Style

LOWE'S

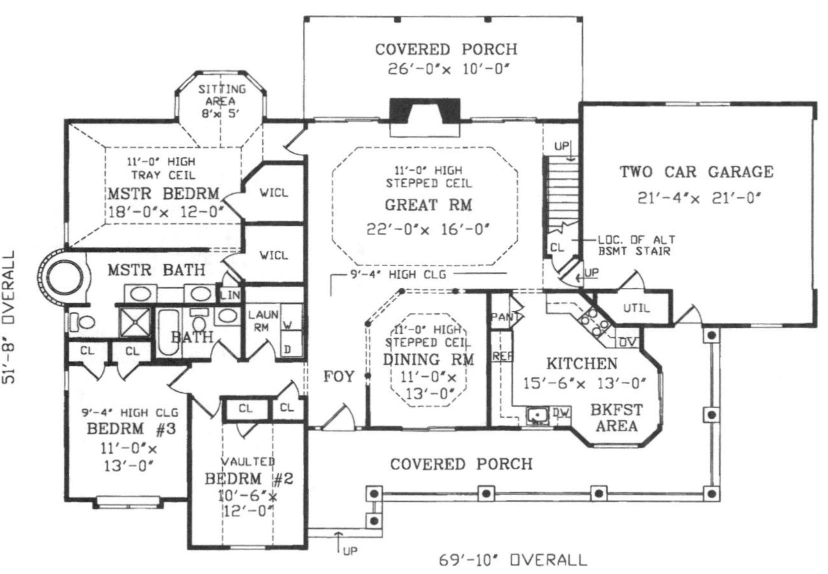
COVERED PORCH
26'-0"x 10'-0"
SITTING AREA
8'x 5'
11'-0" HIGH TRAY CEIL
MSTR BEDRM
18'-0"x 12-0"
WICL
11'-0" HIGH STEPPED CEIL
GREAT RM
22'-0"x 16'-0"
UP
TWO CAR GARAGE
21'-4"x 21'-0"
CL
LOC. OF ALT BSMT STAIR
WICL
MSTR BATH
9'-4" HIGH CLG
UP
LIN
LAUN RM
W
D
BATH
11'-0" HIGH STEPPED CEIL
DINING RM
11'-0"x 13'-0"
PANT
REF
KITCHEN
15'-6"x 13'-0"
DW
UTIL
BKFST AREA
CL
CL
CL
CL
FOY
9'-4" HIGH CLG
BEDRM #3
11'-0"x 13'-0"
VAULTED
BEDRM #2
10'-6"x 12'-0"
COVERED PORCH
UP
51'-8" OVERALL
69'-10" OVERALL

Plan #531-AX-93308

Price Code B

Total Living Area: 1,793 Sq. Ft.

Home has 3 bedrooms, 2 baths, 2-car side entry garage and basement, crawl space or slab foundation.

Special features

- Beautiful entrance foyer leads past a stepped ceiling and a fireplace flanked on two sets of beautifully transomed doors that lead to large covered porch
- Dramatic eat-in kitchen includes an abundance of cabinets and workspace in an exciting angled shape
- Delightful master suite has many amenities

Plan #531-JA-81098

Price Code B

Total Living Area: 1,537 Sq. Ft.

Home has 3 bedrooms, 2 baths, 2-car garage and basement foundation.

Special features

- Vaulted ceilings in foyer and living room welcome guests
- Kitchen offers eating bar and pantry
- Living room features a fireplace flanked by large windows

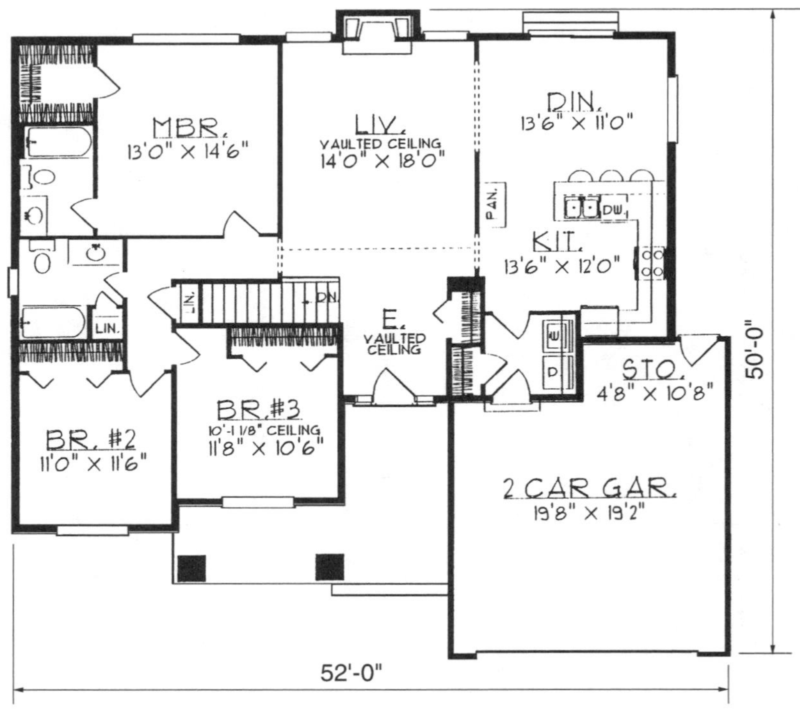
MBR.
13'0" X 14'6"
LIV.
VAULTED CEILING
14'0" X 18'0"
DIN.
13'6" X 11'0"
PAN.
DW.
KIT.
13'6" X 12'0"
LIN.
DN.
E.
VAULTED CEILING
LIN.
BR. #3
10'-1 1/8" CEILING
11'8" X 10'6"
BR. #2
11'0" X 11'6"
STO.
4'8" X 10'8"
2 CAR GAR.
19'8" X 19'2"
50'-0"
52'-0"

 TO ORDER BLUEPRINTS USE THE FORM ON PAGE 290 OR CALL TOLL-FREE **1-800-DREAM HOME** (373-2646)

Trendsetting Home For The Country

LOWE'S

Plan #531-1254-1
basement

Plan #531-1254-2
slab

Price Code B

Total Living Area: 1,704 Sq. Ft.

Home has 3 bedrooms, 2 1/2 baths, 2-car rear entry garage and basement or slab foundation, please specify when ordering.

Special features

- Sensational large front porch for summer evenings and rear breezeway for enjoying outdoors
- Entry leads to living/dining area featuring sloped ceilings and second floor balcony overlook
- Sophisticated master suite complemented by luxury bath with separate shower and toilet area
- Two good-sized bedrooms with centrally located bath

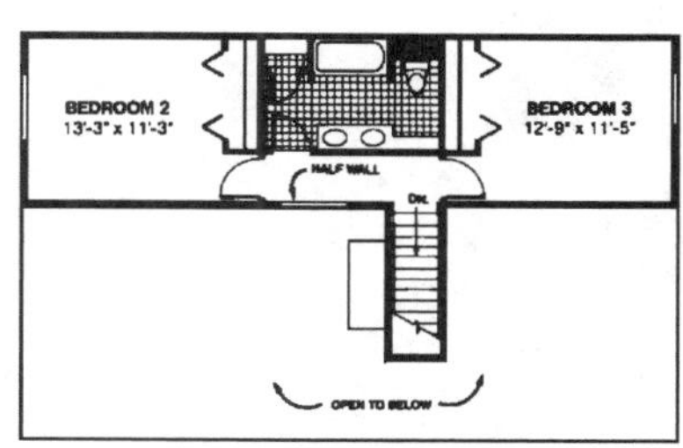
BEDROOM 2
13'-3" x 11'-3"
HALF WALL
BEDROOM 3
12'-9" x 11'-5"
DN.
OPEN TO BELOW

Second Floor
480 sq. ft.

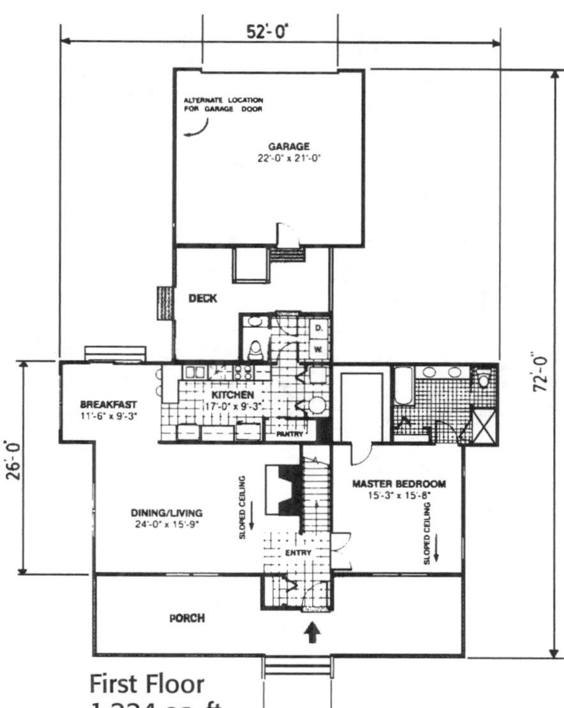
52'-0"
72'-0"
26'-0"
ALTERNATE LOCATION FOR GARAGE DOOR
GARAGE
22'-0" x 21'-0"
DECK
D.
W.
BREAKFAST
11'-6" x 9'-3"
KITCHEN
17'-0" x 9'-3"
PANTRY
MASTER BEDROOM
15'-3" x 15'-8"
DINING/LIVING
24'-0" x 15'-9"
SLOPED CEILING
SLOPED CEILING
ENTRY
PORCH

First Floor
1,224 sq. ft.

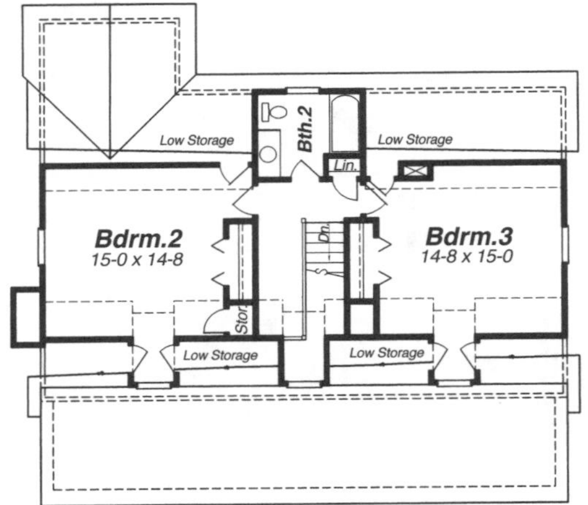
Low Storage
Bth.2
Low Storage
Lin.
Bdrm.2
15-0 x 14-8
Bdrm.3
14-8 x 15-0
Stor.
Low Storage
Low Storage

Second Floor
711 sq. ft.

Plan #531-JV-1870-A

Price Code C

Total Living Area: 1,870 Sq. Ft.

Home has 3 bedrooms, 2 1/2 baths, 2-car drive under garage and basement foundation.

Special features

- Kitchen is open to the living/dining area
- Breakfast area has cathedral ceiling creating a sun room effect
- Master suite is spacious with all the amenities
- Second floor bedrooms share hall bath

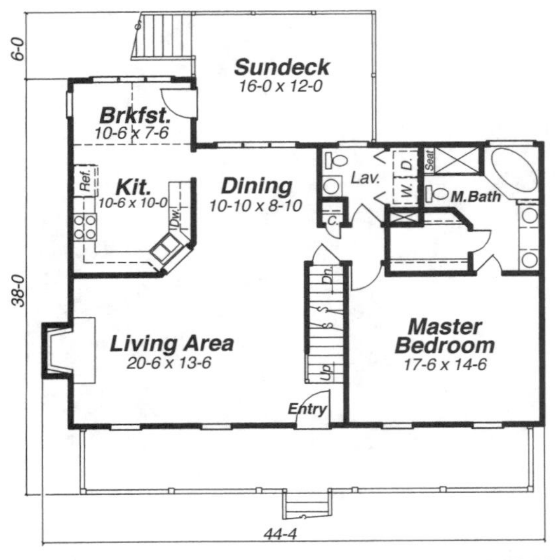
6-0
Sundeck
16-0 x 12-0
Brkfst.
10-6 x 7-6
Kit.
10-6 x 10-0
Ref.
Dw.
Dining
10-10 x 8-10
Lav.
W
D
Seat
M.Bath
C
Dn
38-0
Living Area
20-6 x 13-6
Master
Bedroom
17-6 x 14-6
Up
Entry
44-4

First Floor
1,159 sq. ft.

 TO ORDER BLUEPRINTS USE THE FORM ON PAGE 290 OR CALL TOLL-FREE **1-800-DREAM HOME** (373-2646)

Arched Window Is Focal Point

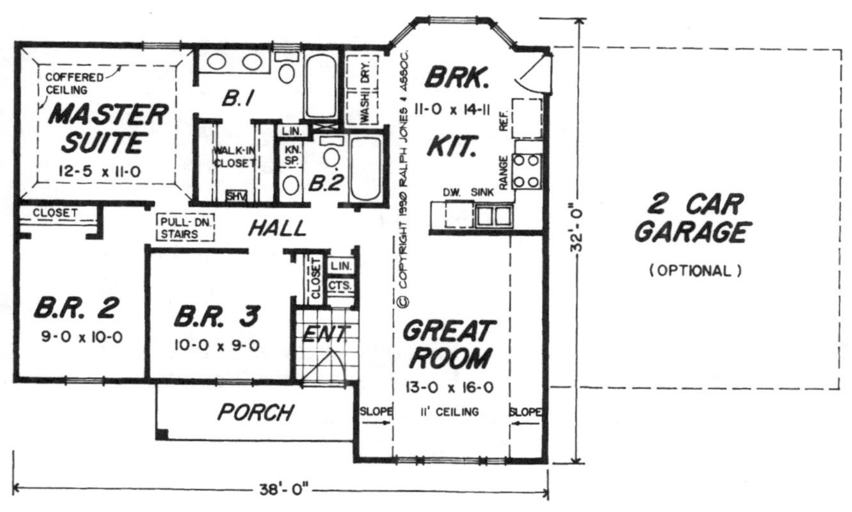
COFFERED CEILING
MASTER SUITE
12-5 x 11-0
B.1
WALK-IN CLOSET
SHV.
LIN.
KN. SP.
B.2
WASH
DRY
© COPYRIGHT 1990 RALPH JONES & ASSOC.
BRK.
11-0 x 14-11
KIT.
REF.
RANGE
DW.
SINK
CLOSET
PULL-DN. STAIRS
HALL
B.R. 2
9-0 x 10-0
B.R. 3
10-0 x 9-0
CLOSET
LIN.
CTS.
ENT.
GREAT ROOM
13-0 x 16-0
11' CEILING
SLOPE
SLOPE
PORCH
2 CAR GARAGE
(OPTIONAL)
32'-0"
38'-0"

Plan #531-RJ-A1079

Price Code AA

Total Living Area: 1,021 Sq. Ft.

Home has 3 bedrooms, 2 baths, optional 2-car garage and slab or crawl space foundation, please specify when ordering.

Special features

- 11' ceiling in great room expands living area
- Combination kitchen/breakfast room allows for easy preparation and cleanup
- Master suite features private bath and oversized walk-in closet

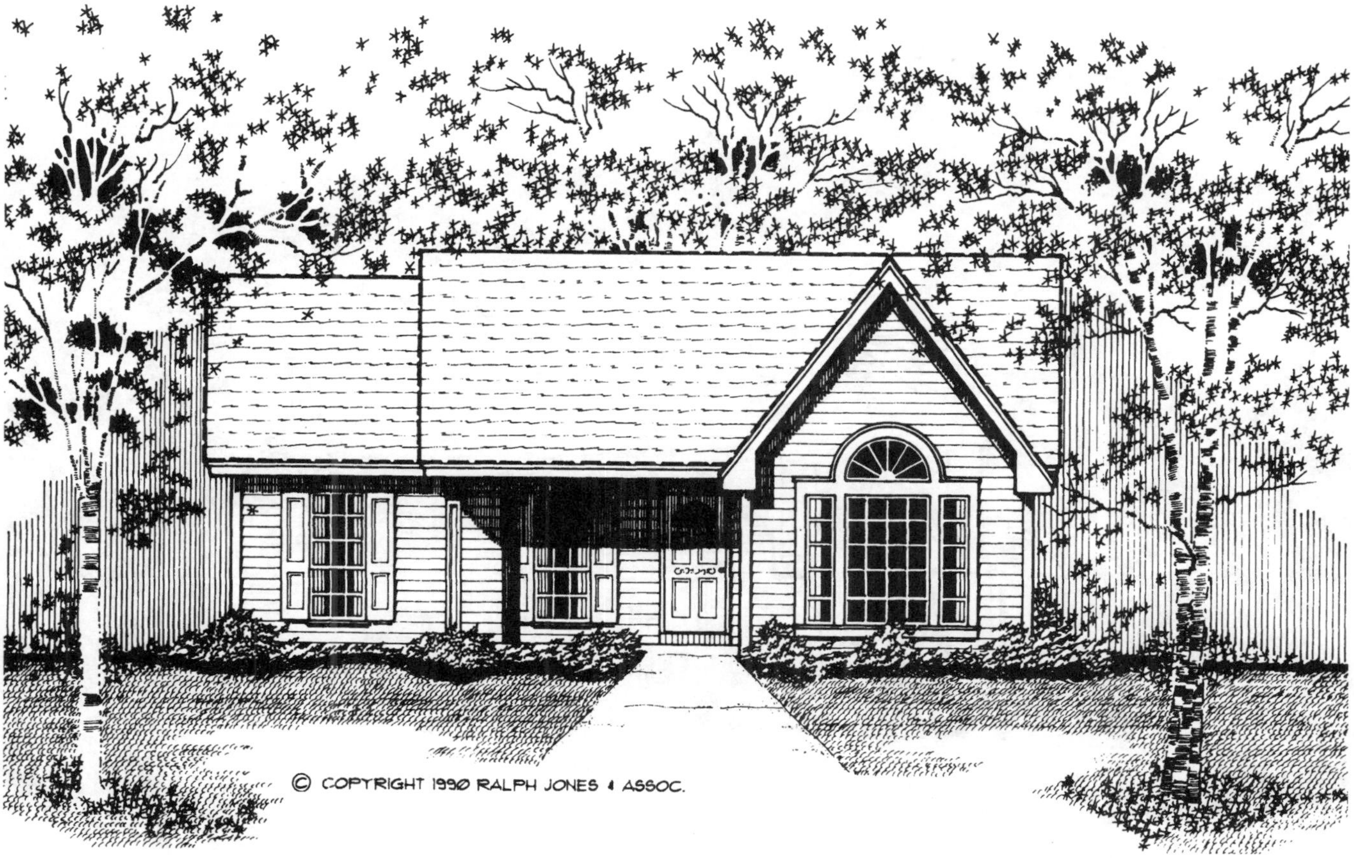

Traditional Styling, Loaded With Extras

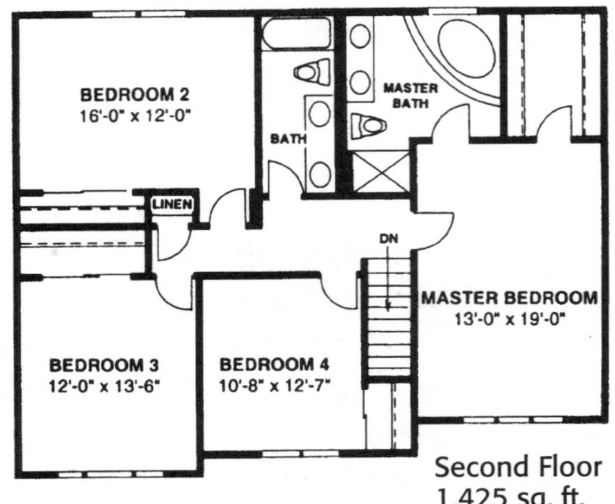
BEDROOM 2
16'-0" x 12'-0"
BATH
MASTER BATH
LINEN
DN
MASTER BEDROOM
13'-0" x 19'-0"
BEDROOM 3
12'-0" x 13'-6"
BEDROOM 4
10'-8" x 12'-7"

Second Floor
1,425 sq. ft.

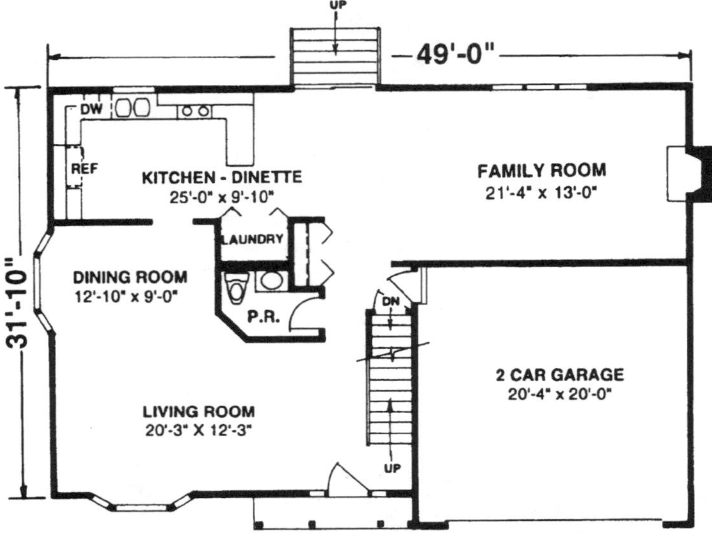
UP
49'-0"
31'-10"
DW
REF
KITCHEN - DINETTE
25'-0" x 9'-10"
FAMILY ROOM
21'-4" x 13'-0"
LAUNDRY
DINING ROOM
12'-10" x 9'-0"
P.R.
DN
2 CAR GARAGE
20'-4" x 20'-0"
LIVING ROOM
20'-3" X 12'-3"
UP

First Floor
1,192 sq. ft.

Plan #531-1425

Price Code E

Total Living Area: 2,617 Sq. Ft.

Home has 4 bedrooms, 2 1/2 baths, 2-car garage and basement foundation.

Special features

- Combination dining and living rooms provide a relaxing atmosphere
- Kitchen/dinette area overlooks large family room with fireplace
- Sunny master bedroom loaded with amenities like walk-in closet and luxurious private bath with step-up garden tub
- Covered front porch is handy feature

Double Dormers Add Country Charm

LOWE'S

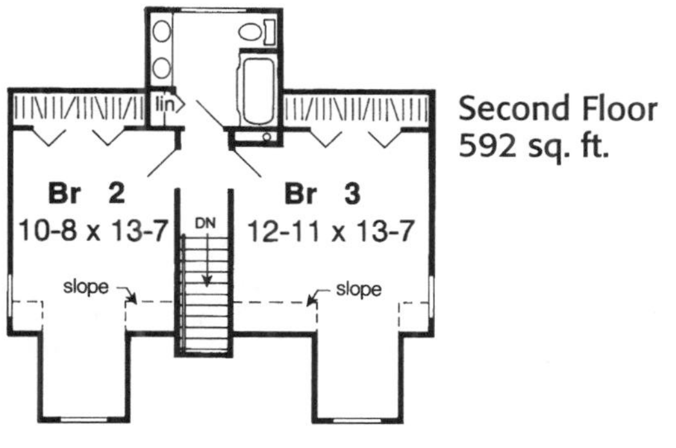
lin
Br 2
10-8 x 13-7
DN
Br 3
12-11 x 13-7
slope
slope

Second Floor
592 sq. ft.

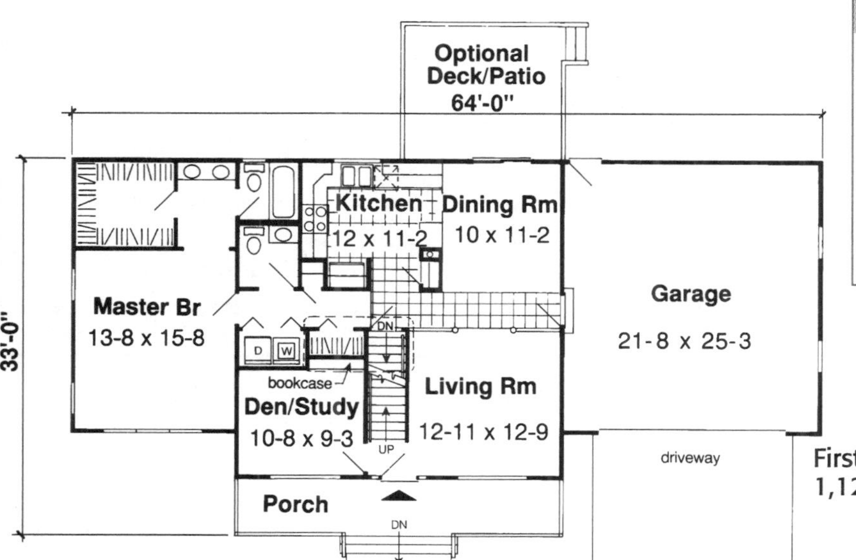
Optional
Deck/Patio
64'-0"
33'-0"
Kitchen
12 x 11-2
Dining Rm
10 x 11-2
Garage
21-8 x 25-3
Master Br
13-8 x 15-8
DN
D
W
bookcase
Den/Study
10-8 x 9-3
Living Rm
12-11 x 12-9
UP
driveway
Porch
DN

First Floor
1,120 sq. ft.

Plan #531-GH-35002

Price Code B

Total Living Area: 1,712 Sq. Ft.

Home has 3 bedrooms, 2 1/2 baths, 2-car garage and basement, crawl space or slab foundation, please specify when ordering.

Special features

- Laundry closet conveniently located near bedrooms
- Formal living room connects to the dining room and kitchen area
- Den/study makes a cozy retreat with built-in bookcases

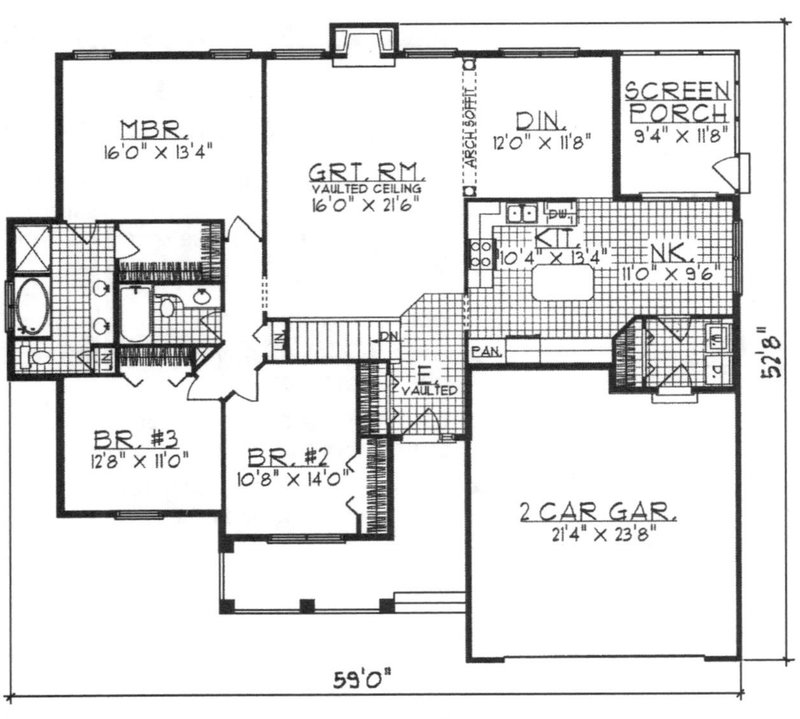
MBR.
16'0" X 13'4"
GRT. RM.
VAULTED CEILING
16'0" X 21'6"
ARCH SOFFIT
DIN.
12'0" X 11'8"
SCREEN
PORCH
9'4" X 11'8"
DW
KIT.
10'4" X 13'4"
NK.
11'0" X 9'6"
DN.
PAN.
E.
VAULTED
BR. #3
12'8" X 11'0"
BR. #2
10'8" X 14'0"
2 CAR GAR.
21'4" X 23'8"
52'8"
59'0"

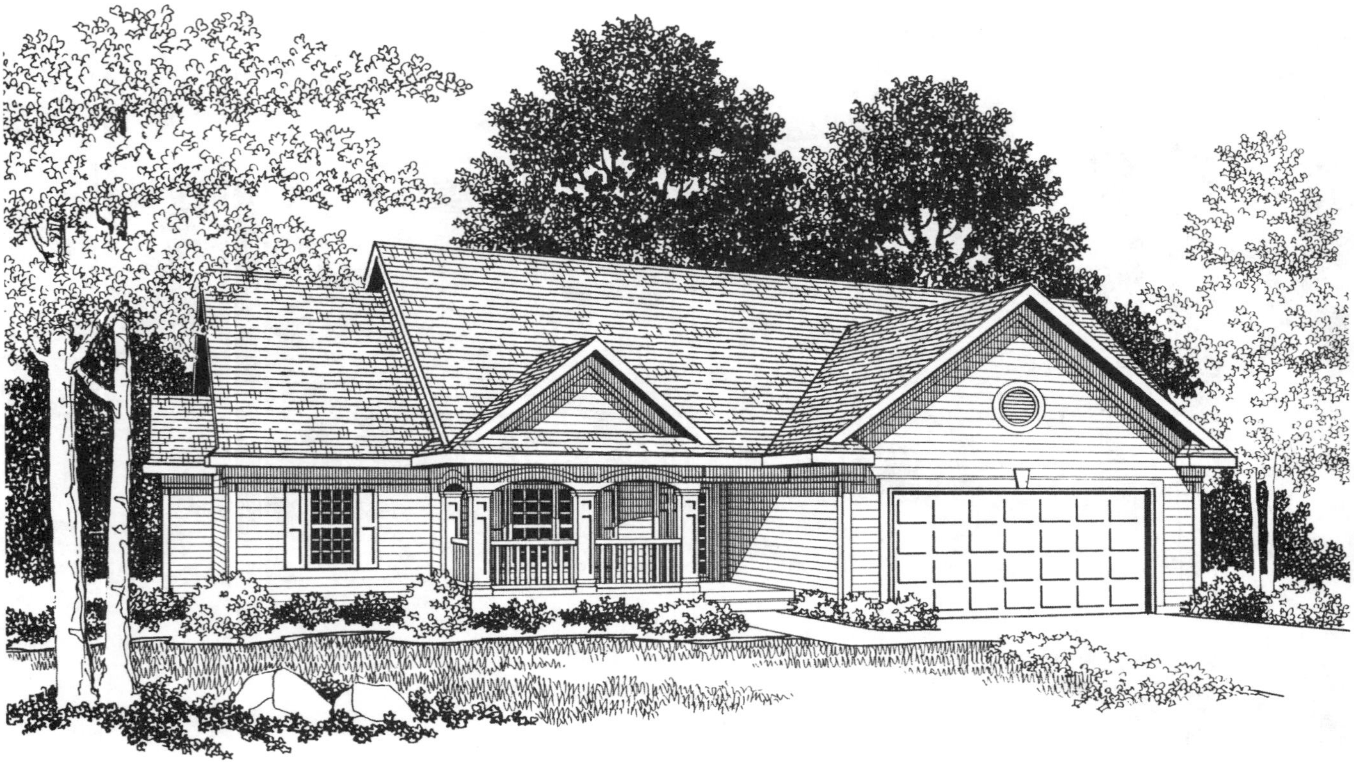

Plan #531-JA-78798

Price Code C

Total Living Area: 1,806 Sq. Ft.

Home has 3 bedrooms, 2 baths, 2-car garage and basement foundation.

Special features

- Large great room has vaulted ceiling, centered fireplace and large windows to let in plenty of light
- Kitchen has direct access to the dining room and nook area
- Two bedrooms share a full bath and linen closet

TO ORDER BLUEPRINTS USE THE FORM ON PAGE 290 OR CALL TOLL-FREE **1-800-DREAM HOME** (373-2646)

Well-Designed Home Makes Great Use Of Space

LOWE'S

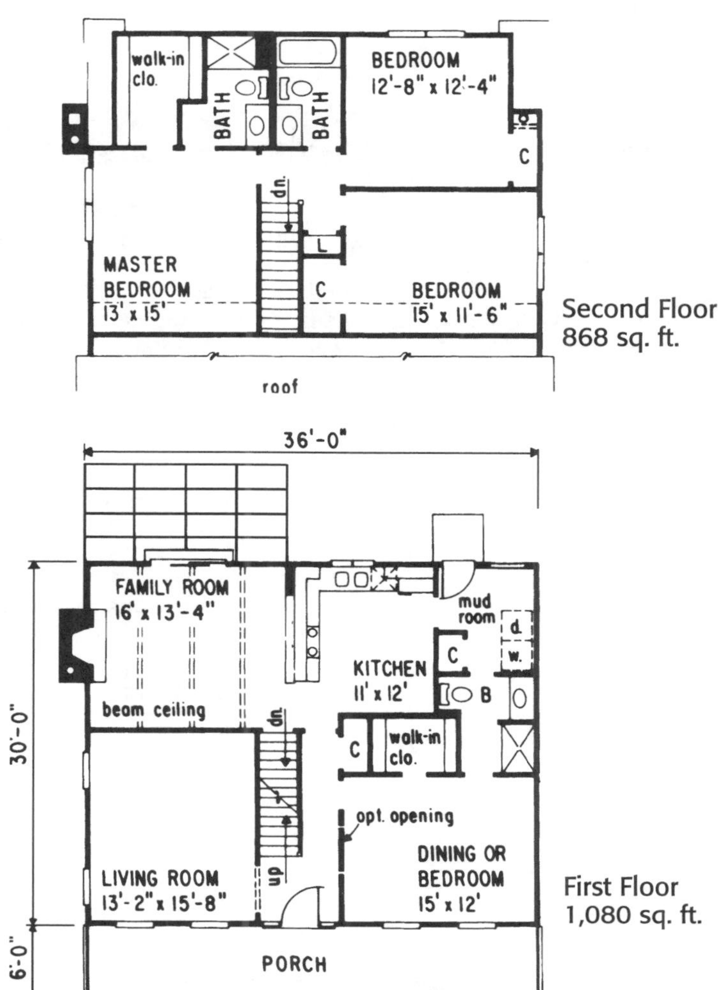
walk-in clo.
BATH
BATH
BEDROOM 12'-8" x 12'-4"
C
dn.
L
MASTER BEDROOM 13' x 15'
C
BEDROOM 15' x 11'-6"
roof
36'-0"
FAMILY ROOM 16' x 13'-4"
mud room
d.
w.
C
KITCHEN 11' x 12'
B
beam ceiling
dn.
C
walk-in clo.
30'-0"
opt. opening
DINING OR BEDROOM 15' x 12'
LIVING ROOM 13'-2" x 15'-8"
up
6'-0"
PORCH

Second Floor
868 sq. ft.

First Floor
1,080 sq. ft.

Plan #531-1233

Price Code C

Total Living Area: 1,948 Sq. Ft.

Home has 3 bedrooms, 2 1/2 baths and basement foundation, drawings also include crawl space and slab foundations.

Special features

- Family room offers warmth with oversized fireplace and rustic beamed ceiling
- Fully appointed kitchen extends into family room
- Practical mud room adjacent to kitchen

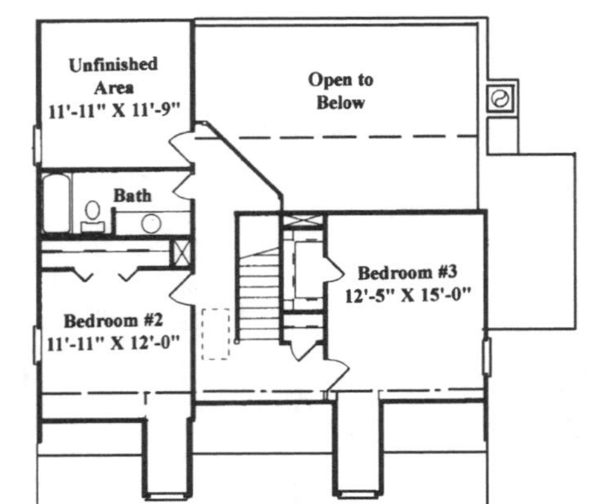
Unfinished Area 11'-11" X 11'-9"
Open to Below
Bath
Bedroom #3 12'-5" X 15'-0"
Bedroom #2 11'-11" X 12'-0"

Second Floor
676 sq. ft.

Plan #531-CHP-2032-A-42

Price Code C

Total Living Area: 2,075 Sq. Ft.

Home has 3 bedrooms, 2 1/2 baths, 2-car side entry garage and slab or crawl space foundation, please specify when ordering.

Special features

- Vaulted family room with fireplace
- Sunny breakfast room
- Private dining perfect for entertaining
- Second floor includes two bedrooms, a bath and an unfinished area that would be perfect as a fourth bedroom, office or play area

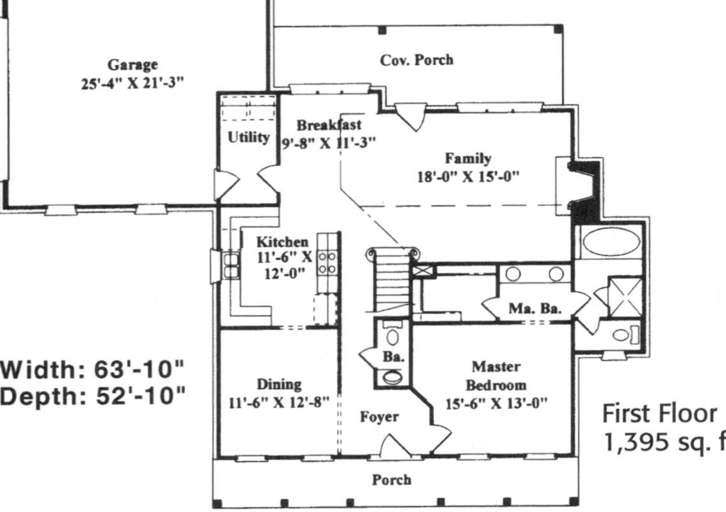
Garage 25'-4" X 21'-3"
Cov. Porch
Utility
Breakfast 9'-8" X 11'-3"
Family 18'-0" X 15'-0"
Kitchen 11'-6" X 12'-0"
Ma. Ba.
Ba.
Dining 11'-6" X 12'-8"
Master Bedroom 15'-6" X 13'-0"
Foyer
Porch

Width: 63'-10"
Depth: 52'-10"

First Floor
1,395 sq. ft.

LOWE'S

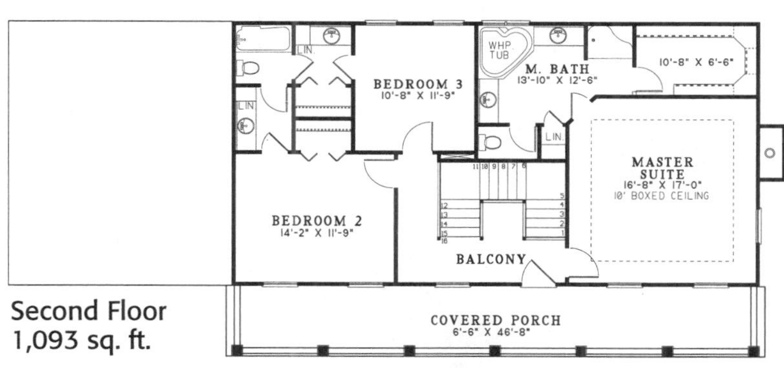
BEDROOM 3
10'-8" X 11'-9"
WHP TUB
M. BATH
13'-10" X 12'-6"
10'-8" X 6'-6"
LIN
MASTER SUITE
16'-8" X 17'-0"
10' BOXED CEILING
BEDROOM 2
14'-2" X 11'-9"
BALCONY
COVERED PORCH
6'-6" X 46'-8"

Second Floor
1,093 sq. ft.

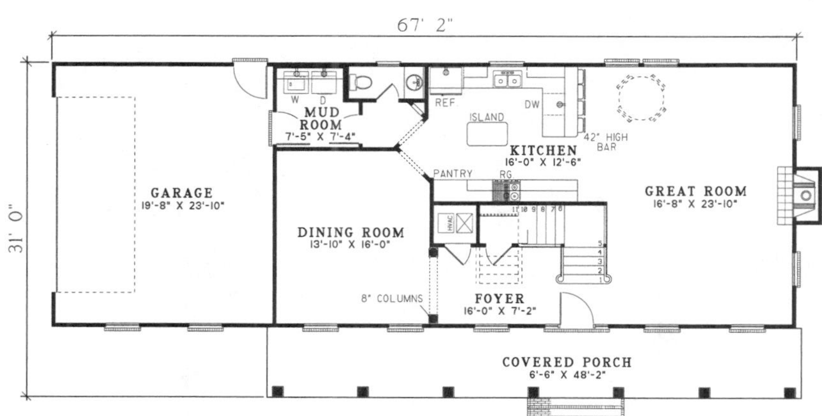
67' 2"
31' 0"
GARAGE
19'-8" X 23'-10"
W D
MUD ROOM
7'-5" X 7'-4"
REF
DW
ISLAND
KITCHEN
16'-0" X 12'-6"
42" HIGH BAR
PANTRY
RG
GREAT ROOM
16'-8" X 23'-10"
DINING ROOM
13'-10" X 16'-0"
8" COLUMNS
FOYER
16'-0" X 7'-2"
COVERED PORCH
6'-6" X 48'-2"

First Floor
1,154 sq. ft.

Plan #531-NDG-275

Price Code D

Total Living Area: 2,247 Sq. Ft.

Home has 3 bedrooms, 2 1/2 baths, 2-car side entry garage and basement, crawl space or slab foundation, please specify when ordering.

Special features

- Enormous great room with fireplace extends into a kitchen with center island
- Formal dining area is quiet, yet convenient to kitchen
- All bedrooms located on second floor maintain privacy

Plan #531-DB2526

Price Code B

Total Living Area: 1,605 Sq. Ft.

Home has 3 bedrooms, 2 1/2 baths, 2-car garage and basement foundation.

Special features

- All bedrooms on second floor for privacy
- Compact yet efficient kitchen is adjacent to breakfast room with access outdoors
- Built-in hutch in formal dining room has a custom feel

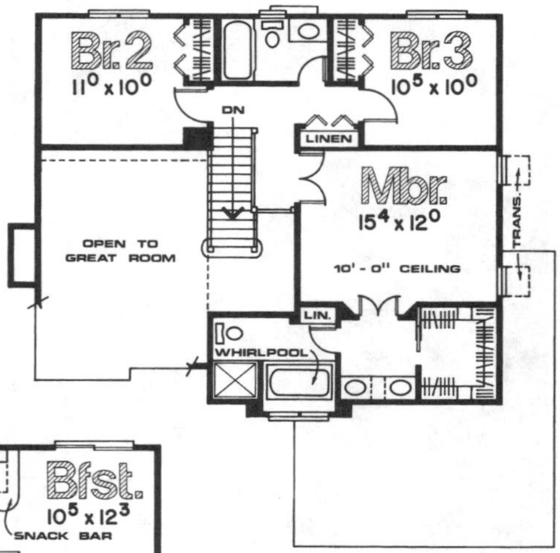

Br.2 11⁰ x 10⁰
Br.3 10⁵ x 10⁰
DN
LINEN
Mbr. 15⁴ x 12⁰
OPEN TO GREAT ROOM
10'-0" CEILING
TRANS.
LIN.
WHIRLPOOL

Second Floor
760 sq. ft.

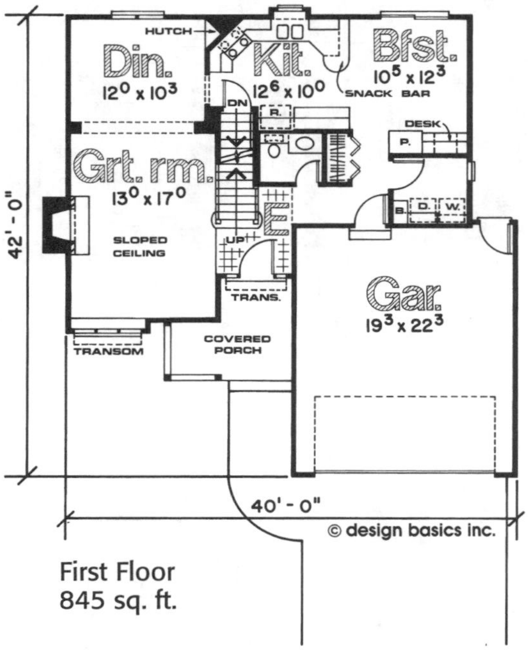

HUTCH
Din. 12⁰ x 10³
Kit. 12⁶ x 10⁰
Bfst. 10⁵ x 12³
SNACK BAR
DN
R.
DESK
P.
Grt. rm. 13⁰ x 17⁰
SLOPED CEILING
B. D. W.
E
UP
TRANS.
Gar. 19³ x 22³
COVERED PORCH
TRANSOM
42'-0"
40'-0"
© design basics inc.

First Floor
845 sq. ft.

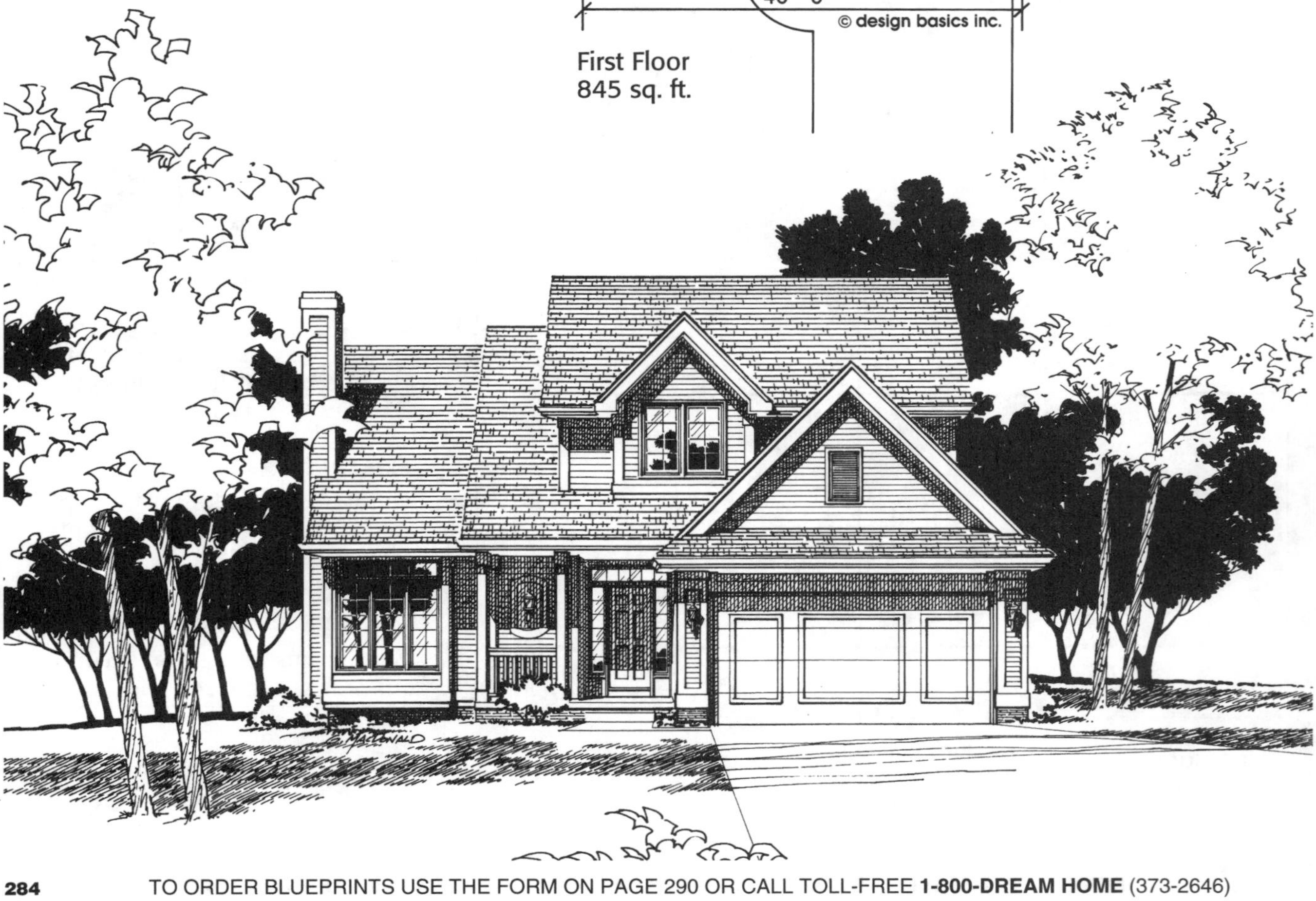

TO ORDER BLUEPRINTS USE THE FORM ON PAGE 290 OR CALL TOLL-FREE **1-800-DREAM HOME** (373-2646)

Warm And Inviting

Plan #531-LBD-19-15A

Price Code C

Total Living Area: 1,955 Sq. Ft.

Home has 3 bedrooms, 2 baths, 2-car side entry garage and crawl space or slab foundation, please specify when ordering.

Special features

- Porch adds outdoor area to this design
- Dining and great rooms visible from foyer through a series of elegant archways
- Kitchen overlooks great room and breakfast room

WIDTH 65-0

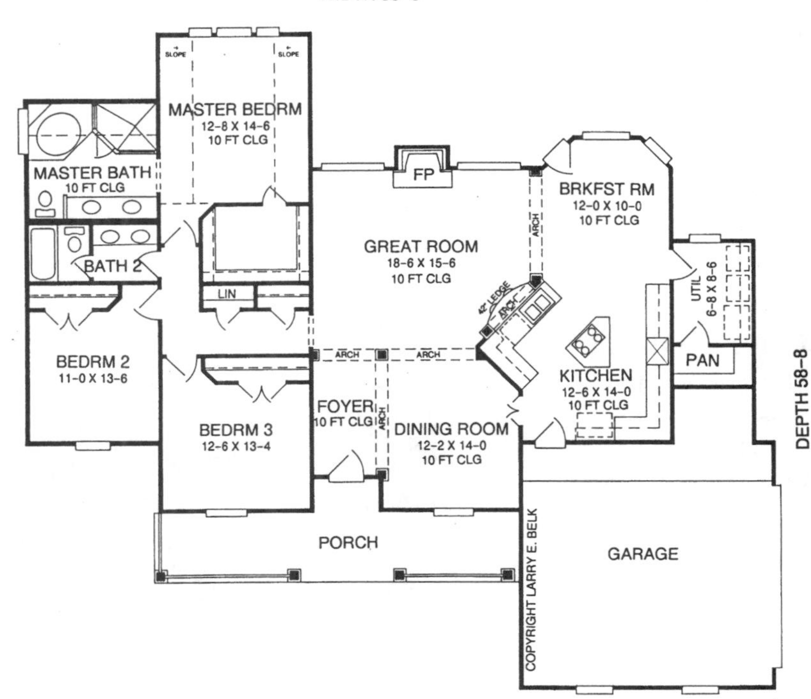
SLOPE
SLOPE
MASTER BEDRM
12-8 X 14-6
10 FT CLG
MASTER BATH
10 FT CLG
FP
BRKFST RM
12-0 X 10-0
10 FT CLG
GREAT ROOM
18-6 X 15-6
10 FT CLG
ARCH
BATH 2
LIN
UTIL
6-8 X 8-6
KITCHEN
12-6 X 14-0
10 FT CLG
PAN
BEDRM 2
11-0 X 13-6
BEDRM 3
12-6 X 13-4
FOYER
10 FT CLG
DINING ROOM
12-2 X 14-0
10 FT CLG
PORCH
GARAGE
DEPTH 58-8
COPYRIGHT LARRY E. BELK

Our Blueprint Packages Offer...

Quality plans for building your future, with extras that provide unsurpassed value, ensure good construction and long-term enjoyment.

A quality home - one that looks good, functions well, and provides years of enjoyment - is a product of many things - design, materials, craftsmanship. But it's also the result of outstanding blueprints - the actual plans and specifications that tell the builder exactly how to build your home.

And with our BLUEPRINT PACKAGES you get the absolute best. A complete set of blueprints is available for every design in this book. These "working drawings," are highly detailed, resulting in two key benefits:

- *Better understanding by the contractor of how to build your home, and...*
- *More accurate construction estimates.*

When you purchase one of our designs, you'll receive all of the BLUEPRINT components shown here - elevations, foundation plan, floor plans, sections, and details. Other helpful building aids are also available to help make your dream home a reality.

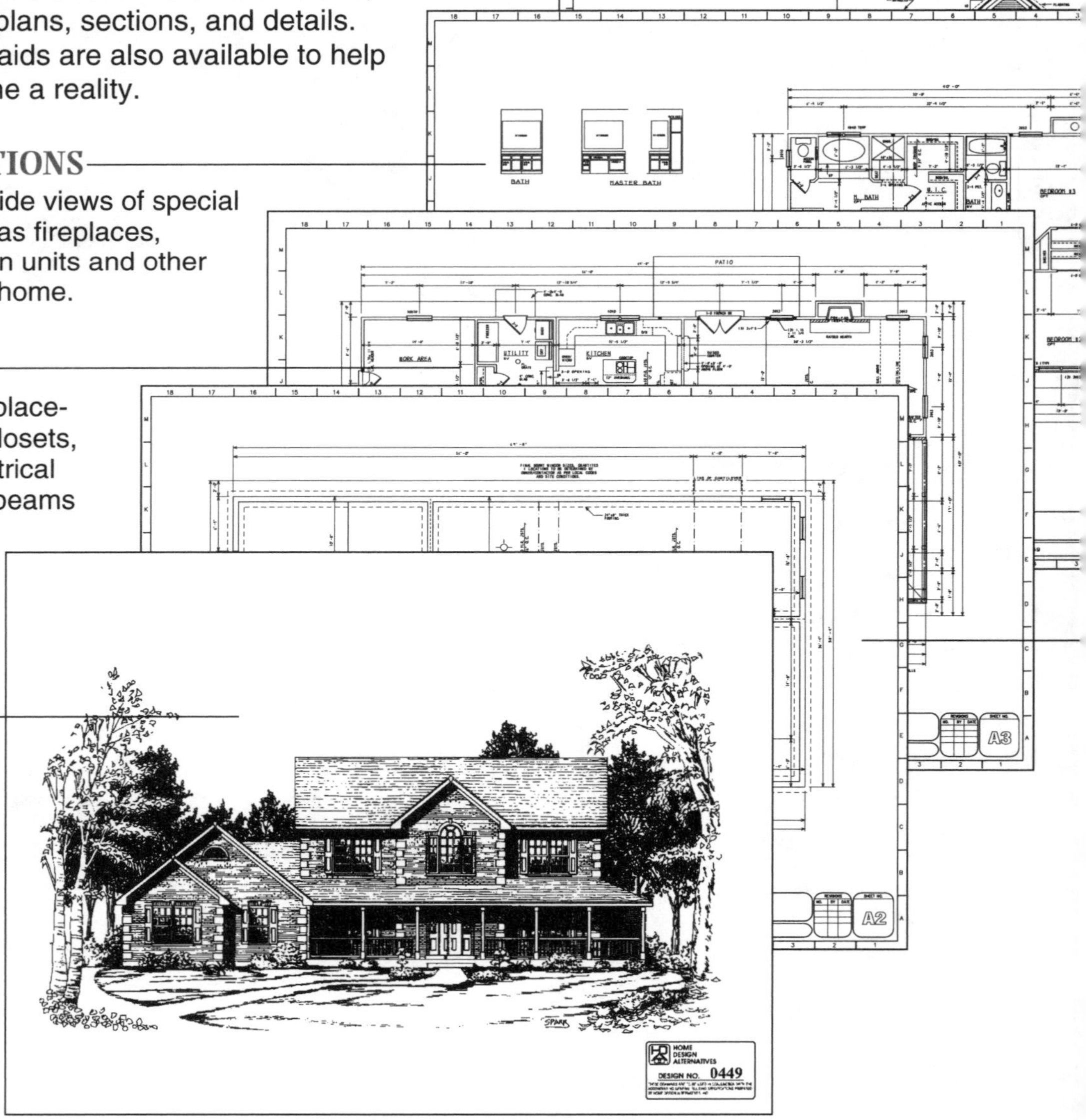

INTERIOR ELEVATIONS

Interior elevations provide views of special interior elements such as fireplaces, kitchen cabinets, built-in units and other special features of the home.

FLOOR PLANS

These plans show the placement of walls, doors, closets, plumbing fixtures, electrical outlets, columns, and beams for each level of the home.

COVER SHEET

This sheet is the artist's rendering of the exterior of the home. It will give you an idea of how your home will look when completed and landscaped.

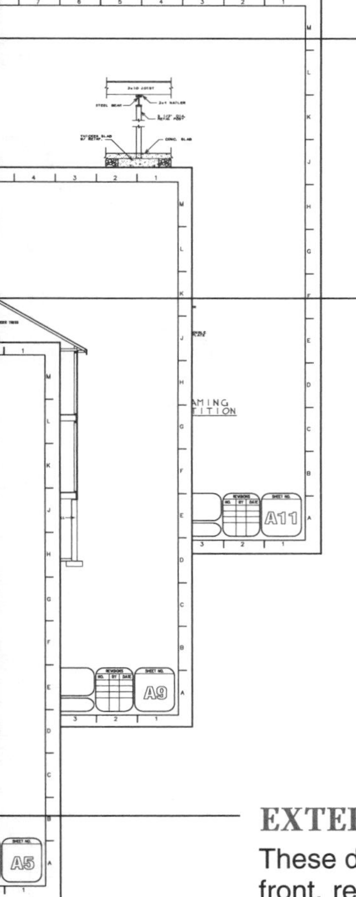

DETAILS

Details show how to construct certain components of your home, such as the roof system, stairs, deck, etc.

SECTIONS

Sections show detail views of the home or portions of the home as if it were sliced from the roof to the foundation. This sheet shows important areas such as load-bearing walls, stairs, joists, trusses and other structural elements, which are critical for proper construction.

EXTERIOR ELEVATIONS

These drawings illustrate the front, rear and both sides of the house, with all details of exterior materials and the required dimensions.

FOUNDATION PLAN

The foundation plan shows the layout of the basement, crawl space, slab, or pier foundation. All necessary notations and dimensions are included. See plan page for the foundation types included. If the home plan you choose does not have your desired foundation type, our Customer Service Representatives can advise you on how to customize your foundation to suit your specific needs or site conditions.

Other Helpful Building Aids...

Your Blueprint Package will contain all the necessary construction information to build your home. We also offer the following products and services to save you time and money in the building process.

Rush Delivery

Most orders are processed within 24 hours of receipt. Please allow 7 working days for delivery. If you need to place a rush order, please call us by 11:00 a.m. CST and ask for overnight or second day service.

Technical Assistance

If you have questions, call our technical support line at 1-314-770-2228 between 8:00 a.m. and 5:00 p.m. CST. Whether it involves design modifications or field assistance, our designers are extremely familiar with all of our designs and will be happy to help you. We want your home to be everything you expect it to be.

Material List

Material lists are available for many of our plans. Each list gives you the quantity, dimensions and description of the building materials necessary to construct your home. You'll get faster and more accurate bids from your contractor and material suppliers, and you'll save money by paying for only the materials you need. Look for the Lowe's Signature Series Logo on the plan pages.

Customizer Kit™

Many of the designs in this book can be customized using our exclusive Customizer Kit. It's your guide to custom designing your home. It leads you through all the essential design decisions and provides the necessary tools for you to clearly show the changes you want made. Customizer Kits are available on all designs that display the Lowe's Signature Series Logo on the plan pages. For more information about this exclusive product see page 5.

HOME PLANS INDEX

Shaded Plans Denote Lowe's Signature Series Plans - Material List and Customizer Kit Available

Plan Number	Sq. Ft.	Price Code	Page
531-0103	1,351	A	57
531-0104	1,359	A	107
531-0106	1,443	A	153
531-0110	1,605	B	98
531-0111	1,582	B	77
531-0112	1,668	C	34
531-0113	1,992	C	31
531-0121	1,976	C	65
531-0122	1,922	C	37
531-0124	1,974	C	126
531-0125	2,468	D	116
531-0129	2,032	C	86
531-0130	2,356	D	80
531-0131	2,336	D	52
531-0132	2,195	C	145
531-0133	2,214	D	135
531-0134	2,216	D	93
531-0135	2,529	E	132
531-0137	2,282	E	122
531-0138	2,286	E	13
531-0139	2,773	F	25
531-0141	2,826	E	50
531-0143	2,449	E	45
531-0151	2,874	E	97
531-0152	2,935	E	110
531-0156	3,050	E	139
531-0158	3,200	F	102
531-0163	1,772	C	72
531-0167	2,282	D	60
531-0168	2,940	E	49
531-0171	2,058	C	8
531-0172	1,643	B	120
531-0173	1,220	A	89
531-0174	1,657	B	68
531-0177	2,562	D	63
531-0180	1,567	B	66
531-0183	2,847	E	40
531-0190	1,600	C	28
531-0194	1,444	A	78
531-0195	988	AA	127
531-0204	2,128	C	84
531-0205	2,665	E	74
531-0206	1,889	C	76
531-0218	1,998	D	42
531-0221	1,619	B	39
531-0225	1,260	A	32
531-0226	1,416	A	81
531-0227	1,674	B	157
531-0231	2,213	E	146
531-0232	2,932	F	17
531-0233	2,772	E	124
531-0237	1,631	B	131
531-0238	2,468	D	108
531-0239	1,496	A	113
531-0241	829	AAA	47
531-0247	2,988	E	20
531-0248	1,978	C	41
531-0249	1,501	B	35
531-0252	1,364	A	30
531-0253	1,458	A	94
531-0254	1,732	B	105
531-0265	1,314	A	111
531-0273	988	AA	161
531-0274	1,020	AA	148
531-0276	950	AA	129
531-0277	1,127	AA	101
531-0282	1,642	B	70
531-0285	2,648	E	61
531-0290	1,700	B	55
531-0291	1,600	B	82
531-0292	1,304	A	103
531-0293	1,595	B	154
531-0294	1,655	B	158
531-0296	1,396	A	119
531-0297	1,320	A	27
531-0298	3,216	F	10
531-0299	3,013	E	62
531-0305	2,605	E	43
531-0306	2,360	D	71
531-0307	3,153	E	44
531-0309	2,106	C	141
531-0310	2,363	D	150
531-0312	1,921	D	90
531-0326	2,539	D	79
531-0358	3,609	F	104
531-0359	2,659	E	155
531-0360	2,327	D	134
531-0362	1,874	C	96
531-0369	2,716	E	117
531-0370	1,721	C	53
531-0374	2,213	D	92
531-0375	1,954	C	144
531-0376	3,019	E	130
531-0378	2,180	C	142
531-0379	1,711	B	88
531-0394	1,558	B	59
531-0396	1,880	C	54
531-0404	2,195	C	159
531-0408	2,498	D	121
531-0413	2,182	C	14
531-0417	2,828	E	11
531-0436	2,801	E	36
531-0437	2,333	D	33
531-0447	1,393	B	56
531-0448	1,597	C	112
531-0449	2,505	D	7
531-0450	1,708	B	15
531-0461	828	AAA	106
531-0462	1,028	AA	99
531-0477	1,140	AA	133
531-0479	1,294	A	64
531-0480	1,618	B	46
531-0483	1,330	A	137
531-0489	1,543	B	85
531-0490	1,687	B	51
531-0491	1,808	C	23
531-0492	1,829	C	125
531-0494	1,085	AA	128
531-0496	977	AA	151
531-0497	1,107	AA	83
531-0515	1,344	A	48
531-0523	1,875	C	152
531-0526	2,262	D	140
531-0528	2,511	D	75
531-0529	1,285	B	67
531-0536	1,664	B	95
531-0540	2,352	D	138
531-0541	2,080	C	87
531-0542	1,832	C	58
531-0598	1,818	C	29
531-0600	3,025	E	156
531-0652	1,524	B	118
531-0672	2,043	C	109
531-0673	1,805	C	100
531-0690	1,400	A	12
531-0692	1,339	A	26
531-0694	1,285	A	143
531-0696	676	AAA	91
531-0704	1,326	B	115
531-0710	2,334	D	6
531-0712	2,029	C	21
531-0722	2,266	D	73
531-0723	1,784	B	69
531-0725	1,977	C	123
531-0726	1,428	A	24
531-0728	2,967	E	9
531-0731	1,761	B	16
531-0732	1,384	A	18
531-0734	929	AA	136
531-0741	1,578	B	162
531-0742	1,883	C	149
531-0747	1,977	C	19
531-0748	2,514	D	38
531-0749	2,727	E	160
531-0751	1,278	A	147
531-0765	1,000	AA	22
531-0767	990	AA	114
531-1065	2,835	E	188
531-1077-1 & 2	2,196	C	236
531-1101	1,643	B	210
531-1102	2,298	D	270
531-1112	2,137	C	261
531-1118-1 & 2	1,550	B	178
531-1120	1,232	A	175
531-1127-1 & 2	2,331	D	248
531-1134-1 & 2	2,212	D	200
531-1207-1 & 2	2,360	D	193
531-1211-1 & 2	2,414	D	214
531-1213-1 & 2	2,554	D	166
531-1219-1 & 2	2,797	E	241
531-1233	1,948	C	281
531-1254-1 & 2	1,704	B	275
531-1293	1,200	A	218
531-1300	2,253	D	196
531-1307	2,420	D	206
531-1308	2,280	D	171
531-1311	2,112	C	257
531-1347-1 & 2	1,948	C	251
531-1396	1,820	C	242
531-1425	2,617	E	278
531-AM2155A	1,958	C	208
531-AM2281	2,730	E	260
531-AMD-2229	2,287	D	181
531-AX-4315	2,018	C	253
531-AX-5380	1,480	A	177
531-AX-90303	1,615	B	165
531-AX-91316	1,097	AA	203
531-AX-93308	1,793	B	273
531-BF-1718	2,665	E	228
531-BF-2108	2,194	C	221
531-BF-3007	3,012	E	198
531-BF-DR1109	1,191	AA	232
531-CHP-1332A	1,363	A	185
531-CHP-1733-A-7	1,737	B	245
531-CHP-2032-A-42	2,075	C	282
531-DB1455	2,594	D	176
531-DB1560	2,879	E	186
531-DB2384	1,948	C	266
531-DB2460	2,695	E	258
531-DB2526	1,605	B	284
531-DB2638	2,103	C	194

HOME PLANS INDEX - *continued*

Plan Number	Sq. Ft.	Price Code	Page
531-DB3097	1,745	B	168
531-DBI-2332	3,775	F	213
531-DDI-95219	1,251	A	172
531-DDI-95220	1,584	B	226
531-DDI-100213	2,202	D	222
531-DDI-100214	2,104	C	252
531-DL-17104L1	1,710	B	238
531-DL-17353L1	1,735	B	246
531-ES-103-1 & 2	1,364	A	169
531-ES-107-1 & 2	1,120	A	225
531-FB-327	1,281	A	164
531-FB-676	1,373	A	205
531-FB-766	1,671	B	268
531-FB-902	1,856	C	243
531-FB-959	1,862	C	216
531-FB-963	2,126	C	179
531-FB-1043	1,692	B	235
531-FB-1148	1,491	A	231
531-FD7410	2,200	D	220
531-FD7507	3,239	F	174
531-GH-24714	1,771	B	207
531-GH-24717	1,642	B	215
531-GH-24724	1,982	C	269
531-GH-24736	2,044	C	259
531-GH-35002	1,712	B	279
531-GM-1253	1,253	A	192
531-GM-1406	1,406	A	197
531-GM-1550	1,550	B	263
531-GM-1815	1,815	C	255
531-GM-1966	1,966	C	180
531-GM-2010	2,010	C	173
531-GM-2235	2,235	D	184
531-GSD-1155	2,355	D	237
531-GSD-1260	2,788	E	224
531-GSD-1748	1,496	A	170
531-GSD-2107	2,422	D	256
531-GSD-2825	3,230	F	264
531-HDS-1167	1,167	AA	223
531-HDS-1558-2	1,885	C	182
531-HDS-1963	1,963	C	254
531-HDS-1993	1,993	C	244
531-JA-53394	1,763	B	202
531-JA-64396	2,196	C	239
531-JA-65996	1,962	C	272
531-JA-70797	1,633	B	262
531-JA-78798	1,806	C	280
531-JA-81098	1,537	B	274
531-JFD-10-1692-1	1,692	B	209
531-JFD-10-1875-1	1,875	C	189
531-JFD-10-2096-2	2,096	C	167
531-JFD-20-17921	1,792	B	195
531-JV-1325-B	1,325	A	240
531-JV-1379	1,379	A	250
531-JV-1617-A-SJ	1,617	B	187
531-JV-1683-B	1,683	B	267
531-JV-1735A	1,735	B	234
531-JV-1865-A	1,865	C	191
531-JV-1870-A	1,870	C	276
531-JV-2012-A-SJ	2,012	C	212
531-JV-2091-A	2,475	D	204
531-LBD-17-14A	1,725	B	271
531-LBD-19-15A	1,955	C	285
531-LBD-19-16A	1,993	C	163
531-NDG-142	2,107	C	219
531-NDG-143	4,237	G	249
531-NDG-275	2,247	D	283
531-NDG-307	2,707	E	211
531-RDD-1815-8	1,815	C	201
531-RDD-1895-9	1,895	C	233
531-RJ-A1068V	1,053	AA	265
531-RJ-A1079	1,021	AA	277
531-RJ-A1175	1,192	AA	183
531-RJ-A1390	1,389	A	247
531-RJ-A1485	1,436	A	227
531-RJ-B123	1,270	A	217
531-VL947	947	AA	229
531-VL2069	2,069	C	230
531-VL2888	2,888	E	199
531-VL3011	3,011	E	190

OTHER GREAT PRODUCTS TO HELP YOU BUILD YOUR DREAM HOME

FRAMING, PLUMBING AND ELECTRICAL DETAIL PLAN PACKAGES

Three separate packages offer homebuilders details for constructing various foundations; numerous floor, wall and roof framing techniques; simple to complex residential wiring; sump and water softener hookups; plumbing connection methods; installation of septic systems, and more. Each package includes three-dimensional illustrations and a glossary of terms. Purchase one or all three. *Cost: $20.00 each or all three for $40.00*

THE LEGAL KIT

Avoid many legal pitfalls and build your home with confidence using the forms and contracts featured in this kit. Included are request for proposal documents, various fixed price and cost plus contracts, instructions on how and when to use each form, warranty statements and more. Save time and money before you break ground on your new home or start a remodeling project. All forms are reproducible. The kit is ideal for homebuilders and contractors. *Cost: $35.00*

Request for Proposal
Time & Materials Contract
Fixed Price Contract
Lien Waiver
Change Order

WHAT KIND OF PLAN PACKAGE DO YOU NEED?

Now that you've found the home plan you've been looking for, here are some suggestions on how to make your Dream Home a reality. To get started, order the type of plans that fit your particular situation.

Your Choices:

The One-set package - This single set of blueprints is offered so you can study or review a home in greater detail. But a single set is never enough for construction and it's a copyright violation to reproduce blueprints.

The Minimum 5-set package - If you're ready to start the construction process, this 5-set package is the minimum number of blueprint sets you will need. It will require keeping close track of each set so they can be used by multiple subcontractors and tradespeople.

The Standard 8-set package - For best results in terms of cost, schedule and quality of construction, we recommend you order eight (or more) sets of blueprints. Besides one set for yourself, additional sets of blueprints will be required by your mortgage lender, local building department, general contractor and all subcontractors working on foundation, electrical, plumbing, heating/air conditioning, carpentry work, etc.

Reproducible Masters - If you wish to make some minor design changes, you'll want to order reproducible masters. These drawings contain the same information as the blueprints but are printed on erasable and reproducible paper. This will allow your builder or a local design professional to make the necessary drawing changes without the major expense of redrawing the plans. This package also allows you to print as many copies of the modified plans as you need.

Mirror Reverse Sets - Plans can be printed in mirror reverse. These plans are useful when the house would fit your site better if all the rooms were on the opposite side than shown. They are simply a mirror image of the original drawings causing the lettering and dimensions to read backwards. Therefore, when ordering mirror reverse drawings, you must purchase at least one set of right reading plans.

ORDER FORM

IMPORTANT INFORMATION TO KNOW BEFORE YOU ORDER YOUR HOME PLANS

❑ **Building Codes & Requirements -** Our plans conform to most national building codes. However, they may not comply completely with your local building regulations. Some counties and municipalities have their own building codes, regulations and requirements. The assistance of a local builder, architect or other building professional may be necessary to modify the drawings to comply with your area's specific requirements. We recommend you consult with your local building officials prior to beginning construction.

❑ **Exchange Policies -** Since blueprints are printed in response to your order, we cannot honor requests for refunds. However, if for some reason you find that the plan you have purchased does not meet your requirements, you may exchange that plan for another plan in our collection. At the time of the exchange, you will be charged a processing fee of 25% of your original plan package price, plus the difference in price between the plan packages (if applicable) and the cost to ship the new plans to you. ***Please note: Reproducible drawings can only be exchanged if the package is unopened, and exchanges are allowed only within 90 days of purchase.***

❑ **Material List -** Remember to order your material list. You'll get faster and more accurate bids while saving money.

Plan prices guaranteed through December 31, 2002

CALL TOLL-FREE
1-800-DREAM HOME
(1-800-373-2646) DAY OR NIGHT

THREE EASY WAYS TO ORDER

1. CALL toll free 1-800-373-2646 for credit card orders. Lowe's, Master Card, Visa, Discover and American Express are accepted.

   — or —

2. FAX your order to 1-314-770-2226.

   — or —

3. MAIL the Order Form to the address below. For proper delivery, make sure to use your street address and not a P.O. Box.

Rush Delivery – if you need to place a rush order, please call us by 11:00 a.m. CST and ask for overnight or second day service.

Questions? Call Our Customer Service Number 314-770-2228

BLUEPRINT PRICE SCHEDULE

Price Code	One-Set	*SAVE $75.00* Five-Sets	*SAVE $150.00* Eight-Sets	Material List*	Reproducible Masters (BEST VALUE)
AAA	$195	$260	$290	$50	$390
AA	245	310	340	55	440
A	295	360	390	60	490
B	345	410	440	60	540
C	395	460	490	65	590
D	445	510	540	65	640
E	495	560	590	70	690
F	545	610	640	70	740
G	650	715	745	75	845
H	755	820	850	80	950

OTHER OPTIONS...

Customizer Kit™* . . . . $ 45.00
Additional Plan Sets* . . . . $ 35.00
Print In Mirror Reverse* . . add $ 5.00 per set
Legal Kit . . . . $ 35.00

Detail Plan Packages: *(Buy 2, get 3rd FREE)*
Framing, Electrical & Plumbing $20.00 ea.
Rush Charges . . . . . . Next Day Air $38.00
Second Day Air $25.00

****Available only within 90 days after purchase of plan package or reproducible masters of same plan.***

ORDER FORM

Please send me Plan Number 531 - ____________
Price Code ____________
(See Home Plans Index)

Specify Foundation Type - see plan page for availability
❑ Basement ❑ Slab ❑ Crawl space ❑ Walk-out basement

❑ Reproducible Masters $________
❑ Eight-Set Plan Package $________
❑ Five-Set Plan Package $________
❑ One-Set Plan Package (no mirror reverse) $________
❑ ____ (Qty.) Additional Plan Sets ($35.00 each) $________
❑ Print ____(Qty.) sets in Mirror Reverse (add $5.00/set) $________
❑ Material List (see index for availability) $________
❑ Customizer Kit (see index for availability) $________
❑ Legal Kit (see page 289) $________
Detail Plan Packages: (see page 289)
❑ Framing ❑ Electrical ❑ Plumbing $________
SUBTOTAL $________
SALES TAX (MO residents add 7%) $________
❑ Rush Charges $________
SHIPPING & HANDLING $ 12.50
TOTAL ENCLOSED (US funds only) $________

❑ Enclosed is my check or money order payable to HDA, Inc.
(Sorry, no COD's)

Mail to: HDA, Inc.
4390 Green Ash Drive
St. Louis, MO 63045-1219

I hereby authorize HDA, Inc. to charge this purchase to my credit card account (check one):

❑ Lowe's ❑ MasterCard ❑ VISA ❑ Discover Novus ❑ American Express Cards

My card number is ____________________
The expiration date is ____________________
Signature ____________________
Name ____________________
(Please print or type)
Street Address ____________________
(Please **do not** use P.O. Box)
City, State, Zip ____________________
My daytime phone number (______) - ______ - ______
I am a ❑ Builder/Contractor ❑ Homeowner ❑ Renter
I ❑ have ❑ have not selected my general contractor.

Please note that plans are not returnable.

Thank you for your order!